Financial Institution Management: Text and Cases

Fred C. Yeager and Neil E. Seitz
Saint Louis University

Reston Publishing Co.
A Prentice-Hall Company
Reston, Virginia 22090

TO HELEN AND BENTE

Library of Congress Cataloging in Publication Data

Yeager, Fred C.
  Financial institution management.

  Includes index.
  1. Financial institutions—Management. I. Seitz,
Neil, 1943–   . II. Title.
HG174.Y4   332.1′068′1   81–15801
ISBN 0–8359–2022–4   AACR2

©1982 by Reston Publishing Company, Inc.
A Prentice-Hall Company
Reston, Virginia

10   9   8   7   6   5   4   3   2   1

Printed in the United States of America

Contents

Preface

This book differs from most other financial institution texts in that it focuses on the management, rather than the description, of financial institutions. More specifically, it focuses on the *financial management* of financial institutions. The concentration is primarily on policy questions, such as the appropriate loan portfolio mix, rather than operating questions such as credit evaluation for a specific loan. This focus was chosen for several reasons:

–Many students taking financial institution courses will eventually seek employment with financial institutions. Thus, a knowledge of the principles guiding their management will help the students to understand the management policies and decisions, and eventually participate in them.

–Recent experience, particularly the plight of the savings and loan industry in the early 1980's, illustrates the fact that financial institution managers face heightened needs for financial skills. They have added to their vocabularies new words such as *unsystematic risk, beta, financial futures hedging*, and *purchasing power parity*. Old expressions such as *inverted curve* have taken on greater importance. Unstable financial markets and high rates of inflation have led to increased needs for financial management skills. Thus, a financial institution management

text aimed at the financial aspects of management is timely and appropriate.

–The management focus gives the book a theme, helping to provide the students with a framework for understanding the material presented. A book which describes without a theme leaves the reader with many facts, but with no conceptual framework within which the facts may be analyzed. A book focusing on policy level management decisions should help even the non-management reader understand why particular institutions choose to do what they do, and therefore why the financial system behaves as it does.

This book differs from other financial institution texts in that it includes both text and cases. The cases serve a number of purposes. First, they reinforce learning by illustrating the fact that techniques discussed in the text have application to real-life problems. Second, they have proved useful in helping the student transfer learning from sterile problems to complex real-life situations. Finally, the cases contain substantial information about the financial institutions involved, helping the students to further understand their operations. The cases were contributed by professors and practitioners around the country who took the time to describe decision problems actually being faced by specific financial institutions.

This book is designed for a one semester course at the graduate or advanced under-graduate level. Prior coursework in elementary economics and statistics would be helpful in understanding the material; the student who has not had these courses, however, should still be able to understand the text and analyze the cases (with a little more work).

Our debts start with our parents and end with our students whose candid comments on earlier drafts helped to improve the final product. We are deeply indebted to Frederic Easter at Reston for his continual encouragement through the evolution of this book. One could not dream of a better editor.

Jeanne-Marie S. Peterson of Reston Publishing Company performed superbly in guiding our material through the production and publication process. What might have been a laborious task became a pleasant one through her involvement.

We, and the users of this book, owe a debt of gratitude to the case writers who took the time to research real business problems and share their information with us. Finally, we thank our colleagues at Saint Louis University for their support during this task. Bouquets will be shared with the above. Brickbats should be aimed only at us.

Chapter 1

Functions and Goals of Financial Institutions

In a primitive economy each household produces what it needs and fulfillment of personal economic needs does not depend on communication between households. A complex modern economy, with its specialized producers and diverse products, requires a vast amount of communication between units. The great depression of the 1930s bears stark witness to what happens when this communication system fails or is inadequate. The smooth functioning of a modern economy is dependent on intermediaries who act as go-betweens, matching the needs of one unit with the output of another. Financial institutions are among the vital intermediaries contributing to economic health.

Financial intermediation is the process of acquiring surplus funds from economic units—business firms, governmental agencies, and individuals—for the purpose of making available such funds to other economic units. Financial institutions exist for the primary purpose of facilitating the intermediation process. Examples of financial intermediaries in the United States include:

Commercial Banks

Savings and Loan Associations

Mutual Savings Banks

Commercial and Consumer Finance Companies

Leasing Companies

Insurance Companies

Credit Unions

Pension Funds

Certain Governmental Units

Trust Companies

Securities Dealers

Investment Trusts

Financial intermediaries play an important role in society. They issue securities[1] to

---

[1] Any form of evidence representing debt or equity is a security.

those from whom funds have been entrusted and accept securities from those to whom funds have been loaned or invested. Thus, intermediaries act as a buffer between suppliers and users of funds, gathering funds in quantities and on terms that are acceptable to savers, and supplying funds in quantities and on terms agreeable to the users. Intermediaries assist society in innumerable ways. Savers and investors benefit in that funds may be left in relative safety, and to the extent securities issued by intermediaries bear interest or dividends, the value of entrusted funds is enhanced. Ultimate users of funds benefit by the availability of capital to purchase homes, acquire durable consumer goods, and finance business operations. In performing these functions, financial intermediaries contribute to a high standard of living for those countries with well-developed financial systems.

THE CIRCULAR FLOW OF INCOME AND MONEY

THE CIRCULAR FLOW OF INCOME

Consider a society without financial intermediaries and with no medium of exchange, i.e., a barter economy. Income earned in a barter economy is paid in the form of goods and services. Income may be earned by the recipient for any of three basic reasons. First, income may be received in return for the provision of labor. Second, income may be received if the recipient allows others to use his physical property, i.e., land, tools, or other goods. Third, income may accumulate if the recipient has provided services of an entrepreneurial nature. Figure 1–1 describes the circular flow of income for a barter economy.

In Figure 1–1, those who are willing and able to do so provide physical property, labor and entrepreneurial ability for production purposes. Note that either products or

Figure 1–1: Circular Flow of Income for a Barter Economy

services may be produced. In return for contributions of property, labor, and entrepreneurial skills, providers of these resource inputs are entitled to receive production outputs, i.e., income. Thus for each round of resource provision, production output is generated.

It should be pointed out that with the barter economy of Figure 1–1, all transactions are "real," i.e., for each unit of resource input, a certain amount of production output is immediately acquired. Thus, "financial assets" such as cash, demand deposits, savings accounts, accounts receivable, and other securities are non-existent. It should also be noted that the barter economy will not function smoothly unless there is a complete willingness on the part of providers of resources to accept production outputs regardless of the nature of such outputs. For the circular flow to continue, resource providers must continue to happily swap their services for the output that streams forth.

A complex economy simply could not operate smoothly based on barter. First, the model assumes a comprehensive and complete coincidence of wants. In other words, it assumes that producers of products and services will require the precise quantities of physical property, labor, and entrepreneurial ability offered, and these resources will be utilized without delay. The model further assumes that production of goods and services is instantaneous and that suppliers of resources will happily accept all production generated, without regard to the nature of such production, as compensation for the use of their resources. In practice, the automobile worker may be reluctant to accept a transmission as compensation for his week's labor. A complex industrial society could not function in this way.

The barter model does, however, illustrate the important point that resources must be supplied if production is to occur. In addition, the model illustrates the fact that in one way or another, those who provide the resources are compensated, ultimately at least, in terms of goods and services.

We will now begin to expand the model with the introduction of money into the circular flow.

THE CIRCULAR FLOW AND MONEY

An important distinction exists in Figure 1–2 as compared with Figure 1–1. The providers of resources are now receiving money as compensation. Note that money so received may now be used to acquire goods and services that are produced as a result of resource provision.

Introduction of money into the circular flow means that "real" transactions, the direct exchange of resource inputs for production outputs, are not the only type of transactions that may occur. Since money exists, resource inputs, products, and services may now be exchanged for money. Thus money is functioning as a standard of value and a store of value. The value of resource inputs or production outputs is defined in terms of money and is stored in money. Since money is accepted in exchange for resources or production, the transactions may be defined as "monetary" transactions.

The introduction of money in Figure 1–2 permits certain other changes to occur. For one, it is no longer necessary to have a comprehensive and complete coincidence of wants. Since money may now be received in exchange for resources or products, the seller has converted these resources or prod-

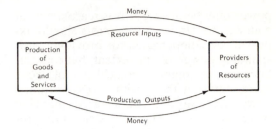

Figure 1–2: Circular Flow of Income for a Money Economy

ucts into "generalized purchasing power." No longer must he accept only those goods or services which the buyer can offer. The introduction of money has made transactions easier and more realistic, thereby more conveniently making the circular flow function. Money can be exchanged for goods and services instead of goods and services being exchanged for other goods and services.

Discussion of the circular flow, to this point, implicitly assumed that all who were willing and able to provide resources would do so. In exchange for resources provided, production outputs in the form of products and services would be provided. As we shall see, a major advantage of money is that it provides a means of accommodating providers of resources who may wish to defer their spending of at least some income derived from their provision of land, labor, and physical property.

To the extent that income recipients defer spending, producers of products and services will find that demand for their production declines and that lower levels of production are thus appropriate. Fewer resources are required to produce the smaller levels of production, and resource unemployment will logically develop; national income will decline. On the other hand, certain of those who defer from spending may find a coincidence of wants with producers or other resource providers who wish to engage in current spending in excess of current income. Should such a coincidence of wants develop, those with excess spending power will find others with whom such spending power may be invested. It is reasonable, of course, that lenders or investors should expect to be compensated for providing such spending power. To the extent that comprehensive and complete coincidence of wants exists between those with excess spending power and those to whom such spending power is transferred, a happy situation prevails. All who are able and wish to refrain from current spending may do so, and receive compensation to boot. Production and national income may continue at high levels.

But once again our model must be re-evaluated. The assumption of comprehensive and complete coincidence of wants on the part of those with surplus funds and those who wish to acquire such spending power is unrealistic. For example, the borrower may need funds for a long time to build a factory while the lender is willing to commit funds for only a short time. The need is evident for financial intermediaries whose purpose is to gather funds in quantities and on terms acceptable to savers and investors, and to supply funds in quantities and on terms agreeable to users.

THE ROLE OF FINANCIAL INTERMEDIARIES

In order to analyze the full benefits of intermediation, it is useful to identify those services that are performed as a result of the intermediation process. These services may be summarized in terms of the following four categories:

1. Asset Transmutation
2. Liquidity
3. Income Reallocation Over Time
4. Transactions Aid

ASSET TRANSMUTATION[2]

Financial institutions hold assets in the

---

[2] The term is that of Basil J. Moore, *An Introduction to the Theory of Finance,* The Free Press, New York, 1968.

form of promises to pay, with terms set to meet the needs of the borrowers. They finance these assets by accepting funds from savers on terms set to meet savers' needs. Thus they convert the borrower's obligation to an asset with a maturity to meet the needs of the saver. This process is known as asset transmutation.

Economic units in need of funds issue *primary securities*. Primary securities include all securities issued by non-financial economic units for the purpose of acquiring funds. Examples of primary securities are mortgages executed by individuals or businesses, stocks and bonds sold by corporations, and United States Treasury bills. In each case, primary securities were issued for the purpose of acquiring funds. They may be either debt or equity (part ownership). The form and maturity of the security is selected to satisfy the needs of the unit acquiring funds.

The securities issued by those acquiring funds may differ in size, maturity, and form from the needs of those with funds. Financial intermediaries solve this problem by acquiring primary securities with funds they have raised through the issuance of *secondary securities*. Secondary securities include all securities issued by financial intermediaries. Examples of secondary securities include demand and time deposits, credit union shares, and cash value of life insurance policies. Table 1–1 contains selected examples of primary and secondary securities held by economic units as a result of the intermediation process. Households are net suppliers of funds and nonfinancial businesses are net users, although some individual households are net users and some individual businesses are net suppliers.

By issuing secondary securities in exchange for financial resources of surplus units and in turn exchanging these resources for primary securities issued by deficit units, intermediaries transmute or convert the securities of business units to obligations desired by households. Through this trans-

Table 1-1:

Selected Primary and Secondary Securities

NET DEFICIT ECONOMIC UNITS (Non-Financial Business Units)		FINANCIAL INTERMEDIARIES		NET SURPLUS ECONOMIC UNITS (Households)	
Assets (Secondary Securities)	*Liabilities (Primary Securities)*	*Assets (Primary Securities)*	*Liabilities (Secondary Securities)*	*Assets (Secondary Securities)*	*Liabilities (Primary Securities)*
		Loans	Demand Deposits		
		Leases	Time Deposits		
		Investments	Life Ins. Reserves		
		Stocks	Pension Fund Reserves		
		Bonds	Investment Co. Shares		
		Mortgages			

mutation process, intermediaries both facilitate the production of real wealth and provide households with the financial rewards associated with such production. In the process, intermediaries generate economies of scale by combining funds received at times and in quantities suitable for producer units. Intermediaries also provide economies of scale by generating knowledge of various alternative investments in producer units, thereby reducing or eliminating the need for individual surplus units to generate independent knowledge of such alternatives. And because intermediaries acquire funds from large numbers of surplus units and provide funds to large numbers of deficit units, substantial diversity is effected and the risk of financial loss is reduced.

LIQUIDITY

Liquidity refers to the ability to generate cash quickly. Some secondary securities are acquired by businesses and households primarily for purposes of liquidity. Secondary securities such as savings and time deposits provide a high degree of liquidity as well as safety and provide income as well. Such instruments are essential to the normal conduct of financial affairs. To the extent economic units acquire secondary securities for purposes of liquidity, intermediaries perform an important financial service.

INCOME REALLOCATION OVER TIME

Many individuals earn satisfactory incomes today, but realize they will eventually face retirement and curtailment of income. They wish to reallocate some of their present income to that future time. They could do this by storing goods, but the acquisition of secondary securities such as savings accounts, pension fund reserves, or investment company shares is more convenient and provides the opportunity to earn a return on these savings. On the other hand, many young individuals and households issue pri-

mary securities, thereby allocating future income to the present or making it possible to pay for assets as they are being used. Primary examples of this latter activity are loans for the purpose of home or automobile purchase.

Business units are also influenced to acquire or issue securities for purposes of income reallocation over time. However, net income reallocation effects on the part of business units differ from those of households in terms of the direction in which income is shifted. Households consist of individuals, many of whom are engaged in the systematic acquisition of secondary securities for no other reason than the expectation of reduced earnings beyond retirement. Business units as a group have no automatic expectation of reduced future earnings. Life expectancy of the typical business corporation is perpetual and future income under normal economic circumstances is not expected to decline.

Business units also differ from the household sector in terms of the purpose for which primary securities are issued. Households normally issue primary securities so as to acquire goods or services for consumption, and not for the purpose of generating future income. Business units normally issue primary securities for the purpose of investment in assets which are expected to increase future income. Secondary securities acquired by business units are obtained primarily to facilitate transactions and to provide liquidity. In contrast to households, business units seek to issue large quantities of primary securities relative to secondary securities acquired, thereby shifting future income to the present.

TRANSACTIONS

Certain secondary securities issued by financial intermediaries represent *money* and constitute a part of the payments system. Traditional demand deposits and certain other deposit accounts function as money and are acquired by households and business units to facilitate the exchange of goods and services. To the extent that economic units acquire secondary securities in order to accommodate day-to-day settlement of financial claims, intermediaries serve a major purpose in facilitating monetary transactions.

AN OVERVIEW OF THE SAVINGS MARKET

Figure 1–3 summarizes the supply and use of savings in the United States economy. As the figure illustrates, households are net surplus units with holdings of financial assets exceeding their financial liabilities. The financial institutions, as intermediaries, have financial assets approximately equal to their financial liabilities. Business and government are the primary users of these funds.

It is evident that households hold substantial quantities of both primary and secondary securities. The proportion of each type varies over time due to a complex variety of economic and social conditions. Fluctuations in the market value of corporate stock, for example, have a heavy impact on year-to-year changes in household wealth.

Another major factor influencing household decisions in their acquisition of debt securities is the relative interest rates prevailing for different classes of securities. For example, generally high market interest rates prevailed for many securities in 1980 and 1981. However, maximum rates for most secondary securities were fixed by law[3] and such maximums or ceilings were less than rates generally available on primary securities. Many households switched from secondary to primary securities during these years.[4]

An overview of the savings market can be completed with a brief look at the relative roles of the various financial institutions. As Figure 1–4 shows, commercial banks continue to be the most important financial institutions. However, banks can be considered a mature industry with a growth rate limited by the growth rate of the economy. Credit unions and pension funds in particular have shown rapid growth in the last decade. This growth is a result of a favorable cost structure for the credit unions and new laws requiring a higher level of funding of pension fund liabilities. Each of these institutions is examined in depth in later chapters.

GOALS OF FINANCIAL INSTITUTIONS

Students and the general public are sometimes confused as to the objectives that guide financial institution managers in their decision making. Because they hold other people's money, financial institutions are probably more closely regulated than any other industry. Furthermore, statements by many critics of the industry seem to reflect the view that financial institutions are quasi-government agencies that should be guided primarily by social objectives. Interviews with executives of financial institutions yield an entirely different perception. For the most part, financial institutions are owned by shareholders who invest their own funds as equity in the institution. They make these investments for the purpose of earning a profit. The management is selected by the board of directors elected by these shareholders. Because they answer to a board of directors elected by shareholders interested in making a profit, financial institution managers view making a profit as their first obligation.

The conflict between the profit objective and the desire to provide services may not be as great as first appears. Like any busi-

---

[3] These regulations will be phased out over a number of years due to the Financial Institution Deregulation and Monetary Control Act of 1980.

[4] This process of shifting from secondary securities issued by financial intermediaries to primary securities is known as *disintermediation*.

ness, a financial institution can only earn a profit by providing a desired service to some group capable of paying for that service. Thus serving the needs of some sector of society is a prerequisite to profitability. In addition, there are many things that managers, as good citizens, can do to help the community without hurting profits. The conflict arises when a critic feels financial institutions should take actions that would decrease profitability but would contribute to some objective deemed desirable by that particular critic. Legislation has occasionally been passed leading institutions to take ac-

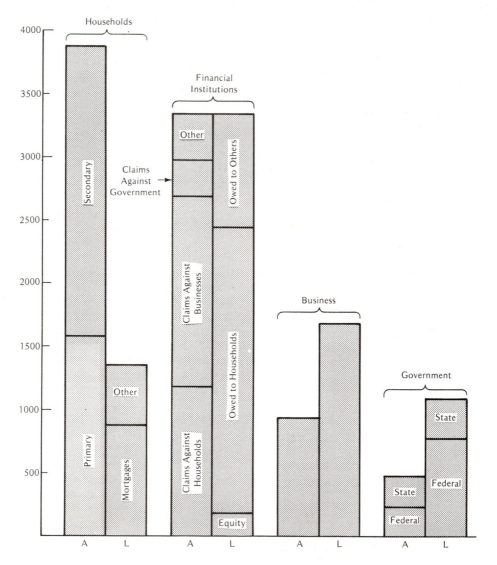

Figure 1–3: Financial Assets, Liabilities, and Equity by Sector, 1979 (in $ billions). Compiled from *Federal Reserve Bulletin,* Federal Reserve *Flow of Funds Accounts, Treasury Bulletin,* and other estimates.

tions that would not be taken in simple pursuit of profit. However, general government policy suggests that, within the limits of the law, financial institutions should behave like other businesses in pursuing their profit objective.

The primary focus of this book is on the management of financial institutions as opposed to a pure description of what they do. A primary interest in profitability and efficient usage of funds is assumed. The book begins with a discussion of the environment in which institutions operate and some general principles used in managerial decision making in financial institutions. Attention is then turned to the principles followed in the management of each major type of fi-

nancial institution. Because of the growing importance of international finance, the final chapter deals with a discussion and analysis of a number of important issues associated with Financial Institution Management on an international scale.

SUMMARY

Financial intermediation is the process of acquiring surplus funds from economic units and of making such funds available to other economic units. In a complex industrial society, a great deal of financial communication and funds transfer is necessary if the economy is to function efficiently. Although

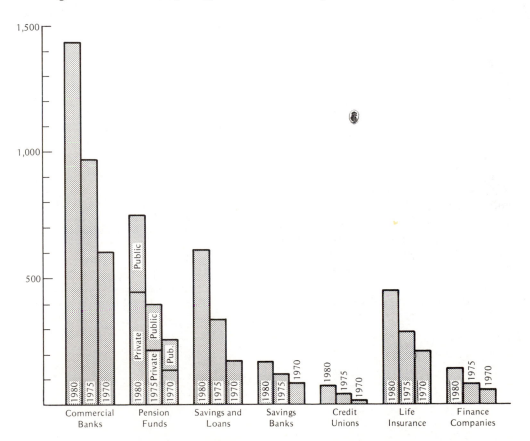

Figure 1–4: Total Assets by Type of Financial Institution, in $ billions

surplus units invest directly in securities issued by deficit units, financial institutions accommodate the majority of funds transfers by acting as a buffer between suppliers and users of funds, issuing secondary securities to funds suppliers and accepting primary securities from funds users. In their role as financial middlemen, intermediaries facilitate the circular flow of income. Services relating to transactions, liquidity, income reallocation, and asset transmutation are among the most important of those performed by intermediaries in facilitating this flow.

Growth and development of any society and the well being of its citizens is clearly influenced by the efficiency and capability of its financial institutions.

QUESTIONS

1. How does financial intermediation facilitate the circular flow of income?

2. Distinguish between primary and secondary securities.

3. In what way or ways does the motivation of households differ from that of business firms in their desire to hold secondary securities?

4. What might be the possible economic consequences of disintermediation? Comment on possible means by which the problem of disintermediation may be resolved.

5. Comment on benefits of financial intermediation in terms of the income reallocation and asset transmutation effects.

SELECTED REFERENCES

Campbell, Tim S., and William A. Kracaw, "Information Production, Market Signalling, and the Theory of Financial Intermediation," *Journal of Finance,* Vol. 35 (September, 1980), pp. 863–882.

Davidson, Paul, *Money and the Real World,* 2d ed. New York: Halstead Press, 1978.

Edminster, Robert O., *Financial Institutions: Markets and Management.* New York: McGraw-Hill, 1980.

Gup, Benten E., *Financial Institutions: an Introduction.* Boston: Houghton Mifflin, 1980.

Kronn, Herman E., and Morten R. Blyn, *A History of Financial Intermediaries.* New York: Random House, 1971.

Murphy, Neil B., and Lewis Mandell, "Consumer Response to Restructured Financial Institutions: The Case of Maine," *Journal of Money, Credit and Banking.* Vol. 11 (February, 1979), pp. 91–98.

Polakoff, Murray E. et. al., *Financial Institutions and Markets.* Boston: Houghton Mifflin, 1970.

Rose, Peter F., and Donald R. Fraser, *Financial Institutions.* Dallas: Business Publications, Inc., 1980.

Sametz, Arnold W., and Paul Wachtel (eds.), *The Financial Environment and the Flow of Funds in the Next Decade.* Boston: Lexington Books, 1977.

Sealey, C. W. Jr., "Deposit Rate-Setting, Risk Aversion and the Theory of Depository Financial Intermediaries," *Journal of Finance,* Vol. 35 (December, 1980), pp. 1139–1154.

Chapter 2

Monetary and Regulatory Environment of Financial Institutions

Financial institutions have an impact on groups far removed from those directly involved in transactions. A bank failure disrupts general commerce and results in loss of jobs, as well as loss of the funds of individual depositors. A decision by a savings and loan company to stop lending in a deteriorating neighborhood leads to further deterioration of the area and limits the ability of present residents to sell their homes in addition to limiting the choices of specific applicants. When the financial institutions create an excessive amount of demand deposit money through their lending activity, everyone suffers from the resulting inflation.

Because of their importance to both the individuals doing business with them and the general public, financial institutions have long received more regulatory attention than most other businesses. Early regulation primarily addressed questions of safety. When a single bank failed, rumors about the safety of other banks tended to arise, with the re-

sulting wholesale withdrawal demands forcing many institutions to close their doors. Lawmakers sought to decrease the number of individual bank failures and to avoid banking panics when single bank failures did occur. It was in the aftermath of a banking panic in 1908 that the Federal Reserve System was created to deal with these problems.

Legislators and the public have also become increasingly aware of how regulating the supply of money determines both the rate of inflation and the overall level of economic activity. The primary form of money in a modern economy is not currency or coin, but "account money" in the form of demand deposits at financial institutions. The institutions increase or decrease the amount of this money through their lending decisions. Because the supply of money is so important to the general welfare, society has chosen to regulate it by regulating the credit policy of financial institutions.

In addition to considering safety and the

money supply, lawmakers occasionally have looked at the way in which savings are allocated by the financial institutions and have attempted to affect that allocation through legislation. Ceilings on interest rates that could be charged on loans are the earliest example of such regulations, while the restrictions on the volume of consumer credit implemented by President Carter in the spring of 1980 are the most recent example as of this writing.

The regulatory environment is a major factor in current planning at every financial institution. In addition, long range strategic planning requires a careful analysis of trends in the regulatory environment as well as the business and competitive environment in which the institution operates. In this chapter, the money supply and its control are discussed. In addition, the general philosophy of financial institution regulation, as well as evidence of trends in that philosophy, are discussed. The specific details for each institution are discussed in the chapter dealing with that institution.

MONEY

A society can only operate without money if transactions are so few that they can be handled through barter. Very early in the development of primitive economies, money began to appear in the form of beads, precious metals, or some other valued item. While money serves as a store of value and unit of account, the primary thing that distinguishes it from other commodities is its use as a *medium of exchange*—prices of other things are stated in terms of the money commodity. In the absence of money, a person who wants leather and holds corn must search the marketplace for the best ratio of corn to leather. Further, it is quite possible that no holder of leather would want corn and a complex series of trades would be needed to move from corn to a product some holder of leather wanted. With a money

economy, the holder of corn can search for the most money he can get for corn and use the money to search for the most leather he can get per unit of money. If this does not seem like a significant convenience, consider an economy in which 10,000 products are bought and sold. The use of money means that the marketplace needs to determine only 10,000 ratios of exchange. If this same economy relied on barter, there would be a need for the establishment of nearly 50,-000,000 ratios of exchange!

In addition to serving as a medium of exchange, money serves as a *store of value*. An individual who does not wish to immediately consume as much as he or she produces can exchange productivity for money and hold the money for later consumption.

It should be pointed out that while individuals can save by accumulating money, society cannot. The savings of a society must be measured in terms of the amount by which production exceeds consumption. The excess production may be in the form of capital, producing goods such as factories, or it may be in the form of stored products such as wheat warehoused against the possibility of a crop failure. If everyone saved by accumulating money, there would be no wheat to buy in the event of a crop failure and even those with the most money might starve. Someone must borrow saved money to acquire goods if true saving is to occur. Modern financial institutions make it possible for individuals to accumulate savings in the form of deposit money while society gains because other people borrow the money for the purpose of acquiring capital goods.

Finally, money serves as a *unit of account or standard of value*. The Gross National Product measure of national economic activity is a good example of this function. Economists wish to reduce the diverse economic activities of the country to some single index. But how do we add up houses, automobiles, breakfast cereals, and haircuts? The solution had been to add them at their dollar values. A byproduct of the primary function of money is its availability as a unit of account for the extensive record keeping needed in a complex economy.

An item to be used as money should be durable and easily transported. It also helps if it can be divided into any number of pieces for transactions of various sizes. Most important, it must be subject to some law—physical or otherwise—that assures its continued scarcity. Otherwise, everyone would choose to produce the money commodity directly rather than other goods, as happened when tobacco was used as money in early colonial America. Gold has the desired characteristics and has been widely used. Other commodities that have been used include silver, grain, fur, spices, salt, fishhooks, and human hair.

As societies developed, paper money began to replace commodity money for many purposes. For convenience, people could entrust gold to a goldsmith who would issue a receipt that could be used to make purchases. The receipts would pass from hand to hand many times without any attempt to redeem them for the underlying gold. This first paper money was only a small transition from the actual commodity because it was totally backed by the actual commodity and only required faith in the honesty of the goldsmith.

The first paper money printed by governments differed little from goldsmith receipts in that it could be exchanged for precious metals at will. Until the Gold Reserve Act of 1934, the U.S. government would purchase or sell any quantity of gold at a price of $20.67 per ounce or 23.22 grams per dollar. Thus a dollar was little more than a gold receipt and the only faith required was in the honesty of the government. The amount of faith required increased sharply when the Gold Reserve Act outlawed private holdings of gold in the United States. Thereafter, gold was used only by the central bank in settling accounts with other countries, at a rate of $35 per ounce. Paper money was no longer exchangeable for anything.

Paper money continued to be used and accepted even though it was no longer redeemable. One reason it continued to be used was that people desperately needed some sort of money to complete transactions. In addition, the government declared paper money to be legal tender, meaning that it could be used to settle any debts, public or private. Finally, and probably most important, paper money continued to be used because people believed that it would not be printed in excessive quantities.

Of course, governments have frequently violated their trust by printing large quantities of money and destroying its value. Pre-World War II Germany printed marks to meet government expenditures in such great quantities that eventually they became worth no more than the value of the paper they were printed on. Even the United States has experienced an 85 percent decline in the value of the dollar since the Gold Reserve Act.

The main change since the Gold Reserve Act of 1934 was the suspension of settlement of private international accounts with gold in 1968, followed by the suspension of gold settlements with foreign central banks in 1971. Paper money now has value only in terms of its ability to purchase goods. This type of money is called *fiat*. It derives value entirely from faith in the government's ability to control its supply and enforce its acceptability.

Most money today is actually removed one step from paper money, with payments being handled through checks—orders to the bank to transfer ownership of a certain dollar deposit to another person. While there are various ways to measure the money supply (as shown in Table 2–1), all counts include coin, currency, and commercial bank transaction accounts. By this relatively narrow money supply measure, currency represents only about 25 percent of the total money supply outstanding in the United States.

In the United States we learned that loss

of faith in the value of money[1] can lead to a collapse of the economic system, with depression following. In other countries, we have seen that failure to control the supply of money can lead to revolution. If money were still primarily in the form of currency, the supply could be controlled by controlling the printing press. With most money being in the form of deposits in financial institutions, controlling the supply is a more complex problem. To understand how the money supply is controlled, it is first necessary to understand how the Federal Reserve System operates.

THE FEDERAL RESERVE SYSTEM

The primary purpose of the central bank is to act as a bank for other financial institutions.[2] The twelve regional federal reserve banks and the controlling Federal Reserve Board comprise the central banking system in the United States. As a bank for other financial institutions, the Federal Reserve System supplies an important clearing house function, providing a means of settling accounts between financial institutions. In addition, it acts as a lender, providing credit to financial institutions when necessary. By granting credit, it can help individual financial institutions meet heavy withdrawal demand and thus maintain faith in individual institutions in the financial system. It was to serve this function that the Federal Reserve System was created following the banking panic of 1907 and 1908.

---

[1] Checking account money in the 1930s and currency in some earlier crises.

[2] The Federal Reserve System was limited to serving and supervising commercial banks until the Financial Institutions Deregulation and Monetary Control Act of 1980 broadened its scope to include other financial institutions.

Table 2-1:

Major Components of Money Stock Measures

M-1A	Demand deposits at commercial banks plus currency in circulation
M-1B	M-1A plus balances in NOW accounts, share draft accounts, and other transaction accounts at financial institutions
M-2	M-1B plus savings and small denomination time deposit accounts, plus money market mutual fund shares
M-3	M-2 plus large denomination time deposits
L	M-3 plus other liquid assets such as commercial paper, Treasury bills, etc.

In the United States, the Federal Reserve System is also the issuer of currency. (It could also be issued by the U.S. Treasury, and was in the past.) A dollar bill or other paper currency displays the words *Federal Reserve Note* and the name of a particular federal reserve bank. The dollar is an interesting obligation in that it only commits the federal reserve bank to pay the holder a dollar. If you took the dollar to the federal reserve bank and demanded payment, you would receive another paper dollar or coins containing metal worth less than one dollar. Again, willingness to accept money comes from faith in the government and status as legal tender.

Still another purpose of the Federal Reserve System is to share responsibility with other government agencies for examining banks to be sure that they are not endangering depositors' funds. Other examining bodies are those agencies providing insurance for depositors' funds at the various types of financial institutions: The Federal Deposit Insurance Corporation for banks;

the National Credit Union Administration for credit unions; and the Federal Savings and Loan Insurance Corporation for savings and loan companies.

Finally, the Federal Reserve System is responsible for the control of the money supply. Since most money is in the form of transaction account balances, banks can generate new checking account money simply by granting loans to customers in the form of credits to their checking account balances. Through several means discussed below, the Federal Reserve System controls the supply of money created in this manner.

OPERATIONS OF THE FEDERAL RESERVE SYSTEM

The Federal Reserve System issues currency, buys and sells U.S. government securities, and serves depository financial institutions by making loans and clearing payments between institutions. These activities are illustrated below with simple balance sheets. As the first sample balance sheet shows, the primary assets are loans to financial institutions and U.S. government securities. The primary liabilities are currency that has been issued and deposits from financial institutions.

SIMPLIFIED COMPOSITE FEDERAL RESERVE BANK BALANCE SHEET
(in $ billions)

Loans to fin. inst.	$ 10	Currency	$100
U.S. government securities	140	Deposits from fin. inst.	50
Other assets	3	Equity	3
Total assets	$153	Total liabilities and net worth	$153

Suppose the federal reserve banks decide to buy U.S. government securities. The securities would probably be purchased directly from a financial institution, but if securities were purchased from an individual, the individual would deposit the check used for payment with a financial institution, achieving the same results. In this example, the federal reserve banks purchase $10 billion worth of U.S. government securities directly from commercial banks. The balance sheet below reflects the changes that occurred. The arrows highlight accounts that have changed. As can be seen, the Federal Reserve pays for these securities by crediting the selling commercial bank's deposit account. Notice that the federal reserve banks do not need money to purchase securities.

FEDERAL RESERVE BANK BALANCE SHEET

Loans to fin. inst.	$ 10	Currency	$100
U.S. government securities	150←	Deposits from fin. inst.	60←
Other assets	3	Equity	3
Total assets	$163	Total liabilities and net worth	$163

The selling commercial bank has now replaced U.S. government securities with liquid funds in the form of a deposit with a federal reserve bank. Because financial institutions can settle accounts with each other by transferring ownership of deposits with the federal reserve banks, the commercial bank can view these federal reserve deposits as money. The commercial bank can take advantage of this new money by making a loan, which is normally accomplished by increasing the borrower's transaction deposit balance. If the borrower then writes a check that is deposited elsewhere and later presented by another bank for payment, the lending bank can use its federal reserve bank deposit to make payment. Thus an increase in its federal reserve bank deposits represents funds that a bank can loan. The federal reserve system can increase or decrease the amount of loanable funds and the money supply by purchasing or selling U.S. government securities.

Continuing with this example, we can observe the process of currency creation. Suppose commercial banks do loan more money and some borrower requests cash. Suppose that the $10 billion Federal Reserve System's

purchase of U.S. government securities eventually results in a demand for an additional $2 billion of currency. Since the cash is being withdrawn from commercial banks, these banks will request $2 billion in currency. The federal reserve banks forward the $2 billion in currency to the individual commercial banks, deducting the amounts from the commercial banks' deposit accounts. Thus deposits from banks decrease by $2 billion and currency liability increases by $2 billion.

FEDERAL RESERVE BANK BALANCE SHEET
(in $ billions)

Loans to fin. inst.	$ 10	Currency	$102←
U.S. government securities	150	Deposits from fin. inst.	58←
Other assets	3	Equity	3
Total assets	$163	Total liabilities and net worth	$163

From the perspective of the federal reserve banks' accounts, currency in circulation and deposits from financial institutions are similar, interchangeable liabilities. Currency is simply physical evidence of a federal reserve bank liability. From the public's point of view, there is little difference between currency and a transactions account deposit since either can be used for payment and one can be readily exchanged for the other. The form in which money is held is based mainly on convenience factors.

A loan to a financial institution is also a matter of offsetting transactions. If commercial banks were to borrow $5 billion from the federal reserve banks, the "loans to financial institutions" account would be increased by $5 billion and the deposits from financial institutions would be increased by $5 billion. Thus the federal reserve banks do not need a source of funds in order to make loans.

The final type of transaction involves clearing accounts between financial institutions. Financial institutions may pay each other by transferring ownership of part of

their federal reserve bank deposit balances. A member bank receives a check written on another bank. The member bank deposits the check with the federal reserve bank, receiving credit to its deposit account for the amount of the check. This amount is then deducted from the balance sheet of the bank on which it was drawn. Of course, each commercial bank may deposit thousands of checks per day, with its deposit balance with the federal reserve bank reflecting the net effect of all checks.

The following example shows the accounts of a federal reserve bank and two member banks before and after a series of checks are cleared. In this example, Bank A deposits checks worth a total of $2 less than checks that are deposited by other banks and written against it. Bank B deposits checks worth $2 more than checks that are deposited against it.

The individual commercial banks show changes in deposit liabilities owed to their customers which offset changes in their accounts with the federal reserve bank. However, total deposit liabilities of commercial

Federal Reserve Bank	*Before checks are cleared*	*After checks are cleared*
Total assets	$163	$163
Liabilities and equity		
Currency	$100	$100
Deposits from financial institutions		
Bank A	6	4←
Bank B	5	7←
All other financial institutions	49	49
Equity	3	3
	$163	$163
Bank A		
Currency	$ 3	$ 3
Deposits with Fed	6	4←
U.S. gov. securities	70	70
Other assets	1	1
Total assets	$ 80	$ 78
Deposits	$ 70	$ 68←
Equity	10	10
	$ 80	$ 78
Bank B		
Currency	$ 2	$ 2
Deposits with Fed	5	7←
U.S. gov. securities	60	60
Other assets	1	1
Total assets	$ 68	$ 70
Deposits	$ 60	$ 62←
Equity	8	8
Total liabilities	$ 68	$ 70

banks and federal reserve banks have not changed.

Most of the functions of the Federal Reserve System could be easily handled by other institutions. In many countries, currency is issued as an obligation of the Treasury department of the government rather than by the central bank. Checks can be cleared through clearing house associations. In fact, private clearing houses are used for stock and commodity trading as well as for a good deal of check processing. Deposit insurance, not Federal Reserve credit, brought an end to banking panics. There is, however, one function the Federal Reserve System is uniquely qualified to provide. The Federal Reserve System is the primary agency responsible for controlling the money supply.

CREATING AND CONTROLLING THE MONEY SUPPLY

To understand the necessity of controlling the money supply, we begin with the process by which new transaction account money is created. Following is a brief financial statement for a bank, though the same process can occur with any institution that offers transaction accounts.

Commercial Bank Balance Sheet

Currency	$ 10	Demand deposits	$500
Loans	1,000	Time deposits	900
Other assets	500	Equity	110
Total assets	$1,510	Total liabilities and net worth	$1,510

A customer wishes to borrow $100, but the institution has only $10 in currency. The institution may simply credit the borrower's transaction account with an additional $100. The balance sheet now appears as follows:

Currency	$ 10	Demand deposits	$ 600←
Loans	1,100←	Time deposits	900
Other assets	500	Equity	110
Total assets	$1,610	Total liabilities and net worth	$1,610

If this were the only bank in existence, it could grant unlimited loans by simply increasing the transaction account balance for each loan. Borrowers would pay others with checks, transferring ownership of transaction account balances, but not changing the total level of these deposits. The only "leakage" would be from people who wanted to hold their new money in the form of currency.

Table 2-2:

Reserve Requirements for Financial Institutions Under The Financial Institution Deregulation and Monetary Control Act of 1980

The First $25 million of transaction account balances	3%
Transaction account balances over $25 million	12%
Negotiable certificates of deposit with maturity less than four years	3%
Eurodollar borrowings	3%

Notes: These requirements are being phased in over an eight year period beginning in November, 1980.

The Federal Reserve system can impose an additional 4 percent reserve requirement if it feels this is necessary.

rency. The bank's only limitation on expansion would be the proportion of new money that was withdrawn in the form of currency.

The example could be expanded to a system of many financial institutions. A borrower may use his loan proceeds to write a check to another person who then makes a deposit with another institution. As we are aware from earlier analysis, this would simply result in changes in who held the deposits and which institution owned deposit balances with a federal reserve bank. The financial system could create money in the same manner as a single financial institution. In the absence of any means of control, the supply of money would increase rapidly, resulting in rapid inflation and possible economic collapse.

The amount of money that can be created is controlled through *reserve requirements*. A financial institution is required to hold reserves in the form of cash or deposits with the federal reserve bank equal to some percentage of its deposits, as summarized in Table 2–2. To create a simple illustration, we will use a bank with only one type of deposit and a 10 percent reserve requirement for those deposits. To begin with, the balance sheet of the bank appears as follows.

Cash	$ 100		
Deposits with Fed	400		
Loans	4,000	Deposits	$5,000
Other assets	1,500	Equity	1,000
Total assets	$6,000	Total liabilities and net worth	$6,000

The bank presently has $5,000 in deposit liabilities and $500 in reserves. With a 10 percent reserve requirement, it is in compliance, but could not make additional loans because this would create a new deposit without creating additional reserves.

Now suppose the bank receives a $100 cash deposit. Cash increases by $100 and deposits also rise by $100. Reserves are now $600 and deposits are $5,100. Required reserves are now $510 (.10 × $5,100) or $90 less than actual reserves. These excess reserves give the bank the ability to make additional loans. If this were the only bank in existence, it could make additional loans of $900, resulting in the balance sheet shown below.

Cash	$ 200←		
Deposits with Fed	400		
Loans	4,900←	Deposits	$6,000←
Other assets	1,500	Equity	1,000
Total assets	$7,000	Total liabilities and net worth	$7,000

The existence of other financial institutions will limit the amount of credit that can actually be given by a single institution to less than that in the above example. The deposits are likely to be used to write checks which will be deposited at other financial institutions, thereby reducing this bank's reserves. Suppose this bank actually makes loans equal to only the $90 of excess reserves. If this $90 is used by the borrower to write a check which is deposited in another bank, the lending bank will lose its excess reserves of $90, but the second bank will gain a deposit of $90. With a 10 percent reserve requirement, the second bank will gain excess reserves of $81. If a loan of $81 is then granted and results in a check for $81 being deposited in a third bank, the third bank will then have excess reserves of $72.90. As this process continues, the result for the system of banks is the same as it was for a single bank: excess reserves of $90 made it possible to increase loans by $900. While the ownership of the loan proceeds may change hands many times, the change will be primarily through transfer of ownership of deposits. Thus the total money supply will remain at a level $900 higher than it was prior to the creation of $90 in excess reserves.

The expansion potential can be formalized in the formula:[3]

$$P = E/r$$

where:
P = Potential expansion in the money supply (or expansion of credit)

E = Excess reserves

r = Percentage reserve requirement

The actual expansion of credit is likely to be less than this potential figure because of "leakage" to cash. If the first borrower of $90 had requested the loan in the form of cash rather than credit to a demand deposit account, the process would be interrupted. If the borrower or some person he paid

---

[3] For a detailed discussion of bank credit expansion, see Paul A. Samuelson, *Economics,* 11th ed., 1980, ch 16.

chose to hold the cash, expansion would be stopped with the first $90. In practice, the creation of $1 of excess reserves appears to increase the money supply by only $2 to $3.

The money supply is controlled by the Federal Reserve System through these required reserves. The simplest approach is to change the reserve requirements. An increase in reserve requirements leads to a curtailment of lending activity and therefore stops the creation of demand deposit money. Likewise, a decrease in reserve requirements gives banks the authority to make additional loans and create more money.

Reserve requirements are actually changed infrequently because a small change in reserve requirements leads to a large change in the money supply. On the other hand, the money supply is adjusted on a day-to-day basis using *open market operations*—the buying and selling of U.S. government securities by the Federal Reserve Banks. Recall that a Federal Reserve purchase of U.S. government securities is normally achieved by simply crediting the selling bank's Federal Reserve deposit account. Thus the commercial bank exchanges U.S. government securities for reserves. With a 10 percent reserve requirement, a $1 billion purchase by the federal reserve banks would increase the potential money supply by $10 billion. By selling U.S. government securities, the federal reserve banks can reverse the process and decrease the money supply.

The *discount rate* is another method used in controlling the money supply. The discount rate is the rate charged by the federal reserve banks on loans to member banks. The importance of the discount rate is limited by the fact that commercial banks are discouraged from regular borrowing from the federal reserve banks.[4] However, the discount rate is frequently used as a signal-

ling device. An increase in the discount rate would lead banks to begin curtailing their lending activity in anticipation of monetary restriction.

In addition to control of the money supply, the Federal Reserve System has available several other tools to use in attempting to control economic activity. *Regulation Q* sets the interest rates that can be paid on many deposits. However, this tool is being phased out, with present legislation calling for an end to deposit interest rate regulation by 1986. *Margin requirements* determine the percentage of value that purchasers of stocks and bonds are allowed to borrow. If there is evidence of excessive speculative pressure in the securities markets, effective demand can be decreased through an increase in margin requirements. The present 50 percent requirement was set in 1974. Finally, the Federal Reserve System operates in the *foreign exchange markets,* buying and selling dollars to smooth out movements in exchange rates.

An important objective of federal reserve policy is economic growth. The Federal Reserve System shares with the U.S. government a statutory obligation to work toward healthy economic conditions. The Federal Reserve System attempts to draw a reasonable balance between the objectives of encouraging economic growth through the provision of adequate credit and avoidance of inflation brought on by excessive money growth.

The governing body of the Federal Reserve System is the Federal Reserve Board. Each member is appointed by the President of the United States with the consent of the Senate for a period of 14 years. This structure was designed to create an "independent" Federal Reserve that would pursue appropriate policy objectives without undue short-term political pressure. However, the chairman only serves a four-year term and is appointed by the President from among the members. Thus the President generally has an opportunity to appoint someone of

---

[4] Borrowing from the federal reserve banks is viewed as a temporary means of meeting unexpected liquidity needs. The main tool used to discourage borrowing is moral persuasion.

his choosing to the Board and then appoint that person chairman sometime during his term. The record of the Federal Reserve System with regard to following the economic leadership of the President or striking its own course is mixed, as is opinion on the degree of independence it should have.

REGULATION OF FINANCIAL INSTITUTIONS

The antecedents of financial institution regulation in the United States date back to the early colonial period. Usury laws were implemented by the colonies to regulate interest charges on loans. Laws were also passed with the goal of regulating the supply of tobacco when it was used as money. Central banks were started in 1791 and 1816, but were forced out of existence when their charters came up for renewal.

At the beginning of the Civil War, all banks were state chartered and regulated. Currency in circulation consisted of notes of these various banks. State authorities did conduct bank examinations, but there was no effective method of controlling the supply and quality of money. At the beginning of the Civil War, there were 7,000 different types of bank notes in circulation. Half were worthless and many more were traded at discounts. The National Bank Act of 1863 and the amendment of 1864 attempted to deal with this problem through a dual banking system—the creation of national banking charters as well as state charters. The attractiveness of national bank charters was enhanced by taxes designed to discourage state chartered institutions from issuing bank notes. National banks were required to maintain reserves behind their bank notes, and the total amount of notes allowed was limited. This did serve to alleviate the problem of heterogeneous monies, but it did not provide a vehicle for controlling the money supply or dealing with liquidity demand and bank runs. These problems were to be left

relatively unattended for another half century.

The banking panic of 1907 and 1908 led to the next major round of regulatory change, and the creation of the Federal Reserve System. On October 22, 1907 savers responded to rumors (apparently true) of financial difficulties at Knickerbocker Trust Company in New York. A "run" began, with depositors demanding their funds in cash. Of course, financial institutions lend or invest most of their despositors' funds and cannot repay more than a small percentage of deposits in cash at any one time. The Knickerbocker was therefore forced to close its doors. The panic spread, forcing other New York banks to close. Within days, the panic spread across the country, forcing many banks to close temporarily. While this was not the first banking panic in history, it came at a time when faith in the ability of government to solve problems was increasing. As a result, the Federal Reserve System was formed in 1913.

The Federal Reserve System was to serve primarily as a bank for bankers, maintaining public confidence and avoiding panics by lending money to banks faced with heavy withdrawal demand. The Federal Reserve System was designed to provide only temporary liquidity; it had no funds to aid ailing banks. Therefore, the Federal Reserve Banks were unwilling to prolong the existence of troubled banks by loaning them money they would not be able to repay. When the 1930s provided the first test of the new system, banks closed, panics followed, depositors lost money, and the economy suffered from the disruption of business activity. This failure led to the development of a regulatory structure that has remained largely intact until the 1980s.

The environment in which the regulatory changes of the 1930s occurred was one in which the economy had been badly hurt by the failures of financial institutions. These failures resulted from actual losses on loans and from the loss of public faith in the institutions. Legislation addressed both of these problems.

The Federal Deposit Insurance Corporation was formed in 1934 to restore public confidence by insuring the value of individuals' savings in the event of a bank failure. The FDIC proved to be a solution, as there has not been a banking panic since, despite the failures of individual banks from time to time. Since then, the Federal Savings and Loan Insurance Corporation and the National Credit Union Administration have been created to provide similar insurance for these institutions.

The assurance of actual financial strength and safety for financial institutions proved to be a more troublesome matter. Two general approaches were followed. First, institutions were examined and regulated to assure that certain standards of soundness were followed in their operations. These standards involve maintenance of certain ratio standards, primarily dealing with liquidity reserves and equity base.

In addition, institutions are limited as to the types of assets they may hold. For example, mutual savings banks are frequently limited to "legal lists" by state regulatory agencies. Insurance companies, while not actually restricted from holding equity securities, are discouraged by the fact that equity values will be written down to reflect market value loss while bonds can be carried at cost even if market value has declined. The specific ratio standards and investment restrictions are discussed in connection with the individual institutions in later chapters.

A second method used to assure safety was the limiting of competition. Since institutions must be chartered by the state or federal government, restriction of charters has been one effective method of limiting competition. When a group applies for a charter to start a new depository financial institution, it must show that there is a community need for its services and that it will not cause undue financial harm to the other financial institutions in the area. In addition

to the denial of new charters, the branching operations of depository institutions were severely restricted, primarily by state law. Many states allowed no branching. Where branching was allowed, the standards of need and protection of existing institutions were imposed.

Competition was also limited through restrictions on services offered. Savings and loans were not allowed to offer checking accounts or make loans other than real estate loans. Savings banks and credit unions were similarly limited from direct competition with commercial banks. Commercial banks were not allowed to offer investment banking services.

While it would be incorrect to say that any institution had a monopoly on business in its area, competition was severely limited. People unhappy with a particular institution might find it necessary to travel a considerable distance to locate another institution offering that service. At a time when a smaller portion of the population lived in cities and transportation was not as well developed, this was a major factor in deterring competition, as indeed was its purpose.

Even with the limitation on the number of institutions, there was still the possibility that institutions would compete vigorously for funds. It was felt that such competition would bid up the price of funds and encourage the institutions to make more risky investments. Regulation Q was created as part of the Banking Act of 1934 to allow the Federal Reserve Board of Governors to set the maximum interest rates that could be paid on deposits by commercial banks. Thrift institutions[5] were not brought under this regulation until 1966. This omission was probably a result of the fact that the thrift institutions were simply not the important factor in the marketplace they were to become later.

The interest rates that institutions are al-

---

[5] Savings and loan companies, mutual savings banks, and credit unions.

lowed to charge on loans (particularly consumer loans) has been regulated since the first usury law was passed in Massachussetts in 1641. Usury laws seem to follow from a belief dating back to at least as far as the classic Greek period, that interest on a loan was a means of taking advantage of a person suffering some misfortune. Today much consumer credit as well as borrowing for business and capital investment purposes has been recognized as arising from other than hardship, but usury ceilings still exist for many types of borrowing, particularly consumer loans. In some cases the state-imposed ceilings are so high as to be of little significance, while in others they are so low as to severely restrict lending. For example, consumer lending in Arkansas has been precluded by a 10 percent usury ceiling.

WINDS OF CHANGE

Recent decades have witnessed the completion of several studies of the structure and regulation of financial institutions by special government commissions. Many of the recommendations of these commissions have become law and represent an important departure from the limited competition philosophy developed in the 1930s. While safety was the primary focus of earlier legislation, quality and price of services has been the focus of this recent legislation.

HUNT COMMISSION

In 1971, the Hunt Commission (formally, the President's Commission on Financial Structure and Regulation) completed a sweeping study of financial institutions and the supply and demand for credit. The commission concluded that attempts to regulate the flow of funds had led to market inefficiency and had generally failed to achieve stated objectives. In general, the commission recommended that competition be increased. The major specific recommendations of the commission were:

1. *Elimination of interest rate ceilings on deposits*. Deposit rate ceilings were supposed to protect the savings of individuals by protecting financial institutions from expensive competition for savings. In addition, they were supposed to assure the availability of funds to the housing industry.[6] This latter objective was pursued by allowing thrift institutions to pay a higher rate (first unrestricted, then 0.25 percent) than banks for deposits. This advantage to thrift institutions has been negated in recent years by disintermediation—investors took their money out of financial institutions and invested directly. Rather than securing a stable, low-cost supply of funds, the interest rate ceilings may have contributed to the lack of stability in the supply of funds.

2. *Allow all depository financial institutions to offer a full range of time deposits*. This is consistent with recommendation No. 1. With the ability to bid at prevailing rates for funds of any maturity, institutions should be in a position to manage the maturity structure of their liabilities. By bidding for longer term deposits, they would also gain in ability to develop more stable sources of funds.

3. *Allow all depository institutions to offer checking account services*. This recommendation followed the general philosophy that the best way to assure low cost services was to allow as many competitors as possible to offer the service.

4. *Broaden lending powers of all institutions*. The commission felt that the public would be better served if more competitors existed for each type of loan. It was also believed that institutions would gain from greater diversity if they were

---

[6] An unspoken "advantage" of regulating interest rates on small savings deposits was that it allowed the federal government to finance part of its debt by selling savings bonds to small investors at an interest rate well below that paid on large denomination U.S. government bonds.

not forced to concentrate on one segment of the market. This recommendation was made against a background of laws that did such things as almost entirely restrict savings and loan companies *to* real estate loans and finance companies *from* real estate related lending in many states.

INSTITUTIONAL INVESTOR STUDY

The Institutional Investor Study, sponsored by the Securities and Exchange Commission, was also completed in 1971. The study was undertaken against a background of complaints that certain institutions, particularly insurance companies, mutual funds, pension funds, and bank trust departments, were distorting the equity capital markets through a tendency to trade large quantities of securities and to buy or sell the same security at the same time. The commission did not find evidence of sheep-like behavior by financial institutions, but it did find that the trading of large blocks of stock caused some distortions in reported prices, primarily because market structure did not lead to an efficient reporting of these prices. Commissions on stock traded on an exchange were fixed at levels that discouraged institutions from using the exchanges. Thus a great deal of trading occurred between institutions not using an exchange. The elimination of fixed commissions and reliance on the market to set commissions was recommended.

NATIONAL COMMISSION ON CONSUMER FINANCE

The National Commission on Consumer Finance was created by the Congress and completed its work in 1972. An important part of this Commission's work was a study of the impact of state usury laws. The Commission concluded that attempts to regulate interest rates charged to individuals had failed to achieve the desired results. Usury laws had led to problems such as circuitous methods of charging higher interest rates.

For example, if restrictive state usury ceilings resulted in reduced credit availability, consumers may go to a so-called credit retailer who sells virtually all of his merchandise on credit and in effect builds interest costs into the price of the product. The effect of the usury ceiling in this case is to restrict the consumer's opportunity to shop for the best interest rate and the best price for the product.

As with other studies, this commission concluded that problems could best be dealt with through encouraging competition. This would require consumer lending authority to be extended to as many lenders as possible and interest charges to be fully disclosed so that people can effectively shop for the best interest cost.

The general thrust of the recommendations from all of these studies is that competition should be relied on to allocate funds to their best use, and to provide the best prices to both consumers and institutions. These recommendations stand in sharp contrast to the regulatory philosophy developed in the 1930s, in which it was felt that elimination of competition was the most effective approach to achieving national goals.[7]

What accounts for the change in attitude about the way in which financial institutions should set prices and allocate resources? In a broad sense, this change is part of a general shift in public attitude, in recent years. Reliance on competition has grown in popularity relative to government control as a means of achieving the goals of individuals and society. Suggestions for financial institution deregulation have paralleled movement toward deregulation in airlines, trucking, and other fields. More specifically, this

---

[7] A continued resistance to the competition-based philosophy is represented by a dissenting statement from Lane Kirkland, then Secretary/Treasurer of the AFL-CIO: "I cannot believe that a financial institution should be encouraged to lend money for only the most profitable purposes." *Report of the President's Commission on Financial Structure and Regulation.* U.S. Government Printing Office, 1972, Stock # 4000–0272.

change of philosophy follows from the realization that many well-intentioned laws simply have not worked. For example, deposit rate ceilings designed to provide a stable, low-cost source of funds actually served to limit the ability of institutions to compete for funds in periods of tight money, thereby destabilizing the major source of funds to depository institutions.

Recent legislation has generally followed the thrust of the recommendations for greater reliance on the marketplace. Brokerage commission regulations were repealed and the result has been the development of a wider variety of services and costs available to individual investors. The brokerage houses previously charged identical commissions and competed by offering other services such as security analysis. Now the conventional brokerage houses compete with discount houses that offer no services other than purchase and sale of securities at the lowest commission possible. The result of freedom from rate regulation has been lower commission rates for many investors and a wider range of available services.

The recommendations of the Hunt commission have largely been brought into law by the Depository Institution Deregulation and Monetary Control Act of 1980, which is being phased in over a period ending in 1988. The act eliminates the interest ceilings on deposits and allows all financial institutions to offer a full range of time deposits. It also gives all thrift institutions the right to offer checking account services and broadens lending powers by allowing savings and loan companies to commit up to 20 percent of their assets to non-real estate loans to corporations and individuals.

The thrust of the recommendations of the National Commission on Consumer Finance have also become law. With the savings and loans authorized to enter consumer lending, the number of competitors has been increased. The Truth in Lending Act, which was passed in 1969, before the commission completed its study, required that the interest rate and the dollar interest charge on consumer loans be stated in writing, thus encouraging shopping for the best rate.

Lest the trend toward deregulation be exaggerated, it should be viewed in light of several recent laws passed with the intention of improving on the allocation occurring in a free market. Beginning in 1975, the Equal Credit Opportunity Act made it illegal to consider sex, marital status, or child bearing plans in making credit decisions. The Community Reinvestment Act of 1977 addressed the outflow of mortgage funds from older neighborhoods. The Retirement Income Security Act of 1974 went beyond requiring full disclosure of pension fund provisions to specify what types of protection must be given to workers covered by pension plans. Last but not least, President Carter acted in 1980 under the power of the little-used Credit Control Act of 1969. The major thrust of the new regulations was to bring additional components of the money supply, such as money market mutual funds, under control and to decrease the availability of consumer credit. Any serious disruption in the financial markets would surely lead to demands for additional controls, and possibly abandonment of the trend toward greater reliance on market forces.

SUMMARY

Because financial institutions manage other people's money, their activities have long been regulated. Regulation is aimed at protecting the wealth of individuals by stabilizing the value of the currency and promoting the solvency of financial institutions. In addition, regulation has sought to smooth out the business cycle and allocate funds to uses deemed socially desirable.

Money has evolved from commodity to gold to gold certificate to specie to accounting entries at financial institutions. Since money is no longer directly backed by anything of value, its supply must be controlled by some agency enjoying a high level of public confidence. In the United States, the Federal Reserve System was structured as an agency free from day-to-day pressures of election politics for this purpose. The Federal Reserve System, which acts as the central bank, controls the supply of money primarily through reserve requirements and open market operations. Its control of the money supply is carried out with the dual (and frequently conflicting) objectives of stable prices and full employment.

Safety of depositors' funds has been protected by requiring financial institutions to maintain certain reserves, by providing for government examination, and by limiting competition to assure a healthy level of profitability. Safety has also been assured by deposit insurance in the event other regulations do not prevent failure of individual institutions. In recent years, there has been some indication of a change in regulatory philosophy, with competition being encouraged as a means of assuring the best service at the best price.

QUESTIONS

1. If money is not directly exchangeable for some valuable commodity such as gold, what must the government do to maintain its acceptability and usefulness?

2. In the summer of 1980, Patricia Harris, Secretary of Health and Human Services, issued a report on the ways people were fighting inflation. Highlighted in the report were do-it-yourself projects, co-op arrangements such as grocery buying co-ops, and barter arrangements in which one person's goods or services are exchanged for another's. In summary, people were finding ways to acquire goods or services without the use of money.

   a. Why would people wish to avoid the use of money in their transactions?

   b. What does this say about the effectiveness of government policy relating to money?

3. What are the three main functions of money? How does inflation affect each of these functions?

4. The Federal Reserve System is operated as an independent agency in the United States, with each director serving a 14-year term. In most other countries, the central bank is directly controlled by the government. What are the advantages and disadvantages of an independent Federal Reserve System?

5. If the Federal Reserve System wishes to buy additional U.S. government securities, where can it get the money to make the purchase? Could the Federal Reserve System get enough money from this source to purchase all U.S. government debt instruments? Would this be a wise policy?

6. Why has competition between financial institutions been discouraged in the past? Why has the legislative attitude toward competition between financial institutions changed?

7. The Financial Institution Deregulation and Monetary Control Act was passed in 1980, but was to be phased in over a number of years. At this writing, there is some question about whether all provisions of the Act will be implemented or whether some aspects, such as deposit interest rate ceilings, will be modified through later legislation. Use the *Federal Reserve Bulletin, Federal Home Loan Bank Board Journal* and other appropriate sources to develop an update on the status of the phasing-in of this law.

PROBLEMS

1. Below are T accounts for the Federal Reserve Banks and a commercial bank. Show how a $10 million sale of U.S. government securities to that commercial bank would change the accounts.

Federal Reserve Bank Balance Sheet
(in $ mil.)

Loans to banks	10,000	Currency	$100,000
U.S. government securities	150,000	Deposits from banks	60,000
Other assets	3,000	Equity	3,000
Total assets	163,000		$163,000

First National Bank of Johnstown
(in $ mil.)

Currency	3	Deposits	70
Deposits with Fed	16	Equity	10
U.S. Government Sec	10		$80
Other assets	51		
	$80		

2. Banks are fully loaned up and face 10 percent reserve requirements. The Federal Reserve System purchases $10 million of U.S. government bonds from a commercial bank. Assume any loans by that bank will be made by increasing the borrowers' transaction accounts and will result in the borrower immediately writing checks against his/her account.

    a) By how much can that bank increase loans?

    b) Ignoring leakage to cash, by how much can all banks in the system increase loans?

SELECTED REFERENCES

Bennett, Robert E., Paul M. Horvitz, and Stanley C. Silverberg, "Deposit Insurance: The Present System and Some Alternatives," *Banking Law Journal,* Vol. 94 (April, 1977), pp. 304–332.

D'Antonio, Louis J., and Ronald W. Melicher, "Changes in Federal Reserve Membership: A Risk Return Profitability Analysis," *Journal of Finance,* Vol. 34 (September, 1979), pp. 987–998.

Edwards, Franklin R., and James H. Scott, "Regulating the Solvency of Depository Institutions," Research Paper No. 210. Columbia University Graduate School of Business, 1977.

Farley, Dennis E., and Thomas D. Sumpson,

"Graduated Reserve Requirements and Monetary Control," *Journal of Finance,* Vol. 34 (September, 1979), pp. 999–1012.

Friedman, Milton, and Anna Schwartz, *A Monetary History of the United States, 1867–1960.* Princeton, New Jersey: Princeton University Press, 1963.

Horvitz, Paul M. "A Reconsideration of the Role of Bank Examination," *Journal of Money Credit and Banking,* Vol. 12 (November, 1980), pp. 654–659.

Kemerschen, David R. *Money and Banking,* 7th ed. Cincinnati, Ohio: South-Western Publishing Company, 1980.

Keynes, John Maynard. *The General Theory of Employment, Interest, and Money.* London: Macmillan, 1936.

Pettway, Richard H., and Joseph F. Sinkey, Jr., "Establishing On-Site Bank Examination Priorities: An Early Warning System Using Accounting and Market Information," *Journal of Finance,* Vol 35 (March, 1980), pp. 137–150.

Spellman, Lewis J. "Deposit Ceilings and the Efficiency of Financial Intermediation," *Journal of Finance,* Vol. 35 (March, 1980), pp. 129–136.

Timberlake, Richard, H. *The Origins of Central Banking in the United States.* Cambridge, Massachusetts: Harvard University Press, 1978.

The Regulation of Financial Institutions. Conference Series No. 21, Federal Reserve Bank of Boston and the National Science Foundation. October, 1979.

Chapter 3

Money Markets

The money and capital markets are similar in that they provide an investment outlet for those with excess funds and a source for those in need of funds. The markets differ with regard to the type of funds involved. The capital markets deal in long-term securities, thereby providing a permanent or semi-permanent outlet for funds. The money markets, on the other hand, provide an outlet and source of short-term borrowing; they are primarily liquidity markets.

The money markets are a group of markets in which short-term, generally high-quality credit instruments are bought and sold. Money market instruments normally mature in one year or less. Because it is necessary to quickly establish the safety of such an instrument, borrowing within this market is limited to large, safe, well recognized organizations. Financial institutions, major corporations, and governmental units are the major issuers of money market instruments.

The major securities bought and sold in the money markets include:

1. *Treasury bills*—obligations of the U.S. Treasury with maturities of one year or less.
2. *Agency securities*—obligations of agencies of the United States government.
3. *Commercial paper*—obligations of large, stable corporations and financial institutions. Maturities normally range from a few days to a maximum of 270 days.
4. *Negotiable certificates of deposit*—Marketable deposit receipts issued by commercial banks and bearing specified rates of interest for a specified period of time.
5. *Banker's acceptances*—an obligation of a firm, guaranteed by a bank. The instruments normally arise through international commerce and carry an average maturity of 90 days.
6. *Federal funds*—loans between commercial banks, typically on an overnight basis.

7. *Repurchase agreements*—sale of one or more securities, normally by a securities dealer, in which the seller agrees to repurchase the same securities within a specified time at a specified price.

8. *Eurodollars*—U.S. dollar denominated deposits held by banks outside the United States, including foreign branches of United States banks.

Each of these instruments and other money market instruments will be discussed in greater depth in this chapter.

There is no central physical location which serves as the money market. Separate market structures have developed for each type of instrument and none of these markets has central meeting places. The primary machinery for bringing together borrower and lender (or buyer and seller) consists of approximately 46 "money market banks" and a handful of specialized dealers and brokers. These "money market banks" include the largest New York banks and banks in other financial centers around the country. There are about 20 government securities dealers, some of which are banks, and about 12 commercial paper dealers. There are also a few banker's acceptances dealers and a number of brokers, such as federal funds brokers. The money markets operate by telephone with brokers and dealers functioning to match supply and demand. The market for each instrument will be discussed in more detail in later parts of this chapter.

The money markets are important because of their sheer size. In early 1981, the volume of outstanding treasury bills, negotiable certificates of deposit, and commercial paper totalled nearly $2,000 for every person in the United States. The money markets are also important because they are a major medium through which the Federal Reserve implements monetary policy. The Federal Reserve increases the money supply by purchasing U.S. government securities and decreases the money supply by reselling these securities.

Many money market instruments do not pay interest directly, but are sold at a *discount*. That is, the instruments are sold at less than their face value with the buyer receiving face value at maturity. Prices and therefore available returns on money market instruments vary with market conditions and the general level of interest rates. The higher the general level of interest rates, the greater will be the yield necessary for a money market instrument to provide its buyer a competitive rate of return.

Most purchasers of money market instruments are large corporations, institutions, or governmental units. Since most money market transactions involve large volumes of money for short time periods, few individuals have the financial capacity to participate in these markets. The main exception to this generalization involves Treasury bills which are presently sold in denominations as small as $10,000. Even in this market, individual participation is quite small relative to total volume.

The bulk of this chapter is devoted to a discussion of the various money market instruments—issuers, holders, market, and volume. Final sections of the chapter are devoted to the determinants of interest rates in the money markets and the impact of Federal Reserve policy decisions on these markets.

TREASURY BILLS

The Treasury bill market is the largest single segment of the money market. From the time of their first issue in 1929 until early 1981, the volume of Treasury bills outstanding has increased from $100 million to $216 billion. Thus Treasury bills provide an important outlet for temporarily idle funds and an important source of borrowed funds for the United States government. In addition, the trading of Treasury bills in secondary markets is a major tool in the implementation of monetary policy.

A Treasury bill is an obligation of the United States government to pay the bearer a fixed sum at a specified date. Treasury bills are regularly issued in maturities of 91 days, 182 days, and 365 days, with the 182-day or six-month bill representing the largest volume. Treasury bills range in denomination from $10,000 to $1,000,000.

A special maturity of treasury bill is the *tax anticipation bill*. Tax anticipation bills are issued to attract corporate funds held in anticipation of tax payments. Tax anticipation bills mature on the 22d of the month, but will be accepted at their maturity value for taxes due on the 15th of the month. Of course, these bills can be sold in the secondary market through a dealer, as can all Treasury bills. Tax anticipation bills help smooth out the Treasury's flow of funds and the timing and quantity of issues depend on the Treasury's assessment of its needs.

Treasury bills are sold in an auction market with the Federal Reserve System handling the sale on behalf of the Treasury. Treasury bills do not pay interest directly, but are sold at a discount, with the amount of discount being determined by the auction process. The actual interest rate earned depends on the amount of the discount. Suppose, for example, that an average accepted bid for 182-day bills is $94.130 per $100 of face value. The published interest rate is based on the amount of discount and on an assumed 360-day year. The quoted interest rate would be:

$$\frac{100 - 94.130}{100} \times \frac{360}{182} = 11.611\%$$

While this method of computing and reporting interest on Treasury bills has become commonplace, it is not comparable to the manner in which the rate is computed for many other instruments. In calculating the yield to maturity on direct interest-bearing issues such as bonds, the denominator is the amount invested rather than the maturity value, and the number of days per year is 365 rather than the 360 used in the above computation. A more accurate computation of the annual yield would be:

$$\frac{100 - 94.130}{94.130} \times \frac{365}{182} = 12.506\%$$

Since the former rate is the one that is normally quoted and the latter procedure represents the method of quotation for interest-bearing issues, this difference must be remembered when comparing interest rates.

Treasury bills are auctioned each week by the Treasury department, with bids being collected and tabulated by the Federal Reserve System. Bids for the weekly offering are accepted at Federal Reserve Banks and their branches until 1:30 P.M. New York time on Monday. Bids for amounts less than $500,000 may be submitted on a noncompetitive basis. Treasury bills are first allocated to noncompetitive bids. Competitive bids are then accepted in descending order until the week's issue has been fully allocated. Successful bidders pay their bid price and bills are awarded to noncompetitive bidders at a price equal to the weighted average of accepted bids. Delivery then occurs on Thursday. The average weekly issue is several billion dollars, with most of the proceeds going to retire existing issues.

Treasury bills provide an excellent temporary outlet for funds held to meet possible liquidity needs. First, they are considered risk-free because they are obligations of the United States government. Second, there is an active secondary market. Government security dealers continually stand ready with bid and ask prices—prices at which they will buy or sell—for all outstanding issues. The typical spread is four basis points[1] or about 1¢ per $100 of a three-month bill. Third, there is no risk of a large shrinkage if the holder needs to sell Treasury bills quickly to meet liquidity needs. Because of the short maturity, even a large interest rate move-

---

[1] The term "basis point" is a short-hand method of describing small fluctuations in interest rates. One hundred basis points represents one percent.

ment will result in only a relatively small change in the price of a Treasury bill.

As an example of how little value loss is risked, we look at the 182-day Treasury bill used above to see how the interest rate is computed. At the time of issue, that particular bill had a quoted interest rate of 11.611 percent and a price of $94.130 per $100 of face value. Normally we would expect the price to rise steadily as the issue gets closer to maturity. However, a rise in the required rate of return or general level of interest rates might prevent this from happening. By the end of 30 days from time of issue, with no change in the quoted interest rate, the price of this issue would rise to 95.098[2]. Suppose, however, that interest rates rise over the 30-day period to the point that the quoted rate is 13 percent, a quite rapid rise in interest rates. The market value would then be 94.511. While this is a small gain over the 94.130 price one month earlier, this price is still above the price originally paid. Thus the chance of a significant loss in market value is quite small.

The identification of holders of Treasury bills is rather difficult, because reporting requirements are such that less than half of total ownership is observed through any kind of reporting requirement. However, it appears that the holders, in descending order or importance, are Federal Reserve banks, commercial banks, state and local governments, non-financial corporations, and individuals. U.S. government trust funds have been substantial holders but are not at the present time. A substantial volume of holdings is also in the hands of foreign holders, both central banks and others.

THE ROLE OF TREASURY BILLS IN ECONOMIC POLICY

In addition to being the largest of the money markets, the Treasury bill market is important because it is the market through which much of the Federal Reserve's monetary policy is implemented. Increases in the supply of money will generally stimulate economic activity if the economy is operating below capacity. Conversely, decreases in the money supply will decrease the ability of financial institutions to lend money and therefore decrease overall demand for goods and services. Through the impact on demand, changes in the money supply also affect the rate of inflation. An increase in the money supply and a resultant increase in demand, when the economy is at or near full capacity, will result in an increase in prices. The Federal Reserve System attempts to control the money supply to create a balance that will encourage a healthy, steady rate of economic growth without encouraging inflation.

While there are several ways that the money supply can be controlled, day-to-day control is primarily maintained through the open market operations of the Federal Reserve. Open market operations consist of buying or selling U.S. Government securities—primarily Treasury bills. When the Federal Reserve buys Treasury bills, the seller receives payment through credit to his demand deposit account. If the seller is a commercial bank, the payment is in the form of a credit to its account with the Federal Reserve. This is an increase in the bank's reserves and an increase in its ability to loan money. For a non-bank seller, the seller ends up with credit to his demand deposit with his bank and the bank ends up with an increase in its deposit account with the Federal Reserve, again resulting in an increase in its ability to make loans. Conversely, the selling of Treasury bills by the Federal Reserve serves to decrease the money supply. The Federal Reserve buys or sells Treasury bills on a daily basis to change the money supply as needed to encourage stable economic growth and avoid encouraging more inflation. In recent years, the Federal Reserve

---

[2] $\frac{100 - P}{100} \times \frac{360}{152} = .1161; P = 95.098$

has held between 20 and 25 percent of outstanding Treasury bills.

U.S. GOVERNMENT AGENCY SECURITIES

The debt of U.S. government agencies has become increasingly important in the money and capital markets. Debt instruments issued by government agencies can be divided into two groups: those directly guaranteed by the U.S. government and those sponsored but not guaranteed by the government. The principal government guaranteed agency issues include obligations of the Federal Housing Administration (FHA), the Farmers Home Administration, the Government National Mortgage Association (GNMA or "Ginnie-Mae"), the Tennessee Valley Authority (TVA), the Export-Import Bank, and certain obligations of the U.S. Postal Service. The Tennessee Valley Authority and the Export-Import Bank owed $11 billion each at the beginning of 1981. The other guaranteed agencies owed a combined total of only $7 billion, a small volume when compared with the outstanding volume of Treasury bills.

The claims of the federally sponsored agencies represent a larger volume of liabilities. These agencies act primarily as financial intermediaries, raising funds for the purpose of loaning to others. Typically, these agencies were originally owned by the U.S. government, with their stock being later sold to private holders. For example, all of the shares of the Federal Home Loan Banks are now owned by members, primarily savings and loan associations. While most of these agency issues are not directly guaranteed by the U.S. government, many observers believe that the government would come to the rescue of any agency facing default. Thus issues of sponsored agencies are generally considered to be almost as safe as those of guaranteed agencies. Because of their importance, the major sponsored agencies are

discussed in more detail in the paragraphs below.

The Federal National Mortgage Association (FNMA or "Fannie Mae") currently represents the largest issuer of non-guaranteed debt. This agency was formed to provide a secondary market for mortgages and issues both short-term and long-term obligations. Thus some of its liabilities qualify as money market instruments. At the beginning of 1981, debt obligations of this agency had expanded to $55 billion.

The Federal Home Loan Bank (FHLB) system was created in part to enhance the flow of credit to the residential housing market. The banks which constitute the system were patterned somewhat after the Federal Reserve System, and were designed to provide a source of liquidity for mortgage lenders (principally savings and loan associations). Funds raised in security markets by the Federal Home Loan Bank System are in turn loaned out to member institutions to support mortgage lending activities. The FHLB varies its mixture of long term and short term issues in response to market conditions. At the beginning of 1981, FHLB debt outstanding totalled $41 billion.

The *Farm Credit Banks* began issuing bonds on a regular basis in 1979 to replace the separate financing operations of the Federal Land Banks, the Federal Intermediate Term Credit Banks, and the Banks for Cooperatives. The Federal Land Banks make mortgage credit available to farmers while the Federal Intermediate Term Credit Banks make credit available by purchasing notes from production credit associations. The Banks for Cooperatives were established to encourage the development of farmers' cooperatives for marketing and related purposes. The total debt of these four agencies was $63 billion at the beginning of 1981.

In addition to these agencies, several smaller agencies owe a total of $6 billion.

Agencies market three specific types of securities: short-term notes (generally discount notes), unsecured bonds, and participation certificates. A participation certificate represents an interest in a pooled group of loans. Rather than selling mortgages to investors, the issuing agency continues to hold the loans and collect payments. The payments are then used to service the participation certificates. Certificates such as these are guaranteed by the federal government and paid from the Treasury if collections from the assets are not sufficient to meet the contractual interest and repayment terms of the certificates.

While agency securities are negotiable and relatively easy to sell, the secondary market for these securities is not as well developed as that for Treasury bills. Thus Treasury bills are more likely to be used for primary liquidity needs. Because of their limited marketability, market interest rates on agency issues are normally a fraction of a percent higher than those for Treasury bills with similar maturities.

Holdings of agency securities are not concentrated in any particular sector. They are fairly well distributed among financial institutions, nonfinancial corporations, state and local governments, and individuals.

To complete this overview, Table 3–1 presents a summary of the outstanding U.S. government debt.

COMMERCIAL PAPER

The commercial paper market is a uniquely American institution. Canada is the only other country with a commercial paper market of any significance and its market is relatively small. Commercial paper is a short-term unsecured promissory note issued by a corporation with a well-known, impeccable credit rating. Maturities range from a few days to 270 days. Most issuers back their commercial paper by maintaining unused bank lines of credit equal to or approaching the amount of commercial paper outstanding.

Commercial paper has advantages for

Table 3-1:

Summary of U.S. Government Debt, January, 1981 (in billions)

	Short term	Inter- mediate and long term	Total
Treasury obligations	$216	$714	$930
Federal National Mortgage Association			55
Federal Home Loan Bank			41
Farm Credit Banks (and related agencies)			63
Tennessee Valley Authority			11
Export-Import Bank			11
Other			13

Source: Treasury Bulletin

both issuer and purchaser. For the issuer, the commercial paper rate is normally below the prime rate—the interest rate charged by banks to their best commercial customers. In some recent years, the commercial paper rate has been more than a full percentage point below the prime rate. From the buyer's point of view, commercial paper offers a return above the rate earned on alternate securities such as Treasury bills with only a small amount of additional risk.

Because of its advantages to both buyer and seller, the commercial paper market has grown rapidly since its inception by General Motors Acceptance Corporation in 1920. The amount of commercial paper outstanding reached $5 billion in 1960, $40 billion in 1970, and over $125 billion by the beginning of 1981.

Like Treasury bills, the vast majority of commercial paper is sold at a discount and redeemed at face value. The computation used in publishing interest rates is the same as that used for Treasury bills.

Only about 600 firms issue commercial

paper, with about two dozen finance companies accounting for approximately half the total. In addition to finance companies, other issuers are bank affiliates and large nonfinancial corporations, especially utilities. This limited number of issuers reflects the nature of the security involved. Purchase of a short-term unsecured obligation cannot realistically be preceded by a lengthy credit investigation if the transaction is to be profitable. This makes it essential that companies issuing commercial paper have well known, impeccable credit ratings.[3]

Commercial paper is sold either directly to lenders (direct placement) or through commercial paper dealers. About 55 percent of the commercial paper is placed directly with almost all directly placed paper being issued by finance companies. The remainder of the commercial paper is sold through dealers. There are about six major dealers in the United States with all but one being New York investment banking houses. The dealers earn their fee in the form of a spread between the price they pay and the price they sell the issue for. The minimum spread amounts to ⅛ of one percent per annum.

The secondary market for commercial paper is quite restricted. Most commercial paper is held to maturity by its original purchaser. However, many direct issuers have "gentlemen's agreements" that they will buy back the paper before maturity (and adjust the interest rate) if the lender suffers severe liquidity problems. The borrowers can do this because they are continually in the commercial paper market in the same way banks continually accept deposits and because they have back-up lines of credit with commercial banks.

Of the $125 billion of commercial paper outstanding at the beginning of 1981, $88 billion was issued by financial institutions and $37 billion was issued by non-financial corporations. Primary holders are banks, non-financial corporations, insurance companies, trust funds, and pension funds.

Despite the fact that commercial paper markets have generally not developed in other countries, this type of market has been very useful in meeting the needs of United States borrowers and lenders as attested by the significant growth and development of this instrument. With the volume in this market more than doubling in the past decade, it appears to be a stable factor in the country's financial structure.

NEGOTIABLE CERTIFICATES OF DEPOSIT

The market for negotiable certificates of deposit (CDs) is the newest of the large money markets. It began in 1961 when First National City Bank of New York issued the first negotiable certificates of deposit and a government securities dealer agreed to make a second market in them. The outstanding amount was $116 billion in early 1981; negotiable CDs now compete with commercial paper as a top volume money market instrument.

A certificate of deposit is a receipt for a bank deposit with a specified maturity and bearing a specified interest rate. This type of deposit has been around since at least the beginning of this century. It was the conversion to a negotiable (saleable) form and the development of a secondary market that made these instruments important ones in money markets. Negotiable CDs can be sold with a fixed maturity, guaranteeing the issuing institution funds for that period of time, and they can be sold in the secondary market if necessary, providing liquidity to the holders.

Negotiable CDs differ from Treasury bills and commercial paper in that they bear interest payable at maturity rather than being issued at a discount. Further, interest is

---

[3] This is not to say that commercial paper has been default free. The commercial paper market was taken by surprise when Penn Central defaulted on its commercial paper in 1970.

based on a 365-day year rather than a 360-day year, as is the case with Treasury bills and commercial paper. Because of these computational differences, quoted rates are not strictly comparable. For purposes of rate comparability, the Treasury bill or commercial paper rate must be recomputed in the manner illustrated within the previous discussion of Treasury bills.

Negotiable CDs are insured only up to Federal Deposit Insurance Corporation limits (currently $100,000). Thus the quality of the bank issuing the CDs is a matter of concern. The largest money market banks are normally able to issue their CDs at ⅛ to ½ percentage point below those issued by smaller regional banks. In addition, secondary markets for CDs issued by smaller banks tend to be less active than those for the large, well known banks. Some corporations divide temporarily idle funds among several different types of money market instruments— e.g., Treasury bills, negotiable CDs of major money market banks, and negotiable CDs of smaller banks—thereby providing different levels of liquidity.

Negotiable CDs also differ from other bank deposits in that certificates of deposit in excess of $100,000 denominations are currently not subject to the Federal Reserve regulations which establish ceiling interest rates that institutions may pay on certain deposits. When banks first began issuing negotiable CDs, maximum interest rates were established by regulation. The result was that during periods of tight money, such as those which existed in 1966 and 1969, banks could not offer CD rates competitive with those available on competing money market instruments. The volume of outstanding CDs declined and the ability of commercial banks to compete for funds was threatened. In 1970 regulations were removed for shorter term large denomination CDs and in 1973 they were removed for all CDs of $100,000 or more. Thus today's rates are set entirely by market conditions. The removal of rate ceilings has resulted in

greater stability in terms of the ability of banks to issue new CDs. However, wide swings in CD volume and rates may be observed as banks' needs for funds and lending opportunities change.

The buyers of negotiable CDs are primarily nonfinancial corporations. Indeed, negotiable CDs came into existence as a means of competing for corporate deposits that were leaving the banks in search of more attractive outlets for temporarily idle funds. CD holders frequently meet day-to-day liquidity needs by adjusting Treasury bill balances while holding negotiable CDs as a secondary reserve asset. Thus secondary market volume in CDs is considerably less than that for Treasury bills.

As previously indicated, the main issuers of negotiable CDs are large money market banks. The majority of the issues are by banks with assets in excess of $1 billion. Approximately 40 percent of the total volume originates with large New York banks. These banks tend to have substantial loan commitments and enjoy the credit and reputations which facilitate sale of large CDs.

The negotiable CD market is an excellent example of the manner in which financial institutions and instruments evolve to meet economic needs. Negotiable CDs were originated in response to a need to compete for corporate deposits that were being lost to other money market instruments. Legislation and regulation gradually changed in response to market needs. Within a relatively few years, this new instrument rose to challenge commercial paper as the second largest volume money market instrument.

BANKER'S ACCEPTANCES

Banker's acceptances, one of the oldest of money market instruments, came into existence primarily through foreign trade. These acceptances provide an alternative to open account credit, primarily when goods are to be shipped across national borders.

Banker's acceptances are negotiable, making them money market instruments. They have grown in importance with the growth in foreign trade, with the volume outstanding at the beginning of 1981 equalling $55 billion.

To understand this somewhat confusing credit instrument, we begin with an example of an American firm wishing to purchase goods overseas for import. The buyer secures a letter of credit for the order from a well known American bank, authorizing the seller of the goods to write a draft on the buyer's bank upon shipment of the goods. The draft instructs the bank to pay a specified amount on a specific date.

The seller may simply decide to hold the draft until the date specified for payment. Alternately, the seller may attach the shipping documents to the draft as evidence of shipment and sell the draft to his bank at a discount from face value. If this is done, the seller's bank then forwards the draft and shipping documents to its American correspondent, which in turn presents them to the buyer's bank. The buyer's bank examines and removes the shipping documents and stamps the draft "I accept," making it a negotiable instrument guaranteed by the buyer's bank. The draft is now the obligation of both the buyer's bank and the seller. Because of these obligations, they are considered nearly as safe as Treasury bills.

Once the draft has been accepted, a number of things can happen to it. Since the seller's bank bought the draft at a discount, it may simply instruct its correspondent to hold the draft until maturity as an investment or it may instruct the correspondent to sell the draft immediately. In this case, it may be sold to the buyer's bank or it may be sold in the market. Thus this accepted draft or banker's acceptance serves as a money market instrument.

This example involves a foreign seller and a United States buyer. Of course, the whole process can be reversed, with the foreign buyer's bank accepting or guaranteeing the draft. Banker's acceptances can also be used as a method of financing domestic trade, although the greatest growth has been in support of foreign trade.

Maturities of banker's acceptances range from 30 to 180 days with 90 being the most common. From the accepting bank's point of view, this procedure represents an attractive means of helping customers with their short-term credit needs. If the accepting bank does not hold the acceptance itself, it is making credit available by lending its name rather than its money. If the accepting bank holds the acceptance itself, it is effectively lending the buyer the amount of the acceptance. However, the acceptance is recorded on the bank's financial statements as a secondary reserve asset rather than a loan.

Banker's acceptances have not experienced as active a secondary market as have most of the other money market instruments previously discussed. Accepting banks hold about one fourth of all outstanding banker's acceptances and foreign financial institutions hold some 60 percent. The remainder are held by domestic owners and by Federal Reserve banks. The secondary market is made up mostly of a few government security dealers that make a market in these securities. One reason acceptances are attractive short-term dollar investments for foreigners is that they are not subject to American income taxes as is the interest on Treasury bills.

FEDERAL FUNDS

The federal funds market arises from the requirement that commercial banks[4] hold certain levels of liquid reserves, primarily in the form of deposits with their federal re-

---

[4] With the Depository Institutions Deregulation and Monetary Control Act of 1980, other institutions having transaction accounts are being brought under these reserve requirements over a period of several years. Thus they may become participants in this market.

serve banks. A bank with excess reserves can lend these reserves to a bank with insufficient reserves. The lending bank instructs its federal reserve bank via check or wire to transfer ownership of part of its deposit to the borrowing bank. As these loans are almost entirely overnight,[5] the borrowing bank sends an order the next day transferring ownership back to the lending bank.

Although the fed funds market is almost entirely restricted to overnight loans, it is still profitable for a bank with excess reserves to make such loans. The denominations are large, with transactions normally being in multiples of $1 million. At an effective annual interest rate of 12 percent, the interest on an overnight loan of $5 million would be in excess of $1,600. Thus it is worth the bank's trouble to make an overnight loan if it has excess reserves. From the borrower's point of view, borrowing in the fed funds market avoids the necessity of less desirable alternatives such as turning down loan applications or selling marketable securities.

Growth of the fed funds market was stimulated over the past two decades by general increases in the level of interest rates and the resultant opportunity cost associated with idle bank funds. While any particular bank could be a net seller (lender) of funds or a net buyer (borrower), large banks as a group tend to be net buyers, with small banks generally being net sellers. While the fed funds market has traditionally served as a means for participating banks to balance reserve requirements, many of the nation's larger banks have been involved as consistent net borrowers, relying on this source of funds on a daily basis.

Federal funds transactions primarily occur on an unsecured basis, because collateral is troublesome for such short-term loans. When security is required, the borrower is typically a smaller bank and U.S. government securities are placed in a special custody account for the one-day period.

The federal funds market, like all markets, depends on some method of bringing buyer and seller together. The role of market maker falls primarily on certain large New York banks because they tend to be net buyers (borrowers) of funds and because most banks throughout the nation maintain a correspondent relationship with a New York bank. The New York banks are normally willing to borrow the funds themselves or have knowledge of who needs them. Other banks, a few stock exchange firms, and some institutional money brokers also act as brokers, collecting information on who has excess federal funds and who needs funds. The federal funds market differs from the money markets previously discussed in that the market makers primarily act as brokers, bringing borrower and lender together. For the other money market instruments, market makers act as dealers, actually purchasing and reselling securities. The fed funds market also differs from other money markets in that direct participation is limited to banks and financial institutions with deposits at the federal reserve banks.

Market rates for fed funds are particularly volatile, reacting to short term shifts in supply and demand conditions. Banks must adjust their position quickly to meet reserve requirements. In periods of tight money these adjustments can result in rapid shifts in fed funds rates. Furthermore, a tendency for some banks to look to the fed funds market as a more or less permanent method of meeting funds requirements has caused demand to be heavy and rates to be high during periods of tight money. Conversely, demand and interest rates can fall sharply in recessionary periods. The fed funds rate is closely watched by the monetary authorities as a barometer of supply and demand for bank credit.

Volume in the fed funds market is a bit difficult to measure because banks report fed funds and repurchase agreements in com-

---

[5] Federal funds transactions occurring on Friday are "three-day" transactions because transactions are not conducted on weekends.

bined form. In early 1981, the sum of these two types of borrowing outstanding on the books of commercial banks was more than $100 billion.

REPURCHASE AGREEMENTS

Repurchase agreements (RPs) are defined as the sale of securities concurrent with an agreement to repurchase them at a later date. The arrangement may call for repurchase at a specific date for a specific price, or it may be open ended with either party able to end the arrangement at any time. In this latter case, the lender would be guaranteed a fixed return per day over the time the agreement remained in effect. Maturities of repurchase agreements range from one day to several months.

While any two parties may enter into a repurchase agreement, this arrangement has served primarily as a method of financing for U.S. government securities dealers. With the growth in U.S. government debt, dealers in U.S. government securities require extremely large sums of money to finance their inventories of securities. These dealers rely primarily on credit, maintaining debt to total asset ratios of 98 percent or more. They meet their financing needs through borrowing and repurchase agreements. Repurchase agreements totalled approximately $42 billion in early 1981.

Because U.S. government securities dealers hold billions of dollars in inventories, their need for funds is quite large and a major part of their daily activity consists of arranging financing at the lowest possible cost. Financing is achieved through direct borrowing, with the securities serving as collateral, and through repurchase agreements.

Lenders (purchasers) include New York banks, regional banks, and other institutions, including nonfinancial corporations. The dealers normally begin their day by seeking funds from sources located outside New York, as New York rates tend to be

slightly higher. Later in the day they complete the financing of their daily needs through the New York banks. Several New York banks post daily rates at which they will meet any desired volume of government securities dealer financing. This posted rate varies from one New York bank to another, depending on how eager each bank is to make additional loans.

Since the dealers are in permanent need of funds, they can tailor maturities to the needs of a particular supplier of funds. Thus corporations view dealer loans and RPs as a flexible method of placing temporarily excess funds. Some funds suppliers prefer direct loans while others prefer repurchase agreements. Repurchase agreements are most likely to be employed when funds are to be advanced for more than a few days. The expense of transferring title for very short periods makes such transfer uneconomical.

The repurchase agreement market is also an important medium for exercise of short-term money supply control by the Federal Reserve. When there is a temporary need for additional funds in the system, the Federal Reserve can buy U.S. government securities under repurchase agreement, assuring that there is a specific date when this agreement will end and the supply of funds to the market can be withdrawn. A reverse RP is also used on occasion. In this case, the Federal Reserve sells security under repurchase agreement to temporarily decrease the money supply.

EURODOLLARS

The Eurodollar market is another relatively young market, tracing its development as an active market to the late 1950s. Eurodollars are dollar deposits in U.S. banks owned by foreign banks, including foreign branches of domestic banks. They represent an important source of funds for businesses and an important market in which banks adjust liquidity.

To come to grips with the operations of the Eurodollar market, we will follow an example of the development and transfer of Eurodollars.

A German exporter has received payment in U.S. dollars and presently holds a demand deposit with Citibank in New York. Because the German exporter expects to need dollars in the future, it converts its asset by making a dollar denominated time deposit with a German bank, with the German bank receiving ownership of the Citibank demand deposit as an offsetting asset. Eurodollars have been created.

Because the German bank is paying interest on its time deposit and receiving no interest on the Citibank demand deposit, it will wish to turn this demand deposit to some profitable use. The German bank may have a customer in need of a dollar denominated loan. If not, it will lend the demand deposit to another bank, which in turn lends it to a customer. A United States bank continues to have the same demand deposit liability, but ownership of this deposit may change many times.

Like the other money markets, the Eurodollar market has no physical location, but is based on wire communications. However, the center of activity is London and the London Interbank Loan Rate (LIBOR) is considered the primary "market" rate. Like the federal funds market, the Eurodollar market is primarily an interbank market, with banks taking deposits from, and loaning to, their customers. Similar markets exist for other major currencies, with London being the center for all currencies except the pound.

A particularly important aspect of the Eurodollar market with regard to the domestic money market is the practice by American banks of borrowing from their foreign affiliates in periods of tight money. The foreign affiliates can borrow Eurodollars in the same way that federal funds or some other short-term credit instrument can be used. The affiliate then deposits the funds with the parent American bank, thereby increasing the parent's reserves of loanable funds. As a foreign borrower, the affiliate (foreign branch) is free of restrictions on the interest rate paid for the Eurodollar deposit, thus providing an avenue for circumventing interest rate regulation.

Reliable statistics on the Eurodollar market are extremely limited. However, it appears that total volume, net of transactions between banks, is probably in the neighborhood of $80 billion. This instrument is discussed in more detail in Chapter 14.

INTEREST RATES IN THE MONEY MARKETS

The general level of interest rates in the money markets moves with the overall credit markets.[6] Interest rate differentials between money market instruments depend on risk, marketability, and supply/demand conditions in particular sub-markets. Among generally available instruments, Treasury bills display the greatest marketability and lowest risk. Thus they normally carry the lowest interest rates. Agency securities normally follow, with similar risk but less marketability. Following U.S. government obligations, commercial paper, negotiable certificates of deposit, and banker's acceptances fall close together and are typically grouped at a rate ¼ to ½ percent above Treasury bill rates. Their individual rankings change from time to time because they are close together in yield and market conditions continually change.

Federal funds represent a special submarket. While rates are not divorced from those in other markets, they do respond to a special set of supply and demand conditions, since they represent the method banks

_____

[6] See chapter 6 for a discussion of general levels of interest rates.

use to adjust their overnight reserve positions. In a recession the fed funds rate will normally lie below all other domestic money market rates. Toward the end of the expansion phase of the business cycle, fed funds typically carry rates above those associated with other domestic money market instruments.

The Eurodollar market represents another special case. Eurodollar rates depend on a host of factors, including perceived strength of the dollar, financial conditions in other countries, and balance of payment considerations. In recent years the Eurodollar rate has been consistently above domestic interest rates.

Figure 3–1 provides a history of interest rate movements for money market instruments, illustrating the factors discussed in the above paragraphs. This figure illustrates the long term trend toward higher interest rates that has been associated with increased inflation. While the present rates seem high, there is no assurance that they have reached a peak.

SUMMARY

The money markets are actually a series of distinct markets in which specific financial instruments are traded. In addition to being

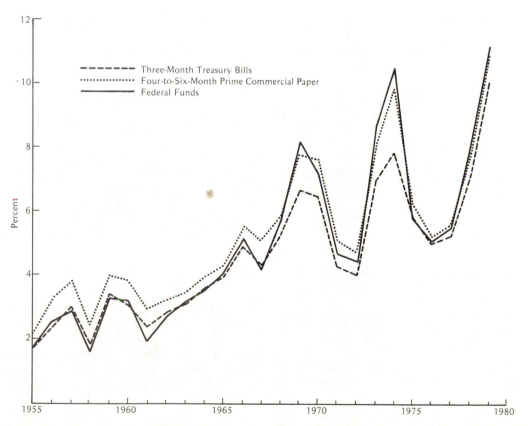

Figure 3–1: Average Annual Interest Rates on Selected Money Market Instruments. Source: *Economic Report of the President, Federal Reserve Bulletin.*

regular sources of funds for certain sectors, the money markets provide a medium for liquidity adjustment. The major money market instruments are summarized below:

Instrument	Issuer (Borrower)	Volume*
Treasury bills	U.S. government	$216 bil
Agency securities	U.S. government agencies	194 bil**
Commercial paper	Large finance companies and nonfinancial corporations	125 bil
Negotiable CDs	Large commercial banks	116 bil
Banker's acceptances	Corporations, normally importers (with the guarantee of a bank)	55 bil
Repurchase agreements	U.S. government security dealers	42 bil***
Federal funds	Commercial banks	100 + bil
Eurodollars	They represent liabilities of major banks	80 bil

*Volumes change substantially with economic and money market conditions.

**Including long term issues.

***Including both loans to dealers and repurchase agreements.

QUESTIONS

1. How could an individual with $10,000 to invest go about purchasing a Treasury bill?

2. Using the *Federal Reserve Bulletin,* find the yields for various money market instruments of three- and six-month maturity. How do you explain the differences between rates?

3. Why does the Federal Reserve System itself hold large quantities of Treasury bills?

4. Where is the secondary market for Treasury bills located?

5. If a decision is made to increase the money supply, what agency acts, and how does the agency act with regard to Treasury bills?

6. What is the primary purpose for which federally sponsored agencies borrow and re-lend money?

7. Why would a company issue commercial paper instead of using bank borrowing?

8 Why would issuers of commercial paper maintain back-up lines of credit with banks?

9. What types of companies are the primary borrowers of funds through the commercial paper market?

10. Why would the regulatory authorities remove interest rate restrictions on large bank deposits (in the form of large denomination certificates of deposit) while maintaining regulation Q ceilings for smaller deposits?

11. For a bank that is "loaned up" and still wants to help a loan customer, what is the advantage of a banker's acceptance?

12. Why are Federal funds rates among the most volatile of money market rates?

PROBLEMS

1. A bid of 97.270 is accepted on three-month Treasury bills. What annual interest rate would be published?

2. For the above Treasury bill, restate the annual interest rate in a way that would make it comparable to rates quoted on bonds.

3. For the Treasury bill in problem 1, assume that the quoted annual interest rate has risen to 12 percent 30 days after

issue. What price will the Treasury bills be selling at? What annual rate would the holder have earned if he bought the Treasury bill when it was first issued and resold after thirty days?

4. At a 14 percent federal funds rate, what would be the dollar interest on a three-day (week-end) loan of $10 million in the federal funds market?

5. A 91-day negotiable certificate of deposit is quoted at annual interest rate of 13.8 percent and 91-day Treasury bills are quoted at 14.2 percent annual rate. Restate these rates on a comparable basis.

SELECTED REFERENCES

Bacon, Peter W., and Richard Williams, "Interest Rate Futures Trading: New Tool for the Financial Manager," *Financial Management,* Vol. 5 (Spring, 1976), pp. 32–38.

Cook, Timothy Q. (ed.), *Instruments of the Money Market.* Richmond, Virginia: Federal Reserve Bank of Richmond, 1977.

Fildes, Robert A., and M. Desmond Fitzgerald, "Efficiency and Premiums in the Short-term Money Market," *Journal of Money, Credit and Banking,* Vol. 12 (November, 1980), pp. 615–629.

James, John A., *Money and Capital Markets in Postbellum America.* Princeton, New Jersey: Princeton University Press, 1978.

Money Market Instruments, Cleveland, Ohio: Federal Reserve Bank of Cleveland, 1970.

Puglisi, Donald J., "Commercial Paper: A Primer," *Federal Home Loan Bank Board Journal,* Vol. 13 (December, 1980), pp. 5–10.

Rendleman, Richard J., and Christopher E. Carabini, "The Efficiency of the Treasury Bill Futures Market," *Journal of Finance,* Vol. 34 (September, 1979), pp. 895–914.

Senchak, Andrew J., Jr., and Donald M. Heep, "Auction Profits in the Treasury Bill Market," *Financial Management,* Vol. 4 (Summer, 1975), pp. 53–62.

Chapter 4

Capital Markets

The capital markets are normally thought of as the markets in which long-term securities, both debt and equity, are bought and sold. The securities involved are corporate stock and bonds; federal, state, and local government bonds and notes; and marketable mortgages. A broader definition would include direct loans, but is not used here because those aspects of the financial system are covered in other parts of this book. While the money markets are primarily liquidity adjustment markets, the capital markets are primarily markets for long-term funds to meet permanent or semi-permanent needs.

Risk is an important factor in the capital markets. While money market instruments are nearly risk-free with regard to default and involve minimal risks of price fluctuation due to their short-term maturities, both types of risk are frequently present in capital market securities. With the exception of U.S. government securities, all capital market instruments involve some risk of default. Even among those with no risk of default,

there is still a substantial risk of price fluctuation with changes in the general level of interest rates. For example, a $1,000 bond with a 6 percent annual interest payment and 20 years to maturity would decline in market value to $657 if the level of required interest rate for this type of security rose to 10 percent.[1]

Because corporations and government units meet a major portion of their external financing needs in the capital markets, the smooth functioning of these markets is important for both. Because financial institutions hold the majority of all capital market securities, the financial institution manager should have a good understanding of the capital markets. In this chapter, we discuss significant aspects of the capital markets: types of securities, the markets in which they are bought and sold, the users of funds, and the suppliers of funds.

---

[1] The mathematics of value are discussed in Chapters 5 and 6.

CORPORATE SECURITIES

In addition to private sources of credit such as trade credit and bank loans, corporations rely heavily on the capital markets to meet their needs for capital. They acquire funds by selling bonds and shares in ownership of their business (stock). For larger firms, both bonds and stock enjoy active primary and secondary markets. Financial institutions furnish a significant amount of funds to corporations through the purchase of these securities, particularly bonds.

STOCK

Stock represents ownership of a corporation. It is sold by corporations at the time of formation and when they need additional equity capital for expansion. It is also regularly resold by investors who need funds or who wish to adjust their investment portfolios. Stock comes in two primary varieties, common and preferred, with common stock representing the largest volume.

Common stock represents residual ownership. The common shareholders own the corporation similar to the way a group of partners would own a business not organized as a corporation. Unlike most other securities, common stock does not promise any particular return to its purchaser. All earnings not specifically owed to others are used for the benefit of the common shareholders, either paid out as dividends or reinvested with the hope of achieving even greater dividends in the future.

Since common shareholders are not promised a specific return, they must have some method of exercising control over the company to enforce their claim. The primary method of exercising control is through the election of a board of directors, who in turn elect the top management of the corporation. In a sense the common shareholders exercise control over the corporation in the same manner citizens of a democracy exercise control over government. In addition to the right to vote for a board of directors, the common shareholders have certain other rights:

1) the right to receive dividends, when voted by the directors;

2) the right to examine the books of the corporation;[2]

3) the right to vote on mergers;

4) the pre-emptive right—the right to be given the opportunity to buy a proportion of any new equity issue equal to the proportion of existing equity presently held;

5) the right to a list of fellow shareholders.

Thus the common shareholders, unlike creditors, are promised no fixed return but enjoy residual claims and exercise control over the corporation.

Preferred stock is an intermediate security with some features of debt and some features of common stock. Typically, preferred stock carries a stated dividend rate, but this dividend is not a legal requirement and is paid only if voted each period by the board of directors. Thus preferred shareholders expect a fixed return but cannot force the company to pay the dividend. Usually their interest is protected in two ways. First, most preferred stock is cumulative, meaning that dividends cannot be paid on common stock until dividends not paid to preferred stockholders during previous periods are paid. Second, preferred stockholders generally have the right to elect a minority of the board of directors if dividends have not been paid for a specific number of quarters. While the pressure that can be applied by preferred shareholders is less than that which can be brought by creditors, it is usually sufficient to assure dividends except in times of hardship. Insurance companies are major purchasers of preferred stock because 85 percent of the dividends received by a corporation are normally excluded from taxable income.

---

[2] The courts have normally ruled that a copy of the annual report satisfies this right.

As illustrated in Table 4-1, the value of new stock sold is much smaller than the value of new bonds. However, the total amount of stock outstanding is several times

Table 4-1:

**Primary Market Volume, 1980
(in billions)**

	Volume of Issues	Net Increase in Amount Outstanding
Corporate Securities		
Bonds	$ 53	$ 36
Stock	20	17
U.S. Government Securities		
Bills	428	
Bonds and Notes	117	127
State and Municipal	48	22
Mortgages	n.a.	125

Source: Federal Reserve Bulletin, Treasury Bulletin

the amount of bonds. The smaller value of new equity occurs because retained earnings are an important source of equity and because stock does not have a maturity date at which it must be refunded. Furthermore, some debt is convertible to common stock, resulting in a further decrease in the amount of new stock that must be sold to increase the equity base.

As illustrated in Table 4-2, stock is primarily held by individuals. More than two-thirds of all common stock is held by individuals, with insurance companies and pension funds holding most of the rest. Most depository financial institutions hold little or no stock because the residual ownership nature causes it to be excessively risky for their portfolios.

CORPORATE BONDS

Bonds are marketable debt instruments of corporations. They are long-term promissory notes, normally with maturities between 5 and 30 years, and normally issued in denominations of $1,000. Bonds represent

Table 4-2:

**Amounts of Outstanding Securities by Type and Owner, 1979
(all numbers in billions of dollars)**

Issuer / Holder	Corporate & Foreign Bonds	Corporate Stock	U.S. Government Securities	State & Local Government Securities	Mortgages*
Total	455.7	1,244.5	916.8	312.7	1,333.7
Households	71.6	906.9	243.0	74.3	123.0
Non-financial Business	—	—	9.5	4.0	—
State & Local Governments	—	—	68.7	8.2	20.7
U.S. Government	—	—	32.1	—	11.3
Monetary Authority	—	—	126.2	—	—
Commercial Banks	7.7	0.1	148.2	135.9	246.8
Nonbank Finance	366.3	287.6	162.9	90.4	727.5
Other	10.2	49.9	124.2	—	204.4

*Including marketable and nonmarketable mortgages. $295 billion of the mortgage debt is owed by nonfinancial businesses.

Source: Board of Governers of the Federal Reserve System

a major source of external capital to American corporations.

There are two primary documents involved with a bond. These are the *bond certificate and the indenture*. The bond certificate is the evidence of ownership of the particular claim and states a limited amount of information, such as when and how interest and principal are to be paid. The certificate may be in either registered or coupon form, with the registered form being more common. With the registered form, the corporation has a record of who owns each bond and mails interest payments to them at the times specified, typically semi-annually. With the coupon form, a coupon must be cut from the bond and turned in to the corporation or a financial institution such as a commercial bank that handles coupons as a customer service. The risk of loss is, of course, greater with the coupon form since interest is paid to whoever has the coupon.

The indenture is a lengthy document, often running to hundreds of pages, and specifying the details of the agreement between borrower and lenders. The indenture covers provisions for retiring the issue, a detailed description of pledged assets, identification and responsibilities of the trustee, and other related matters. In addition, it contains a set of restrictive covenants such as a restriction on the issuance of additional debt, restriction on the sale of assets, and a requirement that a particular level of liquidity be maintained. While the indenture represents an agreement between the company and the lenders, it is not an agreement reached through negotiations with them. The indenture is prepared before the bonds are issued and contains the provisions that are felt to be necessary to successfully sell the issue. The trustee, normally a bank or trust company, acts as the representative of the bondholders in enforcing the provisions of the indenture.

Bonds differ with regard to a number of features. One such feature is *callability*. The company frequently retains the right to retire the bonds before maturity by repurchasing them from the holders. Such a provision is usually seen as important to the issuing company because it gives the flexibility to change the financial structure as necessary. If a bond is callable, the call price that must be paid by the company is normally higher than the face value of the bond by a premium equal to between six months' and one year's interest. Thus, bondholders receive some compensation in the event of early retirement.

Bonds also differ with regard to security offered. A *debenture* is a bond that is secured only by the general good name of the company. Because many debentures are issued by the more credit-worthy companies, the default rate is frequently lower than on bonds secured by the pledge of specific assets. Pledging generally takes one of two forms. The mortgage bond is based on the pledge of specific real assets—land and buildings—as collateral. Equipment trust certificates are based on the pledge of equipment such as railroad cars rather than on land or buildings.

Convertibility is another important feature of many bond issues. A convertible bond can be exchanged for a fixed number of shares of common stock at the option of the bondholder. This feature gives the bondholder the potential for a capital gain if the value of the company's stock rises while still offering the contractual payment of a bond. It is used either as a "sweetener" to sell a risky bond issue or as a sequential method of financing for a company constantly in need of funds. As one issue is converted, it provides the equity base for a new debt issue.

Repayment of bonds can take one of several forms, with a sinking fund being a common method. With a sinking fund provision, the indenture calls for annual payments to a sinking fund managed by the trustee. Depending on the conditions specified in the indenture, payments are invested in safe securities to accumulate funds for repayment at maturity or used to purchase a certain amount of the issue each year and retire it. If part of the issue is to be retired each year, it will be purchased in the open market if the market price is below the call price and will be called if the market price is over the call price.

Alternatives to the sinking fund arrangement include a balloon arrangement and serial bonds. Under a *balloon arrangement,* a large portion or all of the issue is repaid at maturity. In such cases, the company frequently issues new debt to retire existing debt. In the case of a *serial issue,* different bonds in the issue have different maturity dates so that the issue is retired systematically over its life. This has an advantage over

the use of the call provision in that the buyer knows how long the bonds will be outstanding.

Bonds also differ with regard to risk, which in turn depends on the credit worthiness of the company issuing them and the quality of collateral provided. Investment advisory services, with Moody's Corporation and Standard and Poor's Corporation being the best known, rate them according to risk. Table 4-3 shows the rating system used by Moody's. Interest rates are affected by rating, with the lower ratings carrying higher interest rates as compensation for risk. A bond with a Moody's Baa rating will typically carry an interest rate from one to two percentage points above that for a bond with

Table 4-3:

Key to Moody's Corporate Ratings

Aaa

Bonds which are rated Aaa are judged to be of the best quality. They carry the smallest degree of investment risk and are generally referred to as "gilt edge." Interest payments are protected by a large or by an exceptionally stable margin and principal is secure. While the various protective elements are likely to change, such changes as can be visualized are most unlikely to impair the fundamentally strong position of such issues.

Aa

Bonds which are rated Aa are judged to be of high quality by all standards. Together with the Aaa group they comprise what are generally known as high grade bonds. They are rated lower than the best bonds because margins of protection may not be as large as in Aaa securities or fluctuations of protective elements may be of greater amplitude or there may be other elements present which make the long term risks appear somewhat larger than in Aaa securities.

A

Bonds which are rated A possess many favorable investment attributes and are to be considered as upper medium grade obligations. Factors giving security to principal and interest are considered adequate but elements may be present which suggest a susceptibility to impairment sometime in the future.

Baa

Bonds which are rated Baa are considered as medium grade obligations, i.e., they are neither highly protected nor poorly secured. Interest payments and principal security appear adequate for the present but certain protective elements may be lacking or may be characteristically unreliable over any great length of time. Such bonds lack outstanding investment characteristics and in fact have speculative characteristics as well.

Table 4-3: Cont.

Ba

Bonds which are rated Ba are judged to have speculative elements; their future cannot be considered as well assured. Often the protection of interest and principal payments may be very moderate and thereby not well safeguarded during both good and bad times over the future. Uncertainty of position characterizes bonds in this class.

B

Bonds which are rated B generally lack characteristics of the desirable investment. Assurance of interest and principal payments or of maintenance of other terms of the contract over any long period of time may be small.

Caa

Bonds which are rated Caa are of poor standing. Such issues may be in default or there may be present elements of danger with respect to principal or interest.

Ca

Bonds which are rated Ca represent obligations which are speculative in a high degree. Such issues are often in default or have other marked shortcomings.

C

Bonds which are rated C are the lowest rated class of bonds and issues so rated can be regarded as having extremely poor prospects of ever attaining any real investment standing.

Source: *Moody's Bond Record*

a Aaa rating. Chapter 6 contains a detailed discussion of these interest rate differentials.

When a company borrows by selling its bonds, the bonds are normally sold through an investment banker. Purchasers of the bonds who later wish to sell them turn to the secondary markets consisting of both the organized exchanges and the over-the-counter market. The operations of both of these markets are covered in some detail in the following sections of this chapter.

Corporations in virtually every industry category finance part of their operations through bonds. The market is, however, restricted to relatively large companies. Fixed administrative costs are such as to rule out small bond issues. On a small bond issue of under $1 million, the cost of issuance can run as high as 20 percent while issue costs can fall to 1 percent or less for an issue of several hundred million dollars.

While individuals do hold corporate bonds as investments, the majority of bonds are held as investments by financial institutions. Only about one-sixth of all corporate bonds are held by individuals. Seventy percent of all outstanding bonds are held by either pension funds or insurance companies.

PRIMARY MARKETS FOR STOCKS AND BONDS

Companies normally employ the services of an investment banker for selling both stock and bond issues to private investors and financial institutions. A major exception is private placement of bonds, which involves an entire issue being sold to one or a few financial institutions. Investment banking services are provided by companies that specialize only in investment banking and by many of the larger brokerage houses.

Investment bankers normally act as dealers, purchasing an entire issue from the issuing corporation and reselling it in smaller quantities to investors interested in holding it. Occasionally a best efforts arrangement will be used, wherein the investment banker does not buy the entire issue but merely sells as much of it as possible for the issuing company. The steps followed in the issuance of securities through an investment banker are discussed on the following pages. Essentially the same approach applies to the issue of stocks and corporate bonds.

Pre-underwriting conference. The company meets with the investment banker to determine if the investment banker is interested in underwriting an issue for it and what type of issue—debt or equity—would be saleable. Investment bankers wish to maintain their reputation and will not sell an issue unless they have carefully evaluated the company and found it to be sound with good prospects for success. In addition, different investment bankers specialize in different types of issues and a particular investment banking house may not be interested in the issue even though a number of others are. If a general agreement is reached, an *underwriting agreement* is signed between the company and the investment banker.

Registration statement. Once an underwriting agreement has been reached, the issue must be registered with the Securities and Exchange Commission (SEC). The issue cannot be sold until the registration becomes effective—20 days after the registration statement is filed unless the SEC objects or asks for more time. The SEC uses this period to study the registration statement and determine if the appropriate information is being furnished. The SEC does not rule on the quality of the investment, but on whether appropriate information about the investment is properly disclosed. The investment

banker cannot sell any of the issue during this period, but can circulate a preliminary prospectus (also called a "red herring") giving all the information in the regular prospectus except the price at which the issue will be sold.

The prospectus is a statement designed to be helpful to a potential investor in deciding whether to purchase some of the securities being offered. It contains a detailed description of the company, detailed financial statements, and a discussion of the way in which the funds will be used. In the case of a debt issue, it also contains the various provisions of the debt instruments, such as restrictions on further borrowing, when and how interest is to be paid, and so on.

Underwriting Syndicate and Selling Group. Issues worth hundreds of millions of dollars are not uncommon and issues worth several billion dollars are not unheard of. Since the investment banker normally buys the issue and then attempts to resell it, capital is being put at risk. Very seldom can a single investment banker absorb the entire issue. Normally an underwriting syndicate is formed by the originating investment banker. With this arrangement, each of a number of investment bankers buys part of the issue and resells it. Each investment banker has its own selling group—typically a group of brokerage firms—acting as a group of retailers while the investment bankers act as wholesalers. While the selling group handles the actual sale, the underwriters accept the risk of the issue not being sold.

Price Setting and Sale. After the registration becomes effective, the price at which the issue is to be sold is set. Typically this is just before issue time because of market volatility. The selling group then proceeds to sell the issue through public advertisements or contact with investors who may be interested. Since potentially interested investors are notified before the offering via preliminary prospectus, the entire issue is frequently sold in a matter of hours once the registration becomes effective. In any event, the investment bankers hope to sell the entire issue within a few days because they cannot accept the capital commitment and risk of a long-term holding.

Market Stabilization. This is the last act of the managing underwriter. The underwriter stands ready to buy at the offering price any part of the issue that investors attempt to resell before the entire issue is sold. Thus there is not a risk of a decline in market price before the entire issue is sold. However, this price pegging is limited to a maximum of 30 days. If all the issue is not sold by that time, the investment banker must simply face losses or hold the remainder of the issue hoping the price will rise.

Costs of flotation depend on the size of the issue, the quality of the issuer, and whether it is debt or equity. A recent study found that the average flotation cost as a percent of net proceeds was 13.4 percent for equity issues of one half to one million dollars. For equity issues over one hundred million dollars, the average cost was 3.95 percent.[3] As indicated earlier, issue costs can fall to less than 1 percent for a large bond issue. The problem for small issues is that because many costs are fixed, they are very high as a percentage of the issue.

SECONDARY MARKETS FOR CORPORATE STOCKS AND BONDS

The secondary markets for corporate securities consist of the organized exchanges, such as the New York Stock Exchange, and the over-the-counter market. The greatest volume of stock transactions in the secondary markets occurs in the organized exchanges, although the vast majority of stocks are not listed (eligible for sale and purchase) on organized exchanges. Stocks of large corporations, particularly those that are frequently bought and sold, are normally listed on an exchange. The majority of corporate bond volume, on the other hand, occurs in the over-the-counter markets.

The secondary market for stock is much more active than the primary market, with annual trading volume equal to 20 times the volume of new issues. Bonds tend to change hands less frequently, often being held to maturity by the original purchaser.

While funds are not furnished directly to users through the secondary markets, these markets are important because they provide liquidity and a continuous test of value. The owner of a security can find the current value by checking yesterday's market price in the newspaper and can sell the securities quickly if funds are needed. Thus the existence of an active secondary market makes corporate securities more attractive and makes it easier for the corporation to raise funds. In this section, the secondary markets are discussed in detail.

Organized Exchanges Most resale of stocks occurs on the organized exchanges. The two major organized exchanges are the New York Stock Exchange and the American Stock Exchange, both located in New York City. The New York Stock Exchange accounts for approximately 80 percent of total stock exchange volume and the American Stock Exchange accounts for approximately 10 percent. The concentration of this business on one street in southern Manhattan has led to Wall Street being synonymous with finance. Large regional exchanges include the Midwest, the West Coast, and the Baltimore-Philadelphia-Washington exchanges.

The primary purpose of an organized exchange is to provide a physical meeting place for the buying and selling of securities by exchange members, either for themselves or for those they represent. Additionally, the exchanges provide communication and bookkeeping systems for recording and re-

---

[3] Clifford W. Smith, Jr., "Substitute Methods for Raising Additional Capital: Rights Offerings Versus Underwritten Issues," *Journal of Financial Economics* (December, 1977), Vol. 5, No. 3.

porting transactions. Finally, the exchanges provide sets of rules and enforcement procedures to insure an orderly market place.

The organized exchanges are *continuous auction* markets. The floor of the exchange consists of a number of different posts—meeting places for transactions in a particular group of securities. For example, the New York Stock Exchange provides a market for approximately 2200 different securities and divides them among 27 trading posts.

Transactions are based on bid and ask prices. For example, a broker carrying an order for a client who would like to purchase 100 shares of IBM at $70 per share would go to the trading post for IBM and call out the bid. If someone accepted the bid, a transaction would occur. Someone wishing to sell would call out his asking price in the same fashion. These orders are described as limit orders because the investor only wishes to buy or sell if a certain price can be obtained. A *market order* would instruct the broker to buy or sell at the best price available. The broker would then take the best price available from those at the trading post. Once a sale has been agreed on, the price and quantity are recorded and reported to the public. Thus there is a continuous test of value.

Anyone who visited an exchange, particularly on a brisk trading day, would question the use of the word "organized." To the casual observer, it more closely resembles a melee. People are rushing to and from the various posts to communicate with or join other people there. Trading consists of a group of people shouting at each other in what appears to be a totally unorganized manner. However, to the trained, quick-witted participant, it provides a swift efficient way of buying and selling securities at the best price currently available in the marketplace.

The people trading in a security at a particular post are of several types. First, there are the brokers trading on behalf of clients around the country who have placed an order to buy or sell through their local brokerage house. Second, there are members who buy and sell for their own accounts, speculating on short-term movements in prices. Third, there are specialists, a group of members who have available to them special information about supply and demand as reflected in unfilled *limit orders*.[4] In exchange for this information, they are required to "make a market" by continually posting both a bid and an ask price. There is only one specialist for each security, although each specialist is responsible for more than one security. The specialist normally quotes an ask price of 12½ to 25 cents above his bid price. He thus guarantees that a continuous market will exist. In exchange for this service he makes a profit through information about supply and demand, and through selling at an asking price above his bid price.

Volume of sales on the organized exchanges far exceeds the volume of new stock sold. The stock of a company, once issued, typically remains outstanding for the life of the company. However, the typical owner of stock may hold it for a few years or less, with some purchasers (called floor traders) holding the stock for no more than a few hours. Annual volume on the New York Stock Exchange alone is in excess of $150 billion a year. More than one-fifth of the shares listed on the New York Stock Exchange are sold each year.

Over-the-Counter Markets A membership in an organized exchange is referred to as a *seat,* though its owner will find no place to sit on the exchange floor. Likewise, the over-the-counter market (OTC) does not involve a counter. The OTC consists of a group of investment houses acting as market makers in certain securities and a commu-

---

[4] A limit order is one for which the price is specified. The alternative is a market order which instructs the broker to buy or sell at the best price presently available.

nication network to tie them together. The stocks of large, well known corporations are generally listed on one of the organized stock exchanges.[5] Stocks of lesser known companies and most bonds are bought and sold on the OTC.

In the OTC, one or more investment houses act as market makers, standing ready to buy and sell like the specialist on an organized exchange. Instead of a physical meeting place, market makers and brokers are tied together through the National Association of Security Dealers Automated Quotation System (NASDAQ). A central computer system and telecommunication lines tie this market together. It has been argued that modern technology has rendered physical meeting places obsolete. Indeed, the present NASDAQ system was designed with enough capacity to handle all organized exchange volume.

EUROBONDS

Eurobonds are a specialized type of corporate debt issue, designed to increase saleability by decreasing the risk of loss from currency devaluation. A Eurobond is defined as a bond denominated in a currency other than that of the country in which it is being sold. Thus an American company doing business in Europe might decide to finance its European operations by selling bonds in Europe but denominating them in dollars.

Eurobonds can be denominated in any currency and some have even given the holder a choice of currencies. Dollars have traditionally been the most popular currency, partly because the Interest Equalization Tax of 1964 encouraged American companies to finance foreign operations by issuing debt overseas.

Like domestic bonds, Eurobonds are issued through investment bankers. The main

difference is that they are not advertised to the public, but are sold entirely through direct contact with potential buyers. They are rarely sold through private placement, as is frequently done in the case of domestic bonds.

U.S. GOVERNMENT DEBT

Beginning with borrowing to finance wars and expanding with increases in social programs, the U.S. government has become a major borrower in the capital markets. U.S. government securities are unique in that they are the only securities in the U.S. capital markets considered risk-free with regard to default. Another factor leading to particular importance of U.S. government debt is its use as part of economic stabilization policy.

U.S. government debt is issued in different forms. First, there are the regular Treasury issues: bills, notes, and bonds. Bills have maturities of one year or less, notes have maturities of one to five years, and bonds have maturities of longer than five years. In 1981, 48 percent of the privately held U.S. government debt was in the form of bills, 37 percent was in the form of notes, and 15 percent was in the form of bonds.

In addition to the regular Treasury issues, several U.S. government agencies issue debt. These agencies were discussed individually in Chapter 3. Most of the agencies act primarily as financial institutions, selling securities and using the proceeds to provide funds to the mortgage markets. The proportion of their debts financed by bonds depends on market conditions. In general, though, the bulk of their financing is long-term.

While interest is earned on treasury bills only through the discount from face value at which they are sold, other securities pay interest based on the face value, normally on a semi-annual basis.

Approximately 44 percent of U.S. gov-

---

[5] Certain types of companies, particularly banks and breweries, have not been listed by tradition, although it appears that this tradition is beginning to break down.

ernment debt is held by U.S. government trust funds, state and local governments, and the federal reserve banks. Thus only 56 percent of the total is in private hands, with 14 percent of the total being held by individuals, mostly in the form of savings bonds. A small amount is held by nonfinancial corporations and the rest is held by financial institutions, with commercial banks being particularly large holders.

PRIMARY MARKETS

Unlike corporations, the federal government does not use underwriting. The Federal Reserve acts as fiscal agent, handling the mechanics of sale, but neither underwrites nor markets the issues. Thus it is important that the yield be set so as to make the issues attractive to investors. The yields are usually set with the objective of achieving a slight increase in price following initial issue. If this is done, a type of unofficial underwriting occurs, with U.S. government security dealers and commercial banks acquiring part of a new issue as a short-term holding, thus easing its absorption into the market.

The issue procedure differs from the auction market for Treasury bills. The yield of the issue is set so that the Treasury is relatively sure the bonds or notes will sell. Press releases are given out and descriptive circulars are sent to potential buyers. The issues are then allocated to those wishing to purchase. On average, approximately two-thirds of the dollar value of new issues goes to commercial banks and U.S. government securities dealers.

Obviously, a large proportion of U.S. government bond sales occur merely to refund maturing issues. Sometimes, because of a desire to increase average maturity of outstanding debt, advance refunding is used. With this technique, new long-term securities of longer maturity are offered in exchange for issues that are close to their maturity date. Yields of the new securities must be higher than those of the existing matur-

ities, since conversion is voluntary and there must be some incentive to convert.

SECONDARY MARKETS

While it was once common practice to buy and sell U.S. government bonds and notes in the organized exchanges, the market has shifted to the U.S. government securities dealers. For each issue, the dealers continually post prices at which they will buy and prices at which they will sell. Thus they provide a continuous market for those wishing to buy or sell U.S. government securities.

STATE AND LOCAL GOVERNMENT BONDS

Bonds issued by state and local governments are called *municipal bonds*. They provide a distinct investment opportunity because the interest received from such bonds is exempt from federal income tax.

Municipals may be guaranteed by the *full faith and credit* of the government unit involved or they may be guaranteed only by *revenue* from a specific investment such as a water system or toll bridge. In recent years, nearly 60 percent of the newly issued municipal bonds have been revenue bonds. The building of schools, roads, and other capital projects has traditionally been financed through the issuance of bonds, although some cities—New York is the most notable example—have used debt to finance current spending.

Because of their tax status, municipal bonds can be sold at yields well below those for other securities, with high grade municipal bonds normally selling to yield several percentage points below U.S. government bonds.

Municipal bonds are attractive only to investors facing relatively high tax rates. At a municipal bond rate of 5.75 percent and a corporate bond rate of 9.50 percent, the tax rate necessary to make municipals an attractice investment is found as follows:

$$9.5(1 - T) = 5.75$$
$$T = .4$$

In the above example, municipal bonds would be an attractive alternative to corporate bonds if the investor faced a marginal federal income tax rate of 40 percent or greater. The primary holders of municipal bonds are wealthy individuals, banks, and property and casualty insurance companies.

Municipal bonds are sold through underwriting in a manner similar to corporate bonds. An important difference is that banks, which do not underwrite corporate securities, participate in the underwriting of municipals. The underwriter of the original issue also normally makes a second market by acting as a dealer.

Municipal bonds are not risk-free, as illustrated by a number of defaults. The rating services that rate corporate bonds also rate municipal bonds, with yields varying according to rating. A sample analysis of a municipal bond by a rating agency appears in Table 4-4.

With state and municipal government spending being the fastest growing segment of government spending in the 1970s, and with state and local government debt already exceeding one-third of the Federal debt in 1981, municipal debt is becoming increasingly important in the financial markets. The fact that municipal debt is primarily long-term while much Federal government financing is short-term further contributes to the importance of municipal debt in the capital markets. Municipal debt can be expected to assume increasing importance in the portfolios of financial institutions. An understanding of the risks and rewards involved will be of continuing importance.

SUMMARY

Capital markets are the markets for long-term securities, both debt and equity. The primary instruments bought and sold in these markets are corporate stock and bonds, U.S. government bonds, state and local government bonds, and marketable mortgages. Companies and government units wishing to raise funds turn to a system of primary markets made up mostly of investment bankers who purchase the issue and resell it. Original purchasers of securities may hold them until

Table 4-4:

Sample Bond Rating

State of New Mexico
Highway Debentures Rated "AAA"

RATING RATIONALE: The Highway Debentures are special obligations of the State, payable from gasoline excise taxes, motor vehicle registration fees, and a limited $1.5 million general property tax which has never been levied or used. This issue is part of a $20 million authorization, of which $5.7 million has been issued and retired. The State may not issue any parity debentures beyond the initial authorization. Presently, there are no plans to issue the remaining authorized debentures. Motor fuel taxes and registration fees covered estimated maximum debt service 44.20 times in 1978. Total pledged revenues, including the $1.5 million tax levy, would have covered estimated maximum debt service 50 times during this period. The state has enacted legislation which, effective in 1980, will provide for the escalation of the gasoline tax. The tax rate, which will use $0.07 a gallon as a base, is determined by reference to the average wholesale price of gasoline plus federal excise taxes. The annual incremental increase/decrease may not exceed $0.01 per gallon for each 12-month period.

Based upon the overwhelming debt service coverage, the limited general property tax pledge and the short maturity schedule, we are rating these bonds "AAA."

PROPOSED ISSUE: $5,000,000 Highway Debentures, Series 1979, selling June 26, 1979.

Dated: July 15, 1979.

Due: Serially 1980–1984; the debentures are not subject to redemption prior to their respective maturities.

Source: Standard and Poor's *Fixed Income Investor*

maturity or resell them in a secondary market system composed of organized security exchanges, the over-the-counter security market, and a number of dealers who buy and sell for their own inventory.

A review of Tables 4-1 and 4-2 is helpful in developing a perspective on the participants in this market and the importance of various instruments. As Table 4-1 shows, U.S. government securities dominate in the primary markets, followed by mortgage debt (much of which is not marketable), state and local government obligations, and corporate securities. Within corporate securities, debt instruments clearly dominate equity securities in the primary markets.

A somewhat different picture is seen when we look at total holdings as opposed to new issues and increases in amounts outstanding. Corporations are dominant in terms of the value of total securities outstanding, followed by mortgages, U.S. government securities, and state and local government securities. Within the corporate securities, equity dominates debt in terms of total amount outstanding. However, it should be recognized that much of the equity is not publicly traded and the table does not include corporate debt other than bonds.

An examination of the holders of various securities in Table 4–2 illustrates the point made in Chapter 1 that households are the primary suppliers of funds. They hold the majority of equity securities directly. While financial institutions hold the majority of debt securities, they are largely using the funds of households.

QUESTIONS

1. What are the primary types of risk involved in the ownership of capital market instruments?

2. What are the rights of a common stockholder?

3. Explain the differences between common stock and preferred stock.

4. Why are lengthy indentures required for corporate bonds when a similar document is not required for commercial paper issued by the same corporation?

5. Select a bond issue listed in the *Wall Street Journal*. Find the bond's Moody's rating. Would you recommend this bond to an investor looking for a safe investment?

6. Summarize the process by which a new stock or bond issue is sold.

7. Leading stocks are traded at a physical location (New York Stock Exchange or American Stock Exchange) while there is no central physical location for the purchase and sale of money market instruments. How do you account for this difference in trading arrangements?

8. Why would a company use underwriting for a stock or bond issue? Why does the U.S. government not use underwriting?

9. U.S. government issues are considered risk-free with regard to default. Is there any way an investor can lose money on an investment in U.S. government bonds?

10. Explain the difference between a full faith and credit bond and a revenue bond. Which type is likely to be more risky?

11. Since municipal bonds are generally considered more risky than U.S. government bonds, why do they sell at lower yields?

SELECTED REFERENCES

Bradford, William D., David J. Hakman, and Andrew H. Field, "Mortgage-Backed Securities: How Profitable Are They?" *Federal Home Loan Bank Board Journal*, Vol. 12 (August, 1979), pp. 3–7.

Butler, H. L., and J. D. Allen, "Dow-Jones Industrial Average Re-examined," *Financial Analysts Journal,* Vol. 35 (November/December, 1979), pp. 23–30.

Chalker, William E., and James E. McNulty, "The Forward Commitment Market for Mortgage-Backed Securities," *Federal Home Loan Bank Board Journal,* Vol. 13 (June, 1980), pp. 2–15.

Dougall, Herbert E., and Jack E. Gaumitz, *Capital Markets and Institutions.* 3d. ed. Englewood Cliffs, New Jersey: Prentice-Hall, 1975.

Grube, R. Corwin, O. Maurice Joy, and Don B. Panton, "Market Response to Federal Reserve Changes in the Initial Margin Requirement," *Journal of Finance,* Vol. 4 (June, 1979), pp. 659–674.

Hendershott, Patric H., *Understanding Capital Markets: A Flow-of-Funds Financial Model.* Lexington, Massachusetts: D.C. Heath, 1977.

Mendelson, M., and J. W. Peake, "Which Way to a National Market System?" *Financial Analysts Journal,* Vol. 35 (September/October, 1979), pp. 31–42.

Chapter 5

Interest Analysis

Interest plays the same role in financial markets that price plays in the market for goods. Funds are allocated to the uses that can pay the highest rent. Interest is thus rent for money. A financial institution manager must have a thorough understanding of its meaning and computation.

Lenders are required to notify borrowers what interest rate they are charging and are sometimes restricted by law as to the interest rate they can charge. Therefore they must understand the impact of such things as service charges on the effective interest rate. Portfolio managers must be able to do such things as determine the interest rate earned on a bond that is purchased for less than its face value. Pension fund and life insurance company managers must be able to determine the amount of money they will have if funds are invested for a set number of years at a particular interest rate. And these are but a few examples of the ways in which managers must use interest analysis. In this chapter, an understanding of interest definitions, principles, and practices is developed.

INTEREST RATE COMPARISONS

Both actual interest rates and methods of computation vary between markets. It is necessary to distinguish between the various ways in which interest rates are quoted or implied and to develop a methodology by which explicit or implicit interest charges may be calculated and directly compared. The difficulties in comparing the true cost of money over time are illustrated by the following situations:

1. A department store charges 1½ percent per month on the average outstanding account balance.

2. A commercial bank offers to lease industrial equipment. Monthly lease payments are 3.38 percent of the equipment purchase price on a 36-month financial lease.

3. An automobile dealer offers to finance $3,000 of the cost of a new car for three years at an annual add-on interest rate of 6 percent. Repayment terms call for monthly payments. In other words,

the dealer charges total interest of .06 × 3 × 3,000 = $540 and the monthly payment is (3,000 + 540)/36 = $98.33.

4. A mortgage payable monthly over 30 years is negotiated. Although the stated annual interest rate is 8 percent, terms of the mortgage call for payment of a service charge equal to three points (3 percent of the mortgage) at the time loan proceeds are disbursed.

5. A bank negotiates a $1,000 commercial loan with the interest rate stated as 7 percent discount. Loan terms call for repayment of the total loan one year hence. With this arrangement, the borrower receives $1,000 less 7 percent interest, or $930, and pays back $1,000.

6. A security originally issued several years ago may be purchased for $918.90. The holder of the security will receive $30 interest twice each year for the next five years. In addition, par value of the security ($1,000) is payable at the end of year five.

Common to the above situations is the fact that each involves the extension of credit and charging of interest, either explicitly or implicitly. Frequently, the decision maker must calculate the true interest rate inherent in such transactions. Once the true rate is known, the creditor or debtor is in a position to compare credit alternatives.

TIME VALUE OF MONEY: THE MATHEMATICS OF INTEREST

To develop an understanding of the techniques used to compare interest rates, it is first necessary to develop the theory of compound interest. That development is completed in this section.

COMPOUND VALUE OF A SINGLE PAYMENT

The first step in understanding interest rates relates to the concept of compound value. Suppose that $1,000 is deposited in a savings account paying 6 percent interest compounded annually. Interest of $60 will be earned during the first year and the account balance at the end of the first year will be $1,060. If the account is left undisturbed for two years, interest for the second year is $1,060 × .06 = $63.60. The account balance at the end of the second year is $1,060 + 63.60 = $1,123.60. This process by which interest is computed against both the original principal and previously accumulated interest is known as compound interest. If a financial institution credited interest on the original deposit but did not compound it, the saver could simply remove and reinvest funds once interest had been credited, achieving the same result. Thus compound interest, or interest on interest, is a normal practice in the case of savings accounts and other investment instruments.

If the funds were to be left for a large number of years in the account described above, it would be possible to find the amount to which the account would grow by continuing a series of calculations like those completed for the first two years. However, it is convenient to take a more systematic approach. The amount in the account at the end of the first year is:

$$\$1,000 + .06(\$1,000)$$
$$= \$1,000(1.06) = \$1,060$$

The amount in the account at the end of t¹ second year equals

$$\$1,060(1.06) = \$1,000(1.06)^2 = \$1,12\ .60$$

and the amount in the account at the end of the third year is:

$$\$1,000(1.06)^2(1.06) = \$1,000(1.06)^3$$
$$= \$1,191.02$$

This process can be generalized for the future value (FV_n) of an investment of P dollars at i percent interest per period for n periods:

$$FV_n = P(1 + i)^n \qquad (5\text{-}1)$$

If the previous investment were allowed to continue growing for ten years, the value at the end of ten years would be

$$FV_{10} = \$1,000(1.06)^{10}$$

While the procedure is the same for ten years as for two, the calculations can be tedious if done manually. To alleviate this problem, Table 5-1 contains values of $(1 + i)^n$ for various combinations of i and n. Table A-1 in the Appendix to this book is a continuation of Table 5-1, containing compound values for additional combinations of i and n. The value of the account at the end of ten years is found by locating the intersection of the ten-year row and the 6 percent column in Table 5-1. A value of 1.7908 is found and the solution to the problem is:

$$FV_{10} = \$1,000(1.06)^{10}$$
$$= \$1,000(1.7908) = \$1,790.80.$$

In the above examples, interest was calculated and added to the account at the end of each year. This is referred to as *annual* *compounding*. In some cases interest is compounded, or added to the principal, more than once a year. The result of compounding more than once a year is to raise the growth rate slightly. The future value formula when interest is compounded k times per year is:

$$FV_n = P\left(1 + \frac{i}{k}\right)^{kn} \qquad (5\text{-}2)$$

Thus investing funds for three years at 12% per year with semi-annual compounding provides the same growth as investing the funds for six years at 6 percent with annual compounding. If $1,000 is invested for three years at a 12 percent annual rate with interest compounded two times per year, the future value is:

$$FV_3 = \$1,000\left(1 + \frac{.12}{2}\right)^{2 \cdot 3}$$
$$= \$1,000(1.06)^6 = \$1,418.50$$

Among compounding periods other than annual, monthly compounding is the most important for understanding interest prac-

Table 5-1:

Compound Value of a Dollar (Annual Compounding)

Years	6.00%	6.25%	6.50%	6.75%	7.00%	7.25%	7.50%	7.75%
1	1.0600	1.0625	1.0650	1.0675	1.0700	1.0725	1.0750	1.0775
2	1.1236	1.1289	1.1342	1.1396	1.1449	1.1503	1.1556	1.1610
3	1.1910	1.1995	1.2079	1.2165	1.2250	1.2336	1.2423	1.2510
4	1.2625	1.2744	1.2865	1.2986	1.3108	1.3231	1.3355	1.3479
5	1.3382	1.3541	1.3701	1.3862	1.4026	1.4190	1.4356	1.4524
6	1.4185	1.4387	1.4591	1.4798	1.5007	1.5219	1.5433	1.5650
7	1.5036	1.5286	1.5540	1.5797	1.6058	1.6322	1.6590	1.6862
8	1.5938	1.6242	1.6550	1.6863	1.7182	1.7506	1.7835	1.8169
9	1.6895	1.7257	1.7626	1.8002	1.8385	1.8775	1.9172	1.9577
10	1.7908	1.8335	1.8771	1.9217	1.9672	2.0136	2.0610	2.1095
20	3.2071	3.3619	3.5236	3.6928	3.8697	4.0546	4.2479	4.4499
25	4.2919	4.5522	4.8277	5.1191	5.4274	5.7535	6.0983	6.4630

tices. A $100 investment pays interest of 7 percent per year, compounded monthly. By the end of one year the investment will grow to:

$$FV_1 = \$100\left(1 + \frac{.07}{12}\right)^{12 \cdot 1}$$
$$= \$100(1.0723) = \$107.23$$

Thus 7 percent compounded monthly would provide the same growth as 7.23 percent compounded annually. Due to the wide use of monthly compounding in such areas as mortgage loan analysis, special tables for monthly compounding are provided. Table 5-2 contains values of $\left(1 + \frac{i}{12}\right)^{12 \cdot n}$ for various combinations of i and n. (Table A-2 in the Appendix contains compound values for additional combinations of i and n.)

A $5,000 investment has a three-year maturity, a 7 percent interest rate and monthly compounding. Principal and interest is payable at the end of the three-year period. To find the amount to which $1 would grow at the end of three years, we locate the intersection of the three-year row and 7 percent column in Table 5-2. The value found there is 1.2329 and in three years the investment will grow to:

$$FV_3 = \$5,000\left(1 + \frac{.07}{12}\right)^{12 \cdot 3}$$
$$= \$5,000(1.2329) = \$6,164.50$$

Frequently, the tables will not contain the precise interest rate desired. A decision maker wishing to find the compound value of a dollar for ten years at 6.4 percent with monthly compounding is faced with the fact that Table 5-2 contains compound value factors for 6.25 percent and 6.50 percent, but not for 6.4 percent. The compound value factor for 6.4 percent can be estimated using *linear interpolation*. The linear interpolation formula, which is imposing to look at but easy to use, is:

$$TVF_I = TVF_b + (TVF_a - TVF_b)\frac{I - I_b}{I_a - I_b} \quad (5\text{-}3)$$

Table 5-2:

Compound Value of a Dollar (Monthly Compounding)

Years	6.00%	6.25%	6.50%	6.75%	7.00%	7.25%	7.50%	7.75%
1	1.0617	1.0643	1.0670	1.0696	1.0723	1.0750	1.0776	1.0803
2	1.1272	1.1328	1.1384	1.1441	1.1498	1.1555	1.1613	1.1671
3	1.1967	1.2056	1.2147	1.2238	1.2329	1.2422	1.2514	1.2608
4	1.2705	1.2832	1.2960	1.3090	1.3221	1.3353	1.3486	1.3621
5	1.3488	1.3657	1.3828	1.4001	1.4176	1.4354	1.4533	1.4715
6	1.4320	1.4536	1.4754	1.4976	1.5201	1.5429	1.5661	1.5896
7	1.5204	1.5471	1.5742	1.6019	1.6300	1.6586	1.6877	1.7173
8	1.6141	1.6466	1.6797	1.7134	1.7478	1.7829	1.8187	1.8552
9	1.7137	1.7525	1.7922	1.8327	1.8742	1.9166	1.9599	2.0042
10	1.8194	1.8652	1.9122	1.9603	2.0097	2.0602	2.1121	2.1652
20	3.3102	3.4790	3.6564	3.8429	4.0387	4.2446	4.4608	4.6880
25	4.4650	4.7514	5.0562	5.3804	5.7254	6.0924	6.4829	6.8983

where: TVF_I = Time value factor for desired interest rate

TVF_b = Time value factor for interest rate below desired rate

TVF_a = Time value factor for interest rate above desired rate

I = Interest rate for which time value factor is desired

I_b = Interest rate below rate for which time value factor is desired

I_a = Interest rate above rate for which time value factor is desired

Applying the interpolation formula to the above problem, the compound value factor for an annual interest rate of 6.4 percent for ten years with monthly compounding is:

$$CVF_{6.4\%} = 1.8652 + (1.9122 - 1.8652)$$
$$\frac{.064 - .0625}{.065 - .0625}$$
$$= 1.8934$$

The same interpolation approach can be used with Table 5-1 when appropriate.[1]

COMPOUND VALUE OF AN ANNUITY (STREAM OF PAYMENTS)

While the decision maker is frequently interested in the amount to which a single payment or investment will grow, other problems involve the growth of a series of payments. Examples where such problems may be found are in areas such as retirement planning, pension fund management, insurance portfolio management, and loan analysis. The procedure used is an extension of that used in the previous section.

A savings program calls for depositing $100 at the *end* of each year for the next three years in an account which pays 6 percent interest compounded annually. The amount in the account at the end of three years can be found using compound value factors from Table 5-1. The procedure is demonstrated in Table 5-3.

---

[1] A pocket calculator with a power function makes possible an exact solution:

$$\left(1 + \frac{.064}{12}\right)^{10 \cdot 12} = 1.8933$$

Table 5-3:

Compound Value of $100 per Year at 6%

Date: End of Year	Deposit	Number of Years Funds are on Deposit	Compound Value Factor (Table A-I)	Compound Value
1	$100	2	1.1236	$112.36
2	100	1	1.0600	106.00
3	100	0	1.0000	100.00
		Value at the end of three years		$318.36

While this approach provides the correct answer, the calculations would be quite tedious if a large number of years were involved. Again, a table has been provided to aid in calculation. Table 5-4 contains compound values of $1 per year for selected combinations of years (n) and interest rates (i) with annual compounding. The formula for Table 5-4 is:

$$CVA(i,n) = 1 + (1 + i)^1$$
$$+ (1 + i)^2 \qquad (5\text{-}4)$$
$$+ \ldots + (1 + i)^{n-1}$$

Table 5-4:

Compound Value of an Annuity of $1
(Annual Payments, Annual Compounding)

Years	6.00%	6.25%	6.50%	6.75%	7.00%	7.25%	7.50%	7.75%
1	1.000	1.000	1.000	1.000	1.000	1.000	1.000	1.000
2	2.060	2.063	2.065	2.067	2.070	2.073	2.075	2.078
3	3.184	3.191	3.199	3.207	3.215	3.223	3.231	3.239
4	4.375	4.391	4.407	4.424	4.440	4.456	4.473	4.489
5	5.637	5.665	5.694	5.722	5.751	5.779	5.808	5.837
6	6.975	7.019	7.064	7.108	7.153	7.199	7.244	7.290
7	8.394	8.458	8.523	8.588	8.654	8.720	8.787	8.855
8	9.897	9.987	10.077	10.168	10.260	10.353	10.446	10.541
9	11.491	11.611	11.732	11.854	11.978	12.103	12.230	12.358
10	13.181	13.337	13.494	13.654	13.816	13.981	14.147	14.316
20	36.786	37.790	38.825	39.894	40.995	42.132	43.305	44.514
25	54.865	56.836	58.888	61.024	63.249	65.566	67.978	70.490

The intersection of the three-year row and 6 percent column in Table 5-4 yields a compound value factor of 3.184 which, when multiplied by $100, yields (except for a 4¢ rounding difference) the $318.36 found above. If $100 were to be deposited at the end of each year for 20 years, the value at the end of 20 years, based on the 20-year, 6 percent factor from Table 5-4, would be:

$$\$100 \times 36.786 = \underline{\$3,678.60}$$

A number of lending and investment situations involve monthly payments with monthly compounding. Table 5-5 (and Table A-4 in the Appendix) contains compound values of $1 per month for n years at an annual percentage rate of i with monthly compounding. The formula for Table 5-5 is:

$$CVA_m(i,n) = 1 + \left(1 + \frac{i}{12}\right)^1$$
$$+ \left(1 + \frac{i}{12}\right)^2 + \ldots \qquad (5\text{-}5)$$
$$+ \left(1 + \frac{i}{12}\right)^{12n-1}$$

A savings program involves investing $100 at the end of each month for the next 20 years at a 6.5 percent annual interest rate with monthly compounding. The amount in the account at the end of 20 years, based on the 20-year, 6.5 percent figure from Table 5-5 is:

$$\$100 \times 490.421 = \$49,042.10$$

As with compounding of a single payment, interpolation can be used when the desired interest rate is not available. $100 is to be deposited at the end of each month for the next 20 years in an account paying 7.30 percent interest per year with monthly compounding. The compound value factor can be estimated by using equation (5-3) to interpolate between the 7.25 percent 20-year factor and the 7.50 percent 20-year factor in Table 5-5:

Table 5-5:

Compound Value of An Annuity of $1
(Monthly Payments, Monthly Compounding)

Years	6.00%	6.25%	6.50%	6.75%	7.00%	7.25%	7.50%
1	12.336	12.350	12.364	12.378	12.393	12.407	12.421
2	25.432	25.494	25.556	25.618	25.681	25.744	25.807
3	39.336	39.484	39.632	39.781	39.930	40.080	40.231
4	54.098	54.373	54.650	54.929	55.209	55.492	55.776
5	69.770	70.220	70.674	71.132	71.593	72.058	72.527
6	86.409	87.087	87.771	88.463	89.161	89.866	90.579
7	104.074	105.038	106.013	107.000	107.999	109.009	110.032
8	122.829	124.144	125.477	126.829	128.199	129.587	130.995
9	142.740	144.479	146.245	148.038	149.859	151.708	153.586
10	163.879	166.122	168.403	170.724	173.085	175.487	177.930
20	462.041	475.975	490.421	505.397	520.926	537.030	553.730
25	692.993	720.273	748.836	778.746	810.071	842.884	877.260

$$537.030 + (553.730 - 537.030) \frac{.0730 - .0725}{.0750 - .0725} = \underline{540.37}$$

The same interpolation procedure can be used with Table 5-4 for appropriate problems.

PRESENT VALUE OF A FUTURE SUM: REVERSE COMPOUNDING

If a dollar invested today will grow to an amount greater than a dollar at some future date, a dollar received at some future date is less valuable than a dollar received today. Financial institutions acquire and issue securities which provide the holder with one or more future cash payments. Sometimes, securities will have a provision whereby a certain cash payment is to be given the holder at the end of a designated period, with no intervening payments prior to maturity. For example, the prospective purchaser of a certificate of deposit issued by a savings institution may wish to know how much he must invest today in order to have a certain sum two years hence. Similarly, a corporate treasurer may be charged with the responsibility of investing sufficient funds from current earnings to insure the firm's ability to meet construction progress payments due several years hence. Numerous other examples could be cited where the investor knew the amount to be realized in the future and would wish to know what that amount is worth today. Today's value depends, of course, on the interest rate implied in the investment and on the frequency with which interest is compounded.

Suppose an investment will pay $5,000 two years from today. If the investor has alternate opportunities paying 6 percent interest, the amount required to have $5,000 two years from today can be found by restating equation (1):

$$P = FV_n \times \frac{1}{(1 + i)^n} \qquad (5\text{-}6)$$

$$P = \$5,000 \, \frac{1}{(1.06)^2}$$

$$= \$5,000 \times .8900 = \$4,450$$

Thus the *present value* of $5,000 received two years from today, given an annual interest or growth rate of 6 percent compounded annually, is $4,450. The present value of $5,000 received five years from today, *discounted*[2] at 7 percent per annum, would be:

$$P = \$5,000 \, \frac{1}{(1.07)^5}$$

$$= \$5,000 \times .7130 = \$3,565$$

This value can be verified by showing that $3,565 invested today at 7 percent compounded annually will grow to $5,000 by the end of five years.

Table 5-6:

Present Value of a Dollar (Annual Compounding)

Years	6.00%	6.25%	6.50%	6.75%	7.00%	7.25%	7.50%	7.75%
1	0.9434	0.9412	0.9390	0.9368	0.9346	0.9324	0.9302	0.9281
2	0.8900	0.8858	0.8817	0.8775	0.8734	0.8694	0.8653	0.8613
3	0.8396	0.8337	0.8278	0.8220	0.8163	0.8106	0.8050	0.7994
4	0.7921	0.7847	0.7773	0.7701	0.7629	0.7558	0.7488	0.7419
5	0.7473	0.7385	0.7299	0.7214	0.7130	0.7047	0.6966	0.6885
6	0.7050	0.6951	0.6853	0.6758	0.6663	0.6571	0.6480	0.6390
7	0.6651	0.6542	0.6435	0.6330	0.6227	0.6127	0.6028	0.5930
8	0.6274	0.6157	0.6042	0.5930	0.5820	0.5712	0.5607	0.5504
9	0.5919	0.5795	0.5674	0.5555	0.5439	0.5326	0.5216	0.5108
10	0.5584	0.5454	0.5327	0.5204	0.5083	0.4966	0.4852	0.4741
20	0.3118	0.2975	0.2838	0.2708	0.2584	0.2466	0.2354	0.2247
25	0.2330	0.2197	0.2071	0.1953	0.1842	0.1738	0.1640	0.1547

Table 5-6 (and Table A-5 in the Appendix) contains values of $1/(1+i)^n$ for selected combinations of i and n. The intersection of the five-year row and 7 percent column in Table 5-6 yields the present value factor .7130 used above. A payment of $10,000 is to be received 20 years from today. An investor who wishes to earn a return of 7.5 percent compounded annually can find the amount he must pay for the investment by referring to the 7.5 percent 20-year interest factor in Table 5-6:

$$\$10,000 \times .2354 = \$2,354$$

Table 5-7 (and Table A-6 in the Appendix) is used for problems of the same type when monthly compounding is involved. If alternate investments pay a 6 percent annual interest rate with monthly compounding, the present value of $1,000 received ten years

---

[2] The term "discounted" as used in this section should not be confused with the term "discount rate." The latter is a rate applied to original loan principal as a method of calculating interest charges. The former relates to the use of a simple interest rate so as to reduce the value of future cash payments in order to determine their present value.

Table 5-7:

Present Value of a Dollar (Monthly Compounding)

Years	6.00%	6.25%	6.50%	6.75%	7.00%	7.25%	7.50%	7.75%
1	0.9419	0.9396	0.9372	0.9349	0.9326	0.9303	0.9280	0.9257
2	0.8872	0.8828	0.8784	0.8740	0.8697	0.8654	0.8611	0.8568
3	0.8356	0.8294	0.8233	0.8172	0.8111	0.8051	0.7991	0.7931
4	0.7871	0.7793	0.7716	0.7640	0.7564	0.7489	0.7415	0.7342
5	0.7414	0.7322	0.7232	0.7142	0.7054	0.6967	0.6881	0.6796
6	0.6983	0.6880	0.6778	0.6677	0.6578	0.6481	0.6385	0.6291
7	0.6577	0.6464	0.6352	0.6243	0.6135	0.6029	0.5925	0.5823
8	0.6195	0.6073	0.5954	0.5836	0.5721	0.5609	0.5498	0.5390
9	0.5835	0.5706	0.5580	0.5456	0.5336	0.5218	0.5102	0.4989
10	0.5496	0.5361	0.5230	0.5101	0.4976	0.4854	0.4735	0.4619
20	0.3021	0.2874	0.2735	0.2602	0.2476	0.2356	0.2242	0.2133
25	0.2240	0.2105	0.1978	0.1859	0.1747	0.1641	0.1543	0.1450

from today, based on the ten-year, 6 percent factor from Table 5-7, is:

$$\$1,000 \times .5496 = \$549.60$$

As with future value of a single payment, interpolation using equation (5-3) can be used if the desired interest rate is not available.

PRESENT VALUE OF AN ANNUITY

If a security is to provide a *stream* of future payments, the present value of that stream and thus the market value of the security, can be found in a manner similar to that discussed for a single payment. At a required return of 6 percent, a security which is to provide cash flow or payment of $500 at the end of each year for the next two years would have a present value (PV) of:

$$PV = 500 \times \frac{1}{(1.06)} + 500$$
$$\times \frac{1}{(1.06)^2} = \$916.70$$

If the investment were to provide the same cash flows each year for twenty years instead of two, the procedure would be the same but the calculations would become quite tedious. Calculations can be aided by generalizing the approach as follows:

$$PV = CF \times \frac{1}{(1+i)} + CF \times \frac{1}{(1+i)^2} + \ldots + CF \times \frac{1}{(1+i)^n} \qquad (5-7)$$
$$= CF \left[\frac{1}{(1+i)} + \frac{1}{(1+i)^2} + \ldots + \frac{1}{(1+i)^n} \right]$$

where: PV = Present value (of the security)
CF = The amount to be received at the end of each year
i = The required rate of return
n = The number of years the cash flows are to continue

Table 5-8 contains values of this function for selected combinations of i and n. (Table A-7 in the Appendix contains values for additional combinations.) The use of the table eliminates a good deal of tedious calculation. A security will provide cash flows of $5,000 a year for ten years. If the required return

Table 5-8:

Present Value of an Annuity of $1.00 (Annual Payments, Annual Compounding)

Years	6.00%	6.25%	6.50%	6.75%	7.00%	7.25%	7.50%	7.75%
1	0.943	0.941	0.939	0.937	0.935	0.932	0.930	0.928
2	1.833	1.827	1.821	1.814	1.808	1.802	1.796	1.789
3	2.673	2.661	2.648	2.636	2.624	2.612	2.601	2.589
4	3.465	3.445	3.426	3.406	3.387	3.368	3.349	3.331
5	4.212	4.184	4.156	4.128	4.100	4.073	4.046	4.019
6	4.917	4.879	4.841	4.804	4.767	4.730	4.694	4.658
7	5.582	5.533	5.485	5.437	5.389	5.343	5.297	5.251
8	6.210	6.149	6.089	6.030	5.971	5.914	5.857	5.802
9	6.802	6.728	6.656	6.585	6.515	6.447	6.379	6.312
10	7.360	7.274	7.189	7.105	7.024	6.943	6.864	6.786
20	11.470	11.241	11.019	10.803	10.594	10.391	10.194	10.004
25	12.783	12.485	12.198	11.921	11.654	11.396	11.147	10.907

is 7 percent, the value associated with ten years and 7 percent in Table 5-8 is 7.024 and the present value of the cash flows or value of the security is:

$$PV = \$5,000 \times 7.024 = \$35,120$$

If payments are to be received monthly, with interest compounded monthly, the present value equals:

$$PV = CF\left[1/\left(1 + \frac{i}{12}\right) \right.$$
$$+ 1/\left(1 + \frac{i}{12}\right)^2 + \ldots \quad (5\text{-}8)$$
$$\left. + 1/\left(1 + \frac{i}{12}\right)^{12n} \right]$$

Table 5-9 (and Table A-8 in the Appendix) contains values of this function for various combinations of i and n.

Suppose a lender wished to grant a loan with monthly payments and an annual interest rate of 7 percent. By referring to Table 5-9, the lender could determine that the present value of $1 received each month for 20 years, discounted at 7 percent per annum

and compounded monthly, is $128.983. Thus a loan of $128.98 repaid in monthly payments of $1 per month over 20 years yields an annual return on investment of 7 percent compounded monthly. If the loan were to be for a larger amount, say $30,000, we would divide the loan amount by 128.983 to find the monthly payment:

$$\$30,000/128.983 = \$232.59$$

If a 7.2 percent return was required, interpolation, using equation (5-3), would result in a present value factor of:

$$128.983 + (126.522$$
$$- 128.983)\frac{.0720 - .0700}{.0725 - .0700} = 127.014$$

and the monthly payment would be:

$$\$30,000/127.014 = \$236.19$$

DETERMINING INTEREST RATES

Analysis of loan and investment alternatives frequently requires that the decision maker determine the true interest rate as-

Table 5-9:

Present Value of an Annuity of $1.00 (Monthly Payments, Monthly Compounding)

Years	6.00%	6.25%	6.50%	6.75%	7.00%	7.25%	7.50%	7.75%
1	11.619	11.603	11.588	11.573	11.557	11.542	11.526	11.511
2	22.563	22.506	22.449	22.392	22.335	22.279	22.222	22.166
3	32.871	32.749	32.627	32.507	32.386	32.267	32.148	32.030
4	42.580	42.373	42.167	41.963	41.760	41.559	41.358	41.159
5	51.726	51.416	51.109	50.804	50.502	50.202	49.905	49.611
6	60.340	59.912	59.489	59.069	58.654	58.243	57.837	57.434
7	68.453	67.895	67.343	66.797	66.257	65.724	65.196	64.675
8	76.095	75.395	74.704	74.021	73.348	72.683	72.026	71.378
9	83.293	82.442	81.603	80.775	79.960	79.156	78.364	77.583
10	90.073	89.063	88.069	87.090	86.126	85.178	84.245	83.326
20	139.581	136.812	134.125	131.516	128.983	126.522	124.132	121.810
25	155.207	151.591	148.103	144.736	141.487	138.350	135.320	132.393

sociated with a given loan or investment. Insurance companies for example, are often asked to invest in major projects such as proposed shopping centers. In a project of this type, the investor may receive future cash flows based at least in part on rental income derived from shopping center tenants. In this illustration, the decision maker will know the amount of investment required and a reasonable estimate of future cash inflows may be projected. It remains then, to determine the interest rate or return inherent in the transaction. Alternatively, suppose that a security which offers a certain series of future cash flows is available for purchase at a specified price. Such a security could be a new or existing bond, a new or existing mortgage, a negotiable certificate of deposit, or one of a variety of other financial instruments. The decision to purchase or reject such securities is influenced by the interest rate inherent in the transaction. It is important therefore, that the decision maker be at least conceptually familiar with the process by which the rate is determined. This process involves use of equations and tables previously discussed.

Assume that a particular investment requires $5,000 and will grow in value to $7,000 at the end of five years. The problem can be restated as a simple compound value problem using equation (5-1):

$$\$5,000(1 + i)^5 = \$7,000$$
$$(1 + i)^5 = \$7,000/5,000 = 1.4$$

Previous use of Table 5-1 involved searching for the compound value factor associated with a particular interest rate. Our objective now is to refer to Table 5-1 and find the interest rate associated with a particular compound value factor. If we proceed to the five-year row in that table, and look for the interest factor 1.4, a value of 1.4026 is found in the 7 percent column. We conclude that the effective interest rate on the investment is approximately 7 percent compounded annually.

This same procedure can be used when a stream of future payments is involved. An investment requires payments of $100 per month and will grow to $9,000 in six years. The ratio of future value to monthly cash flow is 9000/100 = 90.00 In Table 5-5 an examination of the six-year row reveals a compound value factor of 89.866 at 7.25 percent and 90.579 at 7.50 percent. The effective interest rate lies between 7.25 percent and 7.50 percent.

Interpolation can be used to prepare an estimate of the exact interest rate in a manner similar to that used with equation (5-3) when an estimate of exact compound value is desired:

$$I = I_b + (I_a - I_b) \qquad (5\text{-}9)$$
$$\frac{TV_I - TV_b}{TV_a - TV_b}$$
$$= .0725 + (.0750 - .0725)$$
$$\frac{90.00 - 89.866}{90.579 - 89.866}$$

$$= .0730 \text{ or } 7.3\%$$

Many times the effective interest rate will be desired for an uneven stream of cash flows. An investment which costs $1,130 today will provide $90 at the end of each year for the next ten years and then $1,000 at the end of ten years. The effective interest rate is the rate which will make the present value of the cash inflows equal to the cost. This rate is found by a trial-and-error process. We decide to start the search with 7 percent. Referring to Tables 5-6 and 5-8, we find the present value factors for 7 percent, ten years, and apply these to determine the present value of the cash flows:

Dates	Cash Flow	× Present Value Factor (7%)	= Present Value
Year 1–10 (annual)	90	7.024	$ 632.16
Year 10	$1,000	.5083	508.30
		Total Present Value	$1,140.46

We are seeking an interest rate which would result in a total present value of $1,130. Since a higher interest rate results in a lower present value, we try a higher rate. We decide to try 7.25%:

Dates	Cash Flow	Present Value Factor (7.25%)	Present Value
Year 1–10 (annual)	90	6.943	$ 624.87
Year 10	$1,000	.4966	496.60
		Total Present Value	$1,121.47

Since we are looking for a present value of $1,130, we know the effective interest rate is between 7 percent and 7.25 percent. We can estimate the exact interest rate by interpolation, using equation (5-9):

$$I = 7.0 + (7.25 - 7.0)\frac{1130 - 1140.46}{1121.47 - 1140.46} = 7.14\%$$

INTEREST PRACTICES AND EFFECTIVE INTEREST RATES

Having developed the general mathematics of interest, we are now ready to examine specific interest practices. This section has two major objectives. The first is to develop an understanding of interest terminology and payment practices which are commonly used. The second is to develop a methodology for comparing interest charges which are quoted or computed in different ways.

ANNUAL PERCENTAGE RATE

Early in this chapter it was noted that different computational methods sometimes result in different interest charges even though stated interest rates are identical. The annual percentage rate (also referred to as the simple interest rate) is normally used as the standard of comparison. Indeed, truth in lending legislation of recent years requires disclosure of the effective annual percentage rate (APR) in virtually all types of consumer lending.

When we identified or computed effective interest rates in the previous section, we were dealing with the annual percentage rate. As an example, take a $1,200 note with a 6 percent annual percentage rate, a one-year maturity, and a lump sum payment. Interest on the note will be $72 ($1,200 × .06) and the amount due at maturity will be $1,272.00. If this same loan were to be paid in equal installments at the end of each month, interest charged each month would be .005 (.06/12) of the balance due at the beginning of the month. The amount required to retire the loan in twelve monthly payments can be found by referring to Table A-8 in the Appendix. The present value of $1 per month for one year at 6 percent is found to be 11.619. The monthly payment required is $103.28 ($1,200/11.619). The allocation of the payment between principal and interest is shown in Table 5-10.

Table 5-10:

Amortization Schedule for a $1,200, 6%, One-Year, Simple Interest Note with Equal Installments Payable at the End of Each Month

Month	Beginning Loan Balance	Monthly Payment	Interest Payment*	Principal Reduction	Ending Balance
1	$1,200.00	$ 103.28	$ 6.00	$ 97.28	$1,102.72
2	1,102.72	103.28	5.51	97.77	1,004.95
3	1,004.95	103.28	5.02	98.26	906.69
.	.	.	.	.	.
.	.	.	.	.	.
.	.	.	.	.	.
12	102.77	103.28	0.51	102.77	0.00
Total		$1,239.36	$39.36		

*Sample interest calculations

	P	×	R	×	t	=	Interest
1st month	1,200.00	×	.06	×	1/12	=	6.00
2nd month	1,102.72	×	.06	×	1/12	=	5.51
3rd month	1,004.95	×	.06	×	1/12	=	5.02

The same approach to finding the payment and constructing an amortization schedule can be used when the life of the security is greater than one year. To find the monthly payment necessary to amortize an 8.50 percent 20-year mortgage, the present value factor for 8.50 percent, 20 years (115.231) is first located in Table A-8. The amount of the loan is then divided by this present value factor. If the mortgage loan were for $50,000, the monthly payment would be $433.91 ($50,000/115.231). Alternatively, if the loan were to be repaid in *annual* installments, we would find the

8.5 percent, 20-year figure of 9.463 in Table A-7 and the annual payment would be $5,283.74 ($50,000/9.463).

ADD-ON AND DISCOUNT RATES

Add-on interest rates are frequently used in consumer installment transactions and, to a lesser extent, in business and other commercial loans. Discount rates are also common to both consumer and business trans-actions. A key distinction between both add-on and discount rates as opposed to annual percentage rates is that calculation of interest charges is based upon the original loan principal and ignores the fact that the principal balance may decline over time as periodic payment of principal and interest is made. Table 5-11 illustrates the fact that the method by which interest charges are calculated can have a dramatic effect on total loan charges.

Table 5-11:

Comparison of Interest Charges and True Annual Interest Rates Applicable to Three Loans, Each Bearing Stated Interest of 6%

	Add-on Method	Discount Method	Simple Interest Method
Stated Annual Rate	6%	6%	6%
Amount Loaned	$1,200.00	$1,200.00	$1,200.00
Loan Maturity	1 year	1 year	1 year
Repayment Terms	Monthly	Monthly	Monthly
Interest Charges	$ 72.00	$ 72.00	$ 39.36
Loan Proceeds	1,200.00	1,128.00	1,200.00
Time Balance	1,272.00	1,200.00	1,239.36
Monthly Payments	106.00	100.00	103.28*
Annual Simple Interest Rate	10.89%	11.58%	6.00%

*Using Table A-8, $1,200 ÷ 11.6189 = $103.28

Suppose someone wishes to borrow $1,200 and is told that the loan is available at an annual interest rate of 6 percent add-on with repayment in equal installments, one at the end of each month. With the add-on method, the total interest charge will be .06 × $1,200 = $72.00 (compared to $39.36 when the rate was 6 percent simple) and monthly payments will be $106 ($1272/12). The effective annual percentage rate for this loan can be found using Table A-8. We know that the time is one year and the ratio of loan value to payment is 11.321 ($1,200/106). Scanning across the one-year row of Table A-8, we find the value of 11.344 at 10.5 percent and 11.315 at 11.0 percent. By interpolation, the annual percentage rate is approximately 10.90 percent. Note that this is close to twice the quoted add-on rate.

If the discount method is used, the interest charge of $72 (.06 × $1,200) is immediately deducted from the amount loaned. In this case, the borrower has initial use of only $1,128. If monthly payments are to be made, they will be $100 per month over twelve months. Interest charges total $72. Obviously, the discount method involves a higher annual percentage rate than the add-on method. With the discount method, the borrower receives $1,128 and pays monthly installments of $100. The ratio of loan to payment is 1128/100 = 11.28. Again, the effective annual percentage rate can be found using Table A-8. Present value factors of 11.285 and 11.255 are found at 11.5 percent and 12.0 percent, respectively. Thus the annual percentage rate lies between 11.5 percent and 12.0 percent. By interpolation, the effective simple interest rate is approximately 11.58 percent.

FINANCIAL LEASES

A specific type of financial instrument and one which has received increased use in recent years is the financial lease. Frequently, financial institutions act in the capacity of a lessor, purchasing assets on behalf of a customer (lessee), and in turn, leasing the assets under terms of a lease agreement. Terms of a pure financial lease differ from those typically associated with an operating or service lease. In the case of the latter, the lessor provides maintenance and other services. Furthermore, operating or service leases are often cancellable on short notice. Financial leases, on the other hand, are simply an alternative method of financing assets. In a financial lease, the lessee assumes all obligations normally associated with ownership. The lessor merely provides the capital necessary for acquisition of the asset, holds title to the asset, and enters into an agreement whereby the lessee promises to make a series of payments sufficient to provide a return of all costs as well as a profit to the lessor.

Since a lease is not a loan, interest charges are technically nonexistent and are thus unspecified in the lease agreement. However, an interest rate is *implied* in the transaction and a financial lease is frequently an alternative to a loan. Thus, the decision maker should evaluate the lease agreement in terms of the annual percentage rate implied in the agreement.

Table 5-12 was drawn from the files of a leasing corporation and provides information relating to one method of quoting lease payments. Specific rates vary over time and the quotations contained in Table 5-12 happened to be in effect for that company in the spring of 1973. Suppose that a prospective lessee wished to lease equipment priced at $30,000 from the company whose rates are represented in Table 5-12. If the term of the lease were three years, monthly lease payments would be (3.38% × $30,000) =

$1,014.00. Thus, $1,014 represents an annuity to be paid (or received) over a 36-month period. The present value of that annuity is $30,000. Expressed in terms of a dollar, the present value factor is:

$$\$30,000/\$1,014 = 29.586.$$

Referring to Table A-8 and looking across the three-year row, we find the factor 29.679 associated with 13 percent and 29.259 associated with 14 percent. We conclude that the interest rate inherent in the lease is between 13 percent and 14 percent. Linear interpolation results in an estimate of 13.22 percent. Thus an annual percentage rate of 13.22 percent is implied in the lease agreement.

Table 5-12:

Financial Lease Terms Quoted by a Leasing Corporation

Asset Cost (including all taxes and charges)	Term (no. of years)	Monthly Rental (% of total cost)
Less than $1,000	1	9.28
	2	5.11
1,000 to 5,000	3	3.53
5,000 to 10,000	3	3.47
	4	2.79
	5	2.44
10,000 to 25,000	3	3.42
	5	2.38
25,000 to 50,000	3	3.38
	5	2.33
50,000 to 100,000	3	3.36
	5	2.30
Over 100,000	3	3.33
	5	2.28

Source: Internal files of a leasing corporation.

POINTS AND SERVICE CHARGES

The collection of a charge payable at the time a loan is granted is a common practice that has the effect of increasing the annual percentage rate. Points will be used as an example although discounts and other service charges have a similar impact. A point, normally used in connection with a mortgage loan, is a service charge or discount equal to one percent of the value of the loan. Thus a $20,000 mortgage with a three-point charge would require a fee of $600 (.03 × $20,000). The financial institution would advance a net $19,400 ($20,000 − $600) but would receive payments and calculate interest charges as if the investment had been $20,000. This procedure obviously raises the true rate above that which is stated.

A $20,000 mortgage loan with a 30-year maturity and an 8 percent stated interest rate would require monthly payments of $20,000/136.284 = $146.75 (from Table A-8). Since the net investment is only $19,400, the ratio of loan to payment is $19,400/146.75 = 132.198. In the 30-year row of Table A-8, an interest factor of 133.109 is found at 8¼ percent, a factor of 130.054 is found at 8½ percent. The annual percentage rate is between 8¼ percent and 8½ percent. By interpolation, it is approximately 8.32 percent.

While points are of some significance if the loan is carried to maturity, they are of much greater significance if the loan is retired early. In general, the sooner a loan is retired, the greater the true annual percentage rate when points or similar charges had been levied against the original loan.

BONDS: VALUE AND YIELD TO MATURITY

Bonds are frequently bought and sold by financial institutions and by other investors long after they are issued. Although interest payments and the terminal value of the bond are fixed, the market value of the security may fluctuate depending on shifts in the market interest rate for that type of security. The relationship between par or face value of the bond and the periodic interest payments paid to the holder is called the *stated* or *coupon* interest rate and does not change. The ratio of annual interest payment to current market value is called the *current yield*.

However, the current yield is not the true interest rate earned because it does not include the capital gain or loss—the difference between the current market value and the amount that will be repaid at maturity. The yield to maturity is the true interest rate earned and is identical with the annual percentage rate. It recognizes both the interest payment received and any capital gain or loss that will occur if the bond is held to maturity.

A typical bond has a face or par value of $1,000 and pays interest twice a year. Thus a $1,000, 6 percent bond pays $30 each six months and $1,000 at maturity. As previously suggested, bonds frequently trade above or below their face value, making the true interest rate or yield to maturity different than the stated or coupon rate. Market quotations are stated as a percentage of face value: a price quote of 91.89 would mean that a $1,000 bond is being traded at $918.90.

Suppose the above 6 percent bond is five years from maturity and interest rates have risen such that bonds of this type are selling to provide a yield of 8 percent. What is this existing bond worth? We can answer this question by turning to Tables A-5 and A-8, assuming semi-annual compounding. The 91.89 figure for the above bond is derived using the present value of $1 per year for ten years at 4 percent and the present value of a single payment of $1 in ten years at 4 percent.[3]

$$\begin{aligned} \$30 \times 8.111 &= \$243.33 \\ 1,000 \times .6756 &= \underline{675.60} \\ &\ \$918.93 \end{aligned}$$

or 91.893 percent of face value

---

[3] Tables A-5 and A-7 assume annual cash flows and thus annual compounding. When flows are received semi-annually, these same tables may be used in their evaluation. It is necessary only to divide the interest rate by two and to double the time periods. Thus, cash inflows discounted at 8 percent per annum over five years, when received semi-annually, may be evaluated at 4 percent per time period over 10 six-month periods, as in the above illustration.

In practice, the yield to maturity on a bond is normally found using a set of bond yield tables, a sample of which is contained in Table 5-13. The bond yield tables contain the sum of the combined values from Tables A-5 and A-8. The price of 91.89 is found at the intersection of the 8 percent row and the five-year column. Conversely, the yield to maturity can be determined if the market price is known. If we knew that the market price was 91.89, we could scan down the five-year column until 91.89 was found and observe that the value is associated with an 8 percent interest rate.

Table 5-13:

Relationship Between Bond Yield to Maturity and Price
Face or Coupon Rate: 6.00%

Yield	1 yr	2 yr	3 yr	4 yr	5 yr	6 yr	7 yr	8 yr
5.00%	100.96	101.88	102.75	103.59	104.38	105.13	105.85	106.53
5.10	100.87	101.69	102.47	103.22	103.93	104.60	105.24	105.85
5.20	100.77	101.50	102.20	102.86	103.48	104.08	104.64	105.18
5.30	100.67	101.31	101.92	102.49	103.04	103.56	104.05	104.52
5.40	100.58	101.12	101.64	102.13	102.60	103.04	103.46	103.86
5.50	100.48	100.93	101.37	101.77	102.16	102.53	102.87	103.20
5.60	100.38	100.75	101.09	101.42	101.72	102.01	102.29	102.55
5.70	100.29	100.56	100.82	101.06	101.29	101.51	101.71	101.91
5.80	100.19	100.37	100.54	100.70	100.86	101.00	101.14	101.27
5.90	100.10	100.19	100.27	100.35	100.43	100.50	100.57	100.63
6.00	100.00	100.00	100.00	100.00	100.00	100.00	100.00	100.00
6.10	99.90	99.81	99.73	99.65	99.57	99.50	99.44	99.37
6.20	99.81	99.63	99.46	99.30	99.15	99.01	98.88	98.75
6.30	99.71	99.44	99.19	98.95	98.73	98.52	98.32	98.14
6.40	99.62	99.26	98.92	98.61	98.31	98.03	97.77	97.53
6.50	99.52	99.08	98.66	98.26	97.89	97.55	97.22	96.92
6.60	99.43	98.89	98.39	97.92	97.48	97.07	96.68	96.32
6.70	99.33	98.71	98.13	97.58	97.07	96.59	96.14	95.72
6.80	99.24	98.53	97.86	97.24	96.66	96.11	95.60	95.13
6.90	99.14	98.35	97.60	96.90	96.25	95.64	95.07	94.54
7.00	99.05	98.16	97.34	96.56	95.84	95.17	94.54	93.95
7.10	98.96	97.98	97.07	96.23	95.44	94.70	94.01	93.37
7.20	98.86	97.80	96.81	95.89	95.04	94.24	93.49	92.80
7.30	98.77	97.62	96.55	95.56	94.63	93.77	92.97	92.23
7.40	98.67	97.44	96.29	95.23	94.24	93.31	92.46	91.66
7.50	98.58	97.26	96.04	94.90	93.84	92.86	91.95	91.10
7.60	98.49	97.08	95.78	94.57	93.45	92.40	91.44	90.54
7.70	98.39	96.90	95.52	94.24	93.05	91.95	90.93	89.99
7.80	98.30	96.73	95.27	93.92	92.66	91.50	90.43	89.44
7.90	98.21	96.55	95.01	93.59	92.28	91.06	89.93	88.89
8.00	98.11	96.37	94.76	93.27	91.89	90.61	89.44	88.35

Anyone who deals in bonds will have a book-length set of bond yield tables readily at hand. If a bond yield table is not readily available, the yield to maturity can be estimated using the approximation formula:

$$Y = \frac{Int + (F - M)/N}{(F + M)/2} \quad (5\text{-}10)$$

where: Int = Dollar interest payments per year

M = Market value of the bond

F = Face value of the bond

N = Number of years until maturity.

Applying this formula to the above bond, the yield to maturity is approximately

$$Y = \frac{60 + (1{,}000.00 - 918.90)/5}{(1{,}000.00 + 918.90)/2} = 7.9\%$$

SUMMARY

Interest is basic to the operation of the financial system. It is defined as rent paid for the use of money. The general structure of interest rates is a function of the quantity and quality of investment alternatives, future expectations of consumers and businessmen, financial and nonfinancial habits which shift over time, and the level of inflation.

TIME VALUE OF MONEY

Compound Value is the amount to which an investment will grow over a particular time horizon at a given interest rate. The amount to which an investment (P) will grow in *n* periods with an interest rate of *i* per period is:

$$FV_n = P(1 + i)^n$$

If interest is compounded or added on *k* times per year, the amount to which a sum (*P*) will grow is:

$$FV_n = P\left(1 + \frac{i}{12}\right)^{nk}$$

Compound Value of an Annuity or stream of payments is the sum of the compound values of individual payments. The compound value of an annuity of $1 per year for *n* years at *i* percent is:

$$CVA(i,n) = 1 + (1 + i) + (1 + i)^2 + \ldots + (1 + i)^{n-1}$$

Present Value of a Single Payment is the inverse of the compound value of a single payment. With annual compounding, the present value of $1 received *n* years from today at interest rate *i,* is:

$$P = \frac{1}{(1 + i)^n}$$

Present Value of an Annuity is the sum of the present values of the individual payments. The present value of $1 per year for *n* years at *i* percent is:

$$PV = \frac{1}{(1 + i)} + \frac{1}{(1 + i)^2} + \ldots + \frac{1}{(1 + i)^n}$$

ANNUAL PERCENTAGE RATE

Many problems faced by financial institutions involve cases where the cash flows are known and the interest rate is desired. For such problems, the annual percentage rate is the discount rate which makes the present value of the cash inflows equal to the present value of the cash outflows.

QUESTIONS

1. Why is it important to convert all methods of computing interest to some common basis?

2. In competing for deposits, financial institutions have taken to compounding interest more than once a year. Why would they do this instead of simply raising the annual compounding rate directly?

3. Why do lenders charge points on mortgage loans rather than just increasing the stated interest rate?

4. Other things being equal, a long-term investment will carry a higher interest rate than one with a short maturity. Why then do automobile loans frequently carry higher effective interest rates than mortgage loans?

5. Determine the interest rate and points being charged on mortgage loans at a local financial institution. Convert this to an effective interest rate, if necessary, and compare it to the prime rate being charged the best business customers. (The prime rate is published in the *Federal Reserve Bulletin*.) How do you account for the difference?

PROBLEMS

1. A five-year certificate of deposit pays 6.25 percent compounded annually. A $5,000 deposit will grow to what amount in five years?

2. A competing certificate of deposit pays 6 percent interest with semi-annual compounding. Which provides the higher return?

3. An investment plan calls for depositing $1,200 at the end of each year for the next 20 years in an account which pays 8 percent interest compounded annually. What will be the value at the end of 20 years?

4. Another investment plan calls for depositing $1,000 at the end of each month for the next 20 years in an account which pays 8 percent compounded monthly. What will be the value at the end of 20 years?

5. A non-interest bearing second mortgage for $10,000 has a maturity of five years. The holder of the mortgage needs cash for another investment and wishes to sell it today. If similar mortgages yield 10 percent annual compound return, how

much could the holder expect to sell the mortgage for?

6. A $1,000 lump sum payment is to be received in one year. What is the present value at 8 percent discounted monthly?

7. A $1,000 bond pays $40 interest at the end of each six-month period and will mature in five years. At 6 percent required return with semi-annual compounding what is the value of the bond?

8. Three alternate loan policies involve simple interest of 8 percent, add-on interest of 7.5 percent, or discount interest of 7.25 percent. In any case, retirement will be through 36 equal monthly installments. A $10,000 note is signed. Compute the net proceeds of the loan, the monthly payments, and the effective annual percentage rate for each method.

9. A bond, which pays a face or coupon rate of 6 percent and will mature in eight years, is quoted at 96.32. What is the yield to maturity?

10. What would happen to the price of the above bond if the yield to maturity were to increase to 8 percent?

11. What size equal monthly payments would be required to retire a $30,000, 8 percent mortgage in 20 years? In 30 years?

12. If the above mortgage required a four-point service charge and was to be retired in 20 years, what would be the annual percentage rate?

13. A $50,000 piece of machinery has a five-year life and zero salvage value. A lease with equal annual payments at the end of each year for five years and a 14 percent annual percentage rate is desired. What will be the size of the annual lease payments?

14. A stock is expected to pay dividends of $20 a year for infinity. At an 8 percent required return, what is the value of the stock?

SELECTED REFERENCES

Bonker, Dick, "The 'Rule of 78'," *Journal of Finance,* Vol. 31 (June, 1976), pp. 877–888.

Kalay, Avner, and Ramon Rabinovitch, "On Individual Loans Pricing, Credit Rationing, and Interest Rate Regulation," *Journal of Finance,* Vol. 33 (September, 1978), pp. 1071–1085.

Kau, James B. and Donald Keenan, "The Theory of Housing and Interest Rates," *Journal of Financial and Quantitative Analysis,* Vol. 14 (November, 1980), pp. 833–847.

Chapter 6

Required Return and Value

In the previous chapter we developed the general principles of interest, frequently referred to as the mathematics of finance. For the manager to apply these principles it is frequently necessary to have an understanding of the factors determining the required interest rate on a particular investment. It is also necessary to have an understanding of the relationship between required return and value. Both topics are developed in this chapter.

There are two related questions in the determination of interest rates. First, there is the question of how the general level of interest rates is established. Second, there is the question of how time until maturity and risk cause interest rate differentials between different securities. In this chapter, we begin with a discussion of factors affecting the general level of interest rates.[1] We then consider certain variables that influence

interest rate differentials between securities. Finally, we discuss the relationship between required return and value.

DETERMINANTS OF THE GENERAL LEVEL OF INTEREST RATES

Modern theory recognizes that interest has a role similar to the role of price in determining the supply and demand for other goods. There is a supply curve for money to loan;[2] the higher the interest rate, the more funds will be available for lending. Likewise, there is a demand curve for funds; the lower the interest rate, the more credit will be desired. Figure 6–1 represents the supply and demand curves for funds. In this section, the

---

[1] While the "general level of interest rates" refers to a spectrum of rates which tend to move in the same direction over time, it is convenient to speak as if there were a single rate during the early part of our analysis.

[2] For convenience, we limit the present discussion to borrowing and lending. A company may choose to sell stock instead of borrow and some savers may choose to buy stock instead of lend. For purposes of studying the overall supply and demand for funds, stock may be viewed as synonymous with debt instruments.

various factors affecting these supply and demand curves will be examined.

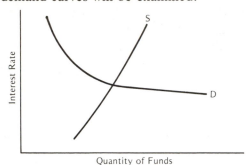

Figure 6–1: Supply and Demand for Funds

SUPPLY OF FUNDS

The supply of funds available within the economy may be viewed as a schedule relating the various quantities of dollars available for loan at different interest rates, given existing economic conditions. Determinants of the supply schedule include the following:

1. Time preference for consumption
2. Expectations concerning future income
3. Desire for money balances
4. Actions of monetary authorities

Time Preference for Consumption This was the first component of the supply schedule to be recognized by economists. It was assumed that consumers were impatient, preferring present to future consumption. One person could consume in excess of his current income only if another consumed less. Compensation in the form of interest would thus encourage one to forego consumption today in return for the prospect of even greater consumption at some future date.

The existence of a multi-billion dollar consumer finance industry bears adequate witness to the fact that there are those willing to pay a premium for the privilege of consuming now rather than later. However, it does not necessarily follow that savers are motivated to save primarily by a desire to earn interest. For example, people continue to save even when the real interest rate—the interest rate after adjustment for changes in buying power—is negative. While high interest rates may serve to encourage some savings, interest is clearly not the only motivation for savings.

Expectations Concerning Future Income Another important determinant of the amount of savings is one's income. If it is expected to fall at a future time, savings today assure some level of consumption at that future time. A significant portion of saving is in the form of contributions to various retirement funds to provide income in the retirement years. Uncertainty about future income, caused by factors such as the possibility of a lay-off or ill health, also encourages savings. This effect is most frequently seen in terms of increased savings in response to concern about the possibility of a recession. Thus expectations of falling future income or uncertainty about future income may lead to an increased supply of savings.

Desire for Money Balances Sometimes a dollar of savings can result in less than a dollar in loans. Savings may be held in the form of money balances—currency and bank demand deposits—or they may be invested in direct loans and securities. One important reason for holding money balances is transactions demand. If a person is paid on a weekly basis, he will hold money at the beginning of the week to handle transactions later in the week. Likewise, businesses hold money for transaction purposes.

In addition to transactions balances, money is held because of uncertainty. Investment in securities, even U.S. government securities, can result in a loss if the interest rate rises sharply. Thus uncertainty about future interest rates will lead to increased desire for money balances. Uncertainty about future income and future investment opportunities are other factors that may lead to increased desire to hold money balances.

The holding of money balances reduces the availability of credit. Money balances held in the form of currency are obviously not available for lending. More importantly, the requirement that financial institutions hold reserves equal to some portion of transaction account balances means that the decision to hold money balances in any form reduces the supply of credit.

Monetary Authorities Government officials have an impact on the supply of credit. Control of credit availability is an important part of government action to stabilize the economy. One form of control is to change the reserve requirements for commercial banks, thus influencing the proportion of bank deposits available in lending markets. Another, more frequently used approach is for the Federal Reserve System to buy or sell U.S. government securities. When the Federal Reserve System purchases securities, it creates money, thereby increasing funds available to loan in credit markets. Of course, the sale of securities owned by the Federal Reserve System has the opposite effect. Thus the Federal Reserve System acts to increase or decrease the availability of credit in response to current economic conditions.

In summary, the supply of credit is affected by the time preference for consumption, expectations concerning future income, the form in which savings are held, and Federal Reserve actions to control credit. Line *S* in Figure 6–1 represents the amount of credit that will be made available at each interest rate under a particular set of economic conditions. The higher the interest rate, the more credit will be made available. A change in conditions can cause *S* to shift. For example, Federal Reserve policy to decrease credit through a change in reserve requirements would cause less credit to be available at each interest rate and would cause the supply curve to shift to the left.

Interest rates are not determined by the supply curve acting alone; they are determined by the interaction of supply and demand. We now turn our attention to the other half of the credit market—demand.

DEMAND FOR FUNDS

The demand for funds within the economy may be viewed as a schedule relating the dollar volume of credit desired at each interest rate, given existing economic conditions. Components of the demand for credit include the following:

1. Demand for consumer credit
2. Government borrowing
3. Acquisition of capital

Demand for Consumer Credit This is generally thought to be relatively insensitive to the interst rate; a rise in interest rates would cause only a small decline in the desire of consumers to borrow. Factors relating to income are believed to have a greater impact. Debt capacity is determined by the ability to make payments. An actual or anticipated increase in income increases the willingness of consumers to borrow so they can enjoy the benefits of that future income today. Stability of income is another factor. If income is viewed as stable, consumers feel more confident of their ability to handle additional debt. Age and family characteristics of the population are also important determinants of the demand for consumer credit. Young people at the family formation age normally demand more consumer credit than older members of the population. While the interest rate has some impact on the demand for consumer credit, these other considerations are of major importance.

Government Borrowing Like consumer borrowing, government borrowing is affected more by revenue expectations and perceived needs than by interest rates. The size of the government deficit is the major determinant of the extent to which government enters credit markets on the demand side. The demand for credit by government is thus insensitive to the rate of interest.

Acquisition of Capital The component of demand which exhibits the greatest sensitivity to interest rates is acquiring capital. Capital goods, such as machinery and factories, make greater production possible. For a capital investment to be attractive, its anticipated return must be at least as great as the interest rate that will be charged. At any time there will be a series of capital investment opportunities, some with higher returns than others. Thus the quantity of credit demanded for the purpose of acquiring capital goods depends on the level of interest rates.

In addition to factories and machinery, another important type of capital good is the residential structure. The quantity of funds demanded for first mortgage loans—characterized by long term maturities—displays some sensitivity to interest rate movements because the interest rate has a major impact on the monthly cost of owning a home. A small shift in interest rates typically results in a relatively large shift in monthly payments for loans of this type. From 1966 to 1981 the monthly payment per $1,000 of principal value of a mortgage loan nearly doubled, solely because of an increase in the interest rate. Thus interest represents a major portion of the cost of residential real estate.

The shape of the demand curve in Figure 6–1 illustrates the shape of a demand curve when some components of demand are sensitive to interest rate levels while other components are relatively insensitive. As interest rates rise to higher levels, demand becomes relatively insensitive to changes in the interest rate, resulting in a near-vertical demand curve at these higher levels.

INFLATION AND INTEREST RATES

The impact of inflation on interest rates has been a matter of growing concern. To understand the impact of inflation, it is first necessary to differentiate between real and nominal interest rates. The nominal interest rate is the contract interest rate paid while the real rate reflects changes in buying power. If the nominal rate is 7 percent and the inflation rate is 5 percent, the real rate is approximately $7\% - 5\% = 2\%$.

Traditional theory has held that the real interest rate will not be affected by inflation and that the nominal rate will increase by the expected inflation rate because savers must be compensated in the form of real returns if they are to be encouraged to lend out their money. In practice, however, the interest rate has not increased by as much as the inflation rate. It appears that this incomplete adjustment is due to uncertainty. As the inflation rate increases, uncertainty about future conditions increases, causing increased savings and decreased demand for credit. Thus inflation causes a shift in both the demand and supply curve. This leads to a decrease in the real interest rate, even though it results in an increase in the nominal rate.

INTEREST RATE DIFFERENTIALS

Up to this point we have treated interest rates as if there were one rate applicable to all securities and loans rather than the array of rates that actually exists at any one time. The rates on securities vary with regard to both risk and maturity. Understanding these differentials is vital for dealing with many financial institution management problems. The two types of differentials are taken up in this section.

TERM STRUCTURE OF INTEREST RATES

The term structure of interest rates represents the relationship between yield and maturity. U.S. government securities can be used to illustrate the impact of maturity as they differ with regard to maturity but not with regard to safety of principal. Figure 6–2 is a yield curve, showing the interest rates on U.S. government securities of various maturities. It represents a more or less typical yield curve, with the interest rate increasing as maturity increases. The three main approaches to explanation of the shape of the yield curve are liquidity premium theory, expectation theory, and market segmentation theory. Each of these is discussed in the following paragraphs.

Liquidity Premium   Even though U.S. government securities are considered virtually risk-free with regard to payment at maturity, there is still a risk associated with an early need for funds. If a holder of long-term bonds should need the funds before maturity, the bonds must be sold in the secondary securities market. If the general level of interest rates has risen in the meantime, the price of outstanding bonds will have fallen. The longer the maturity of a bond, the greater will be the change in the price resulting from a change in interest rates.[3] Thus, even among securities that are risk-

free with regard to payment at maturity, longer maturities result in greater risk. Under normal conditions, higher return is necessary to encourage people to accept the greater liquidity risk associated with long term securities.

Expectation Theory   Another factor affecting the shape of the yield curve is the set of expectations with regard to future interest rates. In the absence of liquidity risk or market restrictions, the yield curve would represent an average of short-term rates expected over each maturity. Thus the yield curve reflects both liquidity risks and expected changes in the general level of interest rates. Figure 6–3 illustrates a yield curve in which short-term rates are higher than long-term rates. This cannot be accounted for with liquidity premium theory. Expectation theory would argue that the difference in shape between Figures 6–2 and 6–3 is explained if January 31, 1978, was a time when

------

[3] A review of bond yield computations in Chapter 5 will confirm this.

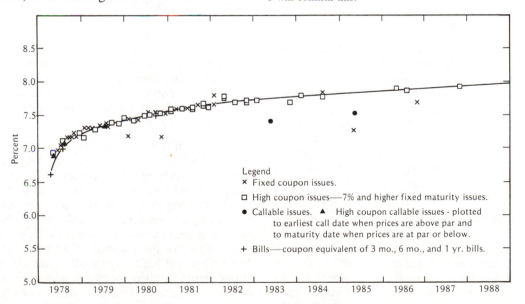

Figure 6–2: Yields of Treasury Securities January 31, 1978 (based on closing bid quotations). Source: *Treasury Bulletin.*

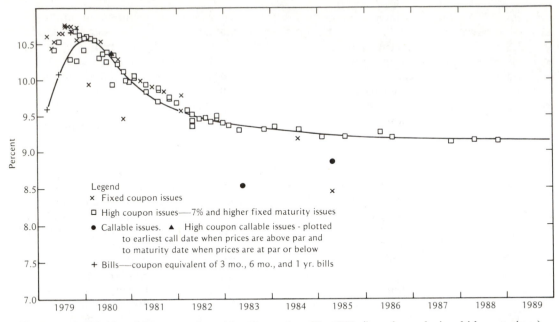

Figure 6–3: Yields of Treasury Securities December 29, 1978 (based on closing bid quotations). Source: *Treasury Bulletin.*

investors were expecting a rise in the level of interest rates and December 31, 1978, was a time when they felt interest rates would decline after about a year. If interest rates were expected to fall, borrowers would tend to avoid long-term borrowing and temporarily borrow short-term with the hope of refinancing through issuance of long-term securities when rates fall. Lenders, on the other hand, would be attempting to acquire long-term securities before rates fell. This combination of actions would tend to drive short-term rates up and long-term rates down until each rate equals the average of expected short-term rates over its maturity.

Market Segmentation Theory A third method is used to explain interest rate differentials. With this approach, the market for funds is looked at as a set of markets, not a single market. For example, the short-term maturity market can be viewed as a liquidity adjustment market while the long-term market can be viewed as a market for capital investment funds. To the extent maturity needs rather than interest rate considerations determine maturity, there are separate markets for each maturity and interest rate differentials are determined by supply and demand conditions in the various maturity markets. Using this approach, the inverted yield curve of Figure 6–3 would be explained by heavy demand in the liquidity adjustment end of the markets.

It is probably most helpful to look at these three approaches to the shape of the yield curve as complementary rather than competing models. First, it is reasonable to expect some compensation for holding longer maturities and giving up some liquidity. Second, it is reasonable for expectations to be reflected in the term structure because some borrowers and lenders can adjust their maturity structure in response to expected interest rate changes. Third, there is some segmentation in the markets. An example of the impact of this is a fed funds rate well

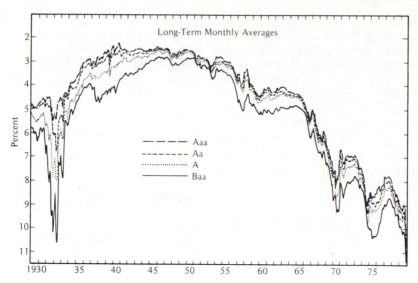

Figure 6–4: Industrial Bond Yields by Ratings.   Source: Moody's Bond Record.

above the rate on maturing Treasury bills. Thus all three reasons should be considered when studying term structure.

Adjusting positions in response to existing and anticipated yield curve shapes can have a substantial impact on profitability. Many borrowers and lenders, particularly portfolio managers of large institutions, study the shape of the yield curves, prepare their own interest rate forecasts, and attempt to pattern their activities in the credit markets in response to these factors.

RISK AND REQUIRED RATES OF RETURN

Another major factor which leads to interest rate differentials is risk[4] with regard to the actual stream of income emanating from a particular security. The value of a share of stock or a bond is a function of the anticipated future cash flows to be derived therefrom and is equal to the discounted

present value of these flows. For a debt instrument, the returns are in the form of principal and interest payments, while for stock the return is in the form of dividends. The present value of this stream of returns and thus the price of the security can change because the general level of interest rates (and therefore the required rate of return) changes. The value of the security will also change if there is a change in the stream of cash flow expected, normally caused by a change in actual or anticipated profitability of the firm. When risk increases, the required return also increases. The bond issuers are rated as to the quality of the issue. The most widely known of these rating agencies are Moody's and Standard and Poor. Moody's rating descriptions appear in Table 4–3.

The rating is one standard measure of the risk level. Figure 6–4 shows average yields of bonds by rating over the past 50 years. An examination of Figure 6–4 reveals that the interest rates are higher for more risky bonds, and that the size of the spread increases as the general level of interest rates increases. It is also known that the spread increases with increased uncertainty about the economic outlook.

---

[4] Risk in this context can be thought of as the probability that the stream of anticipated returns will not be realized. More generally, risk can be thought of as the probability of a financial loss.

The data on bond yields do not provide any specific information about the relationship between risk and required return. Studies of the specific relationship between risk and required rate of return have, for the most part, been based on common stock returns, although the results can be generalized to investments of any kind. A major result of these studies—the mean-variance capital asset pricing model—is summarized in Appendix 6–A.

FORECASTING INTEREST RATES

Future interest rate movements are of vital concern to institutions. Profits can be favorably influenced through accurate projection of interest rates followed by appropriate policy decisions. The savings and loan industry has at times found its profits severely eroded by being on the wrong side of a change in interest rates, granting long-term loans while relying on short-term deposits in periods of rising interest rates. The industry has responded to these losses by increasing its efforts to acquire long-term funds, such as long-term certificates of deposit. If this action had been taken earlier in anticipation of rising interest rates, substantial losses could have been avoided.

Most efforts to forecast interest rates concentrate on what is considered the intermediate term by forecasters: from one quarter to several years in the future. Over the intermediate term, interest rates respond primarily to a set of economic variables discussed in this section. Short-term forecasts of a few days to a few weeks are normally prepared by forecasting the recent trend of interest rates. Long-term forecasts involve such factors as changing age characteristics of the population.[5] Both because of the type of factors involved and because of the importance to institutions, this section will concentrate on intermediate term forecasting.

Methods of preparing forecasts of the general level of interest rates range from application of judgment to mathematical models. Regardless of the method used, the major factors studied in preparing interest rate forecasts are:

1. Federal Reserve policy
2. Changes in Gross National Product
3. The liquidity of the economy
4. The outlook for the supply and demand for funds
5. The inflation rate[6]

Federal Reserve Policy This factor can be measured primarily in terms of the money supply. Target rates of growth are announced by the Federal Reserve and are widely published in the general press. Target growth rates are compared to actual growth rates in preparing forecasts of the money supply. Money supply figures are published monthly in the *Federal Reserve Bulletin* as well as in the business press generally.

Gross National Product Increases in the growth rate of Gross National Product generally cause increased demand for funds for both consumer credit and capital acquisition. Thus increases in the growth rate of Gross National Product cause interest rates to rise while declines in the growth rates typically have a downward impact. While one can prepare his own GNP forecasts, they can also be obtained from publicly available sources.

The Liquidity Position of the Economy As was mentioned earlier, savings do not automatically result in a direct increase in the

---

[5] See, for example, John S. Burton and John R. Toth, "Forecasting Secular Trends in Long-Term Interest Rates," *Financial Analysts Journal*, September-October, 1974, pp. 73–87, or the series of papers on long-term trends in interest rates published in the January, 1970 issue of *Business Economics*.

[6] Francis H. Schott, "Interest Rate Forecasting in Theory and Practice," *Business Economics*, Vol CII (September, 1977), pp. 55–60.

supply of credit. The amount of credit supply increase actually achieved depends on the desires of people and business to hold money balances. For example, if there is a general desire for increased money balances, an effort by the Federal Reserve to increase the money supply may be offset by increased liquid balances, not increased economic activity.

Obviously, the trick here is to forecast the demand for money balances in comparison to present measures of the money supply and adjust the credit supply forecast accordingly. This is, of course, easier said than done. As was discussed earlier in this chapter, desired money balances depend on various factors such as transactions needs and uncertainty about future conditions. A good deal of experienced judgment is required and errors in this area are frequent.

Outlook for the Supply and Demand for Credit A major part of the interest forecasting problem, the outlook is usually prepared by using the sources and uses of credit data published monthly in the *Federal Reserve Bulletin*. A condensed version appears in Table 6–1. The individual components of the supply and demand for credit can be forecast using the outlook for GNP growth, government budgets, capital spending plan surveys, housing construction forecasts, etc. It is then possible to make a prediction as to whether supply or demand will increase more rapidly, and thus whether the pressure on interest rates will be upward or downward.

Expected Inflation As indicated previously, the interest rate includes a real return and some compensation for expected inflation. Thus the interest rate will be expected to rise with an increase in the expected rate of inflation. Many forecasting models use an average of inflation rates for previous years to forecast interest rates for the coming period. Others use surveys of economists.

The various factors can be weighed in the mind of the interest rate forecaster, who relies on his judgment and past experience to develop actual forecasts, or they can be combined using mathematical models.

VALUE

The pursuit of the profitability objective normally involves two steps: the selection of assets with the highest value relative to their cost, and the management of liabilities to achieve the lowest cost of funds. Valuation principles are used to determine what a financial asset is worth, to determine the quality of collateral, and to determine the vulnerability of an asset's price to interest rate changes. Thus valuation is important for both profitability and risk analysis. It is particularly important for financial institutions because most of their assets are financial instruments.

The valuation principles discussed here are limited to revenue producing assets. We do not deal with approaches such as replacement value, sometimes used in the case of residential property, or aesthetic value, which may have some application in the world of art. We do concern ourselves with market value to the extent that we are discussing the market value of a revenue producing asset.

Valuation principles are primarily an application of interest and required return principles discussed in this and the previous chapter. A financial asset has three primary characteristics for this type of analysis: a stream of expected cash flows, a required rate of return, and a value. If two of these variables are known, the third can be inferred from the other two. Thus valuation is the topic that brings interest and required return analysis together in a useful form.

FIXED INCOME ASSETS

To begin the analysis of value, an asset having no maturity and paying a constant stream of cash flows provides a good illustration. An example of this type of asset is

Table 6–1:

Sources and Uses of Funds in U.S. Credit Markets
(in $ billions)

	1978	1979	1980
Users of Credit Funds			
Total credit funds raised	398.3	390.6	349.8
Foreign uses	32.3	21.2	29.9
Total domestic uses of funds	366.0	369.4	319.9
U.S. government uses	53.7	37.4	79.2
Total private domestic uses	312.3	332.0	240.7
State and local government*	28.3	18.9	22.2
Corporate bonds	20.1	21.2	27.6
Mortgages	148.3	159.9	125.8
Consumer credit	50.6	44.2	3.1
Bank loans n.e.c.	37.3	50.6	37.9
Open market paper	5.2	10.9	5.8
Other	22.2	27.3	20.4
Sources of Credit Funds			
Total credit funds raised	398.3	390.6	349.8
Noninstitutional sources			
Lending by U.S. government	65.0	80.0	74.6
Monetary authorities	7.0	7.7	4.5
Foreign lenders	37.7	−7.7	16.7
Other	−8.3	18.1	−11.6
From domestic financial institutions	296.9	292.5	265.6
Commercial banks	128.7	121.1	103.5
Savings institutions	75.9	56.3	57.6
Insurance and pension funds	73.5	70.4	76.4
Other financial institutions	18.7	44.7	28.1
Sources of domestic financial institution funds	296.9	292.5	265.6
Private domestic deposits	142.5	136.7	163.9
Credit market borrowing	38.3	33.8	19.8
Foreign funds	6.3	26.3	−20.0
Insurance and pension fund reserves	62.7	49.0	58.5
Treasury balances	6.8	.4	−2.0
Other	40.3	46.3	45.4
Memo: Corporate equity issues not included in above figures	2.1	4.3	13.5

*Classification of state and local government as "private" is the work of the Federal Reserve statisticians, not the authors.

Source: Condensed from *Federal Reserve Bulletin*

the British Consul, a bond issued to finance the Napoleonic wars. It carries no maturity date but pays a fixed amount of interest each year. Preferred stock, of course, has similar characteristics. For such an instrument, the value (V) is based on the annual cash flows (CF) and the required rate of return (r):

$$V = CF/r \qquad (6\text{--}1)$$

For an instrument with an $80-per-year cash flow and a 6 percent required return, the value is

$$V = 80/.06 = \$1,333$$

This basic valuation principle can be readily verified from common observation. If a savings account pays 6 percent interest, a $1,333 deposit would yield interest of $80 (.06 × $1,333) per year. Thus a promise to pay $80 per year would not be worth more than the amount that you would need to deposit in a savings account to achieve the same result.[7]

The simple problem above can be used to illustrate the relationship among the three characteristics. For example, if we know that the value is $1,333 and the annual cash flow is $80, then the rate of return is found by solving for r in equation 6–1. In this case, the answer would be 6 percent.

The value of an asset with no maturity is particularly sensitive to interest rate changes. If we wanted to test the sensitivity of value to interest rate changes, we could simply solve equation 6–1 for various levels of required return as is done below:

$$V = 80/.02 = \$4,000$$
$$V = 80/.06 = \$1,333$$
$$V = 80/.07 = \$1,143$$
$$V = 80/.15 = \$\ 533$$

Even a one percentage point change in interest rate leads to a 14 percent change in value. Interest rates of such obligations have risen from the 2 percent range to the 15 percent range, resulting in a loss of nearly ninety percent of the previous value with no decline in the credit worthiness of the borrower.

The same general principles apply to the valuation of all financial assets. The value equals the present value of all cash flows, discounted at the required rate of return. However, the existence of a maturity increases the difficulty of computation, requiring the use of the present value tables. A bond with a maturity of 10 years, an $80 annual interest paid in semi-annual installments, and a $1,000 maturity value will be used as an example. If the required return is 6 percent, the 20-year, 3 percent tables are used instead of the ten-year, 6 percent tables because payment is semi-annual. The value of the bond would be

14.877 × 40 + .5537 × 1,000

$$= \$1,148.78[8]$$

To test the sensitivity of the value of this bond to various interest rates, we can simply repeat the calculation at other rates:

2%: 18.046 × 40 + .8195 × 1,000 = $1,541.34
6%: 14.877 × 40 + .5537 × 1,000 = $1,148.78
7%: 14.212 × 40 + .5026 × 1,000 = $1,071.08
9%: 13.008 × 40 + .4146 × 1,000 = $ 934.92

The existence of a fairly limited maturity decreases the sensitivity of value to interest rate changes. In this case one percentage point increase in the interest rate causes the value of the bond to decline by less than 7 percent as opposed to over 14 percent for the perpetual bond.

Sensitivity of the market values of mortgages can be treated in a similar manner. Using Table A–8, we find that the monthly

---

[7] This comparison ignores the fact that the savings account would normally carry a lower required return because it is more liquid. Unless the yield curve were perfectly flat, there would be some difference between the required return on the Consul and the savings account interest rate.

[8] Based on Tables A–5 and A–7. Review the present value methods in Chapter 5 if the reasons for this are not clear.

payment for a 30-year, 9 percent, $50,000 mortgage would be $402.31 ($50,000/ 124.282). If the interest rate were to rise to 12 percent, the value of such a mortgage would decline to $39,112 ($402.31 × 97.218) (again using Table A–8), a loss in value of 22 percent. By way of contrast, a 15-year mortgage would have suffered only a 15 percent decline in value under the same circumstances.

Any fixed income security can be converted to a stream of cash flows and its value can be determined by discounting this stream at the appropriate required return. Alternately, the rate of return can be found if the value and the stream of cash flows are known. This was illustrated for bonds in Chapter 5.

Certain nonfinancial assets, such as rental property, can be valued in a similar manner. The value of rental property, for example, equals the present value of the cash flows generated. These include rental income, net of expenses, and terminal value. An income property will cost $25,000 in cash and will require the assumption of an $80,000 mortgage. Annual cash flow, net of all cash expenses including tax and mortgage repayment, would be $3,000 per year and the value of the property at the end of the 20-year period would be $20,000. At a 12 percent required return, the value would be

$$3,000 \times 7.4694 + 20,000$$
$$\times .1037 = \$24,482$$

The value of the cash flows is less than the amount required to purchase the building. Thus it provides a return below 12 percent and would not be an attractive investment.[9]

---

[9] The same approach could be applied to speculative real estate providing no current income. If the required return is 12 percent, the property is expected to be worth $100,000 in five years, and annual holding expense (tax and insurance) is $2,000, the value of the property today is

$$-\$2,000 \times 3.6048 + \$100,000 \times .5674 = \$49,530$$

EQUITY SECURITIES

While the same principles apply to equity securities, the problem is complicated by the fact that equity securities do not provide a contractual payment, but provide returns based on profits of the firm whose ownership they represent. It is necessary to develop some indirect method of determining value. Two frequently used approaches are discussed here.

The *price-earnings ratio* approach provides one such method of valuation. The price-earnings ratio is simply the ratio of market price to earnings per share for a company's common stock. It can be used as a multiplier like a present value factor. Its use is based on the argument that the earnings, whether paid out or reinvested to provide future dividends, are the return to shareholders. The multiplier applied to these earnings depends on the stability and expected growth of the earnings as well as other opportunities for investment. While the average price-earnings ratio is presently about 9, the range is so broad that ratios of 50 or more are not unheard of.

As an example of the use of this approach, suppose the stock of a company that is not publicly owned is to be given an estimated value. Earnings per share for the company are $3.20. We would begin by looking at the price-earnings ratios for companies in similar business lines whose stock was publicly traded. Suppose that we find a range of 12 to 15. We would then multiply $3.20 by each of these numbers and establish a value range between $38.40 and $48.00. The location of the value within this range would depend on the prospects for this company versus the others in the same business area, as well as factors such as marketability of shares.

The *dividend growth model* is another method of valuing common stock. It is most likely to be applied in a case such as a utility where the dividend level is stable and the growth rate is moderate. In this case, the value of a share of stock equals the present value of the dividends directly:

$$V = \frac{d}{r - g} \qquad (6\text{--}2)$$

where: d = Expected dividends over the next year

r = Required rate of return

g = Anticipated growth rate of dividends

For example, a company is expected to pay dividends of $2.38 over the next year and dividends are expected to grow at the rate of 4 percent a year. At a required return of 14 percent, the value would be:

$$V = \frac{2.38}{.14 - .04} = \$23.80$$

The use of this approach involves two problems. First, there is the problem of a growth rate. The model assumes a stable, continuous growth rate. Since growth rates greater than the overall economy are not sustainable, it can only be used with low, stable growth rates. Second, there is the problem of determining the appropriate rate of return. The mean-variance capital market model, discussed in Appendix 6–A, is frequently used to determine the required rate of return.

The valuation of common stock is made difficult by the fact that there is no accurate way to predict the stream of cash flow. Sometimes these estimating problems are avoided by assuming that the book value per share represents the actual value. This approach ignores the fact that the earnings stream, not historical cost, determines value.

SUMMARY

We have examined both the factors affecting the general level of interest rates and the factors affecting interest rate differentials. The general level of interest rates is determined by supply and demand. The primary factors affecting the supply of credit are

1. Time preference for consumption
2. Expectations concerning future income
3. Desire for money balances

The primary components of demand for credit are

1. Demand for consumer credit
2. Government borrowing
3. Acquisition of capital

The general level of interest rates is also affected by the anticipated rate of inflation. Although the adjustment appears to be less than complete, with the nominal interest rising by less than the anticipated increase in inflation. The interest rate will nevertheless increase in response to an increase in expected inflation.

Interest rate differentials between securities are attributed to risk and time until maturity. The yield curve shows the relationship between interest rate and time until maturity. The shape of the yield curve depends primarily on liquidity preference, expectations concerning future interest rates, and conditions in various sectors of the market for funds.

Interest rate forecasters study the factors leading to changes in interest rates discussed in the first part of the chapter. The five major factors studied are

1. Federal Reserve policy
2. Changes in Gross National Product
3. The liquidity of the economy
4. The outlook for supply and demand for funds
5. The inflation rate

These factors are combined using either the judgment and experience of the forecaster or mathematical models.

Valuation is an application of interest and required return analysis. The value of a financial asset equals the present value of the cash flows discounted at the required rate of return. For fixed income securities, the calculation is relatively straightforward. For equity securities, the problem is complicated by the fact that cash flows are not known and must be estimated.

Required return and valuation principles are useful to institution managers in gauging profitability and risk exposure. Thus they play a vital role in asset management. As we will see in the following chapter, they also play an important role in management of sources of funds.

QUESTIONS

1. Why does a yield curve generally slope upward? What factors would lead to other shapes?

2. As a library project, trace the volume of demand for funds. Which use—government, consumer, capital investment—appears to be the most volatile?

3. Locate at least two recent articles discussing the expected trend in interest rates. Compare and contrast the conclusions and the reasoning.

4. What are the primary sources and uses of credit in the United States?

5. We rely on the rate of return as the method of allocating funds in a free economy. Does this method lead to any problems? What other methods are possible?

PROBLEMS

1. Construct a figure illustrating the downward sloping demand curve and upward sloping supply curve for funds. Illustrate, by showing shifts in the curve, the impact of
    a. An increase in government deficit spending.
    b. A decrease in the savings rate.

2. Construct a yield curve for the most

recent date available using information from the Federal Reserve Bulletin. Do you find evidence of any anticipated changes in interest rates?

3. The nominal interest rate for a particular year was 8 percent and the inflation rate was 5 percent. What was the real rate of interest?

SELECTED REFERENCES

Ben-Horim, Moshe, and Haim Levy, "Total Risk, Diversifiable Risk and Non-Diversifiable Risk: A Pedagogic Note," *Journal of Financial and Quantitative Analysis,* Vol. 15 (June, 1980), pp. 289–297.

Bowsher, Norman N., "Rise and Fall of Interest Rates," *Federal Reserve Bank of St. Louis Review,* Vol. 62 (August/September, 1980), pp. 16–23.

Dobson, Steven W., Richard C. Sutch, and David E. Vanderford, "An Evaluation of Alternative Empirical Models of the Term Structure of Interest Rates," *Journal of Finance,* Vol. 31 (September, 1976), pp. 1035–1066.

Dothan, Uri, and Joseph Williams, "Term-Risk Structures and the Valuation of Projects," *Journal of Financial and Quantitative Analysis,* Vol. 15 (November, 1980), pp. 875–905.

Elliott, J.W., and Jerome R. Baier, "Econometric Models and Current Interest Rates: How Well Do They Predict Future Rates?" *Journal of Finance,* Vol. 34 (September, 1979), pp. 975–986.

Friedman, Benjamin M., "Interest Rate Expectations Versus Forward Rates: Evidence from an Expectations Survey," *Journal of Finance,* Vol. 34 (September, 1979), pp. 965–974.

Friedman, Benjamin M., "Substitution and Expectation Effects on Long Term Borrowing Behavior and Long Term Interest Rates," *Journal of Money, Credit and Banking,* Vol. 11 (May, 1979), pp. 131–150.

Langetieg, Terence C., "A Multivariate Model of the Term Structure," *Journal of Finance,* Vol. 35 (March, 1980), pp. 71–98.

Pesando, James E., "On Forecasting Long Term Interest Rates: Is the Success of the No-

Change Prediction Surprising?" *Journal of Finance,* Vol. 35 (September, 1980), pp. 1045–1048.

Mossin, Jan, *Theory of Financial Markets.* Englewood Cliffs, New Jersey: Prentice-Hall, 1973.

Saving, Thomas R., "Money Supply Theory with Competitively Determined Deposit Rates and

Activity Changes," *Journal of Money, Credit and Banking,* Vol. 11 (February, 1979), pp. 22–31.

VanHorne, James C., "The Term Structure: A Test of the Segmented Markets Hypothesis," *Southern Economics Journal,* Vol. 46 (April, 1980), pp. 1129–1140.

Appendix 6-A

Mean-Variance Capital Asset Pricing Model

Students of finance have long recognized that the required returns are higher for risky assets. However, conversion from this general observation to a specific relationship between risk and required return proved to be an elusive goal. Mean-variance portfolio theory, developed by Harry Markowitz in the early 1950s,[1] provided the foundation for a more precise approach to risk. The work of Sharpe,[2] Treynor,[3] and Jensen,[4] in the 1960s was largely responsible for building from the foundation provided by Markowitz to a specific model of the relationship between risk and the required rate of return.

The model has proved to have numerous uses in practice. First, it provided a method of adjusting for risk in evaluating returns from investment portfolios. Second, it has been used in determining required returns for investments by profit-seeking corporations. Additional uses have been in areas such as public utility rate case hearings.

The model begins with the observation that investors are, in general, risk averse. Therefore, at any given level of expected return, the typical investor prefers less risk to more. Figure 6A–1 represents the spectrum of all portfolios available to investors at a particular time. Each point in Figure 6A–1 represents a given combination of securities (a portfolio) identified as to risk and expected return. Portfolios represented by points B and C, for example, are expected to produce the same return, but portfolio B is more risky. Because investors prefer less risk and more expected return, a particular portfolio will be preferred to any portfolio directly above it or above it and to the left. Portfolio M will be preferred over portfolio B by all investors. However, the choice between M and C is not so obvious. C involves less risk and less expected return. The choice would depend on how risk averse a particular investor is, i.e., his *risk preference function*. A portfolio like M or C, for which there exists no portfolio providing less risk without less return or more return without more risk,

[1] Harry Markowitz, "Portfolio Selection," *Journal of Finance* (March, 1952), pp. 77–91.

[2] William Sharpe, "Capital Asset Prices: A Theory of Market Equilibrium Under Conditions of Risk," *The Journal of Finance* (September, 1964), pp. 425–442.

[3] Jack Treynor, "How to Rate Management of Mutual Funds," *Harvard Business Review* (January-February, 1965), pp. 63–75.

[4] Michael Jensen, "Risk, the Pricing of Capital Assets, and the Evaluation of Investment Portfolios," *Journal of Business* (April, 1969), pp. 167–247.

Figure 6A–1: Investment Opportunity Set.

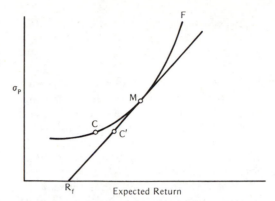

Figure 6A–2: Efficient Frontier Analysis.

is referred to as an *efficient portfolio.* The set of all such portfolios is referred to as the efficient frontier.

Thus far we have spoken of risk only in general terms. In practice, standard deviation, a widely used statistical measure, is normally used as a risk measure. The standard deviation of the probability distribution of expected returns (σ_p) is normally used as a measure of risk. The formula for the standard deviation is

$$\sigma_p = \sqrt{\sum_{i=1}^{n} p_i(R_i - E_p)^2} \quad (6A\text{--}1)$$

where: R_i = Return for the portfolio if outcome *i* occurs

p_i = Probability of outcome *i* occurring

n = The number of different possible outcomes

E_p = Expected return for the portfolio[5]

We now introduce a very important type of investment—a risk-free security such as a Treasury bill. Line F in Figure 6A–2 represents the efficient frontier shown in Figure

6A–1. The efficient frontier can be drawn as a line rather than a series of points because a near-infinite number of different portfolios is possible. By investing a portion of his funds in risky portfolio *M* and the remainder in a risk-free asset, an investor can create a new portfolio on the straight line connecting *M* (referred to as the *tangent portfolio*) and point R_f. By varying the proportion of his funds invested in *M* and putting the remainder in the risk-free asset, the investor can achieve a portfolio anywhere on the line connecting *M* and R_f. Furthermore, he can achieve points on this line above *M* if he can borrow at a similar interest rate. Thus, these various combinations of *M* and the risk-free security provide portfolios superior to all other portfolios on the efficient frontier, such as *C*. *M* would be preferred by all investors and they would adjust for their individual degree of risk aversion by varying the proportion of funds invested in *M* and the proportion invested at the risk-free rate.

As an example, suppose the risk-free rate is 6 percent, the expected return for portfolio *M* is 10 percent, and the standard deviation of expected returns for portfolio *M* is 4 percent. Portfolio *C'* consists of ⅔ of the investor's funds invested in portfolio *M* and ⅓ invested in the risk-free asset. The expected return and standard deviation for portfolio *C'* are

---

[5] The expected return for the portfolio is computed as follows:

$$E_p = \sum_{i=1}^{n} p_i R_i$$

$$\text{Expected return} = \frac{2}{3} \times .10 + \frac{1}{3} \times .06 = 8.6\%$$

$$\text{Standard deviation} = \frac{2}{3} \times .04 = 2.67\%$$

Portfolio C' would be preferred over portfolio C by all investors; C' has the same standard deviation but has a higher expected return. Thus an investor wishing to accept a different amount of risk than M would move to a portfolio such as C' rather than a portfolio such as C.

If investors are in agreement about the prospects for particular securities, M must eventually contain all risky securities. The prices of individual securities will rise or fall so that demand for each, as a component of M, is neither greater nor less than the supply available. M is referred to as the *market portfolio*.

From the foregoing analysis it follows that the important aspect of risk for an individual security is its contribution to the risk of the market portfolio. The total risk of a security can be divided into two parts: diversifiable and non-diversifiable risk. For example, the purchaser of stock in one automobile company faces the risk that that company's new model will be unpopular. That risk can be diversified away by dividing funds among all automobile companies. Likewise, the possibility of a change in taste or technology resulting in a shift from products produced by one industry to those of another can be diversified away by including in the portfolio securities issued by firms in different industries. Eventually though, there are risks that cannot be diversified away. The possibility of a recession or restrictive monetary policy leading to decreased return on all security investments can only be avoided by choosing the risk-free security instead. Aggregate risks of the type that tend to affect the economy in general cannot be diversified away.

If a group of stocks had only diversifiable risk, they could be combined in a portfolio and the portfolio would be risk-free. If this risk-free portfolio had a higher return than the risk-free rate, all investors wishing to hold a risk-free investment would choose the portfolio rather than the single risk-free asset. Thus it is necessary for market equilibrium that the return on such a portfolio be the same as the risk-free rate. Therefore, risky portfolios and risky securities pay a higher return than the risk-free rate as compensation for accepting *nondiversifiable* risk.

Nondiversifiable risk is caused by the tendency of certain factors to affect all securities in the same way. An increase in the general level of interest rates, for example, will cause an increase in required returns for all securities and will drive the prices of all securities down. Likewise, a recession will decrease the profitability and increase the riskiness of most business enterprises. The degree of nondiversifiable risk for a particular security is measured in terms of the tendency of returns for the security to move in the same direction as other securities.

The most widely used method of measuring nondiversifiable risk is *beta*. Beta is a measure of the sensitivity of return for a particular investment to returns for investments in general. The beta can best be explained using a graph. It is illustrated for the common stock of a particular company in Figure 6A–3. Over a period of time, we observe that when returns on securities in general rise, returns for this particular security rise, and when returns for securities in general decline, returns for this particular se-

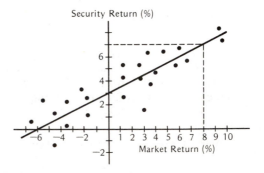

Figure 6A–3: Relation of Security to Market.

curity decline. We observed the returns (dividends and price appreciation) a holder of this security would have received during each of a number of periods and observed the return that an investor would have received during each of these periods if he had held some broad-based portfolio, representing all common stocks. Each dot in Figure 6A–3 represents one such pair of observations. The line is drawn to fit the dots as closely as possible. The line, then, represents the return we might expect from the security at each possible level of return for stocks in general. The greater the slope of this line, the greater the sensitivity of the investment to overall conditions, and the greater the nondiversifiable risk.

Beta provides a measure of the slope of this line, and therefore of nondiversifiable risk. Beta is defined as

$$\text{beta} = \frac{\text{change in expected return for the security}}{\text{change in expected return for all stocks}} \quad (6A\text{--}2)$$

From Figure 6A–3, expected return for the security is 3 percent if expected return for stocks in general is 0 percent. Expected return for the security is 7 percent if expected return for stocks in general is 8 percent. The beta for the security is then:

$$\text{beta} = \frac{.07 - .03}{.08 - .00} = 0.5$$

Obviously, for any particular security during any particular time period, these relationships will not hold precisely. Factors affecting a particular security may cause actual return to be above or below what would be expected based on overall market conditions. For example, return to investors holding the stock of a particular company will depend on acceptance of that company's products as well as overall market conditions. Once again, a well diversified portfolio will cancel out the risks associated only with a particular security. However, the expected relationship between the security and

securities in general cannot be offset through diversification.

The higher the beta, the greater is the nondiversifiable risk. A beta of two indicates that if returns for stocks in general increase, return for the particular security will be expected to increase twice as much and if returns for stocks in general decrease, return for the particular security will be expected to decrease twice as much. Betas for publicly traded common stocks are regularly reported by investment advisory services such as Value Line.

As stated earlier, the required return for a particular investment is a function of the general level of interest rates and the nondiversifiable risk associated with that particular investment. The interest rate on risk-free investments, such as U.S. government securities, is normally used as a measure of the general level of interest rates and beta is used as the measure of nondiversifiable risk. Thus, an individual security's beta measures its contribution to portfolio risk. The required rate of return is a function of the interest rate on risk-free assets, return for other risky assets, and the security's beta. It can be shown[6] that the required return, or interest rate necessary to attract investors to a risky asset is

$$K_e = R_f + b(E_m - R_f)$$

Where:
K_e = The required rate of return
R_f = The rate on risk-free securities
b = Beta
E_m = Expected average return for common stocks in general

The term $(E_m - R_f)$ is the difference between expected average return for all stocks and the risk-free interest rate. It is the average compensation for risk in the security

---

[6] A proof and detailed discussion can be found in any advanced investment text. For example, see Jack Clark Francis, *Investments: Analysis and Management,* New York: McGraw-Hill, 1980.

market, or the risk premium. As the formula shows, the risk premium for a particular security is a function of its beta and the risk premium for stocks in general.

Thus we have a concise measure of security risk as well as a concise statement of the relationship between risk and the required return. The model has proved to be quite useful for evaluating portfolio managers and determining the required returns for specific assets.

AN EXAMPLE

First National Bank is considering a new equity issue to expand its capital base. To decide if this action is in the best interest of the present stockholders, the bank must determine whether the return required by equity investors is above or below the return it can earn with additional funds. The required return on equity cannot be observed directly in the market place as can the return on Treasury bills or corporate bonds. The returns expected from investments of the latter type can be determined because they carry a fixed, contractual obligation and have an observable market price. Common stock has an observable market price, but does not carry a fixed obligation. Therefore, the return required by investors is not directly observable. It must be estimated using available information about general levels of return and risk premiums.

To estimate the required return, the bank must first develop measures of the risk-free interest rate, the average risk premium for the market in general, and the beta for the bank's stock. Studies covering extensive time periods (up to 50 years) have shown that the difference between the interest rates on long-term U.S. government bonds and the realized return on common stock—the realized risk premium—has averaged approximately 5.4 percent. According to the *Value Line Investment Survey,* the beta for the average commercial bank listed there is approximately .90. Assume that the Treasury bond rate is presently 8.6 percent. Thus,

the estimate of the required return for common stock in general is:

$$E_m = .086 + .054 = 14\%$$

The required return for the bank's stock would then be:

$$K_e = .086 + .90(.14 - .086) = 13.5\%$$

Therefore, according to this model, the equity issue would be in the long-run best interest of investors if the bank is successful in producing a return in excess of 13.5 percent for its equity investors.

QUESTIONS

1. Explain the difference between diversifiable and nondiversifiable risk.

2. What are the characteristics of an efficient portfolio?

PROBLEMS

1. Returns for ABC common stock and the market in general for each of the last ten years appear below. What is the beta?

Year	1	2	3	4	5	6	7	8	9	10
Mkt.	.10	.15	−.05	.05	.00	.20	.12	.06	.07	.10
ABC	.13	.20	−.10	.05	−.05	.25	.15	.06	.10	.12

2. Returns for stocks in general are expected to be 12 percent and the risk-free rate is 6 percent. Middle American Finance has a beta of 1.3. Compute the required return for Middle American common stock.

3. Over a particular five-year-period, common stock in general provided an average return of 12 percent per year and the risk-free rate averaged 6 percent. A pension fund managed by Southwest Trust had a return of 15 percent over the same period. It was managed aggressively and had a relatively high beta of 2.0. Evaluate Southwest's performance.

Chapter 7

Financial Structure and the Cost of Funds

We have seen that financial institutions differ from other types of business in that they deal primarily in financial obligations, accepting funds for which a return is promised and reinvesting these funds in financial obligations of others. While the cost of funds used is one of many costs faced by the typical non-financial business, it is a major cost faced by financial institutions. Thus knowledge of the cost of funds and the factors affecting it are of particular concern to the financial institution manager.

While a non-financial business may fail for any number of reasons, such as unacceptance of its major products, the primary danger to the financial institution lies in the structure of financial obligations. Failure results primarily from the inability to earn a return on assets sufficient to meet obligations to suppliers of funds; in general, the greater the fixed obligations and the shorter the maturity, the greater the risk of failure.

More generally, a financial institution can be considered successful only if it meets fixed obligations and provides a return to equity investors that equals or exceeds returns available to these investors elsewhere. Thus the cost of funds consists of fixed obligations and the opportunity cost of funds for which a fixed return is not promised. The total cost of funds, then, represents an important obligation of the institution. The identification of the overall cost of funds is one of the objectives of this chapter.

We are interested in more than understanding the cost of funds and risk of failure associated with a particular financial structure. We are interested in managing and controlling these variables. By varying the financial structure—the proportion of total funds coming from each potential source—management is able to affect both risk and the cost of funds. A second objective of this chapter is to develop the main principles involved in management of the financial mix to control the level of risk and the cost of funds.

This chapter is divided into two main sections. The first section deals with the decision as to what is the appropriate mix of sources of funds and the second section deals with measuring the cost of funds.

FINANCIAL STRUCTURE

By financial structure, we refer to the mix of sources of funds to the institution. These sources can be roughly divided into three main categories. *Short-term liabilities* are those that are due on demand or within a short time period, typically defined as less than one year. *Long-term liabilities* have a maturity of more than one year. *Equity,* the third category, has no maturity at all. For an institution with stockholders, equity consists of the stockholders' direct investments in the firm and the retained earnings. For a firm lacking stockholders, such as a mutual savings and loan association, reserves serve the same function as equity. Sources of funds can also be classified as to whether or not contractually binding payment is required. Contractual—fixed—payments are required in the case of bonds, certificates of deposit, and passbook savings accounts. Returns to stockholders, dividends to holders of life insurance policies, and returns to mutual fund shareholders on the other hand, are related to the return earned on the institution's assets.

When we talk about the debt capacity of an industrial corporation, we normally think in terms of some optimum combination of debt and equity used to support a certain asset structure. For most financial institutions, we tend to think in terms of how much equity is required to support a given set of assets and liabilities. We use the term *capital adequacy.* This difference in emphasis is a result of the management problems faced by the different types of firms. For an industrial

corporation, the primary limitation on growth is found in the asset structure. The size of the corporation is normally determined by the ability to find and manage profitable asset investments. The financial structure is developed in response to this set of opportunities. For the financial institution, the liability structure is more likely to be the determinant of the total size. The total asset level of an insurance company, for example, is largely determined by the ability to sell insurance policies, not by the availability of profitable investments. Likewise, over the long term the size of a bank is heavily influenced by its ability to attract deposits.

While different types of business stress different aspects of the problem, the interactive aspect should not be ignored. The attractiveness of a particular investment depends on both its expected rate of return and the cost of funds. The cost of funds, in turn, depends on the riskiness of assets and the financial structure. The equity capital and liquid reserves judged to be necessary depend on the nature of *both* the assets and liabilities.

Various considerations are included in the financial structure decision:

1. Regulatory requirements
2. Cost of funds
3. Liquidity
4. Risk of insolvency
5. Flexibility

Regulatory limitations are frequently stated in terms of minimum acceptable levels of liquid assets and equity capital, as determined by the asset and liability structure of the institution. This section begins with an examination of the relationship between financial structure and the cost of funds. Then the concepts of liquidity, insolvency risk, and flexibility are developed to complete the general principles followed by all financial institutions in developing financial structure policy.

FINANCIAL STRUCTURE AND THE COST OF FUNDS

Central to our analysis is the fact that the average cost of funds is influenced by the mix of funds employed by an institution. One important objective of financial structure management is the minimization of this cost. Decreasing the cost of funds is one method of increasing the spread between the cost of funds and the return on assets, thus increasing profitability.

Fixed liabilities, such as debt and deposit liabilities, normally cost much less than equity or other non-specific claims. Investors and savers as a group are averse to risks and can be expected to invest in more risky non-specific claims only when returns anticipated from such claims exceed those available from debt and deposit claims. Furthermore, interest payments to fixed claims are an expense for tax purposes while dividends to equity holders must be paid from after-tax income.

Since debt funds tend to have a lower cost than equity funds, we would expect that the average cost of funds could be decreased by increasing the ratio of debt to equity. Indeed, this will happen over some range. However, as the ratio of debt to total assets continues to increase, the institution's debt becomes an increasingly risky investment and the return required to attract such funds rises.[1] Furthermore, continual addition of debt increases the risk to equity investors, driving up the required return on equity. Thus there are limits beyond which the addition of fixed obligations increases, rather than decreases, the average cost of funds.

While the general relationship between capital structure and cost of funds is fairly well understood, the identification of the exact combination which will minimize the

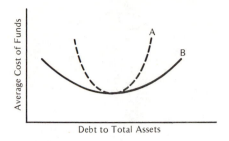

Figure 7–1: Illustrative Cost of Funds Curves.

average cost of funds for any given firm is elusive. Numerous studies of financial and non-financial corporations have failed to identify such a point.[2] However, what such studies have done is to give us a feel for the shape of the relationship between financial structure and the cost of funds. Figure 7–1 shows two possible relationships between capital structure and the cost of funds. The actual relationship appears to be more like curve *B* than curve *A*. The cost of funds curve appears to be fairly flat over a broad range, indicating that within that range modest changes in the financial structure will not have a major impact on the cost of funds.

While the relatively flat cost of capital curve makes it difficult to locate the precise optimum cost of funds, it does indicate that within fairly broad ranges the institution is free to consider other factors in selecting a financial structure. The considerations of liquidity, insolvency risk, and flexibility can be given proper consideration without unduly impairing profitability.

LIQUIDITY

Liquidity refers to the ability to meet financial obligations as they come due. A depository institution must stand ready to meet demand and passbook account withdrawal requests. An insurance company must stand ready to meet claims and the pension funds must make monthly payments on schedule.

---

[1] Of course, many deposits are insured, meaning that they do not become more risky. But financial institutions do borrow in the money markets and these loans are not insured.

[2] See, for example, S. D. Magen, *The Cost of Funds to Commercial Banks,* New York: Dunellen, 1971.

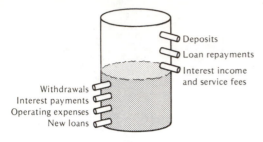

Figure 7–2: The Liquidity Reservoir.

A company with a strong equity base and a strong profitability position can still face liquidity problems if all funds are tied up in non-marketable assets.

Historically, liquidity needs have been determined by studying the liabilities, while cash and near-cash items have been relied on to meet these needs. Analysis has traditionally relied on static ratios. For example, an institution might follow a policy requiring cash items equal to 10 percent of demand deposits, plus 5 percent of passbook accounts, and so on.

More current approaches recognize two important factors. First, liquidity is a dynamic problem, resulting from instability of cash inflows and outflows, not from the absolute values of certain accounts. Second, many depository institutions have increasingly looked to new liabilities as alternatives to assets in meeting liquidity needs.

Liquidity reserves can be thought of as similar to a reservoir in a water system, as illustrated in Figure 7–2. Water constantly flows into and out of the reservoir, with the net flow being the difference between inflow and outflow. The amount of water needed in the reservoir is determined by the variability of the net flow, not by the absolute level of flow. Furthermore, any reservoir will eventually be drained if inflow steadily lags behind outflow. Thus the reservoir serves to offset difference in flow rates during limited periods of time.

To determine the amount of liquid reserves needed, historical patterns of cash inflows and outflows are studied to determine variability. The degree to which cash inflows and outflows move in the same direction at the same time—the covariance—is an important determinant of variability.

This interactive aspect of the liquidity problem heightens the importance of financial structure in liquidity management. The creation of liabilities which coincide in maturity with assets can greatly reduce the amount of assets which must be held in liquid reserves. Thus, financial structure management has a major impact on the pattern of liquidity demands.

It has been traditional to think in terms of meeting liquidity demands by selling short-term assets. However, many financial institutions frequently use short-term borrowing to meet unexpected liquidity demands. The use of negotiable certificates of deposit during recent periods of credit stringency is probably the most widely advertised example of this use of liability management. Eurodollar loans and commercial paper issued by financial institutions are other examples of the use of liabilities to meet liquidity demands, as is borrowing in the federal funds market. Thus liability management is an important part of liquidity management in terms of both creating and meeting liquidity needs.

RISK OF INSOLVENCY (CAPITAL ADEQUACY)

Insolvency occurs when the liabilities of a business exceed the value of its assets. The amount of shrinkage in assets value that can occur without leading to insolvency is related to the amount of equity capital in the financial structure. Thus the risk of insolvency depends on the risk of asset value shrinkage and the amount of equity in the financial structure.

When one thinks of shrinkage in the value of assets of a financial institution, default or credit risk is normally the first thing to come to mind. A loan, for example, may become questionable in value or worthless if the loan collateral loses its value and the borrower loses his ability to repay. Additionally, interest rate change is an important cause of asset value shrinkage. In Chapter 6 it was shown that a rise in the general level of interest rates would cause the value of existing securities to decline. For example, a 20-year, $1,000 U.S. government bond issued in 1975 had declined in market value to $680 by 1980. This decline in market value was entirely the result of a rise in the general level of interest rates over the five-year period. Fluctuations in the prices of equity securities are even more extreme. For example, the value of an average share of common stock fell 11 percent from October 13, 1978, to October 31, 1978, as a result of rising interest rates and a declining profitability outlook. Finally, operating losses caused by such factors as rising interest and operating expenses lead to erosion of total asset values. Thus all assets except the shortest term, highest quality money market instruments are subject to shrinkage in total value. Many financial institutions have found themselves in the embarassing position of holding an excessive portfolio of long term securities or loans, purchased or made when interest rates were viewed as "high," only to find later that interest rates rose further and the value of these assets fell sharply.

One method of dealing with the risk of loss in value is through matching maturities of assets and obligations. The U.S. government bond previously discussed still has a maturity value of $1,000. The loss in value occurs only if the asset is sold before maturity. By matching maturities of assets and liabilities, this risk of loss can be largely eliminated. Unfortunately, this is not always possible. While the primary assets of a savings and loan company are mortgages with maturities of 20 to 30 years, these firms rely on deposits with much shorter maturities as their primary source of funds.

In the case of loans, fixed assets, and equity securities, the risk of loss in value cannot be escaped. Obviously, such risk can be reduced by selecting higher quality loans and securities, and settling for commensurately lower returns. But risk cannot be eliminated if the institution is to invest in the types of assets which traditionally make up the bulk of its portfolio. Equity must serve to protect the institution's depositors and other creditors from loss in the value of assets.

One approach determining total equity requirements is to evaluate each category of assets and to estimate the potential decline in value.

The total equity requirement would thus be estimated by computing the equity needed for each category of assets and by summing the results. This approach is commonly used by regulatory authorities for deposit-type intermediaries. The standards set by regulators are, of course, minimum standards. The institution seeks to avoid the risk of falling to what regulators consider an inadequate equity position.

Another approach to the capital adequacy problem is the portfolio approach. Just as liquidity reserves can be thought of as a reservoir in the cash flow system, equity capital can be thought of as a reservoir in the income system. If net income after adjusting for gains or losses in the value of assets were positive every period, no equity reserve would be needed. It is variability of net income that leads to the need for equity capital. Just as the variance and covariance of the various sources and uses of cash determine liquidity needs, variance and covariance of various sources of income and expense determine the equity capital need. For example, assume that an institution makes automobile loans and invests in long-term U.S. government bonds. Losses in the automobile loan portfolio will occur primarily because of defaults while any losses in the bond portfolio's value will arise from market value losses resulting from rising interest rates. In a recession the default rate on automobile loans may rise, leading to losses in this portfolio. However, the general level of interest rates may fall, leading to an increase in the market value of the bond portfolio. Thus the tendency for the market value of the bond portfolio to increase at the time losses are being experienced in automobile loans makes it unnecessary to have equity equal to the entire potential loss in each category of assets. Portfolio analysis is a method of examining the relationships between these various income and expense factors and selecting assets so as to minimize the variance for a particular level of income. Portfolio analysis is taken up in more detail in Chapter 8.

We have seen that equity capital is the reserve used to reduce insolvency risk. The amount needed is determined not by a simple ratio of debt to equity, but by the variability of the various income and expense factors as well as their interrelationships. As with liquidity, insolvency risk management is a dynamic and interactive problem.

FLEXIBILITY

Flexibility in financial institution management is the ability to deal with unanticipated problems and opportunities that arise from time to time. While attempts to foresee future opportunities and problems are helpful, the simple fact is that the future is unknown. Both unanticipated problems and unanticipated opportunities will arise. Flexibility—the ability to deal with these situations—is very important to both profitability and risk.

The failure of Penn-Central Railroad in 1970 provides an excellent example of the importance of flexibility. The consumer finance companies relied on commercial paper as a means of financing. Because the maturities of their loans were greater than the maturity of commercial paper, they counted on paying off one issue of commercial paper by issuing another. When Penn-Central defaulted on its commercial paper, the entire market for commercial paper virtually dried up overnight. The finance com-

panies were not able to sell new issues of commercial paper in sufficient volume.

This situation would have resulted in massive defaults if it were not for flexibility planning. The finance companies had maintained lines of credit with banks as back-up sources of funds in case of difficulties in the commercial paper market. Thus, when they were faced with this difficulty, there was an alternative source of funds readily available. The banks, with some help from the Federal Reserve System, honored their lines of credit and default was avoided.

While asset management is a major part of flexibility management, management of the maturity structure of liabilities can also contribute to flexibility. Short-term maturities allow the institution to change policy quickly, but carry the risk of liquidity problems if maturing liabilities cannot be replaced with new sources of funds. Again, a distribution of maturities provides the optimum trade-off between flexibility gains and liquidity risks. Additional flexibility can be gained through the use of lines of credit. For example, consumer finance companies normally maintain bank lines of credit equal to their outstanding commercial paper, allowing them to move back and forth between bank debt and commercial paper as market conditions change.

Finally, management of the equity portion of the balance sheet affects flexibility. An institution with the minimum acceptable level of equity capital may find itself unable to take advantage of growth opportunities or may find itself accidentally in violation of regulatory requirements. Flexibility is normally gained by maintaining a capital structure with equity capital somewhat in excess of the minimum required.

As we have seen, flexibility is an important concept in the management of a financial institution. Flexibility is the response to the uncertainty inherent in a dynamic business environment. It is achieved through careful management of both assets and liabilities so that management has the opportunity to adjust the institution's financial position in response to changing problems and opportunities.

COST OF FUNDS FOR DEPOSITORY INSTITUTIONS

The cost of funds may be thought of as the opportunity cost, or the return stockholders, depositors, and other investors could expect from alternative opportunities of equal risk. The cost of funds provides a standard against which proposed uses of funds and past performance can be measured. If an institution is to successfully compete for funds, it must be capable of providing returns that are at least equal to the returns available from competing instruments available to investors. In order to evaluate investment alternatives, it is necessary to have an estimate of the cost of funds that will be invested. Overall profitability and stability of the institution may depend heavily on the cost of funds estimates.

Several important factors affect the institution's cost of funds. As mentioned previously, the cost of funds is an opportunity cost, or the return that investors and depositors could expect from alternative opportunities of equal risk. One factor in the cost of funds is the general level of opportunities which influence the overall level of competitive interest rates. Also, investors must expect a higher rate of return if they are to be pursuaded to invest in assets subject to risk. The more risk associated with the asset and liability structure of the firm, the higher will be the return necessary to attract funds.

Deposit funds, to the extent insured, are essentially risk free. However, financial institutions derive funds through issuance of securities and creation of liabilities, many of which are not covered or are covered only partially by insurance. Examples of these are large certificates of deposit, commercial paper, capital notes and debentures, federal funds borrowed, Eurodollars, preferred stock, and common stock. The required return for such funds, if all other factors such as size and location of the institution are held constant, may be expected to increase as perceived risk in the asset and liability structure increases.

In this section, the costs of the individual sources of funds are computed and the method of combining these costs to develop a weighted average cost of funds is explained.

COST OF EQUITY

The cost of equity is the return required by holders of the common stock. This cost is a function of investment opportunities elsewhere and the perceived risk associated with that particular institution's common stock. Unfortunately, it is seldom possible to directly observe the required return for equity investors. Some method for estimating their required return from available information must be used.

One widely used method of computing the cost of equity is the dividend growth model:

$$K_e = \frac{D}{P} + g$$

where: K_e = Required return on equity

D = Dividends expected over the next year

P = Current market price of the stock

g = Constant annual growth rate of dividends (expected to continue indefinitely)

Suppose, for example, that Southwest Bank's common stock is presently selling for $50 per share. Dividends are expected to be $4 per share next year and are expected to grow 4 percent a year thereafter. The cost of equity for Southwest is

$$K_e = \frac{4}{50} + .04 = .12 \text{ or } 12\%$$

If dividends grow as expected, an investor purchasing Southwest stock today for $50 will enjoy a 12 percent return on the investment.

Another approach to measuring the cost of equity is the risk-adjusted required-return approach developed in Appendix 6–A:

$$K_e = R_f + b(E_m - R_f)$$

where: R_f = Rate available on risk-free investments, such as treasury bills

b = A measure of sensitivity of returns for the particular security to conditions affecting common stock returns in general

E_m = Expected return for securities in general

The application of the dividend growth model requires stable dividend growth and the risk-adjusted return method requires historical market price data for the stock. Lacking these, an institution may consider returns available on comparable securities for which there is an active market to estimate the returns available to investors in opportunities of equal risk. For mutual institutions there is no possibility of a market price for equity. The reserves of such institutions can be thought of as a form of equity and the required return as a rate that could be earned on equal risk investments elsewhere if the institution did not exist. The returns available on common stocks of comparable risk would be a reasonable basis for an estimate. Suppose, for example, expected return for the market in general were 12 percent and the risk-free rate were 6.6 percent. Citizens Mutual Savings and Loan has no equity, but has reserves which serve that purpose. Equity securities of similar companies have betas of approximately 0.8. The required return for Citizens' is estimated to be

$$K_e = .066 + 0.8(.12 - .066) = 10.9\%$$

COST OF CAPITAL NOTES AND DEBENTURES

The cost of capital notes and debentures begins with the yield to maturity of existing notes or debentures (yield to maturity computation is covered in Chapter 5) or the interest rate that would be required to sell new securities of this type. Since interest is a tax-deductible expense, the effective interest cost is less than the yield to maturity. The after-tax cost of debt is

$$K_d = Y(1 - T)$$

where: K_d = After-tax cost of debenture debt

Y = Yield to maturity on existing debenture or required yield on new debentures

T = Effective marginal corporate tax rate

Southwest Bank has a debt series outstanding with a 9 percent yield to maturity. The after-tax cost is

$$K_d = .09(1 - .48) = 4.7\%$$

Financial institutions frequently have other negotiated cost funds such as Eurodollar borrowings and fed funds. The cost of each such source is computed in the same way as was done for capital notes and debentures. The yield to maturity is computed and then multiplied by $(1 - T)$ to create an after-tax cost measure.

COST OF TIME AND SAVINGS DEPOSIT FUNDS

The direct cost of interest-bearing deposit funds is the annual interest paid divided by the amount of interest-bearing deposit funds. Southwest Bank had average interest-bearing deposits of $100 million during its most recent fiscal year and paid total interest of $5.5 million. The direct cost of deposit funds would be

$$K_{sd} = \frac{5.5}{100} = 5.5\%$$

This direct cost actually underestimates the cost of deposit funds substantially. First, the cost of attracting and servicing funds should be added to direct interest payments. In addition, reserve requirements limit the amount that is available for investment. To adjust for this, the required reserves should be deducted from the $100 million and any return earned on reserves should be deducted from the cost. For Southwest Bank, the required reserves were $4 million, interest earned on reserves was $40,000, and the cost of serving these deposits was $1.5 million. The cost of interest bearing deposit funds was therefore

$$K_{sd} = \frac{5.5 + 1.5 - .04}{100 - 4} = 7.3\%$$

The only remaining step is to convert the cost to an after-tax cost:

$$K_{sd} = .073(1 - .48) = 3.8\%$$

The cost of interest-bearing deposit funds can therefore be summarized in one formula:

$$K_{sd} = \frac{I_e + E - Ir}{S_d - R}(1 - T)$$

where: I_e = Dollar annual interest paid on interest-bearing deposits

E = Annual cost of attracting and servicing accounts

I_r = Annual interest received on reserves, if any

S_d = Average value of interest-bearing deposits

R = Amount of required reserves for these deposits

COST OF NONINTEREST-BEARING DEPOSITS

The direct cost of noninterest demand deposits is zero since no interest is paid. The indirect costs of attracting and servicing accounts are real as are the reserve requirements. The cost of noninterest-bearing deposits (K_d) is computed in the same manner as the cost of interest-bearing deposits with the exception that the direct interest expense is zero. Southwest Bank has demand deposits of $60 million. Costs of attracting and servicing these deposits are estimated to be $3 million and required reserves for these deposits are $7 million. No interest is earned on the required reserves. The cost of demand deposits for Southwest is

$$K_d = \frac{3}{60 - 7}(1 - .48) = 2.9\%$$

WEIGHTED AVERAGE COST OF FUNDS

The next step is the computation of an average cost of funds. This requires the com-

Table 7-1:

Southwest Bank Capital Structure Information

Source of Funds	After-Tax Cost	Amount of Funds (Net of Reserves)	Proportion of Total
Demand Deposits	2.9%	$ 53 million	.31
Time and Savings Deposits	3.8	96 million	.55
Debentures	4.7	10 million	.06
Common Equity	12.0	14 million	.08
Total		$173 million	1.00

Table 7-2:

Southwest Bank Weighted Average Cost of Funds

Source of Funds	After-Tax Cost	×	Proportion of Total	=	Weighted Cost
Demand Deposits	.029		.31		.009
Time and Savings Deposits	.038		.55		.021
Debentures	.047		.06		.003
Common Equity	.120		.08		.010
	Weighted Average Cost of Capital			=	.043 or 4.3%

bining of individual sources of funds in some manner. The information concerning the individual sources is summarized in Table 7–1.

Since funds invested are a combination of funds raised from various sources, the cost of funds is an average of the costs of the various individual sources of funds. Since some sources of funds represent a greater portion of the total than others, a *weighted average* must be used. The weighted cost of a source of funds is found by multiplying the after-tax cost by the proportion of total funds represented by that source. The weighted average cost of all sources is found by adding the individual weighted costs. This is illustrated in Table 7–2 for Southwest Bank.

Since this is an after-tax cost, the after-tax return from an investment would need to be 4.3 percent. A loan, for example, would need to have an interest rate of 8.3 percent, net of service costs, to be left with an after-tax return of $.083(1 - .48) = .043$.

COST OF FUNDS FOR NON-DEPOSITORY INSTITUTIONS

For many non-depository financial institutions, the problem of cost of capital is altered by the fact that the most important sources of funds fall into neither the equity nor the fixed obligation category. This does not imply that the funds are costless.

While the payouts from many pension funds depend on the rate earned on the fund's investment portfolio, the beneficiaries still have the right to expect a return as high as that available from alternative investments of equal risk. Thus the required return or cost of these funds also depends on the opportunities available elsewhere.

Take, for example, a hypothetical employee pension fund at Alrite Products Corporation. Contributions to the employee pension fund are primarily divided between mortgages insured by agencies of the U.S. government and common stocks, with half of the funds being invested in each category. If individuals did not contribute to the pension fund they could invest directly in assets of similar risk. Thus the required return for the pension fund is the return investors could earn by dividing their funds between insured mortgages and a common stock portfolio with equal risk to that of the common stock portfolio held by the pension fund. The evaluation of pension fund performance is covered in more detail in Chapter 12.

Insurance companies collect a pool of premiums from which they expect to pay claims. Policy reserves—funds held to meet claims—are the primary source of funds to an insurance company. As an example of the cost of funds to such an institution, we look at a life insurance company writing whole life policies. The whole life policy is generally in force from the time of purchase until the death of the policy holder and pays its face value at the time of death. While the timing of the individual claim is unknown, its eventual payment is certain. Thus the company must build up reserves over the life of the policy holder. As the insured is aware of his eventual death, a policy of this type can be thought of as a combination of a savings plan to provide funds to heirs and insurance against the possibility of death before the savings plan has been completed.

Alternatively, the insured can purchase temporary life insurance at a lower cost and invest the difference directly. The premiums charged and the dividends paid to policy holders depend on the return earned on these reserves. Thus, the ability to compete in the sale of policies depends on these returns. The reserves must earn a return similar to those available on other long-term savings instruments if the company is to be competitive.

While the determination of the cost of funds is somewhat different for a non-depository financial institution, the general principles are still the same. Each type of funds must earn a return that is at least equal to what the furnishers of those funds could have earned from alternative investments.

MANAGEMENT USE OF THE COST OF FUNDS

The cost of funds serves two purposes in the financial institution. First, it serves as a standard against which past performance can be measured. The institution should have earned a return on assets at least equal to the cost of funds. An analysis of returns in comparison to the cost of funds can be a regular part of performance review.

Second, the cost of funds represents a standard against which proposed uses of funds can be evaluated. The after-tax cost of funds represents an average return, expressed on an after-tax basis and net of servicing cost, which must be earned on total assets. Some assets, such as highly liquid securities, will normally earn a return lower than the average required. Further, some investments, such as an employee lounge, generate no direct revenue. These low returns must be compensated for with higher returns on other assets so that the weighted average return for all assets equals the weighted average cost of funds. The assignment of these higher costs to specific asset categories is somewhat difficult and requires a certain amount of managerial judgment.

One method is to consider the return on certain low yielding assets as fixed; arbitrarily adjusting the required returns on other assets upward so as to generate an average overall required return equal to or greater than the cost of funds. While this approach can be used successfully, it is difficult to decide the required return which should be assigned to each asset category.

Another approach is to match each asset to particular sources of funds. For example, Southwest Bank might see 70 percent of funds for consumer loans coming from savings deposits and 30 percent coming from equity capital. The required return for consumer loans would then be computed as shown in Table 7–3. In this case, the required after-tax return net of expense on consumer loans would be 6.3 percent. An

Table 7-3:

Required Return for Consumer Loans

Source of Funds	After-Tax Cost	×	Proportion of Total	=	Weighted Cost
Time and Savings Deposits	.038		.70		.027
Common Equity	.120		.30		.036
			Required Return	=	.063 or 6.3%

effective interest rate of approximately 12 percent would be required to provide a 6.3 percent after-tax return. This approach gives a good first approximation but still leaves difficulties. For example, short-term government securities are seen as necessary for liquidity purposes even though they may not meet the cost of funds against which they are matched. Thus, management judgment continues as a necessary ingredient in adjusting and assigning required rates of return in asset selection.

SUMMARY

In this chapter, we have concentrated on the factors guiding decisions with regard to the financial structure of the financial institution. The costs of individual sources of funds and the average cost of funds have been covered. In addition, we have covered the factors guiding the decision as to what particular financial structure an institution will have. These include regulatory limitations, insolvency risk, liquidity needs, and the cost of funds. These various objectives are frequently contradictory. For example, the structure giving the greatest flexibility and lowest risk of default would undoubtedly result in a high average cost of funds and low profitability. The financial structure decision cannot be reduced to a simple formula.[3] The job of management is to weight these various factors and apply its own judgment and experience in selecting a financial structure which gives adequate consideration to each of these factors.

QUESTIONS

1. Industrial corporations are free to use whatever financial structure they prefer, subject only to the willingness of lenders to furnish funds. On the other hand, the financial structure of a financial institution is closely regulated by government regulatory bodies. Why are the financial structures of financial institutions regulated while the structures of industrial corporations are not?

2. Financial institutions typically have much higher proportions of their total funds furnished by depositors and other lender groups. Such large volumes of fixed obligations are normally considered risky, yet financial institutions typically have lower failure rates than industrial corporations. Why?

3. A typical bank has 15 to 20 percent of its assets in the form of cash and demand deposits with other institutions. A typical savings and loan company, on the other hand, holds only 2 to 3 percent of its assets in similar liquid forms. How do you account for this difference?

4. Why do we emphasize debt capacity when analyzing industrial corporations and capital adequacy when analyzing financial institutions?

5. For which financial institutions is liquidity planning easiest and for which institutions is it likely to be the most difficult? Why?

6. Five types of considerations involved in the financial structure decision are discussed in this chapter. Compare the importance of each of these for financial and non-financial corporations.

7. The cost of funds curve appears to be relatively flat over a broad range. What are the implications of this for managerial decision making?

8. What determines the liquidity needs of a financial institution, and how are these liquidity needs met?

---

[3] One now-successful banker reports that, as an enthusiastic new employee, he developed a massive 800 constraint linear programming model for managing the bank's assets and liabilities. His solution was returned from the president with a short, but unprintable response. The model would have led the bank to failure in less than two years if it had been followed.

PROBLEMS

1. First City Bank has 300,000 shares of common stock outstanding. The stock is traded in the over-the-counter market (there is a market for the stock through local brokerage firms, but it is not traded on a stock exchange) where the present price is $40 per share. Dividends per share for the next year are expected to be $3 and have been growing at the same rate as earnings, 4 percent a year. The present rate on Treasury bills is 6 percent and the expected future return for stocks in general is approximately 12 percent. First City Bank's stock has a beta of 0.9. Compute the cost of equity capital.

2. Community Federal plans to raise additional funds through the sale of one-year certificates of deposit. The certificates will carry 9 percent interest, with annual compounding, and the estimated average cost of attracting one $1,000 certificate is $20. The marginal tax rate is 48 percent. The reserve requirement is 10 percent and reserves will earn 4 percent. Compute the after-tax cost of this source of funds.

3. Old Reliable Life Insurance Company's financial structure consists of $1 billion in policy reserves and $100 million in equity. The company faces a 48 percent tax rate. The required return for equity is estimated to be 12 percent and long-term low-risk debt instruments have returns of 8 percent. Compute the average after-tax cost of funds for Old Reliable.

4. Old Reliable (Problem 3) has office facilities, which earn no direct return, of $6 million. In addition, $50 million is put in liquid reserves that earn an after-tax return of 3 percent. The remainder of their funds are available for investment. What return must be earned on the remainder of the portfolio if the overall cost of funds is to be met?

5. Neighborhood Bank has total assets of $100 million, with 90 percent of funds coming from deposits and 10 percent coming from equity. The after-tax cost of deposit funds is 3 percent and the after-tax cost of equity is 10 percent. The bank faces a 48 percent marginal tax rate.

a. Compute the weighted average cost of funds.

b. The bank is required to maintain non-interest bearing liquid assets equal to 8 percent of deposits. In addition, liquidity needs are met through holdings of low interest (after-tax interest of 3 percent) liquid assets equal to 12 percent of deposits. Physical facilities equal 2 percent of total assets. The service fees collected, net of related expenses, can be thought of as a return on physical assets. By this measure, the return on physical assets is 5 percent after tax. Remaining assets are in the form of the loan and investment portfolio. What after-tax return must be earned on the loan and investment portfolio if the bank is to earn an average return on all assets equal to the cost of funds?

c. The investment portfolio is seen by the bank as an outlet for funds for which no loan demand exists. It is invested primarily in government securities. There is little the bank can do to improve the return on these securities. Yields on these securities, which represent 30 percent of the bank's total assets, are presently 5.0 percent. To meet its cost of funds, what after-tax return must the bank earn on its loan portfolio?

d. Administrative and collection expenses equal 4 percent of the average balance in the loan portfolio. What is the average interest the bank must charge on loans to meet the cost of funds?

6. The balance sheet of Rosewood National Bank appears below.

Cash and Deposits with Other Banks	$17,000,000
Securities	27,000,000
Loans	53,000,000
Other Assets	1,000,000
Bank Premises	2,000,000
Total Assets	$100,000,000
Deposits	
Demand	$45,000,000
Time	37,000,000
Owners' Equity and Reserve Accounts	18,000,000
Total Liabilities and Net Worth	$100,000,000

a. Evaluate the bank's financial structure compared to an average equity to asset ratio of 0.9. According to the average, does the bank have sufficient equity capital?

b. Does compliance with the average assure that liquidity needs will be met?

c. Does compliance with the average assure that flexibility needs will be met?

SELECTED REFERENCES

Beranek, William, "The Weighted Average Cost of Capital and Shareholder Wealth Maximization," *Journal of Financial and Quantitative Analysis,* Vol. 12 (March, 1977), pp. 17–31.

Biederman, Kenneth R., "Capital Adequacy: Problems and Prospects," *Federal Home Loan Bank Board Journal,* Vol. 12 (November, 1979), pp. 13–15.

Gordon, Myron J., and L. I. Gould, "The Cost of Equity Capital with Personal Income Taxes and Flotation Costs," *Journal of Finance,* Vol. 33 (September, 1978), pp. 1201–1212.

Hehman, David H., and Alan R. Winger, "Measuring the Cost of Money Market Certificates," *Federal Home Loan Bank Board Journal,* Vol. 12 (July, 1979), pp. 8–10.

Koehn, Michael, and Anthony M. Santomero, "Regulation of Bank Capital and Portfolio Risk," *Journal of Finance,* Vol. 35 (December, 1980), pp. 1235–1244.

Pringle, John, "The Capital Decision in Commercial Banks," *Journal of Finance,* Vol. 29 (June, 1974), pp. 779–795.

Santomero, Anthony M., and Donald D. Watson, "Determining Optimal Capital Standard for the Banking Industry," *Journal of Finance,* Vol. 32 (September, 1977), pp. 1267–1283.

Chapter 8

Asset Management

Good asset management has always been important for the profitability and liquidity of financial institutions. In recent years, however, its importance has increased due to shortages of funds, higher interest rates, and more aggressive competition. When there was little competition for funds and lower interest rates, a depository institution could make only the safest loans and invest the remainder of its funds in U.S. Treasury obligations. Today, such a policy would not allow the institution to meet costs, compete for funds, and meet its other obligations. Thus institutions have sought profits through a more aggressive loan and investment policy. Aggressive policy reduces the margin for error and requires greater skill in asset management.

Inflationary pressures and erratic behavior of economic and financial variables, especially interest rates, are other factors which have led to greater importance of asset management. Changes in the prime rate—the interest rate banks charge their best commercial loan customers—provide a good ex-

ample. From 1950 through 1969, the prime rate changed 16 times per decade, a significant increase from the two changes that occurred in the period from 1934 to 1949. In the decade of the 1970s, the prime rate changed over 100 times![1] The rapid rate of change in financial variables adds a new dimension to asset management. Flexibility in meeting such changing conditions has become an important consideration.

Another important factor is the increasing emphasis on allocation of assets to uses deemed socially desirable. In recent periods of monetary tightness, the Federal Reserve encouraged banks to allocate credit to firms that could not directly compete for funds. Legislation such as the equal credit opportunity act is aimed at requiring institutions to grant some loans they would not voluntarily choose to make. Other legislation of

---

[1] James V. Baker, Jr., "Why You Need a Formal Asset/Liability Management Policy," *Banking,* June, 1978, p. 33.

Table 8-1:

Categories of Financial Institution Assets

	Short Term	Long Term

Impersonal	U.S. government
	    Treasury notes
	    Agency notes
	State and local notes
	Commercial paper
	Negotiable certificates of deposit
	Federal funds
	Banker's acceptances
		U.S. government
		    Treasury bonds
		    Agency bonds
		State and local government
		    General obligation
		    Revenue
		Corporation bonds
		Corporation equity

Personal	Commercial loans Consumer loans	Commercial loans Consumer loans Mortgages
Other	Cash and deposits	Physical plant

this type is pending.[2] Responding to these requirements without jeopardizing profitability or unduly increasing risk requires new management skills.

TYPES OF ASSETS

Assets of financial institutions vary by maturity, ranging from overnight loans in the fed funds market to long term securities and fixed assets. They also differ according to whether they are personal debt instruments, such as most loans, or impersonal instruments such as Treasury obligations and corporate bonds. The major categories of assets are shown in Table 8–1.

Table 8–2 gives an indication of the relative importance of various classes of assets to selected types of financial institutions. The data for Table 8–2 came largely from reports to the government agencies overseeing the institutions. Since each agency con-

solidates information in a different manner, comparability between types of institutions is somewhat limited. However, some general observations are possible. We note, for example, that commercial banks held substantial cash, deposits, and government securities while savings and loan companies had a total of less than 2 percent of their assets in these categories. Traditionally, savings and loan companies have maintained a less liquid asset structure because their sources of funds were more stable. Their deposits are less volatile compared with banks. Note also that equity holdings are low for all depository institutions. The unstable nature of equity security values largely precludes their use as assets for depository financial institutions.

CONSIDERATIONS IN ASSET MANAGEMENT

There are five primary objectives or areas of consideration in asset management. These include profitability, liquidity, risk, flexibility, and regulatory requirements. This same set of considerations guides all businesses, but with different degrees of emphasis.

---

[2] These responsibilities are in addition to the long-recognized social responsibility of all financial institutions: the responsibility to customers and the general public to stay liquid and solvent through careful selection of assets appropriate to the particular liability structure.

Table 8-2:

Asset Structures of Major Types of Financial Institutions

	Commercial Banks	Savings & Loan Companies	Mutual Savings Banks	Credit Unions	Life Insurance Companies
Cash	18.0%ᵃ	1.3%	1.9%	4.4%ᵃ	
U.S. Government Securities	11.5	}	6.2	}	} 40.0%
State & Local Gov. Securities	9.8	} 0.5	1.2	} 20.5ᵇ	}
Private Debt Securities	} 0.5	}	17.5	}	}
Equity Securities	}	}	3.5	}	9.3
Loans	56.2	89.0	67.0	75.1	44.4ᶜ
Other Assetsᵉ	4.1	9.2	2.6		6.3ᵈ

ᵃCash and deposits with banks

ᵇand other assets

ᶜand private debt securities

ᵈIncluding cash

ᵉIncluding fixed assets

Source: *Federal Reserve Bulletin*

PROFITABILITY

While financial institutions are important to the economy and society, this should not cloud the fact that individual institutions are normally profit-seeking businesses. With certain exceptions, they are owned by stockholders who have invested in the firm with the expectation of earning a rate of return commensurate with the risk involved. Maximization of shareholder wealth is frequently cited as the primary goal of any privately owned business[3] and the value of equity is primarily a function of the firm's profitability. If the institution is to attract equity capital, it must earn a competitive rate of return. Thus asset investments must yield certain minimum required rates of return to be acceptable.

LIQUIDITY

Liquidity—the ability to meet all legitimate demands for cash—is more important for financial institutions than for other firms. The public confidence that institutions must have to attract funds is closely related to their ability to meet legitimate demands for cash, such as deposit withdrawals and insurance claims. While liability sources, including lines of credit and the fed funds market, are frequently used to meet liquidity needs, the primary source continues to be assets that can be sold or converted to cash quickly. Thus, institutions hold a certain amount of funds in cash or in short term, marketable assets to meet liquidity needs.

RISK

Since most of the typical institution's obligations are fixed and the equity base is gen-

[3] A frequently heard debate about the role of business in society can be avoided by differentiating between the goals and results of business activity. A financial institution can only earn a profit if it provides some service for which society is willing to pay. This service results from the financial institution's pursuit of its profitability objective. For example, the availability of credit to automobile buyers results from conclusions by banks and finance companies that they can profit from these loans.

erally small, it must be concerned about the risk of shrinkage in the value of its assets. A level of asset value shrinkage that would cause little difficulty in another type of business can reduce the institution's capital to the point where further expansion must be curtailed. Thus the financial institution must pay very close attention to risk.

FLEXIBILITY

As discussed in Chapter 7, flexibility is an important concept related to both risk and return. Flexibility is essentially the ability to respond to unexpected changes, either problems or opportunities for investment. Profitability can be enhanced and risk can be reduced by managing assets so as to provide such flexibility.

REGULATORY REQUIREMENTS

Regulatory requirements are designed to encourage safety and liquidity as well as to promote the accomplishment of certain public policy goals. Regulatory agencies accomplish these objectives in at least three ways:

1. By specifying the nature of the assets which may be held.

2. By specifying certain general relationships among assets, liabilities, and equity capital.

3. By encouraging investment in assets designed to promote goals of a public policy nature.

The effects of regulatory requirements on the asset structure of selected categories of financial institutions are shown in Table 8–2.

Comparing savings and loan companies with mutual savings banks, for example, the substantial holdings of private debt and equity securities by mutual savings banks and the nearly total absence of these assets from the portfolios of savings and loan companies result from differences in regulations affecting the two types of institutions. Savings and loan companies were created for the purpose of making mortgage money available while mutual savings banks were created as a service to savers.

The regulatory environment has already been discussed in some detail in Chapter 4. For the purposes of this chapter, regulatory considerations can be thought of as constraints that may limit the institution's actions in pursuing its objectives.

PRINCIPLES OF ASSET STRUCTURE MANAGEMENT

Once the objectives to be pursued in asset management are identified, the question of how to achieve these objectives must be faced. In this section, some methods of achieving specific objectives and methods of analyzing the asset structure with regard to these objectives are presented. In studying these methods, it must be kept in mind that pursuit of one objective almost always involves a trade-off in terms of some other objective. The appropriate trade-off is always a difficult policy question for management.

PROFITABILITY

The profitability objective permeates much of what has been discussed. In Chapters 6 and 7, the methods of finding the required return and of comparing it to returns on available assets were developed. Thus those two chapters provide the basis for profitability analysis.

In general, the profitability objective requires that the institution invest only in those assets that earn a return higher than the cost of funds. Among investments meeting this criterion, the highest return possible is desired, all else being equal. Unfortunately, with most investment alternatives, all else is not equal. Problems involving risk and the assignment of costs frequently arise. The assignment of costs is discussed in the following paragraphs and risk is taken up in the next section of this chapter.

Table 8-3:

Second Mortgage Profitability Analysis

Monthly payment (7 year, 12%, $8,000 loan)	$141.22
Processing cost	.50
Net monthly payment received	$140.72
Loan amount	$8,000.00
Solicitation cost (8 × $5)	40.00
Processing cost	120.00
Net outlay	$8,160.00
Amount received at the end of three years ($141.22 × 37.975)	$5,362.83

		10.5%		11.0%		11.5%	
Period	Payment	Present Value Factor	Present Value	Present Value Factor	Present Value	Present Value Factor	Present Value
1–36	$ 140.72	30.767	$4,329.53	30.545	$4,298.29	30.325	$4,267.33
36	5,362.83	.7308	3,919.16	.7200	3,861.24	.7094	3,804.39
			$8,248.69		$8,159.53		$8,071.72

The return on an asset is not just the directly computed rate of return. It must be adjusted for the costs of acquiring and servicing the asset. While the administrative costs of acquiring and holding U.S. government bonds are quite small, a loan involves processing costs, credit examination costs, and general office overhead costs in addition to the cost of funds. Failure to consider these other costs will lead to biased decisions.

Example Friendly Neighborhood Savings and Loan is experiencing insufficient demand for first mortgage loans. Alternative investments including second mortgage lending[4] to existing customers are being considered. While Friendly has not previously been involved in this type of lending, other institutions in the area have, and data on their experience is available. The average

second mortgage loan carries an interest yield of 12 percent, net of bad debt losses, while U.S. government bonds are currently yielding 9 percent. The second mortgage loans appear on the surface to be more attractive. However, the cost of servicing such loans must be considered.

The loans would be promoted through "stuffers" included with statements to regular customers. The cost would be relatively low, an estimated $5 per $1,000 of second mortgage loans made. Credit investigation and other administrative costs associated with granting a loan would average $120 per loan. Ongoing administrative costs would average $.50 per month per loan. Although management anticipates that the original maturity of a typical second mortgage loan would be seven years, the experience of others has shown that the average loan is repaid after three years. No penalty will be charged to people who repay early.

The profitability analysis is summarized in Table 8–3. The monthly payment of $141.22 was found using Table A–8. The outlay by the savings and loan equals the

---

[4] A second mortgage is a security claim against a property that falls after another claim, the first mortgage, in the event of bankruptcy. Second mortgage loans on houses are used for remodeling or to borrow money for unrelated expenses such as education or medical.

$8,000 loan amount plus the solicitation and processing costs for a total of $8,160. The amount still owed (and therefore repaid) at the end of three years is determined using Table A–8. It is the present value of $141.22 per month for four years, discounted at 12 percent per year.

The rate earned on these loans is found by taking the present value of the net monthly payments and final payments—using Tables A–6 and A–8—at various interest rates to find the rate that generates a present value as close as possible to $8,160. This rate (yield) turns out to be about 11 percent, as shown in Table 8–3. In other words, after taking into account the additional expenses associated with the second mortgage loan program, a return of 11 percent is expected. The second mortgage loans are more profitable than U.S. government bonds.

ASSIGNMENT OF JOINT COSTS

One difficult problem in profitability analysis is the assignment of joint costs. In the above problem, for example, should part of the cost of maintaining the savings and loan building be assigned to second mortgage loans since the existence of the building and other services makes the second mortgage lending possible? Or should these costs be ignored because they will continue whether or not the institution enters the second mortgage market?

The traditional argument, and probably the appropriate one in this example, is that only the costs that will change—the marginal costs—should be considered. However, the typical financial institution offers a range of services supported by an organization and structure that will not change significantly with the addition or deletion of one service. Although certain costs are fixed, they must still be seen as a cost of the total package of services and must be met through charges for that package of services. Furthermore, certain services are offered below cost as a means of attracting more profitable business. Thus the marginal cost approach must

be applied with a strong dose of judgment as the institution must price its services competitively and still meet fixed costs from some source.

LIQUIDITY

Although profitability is of paramount importance, the financial institution needs to maintain a sufficient volume of liquid assets. The institution must stand ready to meet all legitimate demands for funds, such as withdrawal demands. Failure to meet such demands on an immediate basis would likely destroy confidence in the institution, without which it cannot survive. On the other hand, liquid assets frequently earn low rates of return, interfering with the profit objective. Thus the institution should seek to maximize profit, but subject to the constraint that adequate liquidity is necessary.

PRIMARY VS. SECONDARY LIQUIDITY RESERVES

In order to evaluate liquidity requirements, it is necessary to differentiate between primary and secondary liquidity reserves. All depository and some non-depository financial institutions are required to maintain some minimum amount of liquid reserves. For example, immediately available cash or "cash-like" assets equal to 12 percent of most transaction account balances must be maintained by commercial banks.

It should be noted that required primary reserves are the minimum level that must be maintained. Use of any of these reserves to meet demands for funds would take the institution below minimum levels and would bring a quick response from the regulatory authorities. Thus primary reserves do not provide a source of usable liquidity for the individual financial institution under normal conditions, although they do provide a certain cushion for the financial system in general.

The funds a financial institution actually uses to meet liquidity needs are called *secondary reserves*. These are assets that earn interest, but can be sold quickly if additional funds are needed. Securities in this category include Treasury bills, bankers acceptances, and federal funds. Financial institutions buy and sell these securities on a daily basis to meet their liquidity needs and primary reserve requirements while avoiding the holding of idle cash.

Liquidity reserves can be viewed from either a "stock" or a "flow" perspective. A stock approach involves looking at the balance sheet and deciding the liquid reserve needs based on the structure of the institution's liabilities. The shorter the maturity of the liability, the higher the proportion of the funds that must be held in liquid reserves. The proportions of each liability that must be maintained in the form of liquid assets is then determined on the basis of past experience. This is the approach used by regulators in determining the amount of required primary reserves. It is also a method used by many institutions in determining the appropriate level of secondary reserves.

A flow approach involves looking at the liquidity reserves as a reservoir, as shown in Figure 7–2. The inflow may not equal the outflow on any particular day and the reservoir serves to offset temporary differences between inflow and outflow. As with a water reservoir, the liquidity reserve cannot offset a permanent imbalance. It can only offset temporary imbalances.

If the flow approach is used, the variabilities of inflows and outflows are studied to determine the amount of liquid reserves that may be needed. The flow approach is similar to certain approaches used in inventory management, and inventory models have been applied successfully to liquid reserve problems. Figure 8–1 illustrates an approach to the problem. It shows the cumulative value of net cash flows (cash inflows minus cash outflows) over time for a particular savings and loan company. There are some periods of time during which cumulative net cash flows decline. These are periods of net cash outflows. Liquid reserves must be held to meet demands for funds during these periods of negative cash flow, or the institution must have some liability source it can call on at such times. For this institution, we see that the largest decline occurred between day 33 and day 43, when cumulative cash flows declined by $76,000. Thus a secondary reserve of $76,000 would have been sufficient to meet demand during the period examined. While the study of data for only two months would not be sufficient for determination of liquidity needs, the method can serve as a useful guide if flows are examined over a sufficiently long time period.

VOLUNTARY VS. INVOLUNTARY OUTFLOWS

A further refinement is to break down the outflow during the negative flow periods into voluntary and involuntary outflows. For example, deposit withdrawal demand must be met while lending can be curtailed when funds are not available. Figure 8–2 shows cumulative net cash flows, including new loans, contrasted with cumulative net cash flows excluding new loans for the two periods of greatest cash outflow.

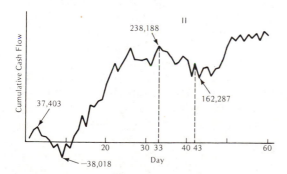

Figure 8–1: Cumulative cash flows.

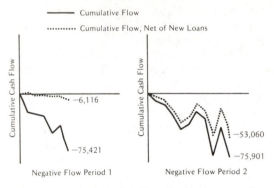

Figure 8–2: Cumulative flow for major negative cash flow periods.

Period 1 in Figure 8–2 was a period when increased loan demand was being met from excess liquid funds. This time period contained no threat to liquidity. However, period 2 was a period of decreasing deposits. It represented the major test of the institutions's liquidity over this time period. Secondary reserves of $53,000 would have been required to meet this demand.

Once the secondary reserve requirement has been determined, the next question is what form these reserves should take. Funds must be held in assets that can be quickly converted to cash without substantial loss. It is also desirable to earn the highest return possible on these funds. Thus secondary reserve assets must be safe, of short maturity, and readily salable. Secondary reserve assets include Treasury bills, bankers acceptances, and other short-term, high quality investments.

In addition to secondary reserves, some temporary liquidity needs can be met through borrowing. Depository institutions can borrow on a temporary, limited basis at the Federal Reserve Discount Window, using such securities as U.S. government bonds as collateral. Depository institutions can also borrow from each other in the federal funds market. Some non-bank financial institutions maintain lines of credit at commercial banks to meet their liquidity needs. For example, finance companies frequently raise funds through the sale of bonds and commercial paper while using bank lines of credit as a back-up source of liquidity.

There are certain dangers inherent in the planned use of borrowing as a means of meeting liquidity needs. Banks and thrift institutions, for example, tend to experience net deposit outflows when market interest rates rise above regulation Q ceilings. When one institution faces heavy withdrawal demand, it is quite likely that other institutions are facing similar problems. Thus it may be very difficult to borrow to meet liquidity needs at the time when these needs are greatest.

Because secondary reserves frequently earn a low return, a reduction in needed secondary reserves will often result in increased profitability. There are several things that can be done to reduce the amount of secondary reserves needed. One method has already been mentioned: arranging lines of credit to provide emergency liquidity. Improved forecasting is another approach. The more accurate the institution in predicting cash flows, the less reserves it needs for potential outflows.

Another frequently used approach to minimizing the secondary reserve need is hedging. Hedging involves matching the maturities of assets and liabilities. To the extent that maturities do match, secondary reserves are not necessary. Unfortunately, the nature of the financial institution limits the degree to which this can be achieved. Deposit funds can frequently be withdrawn on demand while loans are granted for specific maturities. Thus the institution must develop asset management policies based on the stability of particular sources of funds, with less reliance on the absolute maturity of funds sources.

RISK

Because of the small proportion of equity in their capital structures, financial institutions are particularly sensitive to the possibility of asset value shrinkage. Both prudent management and regulatory requirements dictate that risk be held to a relatively low level. The recognition, management, and control of risk are important roles of management in all financial institutions. There are two important sources of asset value shrinkage for a financial institution: interest risk and credit or business risk.

INTEREST RATE RISK

Interest risk refers to the fact that the value of a fixed stream of returns from a financial asset declines as the general level of interest rates rises. For example, the value of a perpetuity of $100 a year would be $2,000 at a required return of 5 percent, but only $1,000 if the required return rose to 10 percent. Thirty-year U.S. government bonds were issued in November, 1972 with a face interest rate of approximately 5.4 percent. In January, 1981, the market interest rate on such bonds was approximately 12 percent and the market value of these bonds had declined to less than 50 percent of face value. While the face value could still be realized by holding the bonds until maturity, anyone wishing to sell one in 1981 would lose over half the original investment.

With increased inflation and the accompanying instability of interest rates, interest risk has become an increasingly serious problem for financial institutions. The problem is aggravated by the fact that the assets of a financial institution frequently have longer maturities than the sources of the institution's funds. Savings and loan companies that made 25-year loans at 5 percent in the early 1960s found themselves paying in excess of 5 percent on virtually all funds sources before these loans matured.

Interest rate risk is difficult to eliminate for many financial institutions. Hedging—matching the maturities of assets and liabilities—is one method of eliminating interest rate risk. Unfortunately this is a difficult task for many financial institutions. An important service of depository financial institutions has traditionally been the provision of immediate liquidity to savers while assuring borrowers of a longer term source of credit (asset transmutation was the name given to this activity in Chapter 1). The problem is particularly severe for mortgage lenders such as savings and loan companies. They face demand for loans with 20- to 30-year maturities while the depositors are generally unwilling to commit their funds for similar periods, particularly at a fixed interest rate.

Depository institutions have tried to deal with the problem by seeking longer term deposits in recent years and have succeeded in increasing the average maturity of deposit funds. They have also worked to reduce the average maturities of their assets. For example, a savings and loan may decide to increase its efforts to market second mortgage loans and take advantage of the 1980 legislation to enter other shorter term lending such as automobile loans. While complete hedging is probably not possible, institutions can take steps to bring the maturity of their assets and liabilities into closer alignment.

Another approach to minimizing interest rate risk is the variable rate loan, a loan with the interest rate tied to some general indicator of interest rates. This type of loan has gained acceptance in several countries and is used on a limited scale by some long-term commercial and mortgage lenders in the United States. A variation is the balloon mortgage loan which is technically due in a few years, but is actually renegotiated to the current market interest rate at its due date. The balloon note has been used increasingly in recent years.

CREDIT OR BUSINESS RISK

Credit or business risk is associated with potential variability of the stream of cash flows from the asset itself. For a debt instrument, credit risk is the risk that the creditor will not meet his obligations under the debt contract. For equity investments such as common stock, the holder faces the risk that the company may suffer from reduced profitability, resulting in a decline in the value of the equity.

Credit or business risk can be controlled by investing in less risky securities, such as U.S. government obligations. Unfortunately, risk-free securities may pay lower returns and a complete portfolio of these would require that the institution essentially forego its profit objective. Risk can be controlled while still allowing reasonable profits through the use of portfolio analysis.

PORTFOLIO ANALYSIS

The central theme of the portfolio concept is that the assets of the institution should be thought of as part of a unified whole, not as the sum of a group of individual entities. By proper management of the asset mix, it is possible to create a group of assets, the total risk of which is less than the sum of the risks of the individual assets. While this concept has long been recognized, it has received particular attention in recent years.

An example serves to highlight both the potential and limitations of portfolio analysis in controlling risk. While 5 percent of the loans made by a particular consumer finance company are expected to default under normal conditions, the portfolio of loans is riskless with regard to these losses. The defaults on 5 percent of the loans are simply one of the costs reflected in the interest rates charged. Thus what first appears to be a group of risky loans can be combined in such a way that the particular risk is virtually eliminated. However, the portfolio is only riskless with regard to this normal level of losses. The company still faces the risk of the loss rate being higher than the anticipated 5 percent. This can occur because of a recession or other economic problem, resulting in higher unemployment among the borrowers. Thus the risk related to individual securities can be eliminated through construction of a portfolio, but certain overall risks remain. We refer to the risk that can be overcome through the use of portfolio approaches as *diversifiable* risk and that which cannot be eliminated in this manner as *nondiversifiable* risk.

To further illustrate the essential nondiversifiability of certain risks, consider the consumer finance company just discussed. While it is possible for the loan company to invest in assets other than consumer loans, the same risks remain. The high default rates occur during periods of economic downturn. At the same time, stock prices normally decline and other types of investments are subject to increased defaults. Thus, further diversification is likely to be unsuccessful in eliminating this type of risk. Nondiversifiable risk can be eliminated only by movement to low-return risk-free securities.

The recognition of diversifiable and nondiversifiable risk can be formal or informal. With the informal approach, we begin by identifying the types of risk involved and determining which are and are not diversifiable. The diversifiable risks must be estimated as carefully as possible so that they can be accurately treated as a cost factor. The degree of nondiversifiable risk can be measured by studying past patterns, if historical data are available, or by estimating the impacts of various conditions.

Example The consumer finance company discussed above makes two general types of loans: loans secured by the item being purchased, such as installment loans for appliance purchase; and unsecured loans for purposes such as medical expenses and bill consolidation. The company has one-half of its funds in each category. Under normal conditions, default rates for the secured loans average 4 percent while default rates for unsecured loans average 6 percent. Normal conditions include a 5 percent unemployment rate. As the primary nondiversifiable risk is associated with unemployment, the default rates experienced for each type of loan during past unemployment periods are shown in Table 8–4.

Table 8-4:

Default Rates at Various Levels of Unemployment

Unemploy- ment Rate	Default Rates		
	Secured	Unsecured	Average
5%	4.00%	6.00%	5.00%
6	4.50	6.60	5.55
7	5.00	7.30	6.15
8	5.60	8.10	6.85
9	6.30	8.90	7.60

The company is considering a change in its mix of loan types. Obviously, average default rates at each unemployment rate depend on the mix of loans. For example, with 30 percent of the funds in secured loans and 70 percent in unsecured loans, the default rate at an 8 percent unemployment rate would be

$$.30(5.6\%) + .70(8.1\%) = \underline{7.35\%}$$

Expected average default rates for a range of unemployment rates and various loan portfolios are shown in Table 8–5.

The information contained in Table 8–5 does not tell the finance company what mixture of secured and unsecured loans would be optimal. However, it does provide a concise summary of the risks associated with each combination. Using the informal approach, the risks for each combination are judgmentally compared to the expected returns in choosing a preferred loan portfolio mix.

The formal approach uses statistical techniques to develop more precise guidelines. The use of beta, first described in Chapter 6, provides one such example. Recall that beta (b) was a measure of sensitivity of returns for the particular asset to conditions affecting common stock returns in general, r_f is the rate available on risk-free securities such as Treasury bills, and E_m is expected return for securities in general. The required return for equity was then

$$K_e = r_f + b(E_m - r_f)$$

This formula was used to develop an estimate of the cost of equity capital. It can also be used to estimate required return for particular assets.

Example The required before-tax return for the loan portfolio of the consumer finance company discussed above is 12 percent. The portfolio has a beta of 1.2, computed by comparing returns for the portfolio to returns in the securities market in general for a number of years. The risk-free rate is 8 percent. What would be the required return if the portfolio beta were reduced to 1.0? By definition, security returns in general (E_m) have a beta of 1. Thus we only need to solve for E_m:

$$12\% = 8\% + 1.2(E_m - 8\%)$$
$$E_m = 11.33\%$$

Table 8-5:

Average Default Rates for Alternative Loan Portfolio Mixes

Unemployment Rate	Proportion of Funds in Secured Loans				
	.3	.4	.5	.6	.7
5%	5.40%	5.20%	5.00%	4.80%	4.60%
6	5.97	5.76	5.55	5.34	5.13
7	6.61	6.38	6.15	5.92	5.69
8	7.35	7.10	6.85	6.60	6.25
9	8.12	7.86	7.60	7.34	7.08

Using this value of E_m, we can then find the required return for any beta. The secured loans have been found to have a beta of 1.0 while the unsecured loans have been found to have a beta of 1.4. Thus the required returns for the two types of loans are

Secured: .08 + 1.0(.1133 − .08) = 11.33%

Unsecured: .08 + 1.4(.1133 − .08) = 12.67%

Using this approach, the company would then compare expected returns for each type of loan with the required return for that type of loan and invest in opportunities exceeding their required return.

One limitation of this approach is that it assumes that diversifiable risk has been eliminated through the holding of a large number of assets (loans in this case). When only a few assets are to be held, or when there is other reason to be concerned about whether diversifiable risk has been eliminated, the mean-variance portfolio model can be used directly. It is briefly summarized in Appendix 8–B.

FLEXIBILITY

Flexibility is the ability to respond to changing conditions. Because of the inherent unpredictability of events, the ability to respond to unanticipated changes in business and economic conditions is an important ingredient of good asset management. An unexpected increase in loan demand (and interest rates) is an example of a situation in which planning for flexibility would be rewarded. Such a situation presents the institution with the opportunity to make highly profitable loans and to gain new customers, if funds are available to lend.

A necessary level of flexibility can be attained through proper management of assets and liabilities. In general, flexibility in asset management is achieved through the management of the maturity structure of securities and loans, and through the holding of marketable assets.

In general, shorter security and loan maturities result in greater flexibility because the institution can make new investment decisions at more frequent intervals. However, this flexibility does not come without cost. Shorter term loans and securities frequently carry lower interest rates. Furthermore, some institutions face only limited demand for short-term credit. A savings and loan company, for example, has little choice but to hold the bulk of its assets in the form of long-term mortgages.

A portfolio with staggered maturities— one with certain proportions of loans or other securities maturing each period on a planned basis—is one method of gaining flexibility without foregoing longer term, higher yielding assets. Properly distributed maturities assure a continued flow of cash to be used in making new loans or investments.

Finally, the existence of marketable securities and loans within the total portfolio increases flexibility while allowing investment in longer term assets. Long-term securities can be sold in the open market if the institution faces a need for funds or if a particularly attractive opportunity for investment becomes available. The existence of interest rate risk and the associated risk of loss in the market value of securities, however, frequently precludes the conversion of this type of asset to cash.

SUMMARY

In this chapter we identified the primary types of assets held by financial institutions. The assets consist primarily of financial obligations of others. They can be classified according to whether they are personal or impersonal and whether they are short-term or long-term. We also noted that the mixture of assets varied by type of institution, depending on institutional objectives, liability structure, and regulatory requirements.

The primary considerations in asset management are:

Profitability—Most financial institutions are private, profit-seeking enterprises.

Liquidity—The ability to meet all obligations on schedule and to meet withdrawal requests immediately is very important for financial institutions. Both regulatory requirements and the need to maintain public confidence make adequate liquidity imperative.

Risk—Loss in asset value is particularly damaging to financial institutions because of their low ratios of equity to total assets. Risk can be recognized through informal methods or through statistical portfolio analysis techniques.

Flexibility—Flexibility is the ability to respond to unanticipated changes in the form of either problems or opportunities. It is achieved primarily through management of maturity structure and marketability of assets.

Regulatory Requirements—Regulatory requirements are designed to control risk and see that the institution provides the service for which it was created.

Regulatory requirements can be thought of as constraints—conditions that must be met. Given the necessity of meeting these constraints, asset management is guided by the desire to achieve the best possible trade-off between the other considerations.

SELECTED REFERENCES

Babcock, Builford, "The Roots of Risk and Return," *Financial Analysts Journal,* Vol. 36 (January/February, 1980),pp. 56–63.

Bates, Timothy, and William Bradford, "An Analysis of the Portfolio Behavior of Black-Owned Commercial Banks," *Journal of Finance,* Vol. 35 (June, 1980), pp. 753–768.

Ferguson, Robert, "Performance Measurement Doesn't Make Sense," *Financial Analysts Journal,* Vol. 36 (May/June, 1980), pp. 59–64

Francis, Jack Clark, *Investments: Analysis and Management,* 3d ed. New York: McGraw-Hill, 1980.

Ibbotsen, R. G., and R. A. Sinquefield, "Stocks, Bonds, Bills and Inflation: Updates," *Financial Analysts Journal,* Vol. 35 (July/August, 1979), pp. 40–44.

Kane, Edward, and Stephen A. Buser, "Portfolio Diversification at Commercial Banks," *Journal of Finance,* Vol. 34 (March, 1979), pp. 19–34.

QUESTIONS

1. Why is the percentage of commercial bank assets held in the form of cash items substantially higher than the percentage of thrift institution assets held in this form?

2. The Financial Institution Deregulation and Monetary Control Act of 1980 instructed the regulatory authorities to move toward equal cash reserve requirements for commercial banks and thrift institutions. Why would it be deemed appropriate for banks and thrift institutions to move toward similar liquid asset percentages?

3. Explain the difference between primary and secondary reserves.

4. Do required reserves provide a source of liquidity to the financial institution? Why?

5. Why is it so difficult for thrift institutions to eliminate interest rate risk?

6. For a life insurance company, list as many types of risk as you can think of. Categorize these risks as to whether they are diversifiable or nondiversifiable.

7. By studying the current news, find an example of a financial institution that has profited from maintaining flexibility or has suffered losses due to the absence of flexibility.

PROBLEMS

1. The Financial Institution Deregulation and Monetary Control Act of 1980 allowed savings and loans to invest up to 20 percent of their funds in assets other than liquidity reserves and real estate mortgage loans. Community Federal Savings and Loan is considering automobile loans. The average automobile loan is for 36 months and carries an interest rate of 14 percent, compared to 12 percent for a first mortgage loan. It costs approximately $50 for promotion and $50 for processing for each loan granted. In addition, it costs Community Federal approximately $0.40 to process each monthly payment. To allow for expected bad debts, Community assumes that actual payments received will be 99 percent of contractual payment amounts. The average automobile loan is expected to be $6,000 and Community's cost of funds is 9 percent.

   a. Are the proposed automobile loans profitable for Community Federal?

   b. Are there any intangible benefits associated with loans of this type by a savings and loan company?

   c. Do you anticipate any problems for savings and loans entering into lending of this type?

2. Following is information on cash flows experienced by Employee's Federal Credit Union over a 26-week period. Analyze these flows and determine the maximum amount of liquid reserves that would have been needed over this period.

Cash Flows Experienced by the Employee's Federal Credit Union

Week	Deposits	Withdrawals	Loan Repayments	New Loans
1	10,000	7,000	3,000	7,000
2	10,600	7,400	3,000	6,000
3	10,900	7,600	3,100	7,000
4	11,800	7,400	3,100	8,000
5	11,600	7,800	3,150	7,000
6	12,000	8,200	3,150	7,000
7	13,000	8,500	3,150	8,000
8	12,500	8,700	3,170	7,000
9	10,000	9,200	3,175	5,000
10	9,600	9,800	3,180	5,000
11	9,400	10,200	3,180	4,000
12	9,200	10,500	3,185	4,000
13	8,400	11,300	3,190	3,000
14	6,400	11,800	3,190	1,000
15	5,200	14,200	3,195	500
16	4,000	15,800	3,195	500
17	4,200	16,200	3,200	300
18	4,400	15,300	3,200	200
19	5,000	12,800	3,200	200
20	5,000	11,700	3,205	0
21	5,200	11,000	3,210	0
22	5,400	10,300	3,210	200
23	5,600	9,000	3,210	200
24	6,000	7,900	3,210	500
25	5,800	6,400	3,210	1,000
26	6,400	6,400	3,215	2,000

Appendix 8-A

Capital Asset Selection

Capital assets are those for which total benefits are expected to be received over a period of more than one year. Examples include a building, a computer, and an electronic funds transfer terminal. Not so obvious examples include projects such as advertising campaigns and investment in a bank leasing department. While the latter examples do not directly appear on the balance sheets of the institution, they involve a cash outlay with benefits expected over a period of more than one year.

The capital investment decision process involves three main steps:

1. *Proposal:* A capital investment is proposed and all expected costs and benefits, as well as other factors to be considered, are identified.

2. *Evaluation:* The unexpected costs and benefits are analyzed to determine if the project is sufficiently profitable to justify investment in light of other opportunities and the cost of funds.

3. *Decision:* Based on the evaluation of costs and benefits as well as considerations of risk, management strategy, and funds availability, the decision as to whether or not to invest is reached.

A complete capital asset management program will also include post-audit of all projects to compare actual with expected results. Only by such follow-up will management assure that objectives are reached and learn from past errors to improve decision making.

The capital investment decision process involves a wide range of considerations. Included in the decision process are many areas of interest such as marketing, personnel, technical, legal, tax, and finance. Furthermore, major projects will be evaluated in light of long-term goals and strategy of the firm. Whether a project is large or small, financial considerations are prominent; the firm must earn a return on total assets that is sufficient to justify the funds invested. In this appendix, the primary emphasis will be on financial considerations including techniques of financial analysis used in successful capital investment programs.

THE PROPOSAL

Proposals originate at various levels within the organization depending on the type of investment being considered. Proposals involving replacement and efficiency as well as limited expansion proposals normally originate at the operating levels. Major expansion proposals and those involving new products, services, or markets normally originate with top management.

Just as capital investments vary in size and complexity, proposals vary from a one-page form for a routine replacement decision to hundreds of pages of information for movement into a new product area or new technology. A proposal for a major project may include, in addition to financial data, such information as technical and engineering data, market research results, legal, tax, and environmental considerations. The present discussion will concentrate on the financial portion of the proposal: estimation of original net investment, annual benefits, and terminal value associated with a capital investment project.

NET CASH INVESTMENT

Net cash investment is the initial outlay required to acquire an investment and place it in service. The items included in the initial outlay for a typical physical asset are summarized below:

Cost of the asset is the direct price paid. This will typically be the purchase price, but may involve a series of expenses including services of institutional personnel, consultants, etc.

Installation and start-up cost includes physical installation costs as well as such items as training expenses and decreased efficiency during implementation.

Working capital increases will normally be required for projects involving expansion or movement into new products, services, or markets. Such projects involve increases in prepaid expenses, accounts receivable, and supplies or other inventory. Failure to properly consider working capital increases is a common error and results in substantial understatement of net cash investment.

Proceeds from sale of replaced assets frequently serve to reduce the net cash investment. The proceeds should be net of any expenses such as brokerage fees and removal costs.

Tax increases or decreases are frequently associated with the acquisition of capital assets for profit-making institutions. The investment tax credit serves to reduce net cash investment by eliminating taxes that would otherwise be paid. Sale of a replaced asset will increase taxes if sale is above book value and will decrease taxes if sale is below book value.[1]

The net investment resulting from this analysis is the *cash* investment. Cash cost is the cost of primary interest. Most evaluation techniques rely on cash costs and benefits as opposed to accounting income and book value.

Example First National Bank of Springfield is considering an expansion of the computer facility. While the existing computer would serve the Bank's projected needs for a number of years, the additional hardware would create sufficient capacity to allow the bank to sell computer services with only modest increases in staff. The new equipment can be purchased for $500,000, including installation. Working capital will be increased by an estimated $20,000. An investment tax credit of 10 percent will apply to the hardware but not the working capital. The initial cash investment is summarized as follows:

Cost of the asset	$500,000
+ Installation and start-up costs	0
+ Working capital required	20,000
− Proceeds from sale of replaced asset	0
− Tax decrease	50,000
= Net cash investment	$470,000

---

[1] Development of expertise in tax law is not one of the goals of this book, and investment of any consequence would not be undertaken without expert tax advice.

ANNUAL CASH BENEFITS

As with the initial outlay, the benefits from an investment are normally measured in cash. The procedure involved in estimating annual cash benefits for a typical physical asset is summarized below:

Expected annual revenue is in the form of sales, service fees, or similar payments. An efficiency project will generate no revenue, but will increase earnings before depreciation and tax by decreasing expenditures.

Expenses include all operating expenses except depreciation, which is treated separately. Interest expenses associated with financing the asset are not included; they are treated separately when the profitability of the project is compared to the cost of funds.

Depreciation is of interest only because it affects taxes. Depreciation, like other expenses, is subtracted from revenue to arrive at taxable income. If replacement is involved, the depreciation figure will be the difference between depreciation on the new asset and depreciation given up by selling the old.

Tax will be based on the firm's marginal tax rate applied to projected earnings before tax.

Expected annual cash benefits are found by adding depreciation to earnings after tax. Depreciation is deducted to find taxes payable even though it is not a cash flow. To arrive at cash benefits, the earnings after tax figure must be adjusted by adding back depreciation to offset previous subtraction of a non-cash expense.

If cash flows are not expected to be the same each year—as when accelerated depreciation is used—the analysis will need to be repeated for each year of the project's expected life.

Example The computer facility expansion described on page 128 is expected to generate annual revenue of $180,000 per year. Expenses, excluding depreciation and taxes, are expected to be $80,000 per year. The equipment will have a ten-year expected life and zero salvage value. Straight line depreciation will be used and the bank is subject to a 48 percent marginal tax rate. The annual cash benefits are summarized as follows:

Expected annual revenue	$180,000
– Operating expenses, except depreciation	80,000
– Depreciation	50,000
Earnings before tax	50,000
– Tax	24,000
Earnings after tax	26,000
+ Depreciation	50,000
Annual cash benefits	$ 76,000

Many capital investments will have some cash value at the end of their useful lives. Typical sources would be sale of a physical asset and recovery of working capital. Tax considerations may be involved if an asset is sold for more or less than book value.

Example The computer expansion discussed previously has an expected life of ten years and no salvage value is anticipated. The $20,000 in working capital will be recovered at the end of the ten-year life. The terminal value is summarized as follows:

Sale price of asset	$ 0
+ Recovery of working capital	20,000
± Tax savings or payment	0
Terminal cash value	$20,000

The procedures and examples which have been presented are applicable to a typical physical asset investment problem. The exact format may need to be modified somewhat to fit unique characteristics of a particular project. The general principles are, however, the same.

Once costs and benefits have been estimated, the proposal is ready to go forward to the next step in the decision process.

EVALUATING COSTS AND BENEFITS

The second step in the analysis of a proposed capital investment is the evaluation of anticipated costs and benefits with regard to the institution's profitability. The two most widely used methods of analysis are the present value method and internal rate of return method.[2] These techinques are defined and discussed in the following sections.

PRESENT VALUE METHODS

It is fairly obvious that a dollar received today is more valuable than a dollar promised several years from now. An amount considerably less than a dollar could be invested today to produce a dollar in several years. Inflation can be expected to reduce the buying power of a dollar received at some later date. Furthermore, there is frequently a greater degree of risk associated with amounts expected at times some distance in the future. The present value techniques use the time value techinques developed in Chapter 5 to evaluate cash flows expected at some future date.

Use of the present value methods requires, as input, all cash inflows and outflows associated with the project. To use the present value method, it is also necessary to have a required rate of return, or cost of capital. The estimation of the cost of capital is discussed in Chapter 7. In addition to other opportunities for investment within the institution, this opportunity concept includes opportunities which investors could choose as alternatives.

---

[2] Other methods occasionally used are the payback and accounting rate of return methods. *Payback period* is the number of years required for total cash inflows from the project to equal the original cash outlay. *Accounting rate of return* is the average annual net income over the life of the project divided by average book value of the investment over the life of the project. These techniques have declined in importance in recent years.

The computation of the present value of the cash flows from an investment is simply an application of the techniques discussed in Chapter 5. The present value of a stream of cash flows is the *value* of the investment to the firm. The value of the asset is a function of the *cash flows* and the *required rate of return*. If the value of the investment exceeds the cost, it would be considered an attractive investment.

For the computer project used earlier in this appendix, there is both a stream of cash inflows and a terminal value. The present value of these components must be found separately and then added to find the present value of the project. This is shown in Table 8A–1 using an 8 percent required rate of return. The project has a present value of $519,220. This value is well in excess of the $470,000 initial cash investment so the project would be considered attractive.

Table 8A-1:

Computer Project Present Value Analysis

Year	Cash Flow	Present Value Factor	Present Value
1–10	$76,000	6.710*	$509,960
10	20,000	.463**	9,260
	Total present value		$519,220

*Table A-4   **Table A-2

Net present value is one method of stating the relationship between present value and cost. The net present value is merely the present value minus the cost. For the computer expansion project, the net present value would be $519,220 − $470,000 = $49,220.

The net present value measures the amount by which wealth will be increased or decreased if a particular investment is taken. By giving up cash of $470,000 to invest in a project with cash flows worth $519,220, the bank has increased its worth by $49,220. The increase in worth, expressed as net present value, is an indication of the degree to which the value of economic resources have been increased. For a profit-making organization, this increase accrues to the shareholders. For a non-profit institution, the increased worth will benefit the segments of society served by the institution.

Profitability index is another measure of the relationship between present value and cost. The profitability index, also called the benefit-cost ratio, is the ratio of present value to cost. For the computer project, the profitability index is $519,220/$470,000 = 1.1.

The profitability index is a measure of the amount of present value created for each dollar invested. The higher the ratio, the better the project. As a profitability index of 1.00 would indicate that present value exactly equals cost, any project with a profitability index greater than 1.00 would be acceptable.

The present value methods are generally considered to be the most theoretically correct techniques for capital investment analysis. In addition to considering both cash flows and timing, the results are stated in terms of value and wealth. However, the present value techniques suffer from several limitations. Computations are somewhat time consuming, the concept is sometimes difficult to grasp, and, most importantly, the use of these techniques requires the cost of funds as an input. While some financial institutions expend considerable effort on cost of capital funds, others use investment evaluation procedures such as internal rate of return that do not rely on the cost of funds.

INTERNAL RATE OF RETURN

Like the present value methods, the internal rate of return recognizes both cash flows and timing. Unlike the present value methods, the internal rate of return formulates expected results in terms of an annual percentage rate. The internal rate of return, also called discounted rate of return, is the rate of return that will actually be earned if the institution invests in the project. It can be compared to rates of return available from comparable projects and available to investors outside the firm.

Financial institutions and investors in general are implicitly familiar with internal rate of return, though it is seldom known by that name. For example, the after-tax yield to maturity on a bond is the internal rate of return for an investment in the bond. Thus the annual percentage rate on a loan or security is comparable to what is termed "internal rate of return" in the case of capital investment projects.

The internal rate of return is the discount rate which will produce a net present value of $0. In the previous section, the required return was known and it was necessary to find the net present value. In this case, the net present value is known ($0) and it is necessary to find the required rate of return. In general, the internal rate of return must be found by a process of trial and error. For the computer project, we know that the internal rate of return is over 8 percent because the net present value was $49,220 at an 8 percent cost of funds. In Table 8A–2 net present values are found at several interest rates. We can see that the internal rate of return is between 10.0 and 10.5 percent.

Special care must be taken when using internal rate of return to compare projects with substantially different lives. A project with a one-year life and an internal rate of return of 16 percent might not be as attractive as a project with a ten-year life and an internal rate of return of 15 percent, particularly if projects in subsequent years promise generally lower returns. The internal rate of return makes no adjustments for such differences in project life and may therefore favor projects with high returns but short lives.

While most theoreticians prefer the present value approach, internal rate of return is the most widely used technique among practitioners. The extra computation involved is offset by the fact that knowledge of the precise cost of funds is not a condition

Table 8A-2:

Internal Rate of Return Analysis

Discount Rate										Net present value
.08	$76,000	×	6.710	+	$20,000	×	.4632	−	$470,000 =	$49,224
.09	$76,000	×	6.418	+	$20,000	×	.4224	−	$470,000 =	26,216
.10	$76,000	×	6.145	+	$20,000	×	.3855	−	$470,000 =	4,730
.105	$76,000	×	6.015	+	$20,000	×	.3684	−	$470,000 =	−5,492

for its estimate. Managers are capable of applying judgments in cases where competing projects have significantly different lives. The widespread use of internal rate of return attests to the fact that financial decision makers have found its advantages sufficient to offset its disadvantages.

PROJECT SELECTION

ORGANIZATION FOR PROJECT SELECTION

As indicated earlier, the proposal for a capital investment may be generated by top management or may come from the operating levels. Proposals dealing with replacement, efficiency, and minor capacity increases will normally be generated at the operating levels while proposals dealing with new products or market areas and major expansion will typically originate with top management. Larger institutions have a decision structure that allows routine decisions to be reached at operating levels while those projects expected to have major impact on overall structure and direction of growth will be decided by top management.

The importance of major capital investment decisions and the myriad of factors that must be considered assure top management involvement. The ultimate vehicle for decision making is the board of directors. But such decisions may fall on an executive committee or the chief executive alone. The board of directors will review and participate

in decisions with the degree of participation depending on the size and importance of the investment.

Typically, the proposal will be screened, evaluated, verified, and analyzed at various levels in the organization prior to reaching the decision making level. Ultimately, top management is responsible for asset selection. There is no mechanical rule which can relieve top management of its decision-making responsibility. Large numbers of considerations must be balanced and decisions made as to whether projects are justified. Examples of factors which management must consider are

1. Goals and objectives: Is the project consistent with the long range goals and objectives of the institution?

2. Marketing: Is the project consistent with the institution's marketing strategy?

3. Profitability: Is the project consistent with the institution's profitability goal?

4. Availability of funds: If limited funds are available, management must allocate funds among worthy projects.

5. Regulatory constraints: For example, physical asset expansion generally must be kept within limits of the institution's capital, surplus, and/or appropriate reserve accounts.

6. Risk: What can go wrong? What is the likelihood of it going wrong? What other options will be available and how badly will the enterprise be hurt if the project does not work out as expected?

7. Personnel and management: Are personnel available and is management talent available to handle the new project?

8. Legal: Will existing or anticipated government action limit the success of the project?

9. Technical: Is the technology involved really feasible and dependable?

FINANCIAL ASPECTS OF THE CAPITAL INVESTMENT DECISION

If the firm has sufficient funds to invest in all attractive projects, it is only necessary to determine whether or not a project is attractive. If a project has a positive net present value, it will also have a profitability index greater than 1.0 and an internal rate of return greater than the cost of funds. If sufficient funds are available to invest in all attractive projects, it will not matter whether present value or internal rate of return is used to evaluate projects.

While there are situations in which an institution has sufficient funds to invest in all attractive projects, such a circumstance is the exception rather than the rule. In the case where funds are limited, the decision

becomes more difficult. It is necessary to develop a ranking system for proposals so that the highest ranked investments may be selected. If competing projects are similar in dollar size and life, it makes little difference which of the discounted cash flow techniques is used. Similar rankings will be achieved using net present value, profitability index, and internal rate of return. However, problems develop when sizes or lives of competing projects differ substantially.

An example will be helpful in pointing up the differences among the discounted cash flow methods as ranking tools. The three competing projects in Table 8A-3 differ in both size and life. Evaluated at an 8 percent cost of capital, they also differ in ranking depending on which discounted cash flow method is used.

The ranking obtained obviously depends on the ranking technique used. Which ranking technique is better? The normal answer is that the goal of financial decision making is wealth maximization and the net present value measures the amount of wealth increase as a result of the investment. The traditional argument is that the capital investment funds should be allocated so as to maximize total net present value created.

Table 8A-3:

Ranking Competing Proposals

Project Cost	A $1,000		B $1,000		C $2,000	
Year	Cash Flow		Cash Flow		Cash Flow	
1	$1,160		0		0	
2	0		0		0	
3	0		0		0	
4	0		0		0	
5	0		$1,925		$3,524	
Present Value (8%)	$1,075		$1,311		$2,400	
Net Present Value (Rank)	$ 75	(3)	$ 311	(2)	$ 400	(1)
Profitability Index (Rank)	1.075	(3)	1.311	(1)	1.200	(2)
Internal Rate of Return (Rank)	16% (1)		14% (2)		12% (3)	

This is the correct approach if the cost of capital is known. Many institutions, however, find that the problems involved in computing a cost of capital cause more difficulty than the ranking inconsistency problem illustrated in Table 8A–3. The dominant measure used for ranking proposals at the present time is the *internal rate of return*.

RISK

Up to this point, the financial analysis of capital investments has been limited to evaluation of expected returns. The future is filled with uncertainty. It is the rare capital investment decision for which risk is not an important factor. It is generally true that projects with higher expected returns also have higher levels of risk. The greatest danger is in failure to explicitly recognize risk in the evaluation and decision making process. If highest internal rate of return or highest net present value projects are chosen with no consideration given to risk, the selection process will move the institution entirely out of low risk projects and into high risk projects over a period of time. Such a change in the structure of the organization is particularly unfortunate when it occurs by accident because of improper project evaluation. Some method of explicitly recognizing risk should be included in the decision-making process.

The *informal approach* to risk is relied on by many decision makers. In addition to expected profitability, risk associated with the project is evaluated on the basis of management philosophy and experience. Information available to management may vary from a simple statement about what could go wrong to a comprehensive analysis using sophisticated statistical measures.

Risk adjusted required return is a widely used formal approach to risk recognition. The required return varies with the level of risk; the riskier the project, the higher the required rate of return. Some organizations categorize projects and use a different required rate of return for each type of project.

For example, a 12 percent rate of return might be required for replacement and cost reduction projects with 16 percent required for expansion projects and, perhaps, 20 percent required for projects involving new products or movement to new markets. The required return for each type of project is normally determined by judgment, based on past experience. A few organizations, however, rely on statistically computed required rates of return for different risk levels.

Other widely used approaches include the use of a shorter payback requirement for risky projects and the downward adjustment of expected cash flows so as to compensate for the degree of risk. Less frequently used approaches to risk evaluation include game theory, utility theory, decision tree analysis, and portfolio theory. In general, companies have not found these techniques particularly useful because their application requires a degree of quantification of the risk situation based on information which is frequently not available.

SUMMARY

The character, financial health, and even the very survival of the organization depends on the quality of its investment decisions. The financial institution is involved in numerous capital investment decisions of its own, and frequently the institution will be asked to finance the capital investments of its customers. Thus, the understanding of techniques useful in capital investment analysis is doubly important for the financial institution manager.

The capital investment decision involves three main steps:

1. *Proposal,* complete with a summary of expected financial costs and benefits as well as considerations relating to risk, technical and engineering factors, market conditions, legal and tax implications, and environmental impact.

2. *Evaluation* of profitability using techniques such as net present value and internal rate of return.

3. *Decision*, based on profitability and other considerations.

Appendix 8-B

The Mean-Variance Portfolio Model

The mean-variance portfolio model is a formal method of recognizing risk in the construction of asset portfolios. It is discussed briefly here, but is presented in more detail in many investments texts.[1]

The mean-variance approach is based on the assumption that investors will choose an investment portfolio with the objective of maximizing expected return and minimizing risk, measured as the variance of the probability distribution of expected returns.[2] The particular combination of risk and expected return chosen depends on the individual's attitude toward risk. However, everyone will be expected to choose a portfolio that provides the lowest variance for its level of expected return. Thus the objective of mean-variance portfolio analysis is the identification of the lowest variance portfolio for each possible expected return.

The expected return for a portfolio can be stated as a weighted average of the expected returns for individual assets:

$$E_p = \sum_{j=1}^{n} p_j E_j \qquad (8B-1)$$

where:

E_p = Expected return for the portfolio

p_j = Proportion of funds invested in asset j

E_j = Expected return for asset j

n = Number of assets in the portfolio

The computation of the variance for the portfolio is complex. It depends on the covariance, a measure of the degree to which the returns for two assets move together. The covariance between two securities is a measure of the tendency for their returns to

---

[1] See, for example, Jack Clark Francis, *Investment Analysis and Management,* 3d ed. (New York: McGraw-Hill, 1980).

[2] The variance (σ^2) is a measure of dispersion. Thus a greater variance indicates a greater range of possible outcomes. Specifically, the variance is computed as follows:

$$\sigma_p^2 = \sum_{i=1}^{m} X_i (R_{pi} - E_p)^2$$

where:

σ_p^2 = Variance of the portfolio

X_i = Probability of condition i occuring

R_{pi} = Return for the portfolio if condition i occurs

E_p = Expected return for the portfolio

m = Number of possible outcomes

be similarly affected by changes in the environment. The formula for the covariance is

$$\sigma_{jk} = \sum_{h=1}^{m} X_h (R_{jh} - E_j)(R_{kh} - E_h)$$

(8B-2)

where: m = Number of different conditions that may occur in the environment

X_h = Probability of condition h occuring

R_{jh} = Expected return on security j if condition h occurs

R_{kh} = Expected return on security k if condition h occurs

The variance for a portfolio is a function of these covariance terms:

$$\sigma_p^2 = \sum_{j=1}^{n} \sum_{k=1}^{n} P_j P_k \sigma_{jk}$$ (8B-3)

Equations 8B-1 and 8B-3 are then the two key equations used in the mean-variance portfolio model. For each possible expected return, we wish to identify the portfolio that minimizes variance. The set of such portfolios is what we identified as the *efficient frontier* in Appendix 6-A. The institution can then choose from among these combinations of risk and return to choose the trade-off between risk and return it feels is most desirable.[3]

We need not concern ourselves with the question of how to actually find the various combinations of expected return and risk that are on the efficient frontier. Computer programs are readily available for this purpose, given the set of expected returns and covariances for the assets.

The main problem in using this method is the set of inputs required. For each asset, the variance and the covariance with each other asset must be computed. For five assets, there are 15 covariance terms required, and for 20 assets, 210 covariance terms are required. To consider 1,000 assets we would require 500,500 covariance terms! Thus the number of covariance terms that must be estimated become quite large if more than a few assets are being used.

One way to overcome the large number of covariance terms needed is to use beta as a risk measure. In doing this, we assume that diversifiable risk will be eliminated by a large number of assets without any attention required. If this assumption is valid, the variance of a portfolio can be computed as follows:

$$\sigma_p^2 = \sigma_m^2 \left[\sum_{j=1}^{m} P_j b_j \right]^2$$ (8B-4)

where: σ_m^2 = Variance of probability distribution of expected returns for a portfolio consisting of all available securities. Variance of returns for an index of stock market returns is normally used as this measure.

b_j = Beta for investment j

Using this approach, the large number of covariance terms can be replaced with one beta for each asset. This approach is applicable when a large number of assets is being considered, such as in a portfolio of bonds and common stock. Again, computer programs are readily available for the purpose of identifying the set of efficient frontier portfolios if expected return and beta for each asset have been computed.

---

[3] A significant body of finance theory would argue that the optimum portfolio is one that maximizes the ratio:

$$(E_p - r_f) \div \sigma_p$$

where: r_f = Risk free interest rate, such as that available on Treasury bills

σ_p = Standard deviation, the square root of the variance

Chapter 9

Bank Management

Like industrial corporations, commercial banks are private businesses operated for the benefit of their owners. The process of establishing management policies in pursuit of this objective is different and, in many ways, more complex than that of a non-financial corporation. Along with responsibilities to owners, management must consider the unique responsibility of a commercial bank to its community and the constraints placed by myriad government regulations. It is thus necessary to consider the special objectives and constraints of commercial banks in developing management principles.

BANK OBJECTIVES AND CONSTRAINTS

BANKS AS PRIVATE ENTERPRISES

Banks, like other private enterprises, establish policy aimed at achieving their primary objective: profitability. Profitability is more than simple profit; it is the level of profits relative to the assets committed. A satisfactory level of profitability is necessary to assure proper returns to creditors and owners.

Like all business firms, banks generate liabilities and assets. Those who provide funds to banks do so by purchasing debt or equity securities issued by the bank or by placing funds on deposit. They provide funds for the purpose of receiving benefits in the form of services or expected future income. Thus banks are liable, as are other private businesses, to those from whom funds have been provided. They are liable to pay interest and ultimately return funds in the case of deposits and debt instruments issued. In addition, they are expected to meet dividend payments on equity as investor expectations dictate. Accordingly, management obligations to those who have provided funds are essentially comparable for commercial banks and private non-financial firms.

It stands to reason then, that bank funds must be invested in those assets that, when taken as a group, generate returns sufficient in amount to satisfy the legal requirements and expectations of depositors, creditors, and owners. A well managed bank will generate a return on assets which not only covers minimum legal requirements and expectations, but also provides retained earnings for support of future growth.

As is true in a non-financial private enterprise, proper management of assets and liabilities is critical to success and growth of commercial banks.

COMPETITION

In a free enterprise system, external constraints are placed on private firms through the mechanism of competition. In competitive markets, firms bid for land, labor, capital and management talent. The interaction of supply and demand determines market prices for those resources. Similarly, prices for products and services are set by the forces of supply and demand. Banks are certainly not immune from competitive pressures. If wage levels are set below those offered in comparable employment circumstances, for example, a bank will not be able to attract and retain competent personnel. Similarly, if compensating balance requirements and loan interest rates consistently exceed those charged by competing institutions, qualified loan customers can be expected to seek accommodations elsewhere. Thus, bank policy must reflect competitive forces in ways which are frequently similar to responses of non-bank firms.

REGULATION

As discussed in Chapter 2, the need to protect the safety of the public's funds has led to financial institutions being more heavily regulated than most other types of business. This has been especially true for commercial banks.

The need for banking regulations has long been justified on the grounds that unbridled competition would lead to massive bank failure and ultimate economic chaos. Consequently, the number of different banks and

banking offices in the marketplace has been restricted. A new bank or branch will not be permitted by the regulatory authority if its existence would threaten the solvency of other banks in the market area. Similarly, to help maintain the solvency of the financial system, bank costs were held to artificially low levels. Prior to the Monetary Control Act of 1980, banks were largely prohibited from paying interest on transaction accounts and competing financial institutions were largely prohibited from offering transaction accounts. This condition, together with Regulation Q restrictions on interest payments for time and savings deposits amounted to a government-imposed cost subsidy that favored commercial banks and that favored borrowers at the expense of savers.

Although the Monetary Control Act of 1980 signalled a shift toward greater reliance on competition in allocating financial resources, the commercial banking industry is still subject to a huge network of regulations. Many of these regulations deal with questions of equity and social justice in credit allocation decisions. Such regulation, in addition to competitive forces and community responsibility, forms the complex of external constraints within which bank assets and liabilities must be managed.

COMMUNITY RESPONSIBILITY

In a non-regulated industry, competition is relied on to assure that needs of society are met. The acceptance of a charter to operate a bank carries with it certain community responsibilities which management must recognize and respond to. Economic growth and stability of an area may depend on the willingness of banks to make necessary credit available. But neither competition nor regulation will assure that community needs are met. One of the most challenging problems for bank managers is the achievement of a proper balance between responsibility to owners and responsibility to the community.

CHOICE OF CHARTER

A group seeking to form a bank must first decide whether to seek a charter from the state or federal government. While most businesses can receive a corporate charter only from the state governmant, banks and certain other depository institutions may choose to apply for either a state or a national charter. This decision was traditionally made in light of the regulatory environment of the particular state vs. regulations by the federal government. If all else were equal, the bank would prefer the charter giving it the greatest freedom.

The second question faced by a bank has been whether or not to be a member of the Federal Reserve System. A national bank was required to be a member while a state bank had a choice. Prior to the Monetary Control Act of 1980, the primary advantage of membership was that the member bank could use the Federal Reserve System's services, such as borrowing at the discount window, wire transfer service, and check clearing. The primary disadvantage was that reserve requirements set by the Federal Reserve System applied only to member banks. Non-member banks had their reserve requirements set by state banking authorities, with state requirements frequently being more lenient than those established by the federal government.

Increasingly, a number of smaller banks and some relatively large ones found that services provided by the Fed did not justify the opportunity cost of required reserves. Indeed, the percentage of all commercial banks which were members fell from 49 percent in 1947 to 37 percent by 1980. The proportion of deposits held by member banks declined from 85 to 71 percent. By 1980, it was believed that this decline in membership, together with the growth in funds held by non-bank financial institutions, was impairing the ability of the Federal Reserve System to effectively implement monetary policy.

The Monetary Control Act of 1980 changed this picture by creating uniform reserve requirements for all depository institutions and by requiring that the Federal Reserve System establish prices for its services and make them available to all depository institutions. Thus the advantages of one chartering system over the other have diminished. There has not yet been enough experience with the new law to observe a trend toward one type of charter over the other.

ASSET MANAGEMENT

Asset management in commercial banks is subject first and foremost to the constraint that assets must be highly liquid. Unlike a non-bank business which might forestall or delay payment without serious consequence, commercial banks must constantly be prepared to meet expected and unexpected demands for cash by depositors. Inability or even suspicion of inability on the part of any bank to meet the demand for funds by depositors could lead to general distrust of commercial banks and ultimately to economic chaos. It is thus necessary that a large proportion of bank assets must be held in cash or in assets easily convertible to cash.

This results in a dilemma of some magnitude for the bank manager. On the one hand, there is the need to keep large sums in cash and low yielding "near cash" assets. On the other hand, there is the need to meet community credit needs and to generate the levels of earnings necessary to meet costs, provide a return to owners, and retain some earnings to sustain future growth. This liquidity-profitability trade-off is the central focus of bank asset and liability management.

ASSET STRUCTURE OF COMMERCIAL BANKS

The first level of asset management policy deals with the allocation of funds among the major categories of assets: cash, invest-

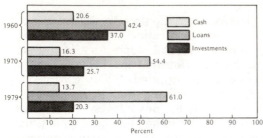

Figure 9–1: Asset structure for all commercial banks, 1960–1979. Graph excludes "other assets." Loans include federal funds sold and securities purchased under agreements to resell. Source: *Federal Reserve Bulletin,* various issues and FDIC Annual Report.

ments, and loans.[1] Cash assets, which earn little or no return, are required to meet withdrawal demand from depositors. Investments, primarily in the form of short and intermediate term U.S. government and municipal securities, provide some income and can be quickly sold to provide additional cash. Loans, which are much less liquid assets, serve the credit needs of the community and provide the greatest source of profit. Figure 9–1 reflects shifts in the relative distribution of these asset categories which occurred during the 1960s and 1970s.

Over the total period covered in Figure 9–1, cash assets declined from 20.6 percent of all assets to 13.7 percent. Moreover, investments declined in relative importance from 37.0 percent of total assets to 20.3 percent. Loans, which in aggregate traditionally yield a higher return but are less liquid, became increasingly important in relative terms. The data suggest that commercial banks, as a group, expanded their loan portfolio and in the process, reduced liquidity over this time period. These changes reflect more aggressive management. As will be seen later, they also reflect an increase in the proportion of funds obtained from time and savings deposits, which are less volatile than demand deposits.

----

[1] Other assets, including physical facilities, amount to a small proportion of total assets for the typical commercial bank.

CASH MANAGEMENT

The most liquid of assets held by banks, and indeed by any firm or institution, is cash. But while cash is unsurpassed as a form of liquidity, the cost of holding cash is equivalent to the income which could have been earned through investment in alternative assets. Cash is held primarily for reserve requirements, day-to-day transactions, and as compensating balances with other banks in exchange for services. Unexpected cash needs are normally met through sale of certain liquid assets rather than through the use of reserves. Since minimum reserve levels are generally fixed by law to assure the solvency of the banking system and to accommodate monetary policy, they are not available for routine liquidity needs.

Effective cash management involves minimizing cash balances over and above minimum required reserves without compromising liquidity. This necessitates management procedures designed to minimize cash balances held for transaction needs and for compensating balance agreements.

Components of Cash The total cash on the balance sheets of commercial banks is divided into four main categories:

1. Coin and currency inside the bank
2. Funds on deposit with federal reserve banks
3. Funds on deposit with other banks and depository institutions
4. Cash items (principally checks) which are in the process of being collected

As shown in Table 9–1, cash represented 13.2 percent of all assets by March, 1980. Currency and coin maintained on the premises represented 8.3 percent of those assets classified as cash. In other words, banks as a group found it necessary to maintain only about 1 percent of total assets in the form of currency and coin on the premises to accommodate day-to-day transactions. Typi-

Table 9-1:

Cash Assets by Domestic Offices of Insured Commercial Banks, March 31, 1980 (in billions)

Cash Assets Held	Amount	Percent
Total cash assets	$185.4	100.0%
Currency and coin	15.3	8.3
Reserves with federal reserve banks	33.0	17.8
Balances with other banks and institutions	58.9	31.8
Cash items in process of collection	78.1	42.1
Memo: All assets and proportion held in cash	$1,402.7	13.2%

Source: *Federal Reserve Bulletin*

cally, coin and currency deposited in a given day is sufficient to accommodate cash disbursements, although local community needs and seasonal factors may result in temporary departure from such a generalization. Funds on deposit with federal reserve banks, funds on deposit with other banks and depository institutions, and cash items in the process of collection constituted a far larger component of total cash than did currency and coin on hand.

Reserve Requirements   Prior to the passage and implementation of the Monetary Control Act, the question of membership in the Federal Reserve System was a significant influencing factor in bank profitability. Advantages of membership were weighed against requirements placed on member banks, chief among which was the stipulation that certain minimum cash balances (required reserves) be maintained. These required balances were usually stricter than those imposed by the states on non-member banks.

The Monetary Control Act addressed these differences. An important provision of the act concerned reserve requirements and virtually eliminated the impact of the Fed membership decision on bank profitability.

Effective November, 1980, sterile reserves were required of all banks, members and non-members alike. Sterile reserves are those which earn no interest. They must be held as cash in the vault or as direct or indirect[2] deposits with the Fed.

The quantity of required reserves for individual banks depends on the types and amounts of deposit liabilities maintained. These include transaction accounts, non-personal time deposits, and Eurocurrency liabilities. Transaction accounts include demand deposits, negotiable order of withdrawal (NOW) accounts, automatic transfer service (ATS) accounts, share draft accounts, and accounts permitting telephone or similar transfers for payments to third parties. Non-personal time deposits are defined as time deposits which are transferable *or* as time deposits held by corporations or by other institutions. Percentage reserve requirements before and after November, 1980, are summarized in Table 9–2.

The purpose of uniform reserve requirements for all depository institutions was to increase Federal Reserve control over the monetary system. The effect was to reduce reserve requirements for member banks and to impose sterile reserve requirements on non-member institutions. In order to provide for an orderly transition, the new reserve requirements will be phased in over a period of several years.

Deposits with Other Banks   Virtually all banks own funds left on deposit with other commercial banks. Generally, such funds are held in the form of demand deposits. If Bank A deposits funds with Bank B, Bank A does so in return for services which Bank B is expected to provide. Bank B, for example, may act as a clearing point for checks

---

[2] Indirect deposits are those which are "passed through" the correspondent network, e.g., Bank A maintains its required reserve balances in the form of deposits with Bank B. Bank B, however, "passes through" these balances by depositing them with the Fed.

Table 9-2:

Depository Institutions Reserve Requirements
(Percent of deposits)

Type of Deposit, and Deposit Interval in Millions of Dollars	Member Bank Requirements Before Implementation of the Monetary Control Act	
	Percent	Effective Date
Net demand		
0–2	7	12/30/76
2–10	9½	12/30/76
10–100	11¾	12/30/76
100–400	12¾	12/30/76
Over 400	16¼	12/30/76
Time and savings		
Savings	3	3/16/67
Time		
0–5, by maturity		
30–179 days	3	3/16/67
180 days to 4 years	2½	1/8/76
4 years or more	1	10/30/75
Over 5, by maturity		
30–179 days	6	12/12/74
180 days to 4 years	2½	1/8/76
4 years or more	1	10/30/75

Type of Deposit, and Deposit Interval	Depository Institution Requirements After Implementation of the Monetary Control Act	
	Percent	Effective Date
Net transaction accounts		
$0–$25 million	3	11/13/80
Over $25 million	12	11/13/80
Nonpersonal time deposits		
By original maturity		
Less than 4 years	3	11/13/80
4 years or more	0	11/13/80
Eurocurrency liabilities		
All types	3	11/13/80

Source: *Federal Reserve Bulletin*

drawn on Bank A. Alternatively, Bank B may provide other services such as advice and assistance in purchase, evaluation, or sale of securities. In fact, Bank A may hold deposits with a large number of other banks (called correspondent banks) in return for a variety of services offered by these correspondents. These deposits are referred to as compensating balances[3] and the size of such balances, in theory at least, is a function of the value of compensatory services performed.

Prior to November, 1980, non-member banks could generally include compensatory balances held with other banks when computing reserves. For this reason, balances held with other banks constituted a far larger proportion of cash assets for non-member banks as compared to members. One consequence of the Monetary Control Act was the fact that compensating balances may no longer be counted for reserve purposes by non-member state banks. Analysis of the value of services provided in relation to the opportunity cost associated with non-interest earning compensating balances is a particularly important component of cash management.

In Chapter 7, we developed methods of determining the cost of funds. If management determines that the cost of balances held in return for services provided is greater than the value of the service, either the size of such balances should be renegotiated or the services should be acquired on a direct payment basis. Evaluation of compensating balances should be an ongoing process and appropriate management policies and procedures providing for their analysis must be developed within the overall framework of cash management.

Evaluating Transaction Needs Just as bankers expect their customers to plan for

future cash needs through development of pro-forma financial statements and cash budgets, banks should also plan for their own future cash needs. The volume of cash required for transactions is frequently predictable on the basis of past experience and future expectations. Too much idle cash results in income foregone, while too little cash may result in forced sale of securities or in expensive borrowing in the money market. In both instances, the impact of poor planning for transaction needs can have a significant impact on profitability. The importance of good forecasts cannot be overemphasized. Good forecasting permits management to determine not only the appropriate size of the secondary reserve, but of the maturity distribution of securities included therein. Since longer term securities normally carry higher yields, knowledge of cash requirements for anticipated future transactions permits management the opportunity to maximize income through investment of excess funds.

Techniques used in projecting transaction needs vary from a simple analysis of seasonal fluctuations based on the experience of prior years to highly sophisticated methods such as construction of econometric models. The appropriate forecasting technique for any given bank depends primarily on the institution's size and on the nature and magnitude of variables which influence changes in the composition of its assets and liabilities.

LOAN AND INVESTMENT MANAGEMENT

The amount of total funds allocated to loans and investments is basically total assets less fixed assets and cash items. By mid-1980, approximately four-fifths of all bank assets were in the form of loans and investments.

The liquidity-profitability tradeoff is most evident in these areas of asset management. Loans provide the primary source of bank earnings and community support. However,

---

[3] Compensating balances refer to demand account balances which are required as a condition in many commercial loan transactions. The balances are to remain idle in the demand account.

loans cannot be converted to cash quickly and economically; and we have seen that required cash reserves are not available to meet expected or unexpected deposit withdrawals. Thus, investments, which normally provide lower returns than loans, must be relied on as the main source of liquidity. Loan and investment policies must therefore be established in light of both profitability and liquidity needs.

Although no two banks are identical in the relative distribution of loan and investment portfolios, all banks must formulate loan and investment policies in relation to liquidity considerations. Liquidity is defined as the ability to meet demands by depositors and to satisfy reasonable loan demands without the necessity of incurring losses or undue expense in the conversion of assets. Variables influencing liquidity requirements for individual banks include the following:

1. Seasonal fluctuation of loans and deposits
2. Quality and structure of bank assets
3. Proportion of large borrowers and depositors
4. Trend and distribution of liabilities
5. Market area competition for the available money supply
6. Trend and distribution of earnings
7. Capital adequacy
8. Local and national economic conditions
9. Monetary policies of the Federal Reserve Board
10. Long range economic trends of the market area

Close examination of the above factors indicates that liquidity policy and hence investment and loan policies cannot be formulated in a vacuum. Investment and loan strategies depend not only upon one another, but upon variables which are influenced both internally and externally. The influence of certain factors may be predicted with reasonable certainty, e.g., seasonal fluctuations. Others require careful study and analysis of conditions based on data generated both internally and externally. It is sufficient to say at this point that variables influencing liquidity policy are constantly changing, and that the well-managed bank is one which is not only informed of such changes, but one which adapts loan and investment policies accordingly. Thus careful analysis of variables which influence liquidity will provide management with the basis for decisions leading to the appropriate mix of loans and securities.

Investment Management Commercial banks maintain investments represented almost entirely by obligations of federal and other governmental units. Reasons for holding these investments include income, liquidity, diversification of assets, and flexibility.

Under normal economic conditions, returns available through investment in securities of comparable quality vary directly with maturity schedules. Thus, investment in Treasury bills maturing in less than one year frequently promises a return lower than that available in Treasury securities maturing several years hence. The primary purpose of investing in short-term securities is to provide for liquidity while earning at least some minimal return. Short-term securities of high quality may be sold quickly in the secondary market without serious risk of capital loss and serve as a backup measure in the event that cash is suddenly needed.

On the other hand, the well-managed bank should also maintain a portfolio of longer-term investment securities. Securities which mature over a period of several years, in addition to providing higher returns relative to short-term investments, provide for asset diversification and offer an outlet for funds still remaining after anticipated loan demand and secondary reserve requirements have been met. Long term securities may be thought of also as an additional line of defense in the event that a totally unexpected need for cash developed and if such need could not reasonably be met through other alternatives. In this unlikely situation, long-term securities could be converted to cash quickly through sale in the secondary market. Typically, however, longer-term investments should be purchased for the purpose of providing asset diversification and reasonably high yields. Forced sale of long-term securities purchased during a period of generally rising interest rates will likely result in capital losses detrimentally affecting bank earnings.

Included in Table 9–3 is a summary of asset structure for insured commercial banks as of December 31, 1979. For all insured banks, investments represented about one-fifth of total assets and, as mentioned earlier, consisted almost entirely of obligations issued by federal, state, and other governmental units.

Notable in Table 9–3 is the tendency for smaller banks to rely heavily on federal securities in calculating their investment strategy. Larger banks, on the other hand, having access to greater investment expertise in evaluating investment alternatives, rely to a greater extent on investment in security issues of state and local governmental units. Noteworthy also in Table 9–3 is the fact that very large banks, those with assets of $5 billion and more, calculated an investment portfolio proportionally smaller than that calculated by smaller and intermediate sized banks. This tendency is explained by two considerations. First, large banks are members of the Federal Reserve System with a larger proportion of their deposits subject to the higher range of reserve requirements.[4] Thus a smaller proportion of assets are available for investment in other alternatives. In addition, as bank size increases, the capability to facilitate credit needs of loan cus-

tomers, particularly those of large and prime corporate borrowers, is improved. Thus a greater opportunity exists on the part of large banks to acquire higher yielding loans in favor of investment securities.

Because commercial banks restrict their investment portfolios to high-grade debt securities issued primarily by governmental authorities, the risk of loss due to default of interest and principal payments is small. For this reason, and because most such securities may readily be converted to cash through sale in secondary markets, potential returns on these securities are less than returns available on loans of comparable maturity. Thus the primary source of earnings for commercial banks, and a primary reason for their existence, is to provide funds to borrowers in the form of loans. It is this important component of asset management, bank lending, to which we now turn.

Loan Management The central focus of commercial banking concerns the acquisition and servicing of loans. Indeed, commercial banks are the primary, if not the only, source of loans for most small and medium sized business firms. But while commercial banks provide a vital service to business organizations and to the community as a source of loans, they are not charitable organizations and cannot be expected to provide loans which may have widespread social merits but which may or may not be repaid. Indeed, banks have primary responsibility to those depositors who have entrusted their funds for safekeeping. Banks also have a responsibility to those who have provided debt and equity capital and are thus expected to operate profitably. It is through returns to equity holders in the form of dividends and through retained earnings that banks are able to continue in operation and to grow along with the communities they serve. Accordingly, the well-managed bank must institute loan policies designed to insure that adequate control exists in the approval and disbursement of loans and that outstanding

---

[4] This condition will continue to prevail for a number of years until reserve requirements are ultimately equalized in accordance with the Monetary Control Act of 1980.

Table 9-3:

Percentages of Assets, Liabilities, and Equity Capital of Insured Commercial Banks Operating Throughout 1979 in the United States and Other Areas, December 31, 1979

(Banks grouped by amount of assets)

Asset, Liability, or Equity Capital Item	All Banks	Less than $5 Million	$5.0 Million to $9.9 Million	$10.0 Million to $24.9 Million	$25.0 Million to $49.9 Million	$50.0 Million to $99.9 Million	$100.0 Million to $299.9 Million	$300.0 Million to $499.9 Million	$500.0 Million to $999.9 Million	$1.0 Billion to $4.9 Billion	$5.0 Billion or More
Total assets	100.0%	100.0%	100.0%	100.0%	100.0%	100.0%	100.0%	100.0%	100.0%	100.0%	100.0%
Cash and due from depository institutions	13.7	10.7	9.6	9.3	9.2	9.6	10.8	13.0	13.2	14.0	18.2
U.S. Treasury Securities[1]	6.3	14.4	12.2	9.4	8.6	8.0	7.8	7.8	7.3	5.7	3.7
Obligations of other U.S. Government agencies and corporations	3.5	9.5	8.5	6.7	5.4	4.7	4.3	4.5	3.4	2.8	1.9
Obligations of states and political subdivisions[1]	9.4	3.3	6.1	10.2	12.4	13.2	13.2	11.4	11.0	9.7	5.3
All other securities	1.1	.5	.5	.5	.5	.6	.5	1.0	1.0	1.1	1.8
Federal funds sold and securities purchased under agreements to resell	4.3	8.1	6.5	5.4	4.7	4.4	4.7	5.6	5.6	4.7	3.0
Loans, net	54.6	50.9	53.8	55.5	55.7	55.8	54.8	52.7	53.9	54.1	54.4
Unearned income on loans	1.5	1.5	1.5	1.9	2.0	2.2	2.0	1.9	1.8	1.2	.8
Allowance for possible loan losses	.6	.4	.5	.5	.5	.5	.6	.6	.6	.6	.8
Loans, gross	56.7	52.8	55.8	57.9	58.2	58.5	57.4	55.2	56.3	55.9	56.0
Real estate loans	17.4	13.7	16.4	20.1	22.3	22.5	22.2	19.3	18.7	15.9	12.8
Loans to financial institutions	3.0	.1	.1	.1	.2	.3	.5	1.2	1.5	3.4	6.5
Loans for purchasing or carrying securities	1.0	.1	.1	.1	.1	.2	.3	.7	.9	.9	1.9
Loans to finance agricultural production and other loans to farmers	2.2	16.1	15.0	10.2	6.0	3.1	1.4	1.1	.8	.7	.8
Commercial and industrial loans	18.3	7.4	8.6	10.3	11.7	13.9	15.6	15.9	17.1	19.4	24.3

Banks with Assets of—

Loans to individuals for household, family and other personal expenditures	11.1	11.1	11.4	12.5	13.2	14.0	13.7	13.5	13.5	11.7	6.9
Single-payment loans for personal expenditures	2.3	3.4	3.3	3.6	3.8	3.6	2.9	2.4	2.6	2.2	1.0
All other loans	1.4	.9	.9	1.0	.9	.9	.8	1.1	1.2	1.7	1.8
All other assets[1]	7.1	2.6	2.8	3.0	3.5	3.7	3.9	4.0	4.6	7.9	11.7
Total liabilities and equity capital	100.0	100.0	100.0	100.0	100.0	100.0	100.0	100.0	100.0	100.0	100.0
Deposits—total	77.8	87.6	89.3	89.6	89.2	88.4	86.3	83.7	81.6	74.7	66.3
Demand deposits	30.8	35.8	30.1	28.9	28.4	28.8	29.1	31.4	32.4	30.9	32.5
Time and savings	47.0	51.6	59.2	60.7	60.8	59.6	57.2	52.3	49.2	43.8	33.8
Individuals, partnerships, and corporations—demand	23.8	32.1	26.6	25.5	25.1	25.4	24.7	24.9	26.1	24.6	21.0
Individuals, partnerships, and corporations—time and savings	41.5	44.8	52.5	54.4	54.6	53.1	50.5	44.9	42.6	38.2	29.7
U.S. Government	.2	.2	.3	.3	.3	.3	.2	.3	.3	.3	.2
States and political subdivisions	5.9	9.6	8.9	8.3	8.1	8.1	8.1	8.4	7.3	6.1	2.5
Certified and officers' checks	1.1	.7	.8	.9	.9	1.0	1.0	1.2	1.1	.9	1.5
All other deposits	5.3	.2	.2	.2	.2	.5	1.8	4.0	4.2	4.6	11.4
Federal funds purchased and securities sold under agreements to repurchase	8.0	.3	.4	.5	.8	1.6	3.6	6.3	7.8	11.5	13.2
Interest-bearing demand notes issued to the U.S. Treasury and other liabilities for borrowed money	2.0	.0	.1	.2	.3	.5	.9	1.0	1.6	2.3	3.7
All other liabilities[2]	4.9	.6	.6	1.0	1.4	1.5	1.6	1.7	1.9	4.6	9.9
Subordinated notes and debentures	.4	.0	.1	.1	.2	.3	.4	.5	.6	.7	.4
Equity capital	6.9	11.5	9.5	8.6	8.1	7.7	7.2	6.8	6.5	6.2	6.5
Number of banks	14,159	728	2,066	4,694	3,365	1,764	1,051	170	149	144	28

[1]Securities held in trading accounts are included in "Other assets."

[2]Includes minority interest in consolidated subsidiaries.

Source: *Annual Report of the Federal Deposit Insurance Corporation*, 1979, p. 180.

loans are monitored so as to insure compliance with terms of the loan and ultimate repayment of principal and interest.

Table 9–3 contains information concerning the distribution of loans at December 31, 1979, for all commercial banks and for banks grouped by size of deposit. Notable in Table 9–3 is the recognition that loans represent the largest single category of assets for commercial banks and amount to more than half of all assets. Inclusion of Federal Funds Sold (loans to other commercial banks) further increases the proportion of loans represented in total assets.

Also with reference to the distribution of loans contained in Table 9–3 is the recognition that commercial and industrial loans are a principal domain of larger banks, which tend to be concentrated in industrial areas. On the other hand, agricultural loans are made in greater proportion to available assets by smaller banks, many of which are located in less industrialized and smaller agricultural communities. Federal Funds Sold, which represent temporary excess reserves, and which are sold (loaned) to other commercial banks, represented a larger proportion of assets for very small banks as compared to that of the larger banks. This condition again reflects the availability of a greater range of alternative uses for funds by large banks and demonstrates the fact that federal funds are an important source of funds in meeting liquidity requirements.

Table 9–4 contains a summary of yields realized on selected categories of loans by banks grouped according to deposit size for 1979. While variations in realized yields occur over time, the data presented in Table 9–4 are helpful in the interpretation of bank lending practices and the relative profitability of different categories of bank lending.

Real estate mortgage loans: Real estate mortgage lending has long been an important component of commercial bank lending. At year end 1979, commercial banks held about 18.4 percent of all real estate mortgages outstanding and over 26.2 per-

cent of mortgages held by financial institutions. In terms of dollar volume, investment in mortgage loans represents the largest single category of loans for intermediate size banks. Large banks, which tend to be located in major money market areas, invest most heavily in loans for commercial and industrial purposes while smaller banks, many of which are located in rural and agriculturally oriented communities, invest heavily in non-real estate loans to farmers in support of agriculture (Table 9–3).

For 1979, according to Table 9–4, real estate loans provided gross yields in excess of 9 percent, a return generally lower than that associated with other loan categories. However, bank expenses associated with making and administering real estate loans in relation to loans outstanding, was substantially lower than that associated with other loan categories. Because of the low expense of administration per dollar invested, real estate lending provided net yields (after allowing for administrative costs) in the range of about 8 percent.

While real estate lending can provide acceptable sources of revenue for commercial banks, the long-term nature of such lending contains inherent risk. Since the cost of generating and servicing such loans is relatively low per dollar outstanding, money cost and possible future increases thereof play a dominant role in the continued profitability of mortgage loans generated in previous years. In 1979, money cost ranged from 5.901 percent for the smallest category of banks in Table 9–4 to 6.296 percent for the largest. Should money cost increase dramatically in any given period, the net yield after money cost associated with real estate loans would obviously decline. The experience of recent years has served to illustrate this point. It is, of course, in the best interest of bank managers to guard against such risk, either through the introduction of variable rate mortgages, where mortgage interest rates would automatically move up or down with the cost of money—or through use of con-

Table 9-4:

Yields on Selected Loan Categories, 1979

Loan Category	Bank Size (Total Deposits for Reporting Banks)		
	358 Banks Under $50M	313 Banks $50M–$200M	80 Banks Over $200M
Real Estate Mortgage Loans			
Gross Yield	9.010%	9.003%	9.228%
Less: Expense	1.111	.817	.988
Loan Losses	.096	.050	.184
Net Yield	7.803	8.137	8.056
Installment Loans			
Gross Yield	12.507%	12.079	12.027%
Less: Expense	3.263	2.901	3.026
Loan Losses	.506	.424	.530
Net Yield	8.739	8.754	8.470
Credit Card*			
Gross Yield			19.616%
Less: Expense			9.376
Loan Losses			1.955
Net Yield			8.285
Commercial and Other Loans			
Gross Yield	10.608%	11.262%	12.015%
Less: Expense	1.871	1.552	1.337
Loan Losses	.377	.300	.307
Net Yield	8.361	9.409	10.371
Money Cost	5.901%	6.094%	6.296%

Source: Board of Governors of the Federal Reserve System, *Functional Cost Analysis: 1979 Average Banks*, p. 2

*Although many small and medium sized banks participate in credit card operations, credit card receivables tend to be held by larger banks.

Note: Money cost is defined as the cost of processing demand deposits, time deposits (including interest expense), and non-deposit funds less any service charge or fee income. It is calculated as a percent of available funds. Net yield shown above is before money cost.

tractual mortgage agreements where interest rates would be renegotiated at fixed time intervals, e.g., every three to five years.

Installment loans: Over the years, installment lending by commercial banks has become an attractive source of revenue for commercial banks. Traditionally, and prior to World War II, commercial banks did not seek significant amounts of installment receivables and displayed little interest in consumer lending.[5] Following World War II,

however, it became evident that yields available on consumer installment receivables were attractive in comparison with those available on commercial and other bank loans. Percentage rates quoted on installment loans were almost always quoted in terms of "add-on" or "discount" as opposed to simple interest. For example, a loan of $1,000 for a one-year period with interest and principal payable in equal money installments, and with a rate of 6 percent applied to the initial amount loaned ($1,000), produced a return of $60. But since the lender's original investment of $1,000 de-

[5] While installment loans may be made to business firms, most installment lending represents loans to consumers.

clines steadily over the time period, the true annual yield is substantially greater than 6 percent and approaches 12 percent. In addition, because of the short-term nature of installment loans, typically maturing within a few years or less, the size of the monthly payments are not materially affected by changes in the interest rate. The evidence suggests that consumers are not particularly sensitive to changes in installment loan interest rates and that such rates do not move freely with money market and mortgage interest rates. By 1980, commercial banks had captured 46 percent of the market for consumer installment receivables. This compares with 30 percent in 1960 and 13 percent at the beginning of the post-World War II era.

Table 9–4 illustrates the fact that net yields for installment loans were higher than those associated with mortgage loans in 1979. In addition, the previous discussion suggests that gross yields could be adjusted as necessary by increasing rates for new installment loans to compensate for increased money cost. Thus the interest rate risk associated with installment loans is not nearly so significant as that associated with fixed rate real estate lending.

Credit card loans: Credit card loans are among the most recent innovations in bank lending practices. Bank credit cards provide the holder with a pre-authorized line of credit in some specified amount. Such cards may be used to acquire cash directly from a bank or to acquire merchandise from participating merchants. Data contained in Table 9–4 suggest that investment in credit card receivables is principally a function of large banks and that gross yields available through credit card loans far outstrip those available through alternative lending categories. The high expense associated with bank credit cards reflects mainly the fact that average loan balances are small and administrative costs high per dollar outstanding. Also, credit card loss chargeoffs are higher than

chargeoffs for other forms of bank lending. But while administrative costs are high in bank credit card lending, significant potential exists for reduction of such costs over the long term. It is in lending programs such as credit card operations, characterized by large volumes of routine transactions, that technological economies may prove to be significant. As technological improvements in this area continue, credit card lending may generate increased contributions to commercial bank profitability.

Commercial and industrial loans: Loans for commercial and industrial purposes have always been the principal domain of commercial banks. While banks have sought to increase market shares for consumer installment receivables and have expanded operations to include credit card loans, commercial lending continues to represent the largest single component of bank lending practices. At year end 1979, commercial and industrial loans constituted 18.3 percent of all loans outstanding for the industry and 24.3 percent of total loans outstanding for the largest banks—those with deposits of $5 billion and more (see Table 9–3).

Traditionally, commercial banks have preferred short-term business loans, designed to meet seasonal needs for working capital purposes. Rates are tied to the prime lending rate with large and established customers borrowing at the prime or best available rate. Loans to less established firms are typically made at interest rates that exceed prime by a margin judged sufficient to compensate for the increased credit risk.[6]

Commercial and industrial loans are essentially of two types. The first and traditional type represents those made for working capital purposes as discussed above. Risk

---

[6] With the volatility of interest rates prevailing in the late 1970's and early 1980's, some banks began the practice of charging less than prime for some short-term loans to certain large business customers. The extent of such lending was unknown.

associated with fluctuating interest rates is minimized in this type loan because maturities are relatively short, averaging a few months at most and with rates adjusted in the event of loan renewal. The second major type of commercial and industrial loans is the *business term loan*. Term loans are those with original maturities of more than one year and are frequently made for the purpose of financing the acquisition of fixed assets. While data describing the extent of term lending in the banking industry are sketchy, available data suggest that the volume of term lending included in commercial and industrial loans increased in the postwar era. Traditionally, term loans have been made at fixed rates somewhat higher than those charged for short-term working capital loans. Higher rates are justified on the grounds that longer term maturities represent increased exposure to the risk of fluctuating money cost.

Beginning with the experience of the early 1970s, when bank money costs increased dramatically as the result of severe fluctuations in money market rates, many banks turned to the practice of allowing term loan rates to vary with money market conditions. Thus many term loans are made with original maturities of several years but with interest rates tied to prime or to some other index with rate adjustments frequently occurring several times per year. Indeed, with the continuing erratic behavior of interest rates in the late 1970s and early 1980s, an increasing proportion of all business loans were made with floating rates. Results of a Federal Reserve survey conducted in August, 1980, indicated that about one third of all short-term commercial and industrial loans were made with floating rates, even though maturities averaged less than three months. About two thirds of the long-term loans had floating rates.[7]

---

[7] *Federal Reserve Bulletin*, December, 1980, p. A–24.

LIABILITY MANAGEMENT

In recent years, commercial banks have devoted increased attention to the concept of liability management. As money costs climbed, and as the demand for bank loans increased, commercial bank managers became increasingly aware of the need to acquire funds to support asset expansion. Thus there developed a general awareness of the fact that desired levels of expansion could be met only through new means of attracting funds. Consequently, the management of commercial bank liabilities took on an importance comparable to that of asset management.

The nature of liabilities and liability management by commercial banks shifted markedly over the decades of the '60s and '70s. Over that period, in response to rising market interest rates and continued loan demand, bankers shifted from a passive role as money gatherers to a role involving active competition for funds in the market place. In 1960, more than 60 percent of liabilities for all commercial banks were represented by non-interest bearing demand deposits. The ratio of demand to time deposits exceeded 2:1 and rates paid on time and savings accounts were low by today's standards. Loan demand during the previous decade was largely supported by available liabilities and by converting investment securities accumulated during the war and during the post-war period. Thus the efforts of bank managers were devoted primarily to asset management with little attention paid to the availability and structure of liabilities.

THE CHANGING NATURE OF BANK LIABILITIES

Table 9–5 summarizes aggregate liabilities of commercial banks for December 31, 1960 and 1970, and for June 30, 1980. While non-interest bearing demand deposits dominated the liability structure in 1960, *time*

Table 9-5:

Liability Structure for Commercial Banks, December 1960, 1970, and June 30, 1980
(in billions of dollars)

	1960		1970		1980	
	Amount	Percent	Amount	Percent	Amount	Percent
Deposits						
Demand	156.4	60.7%	247.9	43.0%	414.8	29.0
Time and Saving	73.4	28.5	233.1	40.4	686.1	48.0
Borrowings	0.2	0.1	19.4	3.4	157.3	11.0
Other Liabilities	20.9	8.1	33.0	5.7	68.6	4.8
Capital Accounts	6.6	2.5	43.0	7.5	102.3	7.2
Total Liabilities	257.6	100.0	576.2	100.0	1,429.2	100.0

Source: *Federal Reserve Bulletin*, various issues.

and savings deposits became increasingly important over the following two decades. By 1980, time and savings deposits were clearly the most important source of funds for commercial banks. At the same time, the proportion of assets financed by demand deposits had declined from 60.7 percent in 1960 to 29 percent by 1980. Commercial bank borrowings, virtually non-existent in 1960, had risen to 11 percent of total liabilities. Factors influencing this condition included a number of innovations in liability management which occurred. Included among these were the following:

1. Development of a secondary market for large denomination certificates of deposit (CDs)

2. Issuance of consumer-type CDs

3. Expansion of the federal funds market

4. Eurodollar borrowings

5. Repurchase agreements

Development of a Secondary Market for CDs A certificate of deposit (CD) issued by a bank is a receipt for funds placed on deposit. The funds must be left on deposit for the time specified on the certificate and bear interest at a rate established at the time of issuance. Prior to 1961, CDS were issued by a few banks. Total CD outstandings prior

to 1961, however, constituted little more than 1 percent of total liabilities and less than 4 percent of total time and savings deposits.

While commercial banks had authority to issue CDs prior to 1961, many felt that to do so would encourage corporations and other large depositors who were precluded by law from holding passbook savings accounts,[8] to transfer funds from non-interest bearing demand deposits to interest bearing CDs. But beginning in early 1961, several large banks began to issue large CDs in negotiable form. At the same time, major securities dealers agreed to make a market for them. Thus the availability of negotiable CDs in large denominations and the liquidity provided by the ready availability of a secondary market provided corporations and other large investors with an alternative and highly liquid means for investment of temporary excess funds. Individual banks found that by varying rates for new issues slightly in relation to current market yields, the volume of new time deposits attracted could be substantially increased or decreased in accordance with current or projected needs for funds. Hence the ability of commercial

---

[8] Effective November 10, 1975, corporations, partnerships, and other profit-making organizations were permitted to hold savings accounts of up to $150,000 per depositor.

banks to manage liabilities was improved dramatically with this turn of events.

Prior to 1973, however, liability management through issuance of new CDs was constrained somewhat by the Federal Reserve's Regulation Q. Regulation Q sets maximum rates payable on time and savings accounts and is applicable to insured commercial banks. At times, throughout the '60s and early '70s, liability management was hindered by the fact that market interest rates exceeded statutory rates permissible for new CDs. This condition caused difficulties for bank managers in attempts to raise funds through issuance of new CDs for the purpose of retiring maturing ones or for the purpose of supporting further asset expansion. Although ceiling rates on certain CDs were modified or partially eliminated from time to time, it was not until mid 1973 that Regulation Q ceilings were suspended for all CDs issued in amounts of $100,000 or more.

Issuance of Consumer Type CDs While large negotiable CDs played an important role in bank liability management during the '60s and '70s, consumer type CDs (savings certificates, non-negotiable CDs, and negotiable CDs in denominations of less than $100,000) took on increasing importance following a change in Regulation Q in late 1965. In December of that year, ceiling rates under Regulation Q were increased for time deposits while rates for passbook savings accounts were held at 4 percent. Subsequent changes in Regulation Q during the '60s and '70s maintained and in some cases expanded the rate differential between consumer savings and time deposits. Finally, because of disintermediation caused by increasingly higher yields on open market securities beginning in 1977, the federal regulatory agencies authorized the sale of certain new consumer-type certificates effective June 1, 1978. The most important of these was the six-month money market certificate, available in minimum denominations of $10,000 and with the interest yield tied to the Treas-

ury bill rate. Thus banks were in a position to provide a variety of time certificates in various denominations and maturity. Table 9–6 contains a summary of maximum interest rates payable on time and savings deposits for commercial banks on November 30, 1980.

Expansion of the Federal Funds Market
Previous discussion has emphasized the need for commercial bank managers to maintain an appropriate balance between liquid investments and higher yielding loans. It has also been suggested that profitability objectives require that a minimum of excess cash over and above required reserves be held. Cash in the vault and deposits with federal reserve banks that exceed necessary requirements may represent evidence of inefficient management. So are balances held with correspondents in excess of that expected or required in return for services provided. On the other hand, it is not realistic to expect loan demand and investment requirements to precisely match the quantity of funds available for the purpose of meeting such demand or requirements. While the volume of deposit liabilities may be managed through variation in interest rates and in the maturity range of offerings, and while lending and investment policies and activities may be adjusted to affect the level and composition of assets, it is likely that too much or too little cash will be available for desired purposes at any given point in time. Further, it may be expected that divergences from the optimal level and composition of assets and liabilities would be an occurrence expected almost daily.

Throughout the '60s and '70s and into the '80s, as interest rates rose and competitive conditions intensified, commercial banks responded to the need for finer adjustment in asset and liability management. A significant mechanism to provide for such adjustment was the *federal funds market*.

Federal funds are deposits held by commercial banks with the Federal Reserve Sys-

Table 9-6:

Maximum Interest Rates Payable on Time and Savings Deposits at Federally Insured Institutions
(percent per annum)

		Commercial Banks	
		In Effect Nov. 30, 1980	
	Type and Maturity of Deposit	*Percent*	*Effective Date*
1	Savings	5¼	7/1/79
2	Negotiable order of withdrawal (NOW) accounts	5	1/1/74
	Time		
	Fixed Ceiling Rates by Maturity		
3	14–89 days	5¼	8/1/79
4	90 days to one year	5¾	1/1/80
5	1 to 2 years	6	7/1/73
6	2 to 2½ years	6	7/1/73
7	2½ to 4 years	6½	7/1/73
8	4 to 6 years	7¼	11/1/73
9	6 to 8 years	7½	12/23/74
10	8 years or more	7¾	6/1/78
11	Issued to governmental units (all maturities)	8	6/1/78
12	Individual retirement assets and KEOGH (H.R. 10) plans (3 years or more)	8	6/1/78
	Special Variable Ceiling Rates by Maturity		
13	6 Month Money Market Time deposit	*	*
14	2½ years or more	**	**

*Money Market Time deposits (certificates) were first permitted June 1, 1978. Maximum interest rates vary with the six-month Treasury bill rates and certain other restrictions apply.

**Effective Jan. 1, 1980. Maximum rates vary with the 2½ year U.S. Treasury Securities and certain other restrictions apply.

Source: *Federal Reserve Bulletin*

tem. The federal funds market refers to the exchange of claims between banks against such balances. Such exchange takes place through the loan of deposit balances by one bank to another. The bank which has borrowed fed funds is said to have "purchased" such funds and the bank which has loaned fed funds is said to have "sold" such funds. From the point of view of the "selling" bank, fed funds constitute an asset and from the point of view of the "buying" bank, a liability.

While federal funds and the federal funds market have existed for a considerable number of years, growth and development of the market began in earnest during the decade of the '60s and was spearheaded, as were many major banking innovations, by major money market banks located principally in New York City. Federal funds transactions are commonly ones which represent loans for a period of only one day, although the length of time may be expanded if desired by the participating parties. Whether or not a bank is a member of the Federal Reserve System is not material insofar as market participation is concerned, since transactions may be handled through a correspondent.

Traditionally, federal funds were looked upon as an alternative to direct borrowing from the Federal Reserve System for the purpose of meeting reserve requirements.

Thus banks needing reserves would borrow from other banks only if such funds were available at lower cost. But in 1965, in the face of strong loan demand and tight money, the fed funds rate began to exceed the discount rate (rate of interest charged by federal reserve banks to member banks). As more and more banks became aware of the convenience and potential of the fed funds market, participation in the market and the volume of transactions increased dramatically.

Table 9–3 provides insight into the importance of federal funds within the structure of assets and liabilities for all commercial banks. The data illustrate the fact that smaller banks tend to be net sellers of federal funds (lenders), while large banks are net buyers (borrowers). Banks with total assets of less than $50 million, while important sources for fed funds, did little borrowing in the market. On the other hand, the largest banks, particularly those with assets exceeding $1 billion, were heavy borrowers of fed funds. In effect, the fed funds market was functioning as a conduit whereby excess funds of small banks were utilized to support cash needs of large banks. Thus, from the viewpoint of bank managers, the fed funds market affords a convenient and flexible means to improve asset and liability management in promoting the goal of profit maximization.

Eurodollar Borrowings Another highly significant development within the framework of liability management occurred with the spectacular growth in Eurodollar borrowings.

Eurodollars are deposits denominated in U.S. dollars and held by any bank located outside the United States—including foreign branches of U.S. banks. Dollars may be on deposit with foreign banks for a variety of reasons. They may exist for the purpose of facilitating trade or they may have been deposited outside the U.S. so as to earn a higher rate of return. Most Eurodollar deposits are held in the form of short-term time deposits and thus earn interest.

Growth in this market became significant in the latter half of the '60s. Impetus to this growth was provided by tight money conditions that prevailed at times over the past 15 years or so, and by Regulation Q ceilings which restricted the ability of banks to acquire desired levels of funds domestically. Hence large banks turned to foreign markets in search of additional funds.

Since Eurodollars represent borrowings rather than deposits, domestic banks were not restricted by interest rate ceilings. Thus a supply of funds from this source was virtually assured for large banks when funds were needed.

Initially, Eurodollar borrowings were not subject to reserve requirements, thus adding to the desirability of this source from the viewpoint of individual banks. Reserve requirements, however, were imposed on certain Eurodollar borrowings in 1969 and the percentage requirement has been changed from time to time in accordance with Federal Reserve System objectives.

Given the continued internationalization of business affairs and the expansion and growing importance of U.S. banks in foreign lands, as well as growth in the presence of foreign owned banks in the U.S., it may be expected that Eurodollars will continue as an important non-deposit source of funds for commercial banks.

Repurchase Agreements A "repurchase agreement" (RP's or "repos") is a financing method by which a bank can acquire relatively large amounts of cash for short term periods, frequently from its corporate customers. A repurchase agreement occurs when a bank sells securities, such as treasury bills, to a securities dealer or to a corporation with an agreement to repurchase the securities at a stated price and a specified time. The sale is usually over a period of a few days. A bank manager, for example, may adjust his bank's reserve position by selling securities to a corporation on Friday with an agreement to repurchase these securities on Monday. The transaction, in this example, would have the effect of increasing the bank's average cash balance for the reserve period. A repurchase agreement is frequently preferable to sale of the securities in the open market with the intent to buy the same securities a few days later because the risk of price fluctuation and brokerage commissions are both avoided.

The use of RP's as a source of funds for commercial banks increased with the surge in short term interest rates in the late 1970's and early 1980's. Indeed, the use of repurchase agreements as a means of attracting *consumer* funds was reported by *The Wall Street Journal* on June 4, 1981.

MONEY-MARKET NOTES will step up bankers' counterattack on money funds.

Reaching out to small investors for financing, the parent companies for Manufacturers Hanover Trust, Chase Manhattan Bank and Continental Illinois Bank all plan $100 million offerings of what they call money-market notes. These variable-rate seven-year instruments will be sold in minimum amounts of $1,000, compared with $25,000 or more for most commercial paper. The interest rate will change weekly.

"These notes were designed with a very specific target in mind—pulling away cash from money-market funds," says Frederick Pape, a Merrill Lynch official promoting the notes. He predicts they'll have higher yields than money funds do, at least most of the time. The funds, whose assets have been declining since early May, already feel pressure as more banks offer "repurchase agreement" certificates (which can be cashed in prematurely without penalty) or check-writing against time deposits.

"Banks are trying much harder to innovate," says Joseph S. DiMartino, president of Dreyfus Liquid Assets. Will the fund be hurt? *"I really don't know, he replies.*

BANK CAPITAL

One of the most important issues which commercial bank managers must face is the question of capital adequacy. We have noted the growth and changing composition of bank assets and liabilities that occurred throughout the '60s and early '70s. Many trends noted thus far suggest that the general composition of bank assets has become less liquid. And with the substitution of a greater volume of loans for cash balances and liquid investments, some would argue that asset structure is characterized by a greater degree of risk as the result of this process.

In addition, increased reliance on CDs, Eurodollars, and other forms of "purchased" funds together with the general reduction in the proportion of funds acquired through interest-free demand deposits, has contributed to upward pressure on the cost of bank funds. Indeed, by the mid '70s, and specifically for each of the years 1975, 1976, and 1979, the number of banks closed because of financial difficulties exceeded the number closed in any given year since 1942 (Table 9–7). Thus bank managers, regula-

Table 9-7:

Number of Banks Closed Because of Financial Difficulties 1934–1979

1934	61	1949	9	1963	2
1935	32	1950	5	1964	8
1936	72	1951	5	1965	9
1937	84	1952	4	1966	8
1938	81	1953	5	1967	4
1939	72	1954	4	1968	3
1940	48	1955	5	1969	9
1941	17	1956	3	1970	8
1942	23	1957	3	1971	6
1943	5	1958	9	1972	3
1944	2	1959	3	1973	6
1945	1	1960	2	1974	4
1946	2	1961	9	1975	14
1947	6	1962	3	1976	17
1948	3			1977	6
				1978	7
				1979	10

Source: *Annual Report*, Federal Deposit Insurance Corporation, 1979. p. 203.

tory agencies, and large depositors have expressed increasing concern over the question of capital adequacy.

For commercial banks, as is true for other business enterprises, capital provides the cushion against which temporary losses may be absorbed. Although the Federal Deposit Insurance Corporation (FDIC) provides protection against loss to depositors for all but a tiny fraction of commercial banks, such protection is subject to an absolute ceiling ($100,000 at present) for each deposit account. Thus insurance protection above that sum is not available through FDIC for holders of large CDs or for holders of savings or demand accounts. Large depositors therefore look to capital as an important factor in evaluating financial strength for individual banks.

THE NATURE OF BANK CAPITAL

Depending on the purpose for which it is calculated or classified, commercial bank capital may be represented in one or more of the following forms:

Equity Capital
  Common Stock
  Preferred Stock
  Surplus
  Undivided Profit
  Reserve for Securities
  Reserve for Bad Debts
  Other Capital Reserves
Debt Capital
  Capital Notes and Debentures

There are, of course, fundamental differences between equity capital and debt capital. In the case of equity capital, there is no legal requirement that payments or dividends be made to holders of equity securities. Thus payment of dividends may be delayed or postponed indefinitely if conditions warrant. In the case of capital notes and de-

bentures, interest must be paid in accordance with legal requirements and the securities must ultimately be retired in accordance with the terms of their issue. But since capital notes and debentures are subordinate to deposit liabilities and other debt obligations of commercial banks, such notes and debentures provide a cushion similar to equity in absorbing losses and asset shrinkage in the event of failure.

CAPITAL ADEQUACY

There is disagreement as to the optimal level of capital which should be maintained by commercial banks. As the casual observor might surmise, regulators would like to see greater levels of capital in relation to assets or deposits for many banks, while at the same time, managers of these same banks frequently believe that existing levels are high enough and perhaps too high. While some would argue that capital should be sufficient to provide for a zero level of bank failures and deposit losses, others suggest that inefficiencies traceable to excessively high capital positions and excessively conservative operating practices would be more harmful to the overall economy than would a limited number of bank failures. Indeed, the evidence suggests that the cause of most bank failures are related to management weaknesses, fraud, embezzlement, speculation, and other factors rather than to an inadequate capital structure.[9]

Differing Views of Capital Adequacy Whether or not a given level of capital is adequate for any particular bank depends upon the vantage point from which the question is viewed. Thus the question must be evaluated from the standpoint of three distinct groups. These include (1) bank regulators and examiners, (2) commercial bank

[9] For a detailed discussion of bank failures see George W. Hill, *Why 67 Insured Banks Failed—1960 to 1974,* Federal Deposit Insurance Corporation.

managers, and (3) large depositors.[10]

Bank Regulators and Examiners: Regulatory bodies such as the Federal Reserve System and the Federal Deposit Insurance System are understandably concerned with the question of capital adequacy. The major function of these regulators is to protect the solvency of the banking system. If the record of bank failures for any given period is zero, regulators may point to such a record as evidence of the fact that their principal responsibilities are being discharged in an optimum fashion. On the other hand, if the number of bank failures looms large, regulators become subject to the criticism that examination procedures are inadequate and that their responsibilities are not being discharged efficiently. Given this system of rewards and penalties, one might expect that regulators would demand capital levels sufficient to provide in-depth protection against bank failure caused by continued and extensive operating losses.

Commercial Bank Managers: While bank managers are concerned with the solvency of their banks and of the banking system in general, their point of view is tempered by the knowledge that increased levels of capital may detrimentally affect returns to holders of bank equity securities. Bank managers may be reluctant to sell additional equity securities if the market for such securities is perceived to be depressed and if earnings dilution may likely result. Management is also aware of the unfavorable reaction of stockholders which may be expected if dividends are restricted for the purpose of strengthening the capital position. Thus, the view of bank managers necessarily takes into account the effect on profitability which may be associated with any effort to strengthen bank capital. The authority of regulators to order increased capital levels for any given

bank is not absolute, and regulators must frequently rely on logic and persuasion in inducing compliance with recommendations concerning capital expansion. Included in a Field Manual published by the Division of Bank Supervision, FDIC (Revised February 23, 1973), for use by bank examiners, is the following passage:

> The Corporation's authority to enforce capital standards in operating banks is limited . . . it would be difficult to prosecute a sustaining case on unsafe or unsound practices where the only major complaint would be continued operation with an insufficient margin of capital protection. Practically, therefore, we have recourse to only two lines of approach:
> a) To induce the bank management, *by logic and persuasion,* to increase capital by sale of new local capital issues; and
> b) To encourage, by the same methods, the conservation of net profits by additions to capital and surplus.

Commercial bank managers, then, can be expected to interpret capital as being adequate if its level is sufficient to protect depositors in the event of normal losses, but not in the event of unexpected, continued, and extensive operating losses.

Large Depositors: Small depositors including most households and those business firms with deposit balances completely or substantially covered by FDIC insurance protection have little cause to worry about loss of deposit funds in the event of bank failure. Large depositors, on the other hand, must rely on the financial strength of banks in which they hold deposits in excess of FDIC insurance ceilings (currently $100,-000). Thus a corporation which purchases negotiable CDs, which represent substantial investments, has cause for concern over the issuing bank's continued solvency. Large investors, therefore, can be expected to consider the question of capital adequacy in deciding whether deposits should be maintained with any given bank. Indeed, the rates

---

[10] We are indebted to Harvey Rosenblum for his analysis of these views. See "Bank Capital Adequacy," *Business Conditions,* Federal Reserve Bank of Chicago, September 1976.

which different banks must pay to attract purchasers of large certificates of deposit are not identical with respect to CD size and maturity. Of course, other factors such as the quality of bank management, bank size, and the range of services made available to large customers are important components in the decision of large investors to place funds with any particular bank. But while conclusive evidence is not available, it is reasonable to believe that the preference of large depositors in terms of capital adequacy would lie somewhere between those of regulatory authorities and commercial bank managers.

Standards of Capital Adequacy Standards of capital adequacy can be classified in terms of two groups: qualitative and quantitative. In evaluating the adequacy of capital for any given bank, both groups of measures must be considered.[11]

1. Qualitative Measures

    a) Management

    b) Assets

    c) Earnings

    d) Deposit Trends

    e) Fiduciary Business

    f) Local Characteristics

2. Quantitative Measures

    a) Ratios of Capital to Total Assets

    b) Ratios of Capital to Risk Assets

Qualitative measures:

1. *Management*—The ability, attentiveness, integrity, and record of management is critical in the evaluation of a bank's ability to withstand risk. Prudent managerial practices and policies are vital in the protection of depository funds.

2. *Assets*—The general character, quality, liquidity, and diversity of assets influence the acceptability or non-acceptability of any given level of capital.

3. *Earnings*—The earnings capacity of a bank and the bank's dividend policy are important aspects in evaluating the adequacy of its capital. Earnings applied first to the elimination of losses and depreciation and to the establishment of suitable reserves prior to disbursement of dividends provide protection against capital impingement.

4. *Deposit trends*—If deposit trends are upward, and if retained earnings reflect the same upward movement, internal additions to capital may be sufficient to support asset expansion. On the other hand, if additions to capital have not kept pace with deposit expansion, and if growth is expected to continue, capital should be augmented through whatever means possible.

5. *Fiduciary business*—The volume and nature of business conducted in a fiduciary capacity must be considered in evaluating capital needs. Contingencies in this area must be carefully appraised.

6. *Local characteristics*—The stability, diversification, and competitive situation of local industries must be considered in the evaluation of capital adequacy.

Quantitative measures:

1. *Ratios of capital to total assets*—The ratio of total capital to total assets or alternatively, the ratio of equity capital to total assets, represents the percent by which the value of such assets could decline without causing losses to depositors. Both the ratio of total capital to total assets and the ratio of equity capital to total assets have declined rather consistently since the early '60s (Figure 9–2), reflecting the fact that for the banking system as a whole, growth in capital has not kept pace with asset expansion.

---

[11] Based on a discussion of capital standards contained in Section D, *Capital* (Revised Feb. 23, 1973), Division of Bank Supervision, Federal Deposit Insurance Agency, pp. 1–2.

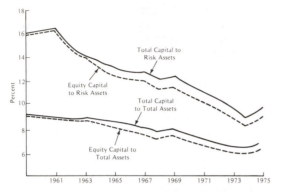

Figure 9–2: Selected Capital Ratios for all Commercial Banks, 1960–75. Equity capital is defined to include the reserve for losses on loans and securities. Total capital equals equity capital as defined above, plus subordinated notes and debentures. Total assets include consolidated foreign and domestic assets. Risk assets equal total assets less cash and due from banks, less U.S. Treasury and government agency securities. Ratios are based on aggregate data for all commercial banks. Source: Reproduced from Harvey Rosenblum, "Bank Capital Adequacy," *Business Conditions,* Federal Reserve Bank of Chicago, September 1976, p. 3.

2. *Ratios of capital to risk assets*—Ratios which are perhaps even more descriptive in terms of a bank's ability to withstand losses include the ratio of total capital to risk assets and the ratio of equity capital to risk assets. Figure 9–2 illustrates the fact that the decline in the value of total capital to risk assets as well as the value of equity capital to risk assets has been rather dramatic since about 1961. Decline in the value of this ratio illustrates the fact that commercial banks expanded loan portfolios largely at the expense of more liquid and less risky investments over the period.

The Optimal Level of Capital Presumably, the optimal level of capital for the banking system as a whole is one where capital is sufficient to maintain overall confidence in the banking system but not so high as to permit a zero level of bank failures. A zero level of bank failures would imply overly restrictive policies and high social costs. From the point of view of bank managers, the capitalization decision must be one which incorporates the goal of profit maximization consistent with the recognition of an acceptable level of risk. Indeed, the bank which seeks to take no risk and to maintain capital ratios sufficient to cover all possible contingencies is performing a disservice to its owners, to its customers, and to the community which it serves.

FUTURE EXPECTATIONS

Commercial banking has long been characterized by competition, but banking has been a regulated and protected industry also. Thus, some contend competition in banking has not been the keen, vigorous, intense type which is found in many less regulated industries. Banking, as a regulated industry, has been protected from complete price and service competition in the market place. By law, non-bank financial institutions were formerly prohibited from offering many bank services, such as checking accounts.

The Monetary Control Act of 1980, however, will likely result in considerably greater competition as many of its provisions become effective over the next several years. Today's bank manager should be alert to the competitive threats represented by the new money market mutual funds, by the recent expansion and aggressiveness of foreign banks, by expanded activities of investment banking firms, by the likelihood of interstate bank branching, by the continued expansion in new electronic technology, by the expanded powers now held by non-bank financial institutions, and by ever increasing price competition for sources of bank funds, particularly in view of the impending phase-out of Regulation Q. The 1980s hold much promise for well managed banks that anticipate and plan for these challenges. Banks that do not anticipate these competitive challenges and that do not develop appropriate strategic responses may well become casualties in this new competitive environment.

SUMMARY

The objective of commercial bank managers continues to be one in which the welfare of the bank and hence the bank's stockholders is maximized. But because of the nature of commercial banking, managers must respond to a number of constraints to which their non-bank counterparts are not subject. A major implication to be drawn in any analysis of bank asset and liability management is the fact that no aspect of such management can stand alone. Asset management policies depend upon the nature and structure of liabilities and capital. In turn, decisions affecting liabilities and capital depend not only upon asset distribution but upon their relationship to one another.

Discussion contained in this chapter illustrates the changing nature of commercial banking; and the need for continued advancement of sound management policies and practices. Successful managers of commercial banks may no longer merely gather funds from inexpensive sources and invest in assets which may be conveniently available. To the contrary, the changing nature of commercial banking implies the need for more and greater expertise in the traditional functions of planning, organizing and control.

QUESTIONS

1. In what way is asset management for commercial banks similar to that of industrial firms? In what way does it differ?

2. What are the three main categories of assets for commercial banks? To what extent have these categories shifted over the past two decades? How do you account for this shift?

3. What are sterile reserves? How did the Monetary Control Act of 1980 influence the quantity of sterile reserves required of member banks? Of non-member banks?

4. What are some differences in *investment* management policies for small banks vs. large banks? How do you account for these differences?

5. What are some differences in *loan* management policies for small banks vs. large banks? How do you account for these differences?

6. Comment on the use of fixed vs. variable interest rates for commercial and industrial loans by commercial banks. Why has the use of variable rates increased in recent years?

7. What were the major innovations in banks' liability management which occurred during the 1960's and 1970's? In general, why did liability management take on such increased importance?

8. Contrast the view of bankers, regulators, and large depositors with regard to the issue of capital adequacy for commercial banks.

SELECTED REFERENCES

Altman, Edward I., "Commercial Bank Lending: Process, Credit Scoring, and Costs of Errors in Lending," *Journal of Financial and Quantitative Analysis,* Vol. 15 (November, 1980), pp. 813–832.

Fielitz, Bruce D., and Thomas A. Loeffler, "A Linear Programming Model for Commercial Bank Liquidity Management," *Financial Management,* Vol. 8 (Autumn, 1979), pp. 41–50.

Gilbert, R. Alton, and Robert H. Rasche, "Federal Reserve Bank Membership: Effects on Bank Profit," *Journal of Money, Credit and Banking,* Vol. 12 (August, 1980), pp. 448–461.

Graddy, Duane B., and Kyle, Rueben, III, "The Simultaneity of Bank Decision-Making, Market Structure, and Bank Performance," *Journal of Finance*, Vol. 34 (March, 1979), pp. 1–18.

Lynge, Morgan J., Jr., and Kenton Zumwalt, "An Empirical Study of the Interest Rate Sensitivity of Commercial Bank Returns: A Multi-index Approach," *Journal of Financial and Quantitative Analysis*, Vol. 15 (September, 1980), pp. 731–742.

Mason, John M., *Financial Management of Commercial Banks*. Boston: Warren, Gorham and Lamont, 1979.

Mayne, Lucille S., "Bank Dividend Policy and Holding Company Affiliation," *Journal of Financial and Quantitative Analysis*, Vol. 15 (June, 1980), pp. 469–480.

Mukherjee, Tarun K., and Larry M. Austin, "An Empirical Investigation of Small Bank Stock Valuation and Dividend Policy," *Financial Management*, Vol. 9 (Spring, 1980), pp. 27–31.

Seaver, William L., and Donald R. Fraser, "Branch Banking and the Availability of Banking Services in Metropolitan Areas," *Journal of Financial and Quantitative Analysis*, Vol. 14 (March, 1979), pp. 153–160.

Spindt, Paul A., and Vefa Tarhan, "Liquidity Structure Adjustment and Behavior of Large Money Center Banks," *Journal of Money, Credit and Banking*, Vol. 12 (May, 1980), pp. 198–208.

Talmor, Eli, "A Normative Approach to Bank Capital Adequacy," *Journal of Financial and Quantitative Analysis*, Vol 15 (November, 1980), pp. 785–811.

Chapter 10

Thrift Institution Management

The thrift institutions—savings and loan companies, mutual savings banks, and credit unions—rank second only to commercial banks in total assets held by a financial institution category. With assets of over $800 billion in 1980, they provide an outlet for savings of individuals and an important source of real estate and consumer credit.

The cumulative balance sheets of these institutions in Table 10–1 provide a quick overview of their characteristics. All three types of thrift institutions have liability structures composed primarily of savings deposits. Both savings and loan companies and mutual savings banks hold the bulk of their assets in the form of mortgage loans. Their mortgage loan holdings are more than double those of commercial banks and account for approximately 60 percent of all mortgage debt not held by government agencies. In contrast, credit unions invest most of their funds in consumer loans, with mortgage loans making up only a small proportion of total assets.

As depository financial intermediaries, the thrift institutions have many character-

istics in common with commercial banks. In fact, as a consequence of the monetary control act of 1980, the similarity is increasing as their services have expanded to include transaction accounts and a wider variety of lending. However, they are more vulnerable to interest rate changes than are commercial banks. With an average asset maturity substantially longer than average deposit maturity, the thrift institutions, and particularly savings and loans, suffered from the effects of rising, unstable interest rates. Thus they have a unique set of management problems.

CHARACTERISTICS OF THRIFT INSTITUTIONS

SAVINGS AND LOAN COMPANIES

The growth in importance of savings and loan companies has been a phenomenon of the last three decades. In 1950, savings and loan assets were only one-tenth those of commercial banks. By 1980, their assets had

Table 10-1:

Total Assets and Liabilities of all Thrift Institutions, 1981
(in $ millions)

	Savings and Loans	Mutual Savings Banks	Credit Unions
Cash		$ 4,135	
U.S. Government Securities	$ 57,383	8,957	
Other Securities		41,695	
Mortgage Loans	504,078	99,900	$47,309
Other Loans	69,585	12,222	
Other Assets		5,091	
Total Assets	$631,046	$172,001	$70,754
Savings Deposits	$512,858	$153,225	$63,874
Other Liabilities	85,042	7,455	6,880
Capital	33,137	11,321	
Total Liabilities and Net Worth	$631,046	$172,001	$70,754

Source: *Federal Reserve Bulletin*

Note: Missing data are a result of differences in reporting requirements and certain data are preliminary.

grown over 30-fold to reach 45 percent of commercial bank assets. This growth can be at least partially attributed to the fact that their primary objectives—encouraging savings and providing loans for home purchase—were consistent with national housing goals and were encouraged by legislation, including favorable tax treatment.

Savings and loan companies are chartered by either the federal government (through the Federal Home Loan Bank Board) or the state in which the institution wishes to set up business. Over half of the more than 5,000 savings and loans are presently state chartered.

A savings and loan may have a mutual or a stock form of ownership, with the mutual form being more common. The depositors and borrowers of a mutual savings and loan elect a board of directors who oversee the company as any other corporate board of directors would do. With the stock form of ownership, stockholders own the company, select the directors, and face returns and risk like stockholders in other firms. Some existing savings and loans have switched from mutual to stock ownership in recent years, primarily to raise capital by selling more

stock. It has also been argued (with some statistical support) that the existence of a group of stockholders interested in profitability leads to greater efficiency.[1]

The primary regulatory body for savings and loans is the Federal Home Loan Bank Board. It examines all federally chartered savings and loans and all state chartered savings and loans that have joined the federally chartered institutions in having their depositors' funds insured by the Federal Savings and Loan Insurance Corporation (FSLIC). Over 98 percent of savings and loans assets are held by institutions insured by the FSLIC. Deposits are presently insured up to $100,-000.

A somewhat confused regulatory structure exists with this dual chartering system. Federal regulations may apply to only federally chartered savings and loans or to all federally insured savings and loans. State regulations may apply to all state chartered savings and loans or only those not insured

---

[1] David L. Smith, Donald M. Kaplan, and William F. Ford, "Profitability: Why Some Associations Perform Far Above Average," *Federal Home Loan Bank Board Journal* (November, 1977), pp. 7–13.

by the FSLIC. For example, variable rate mortgages began in California with state chartered savings and loans being allowed to grant variable rate mortgages. The Federal Home Loan Bank Board did not try to stop insured state chartered institutions from extending variable rate mortgages, but federally chartered institutions were not given authority to enter the market until six years later.

Sources of Funds The major historical source of funds to savings and loans has been passbook savings accounts. However, rising interest rates, increased competition, and the low interest ceilings on passbook accounts mandated by regulatory authorities led to a decrease in this source of funds. The rate that thrift institutions were allowed to pay on passbook deposits has been held at ¼ percent more than the ceiling for commercial bank passbook deposits. The ceiling was held nearly constant through the 1970s, reaching only 5½ percent by the end of the decade, while other interest rates rose rapidly. Savings and loans found it necessary to compete for funds by offering time deposits with specific maturities and six-month "money market certificates" on which they have been allowed to pay interest rates more closely related to those found in competitive markets.

Until the mid-1960s, approximately 90 percent of deposits were normal passbook accounts. This percentage declined to 60 percent in 1970 and 20 percent in 1980. The phasing out of all deposit interest rate regulations by 1986 and the authority to offer transaction accounts, under the authority of the Financial Institutions Deregulation and Monetary Control Act of 1980, will undoubtedly change the sources of funds again. We have already observed vigorous competition between banks and savings and loans for transactions accounts.

In addition to raising funds from depositors, savings and loans may borrow from their regional Federal Home Loan Banks.

The Federal Home Loan Bank System was formed in 1932 and organized into 12 regional banks. These banks, which are public corporations similar to the Federal Reserve Banks, grant savings and loan companies direct loans with maturities from a few months to ten years.

The Federal Home Loan Banks have three sources of funds to loan to member savings and loans. Capital is supplied by member savings and loans, which must purchase capital stock equal to 2 percent of their mortgage loan balances. In addition to capital stock, members are encouraged to make deposits of excess funds. Federal Home Loan Bank capital stock and deposits totalled about 3 percent of savings and loan assets in 1980. Supplementing these funds, the system sells consolidated debentures which are the joint obligations of the 12 banks.

Federal Home Loan Bank lending is supplemented by Federal Home Loan Mortgage Corporation purchases of mortgages from savings and loans and mutual savings banks. The Federal Home Loan Mortgage Corporation finances these purchases by selling public bond issues secured by packages of mortgages purchased from savings and loans. Federal Home Loan Bank debentures and mortgage backed bonds outstanding totalled $52 billion in 1980, or over 10 percent of total real estate loans by savings and loans. Thrift institutions also gained the right to borrow from the Federal Reserve System under provisions of the deregulation act.

Assets On the asset side, the primary savings and loans asset is the mortgage loan, which accounts for about four-fifths of total assets. Of the mortgage portfolio, 75 percent consists of loans for single family homes and 16 percent for multifamily buildings. The remaining 9 percent is for commercial property. These percentages have remained fairly steady over the years.

In addition to mortgage loans, savings and loans must maintain liquidity reserves to meet unexpected demands for withdrawal. Liquid assets are held in the form of short to intermediate term government obligations and certain obligations of other financial institutions.

Funds not needed to meet present loan or liquid asset demand are deposited with the district Federal Home Loan Bank or invested in debt instruments such as U.S. government or corporate debt securities.

Recent regulatory changes, including the Depository Institution Deregulation and Monetary Control Act of 1980, have given savings and loans the authority to greatly expand the scope of their business. The deregulation act allowed savings and loans to invest up to 20 percent of their assets in consumer loans and corporate debt instruments. In addition, savings and loans are presently authorized to offer charge card services, safe deposit services, and trust services. They now have the authority to pursue their frequently stated goal of becoming complete family financial centers.

MUTUAL SAVINGS BANKS

Mutual savings banks presently serve purposes similar to those of savings and loans, but have some differences resulting from their historical development. The savings and loans were formed by people who wanted to purchase homes. In some cases, the savers even drew lots to determine when each one would be allowed to borrow. The mutual savings banks, on the other hand, were started to serve small savers and encourage thrift.

Savings banks operate in only 17 states, with 90 percent of their deposits being in five Northeastern states: New York, Massachusetts, Connecticut, Pennsylvania, and New Jersey. All savings banks presently operate under state charter, though federal charter is available. Their total asset size—27 percent of that of savings and loans—indicates that they are an important factor in the few states in which they do have substantial operations. However, their growth has not

been dramatic, approximately paralleling that of commercial banks and falling well behind that of savings and loans.

In contrast with savings and loans and most other corporations, the savings bank board of directors is not elected by owners. It is a self-perpetuating organization with existing members of the board electing a new board member if a former member resigns. While this situation may seem unusual, new board members of other businesses are frequently selected by management or the existing board, with the vote of the shareholders being little more than a rubber stamp. In any case, the board of a savings bank is held accountable under the standards of fiduciary responsibility.

The liabilities of savings banks are similar to those of savings and loans. They offer passbook savings accounts as well as various time deposit accounts. They were the first institutions to offer NOW accounts.[2] Like the other thrift institutions, their deposits are insured to $100,000.

Savings banks show more significant differences in their asset mix. Mortgage loans comprise less than 60 percent of their assets compared to about 80 percent for savings and loans. They commit approximately 15 percent of their funds to corporate securities, both debt instruments and stock. The proportion of their funds invested in mortgages has gradually increased over recent years, making them more like savings and loans in asset structure. As the Deregulation Act goes into effect, differences between savings and loans and mutual savings banks will probably decrease further.

CREDIT UNIONS

Credit unions have been the fastest growing type of depository financial institution in recent decades, with assets in 1980 being 65 times their 1950 level. However, in total

---

[2] Negotiated Order of Withdrawal accounts. These essentially serve as checking accounts and are now included in the general heading "transaction accounts."

assets, credit unions are still only 5 percent of the size of commercial banks and 11 percent of the size of savings and loans.

The key requirement for a credit union is *commonality*. All members of the credit union must have some common bond, with the most frequent bond being place or means of employment. A physical location is frequently provided by the employer and much of the work is contributed by the employee members. It is also common practice for loans to be repaid through witholding from the borrower's pay, thereby minimizing collection problems. Credit unions have been exempt from taxes, with federal taxation of their income becoming effective in 1984. With minimal operating costs, no taxes, and limited collection problems, credit unions were able to offer competitive interest rates on deposits and still provide loans at rates below these available from other lenders. With these advantages, it is little wonder that their growth has been rapid.

While the type of credit union described above still exists, another type has also evolved, serving interest groups with many thousands of members, such as all people who are employed by educational institutions in a major city. In at least one case, residence in a particular state senatorial district has been used as the common bond. Credit unions of this type have offices resembling those of other depository institutions and rely on professional managers. Their cost structures are also more closely aligned with those of the other depository institutions. As their tax advantages disappear and their cost structures rise to meet those of other institutions, their growth rate may slow.

Credit unions may be chartered by the state or federal government, with slightly over half of the charters presently being federal. Charters, supervision, examination, and deposit insurance are provided by the National Credit Union Administration. Depositors are protected by deposit insurance provided by the National Credit Union As-

sociation for up to $100,000 per account. Credit unions can borrow from the Federal Intermediate Term Credit Bank.

As with other thrift institutions, credit unions take deposits from their members and make loans to them, investing liquid reserves and excess funds in other securities, primarily U.S. government obligations. Credit unions offer time and passbook savings accounts like the other thrift institutions. They also offer share draft accounts, which serve as checking accounts for members. The average credit union deposit in 1980 was about $1,600.

The credit unions differ sharply on the asset side. While they have authority to make mortgage loans, only about 3 percent of their assets are presently invested in mortgages, primarily because they generally lack the capital to make such loans. They concentrate on consumer loans, with automobile loans being the most common. A breakdown of their lending proportions appears in Table 10–2.

Table 10-2:

Credit Union Loan Portfolios

	Percent
Automobile loans	33.6
Other durable goods loans	11.4
Personal expense loans	32.1
Home improvement loans	11.5
Real estate loans	7.6
Business loans	3.8

Source: Above data based on a sample of Federal Credit Unions in 1978 and reported in the *1978 Annual Report of the National Credit Union Administration*, Table 5, p. 8

MANAGEMENT PRINCIPLES FOR THRIFT INSTITUTIONS

As with any other business, the financial management of a thrift institution involves a profitability/risk trade-off. Profitability is the primary motive for most business ventures and additional risk is frequently the cost of added profit. Like other businesses, the thrift institution faces various alternatives, each with different risk and return characteristics. The appropriate risk/return combination is both a management decision and a matter for regulatory control.

At first glance, there may be some question about the appropriateness of the profitability objective as there are seldom any stockholders to benefit from such profitability. However, as economists have long pointed out, competition forces all business in the direction of profitability maximization. In perfect competition, each business will operate in such a way as to minimize its cost per unit of output and market competition will force the price to a level just sufficient to meet these lowest possible production costs plus a profit sufficient to attract the necessary capital. In perfect competition, individual firms cannot affect selling price. They can affect profitability only by minimizing unit production cost. In such an environment, only firms that maximize profitability will earn enough to continue producing.

Recent experience of thrift institutions has underscored the effectiveness of market forces in requiring profitability maximization. When general interest rates rose rapidly and the interest rates that financial institutions were allowed to pay on passbook deposits were not increased correspondingly, the process of disintermediation began. Savers removed their funds from thrift institutions and invested them directly with purchases such as Treasury bills. When Treasury bills in denominations of less than $10,000 were eliminated to discourage disintermediation, money market mutual funds arose to serve the needs of small savers by offering each investor an interest in a large portfolio of money market instruments. Institutions then found themselves bidding in relatively free markets for funds held by the money market funds. Regulation was not very successful in protecting the thrift institutions from competitive forces.

Even the limited protection from competition provided by past legislation is being phased out with the 1980 Deregulation Act. In addition to broadening lending authority, the law phases out most limitations on interest rates paid and some limitations on interest rates charged by institutions, leaving the setting of these rates to market forces. As a result, the profitability objective will become increasingly dominant for financial institutions as they compete in freer markets for both loans and deposits.

Risk for the thrift institution arises from three sources. *Default risk* refers to the failure of borrowers to repay loans. Default losses on first mortgage loans must be held to very low levels because of the small margins traditionally existing between the cost of funds to thrift institutions and the interest rates on these loans. *Interest rate* risk arises from the fact that thrift institution loans are frequently for longer maturities than are their liabilities. Rising interest rates have forced thrift institutions to pay more for some deposits than is being earned on many of the older loans that are still on the institutions' books. With rising and fluctuating interest rates in recent years, interest rate risk has been greater than default risk. It permeates almost every aspect of thrift institution management. *Liquidity risk* also arises from the short-term nature of liabilities. While an industrial corporation may be a few days late with its payments and experience no substantial difficulties, a thrift institution would be seriously damaged if it were unable to meet withdrawal demands. The risk of being unable to meet withdrawal demand must be kept in mind when developing the asset structure.

Finally, the *service obligation* of a thrift institution creates another problem and set of trade-offs for management. Charters are not granted for the benefit of institution stockholders or managers. They are issued for the benefit of the community the institution is expected to serve. The supposed purpose of deposit interest rate regulations was not to insure a happy level of profitability, but to assure the safety of depositors' funds and to assure a steady supply of money to the housing industry. Laws such as the Community Reinvestment Act are aimed at assuring that thrift institutions meet their social responsibility as defined by legislators. Should a thrift institution pursue its own profitability within the constraints created by such laws? Or should it go beyond this and make its own judgments about the social objectives it should be striving for? These issues have been frequently debated but never settled. However, growing competition may decrease the ability of institutions to make decisions on other than profitability grounds.

In pursuing its objectives, the thrift institution must answer five primary asset and liability management questions:

1.   Which loans should be made?

2.   What quantity and specific type of liquid reserves should be held?

3.   What investment outlet(s) should be used for funds not committed to loans or liquid reserves?

4.   What mix of liabilities should be used?

5.   How much equity capital is needed?

While these various questions typically represent separate areas of management within the institution, the policy decisions are not made in isolation. For example, interest rate risk depends on the relative maturities of assets and liabilities. The investments chosen as outlets for idle funds should be considered in light of the asset/liability mix to decrease overall risk. These and other interrelationships must be considered in developing policy so that the sum of the management decisions in the various areas results in a harmonious whole. These interrelationships are stressed in the following discussion.

LOAN MANAGEMENT

As indicated earlier, thrift institution lending is dominated by mortgage loans. As shown in Table 10–3, thrift institutions also

Table 10-3:

The Mortgage Loan Market (in $ millions, 1980)

	Dollars	*Percent*
Commercial banks	264,602	18.3
Mutual savings banks	99,827	6.9
Savings and loan companies	502,718	34.7
Life insurance companies	130,878	9.0
Federal agencies* (General)	114,325	7.9
Federally guaranteed mortgage pools*	142,498	9.8
Individuals and others	194,785	13.4
Total	1,449,633	100.0

*Government National Mortgage Association, Federal National Mortgage Association, Farmers Home Administration, Federal Home Loan Mortgage Administration, FHA and VA direct loans.

Source: *Federal Reserve Bulletin*

dominate mortgage lending by financial institutions and are an important factor in mortgage lending overall. Consumer loans, the second important category, are discussed in detail in Chapter 13 and are discussed here only in terms of the contribution to the risk/returns characteristics of the overall loan portfolio.

Types of Mortgage Loans The most common mortgage loan made by a thrift institution is the *conventional mortgage*. Conventional mortgages involve no guarantee by a third party such as a public or private insurance agency. The institution relies on the credit worthiness of the borrower and the value of the property. A 20 percent down payment is normally required, but loans for up to 95 percent of the value of the property are permitted by regulators if the amount over 80 percent is insured by a separate agency or is covered by a special reserve account. Loans for over 80 percent of property value frequently carry higher interest rates.

A typical conventional loan has traditionally involved a fixed interest rate and equal monthly payments for a maturity of up to 40 years. However, there have been some recent changes aimed at dealing with current market conditions. The *graduated payment loan* is one such adaptation, designed to help house buyers deal with the higher house payments associated with inflation and higher interest rates. With the graduated payment loan, the payments are smaller during the early years. Typically, interest only is paid during the early years, up to five years. Payments necessary to amortize the mortgage then begin after this initial period.

The *variable rate mortgage* (VRM) is a type of conventional loan designed to protect the lender from problems caused by fluctuating interest rates. One type of variable rate mortgage is issued with a maturity similar to that of a conventional mortgage, but with the interest rate on the loan varying with the average cost of funds to savings and loans as published monthly in the *Federal Home Loan Bank Board Journal*. There is a limit as to how much the interest rate can be increased and institutions that choose to offer variable rate mortgages must also decrease interest rates on these mortgages if the cost of funds declines. Changes in interest rates may be handled by increasing the monthly payments or by changing the maturity of the loans.

The *adjustable mortgage loan* (AML) was introduced effective April 30, 1981, by the Federal Home Loan Bank Board. Unlike the variable rate mortgage discussed above, AML's have no limitation as to the amount of increase or decrease in the interest rate. The lender can adjust the interest rate as frequently as once each month and the rate can be tied to virtually any interest rate index which can readily be verified by the borrower. The main restriction on choice of index is that it cannot be one over which the lending institution can exert any direct control. As was the case with VRM's, the interest rate must be decreased if the index falls and the interest rate change can be accommodated by extending loan maturity, changing the payment, adjusting the principal loan balance through negative amortization, or some combination of these. Federal Home Loan Bank Board regulations called for the phaseout of VRM's by July, 1981, with replacement by AML's.

The *rollover loan* is another means of responding to interest rate risk. A rollover mortgage loan may be made for a period of only three to five years, with monthly payments set as if it were a 30-year mortgage. This leaves a large balance still owed at maturity. The loan is then renegotiated at prevailing interest rates.

Adjustable rate mortgage arrangements do not eliminate interest rate risk; they simply pass it on to the borrowers. Even a two-percentage point increase in the interest rate can result in a 20 percent increase in monthly payments. As long as short-term deposits are used as a source of funds for long-term loans, someone must bear the interest rate risk.

While indexing the mortgage rate has been widely heralded as the solution to the thrift institutions' interest rate risk problem, its future is still in doubt. In California, where state chartered institutions have been allowed to offer variable rate mortgages for some years, results have been mixed. A study of the California experience showed that variable rate mortgages peaked in 1976 with only 17 percent of California savings and loans offering variable rate mortgages and 46 percent of the mortgages granted by these institutions being variable rate. The use of variable rate mortgages in California declined from 1976 to 1978, when the study ended. One reason for the decline was that institutions were only willing to offer beginning interest rates approximately 0.25 percent lower for variable rate mortgages. Because this was not enough to encourage voluntary selection of a variable rate mortgage, variable rate mortgage borrowers tended to be lower income, lower down payment borrowers who had no alternative in a tight market. If variable rate mortgages are going to be issued to people other than poorer credit risks, and be issued when money is readily available, they will need to be offered at lower initial interest rates. They offer the institution little protection if they are only offered when interest rates are high.

In addition to conventional first-mortgage loans, the thrift institutions also make second-mortgage loans. Second-mortgage loans are based on a claim to the property which is subordinate to a first-mortgage loan against that same property. These loans are used for purposes such as remodeling, educational expenses, and investment. They are normally of shorter maturity than first-mortgage loans, thereby reducing interest rate risk.

Besides conventional mortgages, the thrift institutions also make *FHA and VA insured* mortgage loans. While the amount thrift institutions have invested in these loans has increased in recent years, they still represent only 14 percent of thrift institution mortgage credit. FHA and VA mortgages traditionally have had the advantage of being more readily marketable than conventional mortgages, thereby providing a source of flexibility and reserve liquidity.

FHA (Federal Housing Administration) loans are made by private lenders, but are insured by the U.S. government through the FHA. There are three types of FHA loans. Title I loans are for home repair and modernization, and are not backed by a mortgage. Title II loans are for home purchase backed by a mortgage. These loans are made for up to 97 percent of the appraised value of the property. Title III loans are for the building of rental housing for military personnel on or near military bases. An insurance fee is collected as part of the monthly mortgage payment and is forwarded to the FHA by the lender.

VA (Veterans Administration) loans are designed to aid military veterans in the return to civilian life. The guarantee is presently for up to $27,500 and the guarantee can be applied to a loan of up to $110,000. The lender would suffer a loss only if a default occurred and the property were sold

for more than $27,500 below the amount owed. As a practical matter, the VA normally acquires and resells defaulted properties, thereby protecting lenders from all losses. Thus the VA guarantee serves to replace the down payment as a source of security, allowing the veteran with minimal funds to buy a house. For the institution, it provides a low-risk asset.

While one might expect high default and delinquency rates in cases where down payments are small or nonexistent, experience with these loans has been relatively favorable. The delinquency rates for FHA and VA loans are not much higher than those for conventional loans, but once trouble does develop, it is more likely to lead to default when the borrower has little or no equity in the property. Defaults have occurred on less than 1 percent of these loans, with VA loans having lower default rates than FHA loans. These default rates are, however, several times higher than those for conventional mortgages with 20 percent down payments. Overall, it can be said that experience with these loans has been favorable enough to encourage thrift institutions and private insurers to move into small down payment lending without government support.

The highest rates allowed on FHA and VA loans have generally been set by the government at rates below those for conventional mortgages. In addition to lower rates, these loans usually involve more paper work and require longer to complete as they must be approved by the VA or FHA. In the past, FHA and VA standards designed to protect would-be buyers frequently disqualifed older homes, further reducing the attractiveness of those loans. Many of the government guaranteed or insured loans are held by financial institutions such as pension funds and insurance companies that do not have retail locations to use in attracting mortgage applications. They typically purchase their mortgages from mortgage banking firms. The mortgage banker grants a large number of mortgage loans and then sells them as a package to a financial institution. FHA and VA mortgages are popular because they are standardized and guaranteed, making it easier to package a salable group of mortgages. FHA and VA loans for houses in new developments are sometimes preferred because the lender can qualify a number of houses through FHA and VA at once rather than having to go through this process for each house separately.

In summary, the FHA and VA loans are most attractive to lenders, without numerous retail locations, making loans for large developments of new homes. They are not very attractive for the sale of existing housing, particularly older existing housing.

Credit Analysis   Mortgage loans differ from other consumer lending in their long-term nature and in the narrow margins between interest rates paid on deposits and interest rates charged. Credit analysis is based on the standard three C's of credit: character, capacity, and collateral. But the application of these factors is different primarily in that the focus must be long term and losses must be held to a very low rate.

Character analysis is little different than that for other loans. Past character is the best evidence concerning future character. The lender checks with the local credit bureau and other financial institutions with which the applicant has dealt to determine if other financial obligations have been treated seriously and honestly. It has been frequently argued that the mortgage payment is the last payment people will default on, while medical bills are about the first category to suffer. Whether these differences result from different senses of obligation or from the importance of protecting the home from foreclosure is not certain, but it is a factor to consider in character analysis. Therefore, special emphasis is placed on any past mortgage loan experience. Of course, it is illegal to consider matters such as sex, marital status, or race in any aspect of the loan analysis. Lenders may not extend their

character analysis to pass moral judgment on such things as living arrangements. The character analysis must focus on the handling of financial responsibilities.

Capacity deals with the ability to meet loan payments. Standard policy for an institution may be that mortgage loan payments cannot exceed 25 percent of income, for example, or that total loan payments cannot exceed 35 percent of income. These policies are based on past experience with regard to default rates. In addition to present income, the stability of income in the future must also be considered. A past record of employment instability or employment in a profession suffering from frequent periods of high unemployment would be a negative factor even if present income were satisfactory. The equal credit opportunity act requires that sex not be considered in evaluating the stability of income and that alimony be considered as income. Questions about childbearing plans are not allowed in evaluating income stability.

Collateral takes on special importance with mortgage loans because it is difficult to forecast an individual's income over the long time periods involved. The loan decision involves both the appraised value (discussed below) and the loan-to-value ratio. Collateral provides protection if an individual's income declines, but the depression of the 1930's showed that it is of little help if everyone's income declines sharply. Experience with VA and FHA loans in the last 30 years has convinced lenders that they can safely lend 90 percent and even 95 percent of the face value. These loan-to-value ratios have not been tested in a depression, but 50 percent loan-to-value ratios provided no protection for the financial system in the 1930s.

The Credit Decision   The loan decision is technically made by a loan committee made up of officers of the institution. However, efficiency and regulatory requirements make relatively standardized policy necessary. The loan committee does not have the time or expertise about individual cases to provide carefully considered judgments in each case. In addition, legislation such as the Community Reinvestment Act and the Equal Credit Opportunity Act require that credit policy be consistent and fair, not arbitrarily considering factors such as race, sex, or property location. In addition, institutions are required to give an answer if an individual inquires as to why his or her application was turned down. A general statement such as "our loan committee voted against it" is usually not adequate. If the institution has specific policy, it can make loan decisions efficiently and without illegal bias.

Institutions do not normally vary the interest rate by risk class, with the exception of variation by down payment size. This is a matter of tradition as well as a matter of regulation. Regulators discourage risk-taking by quickly downgrading delinquent loans and requiring extra capital to support them, thereby decreasing the ability to make further loans. In addition, it is illegal to quote different rates or terms based on race, sex, marital status, or property location. The institution can protect itself from inadvertently developing an illegal policy by quoting the same terms for all first-mortgage loans.

Market forces also discourage the offering of different rates for different risk classes. Because more than 90 percent of applicants are typically approved, higher rate, high-risk loans would have to come from this additional 10 percent. Many of these would not be acceptable credit risks at any additional rate they could possibly afford to pay. In addition, credit analysis is not so precise an art as to make risk classification precise, opening up problems of bias charges and general ill will. In competitive markets, these are costly problems.

Setting credit standards that are expected to result in low default rates has traditionally been a matter of judgment based on senior management's experience (and bias) as to what characteristics lead to default. Recently, this approach has been supplemented by statistical studies aimed at increasing the objectivity and accuracy of policy determination. The most widely used statistical approach is *discriminant analysis*. The analysis begins with loans that have been made in the past and classifies them as good or bad based on payment experience. For each of these loans, information is collected on a number of factors that are believed to be important in determining failure rates. Based on a statistical procedure beyond the scope of this discussion, but readily available on most computers, a *discriminant function* is developed. Rakes[3] developed the following discriminant function for a group of mortgage loans:

$$Z = 1.647 - .442I - .0398C + .218A - .136E + .066W$$

where:
- I = Loan-to-income ratio
- C = Number of unsatisfactory credit indications from previous creditors
- A = 0 if the wife is as old as or older than the husband
  1 if the husband is older than the wife
- E = 0 if a borrower is classified as having stable employment
  1 if a borrower is classified as having unstable employment
- W = Wife's age

If the Z score is above 0.5, the loan is expected to be good and if the score is below .5, the loan is likely to be bad. This particular model was developed from considerations of a large number of variables that did not turn out to be good predictors. The model should be taken as illustrative only since it was based on data from one city and is based

[3] Ganas K. Rakes, "A Numerical Credit Evaluation Model for Residential Mortgages," *Quarterly Review of Economics and Business,* Autumn, 1973, pp. 73–84.

only on applications from families. In addition, the two age variables might be considered unfair discrimination under present laws.

Statistical methods have the benefit of potential increases in accuracy and increased objectivity, thereby increasing the fairness and profitability of credit decisions. The fact that losses continue to occur is an indication of the limits of precision. Nobody can predict exactly who will lose their job, suffer ill health, etc. It is only possible to predict these things in terms of probabilities.

Appraisal Because collateral is important, and because houses are not standard units like stocks or bonds, an accurate estimate of property value is necessary. As loan-to-value ratios have risen, the accuracy of the appraisal has become increasingly important. The fact that most defaults occur early in the life of the mortgage increases the importance of accurate value estimation. The appraisal is normally performed by a professional appraiser who either works for the institution or works independently, performing appraisals for various institutions. There are various approaches to appraisal, depending on the situation.

Replacement cost is an approach that can be used with newer properties. If similar structures are being built, the replacement cost is both easily determined and relevant. The appraiser examines construction costs and land costs in the area, making adjustments for any particular features of the individual property. The replacement cost can also be adjusted for depreciation, if any. The approach is of little use in evaluating older homes, many of which are selling at fractions of their replacement costs.

Present value of benefits is an approach used primarily for income properties. Essentially, the appraiser estimates the useful life of the property, the rental income over that life, and the expenses that will be incurred. The value of the property then equals the present value of the benefits minus the present value of expenses.

Market value is the ultimate objective of all lender appraisals since the lender wants to estimate what the property could be sold for if the borrower were to default. With an older house, a direct market value appraisal is often the only method that can be used. The property is not expected to generate income and may be selling below its replacement cost because houses of its type are not being built any more. The appraiser begins by studying recent transactions in the area to determine the prices other properties have sold for. Adjustments are then made for differences between the particular property and others in the area. Price per square foot is an important part of this approach, with adjustments then being made for location and other features of the property. Needless to say, the skill and experience of the appraiser is very important in going from prices other properties have sold for to an estimate of the likely market value of the property under consideration.

Appraisers have frequently been accused of contributing to the decline of older neighborhoods by appraising property at less than a potential buyer is willing to pay, making it impossible to obtain a loan. Appraisers do consider the present condition of the neighborhood and apparent trends in property condition in preparing their estimates. Therefore, it is likely that a previously deteriorating neighborhood will find appraisals lagging behind redevelopment efforts. Critics of appraisal practices argue that property is worth what someone will pay for it, and therefore cannot be appraised at less than the currently agreed-to sale price. However, the lender is interested in the price the property could be sold for if the buyer should default.

Interest Charges Interest charges on mortgage loans are set in light of the institution's profitability objective. The limit on how much the institution can charge is set by competitive market forces. If the institution sets its interest charges on mortgage loans above those for competing institutions, it is

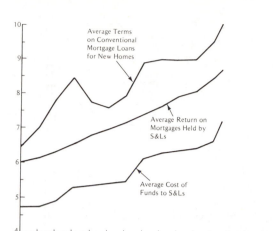

Figure 10–1: Average mortgage interest rates and S&L cost of funds. Source: *Federal Home Loan Bank Board Journal.*

likely to attract only those high-default risk borrowers who do not qualify for a loan at another institution. The lowest rate that could possibly be charged is determined by the cost of funds to the institution plus costs of processing, administering, and collecting loans. Again, competition causes these charges to be quite similar for institutions. The average cost of funds and interest rate charged by savings and loans in Figure 10–1 illustrate the relatively stable relationship between the cost of funds and the interest rate charged.

In addition to direct interest charges, points are a common requirement with mortgage loans, conventional or otherwise. Points are a form of initial service charge for granting a loan. Each point is 1 percent of the loan amount. Points raise the effective interest rate, especially if the loan is repaid early.[4] Thus they provide a means of assuring recovery of fixed costs when a loan is repaid soon after being granted. They also provide a means of raising the effective interest rate if there is some reason it cannot

be raised directly. The average mortgage loan presently carries points and service charges equal to 1.7 percent of its value. These charges, which raise the effective annual interest rate by approximately 0.3 percent, are included in the loan interest rates in Figure 10–1. Prepayment penalties of six months or more of interest may also be required if the loan is prepaid.[5]

Escrow payments provide both decreased risk and a bit of extra return. In addition to loan repayment, the borrower pays an amount each month equal to $\frac{1}{12}$ of the estimated annual tax and insurance expense for the property. Escrow payments decrease risk by assuring that borrowers are saving money to pay insurance and taxes. Since interest is not normally paid on these funds, they provide interest-free deposits.

Mortgage Loan Risk An analysis of mortgage loan risk requires that a distinction be drawn between diversifiable and nondiversifiable risk. Because a life insurance company can accurately predict the number of deaths among a group of insured each year, benefit payments are an expense rather than a risk. The same thing could be said for mortgage loans if the loss rate were steady from year to year. The risk of default for an individual loan would simply be an expense for the portfolio of loans. Unfortunately, the chargeoff rate may be three times as high during a recession as during periods of economic expansion. The loss rates during normal times are a diversifiable risk and can be treated as an expense, but the fact that default rates vary with economic conditions cannot be diversified away within the conventional loan portfolio.

Other risks may be related to specific lending areas. In the 1950s, some thrift institutions that were heavily committed to lending in the older parts of cities suffered

---

[4] See page 73 for a detailed discussion of this relationship.

[5] Federal Home Loan Bank Board regulations prohibit prepayment penalties for adjustable mortgage loans (AML's) made by member institutions.

large losses as those neighborhoods declined with migration to the suburbs. At other times, lenders have suffered losses because a factory or industry in their area suffered a decline. This happened in Cape Canaveral with the phasing down of the space program. This type of risk can be at least partially diversified away by investing some funds in nonmortgage loans and investing in mortgages over a broader lending area.

As indicated earlier, interest-rate risk is another type of risk that is of particular importance to thrift institutions. In the 1950s and early 1960s, thrift institutions received most of their funds in the form of short-term passbook deposits and loaned an increasing proportion of these deposits in the form of long-term mortgage loans. During this period, the yield curve generally had a "normal" shape, with short-term rates being below long-term rates. The institutions earned steady profits by taking deposits at the short-term rates and making loans at the higher long-term rates. Beginning in the mid-1960s, a period of rising and volatile interest rates developed and the nation experienced many periods in which short-term rates were higher than long-term rates. To keep deposits, the institutions found it necessary to pay interest rates which were, at times, more than double the interest rates on older loans. If the older loans were sold to meet withdrawal demand, they could only be sold at substantial discounts from their face values. As Figure 10–2 shows, the value of an outstanding mortgage loan can easily decline by 30 percent or more if the general level of interest rates rises.

This type of risk cannot be eliminated through diversification since a rising interest rate affects all outstanding fixed-interest rate loans in the same general manner. However, it can be dealt with through the new AML's or through maturity hedging: matching the maturity of assets and liabilities. Unfortunately, the thrift institutions have been less than completely successful in doing this.

While wishing to maximize profitability, the thrift institution also desires to minimize

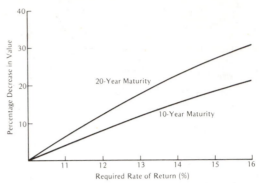

Figure 10–2: Percentage decrease in the value of a 10% mortgage loan with various required rates of return.

risk. This can be partially achieved by eliminating diversifiable risk through diversification. However, interest-rate risk and nondiversifiable default risk remain problems that are dealt with at least partially through a profitability/risk trade-off.

Mortgage Loan Documents Once it has been decided that the risk and costs associated with a mortgage loan are low enough to make the loan profitable at the interest rate that can be charged, the necessary documents must be prepared.

The lender is first concerned with the title to the property, wishing to be sure that the borrower has a clear title. This is normally provided by a title company which searches the records at the county recorder's office for liens or other claims and provides a certificate of insurance against any undiscovered claims. Of couse, the new mortgage must also be filed in the recorder's office if the lender's claim is to be protected.

The borrower's debt is represented by a simple promissory note indicating the amount owed, interest, and repayment schedule. The note also makes reference to the mortgage. The mortgage is essentially a transfer of title to the lender with the provision that the transfer is voided if the borrower repays the loan and interest as called for in the note. Court decisions have interpreted the mortgage as only giving the lender the right to satisfy his claim through sale of the property. Any excess over the debt and reasonable expenses must be returned to the borrower.

Consumer Loans   Except for credit unions, thrift institutions have had little experience with consumer loans. However, the Deregulation Act has now given savings and loans authority to invest up to 20 percent of their assets in consumer loans, commercial paper, and corporate debt instruments. The authority to make consumer loans makes the profitability/risk aspects of these loans of interest.

There is probably a general misperception that consumer loans are much more profitable than mortgage loans because their face interest rates have traditionally been higher. However, analysis of the profitability of consumer finance companies does not bear this out. The higher interest rates charged are offset by higher loan origination and servicing costs plus higher default rates. Profits end up being similar to those of other financial institutions.

However, consumer loans have an attraction other than high profitability. If they provide profits as high as those of mortgage loans, they can be useful as a source of risk reduction. First, they may provide some limited diversification with regard to default risk. Though mortgage and consumer loans both suffer default rates during economic downturns, consumer loans provide some diversification from risk associated with the value of real property in a specific lending area. This diversification is, however, likely to be limited by the fact that many consumer loans are made to existing mortgage customers. Consumer loans may also provide some diversification in times when demand for real estate loans is limited. However, consumer loan and mortgage loan demand tend to be correlated, again limiting the diversification advantage.

The major contribution of consumer loans to risk reduction is not from diversification, but from maturity hedging. The average maturities of consumer loans are a fraction of those of mortgage loans. These shorter maturities can reduce the average maturity of the loan portfolio, matching it more closely to the maturity of the institution's liabilities. Consumer loans may prove to be an important source of interest rate risk reduction.

INVESTMENT PORTFOLIO MANAGEMENT

A depository institution faces the expenses associated with having an office facility readily accessible to the public. One way of recovering these expenses is by making direct loans at rates above what could be earned by investing in securities. A depository institution simply could not earn enough to survive by taking deposits and investing only in securities. However, depository institutions do place part of their funds in securities for a number of reasons. First, institutions hold securities as a source of liquidity because they can be sold quickly if cash is needed to meet withdrawal demand. Institutions may also hold securities as a means of decreasing interest rate risk or default risk. Finally, institutions invest in securities when they do not have sufficient loan demand for all their funds. The excess is invested in securities until needed.

Recent changes in authorization to hold securities other than U.S. government securities have increased the usefulness of the investment portfolio as a source of diversification. Unfortunately, the fact that all credit losses vary with the business cycle tends to limit diversification to specific risks associated with real estate values in limited geographic areas. Like consumer loans, securities make their greatest contribution to risk reduction by reducing the average maturity of the institution's assets, thereby decreasing interest rate risk. Since interest rates on short-term assets are lower than those for longer maturities during most time periods, the shorter maturities and associated decreases in interest risk come at the expense of lower returns. The thrift institution that does not recognize this when short-term rates are low will find these securities of no help in dealing with interest rate risk.

LIQUIDITY RESERVES

The liquidity needs of thrift institutions have traditionally been less than those of commercial banks because their deposit levels have been more stable. However, that situation will bear close watching in the years ahead. Transaction account services, into which thrift institutions are expanding, normally represent unstable account balances. In addition, depositors are showing increasing willingness to move their funds in response to a small change in interest rates.

The thrift institutions have constant inflows from loan repayments and interest payments. Likewise they have constant, predictable outflows in the form of expenses and interest on deposits. They also have less predictable cash flows in the form of loan demand and not deposit flows (deposits less withdrawals). Since the institution can reject all loan applications if it lacks funds, these may not seem like a source of unexpected liquidity demand. However, institutions prefer to meet loan demand in their area when possible. Failure to meet loan demand will detract from their present ability to attract deposits and their future ability to attract loan applications. A net outflow of deposits represents a higher priority liquidity demand. Failure to respond instantly to any withdrawal demand would seriously jeopardize the institution's ability to attract funds.

Liquidity needs can be set by ratio standards, such as a certain percent of total deposits or certain percentages of each type of deposit. However, this type of approach does not really capture the cash flows experienced by an institution. A cumulative cash flow chart, as illustrated in Figure 8–2 on page 120 is a more useful approach. Past

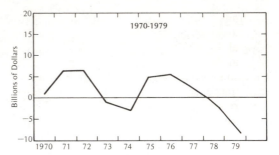

Figure 10–3: Net deposit flows, excluding interest, in mutual savings banks, 1970–1979. Source: *1980 National Fact Book of Mutual Savings Banks.*

experience as illustrated in the chart can be modified by adjusting for changes in the asset and liability structure. For example, daily cash inflow will be greater if the institution has changed its loan mix to reduce the average maturity.

Likewise, outflow can be reduced through a change in the mix of deposits, with increases in long-term deposits leading to decreased outflows and increases in transaction accounts to increased potential outflows. Increased liquidity reserves invested at low interest rates are one of the costs of short-term deposits. Net deposit flows of mutual savings banks appear in Figure 10–3 and give an illustration of the cash flow effects of various economic conditions. With their asset and liability mix undergoing rapid change, the thrift institutions will need to re-examine their cash flow assumptions carefully in the years ahead.

When the thrift institution faces a demand for liquidity, it can sell securities. The first act would normally be to sell short-term securities as these can be sold at or near their face value. Longer-term securities can also be sold, but they will be sold at a loss if interest rates have risen since they were purchased. The institution can also bid for extra funds by raising the interest rates on deposits. It can presently bid for deposits over $100,000 in a free market and will be able to bid as well for smaller deposits as the Deregulation Act goes into effect. The institutions can also borrow money from their respective federal credit sources—e.g., the Federal Home Loan Bank—and from the Federal Reserve System. The institutions can also sell loans. FHA and VA loans have been traditionally the most salable because they are guaranteed and standardized. However, the Federal Home Loan Mortgage Corporation is increasingly moving into the purchase of conventional loans.

Regulatory liquidity requirements are probably of more importance for monetary policy and system liquidity than for the liquidity of the individual institution. They are based on relatively simplistic ratio approaches. As discussed in Chapter 2, we are presently in transition from reserves for each institution being set by its regulatory agency to reserves for all depository institutions being set by the Federal Reserve System.

LIABILITY MANAGEMENT

In the last two decades, liability management at thrift institutions has undergone two revolutions and is in the midst of the third. In the 1950s and early 1960s, interest rates remained relatively steady and rate ceilings on deposits were not significantly below market rates, if at all. Thrift institutions profited from the yield curve by paying the market rate for passbook savings accounts and loaning these funds to purchasers of residential real estate at the higher long-term rates.

Beginning in the mid 1960s, the environment changed in five important ways:

1. Interest rates began an upward trend.

2. Because interest rate ceilings were not increased correspondingly, the rate paid on deposits became fixed by regulation rather than determined by market forces.

3. Free market interest rates fluctuated substantially from year to year.

4. In the absence of ability to compete for funds, the thrift institutions experienced erratic deposit flows.

5. There were many periods in which short-term interest rates rose above long-term rates.

These changes caused frequent periods of sharp savings outflows and sometimes pushed the cost of funds above the interest rates on loans still outstanding. It was a major change in the liability management environment from a stable, free market to an administered, erratic market.

Following the change in market stability, a revolution in liability maturity developed. The thrift institutions and commercial banks asked for, and received, authorization to offer large denomination and long-term certificates of deposit at higher interest rates to allow them to compete for funds. While rate ceilings for these accounts existed, these ceilings reached levels almost triple those for passbook accounts. Certificates of deposit for more than $100,000 carry no interest rate ceilings at all. The differences in interest rate ceilings resulted in major changes in the liability structure of thrift institutions. For example, passbook accounts, which accounted for 90 percent of savings and loan deposits until the mid 1960s, accounted for less than 20 percent in 1980. Savers have moved their funds to the longer term deposits or to money market funds which can pool funds and purchase the $100,000 certificates of deposit without interest rate restrictions.

With the phasing in of the Deregulation Act, a third revolution in liability management is unfolding. With the removal of most interest rate restrictions, thrift institutions will be free to bid for funds over the full yield curve. They will be able to bid for quantities of funds needed at the maturities desired. This will present major new challenges and opportunities in the area of liability management.

The new law will give thrift institutions the opportunity to integrate asset and liability management to a greater extent. With a complete yield curve available, the thrift institution can bid for funds of any maturity and price loans of each maturity in relation to the cost of funds of that maturity. The thrift institution can truly act as a financial intermediary, offering the borrower the full range of maturities and rates available in the financial markets. For example, the choice between fixed and variable rate mortgages can be determined by offering fixed rate mortgages at the cost of long-term money and variable rate mortgages at the rate presently charged for short-term funds. The borrower can decide whether to pay the long-term rate or pay the short-term rate and take the risk of rates rising later. The thrift institution can experience the same risk and return from either loan.

In addition to bidding for funds of different maturities to match the maturities of assets, the thrift institution can use the recently developed financial futures market to decrease interest rate risk. A futures contract is simply a contract between two parties for the sale of a commodity at a fixed price at a specific future date. Financial futures are simply contracts for future sale of certain financial instruments. A marketplace for trading financial futures is provided by the Chicago Board of Trade. The most active trading is in U.S. government obligations, but GNMA (General National Mortgage Association) certificates are probably more appropriate for thrift institutions. GNMA certificates are marketable shares in pools of FHA and VA guaranteed mortgages. Futures contracts are for minimum denominations of $100,000. Traded contracts are for standard delivery dates of March, June, September, and December. An increase in interest rates would cause a decrease in the value of a lender's loan portfolio. But an increase in interest rates would result in a profit from a forward contract to sell, thereby offsetting losses in loan portfolio value. A major limitation of this market is that the short-term nature of the contracts allows protection for a period of less than one year.

A thrift institution that has deposits with average maturities less than its loans and in-

vestments can use the GNMA futures market to decrease interest rate risk. The institution enters into a futures contract to sell GNMA certificates. If the future price is less than the current value, the difference is the cost of decreasing interest rate risk. For a price, the institution assures itself a fixed price at which it can sell a certain package of mortgages at a specific future date.

The institution need not actually own GNMA certificates to take advantage of this method of reducing interest rate risk. It can effectively cancel the contract with an offsetting contract to purchase the same quantity on the same date. The profit or loss on the futures contract will serve to offset gains or losses in the value of the institution's loan portfolio arising from changes in the general level of interest rates.

GNMA futures have not been widely used by thrift institutions up to this point. They have been more frequently used by mortgage bankers who wanted to avoid interest rate risk during very short time periods. One reason for their lack of use is a bad reputation they developed when some institutions used them as a means of speculating on interest rate movements rather than as a means of risk reduction. Several institutions suffered large losses and one institutional trader committed suicide after major losses. However, used properly, financial futures are a proper and effective method of reducing interest rate risk. With the removal of interest rate restrictions, financial futures will probably be used as an alternative to hedging by bidding for higher cost, long maturity deposits.

CAPITAL

Determing the amount of capital needed and the method of acquiring it is an especially difficult problem for most thrift institutions. Non-financial corporations that raise both debt and equity capital in relatively unrestricted markets can observe the market's response to changes in their proportions of debt and equity. Most thrift institutions have no stock, so there is no equity market to observe. Since deposits are insured, it is difficult to observe the debt market's reaction to risk. Thrift institution managers rely on their own judgment and on regulatory requirements.

As in any other business, capital serves to protect creditors in the event of shrinkage in asset value. Shrinkage can derive from loan defaults, interest rate risk fraud and mismanagement, or declining volume of business in the institution's market area. Since most deposits are insured, the primary losers from any such shrinkage would be the deposit insuring agencies.

The question of the appropriate amount of capital is not different in concept than that of the appropriate quantity of liquidity reserves. Just as the liquid assets serve in periods in which cash outflow exceeds cash inflow, capital serves in periods in which expenses (and asset value shrinkage) exceed income. The two key factors that are watched in this regard are loan losses over the business cycle and interest rate risk exposure.

On average, thrift institutions' profits are approximately 0.5 percent of assets. A relatively small change in loan defaults such as that which routinely occurs at the bottom of the business cycle can quickly turn profit to loss. By estimating the worst loss rate that might occur during a business downturn, the necessary cushion for loan default can be estimated. Loan default rates rarely exceed 1 percent for thrift institutions, with losses being a small fraction of defaulted amounts. Thus a relatively small equity capital base would protect against defaults.

Interest rate risk holds the potential for larger losses. This, coupled with the fact that interest rate risk and default risk are not positively correlated causes interest rate risk to be the dominant factor. As shown in Figure 10–2, the percent shrinkage in asset value with a rise in the general level of interest rates can be substantial. Suppose a thrift institution has 80 percent of its assets in loans and the rest in short-term invest-

ments. All but 20 percent of the loans for this institution are offset by equity or liabilities of a maturity similar to that of the loan. The remaining 20 percent of loans—16 percent of assets—has an average maturity of 20 years. As Figure 10–2 shows, a 5 percent rise in interest rates would cause a 26.7 percent decline in the value of these loans. This would be a 4.3 percent ($.16 \times .267$) decline in total asset value. Obviously, the percent of assets not covered by maturity hedging and their average maturities has a major impact on the equity capital needed.

While the institution may develop its own estimates of its capital needs based on measurements of its own potential asset shrinkage, the regulatory authorities make their determinations based on ratio analysis.

Once the amount of equity capital needed has been determined, the method of raising it must be decided. This is particularly troublesome since most thrift institutions cannot sell equity capital. Presently, the primary source of capital is retention of profits. However, rapid growth in recent years has eroded the ability of thrift institutions to create adequate capital through this source. If an institution earns 0.5 percent on assets and wishes to maintain equity equal to 5 percent of assets, it can grow at only 10 percent per year. If no other source is available, the institution would then need to limit growth to this rate. For savings and loans, another approach is to convert to stock form and sell additional equity. It is not coincidental that conversions have been most frequent in areas experiencing rapid growth. A final approach would be the issuance of capital notes. However, thrift institutions are not authorized to offer such notes at present.

DETERMINANTS OF PROFITABILITY

A recent study has shed some light on the specific characteristics of savings and loans that are associated with high profitability.

Table 10-4:

Key Ratios for Highly Profitable and Other Savings and Loans
(All figures in percent)

Item	All Associations	High Performance Associations
Mortgage loan yield:		
Excluding fees	7.74	8.22
Including fees	8.15	8.80
Securities yield:		
Excluding gain or loss	6.68	6.80
Including gain or loss	7.04	7.46
Total yield on investments	8.04	8.71
Total cost of money	6.36	6.38
Cost of savings	6.32	6.32
Cost of borrowings	7.01	7.12
Yield cost spread	1.68	2.33
Operating expenses/ operating income	16.14	14.14

Source: *Federal Home Loan Bank Board Journal*, November, 1977

The most profitable institutions tended to be of the stock form and located in areas of rapid growth. Their cost of funds was almost identical with that of lower profitability institutions. However, their personnel costs were lower and their revenues were higher. The higher revenue came from a higher loan to deposit ratio and a higher percentage of conventional loans relative to FHA and VA loans. Table 10–4 shows key operating ratios for 347 highly profitable savings and loans versus all savings and loans.

Curiously, size is not a clear determinant of profitability. The profitability of federally chartered savings and loans decreased with increased size while the profitability of state chartered stock savings and loans increased with size.[6]

---

[6] David L. Smith, Donald M. Kaplan, and William F. Ford, "Profitability: Why Some Associations Perform far Above Average," *Federal Home Loan Bank Board Journal*, November, 1977, pp. 7–13.

SUMMARY

The thrift institutions have historically specialized in taking passbook deposits and making loans; real estate loans for savings banks and savings and loans; and consumer loans for credit unions. However, the deposit mix has increased to include transaction accounts and time deposits. Recent legislation expanding the lending authority of savings and loans gives most thrift institutions the authority to serve all of the typical family's deposit and lending needs. These traditional limited scope depository institutions are undergoing transition to complete family financial centers.

Like all financial institutions, the thrift institutions are regulated. The regulatory agencies for the various thrift institutions are as follows:

Savings and loans: Federal Home Loan Bank Board

Credit unions: National Credit Union Administration

Savings banks: Various state authorities

However, the Federal Reserve System is taking over the setting of reserve requirements. Regulation has concentrated on assuring safety of depositors' funds by requiring certain liquid asset and equity capital ratios. In addition, safety has been pursued through regulation of the interest rates depository institutions could pay. However, these regulations will be phased out by 1986 and the thrifts will then compete for deposits in a relatively free market.

Like all businesses, the thrift institutions seek to maximize profitability. This can be achieved by minimizing the cost of funds, maximizing return on assets, and maximizing operating efficiency. Unfortunately, increased asset return frequently results in increased default risk. Increasing the spread between asset return and funds cost frequently requires the acceptance of interest rate risk and liquidity risk. These risk-return trade-offs are a major factor in thrift institution management.

Asset return is usually maximized by maximizing the percent of assets committed to conventional first mortgage loans. These loans are the primary lending outlet for funds, with total mortgage loans exceeding 100 percent of deposits for the most profitable institutions.

Default risk is dealt with primarily through careful loan analysis, though some diversification is possible through such things as broadening the lending area. Interest rate risk and liquidity risk are dealt with primarily through matching of asset and liability maturities. Complete matching is seldom possible, with the difference primarily being a cost of doing business, though it can be reduced through contracts in the financial futures markets.

QUESTIONS

1.   Find the most recent asset and liability structures for thrift institutions in the *Federal Reserve Bulletin*. Have the proportions changed since the 1981 data reported in Table 10–1? If so, what do you think has caused these changes?

2.   What are the major differences in financial structure between savings and loans and savings banks? What has caused these differences?

3.   Visit a thrift institution in your area and ask for a copy of its balance sheet. Compare its asset and liability proportions to those shown in Table 10–1. How do you account for the differences? Go back to the institution and inquire if necessary.

4.   If you were a depositor at a savings bank and were unhappy with some management decision, what could you do? What would be your most likely reaction if you were unhappy with the management of a savings and loan at which you had an account?

5.   We noted that the cost of funds differed very little between different savings and loans. Is this evidence that competition is working to effectively control rates paid on deposits, or evidence of an absence of competition?

6.   Why did the government want to regulate the interest rates paid on deposits, and why has the effort to regulate these rates been abandoned?

7.   Describe the type of risk faced by a thrift institution.

8.   Do you feel that a thrift institution has a service obligation beyond things specifically required by law? Why? If your answer is yes, what obligations do the thrift institutions have?

9.   It was once believed that a down payment of up to 50 percent was needed for a mortgage loan. Now thrift institutions are willing to make mortgage loans for up to 95 percent of appraised value. How do you account for this change in attitude?

10.   Explain the difference between a variable rate loan and a rollover loan.

11.   Describe the three methods of appraisal. Which method is most important for existing single-family housing?

12.   What courses of action are available to a thrift institution wishing to reduce interest rate risk?

PROBLEMS

1.   A 9 percent, 30-year loan with annual payments carries a service charge of 3 points. If the loan is repaid after the second annual payment, what is the effective interest rate?

2.   A 7 percent, 30-year loan for $50,000

was made ten years ago. The loan called for equal monthly payments. How much is still owed today? If the current interest rate level for this type of loan is 12 percent, what could this loan be sold for? What is the percentage decrease from face value?

SELECTED REFERENCES

Biederman, Kenneth R. "Savings and Loan Taxation: Historical Perspectives and New Directions," *Federal Home Loan Bank Board Journal*, Vol. 11 (January, 1978), pp. 2–7.

Cox, John C., Johnathan E. Ingersoll, and Stephen A. Ross, "An Analysis of Variable Rate Loan Contracts," *Journal of Finance*, Vol. 35 (May, 1980), pp. 389–403.

Epley, Donald R., and James A. Millar, *Basic Real Estate Finance and Investments*. New York: John Wiley and Sons, 1980.

Hadaway, Beverly L., and Samuel C. Hadaway, "Converting to a Stock Company: A Review of Recent Experiences," *Federal Home Loan Bank Board Journal*, Vol. 13 (October, 1980), pp. 20–22.

Halloran, John A., "A Note on the Impact of FHLB Advances on the Cost and Availability of Funds to S & Ls," *Journal of Finance*, Vol. 34 (December, 1979), pp. 1255–1261.

Kent, Richard J., "A Disaggregated Model of the Residential Mortgage Market," *Southern Economic Journal*, Vol. 47 (January, 1981), pp. 714–727.

_____. "Credit Rationing and the Home Mortgage Market," *Journal of Money, Credit and Banking*, Vol. 12 (August, 1980), pp. 488–501.

Melton, William C., "Graduated Payment Mortgages," *Federal Reserve Bank of New York Quarterly Review*, Vol. 5 (Spring, 1980), pp. 21–28.

Rochester, David, "Savings and Loan Reserves: An Analysis of Capital Adequacy," *Federal Home Loan Bank Board Journal*, Vol. 12 (December, 1979), pp. 7–13.

Rosen, Kenneth T., and David E. Bloom, "A Microeconomic Model of Federal Home Loan Mortgage Corporate Activity," *Journal of Finance*, Vol. 35 (September, 1980), pp. 959–972.

Welch, Jonathan B., "Explaining Disintermediation at Mutual Savings Banks," *Financial Analysts Journal*, Vol. 36 (May/June, 1980), pp. 71–76.

Wilson, J. Holton, "A Note on Scale Economies in the Savings and Loan Industry," *Business Economics*, Vol. 16 (January, 1981), pp. 45–49.

Woerheide, Walt., "S & L Operating Expenses—A Historical Record," *Federal Home Loan Bank Board Journal*, Vol. 13 (June, 1980), pp. 24–29.

_____. "The Reduction of Interest Rate Susceptibility at S & Ls: How It Can Be and Has Been Done," *Federal Home Loan Bank Board Journal*, Vol. 13 (September, 1980), pp. 16–19.

Chapter 11

Insurance Company Management

The primary business of insurance companies is the elimination of certain financial risks for individuals. Most events insured against occur to a stable, predictable percentage of a certain population group on a regular basis. The events may represent risk for individuals, but they are a predictable expense for the population as a whole. The insurance company serves by converting the individual's risk to an individual expense. The premiums it charges those who choose to be insured are sufficient to pay benefits to that proportion of the insured group that suffers the loss insured against.

In addition to the insurance function, many insurance companies also serve a financial intermediary function. A whole life insurance policy is an important example of this function. Since the whole life policy normally remains in force until eventual death and pays a benefit at death, the eventual payment for each insured person is a certainty. The only real insurance provided is against the financial loss associated with premature death. Thus the policy serves as both an insurance against premature death and a savings program. In this provision of a savings program, the insurance company acts as a financial intermediary, accepting and reinvesting savings.

Because of these dual roles, there are two distinct management areas in an insurance company. The insurance function is typically the most visible and employs the greatest number of persons. It involves the retail sale of insurance as well as the determination of the probabilities of certain events, payment of claims, and the recording of the millions of transactions involved. The other aspect of management deals with equally large sums of money, but is less visible and requires fewer employees. This is the management of the nearly $600 billion in assets, which place insurance companies only slightly behind savings and loans in total asset size. The insurance and asset management functions are treated separately in this chapter.

SCOPE OF THE INSURANCE BUSINESS

INSURANCE CONCEPTS

Diversifiability is the essential concept underlying most insurance activity. Death may result in financial hardship to a family.

Since no one knows if he or she will die in the next year, the family faces financial risk. This risk can, however, be eliminated through a type of group diversification. For example, one could get together with a group of other people of the same age and agree that each will contribute to a pool with the funds being divided among the dependents of those who do die during the year. Under normal conditions, the percentage of a particular age group that dies during a year remains quite stable (unless, for example, the cooperating group were all serving on the same battleship in wartime). Therefore, one could predict the amount his or her dependents would receive in the event of death and the individual risk would be converted to an expense.

In earlier times, associations such as burial societies did collect funds from their members and redistribute the funds like an insurance company. However, this service is now provided primarily by insurance companies. They estimate the percent of the population that will suffer some particular financial loss. They then sell policies to individuals, with a price set to provide benefits to those who suffer the loss, cover operating expenses, and provide a reasonable profit.

While diversification is the key to most insurance, we should note that there are insurance policies written in cases where the risk is not really diversifiable. Lloyds of London, for example, frequently provides insurance in cases in which there may not be enough people facing the risk to provide diversification. Wealthy individuals simply place large amounts of capital at risk, betting on such things as the possibility of rain in Sikeston on the day of the Bootheel rodeo. However, this is a relatively small part of the total insurance picture. Even Lloyds does most of its business in the more mundane field of marine insurance. Earthquakes and floods represent more important areas in which diversification is difficult to achieve. Frequently the participation of government has been necessary in order to provide insurance in such cases.

Like all companies, the insurance companies wish to maximize return and minimize risk. Income comes from premiums and from return on the investment portfolio. The insurance company's risk is not that of an individual claim; this is a programmed expense. The primary risks arise from possible loss in investment portfolio value and the possibility that the company's estimates of total claim payments for the population insured are too low. If their estimates of the dollar claims paid out are wrong, the insurance companies can suffer large losses. For example, a particularly severe winter combined with a rapid inflation of health costs can cause a health insurance company to experience more claims than predicted and a higher dollar cost per claim. Since rising interest rates have caused the value of some outstanding stock and bond issues to decline in value 50 percent or more, the risk of portfolio value loss is also great.

TYPES OF INSURANCE COMPANIES

Insurance companies can be classified according to the type of insurance provided. Some insurance companies specialize while others are willing to insure life, health, home, automobile, and business. Multiple offerings are frequently handled through wholly-owned subsidiaries. For example, Prudential Insurance Company sells life insurance and its subsidiary, Prudential Property and Casualty Company, sells property and liability insurance.

Insurance companies can also be classified according to how they market their services. Some companies serve only a special group and promote their services only to members of that group. Teachers' Insurance and Annuity Association is one such example of this. Other companies have groups of agents that sell only insurance offered by them. Still other companies market their insurance through general agencies that sell their insurance plus that offered by other companies. This latter approach is particularly common for companies that do not offer a full range of insurance. A growing amount of insurance is sold through group sales, particularly to groups of employees. Some group sales are handled by agents and some are handled by employees of the insurance company involved. Group sales lower the sales cost per insurance dollar and create the opportunity to price insurance according to the characteristics of a particular group rather than the general population.

Insurance companies can also be classified according to type of ownership. A *stock insurance company* is formed like most other corporations. Common stock is sold to investors who risk the loss of all or part of their investment if the insurance company does not profit, and enjoy the benefits of higher returns if the company does profit.

Mutual insurance companies have no stockholders and are owned by the policy holders. They typically charge a higher premium than a stock company to provide a cushion for larger than expected losses, but then pay a dividend each year based on the actual loss experience for that year. Since the policy holders accept the risk of greater than expected loss experience in this manner, they enjoy lower insurance costs when loss experiences are favorable. In the life insurance field, where mutual insurance companies are most important, 90 percent of the companies are stock companies, but 51 percent of the face value of policies and 60 percent of the assets are held by mutual companies.

TYPES OF INSURANCE

Insurance business can be divided into three broad categories: life insurance, property and liability insurance, and health and disability insurance.

As shown in Figure 11–1, a comparison of the relative importance of these types of insurance can be made in terms of assets held or premiums received. Life insurance

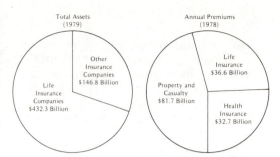

Figure 11–1: Selected finanical data for life and non-life insurance companies. Source: *Statistical Abstract of the United States*. Health insurance data excludes Blue Cross-Blue Shield and certain other plans.

dominates in terms of assets held because life insurance business involves receipt of premiums during one year with payments from those premiums to occur many years in the future. Many other types of insurance involve collection of premiums during a year and payment of claims from those premiums during the same year.[1] Premiums received through sale of life insurance do not dominate so clearly in terms of total insurance premiums received, with life insurance premiums being far less than those for property and liability insurance.

Life Insurance   Life insurance policies can be broken down according to the method by which they were sold. The categories are:

Ordinary: Life insurance sold to an individual by an agent or employee of the life insurance company, with premiums normally being paid by mail monthly, quarterly, semi-annually, or annually.

Group: Life insurance sold to cover all members of some group. The most common group would be all employees of a firm, who receive the insurance as a fringe benefit. The group policy may still give

---

[1] Assets of health insurance companies are not reported separately because health insurance is written by life insurance companies and property and liability companies as well as by separate companies.

some options to individual members of the group.

Credit: Life insurance sold in connection with a loan. The policy is normally for the amount of the loan and is normally marketed to borrowers by lenders. The lender may or may not own a captive insurance company for the purpose of selling these policies.

Industrial: Insurance sold in small amounts to relatively low income buyers. Collection of premiums is normally on a weekly basis with the agent calling on the insured rather than relying on them to mail in premiums.

surance in force, requires payment each period (year, quarter, and so on) until death. *Limited pay life* requires payment for a certain number of years and then continues to provide coverage until the insured dies and benefits are paid. Of course, premiums are higher for limited pay life than for straight life.

Since benefits are paid at eventual death, the payment of benefits from these policies is a certainty unless the policy is cancelled. In the early years of the policy, when very few people in the age group are dying, most of the premiums must be invested to provide funds to pay claims as the insured people get older and the death rate for that group in-

Table 11-1:

Growth of Life Insurance in Force
($ billions)

	Whole Life		Endowment		Term		Total		
	1974	1977	1974	1977	1974	1977	1974	1977	1979
Ordinary	654.0	807.3	43.0	52.2	312.0	429.8	1,009.0	1,289.3	1,585.9
Group	6.6	7.6	0.1	0.1	820.9	1,107.4	827.6	1,115.1	1,419.4
Industrial	33.1	32.7	2.9	2.4	3.4	3.9	39.4	39.0	37.8
Credit	—	—	—	—	109.6	139.4	109.6	139.4	179.3
Total	693.7	847.6	46.0	54.7	1,245.9	1,680.5	1,985.6	2,582.8	3,222.3

Source: *Life Insurance Fact Book*

As shown in the last column of Table 11–1, ordinary and group sales together accounted for 93 percent of all life insurance in force in 1979. Group sales represented the fastest growing sales category and industrial insurance sales declined over the time period considered in Table 11–1.

Probably more important than method of sale, life insurance differs in type of coverage and pattern of payment. *Whole life* insurance is expected to remain in force for the life of the insured and pay the contracted-for benefit upon death. *Straight life*, which represents over 80 percent of the whole life in-

creases. Total lifetime premiums are frequently less than death benefits because the life insurance company has the premiums to invest for most of a century. Most of these policies have cash values based on these savings that are being built up. The insured member can normally either cancel the policy and receive the cash value or borrow against the cash value and keep the insurance in force, with any amount borrowed being deducted from the benefit in the event the insured person dies while the loan is outstanding. Many people who purchase such policies keep them in force until retirement, when their dependents no longer need protection from the financial loss of their death, and then cash them in. Thus these policies serve as both insurance programs and savings programs. From the other side, these policies put the insurance company in the position of acting as a financial intermediary, accepting funds that it must return to the insured persons at some later date and investing these funds to earn a profit in the meantime.

Endowment policies also put the insurance company in the position of acting as a financial intermediary. An endowment policy pays the insured a specific amount at a specified future date. If the insured dies before this date, the same amount is still paid. These policies are frequently sold as a combined savings program to help sons and daughters with their education and insurance programs to guarantee that funds for education will be there in the event the parent dies before the children reach college age.

Term policies are pure insurance. If the premium is paid on a term policy and the insured does not die during the year, there is no cash value, although the policy may frequently be extended simply through payment of another premium. In brief, term insurance is similar to automobile, health, and home insurance in that the only benefit received is insurance against certain risks over the period covered by the premium.

From the buyer's point of view, term and whole life policies can be compared by deducting the premiums required for term insurance from the premiums on a whole life or endowment policy to determine the amount effectively being placed in a savings plan. The cash value at the time the policy will likely be cashed in can be compared to the effective savings plan contributions and the rate of return earned on the savings plan can then be computed. This return can be compared to alternative savings or investment program returns to determine if the whole life or endowment policy is more attractive than a term policy with the savings invested elsewhere.

Term policies come in two main varieties: regular and decreasing. Regular term may be purchased for one year, five years, or with guaranteed right of renewal for any number of years in the future. Premiums will normally rise each year as the insured becomes a greater risk. With decreasing term insurance, payments remain fixed and the amount of death benefit decreases each year. These policies are used in connection with credit insurance as the amount owed also declines each year. They are also used in cases where people feel their insurance needs are declining each year. An endowment policy is really a savings program with a certain savings goal and a decreasing term policy to cover the difference between the amount saved and the goal. An insured person who has a savings plan separate from the insurance plan may also want to cover the difference between present savings and the goal with a decreasing term policy. In addition, the present value of financial obligations such as child support decline over the years as the number of years for which support is required also decrease.

As term insurance, particularly group term insurance, has gained in popularity, marketers of whole life insurance have competed by offering packages which include whole life or endowment policies and term insurance. For example, the insurance agent may convince a young couple that they need $100,000 of life insurance on the primary wage earner and that whole life insurance is a good investment. However, the couple may not be able to afford the $1,200 in annual premiums for such a policy and may be tempted to buy a term policy, which would cost only $400. The life insurance agent may then recommend $20,000 of whole life insurance and $80,000 of term insurance for $560, with a plan calling for gradual conversion of the term insurance to whole life insurance over the years. Various combination packages have increased in popularity as insurance companies have found the lower profit term insurance increasing at the expense of growth in whole life insurance.

Life insurance companies also offer *annuity plans*. The purchaser of an annuity makes a single payment or a series of payments for which the life insurance company then agrees to make monthly payments for the rest of the insured's life. Annuities are used primarily as a means of providing retirement income. They are purchased by individuals who want more retirement income than that provided by their employers or by small employers as a means of providing a pension plan. In addition to providing a regular savings program, the annuity may allow greater monthly income than the individual could achieve by investing funds elsewhere. For a 65-year-old female retiree, a conservative (from the annuity payer's viewpoint) life expectancy is 20 years. If the interest rate on Aaa rated bonds is 10 percent, a retiree with $100,000 could invest in high grade bonds and receive $10,000 a year without reducing the principal. As Table A–7 shows, $100,000 at 10 percent would provide $11,746 a year with the principal being gone by the end of the twenty years. An individual, not knowing when he will die, cannot really afford to consume the principal of his funds if he wishes to be sure of the income for his entire life. However, the insurance company can make payments based on average life expectancy, with losses from those who live longer being offset by gains from those who die sooner. Even after subtracting its operating expenses, the insurance company may be able to offer a greater payment than could be earned by private investment. With whole life policies, it is generally possible to exchange the cash value for an annuity at age 65. Annuity plan premiums received by life insurance companies were $16.3 billion in 1978, or 45 percent of life insurance premiums. This is an increase from 15 percent of life insurance premiums in 1969, with much of the increase being in

the form of pension plans for small companies.

Property and liability insurance   The property and liability insurance field provides protection against financial losses to property and against lawsuit. Most things insured against in this category would be considered accidental, though theft is certainly not an accident to the thief and negligence of some type is normally argued in liability cases.

As previously noted, premiums for property and liability insurance exceeded those for life insurance. A detailed listing of types of property, liability, and allied insurance and annual premiums appears in Table 11–2.

Automobile insurance is the single largest category, accounting for a large portion of total property and liability insurance. Included is protection against damage to the policy holder and his or her own automobile in an accident, as well as insurance against lawsuits arising from an accident.

Multiple peril and *fire and allied lines* make up a group of insurance programs protecting property owners from financial loss from fire, theft, storm damage, etc. The trend among these policies is for writing single policies providing combined coverage for storm, theft, and certain other risks as well as fire.

Table 11-2:

Premiums for Selected Property, Liability, and Allied Insurance, 1979 (in $ millions)

Type of Coverage	Premiums
Automobile	$36,640
Liability other than automobile	7,817
Fire	4,781
Homeowners multiple peril	8,792
Commercial multiple peril	6,667
Workmen's compensation	13,164
Marine	3,070
Surety and fidelity	1,155
Other	1,575

Source: *Insurance Facts*

Worker's compensation is insurance by the employer against claims for injuries by workers. Benefits provided are determined by state law, and employers are required to carry this insurance in most cases.

Liability, including malpractice but excluding worker's compensation and automobile, was an important source of premium income in 1979. This includes personal liability insurance carried by many professionals.

Marine insurance covers risks its name implies. Protection against financial loss from theft, storm damage, and other types of risk is provided for ships and their cargoes. Insurance against political loss is covered separately (see Chapter 14).

Surety and fidelity insurance generally provides a guarantee that a certain course of action will be carried out. This may be required when late or inadequate completion of work would cause serious financial losses to one party to a contract. In such a case, insurance may be required to protect one party to a contract from loss if the other party should fail to complete work as agreed to.

Health Insurance Health insurance covers medical expenses and income loss associated with accident and illness. Insurance premiums in this field have increased rapidly in recent years, with increases in the number of people insured and increases in medical expenses.

Blue Cross and Blue Shield organizations presently account for slightly under half of total health insurance premiums. Blue Cross was started by hospitals as a means of decreasing their collection problems and Blue Shield was started by doctors for the same purpose. The plans are incorporated separately in each state, with premiums and benefits varying by state. The point is sometimes made that these programs are not technically insurance, but are prepayment programs started by hospitals and doctors with payments to them rather than the insured. However, this is hair splitting from the point of view of the insured who receive protection from unexpected medical expenses. Life insurance companies are the dominant factor in health insurance not written by Blue Cross and Blue Shield.

Property and liability insurance companies provide the remainder. Approximately 20 percent of health insurance premiums paid to life insurance companies are for loss of income protection. Blue Cross and Blue Shield provide no loss of income protection.

General health insurance is primarily sold in the form of group policies. Group sales account for 80 percent of private health insurance and a higher percentage for Blue Cross and Blue Shield. "Special" policies such as cancer insurance are more frequently sold as individual policies.

REGULATION OF INSURANCE COMPANIES

Most regulation of insurance companies is carried out by the individual states, with federal regulation limited to matters such as antitrust and fraud. Each state creates its own laws and regulates insurance companies selling insurance within its boundaries as well as those with headquarters there, causing national insurance companies to face 50 different sets of regulations. While specific rules vary from state to state, the same general areas—finance and investment policy, premium rates, contract provisions, and sales practices—are regulated in all states.

Finance and investment policies are regulated to assure that funds will be available to honor claims. Minimum amounts of capital and surplus are needed to start selling insurance and certain ratios of capital, surplus, and reserves must be maintained for all additional insurance written. In addition, the types of investments the insurance company can make are regulated. Life insurance companies are generally required to invest in bonds and mortgages, with only a limited investment in equity securities. Property and liability insurers, on the other hand, are normally allowed to invest in equity securities in amounts up to the value of the company's capital and surplus.

Premium rate regulations require that rates be adequate but not excessive. In addition, rate structures must not discriminate unfairly. In some states, all rates must be approved by the insurance commissioner in advance. In other states, rate increases do not need to be approved in advance, but the insurance commissioner can reduce premiums retroactively if they are found to be unjustified.

Contract provision regulation has resulted in a good deal of standardization across states. Regulation in this area followed complaints from people who filed claims and found out too late that the "fine print" excluded many things they thought were covered. Comparison shopping for policies is much easier when standard language is used.

Sales practices are also regulated, although it is not always clear whether the purpose of regulation is to protect consumers or those in the insurance business. Laws banning deceptive advertising are clearly for the purpose of protecting consumers. However, the benefit from laws that forbid agents from returning part of their commission to the policyholder as a means of price competition is not so clear. Laws requiring testing and licensing of those who would sell insurance are supposed to assure that insurance agents are knowledgeable, but the tests in some states are so easy as to be of little value.

MANAGEMENT CONSIDERATIONS

Management of an insurance company involves the actuarial job of accurately determining the risks involved, the marketing job of selling insurance to groups or the public, the operations management job of processing premiums and claims as efficiently as possible, and the financial management job of investing funds and maintaining an appropriate capital base.

OPERATIONS MANAGEMENT

The insurance company essentially acts as an intermediary by accepting premiums, deducting its expenses and a reasonable profit, and returning the remaining funds in the form of benefits. While the exact amount to be paid in benefits is not known in advance, premiums are set in light of anticipated operating expenses and benefit expenses. Operating and marketing expenses can be a substantial portion of total premiums. Holding these costs to a minimum is an essential part of successful insurance company management. Insurance companies have dealt with these costs by being leaders in the use of such things as computerized data processing and lockbox collections[2] to operate at maximum efficiency.

MARKETING MANAGEMENT

Successful marketing involves packaging the insurance in forms that are attractive to customers and reaching the customers in the most cost-efficient way possible. A major portion of total operating costs can relate to the marketing effort. For example, 40 percent of life insurance company operating costs are for commissions to agents, who may receive 100 percent or more of the first year's premium as the commission for selling a whole life policy. Agent commissions are only part of the marketing expense, as they do not include advertising or the expense of the marketing staff that helps to design policies, supervise and train agents, and so on.

---

[2] A lockbox collection plan involves establishment of a post office lockbox where customer payment is received. The firm's bank picks up the checks, notifies the firm, and begins the check-clearing process, thereby reducing check collection time and speeding cash flow.

As insurance buyers have become sophisticated and price conscious, the emphasis has switched from developing attractive packaging methods to the development of efficient marketing methods. Group insurance has shown substantial increases in market share because of the economies of scale involved. A group life insurance program can be sold to 2,000 employees of a company in a small portion of the time required to sell a policy to each individual. Physical examination costs are eliminated for health and life insurance policies since a large group is involved and the group's health characteristics can be estimated without individual physicals. Group life insurance increased from 20 percent of life insurance in force in 1950 to 44 percent in 1979. Group health insurance policies have also grown dramatically and group automobile insurance is beginning to grow. The decreased costs are reflected in decreased prices. Insurance companies that do not keep pace with these cost reductions will be unable to compete effectively on a price basis.

ACTUARIAL SCIENCE

The work of the actuary is key to the profitable operation of an insurance company. The actuary is primarily a statistician, working with past loss experience and other factors to predict future losses for a particular group. For example, Table 11–3 contains widely used projections of life expectancy and annual death rates for the population as a whole. The life insurance company can use this information to set rates for life insurance.

If actuaries only worked with experience for the total population, such as that in Table 11–3, there would be little need for the thousands of people presently employed as actuaries. The actuaries must deal with several sub-groups of the population and use this information to construct policies that will be cost-competitive in the marketplace and profitable to the company. For example, it is recognized that college professors have lower mortality rates than the population as a whole (despite the wish of an occasional student). A separate mortality table for this particular profession makes it possible to market a policy specifically to this profession at a premium cost below what would have to be charged to the general population and still make a profit. The growing importance of group sales has heightened the importance of separate actuarial computations for each group. Likewise, the sale of insurance to special low-risk groups means that the general population not included in some low-risk group has a higher incidence of loss than the total population, including these various low-risk groups. Thus the expected loss rate for the general population changes continually and must be watched carefully.

Variations in loss ratios are not limited to life insurance. For example, automobile insurance rates incorporate a number of factors that result in higher or lower loss experience. Classifying people as lower accident risks than they actually are will result in losses for the company. Classifying them as higher risks than they actually are will result in the policy being overpriced and business being lost to competing companies.

In addition to predicting the incidence of unfortunate events, the actuary must also predict their costs. The amount to be paid is fixed for most life insurance policies, but must be estimated for health insurance and property and liability insurance. The importance of the actuary in these areas has been particularly important during periods of rapid inflation.

In addition to predicting costs, it is also necessary to predict security returns. Because many life insurance policies and annuity plans involve a period of many years between premium receipt and benefit payment, premiums are based on assumptions about the rate at which funds can be invested. One thousand dollars invested for 40

Table 11-3:
Mortality Tables

Ages 0–23

Age	Individual Annuity Table for 1971—Male (1960–1967)		Individual Annuity Table for 1971—Female (1960–1967)		United States Total Population (1969–1971)	
	Deaths Per 1,000	Expectation of Life (Years)	Deaths Per 1,000	Expectation of Life (Years)	Deaths Per 1,000	Expectation of Life (Years)
0	—	—	—	—	20.02	70.75
1	—	—	—	—	1.25	71.19
2	—	—	—	—	.86	70.28
3	—	—	—	—	.69	69.34
4	—	—	—	—	.57	68.39
5	.46	71.69	.23	76.99	.51	67.43
6	.42	70.73	.19	76.01	.46	66.46
7	.40	69.75	.16	75.02	.43	65.49
8	.39	68.78	.14	74.03	.39	64.52
9	.39	67.81	.13	73.04	.34	63.54
10	.39	66.84	.13	72.05	.31	62.57
11	.40	65.86	.14	71.06	.30	61.58
12	.41	64.89	.16	70.07	.35	60.60
13	.41	63.91	.17	69.08	.46	59.62
14	.42	62.94	.18	68.10	.63	58.65
15	.43	61.97	.19	67.11	.82	57.69
16	.44	60.99	.21	66.12	1.01	56.73
17	.46	60.02	.22	65.13	1.17	55.79
18	.47	59.05	.23	64.15	1.28	54.86
19	.49	58.07	.25	63.16	1.34	53.93
20	.50	57.10	.26	62.18	1.40	53.00
21	.52	56.13	.28	61.19	1.47	52.07
22	.54	55.16	.29	60.21	1.52	51.15
23	.57	54.19	.31	59.23	1.53	50.22

Ages 57–80

Age	Individual Annuity Table for 1971—Male (1960–1967)		Individual Annuity Table for 1971—Female (1960–1967)		United States Total Population (1969–1971)	
	Deaths Per 1,000	Expectation of Life (Years)	Deaths Per 1,000	Expectation of Life (Years)	Deaths Per 1,000	Expectation of Life (Years)
57	9.85	23.13	4.83	26.83	13.41	20.49
58	10.61	22.35	5.41	25.96	14.52	19.76
59	11.41	21.59	6.02	25.10	15.70	19.05
60	12.25	20.83	6.63	24.25	16.95	18.34
61	13.13	20.08	7.22	23.41	18.29	17.65
62	14.07	19.34	7.77	22.57	19.74	16.97
63	15.08	18.61	8.29	21.74	21.33	16.30
64	16.19	17.89	8.78	20.92	23.06	15.65
65	17.41	17.17	9.29	20.10	24.95	15.00
66	18.77	16.47	9.89	19.29	26.99	14.38
67	20.29	15.77	10.62	18.47	29.18	13.76
68	21.99	15.09	11.54	17.67	31.52	13.16
69	23.89	14.42	12.66	16.87	34.00	12.57
70	26.00	13.76	14.03	16.08	36.61	12.00
71	28.34	13.11	15.65	15.30	39.43	11.43
72	30.93	12.48	17.55	14.53	42.66	10.88
73	33.80	11.86	19.74	13.79	46.44	10.34
74	36.98	11.26	22.26	13.05	50.75	9.82
75	40.49	10.67	25.12	12.34	55.52	9.32
76	44.39	10.10	28.37	11.64	60.60	8.84
77	48.72	9.55	32.05	10.97	65.96	8.38
78	53.50	9.01	36.23	10.32	71.53	7.93
79	58.79	8.50	40.98	9.68	77.41	7.51
80	64.60	7.99	46.39	9.08	83.94	7.10

24	.59	53.22	.33	58.25	1.51	49.30
25	.62	52.25	.35	57.27	1.47	48.37
26	.65	51.28	.37	56.29	1.43	47.44
27	.68	50.32	.39	55.31	1.42	46.51
28	.72	49.35	.41	54.33	1.44	45.58
29	.76	48.39	.44	53.35	1.49	44.64
30	.81	47.42	.47	52.37	1.55	43.71
31	.86	46.46	.50	51.40	1.63	42.77
32	.92	45.50	.53	50.42	1.72	41.84
33	.98	44.54	.57	49.45	1.83	40.92
34	1.05	43.58	.61	48.48	1.95	39.99
35	1.12	42.63	.65	47.51	2.09	39.07
36	1.20	41.68	.70	46.54	2.25	38.15
37	1.30	40.73	.75	45.57	2.44	37.23
38	1.40	39.78	.81	44.60	2.66	36.32
39	1.51	38.83	.87	43.64	2.90	35.42
40	1.63	37.89	.94	42.68	3.14	34.52
41	1.79	36.95	1.01	41.72	3.41	33.63
42	2.00	36.02	1.09	40.76	3.70	32.74
43	2.26	35.09	1.19	39.80	4.04	31.86
44	2.57	34.17	1.29	38.85	4.43	30.99
45	2.92	33.25	1.40	37.90	4.84	30.12
46	3.32	32.35	1.52	36.95	5.28	29.27
47	3.75	31.46	1.65	36.01	5.74	28.42
48	4.23	30.57	1.80	35.06	6.24	27.58
49	4.74	29.70	1.97	34.13	6.78	26.75
50	5.29	28.84	2.15	33.19	7.38	25.93
51	5.86	27.99	2.37	32.26	8.04	25.12
52	6.46	27.15	2.64	31.34	8.76	24.32
53	7.09	26.33	2.97	30.42	9.57	23.53
54	7.74	25.51	3.35	29.51	10.43	22.75
55	8.42	24.71	3.79	28.61	11.36	21.99
56	9.12	23.91	4.28	27.71	12.36	21.23

81	7.51	70.90	52.51	8.49	91.22	6.70
82	7.05	77.67	59.41	7.94	98.92	6.32
83	6.60	84.94	67.16	7.41	106.95	5.96
84	6.16	92.87	75.90	6.90	115.48	5.62
85	5.74	101.69	85.77	6.43	125.61	5.28
86	5.34	111.65	96.90	5.99	137.48	4.97
87	4.95	123.05	109.34	5.57	149.79	4.68
88	4.57	136.12	122.98	5.20	161.58	4.42
89	4.21	151.07	137.51	4.86	172.92	4.18
90	3.87	168.04	152.47	4.55	185.02	3.94
91	3.55	187.15	167.37	4.28	198.88	3.73
92	3.26	208.46	181.78	4.04	213.63	3.53
93	2.98	231.89	195.39	3.83	228.70	3.35
94	2.73	257.15	208.07	3.63	243.36	3.19
95	2.50	283.84	219.90	3.46	257.45	3.06
96	2.30	311.57	231.10	3.29	269.59	2.95
97	2.11	340.21	242.21	3.13	280.24	2.85
98	1.94	369.77	253.82	2.97	289.77	2.76
99	1.79	400.19	266.45	2.81	298.69	2.69
100	1.65	431.41	280.54	2.65	306.96	2.62
101	1.53	463.31	296.45	2.49	314.61	2.56
102	1.41	495.76	314.54	2.33	321.67	2.51
103	1.31	528.60	335.12	2.17	328.17	2.46
104	1.21	561.69	358.54	2.01	334.14	2.41
105	1.13	594.88	385.12	1.85	339.60	2.37
106	1.05	628.02	415.24	1.70	344.60	2.34
107	.98	660.95	449.27	1.55	349.17	2.30
108	.92	693.60	487.65	1.41	353.33	2.27
109	.86	725.52	530.79	1.27	357.12	2.24

Source: *Life Insurance Fact Book*

years at 10 percent per year will grow to $45,259 while the same amount invested for the same time period at 15 percent would grow to $267,864. Companies' profits and losses can be dramatically affected by failures in these projections.

A discussion of the skills necessary to perform competently as an actuary is well beyond the scope of this book. Many universities have degree programs in actuarial science, and there are a number of professional associations devoted to maintaining high standards of actuarial practice. The primary actuarial associations are:

American Academy of Actuaries, 208 South Lasalle St., Chicago

American Society of Pension Actuaries, 1700 K St., N.W., Washington, D.C.

Conference of Actuaries in Public Service, 208 S. Lasalle St., Chicago

Society of Actuaries, 208 S. Lasalle St., Chicago

ASSET AND LIABILITY MANAGEMENT

LIABILITIES AND CAPITAL

An understanding of the liabilities of insurance companies is necessary to develop an appropriate approach to management of assets. The dominant liabilities for both life and non-life insurance companies are reserves based on the fact that premiums are collected as much as a year ahead for non-life insurance companies and most of a lifetime ahead for life insurance policies. The amounts expected to be paid out over the period covered by the premium is carried as a reserve when that premium is first received. As claims are paid, both cash and reserves are reduced. If claims exceed reserves, capital and surplus are decreased, and vice versa. The long lives of many life insurance policies versus those of non-life insurance companies result in much larger

policy reserves for life insurance companies.

In addition to the higher absolute amount of reserves, life insurance companies have a much higher ratio of reserves to equity. The lower capital levels for life insurance companies result from both management decisions and regulatory requirements. They are based on recognition of the fact that life insurance obligations are easier to predict than the obligations of most other insurance companies. In addition, the accumulation of funds for certain death benefits means that the dollar value of liabilities per face value of insurance is higher for life insurance than for other insurance. Therefore, a higher ratio of liabilities to equity does not necessarily mean a higher ratio of insurance face value to equity. Accident rates and the amount of settlement per accident have varied. This has been particularly true with high inflation.

The size of the equity base has important implications for asset management. With a limited equity base, the life insurance companies can endure less asset value shrinkage than can non-life companies.

ASSETS

Table 11–4 shows that the primary assets of insurance companies are investment portfolios in the form of government and corporate securities. Investment portfolios are held for two reasons. Because the insurance companies collect premiums with insurance coverage provided for some time after collection, they have these funds to invest until they are paid out as benefits. On the liability side, this shows up as reserves. The second category of funds are held as protection against losses due to factors such as excessive benefit expense or shrinkage in the value of assets. On the liability side of the balance sheet, these funds are represented by surplus and equity accounts. The investment policy is determined by the two purposes the portfolio serves.

The liquidity needs from the investment portfolio are minimal. Most insurance companies are continually expanding in size,

Table 11-4:

Asset Structure of Insurance Companies, 1979
(in $ billions)

Assets	Life	%	Non-life	%
Government securities	$ 29.7	6.9	$ 83.7	57.0
Corporate securities				
Bonds	169.0	39.1	26.3	17.9
Stock	39.8	9.2	25.9	17.6
Mortgages	118.4	27.4	1.1	0.7
Real estate	13.0	3.0	—	—
Policy loans	34.8	8.0	—	—
Other assets	27.6	6.4	9.8	6.7
Total	$432.3	100.0	$146.8	100.0

Source: *1980 Life Insurance Fact Book* and Board of Governors of the Federal Reseve System, *Assets and Liabilities Outstanding, 1969–1979.*

with premiums received during any month being more than sufficient to meet all cash outflows for that month. Actual sale of securities would be necessary only if premium revenue declined. The company will add to its portfolio and reserve accounts from month to month unless its volume declines or disintermediation occurs. Table 11–5 shows the allocation of the life insurance dollar for U.S. life insurance companies for 1979.

This is not to say that day-to-day cash management is not an important function in an insurance company. A large insurance company will have cash flows of several million dollars a day. A company may be able to improve profit by half a million dollars a year or more by reducing idle cash equal to one day's cash flow. Therefore, the companies follow cash flow over the week and month very closely to keep as much cash as possible invested. If premiums for a particular company tend to come in around the first of the month, with claims paid at an even rate over the month, the company will have idle cash during the early part of the month. These funds will be invested in money market instruments, with adjustments being made on a daily basis. Because these day-to-day cash flows vary with such things as mail delivery and are not totally

Table 11-5:

Life Insurance Company Dollar 1979: U.S. Life Insurance Companies

Income

Premiums	73.8¢
Net Investment Earnings and Other Income	26.2
	100.0

How Used

Benefit Payments and Additions to Funds for Policyholders and Beneficiaries	
Benefit Payments in Year	48.5¢
Additions to Policy Reserve Funds .	27.2
Additions to Special Reserves and Surplus Funds	2.9
	78.6
Operating Expenses	
Commissions to Agents	6.2
Home and Field Office Expenses ..	9.5
	15.7
Taxes	4.4
Dividends to Stockholders of Stock Life Insurance Companies	1.3
	100.0

Source: *1980 Life Insurance Fact Book*, p. 62

predictable, there may be short-term liquidity demand that requires the sale of money market instruments. This short-term money management problem is linked to management of the investment portfolio only to the extent that the company must decide how much to invest in money market instruments for liquidity reserve purposes.

Liquidity demands of a more serious nature arise from disintermediation. Whole life and endowment policies normally give the holder the right to borrow a large portion of the reserve attributed to the policy at an interest rate stated in the contract. With rising interest rates, people have found these *policy loans* to be a low-cost source of funds and have borrowed heavily, either to meet credit needs or to invest at higher interest rates. In addition, whole life and endowment policies can normally be cancelled, with the insured being paid most of the reserve associated with that policy. This is the *cash value* spelled out in such policies. Cancellation of whole life policies, to be replaced with term policies, has also occurred during periods of high interest rates. The relative stabilities of cash flow demands for death benefits and loan and cash surrender payments are shown in Figure 11–2. Downturns in loan and cash surrender demand are in periods when interest rates are falling, while rapid increases in this demand are during periods of rising interest rates. Outflows have not been sufficient to cause net outflows for all insurance companies, but they have been sufficient to lead to substantial net outflows for individual companies.

The pressures to earn returns on portfolios come from two sources. First, insurance companies are clearly profit-seeking ventures, and portfolio return is an important source of revenue, equalling 26.2 percent of the life insurance dollar in 1979. Unlike mutual thrift institutions, even mutual insurance companies pay profit-based dividends to members who also elect directors. Thus, virtually all insurance companies are overseen by directors elected by people who

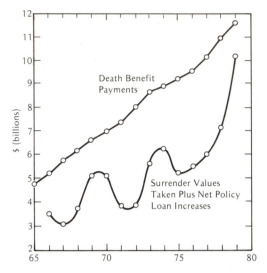

Figure 11–2: Cash outflow demands on life insurance companies. Source: Based on data in *1980 Life Insurance Fact Book.*

share in profits. In addition to direct profitability to the owners, investment portfolio return indirectly affects profitability through the ability of the company to price policies competitively. For all insurance companies, and particularly for a life insurance company, the premiums depend on an assumption about rates of return on the firm's investments and on an assessment of risks. For a $10,000 benefit payment fifty years in the future, the annual investment necessary to accumulate this amount is $8.59 if the interest at which funds can be invested is 10 percent and $1.39 if the interest rate is raised to 15 percent. If a 20 percent rate of return could be assumed, the payment would fall to $0.22. Premiums required for some life insurance policies are therefore quite sensitive to the return that can be earned on the investment portfolio. The assumption of a low long-term investment return at a time when interest rates were high was one factor leading to the increased portion of the life insurance premium dollar going to term insurance.

For life and non-life insurance companies, the amount of new insurance which a particular company can write is limited by the amount of equity and surplus. Return on the investment portfolio increases the amount of surplus.

Tax considerations differ by type of insurance company and lead to different policies with regard to the investment portfolio. The two main forms of tax paid are state premium taxes—a percentage of all premiums collected in a particular state—and income tax. Income tax is the most important of the taxes for both life and non-life companies. All insurance companies are taxed at standard corporate income tax rates (presently 46 percent). However, the tax base income to which this rate is applied varies according to the type of insurance being sold.

Life insurance companies can allocate half their underwriting profits[3] for each year to policyholders' surplus with the balance being allocated to a shareholders' surplus account. The amount allocated to the policyholders' account is recognized as taxable income only if it is transferred to the shareholders' account. Since it would be transferred to the shareholders' account only if it were to be used to pay dividends, the life insurance company can effectively retain half of its underwriting earnings without paying income tax on them. Other insurance companies pay tax on all their profits, whether or not they are retained. In effect then, the marginal federal income tax rate for a life insurance company can be half that for a non-life company or industrial corporation.[4]

Because of this difference in tax treatment, non-life companies hold a substantial proportion (almost half) of their assets in the

form of state and local government obligations while life insurance companies hold less than 2 percent of their assets in this form. State and local government securities pay lower returns than do other securities, but returns associated with these municipal securities are not subject to federal income tax. The yield spreads between municipals and other securities are such that they are attractive only to investors with effective income tax rates in the neighborhood of 40 percent or higher. Thus they are attractive to non-life companies but not to life insurance companies.

Regulation of portfolio policy by state authorities is aimed at protecting the insured by protecting the portfolio from shrinkage in value. Life insurance companies are severely restricted with regard to investment in equity securities, direct investment in real estate, and with regard to other investments perceived to be risky. Non-life companies are usually allowed to invest in equity securities up to the amount of their own equity and surplus. However, the attractiveness of equity securities is decreased by procedures the regulators use in computing the insurance company's equity and surplus. Equity securities are carried at their current market values, whereas bonds can be carried at their face values or original cost. If rising interest rates cause both stock and bond values to decline, the company holding only bonds will not suffer a decline in portfolio value from the regulators' viewpoint, but losses will be recorded for the company with equity investments. The consequent reduction in recognized capital can impair the company's ability to sell additional insurance since certain ratios of capital to insurance face value are required. Non-life insurance companies hold 18 percent of their assets in equity securities while life insurance companies hold 9 percent of their assets in this form.

Risk As with any other company, the insurance company cannot think of the riskiness of a single security in isolation from the

---

[3] Underwriting profits (or losses) are premiums earned less losses and expenses. They do not reflect investment earnings.

[4] For a detailed discussion of insurance company tax treatment, see Keith Tucker and Dennis Van Mieghem of Peat, Marwick, Mitchell & Co. *Taxation of Insurance Companies—Problems and Planning.* Englewood Cliffs, N.J.: Prentice Hall, 1981.

investment portfolio; nor can the investment portfolio be viewed in isolation from the other aspects of the company's business. An insurance company faces four major types of risks.

Excessive benefit costs are the first type of risk. They can occur because of a natural disaster, because inflation drives average claim amounts to higher than anticipated levels, or simply because the company's original estimates of losses were wrong.

Sales declines represent the second type of risk. They can occur because a severe economic downturn eliminates either the ability to pay for premiums or the need for certain types of insurance. Business insurance would be the most obvious example as the need for it decreases during a recession when business activity declines or businesses close. Demand for life insurance, particularly whole life, may also decline in inflationary periods as people look for investments that will provide some protection from inflation.

Portfolio value loss is a risk that results from a similar set of factors. As inflation rates rise, the general level of interest rates rises as well. A rise in the general level of interest rates results in a decline in the market value of existing fixed income securities. In addition, common stock returns have been negatively correlated with the inflation rate in recent years. An economic downturn can also have a negative impact on portfolio value through defaults on bonds and mortgages, and through a reduction in common stock values as profits decline. Default rates on the types of securities that insurance companies hold have remained low even in economic downturns, but losses in market value have been substantial. For example, a bond with an 8 percent coupon rate and 20 years to maturity would be selling at 70 percent of its face value if the general level of interest rates for this risk class were to increase to 12 percent. Likewise, but less surprisingly, we have seen the average value of a share of common stock decline 40 percent or more. With their low ratios of equity capital to total assets, the insurance companies cannot absorb large losses of this type.

Cancellation and policy loan risks are primarily problems faced by companies offering whole life or endowment policies. These withdrawals generally occur during periods of high interest rates, but could also occur in severe economic downturns. Of course, high interest rate periods and economic downturns are both periods when the values of securities may be low. For fixed income securities, the maturity value is not affected by a decline in current market value. The decline in market price is significant because: 1) it reflects an opportunity loss in that higher yielding securities are currently available, and (2) if the company should need cash, the bonds would have to be sold at a loss. As indicated earlier, a loss in the value of equity can have an immediate negative impact on equity and surplus ratios, even in the absence of a need to sell the securities at depressed prices.

The conditions which might lead to each of the various types of losses are summarized as follows:

Problem	Causes		
Excessive claim losses	natural disasters	inflation	
Sales declines		inflation	economic downturn
Losses in investment portfolio		inflation	economic downturn
Policy loans and cancellations		inflation	economic downturn

Since inflation and economic downturn are factors influencing most types of losses, particularly for life insurance companies, the investment portfolio does not provide significant opportunity to diversify away risks from other aspects of the business.

Portfolio Strategy Because of this limited opportunity for diversification, insurance companies pursue a conservative portfolio strategy. Long term fixed income securities are the primary investment for both life insurance and non-life companies. Because of previously discussed tax differences, life insurance companies hold large quantities of corporate bonds and mortgages while non-life insurance companies hold larger quantities of state and local government securities. There has been a switch in emphasis in mortgage holdings, away from FHA and VA mortgages and toward commercial mortgages. In addition to higher return, commercial mortgages create the opportunity for "equity participations" through which the insurance company can participate in profits if the venture is successful.

Within the investment portfolio, the normal principle of eliminating diversifiable risk is followed to the extent possible. Unfortunately, legislation designed to assure safety may actually increase the difficulty of achieving proper diversification. Regulations are based on the view that high grade, fixed-income securities are nearly risk-free. Restricting insurance companies to heavy investment in these securities and restricting them from such areas as direct investment in real estate has left them exposed to the full effect of interest rate risk associated with inflation. Portfolio managers have sought to diversify within these regulatory limits. The movement to commercial mortgages with equity participations is one such example, giving some of the diversification benefits of real estate ownership without violating restriction on direct real estate ownership or direct common stock purchase. Convertible

bonds are another investment medium providing similar opportunities.

To deal with interest rate risk, it must be remembered that the life insurance companies base their premiums on expected investment return. If management knew the policy would not be cancelled or borrowed against, investment maturity could be based on expected eventual payment date, thereby insuring a rate of return. This would not be entirely possible for payments expected to be made 60 years in the future, but 40-year maturities are available and would be sufficient to cover most commitments. Unfortunately, the picture is complicated by a number of uncertainties, including the fact that bonds can be called and policies can be cancelled or borrowed against. The problem of high yield bonds and mortgages being repaid when interest rates fall could be dealt with through increased holdings of U.S. government securities, which are generally not callable. However, with the experience of two decades of rising interest rates and almost no bonds being called, the insurance industry seems content to accept call risk. Convertible bonds and equity participation in real estate loans provide at least some diversification in this regard.

Portfolio strategy to deal with the possibility of excessive withdrawals through loans and cancellations is primarily dealt with through a balancing of the maturity structure so that any demand can be met through maturing securities rather than selling securities at a discount. This has been combined with some movement toward raising the policy loan interest rate in new contracts or making it a floating rate tied to some money market indicator.

An insurance company that temporarily finds itself with an insufficient supply of shorter term securities can hedge in the financial futures markets. By entering into forward contracts to sell, it can effectively convert some long term U.S. government securities or mortgages to short-term securities.

In summary, insurance companies face significant risks tied to the inflation rate and economic conditions. These risks cannot be very effectively diversified away, but they are problems of the short and intermediate term, in which securities might have to be sold below cost. If a company has its maturity structure designed evenly so that it can avoid the necessity of selling securities before maturity, the risks are manageable. A poorly designed maturity structure could quickly result in insolvency in the face of withdrawal demand.

SUMMARY

Insurance companies act as intermediaries for risk. They do so by collecting funds from all members of a large group in order to pay benefits to certain members of the group who suffer some consequence. This consequence is diversifiable from the point of view of the general population but not from the point of view of individuals. The three main types of insurance and annual 1978 premiums are

Life insurance	$36.6 billion
Property and liability insurance	81.7 billion
Health insurance	32.7 billion

The life insurance companies are a larger factor than these premium levels indicate. Life insurance companies receive almost half the health insurance premiums and billions more in payments toward annuity plans. In addition, life insurance company assets are much greater than those of all non-life insurance companies.

Insurance companies also act as financial intermediaries in collecting savings from individuals and reinvesting them. Their investments of some $600 billion make them an important source of investment capital.

Regulation is left almost entirely to state governments. Regulations vary by state, with insurance companies required to meet regulations of states in which they sell insurance. Regulations cover investment and finance policies, premium rates charged, contract provisions, and sales practices.

Like most companies, insurance companies are guided by the profitability objective in the four main areas of management: operations management, actuarial science, marketing management, and financial management. Operations management consists of efficiently and economically handling the millions of transactions involved. Actuarial science consists of accurately estimating the percent of the population that will suffer a particular insurable event. Marketing management involves designing policies that fit buyers' demands, but increasingly involves the development of cost efficient methods of sales. Financial management consists of determining and maintaining the proper amount of equity, and managing the investment portfolio.

The portfolio manager attempts to maximize profitability while dealing with four types of risk: 1) excessive benefit costs; 2) sales declines; 3) portfolio value loss; 4) cancellation and policy loan demands. These risks must be met within the constraints of regulations which affect investment policy. Such regulations tend to restrict equity investments and tax laws have the effect of favoring state and local government securities for non-life insurance companies but not life insurance companies. The fact that most types of potential losses tend to occur in periods of high inflation or economic downturn make them difficult to eliminate through any portfolio strategy, especially in the face of regulatory restrictions. Balancing maturities to avoid the necessity of selling securities at a loss and purchasing fixed income securities with equity participation options are important strategies.

QUESTIONS

1. What pressures would cause a mutual insurance company to pursue a profitability objective? How do these pressures differ from those on a mutual savings and loan company?

2. Why do life insurance companies dominate in asset size, even though they receive less than half of total insurance premiums?

3. For regulatory purposes, bonds can be counted at their face value even if their current market price has declined. If bonds were revalued to current market price, some insurance companies would be insolvent.

   a) Which type of company—life or non-life—would be more likely to be pushed into insolvency by a revaluation of fixed income securities to current market value?

   b) What is the effect of this situation on the protection offered to policyholders?

4. As a regulator, what portfolio management rules would you suggest to improve diversification by insurance companies?

5. Why is it difficult to purchase insurance for damage due to acts of war?

6. For an insurance buyer, which type of insurance company—stock or mutual—would be expected to provide lower total costs if claims expense is lower than anticipated? Higher than anticipated?

7. Why can a life insurance company operate with a higher liability to equity ratio than a non-life insurance company?

8. Under what conditions would a property and liability insurance company find it necessary to sell assets from its portfolio? What is the appropriate maturity structure for property and liability insurance company assets?

PROBLEMS

1. New Horizons Life Insurance company has equity equal to 8 percent of total assets. The company's assets are as follows:

Item	Maturity	Coupon or face rate	Yield to* Maturity	Face value
Bonds	30 yrs	8.0%	10.0%	$2,000,000
Bonds	10 yrs	9.0	9.5	3,000,000
Bonds	5 yrs	9.0	9.25	3,000,000
T-bills	90 days	8.0	8.0	5,000,000
Mortgages**	20 years	8.0	10.0	5,000,000

*Based on market price; assume annual interest payments for bonds.

**These involve monthly payments over the twenty-year period.

   a) If these assets were revalued to market value, would the company be solvent?

   b) If yields to maturity on all securities rose one more percentage point, would the company still be solvent?

   c) If requirements were changed to require that fixed income securities be carried at market value, what would be likely to happen to the average maturities of insurance company assets?

2. Your insurance company can invest funds at 4 percent. 90 percent of the first year's premium is paid as a sales commission and operating expenses are 10 percent of premiums. For someone who lives for 30 years (and pays 31 premiums, with the first being paid today):

a) What would be the annual premium necessary for a straight life insurance policy for $20,000?

b) What would be the annual premium necessary for a 20-year limited payment life insurance policy for $20,000?

c) Rework (a) and (b) on the assumption of a 7 percent return on invested funds.

3. Following are financial statements for Old Reliable Life Insurance company. The board of directors has noted that the profitability of the company is below average. Compare the financial statements of Old Reliable to those for life insurance companies in general, and suggest methods for improving profitability.

Old Reliable Life Insurance
Income Statement
Year ending   **December 31, 1980**
(000,000 omitted)

Premium revenue	$146
Investment portfolio income	44
	190
Benefit payments and reserve additions	145
Operating expenses	41
Income tax	1
Net income	$ 3

Balance Sheet
December 31, 1980
(000,000 omitted)

Demand deposits and currency	$ 8
Corporate equity	70
Treasury bills	12
U.S. government bonds	40
State and local government bonds	21
Corporate bonds	281
FHA and VA mortgages	190
Commercial mortgages	20
Policy loans	60
Other assets	40
Total assets	$742
Policy reserves	$550
Other liabilities	50
Equity and surplus	142
Total liabilities and net worth	$742

SELECTED REFERENCES

Campbell, Ritchie A. "The Demand for Life Insurance: An Application of the Economics of Uncertainty," *Journal of Finance,* Vol. 35 (December, 1980), pp. 1155–1174.

Foster, George. "Valuation Parameters of Property-Liability Companies," *Journal of Finance,* Vol. 32 (June, 1977), pp. 823–836.

Geehan, Randall. "Returns to Scale in the Life Insurance Industry," *The Bell Journal of Economics and Management Science,* Vol. 8 (Autumn, 1977), pp. 497–514.

Life Insurance Companies as Financial Institutions. Englewood Cliffs, New Jersey: Prentice-Hall, 1962.

Shick, Richard A., and James S. Treischmann, "Some Further Evidence on the Performance of Property-Liability Insurance Companies' Stock Portfolios," *Journal of Financial and Quantitative Analysis,* Vol. 13 (March, 1978), pp. 157–166.

Chapter 12

Pension Fund Management

"If 'socialism' is defined as 'ownership of the means of production by the workers'— and this is both the orthodox and the only rigorous definition—then the United States is the first truly 'Socialist country.' . . . Indeed, aside from farming, a larger sector of the American economy is owned today by the American worker through his investment agent, the pension fund, than Allende in Chile had brought under government ownership to make Chile a 'Socialist country,' than Castro's Cuba has actually nationalized, or than had been nationalized in Hungary or Poland at the height of Stalinism." Peter Drucker, *The Unseen Revolution,* Harper and Row, 1976.

Private pension plans, with assets in excess of $400 billion, are the third largest type of financial institution, being exceeded only by banks and savings and loan companies. Combined assets of public and private pension plans—over $600 billion—are exceeded only by assets of commercial banks. Thus, pension plans have come to the fore as a major type of financial institution in the United States and an important factor in its economy.

The growth in importance of pension funds has been such a recent phenomenon that the *Federal Reserve Bulletin,* which carries 70 pages of detailed statistics on financial markets and institutions, does not have a single entry for pension funds. In the 1930s pension fund assets amounted to only about $2.5 billion and as late as 1950 private pension fund assets amounted to only $12 billion. However, these assets had grown to $138 billion by 1970, making pension funds major financial institutions. From this level, the growth rate increased sharply following Labor Day, 1974, when ERISA—the Employee Retirement Income Security Act— was signed into law, increasing required pension fund reserves and leading to projections of a continued high rate of growth in pension fund assets.

As Drucker points out, even these growth numbers may understate the importance of pension funds to the United States economy and society. In combination, the pension funds hold controlling interest in the common stock of most large American corporations.[1] Their continued growth and potential use of that control could lead to major changes in the economic structure of the country. Proper management of pension funds is a matter of concern for the welfare of the country, not to mention the welfare of the individuals covered by the plans and the companies contributing to them.

TYPES OF PENSION FUNDS

Pension plans are operated by private companies, private associations, insurance companies, state and local governments, and the federal government. Government sponsored funds are normally controlled by legislation of the sponsoring government unit while private funds are regulated through ERISA. Regardless of the sponsor or guiding legislation, certain common principles underlie the management of the assets of any pension fund. Following an overview of the types of funds and types of regulation, the principles of fund management will be developed.

As a prelude to examining the various types of funds and sponsors, it is necessary to understand the difference between a funded and an unfunded pension plan. A funded plan maintains assets sufficient to meet its remaining obligations over the lives of the persons covered by the plan. The plan's obligations rise from payments already received and it would be in a position to meet those obligations if no further contributions to the fund occurred. All private pension plans and some government sponsored plans are now of the funded variety. An unfunded plan counts on current payments to meet current obligations and maintains assets sufficient to meet obligations for

only a short time. Because it can guarantee payment through its taxing ability, the U.S. government can sponsor unfunded pension plans. However, private firms and most state and local governments have no way, other than funding, to guarantee that commitments will be honored.

SOCIAL SECURITY

Social Security (Old Age, Survivors, and Disability Insurance Program) is, of course, the broadest pension program, providing coverage to about 150 million people employed in the private sector and state and local government. While it was started as a program to provide a floor level of retirement income to contributing workers, it has been expanded to serve a number of other needs including disability and survivors dependent benefits. Many private pension plans are designed to mesh with social security, providing a supplement to fill the gap between social security and some desired level of retirement income. Social security payments are adjusted for inflation each year, an important consideration and a source of security in periods of high inflation. Because portfolio value may not increase with inflation, few private plans are in a position to promise payments adjusted for inflation. Social security obligations are primarily unfunded, with total assets of the social security trust fund presently being equal to only a few months of benefit payments.

CIVIL SERVICE RETIREMENT SYSTEM

Federal civilian employees are covered by the United States Civil Service Retirement System, which presently has approximately 2.9 million active workers and 1.4 million retired recipients. Civil service employees do not participate in the social security system. The civil service retirement system is one of the few plans with benefits completely adjusted for inflation.

---

[1] Peter Drucker, op. cit., p. 2.

The Civil Service Retirement System is designed to be a fully funded system, with contributions by both the United States government and its employees. Unfunded liabilities are to be made up from appropriations over a 30-year period. At the present time the fund has assets of $38.6 billion and the discounted present value of unfunded liabilities is approximately $108 billion. Thus the bulk of its liabilities are actually unfunded at this time. The assets of the fund are invested in U.S. government securities.

STATE AND LOCAL GOVERNMENT PENSION FUNDS

Pension plans of state and local governments have increased in importance with the increase in the number of persons employed by state and local government. Legislation in 1950 and 1954 made state and local government employees eligible to participate in social security and most have done so. State and local governments have been slow to integrate their pension plans with social security, creating systems in which some employees can actually increase their income by retiring. State and local government pension plans are not covered by all the federal laws that govern the management of private pension funds. They are controlled primarily by state and local legislation. For private plans, the idea of investing corporate pension funds in the company involved has been largely rejected because of the risk of the employee if both the company and the pension fund fail. However, state and local employees do not seem to have similar protection. Their assets have sometimes been used to underwrite unsound fiscal policies by purchasing the debt instruments of the local government when other lenders were unwilling to hold the debt.

PRIVATE PENSION FUNDS

Private funds represent the bulk of pension fund assets to be managed, though they do not provide coverage to as many people as does the Social Security System. Private plans can be further divided into the following categories:

Insurance company sponsored plans

Non-insurance company plans

Single company plans

Multi-company plans

Life insurance-related plans are normally used by small firms as these firms have found the costs of managing their own plans to be excessive. The plan sponsored by a life insurance company has the advantage, particularly for the small fund, of being guaranteed by the life insurance company itself and not merely by the assets of the particular fund. The most common life insurance arrangement is the "group deferred annuity." With this plan, a paid-up annuity[2] is purchased for each employee each month and the policies are held by a trustee (usually a bank or trust company). The employee is protected by the pension plan and the plan requires minimal management time on the part of the company. Assets of life insurance related funds are approximately one-third of all private pension plan assets. Approximately 17 million people are covered by such plans.

The non-life insurance funds represent $200 billion of assets, including both single company and multi-company funds. Contributions to private plans are made by employers (or employers and employees) with the contribution typically being made to a fund administered by a bank or trust company. Because these plans are designed to be fully funded, their assets are quite extensive. The trustee invests the funds and makes

---

[2] An annuity is a simple promise to pay a specific amount per month for life, beginning at a particular age. A paid-up annuity requires no further payments on the part of the recipient. As an example, suppose a company buys a $1 paid up annuity for each employee each month. An employee who works 40 years before retirement will receive $480 per month at retirement.

payments to the retirees in accordance with the provisions of the plan. Some large companies have their own investment staffs that handle the investment of the fund directly. The amount of contribution and the investment policy are directed by legislation as well as company policy and possible agreements between employer and union. Because funds are invested in relatively safe assets, employees can expect to receive their pensions even if the company should fail. Like life insurance-sponsored plans, these plans cannot make commitments unless they can be justified by actuarial experience and the value of the assets on hand.

Multi-company plans normally arise from union contracts, although there are exceptions such as the Teacher's Insurance and Annuity Association, started by the Carnegie Foundation to provide a multi-employer pension plan for teachers. Multi-company plans are particularly popular in industries where employees tend to continue in the industry for long periods of time, but change employers frequently. The multi-company plan provides job mobility—a desirable feature from an economic efficiency viewpoint—without jeopardizing pension protection. Industries with multi-employer plans include construction, motor transportation, trade (wholesale and retail) and some service industries. With a multi-employer plan, contributions are made to a pension fund managed by a board of trustees. The board may be made up of representatives of both management and labor.

Unfortunately, several major multi-company pension funds have been racked with scandal resulting from misappropriation of funds to the benefit of trustees. A number of prison sentences have been imposed for improper use of funds. Despite some problems and the necessity for continuous supervision, these funds provide needed pension protection in mobile professions.

Keogh plans are a special arrangement allowed to individuals who are self-employed or are not covered by a pension plan at their place of employment. An individual is allowed to deduct from his or her taxable income contributions to a private pension plan in amounts up to 15 percent of earned income (up to a limit of $1,500 for an employee and $7,500 for a self-employed person). Funds may be placed with a bank or thrift institution, a life insurance company, a mutual fund, or in certain government bonds.

REGULATION OF PENSION FUNDS

Most pension fund regulation now in effect traces from the 1974 Employee Retirement Income Security Act (ERISA). The objectives of the act were the encouragement of increased pension benefits and protection of benefits. The act does not require employers to have pension plans, but sets standards for plans that do exist. The act covers seven major areas:

1. Who must be covered by pension plans.

2. Status of accrued benefits when an employee leaves an employer (vesting).

3. The pension rights of an employee's spouse.

4. The amount of assets that must be accumulated to vest projected pension benefits (funding).

5. Standards of conduct and responsibility for pension fund managers (fiduciary responsibility).

6. Plan termination insurance to protect employees in the event a cancelled plan has insufficient assets to meet its commitments.

7. Reporting and disclosure requirements.

Who must be covered A very important feature of the coverage aspect of the legislation is that it does not require employers to have pension plans. It also does not require that existing plans be continued. It only requires that any plan that does exist meet certain standards. Basically, a plan must cover any full-time employee who has worked for the company one year and is 25 or older.[3] While issues such as the definition of "full time" are sufficient to keep a battery of attorneys employed, they need not concern the reader interested in the general principles guiding pension fund management.

Vesting An employee is vested on the day his or her right to pension benefits becomes certain. Before ERISA, there were cases of companies discharging employees in their early sixties to negate 40 years of accumulated pension benefits. Under present legislation, there are several allowed vesting plans. The simplest is complete vesting of all employees no later than ten years after beginning employment with the particular employer. Other plans are permitted to include age as a factor when setting the time vesting must occur or be phased in, starting no later than the fifth year of employment.

Vesting does not guarantee benefits at retirement equal to what would have been earned if the employee had stayed with the company. Most pension plans base benefits on years of employment and income. The vested employee receives benefits based on the amount of service up to departure from the employer. For the employer who receives vested rights in the form of a cash settlement when leaving the employer, the law allows the employee to defer tax on the payment if it is reinvested in an individual retirement annuity or invested in the new employer's plan.

Spouse rights An employee covered by a pension plan must be given the option of providing that pension benefits be paid to his (her) spouse if the spouse lives longer than the employee. Of course, choosing this option results in smaller benefits; the amount of adjustment is determined by the relative ages of the two people and other actuarial factors.

Funding Private pension funds are required to maintain assets equal to the present value of future benefits. This requirement is designed to assure that benefits will be paid as provided. Unfunded plans simply pay current benefits from current operating revenues. If the company sponsoring an unfunded plan ceased operation, employees and retirees would simply lose their benefits. Thus ERISA required that all plans be funded. Pension plans are given 30 years to amortize obligations for past services and become fully funded. Because determining the amount of funds needed and the best method for achieving funding are major management problems, these topics will be considered in a separate section.

Fiduciary responsibility This refers to the standards that must be followed in managing pension fund assets. A fiduciary is a trustee, investment adviser, or other person who has the authority to make decisions with regard to investment of the fund's assets. First, fiduciary responsibility standards prohibit transactions that would involve a conflict of interest. A fiduciary cannot invest the funds for any purpose other than the benefit of those covered by the plan. Specifically, transactions from which the trustee may personally gain are prohibited.

The second aspect of fiduciary responsibility is the "prudent man" rule. The fiduciary is required by the law to act "with care, skill, prudence, and diligence under the circumstances then prevailing that a prudent man acting in a like capacity and familiar with such matters would use. . . ." Managing the investment portfolio in consideration of this rule and other objectives is another major aspect of pension fund management and will be discussed as a separate section.

---

[3] If a plan provides immediate vesting, it can require three years of employment before eligibility.

Plan cancellation insurance ERISA called for the creation of the Pension Benefit Guarantee Corporation (PBGC) to protect pension fund beneficiaries in the event a plan was terminated and its assets were not sufficient to meet its future obligations. The PBGC was modeled after the Federal Deposit Insurance Corporation, which guarantees bank deposits. The employer is responsible for unfunded liabilities at plan termination time up to a limit of 30 percent of net worth, with the PBGC making up the difference.

The law also called for Contingent Employer Liability Insurance (CELI) to which employers could subscribe, protecting them from the liability not covered by the PBGC. Unfortunately, the risks turned out to be non-insurable because unfunded liabilities rise and fall with changes in overall security values. Thus no private insurers could absorb the risk. The PBGC, as a government corporation, has been working on a CELI plan, but progress has been slow and no plan is yet in existence. The plan that is finally introduced is likely to be quite limited in scope.

Reporting and disclosure requirements Disclosure regulations, like other aspects of ERISA, arose from prior abuses. Employees were often surprised to find that after 30 years of employment, they had no vested interest when a plan was terminated or they were dismissed; they had built their retirement security upon a false assumption about their pension coverage. Additionally, the lack of oversight to assure that fiduciary standards were being met resulted in millions of dollars in benefits being lost. The present reporting requirements set standards for reports to both the government and covered employees. Plans must now submit to the Secretary of Labor each year an audited financial report similar in detail to the reports companies issue to their shareholders. Employees must be given a description of the plan, written in language that the aver-

age person can understand. The employee must be given a new copy of the description every ten years if no changes have occurred and every five years if changes have occurred.[4]

The reporting requirements have been frequently criticized. The cost and time required for an annual audit has been blamed for the cancellation of many plans. In response, plans with fewer than 100 participants have been exempted from a large portion of the reporting requirements and plans with individual benefits fully guaranteed by an insurance company have been exempted from the auditing requirement. Reporting requirements continue to be an area of debate, with several changes having occurred and more likely to occur.

MANAGEMENT POLICY

Pension fund assets have become large relative to total corporate assets and pension fund expenses have become a substantial portion of total labor expense. Additionally, many people depend on pension plans as an important employee benefit and source of retirement security. From the point of view of both employees and the company, proper management decisions are important. In this section, we discuss the four major areas of management policy:

1. Benefits to be received
2. Vesting procedures
3. Funding of liabilities
4. Investment policy for the fund portfolio

BENEFITS

Interestingly, government regulation has much less to say about the benefit formula than other aspects of the pension plan. This

---

[4] Of course, participants must also be notified of any changes as they occur.

is partly explained in terms of the types of problems prompting ERISA. Failure to receive expected benefits was the major problem addressed. In addition, full disclosure and assurance of ability to meet commitments has been the thrust of most financial regulation.

Since there is considerable freedom in establishing a benefit formula, this provides a rich area for gains through proper decision making by management. Most pension plans are tied to years of service and there is an increasing trend toward tying the plan to income levels as well. The exceptions to income relationship normally occur in plans negotiated with unions where income levels do not vary greatly. Where benefits are tied to income, there is the additional question of whether it should be tied to average income for all years of employment or only the few years immediately preceding retirement. Additional problems involve integrating with social security and dealing with inflation.

To begin, there is the basic question of what amount of income a retiree needs. Many experts feel that a retired person needs income, including social security, of 60 percent to 70 percent of pre-retirement income to maintain the pre-retirement standard of living. Savings come from decreased taxes and elimination of the expenses associated with going to work. Higher income employees need a lower replacement ratio as they consume a smaller portion of their take-home pay and will recognize greater tax savings in retirement.

While needs do not necessarily depend on years of employment, most benefit programs are based on income and length of service. After all, wages themselves are based on service rather than need. Programs are normally designed to provide a "satisfactory" level of retirement income to an employee who has spent a large number of years with the employer or covered by the multi-employer plan.

A major problem in benefit plan development is the question of how to integrate the plan with social security. A company sponsoring a plan will reasonably view its contributions to the pension fund and to social security as a package of retirement benefits. Companies that started pension plans years ago with no effort to integrate them with social security have found their total pension costs rising sharply as social security benefits and taxes have increased. In some cases, the situation has reached the point where employees can increase their after-tax income by retiring. Thus the need to integrate pension benefits with social security is widely recognized. There are three approaches to integration: the excess approach, the offset approach, and the cap approach.

The excess approach ties pension benefits to the social security contributions made by the employer. Social security taxes are based on income up to a certain level, referred to as the base. A typical excess formula for annual pension income is

$$P = .01I_1 + .02I_2$$

where: P = Annual pension benefit

I_1 = Total income earned during employment to which social security tax was applied

I_2 = Total income during employment to which social security tax did not apply (income above the base)

The formula might be modified to consider average income for the last few years of employment multiplied by years of employment instead of actual total income. When the pension is based on income for the last few years, it is also common practice to redefine I_1 and I_2 in terms of income above and below the base during the last few years of employment. Regardless of the precise formula used, the objective of the excess approach is to integrate employer pension fund and social security expenses.

The offset approach is designed to integrate employee social security income and pension income. A typical offset formula would be

$$P = .04I - S$$

where: I = Total income during employment

S = Annual social security benefits

Modifications would involve using average income for recent years or only subtracting some percentage of social security benefits.

On first glance, an offset approach might seem more fair to the employee in that it focuses on achieving a total employee income goal rather than a total company expense goal. However, an offset approach results in serious distortions during a period of rapid inflation. Social security benefits are tied to the cost of living, thereby providing at least some protection from inflation. The offset approach eliminates this protection by decreasing the company pension by an amount equal to any increase in social security cost of living adjustment. At present inflation rates, the offset approach would move a pension plan participant from a comfortable level of income to poverty within a normal post-retirement life span. Thus the offset method appears to be unsuccessful in either assuring retirement income or integrating company costs.[5]

The cap approach is a modification of the offset approach. A typical cap formula would be

$$P = .02I \text{ or } (.8I/n) - S, \text{ whichever is less}$$

where: n = Number of years of employment

Again, income for recent years might be used in place of total income. This approach effectively establishes a cap on total benefits, becoming an offset approach when combined benefits would otherwise exceed some percentage of pre-retirement income.

As with the regular offset approach, the cap approach leads to serious distortions during inflationary periods. If the cap is at 80 percent of pre-retirement income and the consumer price index triples during a participant's retirement years, the total benefit ceiling, in real dollars, would fall to approximately *one-fourth* of pre-retirement income. Under present social security practices, this would mean a complete halt in pension income. Like the offset approach, the cap approach fails to integrate company expenses or provide retirement income security.

Inflation is, of course, the problem that makes the development of a sound benefit formula so difficult. Failure to include an inflation adjustment provision in the benefit formula leaves the employee exposed to the risk of having retirement income badly eroded by inflation. However, it is very difficult for a pension plan to provide inflation protection. If a company knew that the plan would continue indefinitely and the ratio of workers to retirees would remain stable, pension benefits could be tied to salary and paid on an on-going basis, as is done with social security. However, pension plans must be funded on the assumption there will be no new employees and existing commitments must be paid from an investment portfolio. There is no sound actuarial basis for determining the amount of expected inflation to use in computing future benefits and present fund contribution needs. In addition, there is a dearth of investments whose value will grow at the inflation rate. Therefore, adequate inflation protection is very difficult to provide.

A number of approaches have been used to attempt to offset the effect of inflation. One of these is the variable annuity approach under which pension income depends on returns earned on the pension plan

---

[5] For an argument in favor of the offset method, see Lloyd S. Kaye, "The Pension Benefit Formula: An Element in Financial Planning," *Financial Executive*, July, 1978, pp. 24–30.

investment portfolio. Unfortunately, portfolio returns have tended to be low during periods of high inflation, compounding the retiree's problems. The use of an excess rather than an offset approach helps to decrease the bite of inflation somewhat and still produces a predictable cost structure. Basing retirement income on income the last few years before retirement rather than overall years of employment serves to provide protection against inflation occurring before retirement. Finally, some pension plans simply promise to adjust pension benefits for inflation. However, it is not clear what resources they would have with which to meet such promises in the face of high rates of inflation, low investment portfolio returns, and a declining ratio of working participants to retired participants.

Development of a benefit formula is much more than a question of how much should be spent on pension benefits. It involves questions of who should receive the greatest share, how other sources of retirement income should be considered, and how to deal with inflation. The development of a rational benefit plan—one that is equitable and safe for both the company and the employee—is the first, and possibly the most important decision, facing the pension fund manager.

CHOICE OF VESTING PLANS

The choice of a vesting plan involves the desire to control costs, the desire to retain qualified employees, and the desire to provide an equitable program. The cost of a pension plan and the benefits that the employer can afford to provide are affected by the vesting arrangement chosen. Within a given dollar cost constraint, the employer can choose between more generous benefits or more generous vesting. ERISA sets the minimum standards that must be met, with some plans providing vesting in excess of the minimum. The plan must meet one of three minimum standards:

1. Total vesting after ten years on the job.
2. Vesting of 25 percent of accrued rights after five years of employment, with vesting being increased by 5 percent each year for the next five years, then 10 percent each year for the following five years.
3. Vesting of 50 percent of accrued rights after age plus service equal 45, or after five years of service, whichever comes later. The 50 percent vesting must occur after ten years of employment even if age plus employment are still less than 45. After vesting begins, it is then increased 10 percent each year for five years to achieve 100 percent vesting.

Table 12–1 illustrates the effect of vesting plan choice on the rate at which vesting is achieved. An employer wishing to minimize cost should choose the plan that would pro-

Table 12-1:

Percentage Vesting Under Alternative Formulas

Years of Employment	4	5	6	7	8	9	10	11	12	13	14	15
10-year full vesting							100	100	100	100	100	100
Phased-in vesting		25	30	35	40	45	50	60	70	80	90	100
Age/Employment												
Hired at 21							50	60	70	80	90	100
Hired at 31				50	60	70	80	90	100			
Hired at 41		50	60	70	80	90	100					

duce the lowest level of vesting for his particular group of employees. As Table 12–1 shows, the age-plus-service formula provides the slowest vesting for young employees and the fastest vesting for older employees. The relative costs of the ten-year and phased-vesting plans would depend on turnover patterns within the particular company or industry, though phased vesting would seem to be more equitable.

We can see from Table 12–1 that the choice of minimum vesting standard does not matter for the employee who leaves before the fifth or after the fifteenth year. However, it is important for the employee leaving between the fifth and fifteenth year. The benefit impacts of the various vesting choices are illustrated below for a worker beginning employment at age 21. The law allows pension funds to exclude income earned before age 25 and during the first year of employment in computing benefits, though time for vesting of benefits begins with the date of actual employment. The company's formula for annual pension benefits is

$$P = V \times .02 \times I$$

where: P = Annual pension benefit, beginning at age 65

V = Vesting percentage from Table 12–1

I = Total income earned after 25th birthday

If the employee leaves at age 27, after six years of employment at a salary of $1,000 per month, cumulative eligible income (I) is $24,000. From Table 12–1, we see that the vested percentage is .30 after six years, using phased-in vesting, and 0 otherwise. Thus, with phased-in vesting, the employee who starts at age 21, earns $1,000 per month, and leaves after six years, will be eligible for an annual pension at age 65 of

$$P = .30 \times .02 \times \$24,000 = \$144$$

Vested pension entitlements for this employee under various minimum vesting standards are summarized in Table 12–2.

Since funding must equal the present value of vested benefits, the cost of the employee's service is clearly affected by the benefit vesting plan chosen. Suppose the company were to choose a more generous program such as complete immediate vesting. At the end of six years, the vested annual benefit for the employee used in the previous example would be

$$P = 1.0 \times .02 \times \$72,000 = \$1,440$$

Thus the vested annual benefit for the employee could be between $0 and $1,440 using the same basic benefit computation but varying eligibility and vesting rules. Cost differences could be increased many-fold by changing vesting provisions for a plan with high turnover in the early years.

Choosing the right combination of benefits, eligibility, and vesting is indeed difficult. First, it is necessary to ascertain the preferences of employees; within a total pension benefit budget, what combination of

Table 12-2:

Illustrative Vested Monthly Benefit Payments Under Alternative Formulas (in dollars)

Years of Employment	4	5	6	7	8	9	10	11	12	13	14	15
10-year vesting							120	140	160	180	200	220
Phased-in vesting		5	12	21	32	45	60	84	112	144	180	220
Age/Employment							60	84	112	144	180	220

benefits, eligibility, and vesting would they prefer. Second, it is necessary to carefully estimate cost impacts of all alternatives, based on estimates of employee income and turnover. Third, it is necessary to consider questions of equity. Fourth, it is necessary to consider risk; a plan involving high benefits offset by slow vesting could be disastrous if turnover declined sharply. Finally, it is necessary to develop the plan within the constraints of the requirements of ERISA.

Types of vesting continue to vary substantially from plan to plan, with some plans offering complete vesting after three years. However, complete immediate vesting is rare and the trend appears to be toward ten-year vesting, a method that delays vesting about as long as is allowed. Ten-year vesting also has the advantage of being easy for employees to understand.

FUNDING OF LIABILITIES

A problem of more concern to pension fund sponsors than managers, but worthy of a brief discussion, is that of the funding of pension obligations. Basically, ERISA requires that pension funds hold assets equal in value to the present value of all future benefits earned to date. Contributions must be sufficient to meet current obligations and amortize past obligations over a 30-year period for a single employer plan and 40 years for a multi-employer plan. In theory, most plans would gradually become fully funded.

Several problems have arisen in the funding area. First, contractual changes in benefit formulas and actuarial assumptions have created new unfunded liabilities. Second, the falling prices of securities have reduced the level of funding. Third, there are various questions as to the definition of an unfunded liability. While ERISA provides for insurance to protect beneficiaries from losses due to insufficient funding, companies are at least partially liable for the unfunded liabilities in the case of plan termination and must make contributions sufficient to amortize the unfunded liabilities as discussed above.

Among other problems, credit ratings are adversely affected by unfunded liabilities.[6]

The assets needed to meet funding requirements depend on actuarial assumptions about employee turnover and beneficiary life span. Fortunately, actuaries have excellent life span data and reasonably good turnover data to work with. Unfortunately, the same cannot be said for salary growth and investment return assumptions. A recent survey revealed that the median salary growth assumption was 5 percent and the median investment return assumption was 6 percent.[7] With salary growth being substantially greater than investment return in recent years, contribution formulas have proved inadequate, creating a stream of new unfunded liabilities.

Without getting into complex details, we should take a brief look at the problem of defining unfunded liabilities. If we hire an employee and ignore, for simplicity of illustration, the possibility of his leaving employment before retirement, we can compute the present value of eventual benefits using appropriate actuarial assumptions. At any given time, some of the amount needed will be on hand with the rest to be accumulated from future contributions. Thus, the present value of projected benefits is divided between assets on hand and present value of future contributions. Most of, a small percentage of, or none of the present value of future contributions may appear as an unfunded liability,[8] depending on accounting method selected. While we are certain, given our actuarial assumptions, what the present value of future needed contributions is, the accounting conventions give wide latitude in choosing what portion of this

[6] Patrick J. Regan, "Credit Ratings and Pension Costs," *Financial Analysts Journal,* March/April, 1979, pp. 6–7.

[7] *Pension and Investments,* January 2, 1978.

[8] Paul A. Gerwitz and Robert C. Phillips, "Unfunded Pension Liabilities . . . The New Myth," *Financial Executive,* August, 1978, pp. 18–24.

present value should be assigned to unfunded liabilities and what portion should be considered "present value of future normal pension costs." While it is generally agreed that not all of the present value of future benefits should be considered a present liability—since much of it is dependent on assumed future employee income—there is substantial room for disagreement.

While the problem of defining unfunded liabilities remains troublesome, it is clear that by most definitions unfunded liabilities have increased rather than decreased. The increases—resulting from changing benefit formulas, poor portfolio performance, and inflation induced wage increases—present a difficult problem. These liabilities decrease value in mergers, decrease cash flow available for reinvestment, and create a potential national problem in the event of a major economic downturn. Methods of dealing with these problems have proven to be elusive.

MANAGING THE PENSION FUND PORTFOLIO

The classic risk/return trade-offs of finance are most clearly seen in the area of portfolio management. A high return on the portfolio can serve to lower pension fund expense to the company and/or increase employee pension benefits. Unfortunately, increased expected return is normally achieved only by accepting increased risk, as was discussed in Chapter 6. If risks are taken and the fund suffers losses, increased contributions are required or pensions are jeopardized. The fund must be guided by a portfolio management policy that gives adequate operational guidelines with regard to risk and return.

In establishing policy, the first thing that must be decided is who will have primary management responsibility. Where the pension plan is negotiated with a union, there is frequently a board of trustees consisting of members from both management and labor. In the case of some large funds, the sponsoring company decides to manage the funds directly, paying investment advisers to provide recommendations and banks to provide custodial services. However, most companies assign funds to a trustee, either providing general policy statements or leaving the trustees to develop their own policies. The division of funds among several trustees is common practice, with funds being periodically reallocated among trustees according to their past performance. When several trustees are used, each may be given different guidelines. For example, an insurance company may be given funds to invest in real estate while a brokerage firm is given funds to invest in common stock.

Parties serving as trustees include banks, insurance companies, brokerage firms, and investment counselors such as those who manage mutual funds. Banks, the institutions that traditionally dominated this area, have experienced increasing competition from these other groups. Services are heavily marketed and competition to achieve the best performance is intense, sometimes leading to concerns about unsound investment policy.

Factors to consider in the choice of trustees include

Investment skill

Costs

Administrative skill

Size and financial strength[9]

In addition to the obvious need to invest profitably and prudently for a reasonable fee, the trustee has complex record keeping responsibilities. Failure to keep proper records and maintain proper administrative controls led to multi-million dollar losses of securities in the late 1960s and early 1970s.[10]

---

[9] Patrick J. Davey, *Financial Management of Pension Plans,* New York: The Conference Board, p. 46.

[10] For an interesting discussion of these problems, see John Brooks, *The Go-Go Years,* New York: Weybright and Talley, 1973, pp. 182–205.

Finally, the standards of fiduciary responsibility cannot be effectively enforced unless the trustee has the size and financial strength to provide at least some backing to commitments made.

Regardless of who accepts responsibility for managing the portfolio, a management policy must be developed. The policy typically specifies, among other things

Types of investments

Risk levels

Performance objectives

Restrictions on investment in sponsoring company's securities.

Modern mean-variance portfolio theory provides a logical starting point for the development of management policy. For these purposes, there are two primary lessons from portfolio theory:

1. Risk should be viewed in the context of a portfolio rather than for each security separately.

2. Higher expected return is normally associated with greater risk.

The portfolio approach to risk is based on the observation that some risks can be diversified away—effectively eliminated—when risky securities are combined in portfolios. For example, the risk that one automobile design will be favored over others can be diversified away by owning stocks in all automobile companies. However, even a well diversified portfolio will move up and down in value with market conditions in general. Thus risk associated with market conditions in general cannot be eliminated through diversification. Portfolio theory argues that rational people will eliminate diversifiable risk by constructing portfolios consisting of a number of different investments. Opinion varies on the number of securities necessary to construct a well diversified portfolio, but most writers agree that no more than 30 securities are required.

A closely related body of literature argues that markets are *efficient,* meaning that no investor has superior information or superior ability to evaluate information. Thus, the *efficient market hypothesis* argues that the investor cannot expect higher returns except through the acceptance of greater risk.

The implications of the above analysis for pension fund portfolio management are quite significant. First, the portfolio should not contain diversifiable risk since there is no reward for such risk. Thirty is probably a sufficient number of securities to achieve this objective unless the 30 are concentrated in certain industries.

We might also consider the point of view in determining risk. To the extent benefits are not insured, risk should be examined from the point of view of the beneficiary. For example, a concentration in real estate would not provide reasonable diversification if most beneficiaries had real estate investments in the form of their homes and did not own other assets. Heavy investment in the sponsoring company would not be wise, as income risk to the employees is already tied to the well-being of the company.

Finally, plans and objectives must consider the risk-return trade-off and should not be based on the assumption that the fund manager can regularly achieve superior results without accepting greater than average risk. Stating return objectives without reference to risk may simply lead to greater risk being accepted in keeping with the risk-return trade-off.

This problem has sometimes been handled in the pension fund area by specifying a weighted average beta[11] level and specifying that the portfolio be well diversified, then attempting to maximize return within these constraints.

ERISA creates a set of standards that must be considered in applying the principles of portfolio theory. Of particular interest are

---

[11] Recall that beta measures the sensitivity of returns for a security of portfolio to returns for securities in general.

ERISA's standards of fiduciary responsibility:

1. The fiduciary must act only for the purpose of providing benefits to the fund's participants and defraying reasonable costs.

2. The fiduciary must act "with the care, skill, prudence, and diligence under the circumstances then prevailing that a prudent man acting in a like capacity and familiar with such matters would use in the conduct of an enterprise of a like character with like aims."

3. The fiduciary must diversify the portfolio to minimize the risk of large losses.

4. The fiduciary must comply with the plan's documents if they are consistent with ERISA.

The prohibition on conflict of interest, requirement that plan documents be followed, and the instruction to diversify cause little difficulty. In fact, portfolio theory tells us something about how to achieve diversification. Unfortunately, the prudent man rule, as presently interpreted, causes some confusion. In its earlier history at common law, the prudent man rule was interpreted as prohibiting equity investments of any type. However, the application has changed over the years and the concept of investment vs. speculative securities has developed. A frequent interpretation is that only the stocks of very safe, well established companies can be included in a portfolio.

While common stock is recognized as a reasonable investment medium, the full benefits of diversification are not recognized. The trustee may be held accountable for each investment individually. Thus the portfolio manager who achieves a normal risk level by holding a few high-risk stocks offset by a large group of low-risk stocks might have problems if one of the high-risk stocks does poorly, even if the portfolio as a whole does well.[12] The portfolio manager would be free of liability if he invested entirely in conservative, well-established companies and the portfolio performed poorly. Portfolio theory suggests that portfolio risk should be the appropriate risk guideline, but the prudent man rule does not adequately differentiate between diversifiable and nondiversifiable risk.[13]

Under ERISA, there has been an attempt to re-interpret the prudent man rule in light of portfolio theory. Unfortunately, it takes years for an adequate base of case law to be built and portfolio managers cannot wait to act. As a practical matter, they frequently limit equity investments to a narrow list of well established companies held by numerous other institutional portfolios. Table 12–3 contains a list of some of the companies whose equities were "institutional favorites" in December, 1979. Investing in such "favorites" provides excellent protection from liability under the prudent man rule. However, the practice results in a two-tier market consisting of a small group of stocks favored by the institutions and the rest of the market, largely ignored by institutions.

One problem with limiting all investment to a list of older, stable companies is that it may not provide complete diversification. Diversification does not come entirely from large numbers of securities. Holding stock of all steel comppanies would clearly leave the portfolio undiversified with regard to factors affecting the steel business. Likewise, the holding of only old, stable companies and the complete exclusion of innovative newer companies leaves portfolios exposed to risks unique to established companies and may limit returns by excluding highly profitable opportunities.

---

[12] Because ERISA is fairly new, this guideline has not been tested well through case law.

[13] For an excellent discussion of this problem, see Roger D. Blair, "ERISA and the Prudent Man Rule: Avoiding Perverse Results," *Sloan Management Review,* Winter, 1979, pp. 15–23.

Table 12-3:

Stocks Currently Favored by Institutional Portfolios

Company name	Number of institutions holding*
American Home Products	488
American Telephone and Telegraph	903
Atlantic Richfield	619
Caterpillar Tractor	461
Citicorp	450
CocaCola	415
Conoco Corporation	405
Dow Chemical	484
duPont	421
Eastman Kodak	739
Exxon Corporation	868
Ford	401
General Motors	689
General Telephone and Electric	433
Gulf Oil Company	417
Halliburton Co.	446
International Business Machines	1246
K-Mart	466
Merck and Company	554
Minnesota Mining and Manufacturing	524
Mobil Corporation	530
Phillips Petroleum	482
Procter and Gamble	425
Schlumberger, Ltd.	510
Sears, Roebuck and Company	510
Standard Oil of California	488
Standard Oil of Indiana	511
Texaco Corporation	599
Union Carbide	419
Xerox Corporation	635

*Standard and Poors Stock Guide, December, 1979. While the data are based on a survey of 2400 institutions, excluding pension funds, it is believed that pension funds do not differ from the other institutions with regard to which particular stocks are favored at a given time.

From society's viewpoint, the use of a list of institutional favorites has important implications for resource allocation. With the growing importance of pension funds and other institutional portfolios, the favored companies have ready access to new capital while other companies are virtually shut off from the capital markets. Specifically, the innovative new companies that traditionally provide a major source of economic growth have had their access to the capital markets severely restricted.

As the above discussion shows, the prudent man rule sets requirements that would be considered unnecessary and even harmful from the perspective of portfolio theory. Because case law is an evolutionary type of law, we can expect that portfolio risk will come to be fully recognized.

In addition to portfolio theory and fiduciary responsibility, the pension fund manager can also expect certain standards to be set by the sponsoring company. The following is a typical example of a performance objective.

> The portfolio should earn an average return over a five year period of at least 20% greater than the S & P 500 stock index and at least 10% per annum.

A beta range may also be specified, though this is less common.

Performance standards of the type illustrated are particularly difficult to meet in light of what we know about portfolio theory, efficient market theory, and fiduciary responsibility. If everyone is to purchase securities from the same restricted list, everyone has the same information, and nobody has superior ability to analyze available data, earning a superior return is going to be a most difficult project. In fact, the theory would tell us that higher return can be earned only through the acceptance of higher risk. There is no evidence that objectives of the type illustrated are attainable. Moving funds from portfolio manager to portfolio manager in search of "superior" performance is likely to be unproductive.

The considerations discussed above have led to some degree of consensus as to what should be included in a pension fund portfolio. Table 12–4 shows the mix of pension fund portfolio assets as it has developed over the years. From a time when equity was almost entirely excluded from trusteed portfolios, thought on the subject evolved to the point that by the end of the 1960s—a decade in which stock prices rose sharply—common stock became the dominant asset. The poor stock market returns of the 1970s caused a further rethinking, with a growing interest in the asset that performed well in the 1970s: real estate.[14] The consensus as to what a "prudent man" would invest in continues to evolve with changing market conditions.

Portfolio Performance Measurement Both for purposes of analyzing past performance and for projecting future returns, performance measures must be developed. First it is necessary to compute an annualized rate of return. This problem is made a bit difficult by the fact that funds are added and deducted periodically. It is necessary to separate performance of the portfolio from the impact of additions and withdrawals of funds. The problem is illustrated below for two pension funds over a two year period.

	Fund A	Fund B
Starting market value	$1,000	$1,000
Cash contributed at the start of the first year	1,000	0
First year return	80%	80%
Cash contributed at the start of the second year	0	1,000
Second year return	10%	10%
Ending value	$3,960	$3,080

Each fund started with $1,000 and received $1,000 in additional contributions over the two-year period. Can we conclude that fund A was better managed because the terminal value was higher? More careful examination shows that return earned by each fund was

[14] Elbert Bressie, "When Will Pension Funds Enter the Real Estate Market?" *Financial Executive*, April, 1979, pp. 26–29.

Table 12-4:

Assets of Private Noninsured Pension Funds At Market Value
(millions of dollars)

	1955	1960	1965	1970	1972	1974	1976	1978	1979
Cash and Deposits	415	546	940	1,804	1,857	4,286	2,199	8,110	8,609
U.S. Gov. Securities	2,938	2,655	2,913	2,998	3,700	5,582	14,918	18,767	21,516
Corporate & Other Bonds	7,702	14,629	21,949	24,919	26,232	30,825	37,858	48,633	51,261
Preferred Stock	624	718	768	1,631	1,869	703	1,212	1,162	1,099
Common Stock	5,461	15,827	39,986	65,456	113,369	62,582	108,483	106,732	122,703
Mortgages	321	1,034	3,391	3,504	2,427	2,063	2,160	2,554	2,664
Other Assets	592	1,398	2,950	4,422	4,908	5,681	7,073	15,585	17,336
Total Assets	18,053	37,077	72,898	104,737	154,363	111,724	173,906	201,545	225,188
Common Stock as a Percent of Total Assets	30%	43%	55%	62%	73%	56%	62%	53%	55%

Source: Security and Exchange Commission, *Annual Report 1979* and *Statistical Bulletin*, May, 1980.

identical for each year. The higher ending value for A was a result of the timing of contributions from sponsors, not differences in performance by portfolio managers.

The *geometric mean return* (time weighted rate of return)[15] is a method used to put returns on a comparable basis. The geometric mean return for a portfolio is computed using the following formula:

(12–1)

$$G = \sqrt[n]{(1+r_1)(1+r_2)...(1+r_n)} - 1$$

where: G = Geometric mean or time weighted rate of return

r_i = Return (price appreciation and dividends) during period i

n = Total number of periods over which evaluation is to occur

For the portfolios illustrated above, the geometric mean return is

$$G = \sqrt[2]{(1+.8)(1+.1)} - 1 = \underline{40.7\%}$$

The geometric mean return, not being affected by the timing of contributions, is the same for each portfolio. Thus it measures the performance of the portfolio manager, not the effects of contribution and withdrawal timing.

While the geometric mean return is a useful method of evaluating returns, it does not include any method of recognizing differences in risk accepted. Based on portfolio theory, a widely used risk adjustment measure is the reward to variability ratio:

$$\frac{R_p - R_f}{\sigma_p}$$ (12–2)

where: R_p = Average return for the portfolio over the periods for which performance is being evaluated

---

[15] In financial analysis, the geometric mean of a series of annual returns over time is viewed as the annual compound rate of growth inherent in the series of returns.

R_f = Average return on risk-free investments over the same period

σ_p = Standard deviation of returns for the portfolio over this period

For one portfolio to outperform another, it should have a higher ratio as defined in equation 12–2.

SUMMARY

Pension fund management involves three sets of trade-offs and one set of contradictions. The first trade-off involves the desire to provide maximum benefits at a minimum cost. The second trade-off involves the desire to provide maximum benefits to individuals and the desire to provide coverage to as many people as possible. Within a particular total cost limit, various combinations of vesting, participation rights, and benefit formulas are possible. The choice involves legal constraints of ERISA, employee desires, union labor contract provisions, and management judgment. The third trade-off is the classic risk-return trade-off faced in virtually all portfolio management problems. Higher returns lower cost and allow improved benefits, but involve greater risk of loss. Most pension funds are managed quite conservatively with regard to risk. Finally, there is a conflict between portfolio risk as recognized by modern portfolio theory and individual security risk as defined through the prudent man rule. Pension fund management consists of developing both benefit and portfolio management policy in line with these off-setting and contradictory considerations.

QUESTIONS

1. Why have pension fund assets grown so rapidly since the passage of ERISA?

2. Do you feel it is appropriate for the

federal government to sponsor unfunded pension plans? Why? Do you feel it is appropriate for state and local governments to sponsor unfunded pension plans? Why?

3. While pension funds together own enough stock to exercise effective voting control over many major U.S. corporations, they have not done so. What reasons can you think of for their failure to attempt to exercise control?

4. What groups of people are *not* protected by ERISA?

5. What factors should be considered in developing a vesting formula?

6. Should a pension fund sponsor give the fiduciary standards such as "outperform the stock market average by at least 2%"? Why?

7. It has been claimed that the prudent man rule "discourages true diversification." Comment on this claim.

PROBLEMS

1. An employee retires after working 20 years and earning total wages of $200,000, with social security being paid on half of this amount. After retirement, the employee will receive $4,000 a year in social security payments. Inflation is expected to average 10 percent per year. How much pension benefit will the employee receive in the first and tenth year under

  a. the excess approach, with annual benefits equal to 1 percent of total income on which social security was paid and 2 percent of total income on which social security was not paid?

  b. the offset approach, with annual pension benefits equal to 4 percent of total income minus social security benefits?

  c. the cap approach, with annual benefits equal to 2 percent of total income or

$$\frac{.8 \times \text{total income}}{\text{number of years employed}} - \text{social security benefits},$$

whichever is less?

2. You begin to work for a company at age 20. Thereafter, you change jobs every ten years, just prior to completing your tenth year of employment, until you retire just before reaching age 70. Assuming your income did not change, you would be vested for what percent of total benefits from all employers using:

  a. ten-year full vesting?

  b. phased-in vesting?

3. A pension fund portfolio received $100,000 from the sponsor at the beginning of the first year. Through investment return, this amount grows to $120,000 by the end of the first year. It then receives an additional contribution of $30,000 from the sponsor, bringing the total value up to $150,000. Through investment return, the value grows to $160,000 by the end of the second year. What is the geometric mean return?

SELECTED REFERENCES

Blair, Roger D., "ERISA and the Prudent Man Rule: Avoiding Perverse Results," *Sloan Management Review,* Vol. 20, No. 2 (Winter, 1979), pp. 15–23.

Bressie, Elbert, "When Will Pension Funds Enter the Real Estate Market?" *Financial Executive,* April, 1979, pp. 27–29.

Cymrot, Donald J., "Private Pension Saving: The Effect of Tax Incentives on the Rate of Return." *Southern Economic Journal,* Vol. 47 (July, 1980), pp. 179–190.

Drucker, Peter, *The Unseen Revolution.* New York: Harper and Row, 1976.

Ezra, Don, "How Actuaries Determine the Unfunded Pension Liability," *Financial Analysts Journal,* Vol. 36 (July/August, 1980), pp. 43–50.

Gerwitz, Paul A., and Robert C. Phillips, "Unfunded Pension Liabilities. . . . The New Myth," *Financial Executive,* August, 1978, pp. 18–24.

Kaye, Lloyd S., "The Pension Benefit Formula: An Element in Financial Planning," *Financial Executive,* July, 1978, pp. 24–30.

Malca, E., *Pension Funds and Other Institutional Investors.* Lexington, Massachusetts: D.C. Heath and Co., 1975.

Regan, Patrick J., "Credit Ratings and Pension Costs," *Financial Analysts Journal,* Vol. 35 (March/April, 1979), pp. 6–7.

Schotland, Roy A., "Divergent Investing for Pension Funds," *Financial Analysts Journal,* Vol. 36, (September/October, 1980), pp. 29–39.

Twardowski, J.M., and Bogle, J.C., "Institutional Investment Performance Compared," *Financial Analysts Journal,* Vol. 36 (January/February, 1980), pp. 33–41.

Chapter 13

Finance Company Management

Finance companies differ sharply from deposit-type financial intermediaries. On the one hand, finance companies have far greater flexibility in the acquisition of assets and liabilities. On the other, they generally do not have access to deposit funds and must compete for higher cost funds in money and capital markets.

TYPES OF FINANCE COMPANIES

Although all finance companies are similar in that their principal function is to make loans, they differ in terms of the loans they specialize in. Some are predominantly *consumer loan companies,* with their principal activity the granting of direct cash loans to individuals or households. Other finance companies are referred to as *commercial loan companies* with all or a major proportion of their loans being made to business units. Still others are *sales finance companies* whose principal function is to purchase retail time sales contracts from non-financial busi-

nesses. Although most finance companies began by focusing entirely on one of the activities described above, many individual finance companies today offer a broad range of financial services to businesses and consumers alike.

Finance companies are "stock" companies in the sense that they are privately owned entities with ultimate control vested in their owners. The nature of ownership differs however. Some are operated as units of bank holding companies or as subsidiaries of conglomerates, and others are "dependent" or "captive" finance companies, formed by parent firms to finance the sale of goods manufactured by the parent. Perhaps one of the more familiar dependent or captive finance companies is General Motors Acceptance Corporation. Still other sales finance companies are "independent," ranging in size from a single office to multiple offices located throughout the nation.

Table 13–1 contains a summary of finance company assets and liabilities for selected years. Table 13–1 suggests that while the dollar value of all asset categories increased

Table 13-1:

Summary of Federal Reserve Benchmark Data on Finance Companies
1970, 1975, 1980
(Millions of Dollars)

	As of June 30		
	1970	*1975*	*1980*
Assets			
Consumer receivables	31,773	40,814	77,260
Business credit	22,999	39,286	86,067
Real estate receivables	*	1,946	11,831
Other receivables	2,342	3,948	8,183
Total gross receivables	57,113	85,994	183,341
Less: Reserves	6,254	9,307	24,232
Total net receivables	50,859	76,687	159,108
All other assets	9,718	12,030	15,917
Total assets, net	60,577	88,716	175,025
Liabilities and Capital			
Short-term borrowing	29,629	36,620	70,840
Long-term borrowing	16,470	29,730	60,471
Other liabilities	4,531	8,416	18,363
Subtotal liabilities	50,630	74,766	149,674
Capital, surplus and undivided profits	9,947	13,951	25,350
Total liabilities and capital	60,577	88,716	175,025

*Real estate receivables not separately reported prior to 1975.

Note: Totals may not agree because of rounding.

Source: Federal Reserve Quinquennial Surveys of Finance Companies. Above data reported in *Federal Reserve Bulletin*, March, 1976, and May, 1981. Prior survey results reported in *Federal Reserve Bulletin* April, 1957; October, 1961; and April, 1967.

over the years, consumer receivables declined and business receivables increased in relative importance. In 1970, consumer receivables represented 56 percent of all gross receivables with business loan activity amounting to 40 percent of the total. By 1980, the former represented 42 percent of gross receivables, while the latter had increased to 47 percent of the total. A notable feature in Table 13–1 is the dramatic increase in real real estate receivables between 1975 and 1980.

On the liability side, Table 13–1 reveals that finance companies are highly leveraged, with debt representing close to 86 percent of the total capital structure. Finance company profitability then, is highly dependent on the difference (spread) between the cost

of borrowed funds and interest revenue earned from loan receivables.

GROWTH AND DEVELOPMENT OF FINANCE COMPANIES

Unlike commercial banks and thrift institutions, finance companies are not dependent on deposits as a source of funds and have had far greater flexibility in choosing the types of loans and investments to be acquired.[1] In addition, banks and thrift insti-

---

[1] Some finance companies operate Morris Plan companies or industrial banks which are permitted in a few states. These institutions are permitted to accept deposits and issue certificate debt to the public. Liabilities of this type are not a major item for the industry.

tutions are generally precluded from branching across state lines while many finance companies operate nationwide. Also, most states severely restrict the number of branches which may be maintained by depository institutions within the state, but don't restrict the number of finance company offices. In contrast to depository financial institutions, finance companies have been relatively free to innovate and to seek out various types of loan and other investment portfolios.

In some cases, finance companies have paved the way in developing profitable lending innovations and in establishing the relative safety of many types of lending operations. Examples of lending activities of this type include direct consumer lending and the development of retail time sales lending activities. However, once the industry developed successful lending programs such as the financing of retail automobile time sales contracts, it experienced severe competitive pressures from other financial institutions such as banks and credit unions. In many cases, other lending institutions entered and eventually overtook certain traditional finance company lending markets once the finance companies had established the relative safety and profitability of those markets.

Table 13–2 documents the growth in consumer installment receivables following World War II. Households expanded their debt obligations not only in an absolute sense but also in relation to their incomes. Installment debt obligations, which totaled $2.5 billion and represented less than 2 percent of disposable income in 1945, grew dramatically over the next three decades. As the decade of the 1970s drew to a close, consumer installment credit represented almost one fifth of consumer disposable personal income.[2]

Although finance companies participated

in this post-war growth of consumer credit receivables, Table 13–2 suggests that the industry's share of total market receivables began to decline. This decline began to appear by the mid-1950s as commercial banks and credit unions experienced ever increasing market domination. Beginning in the 1950s, commercial banks and credit unions became more aggressive in consumer credit markets. This, combined with their ability to attract lower cost (deposit-type) funds and therefore offer consumer financing at lower rates, resulted in a strong competitive advantage for commercial banks and thrift institutions.

ASSET STRUCTURE

Table 13–3 is a listing of the major categories of consumer and business receivables held by finance companies. A review and discussion of the various asset items represented in that table is useful in the development of an understanding of finance company operations. Each of these will be discussed in turn.

CONSUMER RECEIVABLES

Retail Passenger Automobile Paper Retail passenger automobile paper refers to receivables generated through the sale of new or used automobiles under terms of a conditional sales (or similar) contract. Receivables such as these are originated through automobile dealers and are subsequently sold or assigned to a financial institution. A typical procedure is as follows:

1. The automobile dealer negotiates the selling price and trade-in allowance for a new or used car with the purchaser.

2. Following agreement on these cash sales terms, the dealer may offer to finance the automobile with the customer to pay monthly payments over time. Given an extended payment arrangement, the sale would be termed a "time sale" as opposed to a "cash sale."

---

[2] During 1980, a federal credit restraint program combined with certain recessionary factors, resulted in a decline in the ratio of consumer installment credit to disposable personal income. The ratio was 16 percent by the first quarter of 1981.

Table 13-2 (a):

Consumer Installment Credit By Holder
(In Millions of Dollars)

Year End	Total	Comm. Banks	Finance Companies	Credit Unions	Misc. Lenders, Retailers & Others
1945	$ 2,462	$ 745	$ 910	$ 102	$ 705
1950	14,703	5,798	5,315	590	3,000
1955	28,906	10,601	11,838	1,678	4,798
1960	42,968	16,672	15,435	3,923	6,938
1965	71,324	28,962	24,282	7,324	10,756
1970	101,161	41,895	31,123	12,500	15,643
1975	162,237	78,703	36,695	25,354	21,485
1980	313,435	145,765	76,756	44,041	46,873

Table 13-2 (b):

Consumer Installment Credit By Holder
(Share of the Market)

Year End	Total	Comm. Banks	Finance Companies	Credit Unions	Misc. Lenders, Retailers & Others
1945	100.0%	30.3%	37.0%	4.1%	28.6%
1950	100.0	39.4	36.1	4.0	20.4
1955	100.0	36.7	41.0	5.8	16.6
1960	100.0	38.8	35.9	9.1	16.1
1965	100.0	40.6	34.0	10.3	15.1
1970	100.0	41.4	30.8	12.4	15.5
1975	100.0	48.5	22.6	15.6	13.2
1980	100.0	46.5	24.5	14.1	15.0

Source: *Federal Reserve Bulletin*, various issues

3. The customer at this point may choose to (a) pay the cash price from his own funds, (b) arrange financing directly through a lender of his choice, or (c) accept the dealer's offer to finance the automobile.

4. If the dealer's financing offer is accepted, the customer will complete a credit application.

5. Information concerning the transaction—e.g., price and description of the automobile, down payment, requested contract maturity, and credit informa-tion—is telephoned or otherwise transmitted to the lending institution.

6. On the basis of information submitted, the lending institution will (verbally) approve, reject, or suggest modification of contract terms (required down payment, maturity, comaker, etc.).

7. If the contract is approved by the lending institution, the sale is consummated. The contract is endorsed by the dealer and sold or assigned to the lender, who in turn issues the dealer a check for the principal balance financed.

Table 13-3:

Major Types of Credit Outstanding Held by Finance Companies

Consumer Receivables	*Business Receivables*
Retail Passenger Automobile Paper	Wholesale Paper
Mobile Homes	Automobiles
Revolving Consumer Installment Credit	Other consumer goods
Personal Cash Loans	Equipment and industrial
Second Mortgage Loans	Retail Paper
Other Consumer Installment Loans	Commercial vehicles
	Business, industrial, and farm equipment
	Lease Paper
	Automobile paper
	Business, industrial, and farm equipment
	Other Business Credit
	Loans on commercial accounts receivable
	Factored accounts receivable

Certain features of the time sales contract and its subsequent sale or assignment to the lender are noteworthy and influence the potential risk and profitability of the transaction.

First, the nature of the dealer's endorsement influences the level of risk inherent in the transaction. The contract may be endorsed "without recourse," with "full recourse," or in some other way so as to partially protect the lender in the event of customer default. If the endorsement is "without recourse," the dealer has no responsibility in the event of customer default and any collection or collateral repossession expense must be borne by the lender. If a "full recourse" endorsement is used, credit risk for the lender is substantially reduced or eliminated, and the dealer is committed to absorb the losses in event of customer default. Under terms of a "partial repurchase" or other limited recourse agreement, the dealer is obligated to absorb losses up to some fixed sum or is perhaps obligated only until a given number of payments have been paid by the customer.

The nature of contract endorsement is thus important from a managerial aspect. Obviously, if all else is equal, the financial institution would prefer to have all contracts endorsed on a "full recourse" basis. Even in the case of full recourse endorsements, however, the financial institution faces certain risks. Full recourse endorsement by financially unsound dealerships may provide little protection to the lender. Even in the case of financially sound dealerships, risk exposure may be substantial if the institution relies excessively on dealer endorsements and relaxes credit standards or regularly accepts contracts with cash advancements in excess of the "quick" or wholesale value of the collateral. The extent to which recourse endorsements may be required by financial institutions varies over time as well as with the nature of the collateral and the geographic location. In larger urban areas where lenders compete vigorously in the retail automobile paper market, a lender who wishes to participate in this market may have little choice other than to purchase the paper on a non-recourse basis, particularly with regard to contracts secured by new automobiles. On the other hand, dealers in rural areas tend to have fewer financing outlets and must frequently endorse time sales contracts on a recourse basis.

A second feature associated with time

sales financing and one with considerable influence on potential profitability associated with the financing of retail paper involves the tradition of dealer participation in finance charges. Because competition among financial institutions for retail auto receivables has been intense, particularly in the post-war era, most financial institutions which seek those receivables offer some program whereby a portion of finance charges from times sales contracts are shared with the dealer. For example, a particular lender might establish a (retail) rate to the public of, say, 7 percent add-on. If the amount financed were $5,000 over 36 months, total finance charges would be $1,050 ($5,000 × 7% × 3 years). Suppose the same institution established a net rate of 6 percent add-on (net rate is the rate retained by the lender). The financial institution would seek to net $900 ($5,000 × 6% × 3 years) and the difference of $150 ($1,050 − $900) would be paid to the dealer as an incentive for offering the contract to the lender. This dealer participation in finance charges is frequently referred to as "dealer reserve." Also, the proportion of total finance charges received by the dealer is influenced by the type of collateral, contract maturity, competition, and other factors.

When the contract is sold or assigned to the lender, the lender may issue an additional check to the dealer in the amount of the finance charge participation. More commonly, however, the dealer reserve is entered as a liability on the lender's books and paid at periodic intervals. Frequently, the reserve account is established in such a way that the account may be charged to cover losses arising through defaults on contracts that had been partially or fully guaranteed by the dealer.

From a managerial point of view, competitive conditions frequently dictate dealer participation in finance charges. The amount of participation and the terms under which reserves are available to offset credit losses should be carefully monitored. Changes in competitive conditions and analysis of the profitability of retail paper should influence policy decisions regarding relationships between the lender and dealers.

Mobile Home Financing Although mobile homes may be financed through mortgage instruments in ways that are similar to the financing of residential real estate, finance companies have traditionally financed mobile homes in a manner similar to that of automobiles, through use of conditional sales (or similar) contracts.

As Table 13–4 shows, several aspects of the financing of mobile homes by finance companies differ from those of new automobile financing. Principal differences include a) higher finance rates, b) larger average amounts financed, and c) longer maturities. By December 1979, consumer mobile home installment credit receivables held by all lenders were about $17.5 billion. Of this, commercial banks held almost $10 billion while finance companies and savings and loans each held about $3.5 billion. Most of the remainder was held by credit unions.

Like automobile financing, conditional sales contracts for mobile homes may be subject to full or partial dealer recourse arrangements. Dealer participation in finance charges is common within the industry. Because mobile homes, unlike residential real property, have traditionally been subject to rapid depreciation, and because of the greater complexity and potential loss in the sale of mobile homes in the event of customer default, management should exercise considerable care in establishing relationships with individual dealers, evaluating credit applications, and selecting terms.

Revolving Consumer Installment Credit Over the decade of the 1970s, revolving credit has perhaps been the fastest growing single segment of the consumer credit market. Accoring to a 1977 Federal Reserve Survey dealing with consumer credit, almost 63 percent of all families surveyed had at least one credit card.[3]

---

[3] Board of Governors of the Federal Reserve System, *1977 Consumer Credit Survey,* 1978.

Table 13-4:

Finance Rates, Maturities, and Average Amount Financed by Finance Companies, 1974–1979

	1974	*1975*	*1976*	*1977*	*1978*	*1979*
*Average Finance Rates**						
Personal loans	20.7%	21.0%	21.0%	20.5%	20.5%	20.5%
Automobiles						
New	12.6%	13.1%	13.2%	13.1%	13.1%	13.5%
Used	17.2%	17.6%	17.6%	17.6%	17.6%	18.0%
Mobile homes	13.3%	13.6%	13.4%	13.6%	13.4%	13.6%
Other consumer goods .	19.1%	19.8%	19.5%	19.2%	19.0%	19.1%
*Average Maturities**						
Personal loans in						
months	34.8	36.3	37.6	42.9	45.8	50.5
Automobiles—percent						
New—Total	100.0%	100.0%	100.0%	100.0%	100.0%	100.0%
% over 42 months ...	—	—	14.5	26.4	45.3	59.2
% 37 to 42 months ..	8.4**	23.6**	17.8	21.2	16.9	11.0
% 31 to 36 months ..	78.4	65.3	55.8	40.4	27.3	21.1
% 30 months or less .	13.2	11.2	11.7	11.9	10.5	8.7
% balloon	0.2	0.1	—	—	—	—
Used—Total	100.0%	100.0%	100.0%	100.0%	100.0%	100.0%
% over 36 months ...	—	—	3.6	8.7	21.9	40.8
% 31 to 36 months ..	52.9***	54.2***	53.3	57.3	43.5	43.5
% 25 to 30 months ..	29.2	31.1	29.9	23.6	19.7	8.5
% 24 months or less .	17.8	14.7	13.2	10.4	14.9	7.2
% balloon	0.1	—	—	—	—	—
Mobile homes	121.2	121.0	123.3	126.9	130.8	133.4
Other consumer goods .	21.1	21.1	22.2	23.6	25.8	25.4
*Average Amount Financed**						
Personal loans	$1,162	$1,260	$1,384	$1,521	$1,572	$ 1,684
Mobile homes	$7,292	$7,686	$8,404	$9,174	$9,999	$11,617
Other consumer goods .	$ 434	$ 464	$ 510	$ 563	$ 605	$ 600
Automobiles						
New	$3,615	$4,096	$4,499	$4,990	$5,590	$ 6,035
Used	$1,996	$2,249	$2,451	$2,720	$3,168	$ 3,555

Note: Parts may not add to totals due to rounding.

*Unweighted means of periodic sample data for each year. Average amount financed excludes precomputed finance charges.

**Over 36 months.

***Over 30 months.

Source: Federal Reserve Board and summarized in *Finance Facts Yearbook*, National Consumer Finance Association, 1980, p. 61

Although the bulk of revolving credit receivables are held by commercial banks and retailers, some finance companies have developed revolving credit programs of their own in recent years. In lending programs of this type, customers are given advance approval for credit extensions up to some maximum limit and may draw against this limit by executing notes and forwarding these to the finance company office. In a few programs, arrangements have been developed whereby finance company credit is extended through use of Visa cards. As the movement toward electronic funds transfer systems continues, scale economies and innovative marketing techniques may well stimulate further expansion by the consumer finance industry into the market for revolving consumer installment credit.

Personal Cash Loans Personal or direct cash loans constitute a major portion of finance company consumer receivables. Loans of this type have amounted to about 39 percent of all finance company consumer receivables in recent years.

Unlike other types of loan receivables such as those secured by automobiles or mobile homes, direct cash loans are typically small in size. They may be secured by household goods and other miscellaneous assets, or may be unsecured. Data contained in Table 13–4 indicate that finance rates for personal loans in the 20 to 21 percent interest rate range are common within the industry. Although these rates have traditionally been high compared to finance rates associated with automobile or mobile home loans, finance company personal loans tend to be relatively small in size and are costly to administer. Also, because of competitive pressures, increasing funds costs, and state mandated interest rate ceilings, the relative profitability of personal loans by finance companies has fallen over the years.

A particular problem area for finance company management with regard to small personal loans is the fact that finance companies must compete for funds in money and capital markets where interest rates are not regulated. At the same time, maximum rates for personal loans are fixed by the various states. In a 1978 study of the consumer finance industry in Missouri, the authors found that the combination of high funds costs and fixed state interest rate ceilings had resulted in a decline of the industry in Missouri.

From a management perspective, the future attractiveness of the market for relatively small personal loans is questionable at best. It is likely that commercial banks and credit unions will continue to increase their respective market shares. On the other hand, if inflationary pressures continue through most or all of the 1980s, and if Federal Reserve Regulation Q ceilings are phased out in accordance with legislation adopted in 1980, it is possible that the cost of deposit funds for commercial banks and credit unions will increase, with a consequent reduction in the competitive advantage these institutions traditionally have had over finance companies.

Second Mortgage Loans A second mortgage loan (sometimes called "home equity loan") is one secured by real estate but where the real estate collateral is subject to some prior lien. The prior lienholder has priority in the event of foreclosure and liquidation of the real estate collateral.

Information concerning the total volume of second mortgage lending is relatively sketchy and frequently inconsistent. There is, however, general agreement that consumer lending of this type was among the fastest growing forms of credit to consumers during the 1970s. Estimates of outstanding and market shares by lenders for 1971 and 1976 were developed by Commercial Credit Economic Services and are reproduced in Table 13–5. Of all lenders represented in Table 13–5, finance companies held the largest single share of second mortgage receivables by 1976.

Reasons for growth in second mortgage lending markets were cited during testimony before the Federal Trade Commission in December, 1977, by C. Stuart LaDow, a director of the National Second Mortgage Association. In his testimony, LaDow indicated that much of the growth in second mortgage lending can be attributed to inflation in at least three identifiable ways:

1. As housing prices climbs, homeown-

Table 13-5:

**Estimated Value of Second Mortgage Loans Outstanding for the United States
(In Millions of Dollars)**

	1971		1976	
	Amount	*Percent*	*Amount*	*Percent*
Individuals	$1,477	33.6	$2,379	26.1
Finance Companies	797	18.1	2,433	26.7
Commercial Banks	461	10.5	1,407	15.4
Savings & Loans	442	10.1	712	7.8
Mortgage Companies	261	5.9	420	4.6
Credit Unions	130	3.0	525	5.8
Others*	826	18.8	1,248	13.7
Total	$4,394	100.0	$9,124	100.0

*Others include real estate and construction companies, mutual savings banks, federal agencies, insurance companies, retirement funds, state and local pension systems, private pension plans, non-profit organizations and organizations and trust accounts administered by banks.

Note: According to Federal Reserve Survey Data summarized in Table 13-1, Finance Company Real Estate Receivables had grown from $1.9 billion in 1975 to $11.8 billion in 1980. Of these $11.8 billion in 1980 real estate receivables, $10.5 billion were second mortgage loans with the remainder secured by first liens.

Source: "Monthly Perspective and Insight on Consumer Financial Behavior," (Vol. 2, Number 3), Commercial Credit Economic Services, March, 1977, p. 8.

ers find that they have increased equity in their homes—equity which may be used as loan collateral.

2. Homeowners who might otherwise have been in the market for new homes are staying where they are and taking out second mortgage loans to make improvements and repairs on their existing homes.

3. (Many of) those who can afford a new home are finding that they cannot afford the higher down payments and closing costs, so they turn to a second mortgage to finance those items.

The representative of the National Second Mortgage Association, in emphasizing the fact that second mortgage loans tended to be relatively large in size, cited average loan sizes made by three of the group's members. Average loan sizes that were cited ranged from $10,000 to $12,900 and loan maturities ranged from 72 to 99 months.

The typical second mortgage borrower appears to be a middle-income person approximately 40 years of age with consider-able residential and job stability. The two primary reasons for second mortgage borrowing are home improvement and consolidation of short-term consumer loans. Borrowers appear to take out second mortgage loans only after a period of contemplation averaging several months. Delinquency rates for these loans appear to be quite low.

Maximum interest rates for second mortgage loans are established by state law. Some states also specify maximum loan amounts and maturities.

Second mortgage lending offers finance companies certain advantages over the more traditional cash loans offered by the industry. Lending of this type offers cost economies since handling and processing costs per dollar loaned are significantly less. Also, credit risk associated with lending of this type is reduced, given customer stability and the nature of the collateral. Finally, it is a market that is growing much more rapidly than the market for other types of loans.

Other Consumer Installment Loans Other

consumer installment loans include finance receivables secured by personal property such as refrigerators or television sets. Goods such as this are sold and financed in a manner similar to that described in the financing of retail passenger automobile paper.

EVALUATING CONSUMER CREDIT APPLICATIONS

The analysis of consumer credit applications is similar to business credit evaluation in some respects and different in others. In both cases, the three C's of credit (character, capacity, and collateral) must be considered.

Character refers to the reputation of the potential borrower in terms of his perceived reliability in repaying the loan. Finance companies, as do other consumer lenders, contact prior or existing creditors, the names of which are typically disclosed by the applicant in his credit applications. These credit references are asked to furnish information concerning the applicant's record with them. Alternatively, or in addition to direct contact with creditors, the lender may communicate by telephone or teletype with the local credit bureau or lenders' exchange, where a file containing the applicant's credit repayment history is maintained. This file frequently contains employment history and residence information in addition to an evaluation of loans and other credit repayment history. The credit evaluation agency will have accumulated this credit information as the result of the applicant's prior requests for credit and subsequent inquiries from other lenders.

The second "C" (Capacity) refers to the applicant's potential ability to repay the loan from current income or existing resources. The credit manager must evaluate the applicant's ability to repay the loan, in view of the borrower's existing financial obligations and income limitations.

Finally, the third "C" (Collateral) represents the security to which the lender may turn in the event of loan default. Collateral

repossession in order to liquidate a loan is viewed as a last resort by finance company lenders. In 1978, about three-fifths of all finance company loans to consumers were secured by automobiles, household goods, or by other chattels. One-fifth were secured by co-makers, real estate, and other considerations. The remainder (approximately one-fifth) were unsecured.[4]

BUSINESS RECEIVABLES

Wholesale Paper Wholesale paper refers to trust agreements or similar legal documents which arise during the course of inventory financing. To induce sellers of "large ticket items" such as automobiles, heavy duty trucks, farm equipment, and other items which are frequently sold on time sales contracts to offer these contracts to a particular lender, a finance company (or other lender) may offer to finance the wholesale value of the dealer's inventory. Such financing—also referred to as "floorplanning"—is typically provided as an accommodation to the dealer.

As an example, suppose that a franchise for a new car or truck dealership is awarded to a businessman in the local area. The dealership will be expected to develop a certain amount of retail time sales finance paper and it is likely that a number of financial institutions will have an interest in purchasing this retail paper. The dealer, on the other hand, will likely carry large inventories of the product and these inventories must generally be financed. Typically, one or more lenders would approach the dealer and offer to finance the inventory in exchange for the opportunity to finance the retail contracts. The lender may agree to establish a "floorplan line of credit" whereby the dealer maintains inventory financed by the lender up to the amount of the established credit line. Once the floorplan arrangement has been negotiated, the manufacturer will be au-

---

[4] *Finance Facts Yearbook, 1980,* National Consumer Finance Association, p. 63.

thorized to draft on or bill the lender for subsequent shipments of inventory items to the dealer. As the dealer sells the floor-planned units, he is expected to remit payment for sold items promptly to the lender.

Because of competitive conditions, wholesale dealer paper is typically financed at breakeven interest rates, with the interest rate tied to the prime lending rate plus, say, 1 percent. Since finance companies frequently borrow at rates which are only slightly less than the floorplan rates offered to dealers, floorplanning in and of itself is not a particularly profitable operation. Wholesale financing accommodations are generally provided to the dealer with the expectation that the dealer will offer "compensating retail paper" to the lender. On the basis of experience, the lender knows that a considerable portion of "big ticket items" such as new cars, trucks, etc., are financed. Since the dealer is in a position to control the placement of a certain proportion of the retail time sales paper, the dealer is expected to offer this paper to the lender who has provided the floorplan accommodation. Of course, if the floorplanning lender rejects a particular financing transaction, the dealer may well seek to sell the time sales contract to some other lender.

Floorplanning can involve considerable risk to the lender and considerable management attention should be given to its control. Even relatively small dealers may require floorplan lines amounting to several hundred thousand dollars. For large dealerships, the value of floorplanned inventory can amount to a million dollars or more; amounts which may be far in excess of the dealer's equity investment.

The risk of potential loss through whole-sale financing is perhaps greatest during depressed economic periods when dealer sales volume may be low. Indeed, examples abound where particular dealers, faced with high fixed costs and working capital requirements, have defaulted on inventory trust agreements. The default may go undetected

by the lender for a considerable period of time because the dealer simply defers payment on sold inventory items and enters into a floorplan "float." The float may at first involve a delay in payment of sold inventory items for a few days with the proceeds from current sales used to pay the lender for floorplanned units sold in the prior time period. If depressed economic conditions continue, the float may build gradually over time, reaching the point where the lender suffers considerable losses.

Although the nature of wholesale financing is such that the risk of a dealer being "out of trust" is always present, controls can be instituted to minimize potential losses. Frequent unannounced floorplan inventory checks by the lender are a critical component of such controls. Insistence on the timely preparation and submission of dealer financial statements, followed by analysis of such statements on an ongoing basis, is another means of control.

Finally, management should systematically evaluate the quantity and profitability of the compensating retail paper purchased from individual dealers. If the quantity and quality of the retail paper is insufficient to justify the investment and risk associated with the dealers' wholesale receivables, and if this condition cannot be improved, the floorplan line should be terminated.

Retail Business Receivables In addition to time sales contracts secured by consumer durables, finance companies also purchase time sales contracts secured by commercial assets such as heavy duty trucks, farm equipment, and other industrial products. Frequently, commercial time sales contracts secured by assets such as these are purchased from dealers in ways that are similar to the procedure described for retail passenger automobile paper.

On the one hand, the financing of commercial equipment carries with it the prospect for enhanced profitability. The amount financed under individual contracts tends to be substantial when compared with consumer durables such as automobiles or household products. On the other hand, collateral such as heavy duty trucks and other types of industrial products is difficult to dispose of in the event of foreclosure. Because of the large balances financed and the lack of a readily available secondary market for most types of industrial equipment, there exists considerable risk of loss on individual time sales contracts.

Large finance companies with branches located throughout the nation have competitive advantages in the financing of certain types of industrial equipment. First, it is possible to diversify portfolio holdings of this paper on a geographic basis, reducing the impact of credit losses caused by regional economic slowdowns. Second, commercial banks are reluctant to purchase contracts secured by "on the road" commercial vehicles such as tractor-trailers financed for "owner-operators," because the equipment may be far away and physically difficult to reposess in the event of default. From a practical point of view, the lender must have the capability to enforce terms of the time sales contract, and as a last resort, to take physical possession of the collateral when it appears that the purchaser is unable or unwilling to meet his contractual obligations. Large finance companies with a national network of branches have this capability.

LIABILITY MANAGEMENT

On average, finance companies carry six to seven dollars in debt for each dollar of equity capital. Lacking deposit funds as a major source of debt, they must bid for funds in a competitive market place. With the cost of these funds being a major part of their total costs, finance companies depend on skillful liability management to minimize interest expense and achieve a satisfactory level of profitability.

However, minimizing the cost of funds is only one consideration in liability management. A second major factor is interest rate risk. The average finance company loan has a maturity of several years. A shorter liability maturity exposes the finance company to the risk of having to refinance maturing liabilities at interest rates higher than the net rates being earned on loans. In a period of falling interest rates, liability maturities longer than loan maturities can leave the institution in the position of being committed to high-cost sources of funds while competition is driving down the rates charged on loans. Thus interest rate risk is a major consideration in liability management.

Finally, availability of funds is a major consideration for finance company management. The money and capital markets are quite impersonal, making no commitment to provide funds. Past experience such as collapse of the commercial paper market following the Penn Central default confirms the importance of assuring that some source of funds will always be available to finance existing loans.

Tables 13–6 and 13–7 summarize the liability management structure of finance companies for selected years. Each of the major sources of funds covered there is discussed in the following paragraphs.

BANK LOANS

Finance companies have traditionally relied on commercial banks as key sources of funds, frequently borrowing against revolving credit lines. Such reliance is particularly true for the smaller finance companies which lack access to national credit markets.

For the industry as a whole, bank loans varied from 8.8 to 12.5 percent of total liabilities and capital over the time period represented in Table 13–6. The aggregated data contained in Table 13–6, however, obscure the fact that liability structure differs markedly for finance companies depending on firm size.

Table 13-6:

Liabilities and Capital Outstanding at Finance Companies, Midyears 1970, 1975, and 1980

Type of liability	Amount outstanding (Millions of dollars)			Percentage change		Percentage of total liabilities and capital	
	Mid-1970	Mid-1975	Mid-1980	1970–75	1975–80	Mid-1975	Mid-1980
Bank loans	7,551	8,617	15,458	14.1	79.4	9.7	8.8
Short-term	6,581	7,900	7,885	20.0	-0.2	8.9	4.5
Long-term	969	718	7,573	-25.9	954.7	0.8	4.3
Commercial paper	22,073	25,905	52,328	17.4	102.0	29.2	29.9
Directly placed	19,247	23,686	43,232	23.1	82.5	26.7	24.7
Dealer placed	2,826	2,218	9,095	-21.5	310.1	2.5	5.2
Other short-term debt ...	975	2,815	10,627	188.7	277.5	3.2	6.1
Other long-term debt	15,501	29,013	52,898	87.2	82.3	32.7	30.2
All other liabilities	4,531	8,416	18,363	85.7	118.2	9.5	10.5
Capital and surplus	9,947	13,951	25,350	40.3	81.7	15.7	14.5
Total liabilities and capital ...	60,577	88,716	175,025	46.5	97.3	100.0	100.0
MEMO:							
Short-term debt	29,629	36,620	70,840	23.6	93.4	41.3	40.5
Long-term debt	16,470	29,730	60,471	80.5	103.4	33.5	34.5
Total debt	46,100	66,350	131,311	43.9	97.9	74.8	75.0

Source: Board of Governors of the Fedeal Reserve System, *Federal Reserve Bulletin*, May, 1981, p. 406

Table 13-7:

Liabilities and Capital Outstanding at Finance Companies, Midyears 1975 and 1980

Size of company (gross receivables outstanding, millions of dollars)

Type of liability	All companies 1975	All companies 1980	25 and over 1975	25 and over 1980	5 to 25 1975	5 to 25 1980	Under 5 1975	Under 5 1980
Loans and notes payable to banks	8,617	15,458	7,314	14,134	783	969	519	355
Short-term	7,900	7,885	6,869	7,183	654	477	377	226
Long-term	718	7,573	446	6,951	130	492	141	129
Commercial paper	25,905	52,328	25,799	52,166	85	143	20	18
Directly placed	23,686	43,232	23,607	43,119	59	95	20	18
Dealer placed	2,218	9,095	2,192	9,047	26	49	*	*
Other short-term debt	2,815	10,627	2,288	10,133	351	257	176	237
Other long-term debt	29,013	52,898	28,429	52,255	292	400	291	243
All other liabilities	8,416	18,363	7,867	17,908	257	283	291	172
Capital and surplus	13,951	25,350	12,911	24,013	423	475	618	862
Total liabilities and surplus	88,716	175,025	84,609	170,609	2,193	2,527	1,915	1,888
MEMO:								
Short-term debt	36,620	70,840	34,955	69,481	1,090	877	576	481
Long-term debt	29,730	60,471	28,875	59,206	422	892	433	372
Total debt	66,350	131,311	63,831	128,687	1,512	1,769	1,009	853

*Less than $500,000.

Source: Board of Governors of the Federal Reserve System, *Federal Reserve Bulletin*, May, 1981, p. 407.

240

Of the 2,775 finance companies that constituted the 1980 survey group represented in Table 13–6, less than 2 percent were responsible for some 80 percent of total industry liabilities. These larger firms tend to rely proportionately less on commercial bank loans and proportionately more on commercial paper. Regional and small firms, however, draw heavily on bank credit lines in financing their operations. More than half the outstanding debt of smaller finance companies (those with receivables of $25 million or less) was owed to commercial banks in 1980, compared to only 11 percent of the debt owed by large finance companies.

Bank borrowing is frequently accomplished by drawing down on a pre-negotiated revolving line of credit. This source of borrowing has the important advantage of assuring availability. However, interest rates on such lines are frequently tied to prime rate, with the cost of bank credit varying from the prime rate for the soundest companies to three or four percentage points over prime for the smaller firms. Thus the interest rate may vary, and the benefit of assured availability is offset by exposure to interest rate risk. Normally, credit arrangements of this type require a compensating balance, and/or a fee of about one half of 1 percent of the credit line. Charges or balances are frequently required regardless of whether or not the line is used. Therefore, a price is paid for availability, making bank credit a sometimes expensive source of funds.

Finance company managers using bank credit should seek to minimize the cost of these funds. It may be possible, for example, to negotiate a reduced commitment fee—or a lower compensating balance—in return for the firm's payroll account. Alternatively, the finance company might suggest a smaller compensating balance, but one which would be kept in the form of a non-interest bearing time deposit (one on which the bank would be required to hold proportionately smaller reserves). In short, the cost of bank credit is an important component of finance company cost and new, innovative financing techniques can have important implications for company profitability.

COMMERCIAL PAPER

The commercial paper market is a major source of funds for large finance companies. According to data contained in Table 13–7, financing of this type represented about 40 percent of outstanding industry debt in 1980. In fact, finance company paper constitutes more than half the entire domestic commercial paper market.

The use of short-term bank loans and commercial paper in financing such a large part of operations is consistent with the principle of matching the maturity of assets and liabilities. Finance companies, as our previous discussion indicated, hold large volumes of short-term self-liquidating retail and wholesale receivables. The commercial paper and bank loans, combined with long-term debt, provide a liability structure with an average maturity similar to that of the assets.

Financing of this type also provides flexibility. The volume of financing requirements can be adjusted on a daily basis, principally by varying the rate of interest that the issuing company is willing to pay.

Of course, a principal reason for the popularity of commercial paper among finance companies is the fact that interest rates for the paper are consistently below the bank prime rate. It should be noted, however, that the rate of interest applicable to commercial paper does not represent the entire cost. Smaller issuers generally place their paper through dealers, who charge a fee. Larger firms place commercial paper directly with investors and thus are faced with the expense associated with the maintenance of commercial paper managers and staff.

In addition to selling costs, commercial paper issuers face the cost of maintaining back-up, unused lines of bank credit, as expected by the investment community. Under normal circumstances, maturing commercial paper is redeemed through issuance of new paper. However, there may exist market conditions under which the issuer would find it difficult to "roll over" maturing paper and would be forced to rely on bank credit to redeem it. Since these lines of credit are paid for with non-interest compensating balances or by direct payment of fees, part of the cost-savings of commercial paper is offset by the cost of assuring availability of funds through banks.

BONDS AND OTHER LONG-TERM DEBT FINANCING

Like industrial corporations, finance companies rely on bonds and other long-term debt as sources of financing. Long-term sources have the advantage of assuring the availability of funds at a fixed interest rate for a specific period of time. Thus they provide a solution to the availability problem.

One major disadvantage of long-term debt is that it has historically been more expensive than short-term funds. However, this disadvantage is somewhat offset by the fact that most bonds are callable; they can be retired early, at the option of the issuer, typically with the payment of a call premium. If interest rates rise after a bond has been issued, the issuer continues to pay interest at the prior low rate. On the other hand, if market interest rates fall, the bonds can be called and replaced with a new, lower interest rate issue. Thus the higher average cost of long-term debt is at least partially offset by inclusion of the call feature or by other features that provide flexibility in adjusting to changes in interest rates.

Given the advantage of assuring availability of funds, and with the cost and interest rate risk problems mitigated by callability, bonds have been an important source of funds to finance companies. Bonds and other long-term debt totalled 35 percent of finance company sources of funds in early 1981.

EQUITY CAPITAL

Finance companies differ from most other financial institutions in that regulators do not impose a minimum equity level requirement on them. They are free to choose a debt-to-equity ratio in keeping with market forces and their own objectives.

Finance companies face two major considerations when choosing a financial structure. First, like any company, they recognize that the value of the owner's investment is affected by financial leverage. A higher debt-to-equity ratio can lead to a higher return on equity if funds are invested in assets which earn a rate of return greater than the cost of debt. However, beyond some point, further increases in debt increase the risk of insolvency, thereby driving up both the interest rate on debt and the required return on equity. Finance companies with less risky and better diversified asset portfolios can use proportionately less equity. The larger finance companies, those with total assets over $25 million, had equity equal to 14 percent of total assets in 1980. At the same time, finance companies with total assets under $5 million had equity of some 46 percent of total assets. These smaller companies normally concentrate in limited types of lending in narrow geographic areas and are not nearly so diversified as are the larger firms.

In addition to the threat of insolvency, finance companies must consider the effect of their equity ratios on their access to the debt markets. Finance companies that allow the equity cushion to fall too low may find it difficult or impossible to market commercial paper. Similarly, a low equity ratio may impair the firm's ability to acquire other short- or long-term debt funds at reasonable cost.

FUTURE EXPECTATIONS

Successful managers of financial institutions are those with the capability to assess conditions which surround them and to formulate policy decisions based on this environment. As was suggested in the opening observations of this chapter, finance companies face fewer restrictions than depository type competitors in the acquisition of assets and liabilities. Finance companies can open new offices and close down former ones almost at will. They can expand across the nation and world with little or no need for regulatory agency approval. Unlike depository institutions, finance companies face almost no legislative or regulatory restrictions in terms of the type of loans made or securities purchased.

On the other hand, finance companies have operated at a disadvantage, having to pay market rates for funds while depository institutions acquired low cost deposit funds. Also, because of the lower funds costs, depository institutions have sometimes been able to offer more favorable terms for consumer and business loans.

Given this competitive background, the shifting regulatory philosophy discussed in Chapter 2, particularly the elimination of deposit rate ceilings, may in fact leave finance companies in an improved competitive condition relative to deposit type financial institutions.

SUMMARY

Finance companies differ in many respects from their major competitors, banks and thrift institutions. These differences, which are reflected in their sources and uses of funds, were shaped by historical development and by the competitive and legislative environment facing all financial institutions.

Finance companies have paved the way for many types of lending activities, particularly in certain consumer lending areas such as time sales financing. In recent years, the industry has expanded its portfolio to include a larger proportion of business loans.

Although certain types of lending programs, such as consumer automobile financing, were abandoned or curtailed by the industry in recent decades, the present regulatory philosophy and environment, by imposing greater funds costs on their depository competitors, may result in an improved competitive climate for the industry.

QUESTIONS

1. Beginning in the late 1950s, the market share of installment credit held by finance companies declined. How do you account for this decline?

2. Should consumers finance large purchases, such as a new or used car, directly through the dealer? Why might this be to the customers' advantage or disadvantage?

3. Distinguish between the various ways in which a time sales finance contract may be endorsed before being sold to a financial institution by a dealer.

4. What is meant by the term "Dealer Reserve"?

5. Why have finance companies emphasized second mortgage lending in recent years?

6. Define the term "floorplanning" and comment on the inherent riskiness of this type of financing from the lender's point of view.

7. Certain types of equipment, such as heavy trucks and trailers, are financed by finance companies. Why might finance companies pursue this type of lending while depository and thrift institutions do not?

8. In addition to interest charges, there may be certain additional costs implied when finance companies borrow from banks. Comment on these.

9. Why are finance companies such heavy issuers of commercial paper? Are

there significant costs associated with the issuance of commercial paper above and beyond interest paid to purchasers of the paper?

10. Suppose that the balance sheets of a large bank were contrasted with that of a large finance company. Would the proportion of assets financed by equity capital tend to be greater for the finance company as compared to the bank? Why or why not?

11. Comment on ways in which the gradual phase-out of Regulation Q ceilings may influence finance companies.

SELECTED REFERENCES

Benston, George, "Graduated Interest Rate Ceilings and Operating Costs by Size of Small Consumer Cash Loans," *Journal of Finance,* Vol. 32 (June, 1977), pp. 695–708.

————, "Rate Ceiling Implications of the Cost Structure of Consumer Finance Companies," *Journal of Finance,* Vol. 32 (September, 1977), pp. 1169–1194.

————, "Risk on Consumer Finance Company Personal Loans," *Journal of Finance,* Vol. 32 (May, 1977), pp. 593–607.

Boczar, Gregory, "Competition Between Banks and Finance Companies: A Cross-Section Approach," *Journal of Finance,* Vol. 33 (March, 1978), pp. 245–258.

Hamburger, Michael J., and Burton Zwick, "Installment Credit Controls, Consumer Expenditures and the Allocation of Real Resources," *Journal of Finance,* Vol. 33 (December 1977), pp. 1557–1570.

Wiginton, John C., "A Note on the Comparison of Logit and Discriminant Models of Consumer Credit Behavior," *Journal of Financial and Quantitative Analysis,* Vol. 15 (September, 1980), pp. 757–770.

Chapter 14

International Aspects of Financial Institution Management

The topic of international finance is extremely broad, including the problems of exchange rate and balance of payments policy, the myriad international financial institutions, and the international aspects of financial management. In keeping with the purpose of this text, we concentrate on the international aspects of financial institution management and the role of financial institutions in facilitating international business. We concentrate on the primary financial problems and needs encountered by business and financial institutions dealing in the international sphere, and discuss the institutions, instruments, and conventions that have been developed to meet these needs.

DEVELOPMENT OF INTERNATIONAL BUSINESS

Economic history is characterized by growing interdependence. The industrial revolution led to interdependence between people and business units, and the growth of international business has led to growing interdependence between nations. The result has been a rising standard of living and a growing challenge to financial managers and policy makers.

REASONS FOR INTERNATIONAL BUSINESS

When asked why international business has expanded so rapidly, economists are quick to cite the *theory of comparative advantage*. Just as income within countries has been increased through specialization by individuals, world income can be increased through specialization by countries. For example, a country with a limited population and substantial potential for hydroelectric energy might concentrate on manufacturing processes requiring high energy inputs and purchase products requiring extensive manual labor from a country with a large, low-skill population. Both countries would gain from the exchange.

The theory of comparative advantage certainly accounts for a substantial amount of export and import activity in a world in which raw materials, energy, capital, labor, and technology are so unevenly distributed. The advanced economies have primarily sold goods requiring highly skilled labor and capital intensive production. Their imports, by comparison, have been raw materials and products requiring a substantial input of low-skill labor.

Technological advantage is a type of comparative advantage which deserves special attention. A country may have a technological advantage because of a sudden breakthrough, a highly educated population, or a heavy investment in a particular technology. It could be argued that United States' domination of the international computer market for a number of years depended on some important conceptual breakthroughs as well as a heavy investment in engineering development and a highly educated population. By comparison, the development of a new class of airplane, such as the Anglo-French Concorde, depends primarily on an engineering application of known technology. The fixed cost of converting this known technology to a tested airplane is measured in billions of dollars. The country that takes the initial risk in making this investment has a decided cost advantage over other countries considering their own production. Had the Concorde proved commercially feasible, the United States and Russia are the only other countries that could have been expected to make the investment necessary to develop a competitive airplane. Other countries wishing to own such airplanes would have purchased them from one of these countries, selling other goods to obtain the necessary funds.

Moving from import-export to internationalization of production, technological

advantage again comes to play. A company with developed technology may take advantage of that technology by producing at home or in other countries. The production of foreign designed automobiles in the United States is one such example. The construction of United States designed calculators in developing countries for sale in the United States is an even more striking example of companies roaming the globe in search of comparative advantage in any one phase of their operation.

Differences in capital accumulation rates and investment opportunities represent other reasons for foreign business. Other things being equal, investors will place their funds where the highest return can be earned. If a country has a mature economy, a non-growing population, and a high savings rate, domestic investment opportunities are likely to be limited and businesses will look overseas for opportunities paying higher returns. Frequently, these may be found in countries with growing populations and limited savings. The overseas investments of oil producing countries can also be explained in terms of an inability to find domestic investments paying a high rate of return. Their economies cannot absorb such huge amounts of capital efficiently.

Diversification and risk control are other motivations for foreign business. Investments or business operations in numerous countries help to diversify away risks unique to a particular country. Both business cycle risks and risks associated with government instability can be at least partially diversified away through international expansion.

Finally, much international business activity is motivated by the desire to avoid taxes or government regulation. For example, production may be moved to a country with minimal pollution laws. By operating in several countries, it is frequently possible, through altering methods of cost allocation, to shift at least some profits to the country with the most favorable tax structure.

Table 14-1:

**Exports, Imports, and Capital Flows of the
United States
(in billions of $)**

Year	Exports	Imports	Capital Outflow	Capital Inflow
1946	12	5	1.6	2.1
1950	10	12	1.4	1.9
1955	14	12	1.5	1.5
1960	20	15	4	2.3
1965	26	22	6	0.7
1970	42	40	9	6
1972	49	56	14	21
1973	71	70	23	18
1974	98	104	35	34
1975	107	98	40	16
1976	115	124	51	37
1977	121	152	36	51
1978	142	175	61	64
1979	182	212	62	38

Source: Department of Commerce, Bureau of Economic Analysis, and summarized in *Economic Report of the President.*

GROWTH OF INTERNATIONAL BUSINESS

Table 14–1 gives an indication of the growing importance of international business to the United States. Particularly in the period since World War II, the United States has grown to be a major power in the international marketplace. Concurrently, the international marketplace has grown to be a major factor in the United States economy.

While the growth in international business is itself impressive, the changing nature of international business is of even greater significance. The trend has been away from the traditional import-export form of business toward truly multinational business, characterized by capital, technology, materials, and people moving across national boundaries with increased freedom. Table 14–1 also shows the dollar value of foreign investment by the U.S. in foreign countries and by foreign countries in the U.S.

Since World War II, exports and imports have grown at a more rapid rate than has the Gross National Product while inflows and outflows of capital have grown at an even faster rate.

Analyses of these international accounts and their rates of growth tend to underestimate the internationalization of business in that they do not capture foreign control of capital raised and invested within a country. For example, the building of a Volkswagen plant in the United States, financed with borrowing in the United States, shows up as neither import nor capital flow. Thus, the growth of international business has been much more rapid than the growth of the domestic economy, with no letup in sight.

Before leaving this overview, we should note that for all this growth, international business remains much less important to the United States than to most other developed countries. Table 14–2 gives one measure of the international business of some other countries in comparison to the United States. Because of its internal resources and diversity, the United States depends on foreign trade much less than any other developed capitalistic country.

Table 14-2:

**Exports as a Percent of
Gross Domestic Product, 1978**

Israel	48
Korea	33
Great Britain	30
Sweden	28
West Germany	27
Italy	25
France	20
Japan	14
United States	8
India	7
Brazil	7

Source: *International Financial Statistics*, International Monetary Fund.

SPECIAL PROBLEMS ENCOUNTERED IN INTERNATIONAL BUSINESS

The company involved in international business faces a number of problems not faced by the domestic company. First, there is the problem of managing exchange rate risk arising from the fact that different currencies are involved and the relative values of those currencies are subject to unexpected change. Second, the exporter or importer faces problems caused by distance, unfamiliarity, and the fact that foreign sales frequently require more extensive credit terms than domestic sales. Finally, the truly international business faces the problem of raising and investing money in the international money and capital markets. Financial institutions aid nonfinancial businesses with each of these problems as well as using the international markets to make investments and raise funds for themselves. Each of the main problem areas of international business is discussed in the following sections.

EXCHANGE RATE RISK

One of the major problems in international finance results from the fact that the value of one currency relative to another is continually changing. Any international contract involving future payment requires that one side agree to transact in a currency other than that of his native country, thereby accepting the risk that the amount involved will, when converted to his own currency, be different than anticipated.

While we usually expect risk to decline as we gain experience in a particular area, foreign exchange risk has increased concurrent with the increased volume of international business. From the end of World War II until the late 1960s, exchange rates were held nearly constant by international agreement. The cornerstone of the agreement was the U.S. commitment to buy or sell any

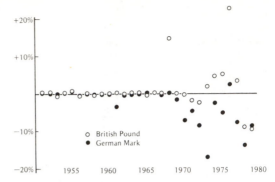

Figure 14–1: Percent change in the value of the dollar with respect to other currencies.

amount of gold at $35 an ounce. Imbalances between exports and imports were cleared through purchase and sale of U.S. dollars or gold. The lack of gold stock growth in relation to business growth led to problems in the 1960s, with the first major break in stability being the devaluation of the British pound in 1967. Figure 14–1 illustrates what has happened since then, using the British pound and the German mark as examples. While the dollar has generally strengthened against the pound and weakened against the mark, it has become more volatile against both currencies. International business continues to grow in the face of this instability because methods of dealing with these risks have been developed.

MANAGING EXCHANGE RATE RISK

The possibility of a change in the relative values of currencies creates two primary types of risk: *translation risk* and *transaction risk*. These risks and methods of dealing with them are discussed in the following paragraphs.

Translation risk arises primarily from accounting conventions. A U.S. firm with interests in several countries must somehow convert all of its assets to dollar values for the purpose of preparing annual reports. The current rules on translation are spelled out in *Financial Accounting Standards Board*

Statement #8 (FASB #8). Essentially, non-monetary assets and liabilities are translated at the exchange rate in effect when they were acquired while monetary assets and liabilities are translated at the current exchange rate. The illustration given below shows the impact of a Deutsch mark devaluation—from 2.0 D.M. per dollar to 2.5 D.M. per dollar—on a company with net Deutsch mark monetary assets at the time of devaluation. Note that fixed assets are not revalued, but monetary assets and liabilities are. The company must report a $200 translation loss. Various methods are available to avoid losses of this type.

Balance sheet hedging (also referred to as money market hedging) provides an effective method of controlling translation risk. Essentially, the company strives to have a

Transaction risk represents a more immediate and more real risk. Transaction risk occurs when there are outstanding contracts calling for payment or receipt in a currency other than that of the home country. They occur because of purchase or sale on credit as well as from contracts for future delivery with the price agreed upon today. Suppose a U.S. firm agrees to purchase French goods for one million francs at a time when the exchange rate is .2459 dollars per franc. The goods are to be delivered and paid for in 90 days and the importer has contracted to re-sell them for $250,000 in the United States. At the present exchange rate, the goods would cost $245,900 (1,000,000 × .2459). Thus the importer expects to sell the goods for $4,100 above cost. However, if the exchange rate should rise to above .2500 by

	Old Exchange Rate		New Exchange Rate		
	Value in D.M.	Value in U.S. $	Value in D.M.	Value in U.S. $	Change in dollar value
Fixed assets	5,000	$2,500	5,000	$2,500	
Accounts receivable	5,000	2,500	5,000	2,000	
Bank loans	3,000	1,500	3,000	1,200	
Net D.M. monetary assets	2,000	1,000	2,000	800	(200)

net exposure (monetary assets minus monetary liabilities) of zero in each currency in which it deals. In the previous example, this could have been achieved by borrowing an additional 2,000 D.M. and investing the proceeds in nonmonetary assets or U.S. dollar denominated money market instruments.

A net liability position in D.M. would result in a translation loss if D.M. were revalued upward vis-a-vis U.S. dollars. The risk associated with a net liability position would be similarly offset by replacing a D.M. denominated loan with a U.S. dollar denominated loan or by borrowing in U.S. dollars and investing the proceeds in D.M. denominated money market instruments. Industrial corporations and financial institutions attempt to offset translation risk in this manner as a routine policy.

the end of the 90-day period, the products will be sold at a loss instead of a gain. Clearly, some method of eliminating these risks is desirable.

Borrowing and lending can also be used to provide a hedge against transaction risk. In the case of the French products discussed above, the risk could have been eliminated by immediately converting U.S. dollars to francs at .2459 and investing the proceeds in franc denominated money market instruments with 90 days to maturity. Likewise, a U.S. company that had agreed to accept payment in francs 90 days hence could hedge against exchange rate risk by taking out a franc denominated loan with a 90-day maturity, converting the proceeds to dollars, and investing the proceeds in United States money market instruments. Of course, the transaction would be completed by using the franc payment to repay the franc loan.

Currency futures provide another widely used method of hedging against exchange rate risks. Currency futures, or forward exchange contracts, are handled in a manner similar to forward contracts for commodities. Two parties enter into a contract, agreeing to exchange a certain amount of one currency for a certain amount of another currency at a specified future date. If we enter into a futures contract for French francs, we assure ourselves a certain number of francs at a specified price while the other party is being assured of a certain amount of dollars at a fixed price in francs.

The use of a forward exchange contract can be illustrated with the French franc example from above. The forward exchange quotes from the *Wall Street Journal* appear in Table 14–3. Our purchaser of French goods sees that he can purchase 90-day forward exchange contracts for French francs at .2472. In other words, he can contract to purchase francs at $.2472 each. This assures him a total cost of $247,200 and secures a profit on the purchase and resale of goods. Of course, we also observe that the spot rate was .2459, meaning that he could have purchased the francs today for $245,900 and invested in franc denominated money market instruments for 90 days. However, this would have required the immediate commitment of funds, a situation which can be avoided through use of forward exchange.

The forward exchange market operates in a manner similar to the over-the-counter securities market. There is no central meeting place.[1] The market consists of a few large banks and a handful of foreign exchange dealers and brokers who make a market among each other. The banks then transact with customers either directly or through their correspondent banks. Participants in the market include industrial corporations

as well as financial institutions covering their own positions and speculators hoping to make a profit by correctly predicting the direction of forward exchange rates.

The forward exchange market is quite limited. There are only a few major currencies involved and the longest contract normally available is for 180 days. Other currencies must be covered using money market hedges—borrowing or lending so that payments due equal payments owed in each foreign currency.

INTEREST RATES AND EXCHANGE RATES

The relationship between exchange rates and interest rates is an excellent example of how the opportunity for arbitrage serves to remove market differentials. We note in Table 14–3 that the "spot" or current U.S. dollar equivalent for Franch francs is .2459 while the 180-day future rate is .2478. This reflects an expectation that the value of the franc will rise relative to the dollar. International finance theory would suggest that changes in exchange rates are primarily (or entirely) a result of differences in inflation rates between countries. A future rate for the franc above the spot rate is evidence that investors expect the French inflation rate to be lower than the U.S. inflation rate over the next 180 days.

Since interest rates normally increase when expected inflation increases, we would expect interest rates to be higher in the United States than in France. However, the forward exchange rate sets a limit on how much higher or lower this rate will be. Suppose, for example, that 180-day U.S. Treasury bills are presently selling at a discount sufficient to provide a 6 percent return over the 180-day period (an equivalent yield of 12 percent on an annual basis). If 180-day French government obligations were selling to yield 4 percent per 180-day period, a French investor or financial institution could improve return with no increase in risk by purchasing a U.S. Treasury bill and selling

---

[1] An exception is the Chicago Board of Options Exchange, which maintains a physical location for dealing in currency futures.

Table 14-3:

Foreign Exchange

Wednesday, February 13, 1980

The New York foreign exchange selling rates below apply to trading among banks in amounts of $1 million and more, as quoted at 3 p.m. Eastern time by Bankers Trust Co. Retail transactions provide fewer units of foreign currency per dollar.

Country	U.S. $ equiv. Wed.	U.S. $ equiv. Mon.	Currency per U.S. $ Wed.	Currency per U.S. $ Mon.
Argentina (Peso)				
Financial	.00060	.00060	1665.00	1665.00
Australia (Dollar)	1.1075	1.1100	.9029	.9009
Austria (Schilling)	.0804	.0803	12.44	12.46
Belgium (Franc)				
Commercial rate	.035511	.035499	28.16	28.17
Financial rate	.034674	.034674	28.84	28.84
Brazil (Cruzeiro)	.0222	.02217	45.11	45.11
Britain (Pound)	2.3084	2.3055	.4332	.4337
30-Day Futures	2.2989	2.2977	.4350	.4352
90-Day Futures	2.2882	2.2867	.4370	.4373
180-Day Futures	2.2792	2.2765	.4388	.4393
Canada (Dollar)	.8608	.8632	1.1617	1.1585
30-Day Futures	.8611	.8630	1.1613	1.1587
90-Day Futures	.8618	.8640	1.1604	1.1574
180-Day Futures	.8631	.8654	1.1586	1.1555
China-Taiwan (Dollar)	.02785	.02785	35.70	35.70
Colombia (Peso)	.0253	.0253	39.50	39.50
Denmark (Krone)	.1843	.1840	5.4250	5.4340
Ecuador (Sucre)	.0404	.0404	24.75	24.75
Finland (Markka)	.2704	.2705	3.6980	3.6975
France (Franc)	.2459	.2456	4.0645	4.0710
30-Day Futures	.2461	.2462	4.0628	4.0625
90-Day Futures	.2472	.2469	4.0450	4.0510
180-Day Futures	.2478	.2474	4.0360	4.0415
Greece (Drachma)	.02618	.0262	38.20	38.15
Hong Kong (Dollar)	.2053	.2064	4.8700	4.8450
India (Rupee)	.1275	.1275	7.843	7.843
Indonesia (Ruplah)	.00162	.00162	618.00	618.00
Iraq (Dinar)	3.397	3.397	.2943	.2943
Ireland (Pound)	2.1270	2.1245	.4701	.4707
Israel (Pound)	.0265	.02665	37.67	37.52
Italy (Lira)	.0012428	.00124	804.65	805.85
Japan (Yen)	.0041322	.004144	242.00	241.33
30-Day Futures	.004151	.004165	240.92	240.09
90-Day Futures	.004188	.004205	238.77	237.79
180-Day Futures	.004252	.004265	235.20	234.45
Lebanon (Pound)	.3033	.30488	3.2975	3.2800
Malaysia (Ringgit)	.4614	.4608	2.1675	2.1700
Mexico (Peso)	.0439	.0439	22.78	22.78
Netherlands (Guilder)	.5231	.5221	1.9115	1.9155
New Zealand (Dollar)	.9870	.9870	1.0132	1.0132
Norway (Krone)	.2059	.2056	4.8570	4.8640

Table 14-3 (continued):

Country	U.S. $ equiv.		Currency per U.S. $	
	Wed.	Mon.	Wed.	Mon.
Pakistan (Rupee)	.1015	.1015	9.852	9.852
Peru (Sol)	.004	.004	250.00	250.00
Philippines (Peso)	.1360	.1360	7.353	7.353
Portugal (Escudo)	.0212	.02128	47.20	47.00
Saudi Arabia (Riyal)	.2977	.2976	3.3590	3.3600
Singapore (Dollar)	.4667	.4649	2.1425	2.1510
South Africa (Rand)	1.2250	1.2250	.8163	.8163
South Korea (Won)	.00173	.00173	580.00	580.00
Spain (Peseta)	.01509	.01509	66.26	66.25
Sweden (Krona)	.2414	.2411	4.1430	4.1475
Switzerland (Franc)	.6190	.6188	1.6155	1.6160
30-Day Futures	.6237	.6236	1.6033	1.6036
90-Day Futures	.6342	.6333	1.5767	1.5790
180-Day Futures	.6489	.6470	1.5410	1.5455
Thailand (Baht)	.05	.05	20.00	20.00
Uruguay (New Peso)				
Financial	.1188	.1188	8.42	8.42
Venezuela (Bolivar)	.2399	.2329	4.2930	4.2930
West Germany (Mark)	.5762	.5753	1.7355	1.7383
30-Day Futures	.5786	.5800	1.7284	1.7300
90-Day Futures	.5850	.5840	1.7095	1.7124
180-Day Futures	.5936	.5926	1.6845	1.6874

Source: *Wall Street Journal*, Feb. 14, 1980

U.S. dollars on a 180-day forward contract. The return on a 3,836,507 French franc investment would be as follows:

Purchase dollars at current spot rate: (3,836,507 × .2459)	$943,396
Purchase U.S. Treasury bills with a face value of $1,000,000, discounted to yield 6% over a 180-day period	943,396
Simultaneously purchase a forward contract for $1 million worth of French francs in 180 days at $.2478 per franc: $1,000,000/.2478	4,035,513 ff
Hold Treasury bills until maturity and receive face value	$1,000,000
Complete forward contract to purchase francs	4,035,513 ff
Return earned: [(4,035,513/3,836,507) − 1] =	<u>5.19%</u>

If French government 180-day obligations are selling to yield less than 5.19 percent, the French investor can improve his position by investing in U.S. Treasury obligations and using a forward exchange contract to protect himself from exchange rate risk. The reverse is also true. If the rate in France were over 5.19 percent, an American investor could improve his position by purchasing French government obligations and hedging against exchange rate risk by contracting to sell francs in 180 days.

The calculation of the interest rate that would prevent investors from either country gaining by investment in the other country can be found using a simple formula instead of the extensive calculation above:

$$R_f = \frac{S}{F}(1 + R_d) - 1 \qquad (14\text{–}1)$$

where: R_f = Interest rate on risk-free obligations in the foreign country

$$S = \text{The spot value of a unit of the foreign country's currency}$$

$$F = \text{The forward value of a unit of the foreign country's currency}$$

$$R_d = \text{The domestic risk-free interest rate}$$

Applying the formula to the previous example, we confirm the previous solution and the correctness of the formula:

$$R_f = \frac{.2459}{.2478}(1 + .06) - 1 = 5.19\%$$

Of course, the fact that everyone could take advantage of this risk-free opportunity to increase return is likely to decrease or eliminate such opportunities. A flow of capital from France to the United States and the offsetting demand for future contracts to buy francs would drive the French interest rates up, the U.S. interest rates down, and the forward value of francs up until the potential profit disappeared. Thus we would expect to find the relationship between interest rates and exchange rates shown in equation 14–1 to hold in general.

FINANCING EXPORTS AND IMPORTS

The purchase and sale of goods across international borders involves several problems that do not exist or are much less difficult to handle for domestic sales. First, a contract calling for future payment requires that payment be specified in some currency. If the contract calls for payment in the importer's currency, the exporter must accept the risk that an unfavorable movement in the exchange rate between the two currencies will result in his receiving less than anticipated, and vice versa. Second, the problem of dealing with noncompliance—failure to deliver goods according to contract or failure to make payment according to con-

tract—is more difficult to deal with because of distance, unfamiliarity, and different legal systems. Third, credit is needed for longer periods of time because of distances and shipping times involved. Exchange rate risk was treated as a separate topic. The second two problems are treated in this section.

ASSURING COMPLIANCE

Every domestic seller of goods on credit must make the sale decision based on knowledge of the credit worthiness of the potential buyer. The decision is normally based on substantial personal knowledge of the buyer or readily available credit information sources. In the international marketplace, information on credit worthiness is limited by distance, language barriers, infrequency of trade, and other factors. Furthermore, a domestic firm's credit manager is likely to be quite knowledgeable with regard to the status of a claim in the courts in the event of a payment default. In the international marketplace, the status of a claim in the courts, and even the proper jurisdiction, is likely to be subject to question. Thus legal remedy is uncertain and expensive. Finally, the distances involved in shipment frequently make longer credit periods necessary, again increasing risk exposure.

From the buyer's point of view, there are also increased risks. A failure to ship goods per contract specifications on a domestic order can be remedied by returning goods or turning to a familiar court system. Again, great distances and unfamiliar court systems decrease the buyer's confidence in his ability to achieve adequate remedies in the case of default. The problem is again complicated by lack of direct knowledge about the seller. The problems cited above must be overcome if international trade is to flourish. The procedures that have evolved for dealing with these problems are outlined in the following paragraphs.

Transaction procedures must deal with the uncertainties suffered by both exporter and importer. Like most business procedures, the ultimate foundation is on trust rather than the availability of legal remedies. Essentially, the procedure is based on the fact that banks know their customers, and the fact that major banks dealing in the international marketplace are considered trustworthy. The reputation of the buyer's bank and the bank's trust of the buyer is substituted for trust between buyer and seller.

The normal procedure used in exporting involves three documents: a letter of credit from the buyer's bank, the bill of lading,[2] and a draft. The process begins with the buyer applying to his bank for a letter of credit. The letter of credit specifies the goods to be purchased, documentation required, and so on. The letter also says that the seller is authorized to write a draft on the bank upon shipment of the goods. Based on this information, the seller can ship the goods, assured that the draft will be honored.

Once shipment has been completed, the seller writes a draft on the buyer's bank, attaches the bill of lading, and forwards these two documents to his own bank. The seller's bank forwards the documents through its U.S. correspondent bank to the buyer's bank. The buyer's bank examines the bill of lading to confirm that shipment was in accordance with the terms of the letter of credit. The letter of credit may have authorized a sight draft, payable upon presentation with appropriate shipping documents. Or it may have authorized a time draft, payable a specified number of days following shipment. If the draft is a sight draft, it is honored immediately. If not, it is marked "I accept" and returned to the correspondent bank of the seller.

Once the correspondent receives the accepted draft (hereafter referred to as a *banker's acceptance*), it notifies the seller's bank which notifies the seller. The seller may then simply wait until the specified due date

---

[2] The bill of lading is the standard shipping document, containing evidence as to what has been shipped and instructions as to disposition of the shipment.

or he may discount the draft (sell it at a discount from its face value) to his bank. In the majority of cases in which the draft is discounted, the seller's bank then instructs its correspondent to hold the draft until maturity. Alternately, the seller's bank may instruct its correspondent to discount the draft in the United States market. The most likely sale is then to the buyer's bank, which simply honors the draft at a discount before maturity. In addition, there is a limited open market with several government securities dealers acting to make a small market in banker's acceptances.

If the buyer's bank does not purchase the draft before maturity, it will have provided credit to a customer by lending its name through a letter of credit rather than through the use of funds. A bank holding a banker's acceptance can use it as a secondary reserve asset rather than as a loan, thereby leaving it free to make other loans.

The use of the above procedure has proved to be a successful method of managing noncompliance risk and providing short-term credit. However, the average banker's acceptance has a maturity of 90 days, with 180 days being the upper limit. Sources of longer-term import-export credit are discussed in the following paragraphs.

EXPORT CREDIT INSURANCE

Export credit insurance provides another method of dealing with the risks involved in export sales on credit. Export credit insurance is used when the seller wishes to provide credit without the use of a banker's acceptance. In the United States, export credit insurance is provided primarily through the Foreign Credit Insurance Association (FCIA), an association of insurance companies working in conjunction with the Export-Import Bank of the United States. FCIA provides insurance against both commercial risk and political risk on American products sold abroad for credit. Commercial risks involve delayed payment or failure to pay for reasons covering the gamut of factors leading to failure to pay in domestic trade. FCIA has paid off in cases of failure running from competitive difficulties to theft, fire, and earthquake. Political risk covers war, expropriation, cancellation of import and export licenses, and so on. Insurance can be provided for short periods of time or for credit terms up to seven years in certain cases. Policies are normally sold for all shipments over a period of time rather than for just one shipment. The percent of loss covered by the policy varies from 90 percent to 98 percent. Premiums depend on length of time involved, category of country, and the riskiness of the credit involved.

SPECIAL SOURCES OF IMPORT-EXPORT CREDIT

While the banker's acceptance has proved to be a very useful method of handling transactions and a satisfactory source of short-term credit, it does not meet all the needs of exporters for extended credit terms. Most developed countries have some government agency which provides credit to encourage exports. In the United States that organization is the *Export-Import Bank*. The Export-Import Bank was started in 1934 to aid companies in importing and exporting. Actually, it was started to encourage the development of trade with Russia.

The Export-Import Bank is a quasi-public agency with a president and vice president appointed by the President of the United States. The bank is financed through the purchase of equity, all of which is owned by the U.S. Treasury.

The Export-Import Bank's primary mode of activity involves support of commercial banks. The Export-Import Bank guarantees intermediate term export obligations with maturities of six months to five years. Additionally, the Export-Import Bank purchases debt obligations of foreign borrowers from United States banks. Both short- and intermediate-term obligations are purchased

in this manner. Through these two routes the Export-Import Bank provides funds or support to banks lending money to exporters.

In addition to the support of banks, the Export-Import Bank also makes direct loans to foreign purchasers of U.S. goods. These direct loans are primarily participation loans with other financial institutions. Finally, the Export-Import Bank makes loans to foreign financial institutions that in turn loan money to small businesses purchasing United States goods.

As the above brief outline shows, the Export-Import bank acts primarily in conjunction with other financial institutions. It serves to increase the ability of financial institutions to serve their customers' needs rather than as a source of competition to financial institutions. The private financial institution can frequently provide greater credit service at lower risk by using the services of the Export-Import Bank.

The Private Export Funding Corporation (PEFCO) can reasonably be thought of as another extension of the services of the Export-Import Bank. The PEFCO was formed in 1970 through the efforts of the Bankers' Association for Foreign Trade. It makes loans to foreign purchasers of U.S. goods. All of its loans are guaranteed by the Export-Import Bank. Because it is privately owned—primarily by a group of large banks—PEFCO provides another source of credit, drawing on the Export-Import Bank guarantee to increase the supply of export credit available. PEFCO borrows in the long-term security markets, issuing secured notes.

INTERNATIONAL CAPITAL MARKETS

Along with the change from concentration on export-import operations to multinational production has come an increased tendency to turn to international capital markets for funds. Companies are motivated to use the international capital markets by considerations of balance sheet hedging, cost, and tax considerations. Funds are raised through Eurobonds, foreign bonds, and financial institutions specializing in international lending.

A *foreign bond* is issued primarily in one country, denominated in the currency of that country, and is the obligation of a corporation headquartered in another country. For example, a foreign automobile producer such as Toyota or Volkswagen might issue dollar denominated bonds in the United States for the purpose of building a plant in the United States. These would be foreign bonds because they are denominated and sold in the United States, but are an obligation of the foreign manufacturer. Such a bond issue might be motivated by cost of capital considerations or a desire for exchange rate hedging.

Foreign bond issues are sold through the services of financial institutions normally handling bond underwritings in the country in which the issue is being sold. In the United States, this would be an investment banking firm. In most other countries, commercial banks are allowed to provide this service and are the institutions primarily involved.

A *Eurobond* is in a sense a more truly "international" issue. The Eurobond is sold principally in countries other than the country of the currency in which it is denominated. It is usually underwritten by an international syndicate of underwriters: major European banks, European branches of United States banks, and banks from other major financial centers. For tax and other reasons, the issue is usually sold to people who are not citizens or residents of the country of denomination. These bonds are usually sold on general reputation rather than financial analysis or bond ratings. Thus, only the best-known international firms are able to use this source of funds. Approximately two-thirds of the amount of Eurobonds outstanding is denominated in U.S. dollars. Not

infrequently, companies headquartered outside the United States use the Eurobond market to raise funds in other non-United States countries, denominated in U.S. dollars.

U.S. companies selling bonds overseas are normally hampered by the fact that there is a United States withholding tax of as much as 30 percent of gross interest. This withholding tax is normally circumvented through the use of an offshore finance subsidiary. The finance subsidiary is incorporated in a tax haven country such as Switzerland, the Bahamas, or the Netherland Antilles. The subsidiary is wholly owned by the United States company and its sole purpose is to borrow money through the sale of bonds and re-lend it to the parent company, thereby paying interest from a foreign country and avoiding the United States withholding tax.

In addition to the above mentioned bond markets, there are a number of financial institutions that specialize in providing capital on an international basis. Most of these specialize in loans to countries, but some also participate in purchases of private debt and equity. Foremost among these is the World Bank Group. The primary institution of the World Bank Group is the International Bank for Reconstruction and Development, also called the World Bank. The World Bank makes loans only to countries. The International Finance Corporation, another member of the World Bank Group, specializes in direct investments in businesses in developing countries. It specializes in participation equity investments in basic industries such as steel and cement. Finally, there are a number of national development banks and private development banks that specialize in private loans. The Atlantic Development Group for Latin America (ADELA) is a good example of these. It is owned by more than 200 large corporations and invests in participations in private business enterprises in Latin American countries.

INTERNATIONAL PAYMENTS SYSTEM

Like the domestic payment system, the international payment system depends on instructions to banks to transfer ownership of deposits rather than through physical transfer of currency or metal. The process can be illustrated with a draft created through import of goods to the United States. Let us say that German goods were purchased with a letter of credit authorizing the German firm to write a draft of $1 million on Morgan Guarantee Trust, the United States purchaser's bank. The German exporter deposits the draft with its bank, Deutsche Bank, acquiring a $1 million deposit denominated in dollars. Deutsche Bank gains an asset of $1 million in the form of a deposit with Morgan and a $1 million liability in the form of a customer deposit. The German exporter may now use the dollar deposit to pay dollar obligations, convert it to marks, or hold it as a dollar investment.

Suppose the German firm owes $1 million to a British firm that wants payment in the form of a deposit at National Westminster Bank in London. The German firm instructs Deutsche Bank to transfer the $1 million to National Westminster in payment. Deutsche Bank carries out this instruction by wiring Morgan in New York to transfer ownership of a $1 million deposit to National Westminster. Morgan then notifies National Westminster by wire that the $1 million has been credited to its account and National Westminster notifies its customers, completing the transaction.

If the German business had no dollar debts, it could decide to convert the funds to Deutsche marks. The German firm would instruct Deutsche Bank to convert the dollars to marks. As a major money market bank, Deutsche Bank will have an inventory of dollar deposits for trading purposes and will be able to immediately quote the German firm a rate. Assuming the conversion rate in Table 14–3, the German firm will be able to exchange a $1 million deposit for 1,735,500 marks (minus the fee charged by the bank). Payment will be made by deducting $1 million from the German firm's dollar deposit balance and adding 1,735,500 to its mark balance. Because the bank made the exchange based on its own position, its dollar deposit assets have remained constant while its dollar liabilities have decreased. Deutsche Bank still has the $1 million deposit with Morgan.

As a continual buyer and seller of deposits denominated in various currencies, Deutsche Bank may decide to simply hold the dollar deposit in its own inventory. If, on the other hand, Deutsche Bank now feels that it is holding excess dollars, its trading department will use its telephone networks to exchange some dollars for marks. Suppose Deutsche Bank feels that its dollar holdings are excessive and Credit Lyonnais in France— one of the money market banks with which Deutsche Bank is in constant contact—feels that its mark holdings are excessive and its dollar holdings are low. Credit Lyonnais' holdings of marks are in the form of a deposit with Dresdner Bank in Germany. Credit Lyonnais and Deutsche Bank agree to an exchange at the presently quoted rate of 1.7355 marks per dollar. Credit Lyonnais wires Dresdner Bank to transfer ownership of a 1,735,500 mark deposit to Deutsche Bank and Deutsche Bank wires Morgan to transfer ownership of a $1,000,000 deposit to Credit Lyonnais, completing the transaction.

The number of banks acting in the foreign exchange market in this manner is quite limited. In the United States, only about two dozen banks maintain positions in the leading currencies. Other banks serve their customers' needs by dealing with one of these leading banks. The leading banks adjust their positions by buying and selling between one another, primarily through one of the six brokers that deal in foreign exchange.

Normally, banks within a particular money center, such as New York, would contract most of their exchanges with other banks in the same area. However, traders in foreign exchange departments will constantly watch rates in other money market centers, ready to buy or sell in one of those markets if the rate is different than that in the local market. Thus while most trades occur within a local market, there is a parity between rates quoted at different locations around the world.

A third alternative is also possible. Either the German exporter or Deutsche Bank may decide to hold the dollar deposit and loan it out to earn interest. When this is done, a Eurodollar deposit is created. The Eurodollar market represents a special international money market, worthy of additional attention.

EURODOLLAR MARKETS

The Eurodollar, as an investment or loan source, follows from the international payment system as described above. The German exporter has received payment in the form of a demand deposit with Morgan Guarantee Trust, credited to the account of Deutsche Bank. The German exporter decides to convert the dollar demand deposit to a time deposit with its bank rather than convert it to marks or use it for payment purposes. Thus, Deutsche Bank, the German firm's bank in this example, continues to have a dollar denominated liability and an offsetting dollar denominated asset in the form of a deposit with Morgan Guarantee Trust. The relevant accounts for the three entities are summarized in the following T-accounts.

German Exporter	
Time deposit with Deutsche Bank $1,000,000	

Deutsche Bank	
Demand deposit with Morgan $1,000,000	Time deposit from German exporter $1,000,000

Morgan Guarantee Trust	
	Demand deposit from Deutsche Bank $1,000,000

At this point Eurodollars have been created. A Eurodollar is defined as a U.S. dollar denominated deposit held by a bank outside the United States, including a foreign branch of a United States bank. Deutsche Bank is now paying interest on a time deposit and holding a non-interest bearing demand deposit. One possible course of action is for Deutsche Bank to exchange the demand deposit for a certificate of deposit, at the interest rate presently being quoted by Morgan. If this is done, the only change in the above T-accounts is the change of the Deutsche Bank deposit with Morgan from demand to time. Deutsche Bank may decide to loan the Morgan demand deposit to another bank. This is the point where the funds enter the active Eurodollar market. The loan to another bank may be for as short as overnight or for as long as six months.

The center of the Eurodollar market is in London, with the London Interbank Offer Rate (LIBOR) being the primary Eurodollar rate. Like the federal funds rate in the United States, the LIBOR represents the rate paid by banks on large ($500,000 or more) dollar deposits from other banks. Besides London, there are active markets in Frankfurt, Paris, Amsterdam, Zurich, Geneva, Basle, Milan, Vienna, Toronto, Montreal, and Singapore.

Suppose Deutsche Bank, lacking a direct dollar borrower, decides to deposit the funds with Barclays, a London bank, at the current LIBOR. Deutsche Bank will contact Barclays by wire to arrange for the desired maturity. Barclays, being a major money market bank, stands ready to make Eurodollar loans or accept Eurodollar deposits. After making arrangements with Barclays, Deutsche Bank wires instructions for the transfer to Morgan. These transactions have not caused any changes in the financial statement of the German exporter, which still holds a dollar denominated time deposit with Deutsche Bank. However, the accounts of the other parties have changed as shown in the following T-accounts.

Deutsche Bank

Time deposit with Barclays bank $1,000,000	Time deposit from German exporter $1,000,000

Barclays Bank

Demand deposit with Morgan $1,000,000	Time deposit from Deutsche Bank $1,000,000

Morgan Guarantee Trust

	Demand deposit from Barclays Bank $1,000,000

Of course, Barclays will want to find a profitable use for the Morgan demand deposit as quickly as possible. Suppose Barclays loans the money to a British importer by crediting the importer's Barclays demand deposit. The only accounts that change are those of Barclays, which now appear as follows:

Barclays Bank

Demand deposit with Morgan $1,000,000	Time deposit from Deutsche Bank $1,000,000
Loan to British importer $1,000,000	Demand deposit from British importer $1,000,000

How much time is required to complete this series of transactions? The funds can flow from the German exporter to the British importer in as little as a few hours through the use of wire transfers.

The British importer will either pay for the goods in dollars or convert the dollars to some other currency for the purpose of purchasing goods. Suppose the British importer decides to purchase American goods worth $1,000,000. Payment is to be made by transferring ownership of a Morgan demand deposit to the American exporter. Thus the British importer instructs Barclays to transfer ownership of his deposit to the American exporter. After this transaction, the accounts of all parties appear as follows:

German Exporter

Time deposit with Deutsche Bank $1,000,000	

Deutsche Bank

Time deposit with Barclays $1,000,000	Time deposit from German exporter $1,000,000

Barclays Bank

Loan to British importer $1,000,000	Time deposit from Deutsche Bank $1,000,000

British Importer

Inventory $1,000,000	Loan from Barclays $1,000,000

Morgan Guarantee

	Demand deposit from American importer $1,000,000

We should now observe several points about the Eurodollar market. First, its entire growth was based on an underlying dollar denominated demand deposit at Morgan. Total credit granted to business firms never exceeded the amount of this deposit. All Eurodollar transactions involved transfer of ownership of this Morgan account. Transfer of ownership of the account back to the United States ends the series of Eurodollar transactions. The remaining dollar denominated accounts are likely to fall to zero within a short time as the German exporter and British importer replace their dollar denominated accounts with accounts denominated in the local currency.

Another point we should notice is that the banks were never exposed to exchange rate risk. Their dollar assets and liabilities were always equal. Exchange rate risks are borne by the German exporter and British importer. These two parties could, of course, eliminate their risks through transactions in the foreign exchange futures market.

There is also the question of why Eurodollar transactions occur at all. The German firm could have held a Morgan time deposit itself and Morgan could have made a loan to the British importer. This does not occur for reasons that include knowledge and convenience of transaction. It is more convenient for the German exporter to deal with its bank and the British importer to deal with its bank. More important, the arrangement allows the banks to circumvent regulations aimed at limiting interest rates and money expansion. We showed Deutsch Bank lending the entire amount of its dollar deposits. In reality, the banks act on a fractional reserve basis, receiving many Eurodollar deposits and loaning out less than they receive in deposits, with the remainder held as reserve. However, reserve requirements are minimal compared to regulations in the United States.

We should also note that the phrase Eurodollar market is a misnomer in two senses. First, the market is not limited to Europe. A dollar deposit in a United States bank owned by anyone outside the United States meets the definition of a Eurodollar. There are active markets outside Europe, particularly in Asia. Additionally, market activity of this type is not limited to dollars. There are active markets in deposits of all major currencies outside their home countries. The market for all currencies is referred to as the *Eurocurrency market*.

BANK USE OF THE EURODOLLAR MARKET

Thus far, we have treated the Eurodollar market as a market in which banks serve the deposit and credit needs of their customers. The Eurodollar market also serves as an important money market in which banks can borrow funds to meet liquidity needs and invest idle funds at a profit.

An American bank facing a liquidity problem can attempt to adjust reserves by using the federal funds market or other sources within the United States. Alternatively, the bank can turn to the Eurodollar market for funds. This is done through an overseas branch of the American bank. Let us go back to the situation as it occurred immediately after Deutsche Bank received the time deposit from the German exporter. Instead of depositing funds in Barclays, Deutsche Bank could have deposited the funds with an overseas branch of an American bank. Suppose Citibank in the United States is presently in need of funds. The London branch of Citibank may accept the deposit from Deutsche Bank and gain, as an asset, the demand deposit with Morgan. The London branch of Citibank then notifies Morgan by wire that it wants the demand deposit transferred to Citibank. We should note that no increase in bank deposits occurred. Citibank simply used its overseas branch to bid for deposits presently with other U.S. banks. While the bidding for funds results in no direct increase in deposits in the United States, it may result in an indirect increase as interest rates are bid up and holders are encouraged to hold their Eurodollar deposits longer.

Instead of a shortage, suppose Citibank has an excess of funds. Suppose further that Eurodollar rates are presently more attractive than domestic money market rates. Citibank can loan funds to its London branch, showing a demand deposit as an asset and a loan as an offsetting liability. The London branch can then loan this demand deposit in the Eurodollar market, earning a favorable rate of return.

SUMMARY

With the increased volume of international business, financial institutions have become increasingly involved in the international financial markets. They are involved in these markets both to serve the needs of their customers and to meet their own liquidity and profitability objectives.

Financial institutions help their customers complete international transactions through such approaches as the letter of credit, draft, bill of lading, and through other specialized arrangements. Financial institutions help their customers exchange one currency for another and hedge against exchange rate risk through their foreign exchange departments. They also help customers in using international money markets to create balance sheet hedges. Additionally, financial institutions provide export credit insurance and certain institutions specialize in providing export credit.

Financial institutions also aid their customers in tapping the international capital markets. While there is no truly international equity market, there are two types of international bonds. A foreign bond is issued primarily in one country, denominated in the currency of that country, and is the obligation of a corporation headquartered in another country. A Eurobond is sold principally in countries other than the country of the currency in which it is denominated. In addition to these international bond markets, certain firms specialize in long-term loans, particularly in developing countries.

The Eurocurrency markets represent the primary international money markets. The Eurodollar is defined as a dollar deposit in a United States bank owned by a person, business, or institution outside the United States. In addition to helping customers through this market, banks use it as a source of liquidity adjustment and temporary investment.

The history of financial system development on the international front is similar to that for the domestic financial system. Institutions and instruments have developed in response to specific needs and the profit opportunities they created. While the growth of international business was not caused by financial institutions, it probably would not have occurred without them.

QUESTIONS

1. Give an example of international business activity that can be explained through the theory of comparative advantage.

2. Table 14–1 shows that capital flows *into* the United States have increased sharply in recent years. What factors have led to this increased inflow?

3. What are the main financial problems faced in international business that are not encountered in domestic enterprise?

4. The data in Table 14–2 provide evidence that international business is relatively less important for the United States than for other developed countries. What are the reasons for this?

5. What is translation risk? How does a company normally protect itself from translation risk?

6. Translation risk only involves accounting entries. Why would a company be concerned about translation risk?

7. What factors have caused exchange rates to become less stable in recent years?

8. Find the most recent spot and 90-day rate for Japanese yen. Are people

expecting the yen to increase or decrease in value relative to the dollar in the next 90 days?

9. An American company will sell goods to a German company, agreeing to grant one-year credit terms and accept payment in marks. How can the company hedge against exchange rate risk?

10. It is common practice for sales between businesses in the United States to be on an open-account basis. Why is this not common practice in international trade?

11. Explain the difference between a foreign bond and a Eurobond.

12. Most domestic payments are made through paper order, in the form of checks. How are international payments normally made?

13. How would a business go about raising funds in the foreign bond market?

14. Explain how a bank uses the Eurodollar market to adjust its liquidity position. Can the banking *system* adjust its liquidity through the Eurodollar market?

PROBLEMS

1. Following is a summary of the Deutsche mark denominated assets on the balance sheet of Allied Products, a United States firm.

Cash	100,000 D.M.
Accounts receivable	500,000 D.M.
Plant and equipment	1,000,000 D.M.
Accounts payable	200,000 D.M.
Bank loans	600,000 D.M.

Recommend a set of transactions that would protect Allied from translation risk.

2. Find the present yield for 90-day United States Treasury bills. Also find the spot and 90-day exchange rate for the

British pound. What would the equilibrium rate for 90-day British government obligations be under these conditions?

3. British government obligations with 180 days to maturity are selling to provide an 8 percent annual yield while U.S. government obligations of similar maturity are selling to yield 8.5 percent. Based on the quotes in Table 14–3, is the relationship between these two interest rates in equilibrium? If not, what type of transaction would take advantage of this disequilibrium?

4. An Italian exporter receives a $1,-000,000 payment from a United States importer in the form of a deposit in the name of the Italian exporter's Roman bank—in dollars at Citibank. The Italian exporter converts its deposits to a time deposit with the Roman bank and the Roman bank deposits the funds with a London bank that in turn loans them to a customer in the form of a dollar demand deposit with the London bank. Show the status of the relevant accounts of the Italian exporter, the Roman bank, the London bank, the London borrower, and Citibank.

SELECTED REFERENCES

Callier, Philippe, "Speculation and the Forward Exchange Rate: A Note," *Journal of Finance,* Vol. 35 (March, 1980), pp. 173–176.

Cornell, Bradford, "The Denomination of Foreign Trade Contracts Once Again," *Journal of Financial and Quantitative Analysis,* Vol. 15 (November, 1980), pp. 933–944.

Finnerty, Joseph E., Thomas Schneeweis, and Shantaram P. Hegde, "Interest Rates in the $Eurobond Market," *Journal of Financial and Quantitative Analysis,* Vol. 15 (September, 1980), pp. 743–755.

Frenkel, Jacob A., and Harry G. Johnson (eds.), *The Economics of Exchange Rates.* Reading, Massachusetts: Addison-Wesley, 1978.

Goodman, Stephen H., "Foreign Exchange-Rate Forecasting Techniques: Implications for Business and Policy," *Journal of Finance,* Vol. 34 (May, 1979), pp. 415–428.

Krugman, Paul. "Vehicle Eurocurrencies and the Structure of International Exchange," *Journal of Money, Credit and Banking,* Vol. 12 (August, 1980), pp. 513–526.

Murphy, J. Carter, *The International Monetary System: Beyond the First Stage of Reform.* Washington, D.C.: American Enterprise Institute, 1979.

Resler, David H., and Anatol B. Balbach, "Eurodollars and the U.S. Money Supply," *Federal Reserve Bank of St. Louis Review,* Vol. 62 (June/July, 1980), pp. 2–12.

Severn, Alan K., and David R. Meinster, "The Use of Multicurrency Financing by the Financial Manager," *Financial Management,* Vol. 7 (Winter, 1978), pp. 45–53.

White, Betsy, and John R. Woodbury, III, "Exchange Rate Systems and International Capital Market Integration," *Journal of Money, Credit and Banking,* Vol. 12 (May, 1980), pp. 175–183.

Case 1

Auburn Bank and Trust Company
The Charter Application

This case was prepared by John H. Hand, associate professor of finance, Auburn University. It is a basis for classroom discussion and is not intended to illustrate either effective or ineffective handling of an administrative situation.

Presented at a Case Workshop and distributed by the Intercollegiate Case Clearing House, Soldiers Field, Boston, Mass. 02163. All rights reserved to the contributors.

Auburn, Alabama is fairly typical of small university towns. With a population of just 23,000, it is economically dependent on Auburn University (enrollment: 15,000). At the same time, the university community relies on the town to provide the necessities and luxuries of life. (Montgomery, the state capital, is 50 miles away, too far to travel except for major purchases.)

Immediately adjacent to Auburn is the city of Opelika, whose economy is based on light industry and whose population is about 19,000. Recent growth of both towns has made their combined population large enough to attract the interest of larger retail establishments based elsewhere. The most viable result of this interest is a new enclosed shopping mall opened in 1973.

Early in 1972, the banking situation in Auburn closely resembled that prevailing in many towns of its size. There were two banks in town of virtually equal size (just under $20 million total assets), neither of which showed any inclination toward aggressive competition in the opinion of many business and individual customers. Loan standards seemed excessively conservative, maximum rates on savings deposits were not paid, free checking accounts were not offered, and the banks were not open evenings and Saturdays. The potential for change was also present, however. Alabama law permits countywide branching. Opelika had three banks, two of which had more liberal loan standards as evidenced by their loan to deposit ratios. (See Exhibit A–9) The most aggressive of the three had opened a branch in Auburn, but it could not be said that the Opelika banks had made a major effort to penetrate the Auburn market.

Another latent force in Auburn banking was a group of business and professional people who were not entirely satisfied with the service provided by the existing banks. Led by a prominent local businessman who had long desired to become active in banking, they considered the possibility of obtaining a charter for a new bank. The first decision they faced was whether to apply for a state or a national charter. The possession of Federal charters by both Auburn banks and all three Opelika banks was the major factor in the decision to explore a state charter first. (The First State Bank of Smiths, the only other bank in the county, had a state charter, but it was located 25 miles from Auburn. Because of its distance and small size, this bank was not a significant factor in the Auburn market.)

In spring 1972, those of the interested businessmen who had tentatively agreed to serve on the board of directors went to Montgomery to discuss the prospects for a new bank with the state banking supervisor. They recognized that the supervisor could not make any firm commitments, but at least they might find out whether it would be worth the time and expense of filing a formal application. If the supervisor had been negative, the men could have dropped the project with no further expense. As it happened, the official was receptive to their plans, and suggested that they file a formal application. The market research department of a large bank in the state was recommended for preparation and analysis of supporting data.

The organizers were not ready to formalize the structure of the proposed bank. A critical decision was selection of officers and directors. Whether or not these people would impress the banking authorities would be a critical factor in the success or failure of the application. Needless to say, these same people would be responsible for the survival and growth of the new bank if the application were successful. All officers and directors must be legally and financially "clean." The top officers should be experienced in banking, with some local connections if possible. The primary criterion for selection to the board was to be of substantial importance in the town. The directors not only would bring their own business to the bank, but they could influence others to do the same. The organizers found little difficulty in drawing up a slate of officers and directors who met these criteria, and their qualifications were never an issue in the application.

The initial capitalization of the bank was set at $750,000. The legal minimum was $500,000, but the state banking officials suggested the larger figure. The stock was to sell at $20 per share, with a par value of $10 per share.

With these preliminaries out of the way, the directors were ready to take the first step of the formal application process. The law requires that a notice be printed in the local press for 15 days announcing the intentions of the undersigned individuals to open a bank with stated capitalization. This notice serves two purposes: to ascertain public interest in the venture, and to allow the existing banks to prepare their opposition to the application if they so desire. Existing banks rarely fail to object to introduction of new competition, and this application was no exception. Banking authorities are interested in public reaction, for this reaction determines if the new bank can attract enough business to survive. Also, the authorities prefer banks to have a broad public participation in ownership. The willingness of the public to purchase stock is a significant test of community interest in a new bank. In this case, the stock issue was oversubscribed by a wide margin.

The structure of the application document and all supporting data is the language of Section 6 of the Federal Deposit Insurance Act of 1950, presented in Exhibit 1. The Federal Deposit Insurance Act is important even in a state application because nearly every bank—including this one—considers

Exhibit 1

An Act

To amend the Federal Deposit Insurance Act (U.S.C., Title 12, Sec. 264), Section 12B of the Federal Reserve Act, as amended, is hereby withdrawn as a part of that Act and is made a separate Act to be known as the "Federal Deposit Insurance Act."

Sec. 6. The factors to be enumerated in the certificate required under Section 4 and to be considered under Section 5 shall be the following: The financial history and condition of the bank, the adequacy of its capital structure, its future earnings prospects, the general character of its management, the convenience and needs of the community to be served by the bank, and whether or not its corporate powers are consistent with the purposes of this Act.

Source: *U.S. Statutes at Large*, Vol. 64, pt. 1, 1950–51.

---

federal insurance of its deposits a necessity. Thus, the application must be considered by two sources, the state banking supervisor and the Federal Deposit Insurance Corporation. The sixth requirement of the Federal Deposit Insurance Act, that the bank's corporate powers be consistent with the purposes of the Act, forces the state to adopt essentially the same standards. Since Alabama requirements are in conformity with federal law, FDIC approval is virtually automatic if the state approves the charter.

The first FDIC criterion, the financial history and condition of the bank, is a simple matter for a proposed new bank. Its history is nonexistent, and its present condition, that is, its current financial condition, includes nothing beyond the capital account. This provision is important mainly for banks already in business which might apply to join the FDIC. The second criterion, the adequacy of the bank's capital structure, is also more appropriate for banks already in op-

eration. Whether the bank's capital is capable of supporting its liabilities is moot when the organization has no liabilities. The question is extended to assess the likelihood of the capital being adequate to cover future liabilities. Since the major part of a bank's liabilities are deposits, a forecast of deposits is needed. A three-year forecast is usual. The applicants reported that they expected total deposits to be $2 million after one year, $4 million after two years, and $6 million after three years. No formal estimation techniques were used to derive this forecast.

The future earnings prospects of a proposed bank are documented by three-year estimates of income and expenses. Revenue estimates are dependent on the deposit forecast. Given the deposit forecast, the amount of loans outstanding are estimated by applying a loan-to-deposit ratio that is reasonable for a bank of its size. In this case, loans were estimated at $1.1 million, $2.2 million, and $3.3 million for the first three years, implying a loan-to-deposit ratio of 55 percent—about average for banks with deposits between $2 million and $5 million. Given an estimate for loans outstanding, revenue from loans can be forecast by multiplying loans by the anticipated average interest yield. A similar procedure for interest and dividends on securities generates an estimate of income from that source. The technique can also provide an estimate of the interest that must be paid on time deposits. Wage and salary expenses were calculated by determining the number and type of employees that would be needed and assuming they would be paid about the average amount prevailing in the area. These calculations showed that the bank could expect to make a small profit even in the first year (a rather unusual feat for a new business), and that profits would expand sharply the following two years thanks to favorable operating leverage.

The applicants also estimated the costs of the land and building, the office furniture, and such expenses of organization as the filing fee, attorney fees, and advertising. The land and building could not cost more than 40 percent of the bank's capital, but recent inflation of construction costs led the banking authorities to be flexible about that requirement. The total of these expenses was estimated as in excess of $450,000.

The FDIC's "convenience and needs" criterion essentially asks the question, "Does this town need another bank?" Two types of evidence are brought to bear on this issue, the potential for economic growth in the area and the state of competition among banks already there. The first type calls for analysis of population, industries (including agriculture), income, and the labor force. This information would determine whether the region could support a new bank. The second type shows whether the present banks are providing adequate service to the commu-

nity. The most important test of service adequacy is the lending practices of the banks: are they providing the financial backing for the area's economic growth? The task of marshalling the needed evidence was assigned to the marketing research consultants. The text of their report and some of the supporting data are presented in the Appendix.

The application form was completed and the supporting data assembled by the end of the summer. The application was formally filed on September 7, 1972. The state would take about six weeks to reach a decision, and until then the would-be bankers could only wait and hope. In the meantime, the other banks had been preparing their opposition, and were ready to carry their case to the state.

Auburn Bank and Trust Company

Appendix: Economic and Market Research Study

INTRODUCTION AND PREFACE

For the purposes of this study, Lee County in general, and the Auburn-Opelika area specifically, will be the topics under consideration since it is consistent that a new bank market its services throughout most of this county. It is realized that bank business could also accrue from adjoining counties; however, this is not taken as a matter of reference in this text.

The data and statistics used in this report are from reputable secondary sources and are as up-to-date as possible. It is the contention of this study that Auburn could use an additional banking outlet. This text is prepared simply as an additional source for the proper banking authorities to make this decision.

TRADE AREA OF THE PROPOSED AUBURN BANK AND TRUST COMPANY

Lee County is the industrial and commercial center of East Alabama. It is sur-rounded by Chambers and Tallapoosa counties to the north, Macon and Russell counties to the south, and the Chattahoochee river, which serves the Alabama-Georgia border, to the east. The county contains 612 square miles.

Auburn is the largest city in Lee County and adjoining Opelika is the county seat. Because of its central location in Lee County, the trade area for the proposed new bank will be defined as the entire county. Although it is not reasonable to expect any great overflow of bank business from the surrounding counties, including Georgia, some business will accrue from these areas.

A look at Auburn and Lee County economic indicators will be a reasonable framework in which to analyze the convenience and needs of the community for the proposed Auburn Bank and Trust Company.

LEE COUNTY

The principal trade centers in Lee County are Auburn and Opelika, a smaller portion of the trade going to Marvyn and other small communities. Items that cannot be obtained within Lee County are secured from nearby trade centers such as Montgomery and Columbus, Georgia. The good road system throughout the county, plus main roads leading to these centers, furnish a means of rapid transportation both within the county and outside it.

Lee County has had an increase in population of 23.1 percent from 1960 to 1970 and Auburn had an increase of 40 percent during the same period.

The remainder of this section will present in table form an excerpted overview of the economy and characteristics of Lee County.

COMPETITION FOR THE PROPOSED AUBURN BANK AND TRUST COMPANY

Data will be given on competing banks within Lee County.

Exhibit A–9 indicates that the loan/deposit ratios for Auburn and Lee County are somewhat low. Also, there has not been a bank chartered in the major trade areas of Auburn or Opelika since 1923 and presently, there is not a state bank in either of these areas. With the economic development activity that needs to be started now and in the future, the Auburn Bank and Trust Company expects to actively solicit loans and keep a vigorous loan/deposit ratio that is more in keeping with a growing and economically potent trade area.

In addition to the banks, other agencies make loans in the county. The Farmers Home Administration has an office located in the county, and makes loans to rural residents. Their loans include operating loans, farm ownership loans, water and waste disposal system loans to small communities under 5500 population, loans to rural groups for soil and water conservation and shifts in land use, rural housing loans, emergency loans, and water economic opportunity loans. These loans vary from one-year loans for production expenses, to long-term loans for farm ownership and other uses.

The Production Credit Association makes loans to farmers for the production of crops, livestock and the purchase of machinery and equipment. Loans from this agency are usually short-term and intermediate type loans up to seven years. The Federal Land Bank also makes loans to farmers. These include real estate, crop and livestock and general farm improvement loans.

The length of the loans depends on the type, usually ranging from five to 35 years.

The Bank for Cooperatives makes loans to farm marketing, service and supply processing, and purchasing cooperatives. Length of loans and terms depend on the type of loans made.

The Small Business Administration, Economic Development Administration, Department of Housing and Urban Development, Federal Housing Administration, and the Department of Health, Education and Welfare, have loans for certain types of commercial, industrial, public utilities, and recreational enterprises. Insurance companies, the Veterans Administration, and individuals also make loans in the area.

SUMMARY

This report has given data on the convenience and needs of the community for the proposed Auburn Bank and Trust Company.

Statistics on Lee County, Auburn, and financial competition have been presented. It is the contention of this study that:

1. Lee County is an agricultural and industrial area capable of sustaining and increasing economic growth.

2. Auburn is showing good population and economic growth. It is the largest city in the county. However, Auburn, with a larger population, has a combined deposit/population ratio of only $1,529 per person while Opelika has a combined deposit/population ratio of $2,509 per person with a smaller population. This is a

possible indicator of an outflow of deposits to Opelika and other cities.

3.   New shopping malls, plazas, and industrial parks are being built in the Auburn area (example: Village Mall, $5 million investment, proposed opening date March 1973). The Auburn-Opelika area is also fast becoming a medical services center for eastern Alabama.

4.   All present economic barometers seem to indicate that the Auburn-Opelika trade area will become one of Alabama's major trade centers. In fact, this area is presently in the top ten trade areas in the state.

5.   As a sidenote, during the spring 1972 Student Government Association election at Auburn University, one of the SGA presidential hopefuls indicated on his platform that the improvement of bank services and bank relations to the student body would be one of his "planks." The proposed Auburn Bank and Trust Company will hopefully meet their needs.

6.   Based on the preceding report, we submit that Auburn can support the proposed Auburn Bank and Trust Company and that this new bank will more than meet the convenience and needs of the community, while providing increased banking competition, increased economic activity, and the ever worthwhile factor of resulting benefits to the people of Auburn and Lee County.

Exhibit A-1:

Population of Primary Trade Areas for Auburn Bank and Trust Company
(Lee County Subdivisions 1960 to 1970)

Area or Town	1970 Population	1960 Population	Population Increase	Percent Change
Auburn	22,767	16,261	+ 6,506	+ 40.0%
Opelika	19,027	15,678	+ 3,349	+ 21.4%
Loachapoka - Roxana	4,242	3,977	+ 265	+ 6.7%
Beauregard - Marvyn	3,557	3,646	− 89	− 2.4%
Opelika - Rural - Pepperell	4,034	3,789	+ 245	+ 6.5%
Smith's Station - Salem	7,641	5,227	+ 2,414	+ 46.2%

Source: U.S. Dept. of Commerce

Exhibit A-2:

Per Capita Income in Lee County, Alabama
1960 to 1970

Year	Per Capita Income	Percentage Change from 1960 to 1970
1960	$1,257	
1970	$2,362	+ 87.9%

Source: U.S. Dept. of Commerce

Exhibit A-3:

Estimated Non-Agricultural Wage and Salary Employment for Lee County, Alabama
September 1971

Category	Unit (000)
Total Wage Salary	$18,020
Manufacturing	$ 6,790
Mining and Quarries	—
Construction	$ 610
Transportation, Communication and Utilities	$ 570
Wholesale and Retail Trade	$ 2,480
Finance, Insurance and Real Estate	$ 510
Services and Miscellaneous	$ 1,760
Government	$ 5,300

Source: Alabama Dept. of Industrial Relations

Exhibit A-4:

Basic Labor Market Information for Lee County, Alabama
September 1971

Category	Unit
Civilian Work Force	23,620
Total Unemployment	870
Unemployment Rate	3.7
Total Employment	22,750
Non-agricultural Employment:	
Wage and Salary	18,020
All other	3,840
Total	21,860
Agricultural Employment	890

Source: Alabama Dept. of Industrial Relations

Exhibit A-5:

Effective Buying Income Estimates by Households, Lee County, Alabama
1970

Breakdown	Percentage of Households
$0 – $2,999	26.3%
$3,000 – $4,999	17.0%
$5,000 – $7,999	20.5%
$8,000 – $9,999	11.6%
$10,000 and over	24.6%

Source: *1971 Survey of Buying Power, Sales Management Magazine*

Exhibit A-6:

General Characteristics of Lee County, Alabama
1970

General Characteristics:	Data
Number of Households	17,600
Effective Buying Income	$156,476,000
Total Retail Sales	$ 73,019,000
Effective Buying Income Per Household	$ 8,891

Source: *1971 Survey of Buying Power, Sales Management Magazine*

Exhibit A-7:

General Housing Characteristics of Auburn (Lee County) Alabama

Category	Unit
Total Population	22,767
Total Housing Units	6,490
Median Number of Persons per Unit	2.3
Percent Owner Occupied	44.8
Owner Median Value (dollars)	$21,800
Renter Median Contract Rent (dollars)	$ 80

Source: *General Housing Characteristics (Alabama)*, U.S. Dept. of Commerce

Exhibit A-8:

Retail Sales, Lee County, Alabama

Kind of Business	1971 ($1,000)	1970 ($1,000)	Percentage Change 1970 to 1971
Food	11,556	9,413	+22.8%
General Stores with Food & Gas	1,228	1,574	−22.0%
General Merchandise	4,868	6,321	−23.0%
Apparel	3,461	3,336	+ 3.7%
Furniture, Furnishings & Appliances	2,393	2,215	+ 8.0%
Automotive	15,728	11,832	+32.9%
Gasoline Service Stations	5,669	5,211	+ 8.8%
Lumber & Building Materials	4,419	3,615	+22.2%
Hardware & Farm Implements	898	794	+13.1%
Eating Places	8,800	7,834	+12.3%
Drug Stores	2,203	2,099	+ 5.0%
All Other Retail Concerns	6,518	5,929	+ 9.9%
Total Retail Sales	67,739	60,172	+12.6%

*Percent of state sales at Retail for 1971 equals 1.1%

Source: Bureau of Business Research, University of Alabama

Exhibit A-9:

Lee County, Alabama, Bank Competition
December 31, 1971

Bank	City	County	Established (Year)	Offices	Total Deposits	Total Loans	Loans/ Deposits	Total Resources
Auburn National Bank	Auburn	Lee	1907	1	$17,821,553	$ 6,289,982	35.3%	$19,865,813
First National Bank of Auburn	Auburn	Lee	1923	2	$17,559,807	$ 7,277,370	41.4%	$19,268,565
First National Bank of Opelika	Opelika	Lee	1886	1	$12,587,939	$ 5,319,323	42.3%	$13,891,535
Farmers National	Opelika	Lee	1909	1	$16,994,608	$ 9,297,036	54.7%	$18,854,555
Opelika National Bank	Opelika	Lee	1869	3	$20,058,377	$14,127,903	70.4%	$22,676,546
First State Bank	Smiths	Lee	1970	1	$ 1,200,000	$ 689,000	57.4%	$ 1,500,000

Source: *Published Call Reports December 31, 1971*

273

Case 2

Jackson County Bank

This case was prepared by Professors Larry E. Price and Lynn E. Dellenbarger, Jr., of Georgia Southern College as a basis for class discussion rather than to illustrate either effective or ineffective handling of an administrative situation.

Presented at a Case Workshop and distributed by the Intercollegiate Case Clearing House, Soldiers Field, Boston, Mass. 02163. All rights reserved to the contributors.

"It is so obvious that the biggest reason for wanting a branch bank is because our competition has one." Thus spoke Martin Thomas, member of the Board of Jackson County Bank, as he left a board meeting in early spring 1972. Thomas served as vice president and cashier of the bank. Some weeks earlier he had been appointed to spearhead a task force to report back to the board on the desirability of alternate locations for a proposed new branch. In giving him this assignment, Randy Holland, chairman of the board, told the members:

"I feel that it is now necessary for us to begin placing branches in different areas, in order that we may not only better serve our customers, but also that we may keep pace with our competition."

Following Holland's comments, the board went on to decide that branching was necessary to insure the continued growth of the bank. Board members felt that a branch should be profitable in its own right and should not be operated at a loss. Nathan Beasley, president of the bank, assured Thomas that he would support the task force study by assigning needed clerical help so that the job of gathering facts and figures for a report to the board could go forward. Because some board members had only recently been elected, Thomas felt it would be helpful to begin his report with a recap of the history of the bank as well as a capsule of the local economic picture. The information he gathered included this rundown:

The Jackson County Bank is located in the county seat of Carnes, Georgia. The bank began operations in 1934 following the reorganization of an earlier failed bank. Local businessmen generally perceive the bank as being more conservatively managed than its competitor, the Adams State Bank. Adams, for example, has already entered the branching field by establishing a branch near the campus of Eastern Georgia College located on the southern edge of Carnes. Adams State has also recently opened a new elaborate downtown home Office just two blocks from the older and less attractive facility of Jackson County.

The town of Carnes, as well as Jackson County, has experienced a period of growth and prosperity during the decade of the 60s. The population of the county rose to 31,585 at the last census. The city population was 14,616, not including the college community. Student enrollment in the current term is at an all-time high of 6,027. The college enrollment has caused state funding to be made available for an extensive building program on campus with four major buildings under construction and two more in the early planning stages.

Carnes is not reliant solely on the college. Several branch plants of major industries have located in the area. Figures supplied by the local Chamber of Commerce show that the six largest employers have a payroll of over $9,000,000 annually. The County remains, however, primarily an agricultural center. Some of the more important crops include tobacco, peanuts, corn, soybeans, pecans, timber, and livestock. Estimated agricultural sales for 1970, the latest figures that Thomas could locate, were $25 million.

Because three major highways intersect in Carnes a substantial tourism related business growth has been experienced. There are 13 motels and one hotel located in town. The 12 local restaurants have a total seating capacity of 1,944. Thomas considered this to be quite remarkable in a town of only 14,000 population.

Thomas next briefed Mr. Beasley on the background information he developed. After reviewing the facts presented, Beasley remarked, "I think we have all been surprised at how rapidly our area has progressed recently, I am particularly surprised at the large revenue from farming. Between agriculture, industry, and the college, I believe that Carnes and Jackson County have a very promising future."

Beasley went on to explain that the action of Adams State Bank in establishing a branch near the college had convinced the board that they must place a branch *somewhere* because of the action of their competitor. As Beasley put it, "There is really no way to know how everyone would feel if the Adams Bank didn't have a branch, but I feel sure that this strong desire of the directors for a branch is quite successful." As Beasley explained it, "Adams definitely got the jump on us with that branch. Now we are trying to find a place to put a branch that will be equally or more effective than *their* branch. After all, that's the name of the game."

Since the Adams branch has been started, the total assets of Adams have outdistanced Jackson County by about $3 million. Thomas was convinced, however, that at least some part of this increase was window dressing of the Adams reports in order to make the operation of their branch seem even more successful than it had really been. The year end statement of condition for Jackson, Exhibit 1, showed resources of about $14 million while Adams was claiming footings of $17 million.

Thomas began a search of the community for possible branch bank locations. One area immediately came to mind. Although it was not yet generally known in the community, Thomas had learned about a shopping center to be built. This new College Plaza Shopping Center would be located about one-fourth mile from the Eastern Georgia College campus. This was on the south side of town, the area that experienced the largest building growth during the last decade. The shopping center site was alongside a major U.S. highway and only about one mile from the center of town. The center, when completed, would have space for 12 stores. Leases had been signed so far with only four businesses, but Thomas believed that as soon as the plans were announced to the business community that some specialty shops would quickly be lined up to fill out the vacancies. Just adjacent to the shopping center was the empty building previously used by a national franchise fast food restaurant that had failed. Only the vacant building was left and Thomas knew that it would be available at a reasonable price.

If Jackson County wanted to place a branch near the shopping center, but not actually in the center proper, a good possibility might be the purchase and conversion of the building into a branch bank. It would be possible to construct a short road that would run from the rear of the building directly into the shopping center parking lot, which would enable customers to go from one lot to the other without entering the major highway. This was an important factor to Thomas because he feared that although a lot of customers would be in the immediate area, traffic congestion might discourage the use of the branch bank. The State Highway Department was working on plans to enlarge the highway at the point where it passed the shopping center. This would make it much easier to enter and leave the parking lots and would probably relieve some of the congestion.

Thomas wished to prepare a pro forma statement of the proposed branch if it were located in the College Plaza Center. Since it was uncertain how many stores, and which ones, would occupy the Plaza, he felt that the uncertainties precluded constructing any kind of meaningful estimated statements.

Thomas was able to locate only one other possible site for the proposed branch. The Carnes Mall was nearing completion. The Mall was located about three miles from the center of town in an easterly direction. As in the case of the Plaza shopping center, the Mall was located on a U.S. highway. The Mall was inconveniently located for students at Eastern Georgia College. It was far from some areas of town but was quite convenient to many county residents in the eastern section of Jackson County. Several national chain stores were located in the Mall. Although the Mall was not yet open to the public for retail sales, the stores were near opening date. Thus, employees had been hired and were already at work stocking shelves and learning the company procedures of their new employers. Thomas talked with several of the store managers as well as with the officials of the newly formed Mall Merchants Association.

Mall merchants projected total retail sales for the first year of operation at $10–12 million. Based on this information Thomas attempted to prepare an estimated statement for a branch located at the Mall. Using some figures taken from averages furnished by his state bankers association, he estimated that the branch would generate $700 thousand in demand deposits and $300 thousand in time deposits. He concluded that the branch would garner 675 new demand deposit accounts and 115 new time deposit customers. He incorporated these estimates in Exhibit 2, which he prepared for presentation to the Board of Directors.

One important factor of concern to Thomas was the distance from the Mall to the college. He wished he had a way of measuring the likely success of drawing students the three miles from the campus to the Mall branch. As Thomas observed to this assistant, "It's not the most convenient location for the students, but since the Mall will be open long before College Plaza, maybe they will get in the habit of driving out to the Mall for shopping."

Thomas estimated that it would cost the same amount to place a branch bank at either location. After consulting bank equipment dealers, he figured that the cost of the branch would be about $125,000. He thought the board would seek the funds from an additional issue of stock offered to existing holders of the bank's common.

After spending several days at his desk looking over all of the data he had gathered, Thomas went into President Beasley's office to see if the two of them could finalize a recommendation for the next meeting of the Board of Directors.

Exhibit 1:

Jackson County Bank
Condensed Statement of Condition

	December 31, 197X
Assets	
Cash & Due from Banks	$ 1,726,814.67
U. S. Government Securities	2,671,819.89
Other Bonds & Securities	1,151,251.50
Federal Funds Sold	None
Loans & Discounts	7,917,236.91
Banking House	247,899.77
Furniture & Fixtures	67,453.93
Other Real Estate	None
Accrued Interest Receivable	48,926.80
Other Assets	5,781.50
Total Assets	$13,837,184.97
Liabilities	
Capital	$ 300,000.00
Surplus	400,000.00
Undivided Profits	136,137.08
Reserves	223,508.63
Reserves for Taxes, Expenses, etc.	108,842.49
Unearned Discounts	193,963.46
Deposits	12,474,733.31
Total Liabilities	$13,837,184.97

Exhibit 2:

Jackson County Bank
Mall Branch Pro-Forma Income Statements

	197X + 1	*197X + 2*	*197X + 3*
Demand Deposits	$700,000	$900,000	$1,200,000
Time Deposits	300,000	400,000	550,000
Number of New Accounts			
Demand	675	1,020	1,560
Time	115	165	225
Total Deposits	$925,000	$1,225,000	$1,625,000
Gross Income	61,050	80,850	107,250
Net Income	8,420	18,665	31,063

Case 3

A Bank IS a Bank—Is a Bank?

This case was prepared by Professor Eleanor Casebier with the collaboration of Professor Manning Hanline at The University of West Florida. It is designed to be used as a basis for class discussion rather than to illustrate either effective or ineffective handling of decision making.

More than 700 stockholders were represented when an application for authority to organize a bank in Pensacola, Florida, was filed in May, 1976. This was the largest group that had ever applied for a bank charter in Florida. The application was unusual also because the seven persons whose names appeared on it were all women. The major purpose of the bank was to serve the financial needs of women. Filing for a charter represented a culmination of intense effort over a ten-month period from August, 1975 to May, 1976. The announcement of the decision by three women to organize a bank appeared in *The Pensacola News Journal* on August 24, 1975. The news item presented this action of the women as another example of feminine invasion of fields traditionally dominated by men. It stated that the first all-women's bank was chartered in Cleveland in 1935. Two such groups in Florida—this one and another in Tallahassee—were working for a bank charter.

Justification for the action can be seen from statements in the newspaper article containing quotes from the three women:

Mrs. Hunter: "We feel the community is ready for it . . . and the brilliant caliber of women right here in this community will help make this a success."

Mrs. Moore: "Women are not given the same consideration in the trust department. . . . The male trust officers don't feel you know enough as a woman to make decisions on what to do with your money. They give advice, instead of listening to any ideas women might have."

Mrs. Hadley: "That's right . . . A man in a pair of pants feels he knows more. But I've been in the business world long enough to know better."

Both Mrs. Hadley and Mrs. Moore were realtors. Mrs. Hunter worked for the city.

Further evidence of a felt need for improving credit facilities for women was the new federal law which was a part of the Equal Credit Opportunity Act passed in October, 1975. The law states, "A creditor shall not discriminate against any applicant on the basis of sex or marital status with respect to any aspect of a credit transaction." According to the December (1975) issue of *American Teacher,* "the ECOA marks the first legislation written to deal with the rampant discrimination against women by banking and loan companies. Some of the regulations go into effect immediately; others will be phased in gradually until February, 1977. Sexist credit applications have to be changed by next June 30. Creditors won't have to explain why they reject a woman's application until next year."

Also, Regulation B, issued by the Federal Reserve Board on October 28, 1975, expressly states: "A creditor shall not discriminate against any applicant on the basis of sex or marital status with respect to any aspect of a credit transaction." Section 202.4 (b) says: "A creditor shall not refuse, on the basis of sex or marital status, to grant a separate account to a credit-worthy applicant."

It appears from the foregoing comments that women have been discriminated against in matters pertaining to credit. A need for the bank in Pensacola could be based on patterns of population growth, as well. Statements supporting this need are quoted from the Pensacola paper under the dateline of November 26, 1975.

Exhibit 1

POPULATION EXPANSION CALLS FOR PLANNING

A POPULATION projection for the Pensacola metropolitan area predicted for the next five years by *Sales Management* magazine, forcefully points up the urgency for sound planning, both economic and environmental.

The Pensacola area, which includes Pensacola Beach and Gulf Breeze in Santa Rosa County, is listed 12th in growth in Florida, with a 15.1 percent increase by 1980 and a population of 325,400, of which 265,200 would reside in Escambia County.

If the magazine's projection is accurate, there will be an influx of approximately 50,000 new residents, most of them living in the extreme southern portion of Escambia County between Pensacola and Perdido bays.

And if this projection is incorrect, it most certainly errs on the conservative side.

Increasing numbers of people seek the mild climate of the South, both the old in search of retirement homes and the young attracted by year-round recreational opportunities, and they all endeavor to get as near the Gulf Coast as possible.

A case analysis is made of the decision points which occurred in the organizational period. It is well to keep in mind that the decision-making group was an interim board of directors that varied in size over time. There were 20 board members at the time the charter application was filed. Only one of them had previous experience in banking, although their backgrounds included many years of business experience.

The ultimate goal was to obtain a bank charter, and this could be accomplished only after an application had been filed. Before that could happen stock subscriptions had to be acquired in the amount of one million dollars and a feasibility study and site analysis had to be completed. Raising required capital was not an easy task, especially since there were no women of great wealth on the interim board for most of the time in which stock subscriptions were sought. Financial strength came from hundreds of individuals (mostly women) in the community who saw the project as an opportunity both to lend support to a women's group and also to make a wise investment.

Obviously, legal requirements had to be met. Most of the activity that is described in this case was an effort to comply with the state laws for organizing a bank. The following steps are necessary to get a charter:

1. Application. The application must be in compliance of regulation (Charter) 659. It must include proof of need and a reasonable promise of success.

2. Field investigation. This is done by the comptroller's office and the FDIC. The State will be looking at the site, speaking to local bankers and businessmen. The FDIC does the same.

3. Actual investigation. This is a very thorough investigation of the charter applicants.

4. Public meeting. This is designed to let residents of the area speak for or against a new bank. This was presented as a great opportunity for local feedback and an opportunity to use the rules advantageously by getting women, men, and blacks to come to the meeting and speak positively about a women's bank.

5. Evaluation. The reports from the field investigation (in the community) are sent back to Tallahassee for evaluation of the business expertise and ability of the proposed charter applicants to manage a bank. Simultaneously, reports of public meeting (pros and cons) are submitted for evaluation. Both of these reports are open for public review.

6. Comptrollers' conference. The comptroller or deputy comptroller hears arguments from each side concerning the advisability of the bank. There is no cross examination. The applicants, the protestants, and public attend.

7. Order. The decision on the application is called the order and the order is made after the comptroller's conference.

Before a charter will be granted, the comptroller must be convinced of three things—management, capital and need. A reasonable chance of success must be proved and the burden of proof is on the applicant. One factor that caused concern was that a branch banking law had been passed and would take effect in 1977. A copy of the Senate Bill revising the law follows:

Exhibit 2

Chapter 76–142
Senate Bill No. 711

AN ACT relating to industrial savings banks; amending s. 656.071(1), Florida Statutes; providing for the establishment of branch banks, the relocation of a parent or branch bank, and the merger of banks; providing an effective date.

Be it Enacted by the Legislature of the State of Florida:

Section 1. Subsection (1) of section 656.071, Florida Statutes, is amended to read:

(Substantial rewording of subsection. See S. 656.071(1), F. S., for present text.)

656.071 Place of transacting business; drive-in facilities.—

(1) (a) Any bank heretofore or hereafter incorporated pursuant to this chapter shall have one principal place of doing business as designated in its articles of incorporation; in addition, with the approval of the department and upon such conditions as the department shall prescribe, including a satisfactory showing by the bank that public convenience and necessity will be served thereby, any bank may establish up to two branches per calendar year within the limits of the county in which the parent bank is located and, in addition, may establish branches by merger with other banks located within the county in which the parent bank is located. The location of a parent bank or of a branch bank may be moved if the department determines that public convenience and necessity will be served by such move, but the location of a parent bank or of a branch bank may not be moved beyond the limits of the county in which it is located. The term "parent bank" shall

be construed to mean the bank or banking office at which the principal functions of the bank are conducted. An application for a branch bank shall be in writing in such form as the department prescribes, supported by such information, data and records as the department may require to make findings necessary for approval. The department shall not act upon a branch application until it has completed consideration of any bank application pending when the branch application was filed if the proposed locations for such branch and bank are within one mile of each other. Provided however, that action upon a branch application shall not be delayed more than six months after its filing due to the pendency of such a prior bank application. When the department has approved an application, it shall issue a certificate authorizing the operation of the branch bank and specifying the date on which it may be opened and the place where it will be located.

(b) This subsection shall be construed to allow the merger of banks within the same county and the operation by the merged company of such banks, and to allow the sale of any bank to, and the purchase thereof through merger by, any other bank in the same county and the operation of such banks by the merged bank, provided that the Department of Banking and Finance shall be of the opinion and shall first determine that public convenience and necessity will be served by such operation.

Section 2. This act shall take effect January 1, 1977.

Approved by the Governor June 15, 1976

Filed in Office of Secretary of State June 16, 1976.

REPRODUCED by FBA

JULY, 1976

Applications take anywhere from one to seven years but can be done in 270 days or nine months. Because the branch banking law was passed, speed in preparing the application was imperative. The decision-making group felt extreme pressure in relation to time. Since *need* for additional banking facilities had to proved, a stronger case could be made for this bank with an application filed prior to those that certainly would be made by existing banks for establishing branches.

Decision Point 1 The first decision was that of the three women to organize a bank which was to be owned, managed, and operated mainly for the benefit of women. After a public announcement in the newspaper, there was quite a lot of interest in the project. Many persons contacted the three women organizers and indicated a wish to support the effort or to be employed by the bank.

Decision Point 2 An open meeting was held for the first time on Monday, October 7, 1975. Prior to that time several decisions had been made by the organizers. There had been agreement about a proposed name and location as well as preliminary plans for design of the building to house the bank. Other areas covered were requirements for directors, proposed capital structure, and statement of purpose. Seven women had been selected to serve on the Interim Board. These early decisions were made primarily by Mrs. Hunter, her husband, who acted as attorney for the group, and Mrs. Imus, who was comptroller of a local motel. At subsequent dates and decision points, many of these items were changed.

The first meeting was conducted by the interim board of directors which was made up of five realtors, Mrs. Imus and Mrs. Hunter. It was well attended and there was obviously great interest and enthusiasm about the bank. Women present were lawyers, teachers, professors, realtors, government employees, and housewives. At the meeting there was a general discussion of the bank project, followed by a distribution of stock subscription forms. Capital stock had a par value initially of five dollars a share—later increased to ten dollars. A subscription fee of 5 percent was assessed at the time of the agreement. This money was to be used as a contingency fund for paying legal fees, application fees, and other expenses incurred in the organization phase. Subscriptions were to be paid in full at the time the charter was granted. Subsequent meetings held from time to time followed the same general format.

Decision Point 3 During October, the number of women named to the Interim Board of Directors was increased from seven to thirteen. One of these was a newcomer to the community, with several years of experience in banking. Two of the new directors were black, both prominent educators. One woman was quite active in state politics and in the women's movement. The number was increased again in March in an effort to include women whose names might be helpful in applying for the charter.

Decision Point 4 On November 6, 1975, a "Notice Required For Proposed New Financial Institution" was mailed to the Division of Securities, Tallahassee, Florida. According to state banking laws, this had to be done prior to application, and renewal was possible in the event that an application was not forwarded within 90 days. One of the benefits of having filed a formal notification was that the Board could deposit checks received as payment for stock subscriptions. Checks were made payable to Ed O. Hunter, Trustee, and the money could not be used prior to the formal notification.

Decision Point 5 A dinner meeting was held for a few interested women on November 25, at the home of Mary Baker, who was corresponding secretary. Several matters of concern were discussed. One of these had to do with the question of selling stock to men. Some of those present felt quite strongly that the bank stock should be owned only by women. Yet, it was obvious that this would be discriminatory and therefore illegal. A decision was made to accept stock subscriptions from men. This policy change was approved by the board on January 12.

The formal motion carried a stipulation that the percentage of stock held by male stockholders would be restricted.

Decision Point 6 Completion of a market study and site analysis was required as a part of the application for a charter. The decision to award a contract for this proved difficult for the board. The problem became an issue in November and was finally solved in late December. Three proposals were examined. One was submitted by the Marketing Department of the local university. Their price was $10,000 and the proposal was rejected because it was too costly. Another bid for the contract was submitted by the Management Department of the same university; their proposal was also rejected. The contract was awarded to a professional team from Miami. Mike Barth, an economist, had ten years of experience in economic and market consulting and had worked on many charters throughout the country, most of them successfully. Mr. Hansen, an attorney, had been general counsel to the State of Florida comptroller's office and helped draft existing rules that applied to this charter. The bank attorney indicated his hearty approval of this choice in a memorandum to the interim board on December 23, 1975. Fees for Barth and Hansen were established at roughly $6,500 each.

Decision Point 7 Barth told the board members that they must make a decision as to whether they intended to be a member of the Federal Reserve System or apply for membership in the Federal Deposit Insurance Corporation. He advised that there are advantages to being a member of the *Fed* but a non-member is less closely regulated. The group voted to apply for membership in FDIC.

Decision Point 8 A pressing problem came to the attention of the board in January and February. On December 2, subscriptions amounted to about a half million dollars. On January 12, a financial report was submitted showing the Bank had about $540,000 in subscriptions. By February the increase had amounted to only $50,000. This represented too little progress and members were disappointed. A decision was made to use a new approach in an effort to acquire the needed minimum of one million dollars in subscriptions. The Board decided to spend money in fairly generous amounts in an effort to increase subscriptions. They began a program of luncheons and parties to attract subscriptions.

On February 26, there was an open meeting at a local country club held in the evening. Coffee was served as well as several kinds of hors d'oeuvres. About 200 attended and the number who showed an interest in subscribing to stock was gratifying. There was a distressing situation that developed in relation to this meeting. The bill from the country club was $700. Board members felt it was excessive for the service rendered. This was a learning experience and was not to be repeated.

Luncheon meetings were held almost weekly. The guest list was provided by various members of the board. The number attending the luncheon was between 15 and 20. Two or three members of the board would explain the bank project and solicit subscriptions. Sales of stock picked up very rapidly and by March 22 it was reported that in excess of $800,000 had been subscribed.

Decision Point 9 A site had to be chosen before an application could be prepared. Barth was responsible for assisting in this decision based on an exhaustive economic study of the area. Several sites were available and were investigated. One of these was a building formerly used as a brewery. It was rejected because that location was not considered to be a favorable one. It was in an old, rundown neighborhood and on a street with only an average traffic flow. A second site was an abandoned grocery store building, available for $360,000. It was on a 1.57-acre tract of land directly across from a ma-

jor bank. One drawback to this location was that on two of the three access streets there was only a one-way traffic flow.

A third possibility consisted of a 4-acre tract of land in a large, new shopping center. The land was available for $310,000, part of which could be paid in stock. Interest payments of $6,000 would be needed quarterly to reserve the tract.

A fourth site carried with it an opportunity to substantially increase stock subscriptions. It was described as "a parcel of land located in the southeast quadrant of the intersection of Bayou Boulevard and 170 feet on the north side of Dodson Drive." It was near a huge shopping complex in the center of the metropolitan area. This possibility was made known to the board on March 24. A wealthy couple, Jim and Christy Sons, who owned this site, had offered to make it available for the bank. They had agreed to subscribe to $400,000 in stock, pay the required 5 percent fee, or $20,000, and in return accept $30,000 as lease payment for one year. Rental for the property was $30,000 annually and the lease agreement was to be for ten years. There was no building on the property.

Board members were concerned about two aspects of this offer. First, there had been an early agreement that no one person would control the bank as a result of holding more than 10,000 shares of stock. It was obvious that the Sons family, with one-third of the capital stock, could easily get enough votes to control all matters including membership on the board of directors as well as chairmanship of the board. This was resolved, on paper at least, by issuing 10,000 shares of stock to each of four members of the Sons family—husband, wife, and two children. The other major concern was that a ten-year lease was insufficient for the purpose of obtaining a mortgage to build a bank structure. This was resolved by obtaining an option to renew the lease for an additional 30 years. With these decisions clearing away any further objections, the offer was accepted and subscriptions were closed at $1.2 million.

One would have expected some members of the board to increase their stock subscriptions after hearing about the Sons' offer. In fact, during the 24-hour period following the disclosure of the offer of the Sons family, two board members increased their subscriptions. One member subscribed to 100 shares and the other subscribed to 300 shares.

A stockholder's meeting was called for the following Monday evening, March 29, at which time affidavits were signed and notarized which was another legal requirement before the charter application could be finalized. On this same date there was a board meeting, and an announcement was made that the sale of stock to the Sons family had been finalized, and the lease agreement had been signed. Mrs. Sons was introduced as a member of the interim board. Members of the board planned a dinner party to celebrate acquiring a charter.

Case 4

First Hawaiian Bank
Formation of a Bank Holding Company

There is not supposed to be any such thing as a free lunch in this world, but it certainly looks like one may have arrived in the mail this morning. A letter and prospectus from First Hawaiian Bank, a company in which you own stock, announced that a special stockholders' meeting would be held on April 19, 1974. At the meeting stockholders will be asked to approve a merger of First Hawaiian Bank into a subsidiary of a bank holding company. Each share of stock in the bank would be exchanged for a share of stock in First Hawaiian, Inc., the bank holding company. Instead of holding stock in the bank only, you would own stock in a larger organization, the holding company, which included the bank as a subsidiary.

In the letter to stockholders, John Bellinger, president of First Hawaiian Bank, pointed to several advantages of the proposal and to the unanimous recommendation for approval by the Board of Directors. The proposal may result in greater growth potential due to an expansion of the banking operations and other financial services currently offered by the bank. There will be new alternative ways to raise funds in financial and monetary markets not now available to the bank. Also, the holding company will have the ability to establish or acquire certain other financial enterprises as authorized recently by the Federal Reserve Board.

In forming a bank holding company, First Hawaiian is following the course taken by its major competitor, the Bank of Hawaii. In 1972 the Bank of Hawaii formed Hawaii Bancorporation, a bank holding company. Rival Hawaii Bancorporation has already set up two new subsidiaries with the bank and issued commercial paper in its own name;

one subsidiary provides computer services while the other is in the leasing business.

First Hawaiian proudly claims to be the "Bank that says yes." What you have to decide is whether you want to be the stockholder who says yes. The proposal certainly looks good. There has been a great deal of talk lately in the financial press about the rapid expansion of the bank holding company movement, and you have seen numerous references to other bank holding companies moving into areas which are closely related to banking yet denied to banks themselves. On the other hand, there might be some disadvantages to the proposal. After all, except for Bank of Hawaii, none of the other banks in Hawaii has set up a bank holding company. Before the April stockholder meeting you plan to consider thoroughly all the advantages and disadvantages so that you can make an intelligent decision.

FIRST HAWAIIAN BANK

First Hawaiaan Bank is the oldest bank in the State of Hawaii, being established in 1858. Known then as Bishop and Co., it was founded by Charles Reed Bishop and William Aldrich. It was a one-room bank in the Makee Building on Kaahumanu Street. For the next 27 years it was the only bank chartered in Hawaii until Claus Spreckels and Co. came along in 1885. Over the past century the bank has grown and prospered, acquiring other banks and adding branches until it now has 40 offices.

Today, First Hawaiian offers a broader range of financial services than any other bank in Hawaii's tough competitive environment. The bank is an active lender in the commercial, consumer, and real estate loan markets. Demand, savings, and time deposits are accepted. Unlike its major rival, the Bank of Hawaii, it has a trust department which handles a full range of trust services. The International Banking Department finances international trade, principally in the Pacific Basin area.

As Exhibit 1 shows, First Hawaiian is the second largest bank in the state with assets well above American Security, the next largest. Only the Bank of Hawaii is larger, but it wasn't always that way. Back in 1956, First Hawaiian Bank was the State's largest bank. Being second biggest is not an easy thing to accept, even if it is large enough to rank 117th nationally, and a number of competitive moves have been taken in recent years. At the start of 1969 the bank switched from a national to a state charter and gave up its membership in the Federal Reserve System. This added substantially to the funds available for use as loans or investments. As a Federal Reserve member the bank could not count money deposited with correspondent banks as part of its required reserves. With a state charter these deposits do count toward the requirement. Later in 1969, the bank introduced the Master Charge credit card to Hawaii. In 1970 the bank entered the field of international banking when it became a member of Allied Bank International. This consortium of 18 U.S. banks is organized to compete effectively with the international banking giants such as Chase Manhattan, First National City, and Bank of America.

Of course, the Bank of Hawaii has not been standing still. In 1972 it became the first bank in Hawaii to form a bank holding company.

BANK HOLDING COMPANY LEGISLATION

In 1956 Congress passed the Bank Holding Company Act. The Federal Reserve was concerned at the time that holding companies were being used to evade the intent of the Banking Act of 1933. Banks were not supposed to engage in business activities unrelated to banking, yet bank holding companies or their affiliates were doing what their subsidiary banks were prohibited from doing. The 1956 Act sharply limited the nonbank activities. Only those which were "a

Exhibit 1:

Asset Size of Hawaii's Banks
December 31, 1973

	Assets $000	*% of Total*
Bank of Hawaii	$1,024,219	37.3%
First Hawaiian Bank	887,972	32.4%
American Security Bank	214,900	7.8%
Central Pacific Bank	208,415	7.6%
City Bank	141,757	5.2%
Liberty Bank	138,174	5.0%
Hawaii National Bank	114,120	4.2%
Bank of Honolulu	13,631	0.5%
	$2,743,189	100.0%

Source: Bank Examiner Reports, State of Hawaii Department of Regulatory Agencies

proper incident to" banking or managing or controlling banks and which were "of a financial, fiduciary or insurance nature" could be undertaken. Holding companies were given a choice of relinquishing all but one of their banks or else getting rid of their nonbanking interests. Significantly, the law only applied to multibank holding companies. This was because many organizations, including Goodyear Tire and Rubber, Hershey Foods, the United Mine Workers, and even Dartmouth College, owned small and relatively insignificant banks.

Exclusion of one-bank holding companies meant they could engage in unrestricted types of business activity. It wasn't long before this loophole was discovered and exploited. By the end of the 1960s the number of one-bank holding companies and their nonbank activities increased greatly. The 1970 amendments to the Bank Holding Company Act restored control over bank holding companies. There were two key aspects of the amendments. First, one-bank holding companies were now included. Second, in a liberalization of the 1956 Act, the Federal Reserve Board, which administered the Act, was directed to determine acceptable non-banking activities for holding companies. Holding companies could not, however, return to earlier ways since these activities were to be "so closely related to

banking or managing or controlling banks as to be a proper incident thereto." Missing was the earlier phraseology "Financial, fiduciary, or insurance [in] nature."

By early 1974 the list of permitted activities for bank holding companies (designated Regulation Y) included the following:

1. Mortgage banking
2. Finance company (consumer or commercial)
3. Insurance
4. Leasing or real and personal property
5. Data processing
6. Factoring
7. Community development
8. Industrial banking
9. Trust services
10. Investment or financial advising

In announcing its intention to form a bank holding company, First Hawaiian stated that the holding company had no present intention to acquire other banks. It might engage through subsidiaries in those activities which are permitted by the Bank Holding Company Act and the regulations of the Board of Governors of the Federal Reserve System, but according to the letter to shareholders, there are currently "no definite plans" to do so. A newspaper report noted that Mr. Bellinger was legally barred from discussing possible holding company ventures, but "the Bank wouldn't be setting up the holding company unless it had some specific ideas, with prospects for near-term results."

THE PROPOSAL

At the meeting called for April 19, 1974, the stockholders would be asked to approve the merger of First Hawaiian Bank into a subsidiary of a bank holding company, First Hawaiian, Inc. The technical details of the transaction would call for First Hawaiian Bank to merge with a newly organized state bank, FHB Bank, whose common stock except for Directors shares is owned by First Hawaiian, Inc. After the merger, FHB Bank would change its name to First Hawaiian Bank, thereby continuing the name of the present bank. The bank subsidiary would carry on the same banking activities as before and keep the same officers and directors.

Exchange Ratio The 3,045,360 shares of Bank stock could be exchanged on a one-for-one basis for shares in First Hawaiian, Inc., the holding company. An additional 24,640 shares of authorized holding company stock would be available for future acquisitions or other corporate purposes.

Required Vote The formulation of the holding company was approved earlier by the Federal Reserve Board. The merger has been approved by the Department of Regulatory Agencies of the State of Hawaii. An application is on file with the FDIC. This application will be acted upon if there is a favorable vote from holders of two-thirds of the bank stock.

Stockholders who reject the exchange Stockholders who do not want to exchange their bank stock for holding company stock may exercise their right to receive the appraised cash value of the bank shares as provided for in Section 404–10 of the Hawaii Revised Statutes. This option is available only to stockholders who vote against the proposal. The amount paid for these shares will be established by the new bank subsidiary and it will represent what is considered to be the fair market value at the time of the stockholders' meeting. If this value is not acceptable to the dissenting stockholders, a second appraisal will be made by three appraisers. One each will be selected by the dissenting stockholders and the bank directors, with these two selecting a third person.

This plan differs from the offer made by Bank of Hawaii when it formed a holding company. The Bank of Hawaii made a tender offer to existing stockholders. Those who did not accept, about 0.5 percent of the stock outstanding, kept their bank shares.

Reasons for the plan The prospectus distributed to shareholders contains the following statement in support of the proposal:

The directors and principal officers of the Bank believe that a bank holding company will be able to enter into more diversified financial activities than the Bank can do directly or through bank-owned subsidiaries. A bank holding company may provide more alternatives in the raising of funds required by the Continuing Bank, or by other subsidiaries of the holding company under changing conditions in financial and monetary markets. A holding company also has greater flexibility than the Bank in structuring the establishment or acquisition of banks and other financial enterprises. A bank is not permitted by law to engage in certain businesses, even though they are closely related to banking. Similarly, it may not own subsidiaries engaging in such businesses. A holding company may do both.

Income tax consequences Shareholders who receive holding company shares will not pay

taxes on the exchange and will contiue to have the same tax basis as with the bank stock. Dissenting shareholders who elect to receive cash will be liable for taxes due on any realized gain.

COMPARISON OF BANK STOCK WITH HOLDING COMPANY STOCK

Dividends   Until other subsidiaries become part of the holding company, dividends of the continuing bank will be the only source of dividends for the holding company. The ability of the Bank to legally pay dividends remains the same.

Voting rights   Hawaii laws require that stockholders in state banks have cumulative voting rights. Stockholders in the holding company will not have cumulative voting rights.

Liquidation rights   In liquidation, stockholders receive pro rata any assets distributed. There is no change.

Amendments to by-laws   Bank stockholders must approve any changes in the by-laws of the bank. The by-laws of the holding company may be amended by the board of directors without stockholder action.

STOCKHOLDERS AND MARKET TRADING

There are approximately 2,250 stockholders who own the 3,045,360 shares of First Hawaiian Bank stock. The bank's officers and directors own a total of 36,910 shares. In addition four of the directors are trustees for the estate of S. M. Damon, which holds 700,000 shares (23 percent) of stock. There are no other stockholders who own more than 10 percent of the stock. The stock has unlisted trading privileges on the Honolulu Stock Exchange and it is traded on the over-the-counter market. The latest closing bid price at the Honolulu Stock Exchange was $23.50. This is just above its recent low of $21 and well below its 1973 high of $36. Exhibit 3 contains more detailed stock prices as well as information about Hawaii Bancorporation stock, the holding company for the Bank of Hawaii.

RELATIONSHIP OF BANK TO OTHER AFFILIATES OF THE HOLDING COMPANY

There would be no direct relationship between the bank and other affiliates of the bank holding company. If the holding company should start or acquire, for instance, a leasing affiliate, the leasing company would be a subsidiary of the holding company and not of the bank. The only factor the bank and the leasing company would have in common would be their common ownership by the holding company.

The ability of the bank to flow funds to other affiliates would also be limited. There are three main devices by which funds could be transferred: by loans to affiliates, through dividends to the holding company, and by the purchase of assets. Each of these has its limitations.

Loans to affiliates   These are limited by the Federal Reserve Act, as amended and the Banking Act of 1933, as amended. Loans of insured banks to individual affiliates may not exceed 10 percent of the bank's capital and surplus. Loans to all affiliates combined are limited to 20 percent. Furthermore, these loans must usually be secured by collateral which has a market value in excess of the amount of the loan.

Dividends   Dividends cannot be paid to the parent company which would endanger the bank. As a state bank, First Hawaiian cannot pay dividends greater than its undivided profits.

Purchase of assets   A bank could try to bail out a troubled affiliate by purchasing assets. There are, however, limitations on the kinds of assets banks can buy. For insured banks, there are laws restricting loans to affiliates which are so broadly defined that the Federal Reserve Board has taken the position it covers the purchase of assets in this situation.

Commenting on the separation of the bank from the other bank holding company activities, one observer notes "It is in the interests of depositors, examiners, and shareholders alike for the capital accounts of individual banks to be protected as much as possible from the risk associated with innovation—and yet innovation is absolutely essential if banks are to keep up with the changing times. The bank holding company structure serves both purposes."

STUDIES OF HOLDING COMPANY PROFITABILITY AND RISK

Although every proposal to change from a bank to a bank holding company is probably a unique situation, it is interesting to look at what has happened in other such situations. A number of studies have examined the change in profitability for banks affiliated to bank holding companies. None of the evidence reported so far, however, concerns bank holding companies that acquired non-bank subsidiaries. The performance studies generally conclude that profitability does not improve significantly. The common methodology of the studies was to identify a set of acquired banks and compare them with a control group of "similar" non-acquired banks. Rose and Fraser, who have published a review of these studies, conclude that "Bank holding companies seem to have much less effect on the performance of their affiliated institutions than both the supporters and the critics of the holding company movement would have us believe."[1]

We've all heard of the statement that a growth company and a growth stock are not necessarily the same thing. Let's look at what happened to stockholder returns. There are two studies available with conflicting results:

1. Upson and Jessup have concluded that for the 1957–1971 period bank holding companies provided significantly higher returns to investors than did banks.[2] Their study compared a group of banks with a separate group of bank holding companies over the same time period.

2. Brewer and Dukes used a different approach and concluded that stockholders who exchanged their bank stock for bank holding company stock between 1965 and 1973 have generally faced a decline in returns, an increase in market risk, or both.[3] Return was measured for 78 weeks before and after becoming a holding company and was adjusted for changes in Standard and Poor's Bank Index. In 34 of 41 cases the bank stock provided the higher return. The mean return during the bank stock period was 2.39 percent compared to minus 1.10 percent for the bank holding companies. The respective standard deviations were 2.14 and 4.58. Ten of 41 sample companies had a significant change in their beta value after becoming a bank holding company. Eight of the 10 were increases in market risk.

Sketchy information is available about the level of risk in some of the areas opened up

---

[1] Peter S. Rose and Donald R. Fraser, "The Impact of Holding Company Acquisitions on Bank Performance," *The Bankers Magazine*, (Spring, 1973), p. 91.

[2] Roger B. Upson and Paul F. Jessup, "Returns from Bank Holding Companies," *The Banker's Magazine,* (Spring, 1972), pp. 59–62.

[3] Virgil L. Brewer and William P. Dukes, "Empirical Evidence on the Risk-Return Relationship Between Banks and Related Bank Holding Companies," *Review of Business and Economic Research*, (Spring 1976), pp. 56–65.

to bank holding company affiliates. The data are difficult to obtain but Heggestad has compiled several measures of risk using 1953–1967 figures published by the Internal Revenue Service.[4] These are presented below in Exhibit 2.

Exhibit 2:

B.H.C. Activity	Avg. Profits to Capital	Variability	Risk Index	Correlation To Bank Profits
Commercial Banks	5.49%	1.21	.220	—
Insurance Agents and Brokers	15.40%	2.71	.176	−.44
Business Credit Agencies	8.95%	1.98	.221	.49
Personal Credit Agencies	9.44%	1.23	.131	.36
Lessors of Agricultural and Public Utility Property	8.51%	1.53	.180	0

Riskiness has traditionally been measured by the variability of profit rates with greater variability being associated with greater risk. The data for profitability in Exhibit 2 are the ratio of net income after taxes to equity capital. This is the relevant measure for bank holding companies since it indicates the return on their investment in affiliates. Variability is measured by the standard deviation of the average industry profit rate over the period 1953–1967. The risk index is the industry's variability divided by its profitability. Two industries with similar profit variability but different profit levels do not have the same risk characteristics. The last risk measure in Exhibit 2 is the correlation of industry profits with bank profits.

OTHER ASPECTS

Some other stockholders have been grumbling a little about the one-for-one exchange they are being offered. When the Bank of Hawaii stockholders voted to change to a bank holding company they received four shares of new stock in the bank holding company for each share of bank stock. "Sure they are a bigger bank, but they certainly aren't four times as big," was the way one First Hawaiian stockholder put it. Another pointed to the two-for-one split-ups of First Hawaiian stock in August, 1972, and early in 1969 as an explanation for the one-for-one exchange. A shareholder already had four bank shares for every one held in early 1969. It wouldn't be fair to reward relatively new stockholders the same as the long-term investors who had been with the bank for a number of years. A third stockholder stated that the one-for-one exchange was actually preferable since it would result in less dilution of earnings.

TIME FOR A DECISION

It certainly seemed that the bank holding company was the current trend in banking, and First Hawaiian should follow along. In 1956 when the First Bank Holding Company Act was passed there were 53 bank holding companies owning 428 banks and controlling 7.5 percent of total bank deposits. At the end of 1971, the year the Amendments to the 1956 Act were passed, 1567 holding companies owned 2420 banks and 58 percent of all bank deposits. Still more banks have made the switch in the last two years.

Nevertheless, a nagging doubt still remains about switching to the holding company strategy. Just because others were doing it doesn't mean it will be good for First Hawaiian's stockholders. Lemmings proba-

---

[4] Arnold A. Heggestad, "The Economist's Corner," *The Banker's Magazine*, (Winter, 1976), pp. 109–12.

Exhibit 3:

Market Price of Bank Stock

	Average of High and Low Bid		
Date	First Hawaiian	Bank of Hawaii[1]	S&P Bank Stock (outside NYC) Index
1971	$26.375	$15.875	88.85
1972			
First Quarter	32.125	16.41	95.2
Second Quarter	33.625	19.00	102.4
Third Quarter	34.00	18.50	111.3
Fourth Quarter	33.625	19.00	117.3
1973			
First Quarter	33.875	18.062	110.3
Second Quarter	28.625	16.375	99.0
Third Quarter	27.50	15.688	105.0
Fourth Quarter[6]	26.625	15.50	107.6
1974			
to March 22	22.25	14.188	106.0
May 27, 1971[2]	28.50	16.125	86.2
January 31, 1972[3]	31.25	16.37	90.1
October 19, 1973[4]	28.50	17.50	115.1
March 22, 1974[5]	23.50	13.50	110.0

[1]Hawaii Bancorporation after April 3, 1972. Adjusted for 4-to-1 split.

[2]Bank of Hawaii announced it would form a bank holding company.

[3]Bank of Hawaii on January 31, 1972, informed stockholders about the bank holding company proposal details.

[4]First Hawaiian Bank's Board of Directors voted on October 20 to form a bank holding company.

[5]Latest price available.

[6]Book value as of December 31, 1973, was $17.18 for First Hawaiian and $8.92 for Hawaii Bancorporation.

bly think they are headed in the right direction too. What about the fact that Bank of Hawaii was the only other bank in the state to form one? Another legitimate question is why those specified activities can't be conducted by the bank directly or through a subsidiary of the bank?

Shareholders need to make up their minds before the stockholders' meeting. Those who do not want to exchange bank shares

Exhibit 4:

Earnings and Dividends Per Share

	First Hawaiian Bank		Bank of Hawaii	
	EPS	Dividends	EPS	Dividends
1971	$2.32	$1.08	$1.18	$.625
1972	2.49	1.22	1.27	.65
1973	2.74	1.27	1.49	.65

for holding company shares will need to cast a negative vote. Unless an affirmative vote of two-thirds of the shares is obtained, the transaction is defeated. If it is passed, anyone who voted no has the right to claim the cash surrender value of his or her shares.

Case 5

Independence Savings and Loan Association

Four months ago the Independence Savings and Loan Association had contracted Don Sandiman of Financial Research Corporation to provide them with a feasibility study on a proposed branch office. Don founded Financial Research with three other colleagues from the business school at State University seven years ago. Among his consulting activities, he had participated in many similar feasibility studies for Independence, other savings organizations, and various banks. He was especially pleased with this report since all signs were favorable for a new branch office in Adamson.

Adamson is a small township located in a semicircle of medium-to-large cities in a southern sunbelt state. Adamson lies ten miles south of Lofton, the state capital, a city with a population of over 250,000. Mason, a city of 24,000 lies eight miles due east of Adamson with the towns of Pilgrim City (population 15,000) and Stafford (population 36,000), seven and twelve miles respectively, to the south. Historically Adams County, in which Adamson is located, has been a farming and rural residential area. Beginning in the late 1950s, however, the area began a pattern of population increase which continues today.

As he reviewed his research, Don felt sure the Federal Home Loan Bank in Atlanta would approve the application for a new branch of Independence Savings and Loan in the area. He knew an application based on his study for Independence would have to show a present and increasing need for a new branch savings institution and that a new office would not cause harm to existing thrift and home-financing institutions. Support for these assertions would have to come from population and per capita increases in incomes and from savings potential in the proposed area.

The major cause for the population increase in the portion of Adams county to be served by the proposed Adamson branch is due to the area's location between two urban land masses. On the northern boundary of the proposed market area lies Lofton, the state capital, with all the attending agencies and departments of government. To the south and east lie the more industrialized cities of Mason, Stafford, and Pilgrim City with a combined population of over 75,000. While some industries are contemplating the construction of new facilities in the proposed market area for the new branch, a metals manufacturer employing between 900 and 1000 and a Department of Defense facility employing 85 are the area's only major current employers. Even so, Adams County is one of the state's fastest growing counties. Between 1970 and 1974 Adams County recorded a gain of 20,600 new residents, earning it a number-three ranking out of the state's 105 counties in terms of absolute population growth. Moreover, Adams County's near 27 percent rate of growth earned it a ranking of number one of all the counties in the state that grew by 5000 or more during the period. The portion of the county which will be served by the proposed savings and

loan branch office has historically grown at approximately the same rate as the county. The county and market area's growth is particularly impressive when compared to the decreases in population in most of the surrounding cities (Exhibit 1). The continued growth in the area may be anticipated from the building permit data (Exhibit 2).

The growth in population in the area has been accompanied by a concomitant increase in income for the county and proposed market area. Total personal income in Adams County grew 80.5 percent between 1970 and 1974. (Exhibit 1)

The analysis of the market area by Sandiman indicated an estimated $51 million in deposit-type savings potential. The estimate was derived by finding the per capita savings deposits for the state, multiplied by the market area population. Thus, with savings and loan deposits in the state equaling $4.8 billion and time deposits in commercial banks of $8.4 billion, the combined savings deposits in the state equal $13.2 billion. With a state population of 4.906 million, the per capita savings deposit for the state is $2,690. Applying this per capita savings deposit figure of $2,690 to the current market area population of 19,200 persons results in an exist-

Exhibit 1:

Population and Income Data

| | | Changes 1970–1974 | | | 1974 |
Jurisdiction	Population	Total Personal Income	Per Capita Personal Income	Per Capita Personal Income
Adams County	26.7%	80.5%	40.2%	117%
Proposed Market				
Area in County	23.8%	80.5%	40.2%	117%
Lofton	−5.5%	30.3%	39.8%	121%
Pilgrim City	11.7%	50.7%	35.3%	107%
Mason	−1.1%	38.5%	40.5%	89%
Stafford	−3.7%	41.7%	52.0%	95%
State	5.5%	51.3%	44.0%	100%

Exhibit 2:

Selected Items

Building Permit Data* Single Family	
1975	2,064
1974	1,520
1973	1,931
1972	2,144
1971	1,662
1970	1,038
Total	10,359

*Approximately 16% of this activity is located in the market area of the proposed branch.

Savings and Loan Deposit Growth*

Conservative Federal Savings (Chartered 1960)

Dec. 31, 1972	$ 7,063,000
Dec. 31, 1973	7,457,000
Dec. 31, 1974	8,033,000
Dec. 31, 1975	9,472,000
July 31, 1976	10,544,000

Adams Savings and Loan (Chartered 1974)

Sept. 30, 1974	$ 187,000
Sept. 30, 1975	1,001,000
July 31, 1976	2,012,000

*Total time and savings deposits in commercial banks (5 offices) totaled $11,424,000 as of June, 1976.

Offices Per Capita*
Market Area

Year	Savings and Loan Offices	Population
1970	1	15,515
1976	2	19,200

State

Year	Savings and Loan Offices	Population
1970	132	4,651,487
1976	337	4,973,000

*As of 1976 there was one banking office for each 3,440 persons in the state.

ing savings potential estimate of $51,648,000.

Sandiman further estimated that during the first year of operation the proposed branch should attract an approximate 5 percent share of the savings potential. Therefore the first-year savings at the new branch should amount to slightly over $2.5 million. In future years savings flows at the proposed branch office should increase as additional savings are created out of the incomes of existing savers, and as new families move into the market area bringing with them their accumulated savings.

In addition to the income and population increases which argued for an additional savings institution, Sandiman felt there was an imbalance of savings and investment in the area for Independence. Total loans outstanding in the proposed market area from Independence Savings and Loan's branches is slightly less than $5 million. Even though Independence has a large dollar volume of investments in the proposed market area, it has been able to attract only about $1 million in savings from that portion of the county. Thus, Sandiman's analysis showed a clear deficit of nearly $4 million in the area. That is, the firm is attracting nearly $4 million less in savings accounts from the area than it is investing in mortgages there. Because of its heavy mortgage activity in this part of Adams County, Independence Savings and Loan felt that when it opened a branch in Adamson it would be able to attract a larger volume of savings from the area which will enable it to balance out its mortgage investment there.

Sandiman's report to Independence also argued for the branch on the grounds that there was an imbalance between the number of savings and loan offices and banks in the proposed market area. There were five commercial banks and, in contrast, only two savings and loans.

Case 6

Warren Federal Savings and Loan Association

This case was prepared by Harold D. Fletcher, Booz, Allen & Hamilton, Inc., William W. McCartney, University of Central Florida, and Philip M. Van Auken, Baylor University, as a basis for class discussion rather than to illustrate either effective or ineffective handling of an administrative situation.

In February 1977, Marion Lyman, president of Warren Federal Savings and Loan Association, was preparing a report for the Association's board of director's meeting. At the last meeting the board had discussed several economic forecasts for 1977 and the forecasts' implications for the Association. The economic forecasts predicted rising interest rates for 1977 beginning in the spring, if not earlier, with one exception—mortgage rates. These were expected to continue in a mild decline for quite a while. The forecasts were also quite bullish for housing. The economic reports were predicting a 15 to 20 percent increase in new housing starts in 1977, coming after a 33 percent increase in 1976. After the discussion of the economic reports, the meeting had adjourned with a request that Mr. Lyman recommend possible courses of action available to the Association in light of these forecasts and the Association's financial resources.

HISTORY OF WARREN FEDERAL

Warren Federal was founded in Bowling Green, Kentucky in 1961 by Richard Hawes, a local real estate broker and builder, and several of his business associates and close friends. Since there was only one other savings and loan association in the city, the association grew quite rapidly from its inception until 1970, paralleling the growth of Bowling Green. By 1970, the total assets of the association were $19 million. From 1970 until 1976 the growth of the association slowed considerably but continued with total assets reaching $27 million in 1976. (See Exhibit 1)

The Association has its headquarters approximately three blocks from downtown Bowling Green in a new modern building with ample parking facilities. The new building was erected in 1972 after the Association's initial building proved to be too small. The association maintains one branch in the downtown area of Bowling Green. This branch, located in a remodeled storefront, was started in 1975 as a service for the Association's downtown customers. Although the branch's performance proved to be disappointing, it was continued for public relations purposes. Its location between the two largest financial institutions in the city was thought to enhance the visibility and prestige of Warren Federal.

THE COMMUNITY

Bowling Green, Kentucky, the fifth largest city in the state of Kentucky, is a growing city with a greater metropolitan population of approximately 70,000 people. The city is also the county seat of Warren County. There are no other major urban areas in Warren County, the remaining incorporated areas being small farming villages. The city has grown quite rapidly in recent years. Since the 1960 census the average rate of population growth has been between 2.5 to 3 percent per annum. The projected population figure for the early 1980s is approximately 100,000 people.

The economy of Bowling Green is diverse. The city and the county area adjacent to the city are the homes of a number of manufacturing and assembly facilities producing such products as chemicals, fertilizers, air conditioning equipment, automotive parts, textiles, clothing, and heavy equipment. The city is also the home of a state university with a student enrollment of 13,000.

The economy has expanded at a rapid rate since the early 1960s. Before 1960, Bowling Green was a typical, small, sleepy southern town with very little manufacturing except some textiles and clothing manufacturing. Beginning in the early 1960s, the city, with the judicious use of municipal bond financing, was able to persuade several disgruntled northern companies to locate plants in the area. Initial successes by these plants provided the encouragement for additional companies to relocate in the Bowling Green area. Also during this period, the university increased enrollments and expanded its facilities. Enrollments rose from approximately 5,000 students in 1960 to approximately 13,000 students in 1976.

The combination of increasing population, growing industry, and an expanding university created problems for the city of Bowling Green. Rapid growth fostered the development of several new suburban neighborhoods and shopping centers. However, the city street system and city services such as sewage, water, and fire protection were not expanded to meet the growing needs. The school systems, city and county, also have felt the effects of this growth. The county schools in particular did not have the resources to meet increased enrollment.

Given these increased service demands, the city and county tax base was forced upward in the face of taxpayer opposition. These increased taxes raised the costs of doing business in Bowling Green, obviously mitigating some of the previous advantages of locating and living in Bowling Green.

In recent years additional problems developed. While demands for increased city services continued, the city faced increased competition from other cities for new plant locations. The rush of new plants to Bowling Green slowed considerably in mid-1970s, leaving the city no choice but to extract higher taxes from existing plants instead of obtaining new taxes from new plants.

Another concern for the city was the decline of the downtown area. The rise of suburban shopping centers with new stores and available parking discouraged downtown shopping. After the closing of several downtown stores, the remaining businesses financed the renovation of the town square, the construction of new sidewalks and benches, and the planting of trees. Parking meters were removed. Unfortunately, the results of the renovation were considerably less than expected. Businesses continued to close and pedesterian traffic continued to decline.

The rapid growth rate of the city also has reduced the "quality of life" in Bowling Green. The cost of housing, the cost of services, and other consumer costs have been forced up to levels found in Louisville, Kentucky's largest city, which is more than ten times the size of Bowling Green. Thus the city has lost some of the appeal and its image of a small town that is a nice place to live. The city is faced with the same complex of urban problems as any other city.

Furthermore, the stabilization of the university enrollments had its effects on the city. The stable student enrollment has resulted in fewer new university employment opportunities, decreased building construction, and less stimulus to the local economy in general.

MANAGEMENT

Warren Federal is headed by Marion Lyman, who is both president and chairman of the board of directors. Lyman, 52 years old, has been with Warren Federal since its inception. He had originally been a partner of Hawes in the real estate business and joined Warren Federal as vice-president at its creation. He became president in 1966 upon Hawes' death. He became chairman of the board of directors in 1968.

The Association is operated on a very informal level. In addition to Lyman, the Association is managed by Anthony Colt, 48 years old, and James Haskell, 61 years old. Both Colt and Haskell have been with the Association from its creation and now carry titles of vice-president. Colt handles mortgages including all appraisals and other details, while Haskell concentrates on internal operations, including personnel. Haskell, a member of an old-line Bowling Green family, also does considerable public relations and civic work.

The three officers have offices next to each other and all decisions are made through a process of informal consultation. In practice, the three men handle all problems as the problems arise as if there were no separately defined areas of responsibility.

In addition to the three executive officers, the Association also employs Mrs. Bonita Jagers, 45 years old, in an executive position. Mrs. Jagers originally joined the Association at its creation as a bookkeeper and currently carries the title of treasurer. She works in the areas of accounting and also does considerable work in the mortgage area. As in the case of the other executives, Mrs. Jagers is a member of the board of directors and participates in all management decisions.

The Association also employs twelve other people, primarily as tellers and bookkeepers. The ranks of tellers change fairly rapidly as the tellers leave for better paying jobs or for marriage and family. The tellers were all women until last year when a young male teller was hired. All record keeping is done with accounting machines since computers are considered too expensive.

The Association is governed by a board of directors that includes four officers, Messrs. Lyman, Colt, and Haskell, and Mrs. Jagers, and ten local residents. The local members are business and professional people, including an attorney, who is also the legal counsel of the Association, a university dean, several local builders, a local real estate broker, a local doctor, several local manufacturers, and Mrs. Viola Lee Hawes, the founder's widow. The board meets monthly and several members are also members of the Association's loan committee.

OPERATING POLICIES OF WARREN FEDERAL

The Association has grown rapidly from its organization in 1961 until 1970 when its assets reached $19 million. Since 1970 the growth has been far less spectacular. During 1969 and 1970, the Association suffered from the effects of tight money, recession, and severe savings competition from local financial institutions. The Association found that while loan demand continued at high levels because of the momentum of the local economy, the influx of savings ceased as savers placed their funds in higher yielding financial instruments. This problem of strong loan demand and slow growth of savings continued to plague the Association throughout the 1970s. The Association raised saving rates in 1973 when allowable, but this did little to alleviate the problem since other institutions raised their rates also. By 1976, the assets had reached $26 million, but the problem of differential rates of growth of loan demand and savings was still unresolved. (Exhibits 1, 4, and 5)

Beginning with Hawes' tenure as president, the Association has sought growth within a simple framework. It had been Hawes' opinion that a savings and loan association had one simple objective: to gather the savings of many small savers and to promise them the utmost safety through lending their savings to build homes. This objective was reinforced when Lyman became president and coined the Association's motto, "Save safely and help build the community." These twin concepts of safety and home building have continued to dominate the asset and liability management policies of the association in recent years.

The asset portfolio reflected this philosophy of safety and home building by emphasizing single family mortgages and the purchase of FHA and VA guaranteed mortgages. The Association did not actively seek any kind of mortgage other than mortgages on single family dwellings. The officers preferred not to make apartment building loans, unless for an old customer, because they felt that apartment lending was riskier than home mortgages. The government-guaranteed mortgages, which were purchased from outside of the area, were maintained for reasons of safety. Although the yields on these guaranteed mortgages were below conventional rates, the Association felt that the increased safety obtained was worth the price. It was the Association's policy to hold all mortgages obtained by either lending or purchasing until maturity. (Exhibit 3)

It was felt that the savings and loan business involved long-term lending and therefore a savings and loan association should not move in and out of various types of assets like a commercial bank. Its function was to lend for home building, not to make short-term loans like a bank. The Association therefore did not seek some of the newer types of loans made by other savings and loan associations. It did not make mobile home loans, and kept a tight hold on short-term construction loans and other types of non-mortgage loans.

The Association set mortgage rates at as low a level as possible in order to make single homes affordable to as many people as possible. In theory, the mortgage rates were set to yield a high enough return to pay adequate dividends, cover costs, and increase reserves without excess profits. In recent years, the Association's mortgage rate was approximately ¼ percent to ½ percent below its competitor. In addition, the Association did not force borrowers to pay property taxes monthly into escrow accounts. Thus the Association's rate-setting policies did not yield any significant increase in profits to build reserves. Almost all profits were paid to savers in the form of dividends. (Exhibit 2)

The Association's liability management policy was also structured around the concepts of safety and home building. The Association sought savings from a variety of savers, but concentrated its efforts on the passbook type of saver. The Association paid competitive rates on passbook savings although it tended to lag behind other institutions in raising its saving rates. The officers felt that savings rates should be raised when prudently possible and when the higher rates could be maintained. Rates should not reflect up and down variations in the financial markets. The longer term and more costly savings certificates were not aggressively sought by the Association. These sources of funds were considered to be too expensive and too volatile. Therefore, the liability policy concentrates on the small saver. The Association has no well-defined marketing or advertising strategy to support its liability management policies other than to run advertising in the local newspaper periodically.

PROBLEMS CONFRONTING WARREN FEDERAL

As a first step in making recommendations to the board, Lyman outlined the major problems the Association faced. After discussion with Haskell, Colt, and Mrs. Jagers, the following concerns were identified as requiring immediate action. These included:

1. *Increased Competition*. Warren Federal faces considerable competition from the other financial institutions in Bowling Green. The major competition is from the three commercial banks, $100 million, $90 million, and $50 million in total assets, respectively, and the other savings and loan association which has assets of $95 million. The commercial banks in particular have been very aggressive in seeking the small saver. The smallest commercial bank has just recently instituted an "Insta-Teller" service in which funds are automatically transferred from the customer's saving account to his checking account by phone. The larger banks will in all likelihood offer this service during

1977 also. The savings and loan competitor has begun a new advertising campaign on local radio and television stressing its higher rates on longer term saving certificates.

2. *Increasing Savings Inflow*. The economic forecasts predict a high level of housing starts, implying greater mortgage loan demands for the Association. This demand can be met only if savings inflow increases. Yet, if interest rates increase as predicted, savings will leave the Association because of disintermediation. The total number of savers at the Association has declined from 6,580 savers with an average account balance of $3,052 in 1975 to 6,420 savers with an average account balance of $3,200 in 1976. The January, 1977, cash flow (Exhibit 6) emphasizes the problem of both high savings withdrawals and high mortgage loans as reflected in changes in cash. If the remaining forecasts of cash flow are also wrong, major revisions in management policies will be necessary. The slower growth trend in saving deposits presents a major area of concern.

3. *Increasing the Profitability of the Association*. The Association's profitability has proven to be disappointing in recent years. Operating expenses and interest on borrowed money are considered to be too high. (Exhibit 2) The additions to net worth (Exhibit 2) have not increased in proportion to other balance sheet items. This does not meet the safety objective of the Association. Without profits, dividends to savers cannot be maintained at a high enough level to attract savers.

With these three specific problem areas in mind, Lyman is considering potential courses of action. Lyman believes the Association must continue to emphasize safety and home building while attracting increasing savings and improving investment performance. These goals must be implemented in the face of changing economic activity and discrepant community needs.

Exhibit 1:

Warren Federal Savings and Loan Association

Statement of Condition (December 31 of Each Year)

(000 Omitted)

	1970	1971	1972	1973	1974	1975	1976
Assets							
Mortgage Loans	$16,631	$17,784	$18,237	$19,942	$20,765	$21,876	$22,612
Loans on Savings	113	117	116	117	121	122	124
Other Loans	40	42	51	61	75	42	54
Investments and Securities	1,943	2,018	2,761	2,451	2,614	2,941	3,198
Cash on Hand and in Bank	577	672	615	418	782	725	773
Office Building (net)	375	361	384	372	368	371	369
Office Equipment (net)	76	81	91	90	93	97	101
Other Assets	83	92	76	69	78	55	68
Total Assets	$19,838	$21,167	$22,331	$23,520	$24,896	$26,229	$27,299
Liabilities and Net Worth							
Total Savings	$16,562	$17,656	$17,614	$18,652	$19,260	$20,084	$20,547
Borrowed Money	773	891	1,442	1,684	2,487	2,997	3,464
Notes Payable - Office Building	150	150	150	150	150	150	150
Loans in Process	393	412	671	703	738	571	710
Other Liabilities	307	390	713	550	584	660	803
Net Worth	1,653	1,668	1,741	1,781	1,677	1,767	1,626
Total Liabilities and Net Worth	$19,838	$21,167	$22,331	$23,520	$24,896	$26,229	$27,299

303

Exhibit 2:

Warren Federal Savings and Loan Association

Operating Statements (December 31 of Each Year)

(000 Omitted)

	1970	1971	1972	1973	1974	1975	1976
Total Operating Income	$1,329	$1,435	$1,570	$1,637	$1,720	$2,136	$2,052
Operating Expense	235	283	302	379	412	464	508
Net Operating Income	$1,094	$1,152	$1,268	$1,258	$1,308	$1,672	$1,544
Interest on Borrowed Money	147	152	211	225	403	435	535
Nonoperating Income (+) or Expense (−)	+18	−18	−12	+6	−10	+12	−9
Income Taxes	35	61	79	82	76	69	73
Net Income After Taxes	$ 930	$ 925	$ 966	$ 957	$ 819	$1,180	$ 932
Dividends Paid Savers	$ 901	$ 910	$ 893	$ 917	$ 923	$1,090	$1,073
Addition to Net Worth	$ 29	$ 15	$ 73	$ 40	$ (104)	$ 90	$ (141)

Exhibit 3:

Warren Federal Savings and Loan Association
Analysis of Mortgage Portfolio - Dec. 31, 1976

Type of Loan	Principal Amount	Interest Payments Received	Amortization (Payments on Principal)	Loan Pay-Offs (Additonal Repayments in Full)
Purchased:	$ 2,736	$ 164	$102	$160
Over Four Years Old				
Single Family FHA/VA				
Less than Four Years Old	3,618	272	60	38
Others Less than Four Years Old	2,126	162	85	55
Total Purchased	$ 8,480	$ 598	$247	$160
Generated by Association:				
Over Four Years Old	$ 8,660	$ 604	$476	$190
Less than Four Years Old	5,472	504	116	49
Total Locally Generated	$14,132	$1,108	$592	$239
Total Loans	$22,162	$1,706	$839	$399

Yields (Annual Rates)	Per-Cent of Total	Interest Yield	Amortization Rate	Pay-Off Rate
Purchased:				
Over Four Years Old	12.1%	6.01%	3.71%	2.45%
Single Family FHA/VA				
Less than Four Years Old	16.0%	7.52%	1.67%	1.06%
Others Less than Four Years Old	9.4%	7.63%	4.02%	2.61%
Generated by Association:				
Over Four Years Old	38.3%	6.98%	5.50%	2.20%
Less than Four Years Old	24.2%	9.21%	2.13%	0.90%
Total Loans	100.0%	7.54%	3.71%	1.76%

Exhibit 4:

Warren Federal Savings and Loan Association
Savings Transactions 1975 and 1976
(000 Omitted)

	Deposits	Dividends Credited	Withdrawals	Net Savings
1975:				
January	$ 229		$ 530	$ (301)
February	209		346	(137)
March	290		45	245
April	205		130	75
May	196		54	142
June	266	$ 548	162	652
July	280		597	(317)
August	219		406	(187)
September	254		392	(138)
October	288		167	121
November	277		171	106
December	216	542	196	563
1975 Total	$2,929	$1,090	$3,195	$ 824
1976:				
January	$ 158		$ 619	$ (461)
February	212		409	(197)
March	179		78	101
April	206		211	(5)
May	239		76	163
June	330	$ 521	173	678
July	168		599	(431)
August	184		387	(203)
September	277		413	(136)
October	439		181	258
November	207		140	67
December	353	552	276	629
1976 Total	$2,952	$1,073	$3,562	$ 463

Exhibit 5:

Warren Federal Savings and Loan Association
Loan Transactions 1975 and 1976
(000 Omitted)

	Loans Closed		Purchased		Total
	Number	Value	Number	Value	Payments (Principal)
1975:					
January	2	43	4	115	103
February	1	31	0	0	92
March	3	97	0	0	74
April	4	160	5	127	91
May	5	213	0	0	100
June	7	280	0	0	118
July	6	243	1	28	80
August	4	86	0	0	130
September	3	91	7	168	105
October	2	38	5	174	85
November	2	56	6	197	97
December	1	39	3	103	103
1975 Total	40	$1,377	31	$912	$1,178
1976:					
January	1	36	0	0	137
February	2	78	0	0	83
March	4	127	2	73	92
April	3	91	1	15	108
May	5	163	1	18	113
June	8	251	0	0	170
July	9	376	0	0	94
August	3	98	5	162	73
September	2	47	4	149	81
October	2	54	3	82	95
November	1	38	2	44	83
December	1	43	1	29	109
1976 Total	41	$1,402	19	$572	$1,238

Exhibit 6:

Warren Federal Savings and Loan Association
Projected Cash Flow January–June 1971
(000 Omitted)

	January Estimated	January Actual	February	March	April	May	June
Beginning Cash Balance	$773	$630	$541	$516	$1,104	$1,007	$1,087
Receipts:							
Mortgage Loans-Interest and Principal	$250	$238	$250	$250	$250	$250	$250
Loans on Savings-Interest and Principal	2	3	2	2	2	2	2
Other Loans	1	2	1	1	1	1	1
Escrow Account	30	21	30	30	30	30	30
Borrowed Money	100	75	—	250	—	150	—
Other Receipts	5	2	5	5	5	5	5
Net Savings	(300)	(400)	(150)	275	100	150	700
Total Receipts	$ 88	$ (59)	$138	$813	$388	$588	$990
Total Cash Available	$861	$571	$679	$1,332	$1,492	$1,595	$2,077
Disbursements:							
Mortgage Loans	$190	$300	$ 40	$100	$350	$375	$400
Loans on Savings	12	16	12	12	12	12	12
Other Loans	6	8	6	6	6	6	6
Interest on Borrowed Money	60	64	55	60	65	65	60
Escrow Payments	—	9	—	—	—	—	—
Taxes	—	—	—	—	—	—	—
Expenses	50	57	50	50	50	50	50
Other Disbursements	2	3	—	—	2	—	—
Dividends on Deposits	—	—	—	—	—	—	600
Total Disbursements	$320	$457	$163	$228	$485	$508	$1,128
Ending Cash Balance	$541	$114	$516	$1,104	$1,007	$1,087	$949

Exhibit 7:

Savings and Loan Association: Selected Assets and Liabilities
(millions of dollars, end of period)

	1970	1971	1972	1973	1974	1975	1976
Assets							
Mortgages	$150,331	$174,250	$206,182	$232,104	$249,301	$278,590	$323,130
Cash and Investment							
Securities	16,526	21,042	24,355	21,027	23,251	30,853	35,660
Other	9,326	10,731	12,590	19,227	22,993	28,790	33,209
Total Assets	$176,183	$206,023	$243,127	$272,358	$295,545	$338,233	$391,999
Liabilities and Net Worth							
Savings Capital	$146,404	$174,197	$206,764	$227,254	$242,974	$285,743	$336,030
Borrowed Money (FHLBB and Other)	10,911	8,992	9,782	17,100	24,780	20,634	19,087
Loans in Process	3,078	5,029	6,029	5,132	3,244	5,128	6,836
Other	3,389	4,213	5,132	6,220	6,105	6,949	8,015
Net Worth	12,401	13,592	15,240	17,108	18,442	19,779	22,031
Total Liabilities and Net Worth	$176,183	$206,023	$243,127	$272,358	$295,545	$338,233	$391,999

(Source: Federal Reserve Bulletin)

Exhibit 8:

**Operating Statements of All Savings and Loan Associations
1970–75* (In Millions of Dollars)**

	1970	1971	1972	1973	1974	1975
Operating Income	$11,039	$13,073	$15,572	$18,692	$21,477	$24,354
Operating Expense	1,967	2,180	2,524	3,026	3,490	4,112
Net Operating Income	$ 9,072	$10,893	$13,048	$15,666	$17,987	$20,242
Interest on Savings Deposits	7,187	8,604	10,266	12,012	14,015	16,460
Interest on Borrowed Money	785	623	493	942	1,731	1,569
Net Income Before Taxes	$ 1,152	$ 1,739	$ 2,378	$ 2,729	$ 2,213	$ 2,145
Taxes	248	448	649	779	681	634
Net Income After Taxes	$ 904	$ 1,291	$ 1,729	$ 1,950	$ 1,532	$ 1,511

Source: Savings and Loan Fact Book, 1976 (Chicago: U.S. League of Savings Associations, 1976).

*Items do not add to totals because of the omission of minor nonoperating income and expense items.

310

Exhibit 9:

Savings and Loan Associations Maximum Interest Rates Payable on Time and Savings Deposits - December, 1976

Type and Maturity of Deposit	December 1976		Previous Maximum	
	%	Effective Date	%	Effective Date
Savings	5¼	7/6/73	5	1/21/70
Negotiable Order of Withdrawal	5	1/1/74	—	—
90 Days to 1 Year	5¾	7/6/73	5¼	1/21/70
1 to 2 Years	6½	7/6/73	5¾	1/21/70
2 to 2½ Years	6½	7/6/73	6	1/21/70
2½ to 4 Years	6¾	7/6/73	6	1/21/70
4 to 6 Years	7½	11/1/73	None	—
6 Years or More	7¾	12/23/74	7½	11/1/73

(Source: Federal Reserve Bulletin)

Exhibit 10:

**Selected Interest Rates - Money and Capital Markets
(Averages, Percent Per Annum)**

	1970	1971	1972	1973	1974	1975	1976
Prime Commercial Paper (4 to 6 Months)	7.72	5.11	4.69	8.15	9.87	6.33	5.35
Treasury Bills (3 Months)	6.39	4.33	4.07	7.03	7.84	5.80	4.98
U.S. Treasury Bond (Long-Term)	6.59	5.74	5.63	6.30	6.99	6.98	6.78
State and Local Bonds (Mixed Issues)	6.42	5.62	5.30	5.22	6.17	7.05	6.64
Corporate Bonds (All Industries)	8.51	7.94	7.63	7.80	9.03	9.57	9.01
Conventional Mortgages (FHLB Series)	8.44	7.74	7.60	7.95	8.92	9.01	8.99

(Source: Federal Reserve Bulletin)

Case 7

D.C. Neighborhood Reinvestment Commission

This case was prepared by Edwin L. Carey, Professor of Finance, and Cecil Howard, Associate Professor of Marketing, in the School of Business and Public Administration, Howard University, as a basis for class discussion rather than to illustrate either effective or ineffective handling of an administrative situation.

Copyright 1977 by Professors Edwin Carey and Cecil Howard.

Presented at a Case Workshop and distributed by the Intercollegiate Case Clearing House, Soldiers Field, Boston, Mass. 02163. All rights reserved to the contributors.

BACKGROUND INFORMATION

The American city has been the hub of industry, commerce, and government, and the center of major cultural activity. The variety of ethnic and racial neighborhoods gave the city its vitality. The city has had a deep and lasting influence over the life of the rest of our country.

Today, many large cities are in deep trouble. They are plagued with high unemployment, a diminishing tax base, increasing crime, greatly reduced commercial activity, high concentration of low-and moderate-income families, middle-class flight to the suburbs, and neighborhood deterioration.

One of the major causes of urban decline is private and public disinvestment, popularly known as "redlining." Redlining is a process used by lending institutions to draw imaginary boundaries around neighborhoods considered to be "bad risks" or "bad investment areas." The immediate result is that families and businesses are unable to obtain loans, because of their geographic location. The non-loan decision is based solely on location and is not due to the credit rating of the applicant or the structural soundness of the property.

As disinvestment continues, mortgage and loan funds flow to the suburbs and more affluent city areas; businesses and middle-class residents leave; and, in the inner city, only low- and moderate-income families—particularly minorities and the aged—remain.

Community groups, city administrations, and civil rights groups have organized to fight the pattern of disinvestment. The U.S. Congress passed a Mortgage Disclosure Act which became effective September 30, 1976. The Act requires annual disclosure by federally insured commercial banks, savings and loan associations, and credit unions of all first-mortgages, home-improvement loans, federally insured loans, and home loans to owner-occupants.

WASHINGTON, D.C.

In the 1940s, and especially after World War II, Washington, D.C.'s surrounding suburbs became the target of development activities and subsequently experienced tremendous growth. The city began to experience disinvestment as housing loans became unavailable to "changing" neighborhoods. Without financing, these neighborhoods began to deteriorate; they changed from racially integrated to predominantly black.

During the 1960s, speculators began purchasing homes in areas where federal housing programs were being initiated. The homes were then sold to unsuspecting homebuyers at artificially high prices. Major repairs were often needed and the homeowners, unable to afford both the cost of repairs and the mortgage payments, often were forced to default on the mortgage. Many abandoned and boarded-up homes followed in their wake.

Similar conditions in several cities led to an investigation by a special "Ad Hoc Subcommittee on Home Financing Practices and Procedures." The main target of the subcommittee's inquiry was Washington, D.C. In 1970, one of the recommendations of the subcommittee was directed toward financial institutions.

> The housing needs of this Nation will never be met by financing from the private sector so long as the commercial banks of the District and the Nation consider that their first and perhaps only responsibility is to make as much money as possible in the shortest amount of time with the least amount of risk, and so long as the savings and loan associations of the District and the Nation conclude they have fulfilled their responsibility to promote thrift and home-ownership by placing most of their energy

and assets at the service of middle- and higher-income families.[1]

By the early 1970s, a new wave of speculation surfaced in the District of Columbia. Many younger, middle-income families and individuals were returning to the city and willing to pay high prices for older townhouses in low- and moderate-income neighborhoods. The higher cost of transportation, combined with disillusionment with suburban living, motivated many of these families to find more conveniently located housing close to the center of the city.

As revitalization of disinvestment neighborhoods continues, many of the existing low- and moderate-income families are forced to move to less desirable areas.

THE D.C. NEIGHBORHOOD REINVESTMENT COMMISSION

In 1974, the D.C. City Council decided to develop a workable housing reinvestment program to assist moderate-income families. Therefore, the Council created what is now the D.C. Neighborhood Reinvestment Commission (NRC). The Commission is composed of 17 members.

> The chairpersons of the Council Committees on Employment and Economic Development, Housing and Community Development, and Finance Revenue; two members of the executive branch of the D.C. government; two representatives of the local savings and loan associations (including one minority representative); one local credit union representative; one member of the mortgage banking industry; one representative of the local real estate industry; one representative of the minority business community; two representatives

---

[1] U.S. Congress, House, Committee on Banking and Currency, *Report and Recommendations of the Ad Hoc Subcommittee on Home Financing Practices and Procedures,* 91st Congress, 2nd session, 1970, p. 1.

of disinvested neighborhoods; and two public members.

Much of the work activities of the NRC are carried out by the executive director and his staff of three people plus consultants.

In July, 1976, the D.C. City Council gave the following mandate to the NRC:

1. Develop and implement a survey of the past and current mortgage, rehabilitation, and commercial investment performance of all local commercial banks, savings and loan associations, mortgage banking firms, credit unions, and life insurance companies.

2. Survey the past and present employment patterns of local lenders.

3. Develop an affirmative marketing and employment program.

4. Help lenders, city and federal government agencies, and community groups to develop reinvestment mechanisms and programs.

5. Work with the D.C. City Council for the enactment of legislation supporting the revitalization of city neighborhoods.

The Commission did a base line survey of all commercial banks and savings and loans (S&Ls) based in the city from 1971 to mid-1975; and a pilot neighborhood study of the total mortgage-lending activity and the relative housing finance demand for 1973 and 1975 in each of the city's 36 neighborhoods.[2]

In this case study it is not possible to present all the findings. Some of the more significant findings and conclusions were:

1. The banks and S&Ls did a disproportionately high number and dollar amount of loans in those areas of the city with high incomes and low percentage of black population.

---

[2] *Strategy for Change: Housing Finance in Washington, D.C.*, Commission on Residential Mortgage Investment, Government of the District of Columbia, (January, 1977), 155 pages.

2. Some areas with relatively high "affordability" of home ownership ("affordability" was determined by comparing the average 1974 family income with the average mortgage amount reported by banks and S&Ls) plus a high percentage of blacks had lower number and dollar amount of loans than lower "affordability" areas with low percentage of blacks.

3. It was possible to rank banks and S&Ls as institutional groups (i.e., total banks compared to total S&Ls), and as individual lenders using a rating system which included such items as Average Mortgage Amounts, Average Interest Rates, Average Monthly Payments, number and dollar amount of loans made to areas with a high percentage of black population, proportion of mortgage loans made on 1- to 4-unit housing, and other factors available in the data.

4. There is a large, untapped demand for mortgage loans in areas populated with moderate income earners who meet basic "affordability" criteria for home-ownership in their area of residence.

THE HOUSING FINANCE PLAN

The NRC proposed a "positive-action plan" to increase the availability of housing for moderate-income families. The major features of this Housing Finance Plan were:

1. Local lenders who join the housing finance plan would, in conjunction with the NRC, review, discuss, and where appropriate, revise all housing-loan policies and procedures to conform with actual neighborhood lending "risk."

2. A new joint lending mechanism would be established through which the local banks and S&Ls would provide home loans to homebuyers traditionally unable to obtain financing from conventional sources. For example, a "mortgage pool" is an aggregation of funds allotted

by two or more lenders, and available to borrowers of a specific geographic area of socio-economic level.

3. A Loan Review Committee, composed of lender representatives and selected Commission members, would be established to review complaints from loan applicants and, where a loan rejection is unjustified, to assure placement of the loan.

4. Local lenders would be asked to participate in neighborhood-based home-ownership counseling programs designed to provide a wide range of home-purchase and maintenance services.

5. Participating lenders would be required to develop and implement a uniform affirmative marketing program to meet the existing and potential home loan demand in the minority community.

6. Local lenders would be required to make mortgage, refinancing, and rehabilitation loans to all qualified homebuyers in every area of the District.

7. Special consideration would be given to all moderate-income home loan applicants, and particularly to those families that have been, or soon will be, displaced because of private or public housing redevelopment.

8. Every prospective homebuyer in the District would have the right to complete a home loan application.

9. Every loan applicant would have the right to receive a copy of the property appraisal report, where the applicant bears the appraisal cost.

10. Local lenders would be required to provide an explanation in writing for the rejection of a home-loan application within 30 days after the lender's receipt of the application, and would guarantee to the applicant the right of appeal to the Loan Review Committee.

A SURVEY OF MORTGAGE LENDING POLICIES AND PRACTICES IN D.C.

Under the mandate from the D.C. City Council, the NRC contracted two consultants to investigate the mortgage lending policies and practices of a representative sample of financial institutions. Interviews were conducted with officers in selected commercial banks, mortgage banks, and savings and loan associations. A by-product of the study was an assessment of the availability of socio-economic and demographic characteristics of loan applicants. The summarized results of that survey are as follows:

Loan Policies Of the three types of financial institutions surveyed, the commercial banks have the most conservative mortgage loan policies. They require the largest down payments (25 percent) in relation to the property value and lend for shorter periods (20–25 years). They seem to experience few delinquency problems and defaults (foreclosures) are rare. These policies and experience indicate the commercial banks expose themselves to very little risk in their mortgage lending activities.

Commercial banks have alternative situations in which to invest funds—commercial loans, bonds, consumer loans—and they may be content to leave the inner city mortgage loan market to those that specialize in mortgages—savings and loan associations and mortgage bankers.

Savings and loan associations (S&Ls) make loans up to 90 percent of property value for periods up to 30 years. Other available data indicate the S&Ls prefer mortgage loans in the more affluent areas in the District.[3]

However, although three of the four surveyed mortgage bankers are not located in the District of Columbia, they seem to pro-

---

[3] Ibid., p. 33.

vide more mortgage loans in the District than do comparably sized commercial banks or S&Ls located in D.C.

Mortgage bank management aggressively seeks out customers for mortgage loans and seems to be more willing to make inner-city loans to higher risk neighborhoods and/or borrowers. The mortgage bank's customers tend to be middle and low-middle income earners and thus the average value of the residential unit tends to be lower than for banks or S&Ls.

Mortgage banks are willing to make larger loans in relation to property value (90 to 95 percent), and lend for longer terms (up to 30 years) than either commercial banks or S&Ls. Thus, the interest yield charged borrowers tends to be higher in the mortgage banks.

All institutions used some ratio of loan to property value to set the limit of the mortgage, and used a ratio of monthly income to monthly payment in determining the basic capability of the borrower. A large flow of mortgage financing to moderate income families would call for more relaxed loan-to-value ratios, and income-to-payment ratios, than are now required by the more conservative financial institutions. Greater effort could be made to relate supplementary information about marginal applicants to the risk involved in the specific loan. It may be that an addition of extra charges could compensate for the extra risk. This higher interest rate might be subsidized by government, if it would help produce an increased availability of credit.

Processing of Loan Applications The processing of loan applications in the main office is basically the same in all the surveyed financial institutions. That is, the application information is verified and a credit check is made. If the applicant meets the basic income and credit requirements, a fee-appraisal is made of the property. The final decision on the loan is usually made by two or more officers and the decision is communicated to the applicant in writing.

However, the mortgage banks have "branch managers" who actively seek borrowers and maintain close contacts with real estate agents. The potential borrower can go through preliminary screening and fill out a loan application in a less formal and institutionalized setting than in the home office. Providing a more relaxed and informal setting for the loan applicant may be a step in meeting (or increasing) the housing finance demands of moderate income families. Also, applications that are initially given an adverse reaction can be more easily reviewed with the loan applicant in an informal setting.

Delinquency and Defaults In comparing the financial institutions, mortgage banks require lower down payments, loan for longer periods and, in general, make loans to those with lower incomes. The mortgage banks also experience higher delinquency rates and more foreclosures. As a consequence they also stress efficiency in following up on delinquent loans and the provision of financial counseling to borrowers who are experiencing problems.

A housing finance program which aims at increasing loans to moderate income families must also provide for financial counseling services and efficient handling of delinquency and foreclosure situations—and the cost of providing these services must be covered.

In general, the surveyed financial officers reported marital problems as the number one cause of delinquent loans and defaults.

Data Availability The formal loan applications (both approved and disapproved) are kept by all lending institutions. However, little of the socio-economic and demographic information contained in the applications is available in a form that can be processed by a machine. A study in which sampling techniques are used could set forth a profile of the socio-economic and demographic characteristics of borrowers and rejected applicants. However, it would be a time consuming and costly study to undertake.

Rehabilitation Loans In general, the surveyed financial institutions make rehabilitation loans, primarily to professional rehabers. Servicing these loans and inspecting improvements as rehabilitation progresses adds to the cost and risk involved in these loans.

Institutions which do not make rehabilitation loans may be reluctant to incur the expenses necessary to employ a staff of inspectors and rehab loan specialists. If these institutions could be encouraged to use a pool of qualified, reliable inspectors, more financing of rehab projects could be forthcoming.

Home improvement loans, which are loans to an owner-occupier rather than to a professional rehaber of a whole building, are handled as consumer loans by some financial institutions with monthly payments extending up to seven years. The lender relies on the reputation and credit-worthiness of the borrower to see that the work is done and the loan repaid. Thus, lender personnel are not involved in inspection of the premises as work progresses.

Conclusion The risks of inner city lending are greater than the risks of suburban lending. However, many District financial institutions are assuming little or no share of this risk, even though they have both social and legal responsibilities to their community. It should be possible to cooperatively increase the availability of housing financing in the inner city and, at the same time, provide benefits to both the community and to the financial institutions involved.

THE SOCIAL RESPONSIBILITY ISSUE

The managers of D.C. banks and S&Ls subscribe to the general aims of the Housing Finance Plan. However, the Plan's provisions would require significant changes in the mortgage lending policies and procedures within the banks and S&Ls. What alternative courses of action are open for the managers, and what do you recommend?

Case 8

Listerhill Credit Union

Credit unions are state or federally chartered nonprofit cooperative institutions designed primarily to provide credit to members. These financial institutions also provide a place for members to save. Members must have a common bond of some type—they must be employees of a given firm, members of a given profession, or somehow joined by a common activity. Credit unions compete with commercial banks, sales finance companies, personal finance companies, and retailers in making loans to finance purchases. In addition, credit unions compete with banks, savings and loan associations, and other financial organizations in providing a place to save.

The Listerhill Credit Union is located in Sheffield, Alabama and was chartered to serve employees of Reynolds Metals Company. It started in 1953 with assets of $83,-407, and a membership of 864. Before the credit union was founded, there were several loan companies in the immediate area and it was known that "loan sharking" was taking place. Also, it was not uncommon for Reynolds to receive as many as 100 wage garnishments each week, a problem for employees and for the company. In the early days, Reynolds provided some support of the credit union, usually in the form of personnel and office space. Listerhill soon became self-supporting, but chose to continue serving only the employees of the Reynolds Metals Company.

Steady growth characterized the first 18 years of operation. A real problem came, however, in 1972 when three local business firms defaulted on a $1.3 million loan from Listerhill. The credit union was forced to borrow $1.5 million to survive. The publicity from this was not favorable. In the following months members withdrew $3.9 million in shares. The credit union did survive, but failed to show new growth in assets and membership until 1975.

At the present time (mid 1976) Listerhill has almost 9000 employee accounts and an additional 2000 family accounts. The principal membership represents 85 to 90 percent of the local Reynolds Metals workforce. In terms of deposit balances, or shares, Listerhill has almost $11 million in various accounts. Of course, some share accounts are more active than others, as shown in Exhibit 1.

In addition to deposit balances, Listerhill has almost 3500 loans outstanding among members. The average loan balance is approximately $3300. Most loans are made for automobiles (48 percent), real estate (10 percent), furniture and appliances (2.6 percent), signature loans (8.7 percent), and two party "co-signer" loans. Following the financial crisis in 1972, loan policies were revised and strengthened to minimize losses from default.

Listerhill communicates directly with its members in a quarterly newsletter. In addition, a small advertising budget is used to promote the credit union. These funds are traditionally spent on radio advertising, matchbooks, and small birthday gifts for members. The advertising messages used have varied, but usually center on making non-members aware of the credit union. There is a general feeling that the best way to recruit members is through present members at the plant level. This seems to have been effective in the past, based on the 85 to 90 percent participation rate among Reynolds employees.

The credit union is considered a non-profit organization. Net earnings are paid to members in the form of dividends or reinvestment in the business. The two main services offered by the credit union are thought to be (a) a place to save, and (b) a place to borrow. Other services offered include safety deposit boxes, free travel checks, free notary service, payroll deduction plans, drive-up windows, insurance services, financial coun-

seling, meeting rooms for various groups, and vacation information.

Al Williams has been the manager of Listerhill Credit Union since 1972. Prior to becoming manager, he served as assistant manager for five years. He is presently 38 years old, holds a college degree in business, and is considered to be an excellent administrator. His acknowledged strengths are in the general management and computer applications area. Williams reports directly to a nine-member board of directors. Each director is a member of the credit union and is elected by the general membership at an annual meeting. The directors represent a reasonably wide range of backgrounds and skills. Most of them, however, work as hourly or salaried employees at the Reynolds plant. The manager has developed good rapport with the directors and with his 27-member staff.

There are eight banks, each with several branches, three savings and loan associations, several finance companies, and other credit unions located in the quad-cities area of North Alabama. The metropolitan area comprised of Florence, Sheffield, Tuscumbia, and Muscle Shoals has a population of 117,000. There are a large number of plants in the area, most are heavy industry—aluminum, chemicals, paper, and textiles. Most of the plants in the area are unionized and there is generally a pro-union attitude among employees.

Listerhill has managed to grow and prosper over the years. While the credit union does not compete directly with many other types of financial institutions, it has managed to carve out a loyal and supportive market segment. It is felt that several factors have provided the basis for this stability and growth; among them are: the "common bond" among credit union members, the payroll deduction plans, convenient location, reasonable dividends on deposits, and reasonable interest rates paid on savings. Listerhill has usually paid around 5 percent based on the dividends declared by the board of directors. Recently, banks and savings and loan associations have begun offering a wide array of savings plans and certificates of deposit bearing different rates of interest. These various savings plans pay from 4 to 7.5 percent interest depending on variable dates of maturity. The Board of Directors at Listerhill has not favored the use of variable interest plans because this seems to conflict with basic union philosophy—"equal treatment for all."

Williams is now starting to develop plans for 1977. He is a progressive individual and feels that Listerhill needs to develop new and better programs to better serve the membership. But change comes slowly and sometimes Williams becomes a little discouraged when he recognizes that the credit union is a non-profit organization. Success is not measured in profits. Also, he recognizes that the membership is very large—85 to 90 percent of the Reynolds workforce—that does not leave much room for growth.

After some thought, Williams decided that Listerhill could benefit from the development of a better marketing program. Since he does not have the time and experience needed to handle the total marketing area, he has decided that an additional staff member with a marketing background could be a valuable addition. Several candidates for this position were subsequently interviewed. If *you* were the one selected to fill the new marketing position, what action would you take?

Exhibit 1:

Share Account Activity

Share Account Balances ($)	Number of Accounts	Percent of Total Accounts	Percent of Total Shares
*Not prime accounts	1,015	9.22	.66
0 to 10.	1,262	11.45	.05
11. to 25.	1,086	9.85	.08
26. to 100.	1,129	10.25	.54
101. to 250.	1,533	13.91	2.56
251. to 500.	1,133	10.28	4.12
501. to 1000.	1,134	10.30	8.20
1001. to 2000.	1,117	10.14	16.05
2001. to 5000.	1,253	11.38	36.60
5001. to 10,000.	268	2.44	17.95
10,001. and up	85	.78	13.19
Totals	11,015	100.00	100.00

*Secondary accounts that show little activity and generally have small balances.

Case 9

Old Reliable Life Assurance Society

This case was prepared by D. Stuart Bancroft of Pacific Lutheran University, Tacoma, Washington, as a basis for classroom discussion and not to illustrate either effective or ineffective administrative action.

Presented at a Case Workshop and distributed by the Intercollegiate Case Clearing House, Soldiers Field, Boston, Mass. 02163. All rights reserved to the contributors.

In July of 1974, Hayden Roberts, an actuarial trainee for the Old Reliable Life Assurance Society, became keenly interested in the effect that increasing short-term interest rates might have on the company's near- and intermediate-term asset structure, earnings rate, and underwriting portfolio. With the prime rate hovering in the 8½ to 11¾ percent range for the two preceding months, and averaging about 9 percent over the period May, 1973, to May, 1974, Roberts felt confident that many policy holders were exercising their legal right to borrow against their cash value life insurance policies. The interest rate charged (i.e., earned) by the company on such policy loans was contractually fixed at the time the policy was issued. The overwhelming majority of policies in the

Old Reliable's underwriting portfolio was issued between 1939 and 1967, and these policies carried a 5 percent loan rate. The borrowing rate associated with policies written after 1967 was, in most state jurisdictions served by the company, increased to 6 percent. For the most part, though, these policies had not yet developed sizable loan values as of 1974 and Roberts believed it would be many years before the company's return on policy loans would average 6 percent.

The potential for intense arbitrage activity by policyholders—encouraged by the differential between commercial bank loan rates and policy loan borrowing rates—was, Roberts believed, heightened by abnormally high money market rates (see Exhibit 1).

Given these concerns, Roberts arranged an appointment with Van Ackerman, Old Reliable's chief actuary. Van Ackerman suggested that John Pershing, a new actuarial trainee, be included in the session. During his conversation with Van Ackerman, Roberts was astounded to learn that the company had taken no steps to clarify either the nature or the consequences of policy loan activity.

"At no time since 1960," he observed, "have we committed less than 9 percent of our total assets to policy loans—and for the last five years, that figure has been closer to 12 percent. So what you are saying, Mr. Van Ackerman, is that the company has a policy of ignoring an increasingly significant proportion of its total assets!"

"Well, that's a pretty harsh way of phrasing the matter," Van Ackerman replied. "After all, you know as well as I do that we are legally obligated to honor a policyholder's legitimate loan request."

"That's true. We can't exercise any discretion when it comes to adding these loans to our investment portfolio," Roberts observed. "But, on the other hand, we are not restrained from attempting to actively manage the policy loan account, just as we do our other asset accounts."

"What do you mean by that?" Van Ackerman asked.

"Well, it seems to me as if the process of managing any investment account consists, essentially, of two things: (1) forecasting the future status of that account, and (2) taking corrective action where the need for it is indicated. For example, we hold a tremendous volume of marketable bonds. Now, for the most part, we don't just sit on these bonds until they've run their course (i.e., matured). Rather, we scrutinize the market, forecast interest rate movements, and on the basis of such predictions, we decide whether a particular bond is a good or a bad investment. Then, we act accordingly. So why shouldn't we scrutinize our policy loans in the same way?"

"Why should we?" Van Ackerman inquired. "There's obvious merit to attempts to discriminate between bonds that constitute 'good' investments and those that are 'bad' investments, because we can sell the bad ones. But in the case of policy loans, we don't hold the initiative—that always rests with the borrowing policyholder. Besides, when market rates exceed the contractual loan rate, *all* policy loans are 'bad' invest-

ments and, if we could, we ought to liquidate the entire policy loan portfolio—something which, of course, we have no way of accomplishing!"

Roberts agreed that everything Van Ackerman had said was true, as far as it went. He continued, "Yes, given current money market conditions, all of the policy loans on our books are bad investments, but irrespective of money market conditions, some policy loans are always going to be worse investments than others and if we could correctly categorize them as such in advance. . . ."

"Hayden, let me make sure that you understand the rudiments of the life insurance business before we go any further," Van Ackerman interrupted. "A loan against the cash value of a life insurance policy is completely secured, with respect to both principal and interest, by the policy's reserve value. . . ."

"I'm quite familiar with these facts," Roberts quickly asserted. "If the borrowing policyholder neglects or refuses to pay the interest due on his loan, we just add it to the loan balance by, in effect, apportioning it from the policy's cash value. And, if the insured dies or surrenders the policy, we deduct the principal sum of the loan, including capitalized interest, from the face value due the beneficiary or from the cash value due the insured, whichever the case might be.

"So you see," he continued, "I'm not advocating that we attempt to differentiate between 'good' and 'bad' policy loans on the basis of the degree of risk surrounding the principal and/or interest—that risk is always zero. Irrespective of whether the policyholder lives or dies, persists or terminates, we'll never lose those sums. However, the policy loan is a source of risk and potential loss to the company in another respect."

"If you're referring to the inducement which policy loans allegedly give to surrender of the policy," Van Ackerman interjected, "I think I'm finally beginning to follow you, Hayden."

"Precisely," Hayden Roberts replied. "But it's more than an 'alleged' relationship—it's actually fairly well documented. I pulled a few figures together the other day which indicate that, of a systematically selected sample of policies which developed loan balances in 1966, nearly 20 percent were surrendered within one year of the time the loan was initiated! That figure is quite a bit higher than the average surrender rate on our overall book of business (underwriting portfolio)."

At this point, John Pershing—the new addition to the staff of actuarial trainees—inquired as to the way in which surrender caused the company to suffer a loss. Van Ackerman explained that surrender values are normally made available to a policyholder before he has contributed, through premiums, an amount sufficient to cover the acquisition expenses incurred by the company in the process of getting his business on the books. Such expenses (primarily sales commissions) are generally quite large relative to other expenses associated with the policy and it is not feasible to recoup them by means of the first-year expense loading. Therefore, life companies are allowed to charge the excess of first-year expenses over first-year expense loading against the policy's surrender value and then amortize this 'loan' against the surrender value out of the expense loading contained in the remaining premiums. If a policyholder surrenders his policy before the acquisition expenses are fully amortized (and this may be 20 years, or more), the company must make up the difference out of surplus and eventually, the persisting policyholders must replenish the surplus out of either gross premiums, dividends, or both.

Van Ackerman now sought to bring the entire discussion into focus by summarizing the critical points that had been raised. "Clearly," he began, "The rise in policy loan activity—which seems to have been arbitrage induced—does not bode well for the company, for two reasons: (1) our rate of return on policy loans is considerably below what we could expect on alternative, riskless investments; and (2) loan-supporting policies stand a better than average chance to result in premature surrender of the policy, thereby leaving the company and its persisting policyholders to absorb the unamortized acquisition expenses. In either case," he continued, "the end result is to increase the net cost of insurance."

The policy loan issue, first posed by Hayden Roberts, constituted, in Van Ackerman's words, "an interesting dilemma for the company." Life companies are legally obligated to honor a policyholder's legitimate loan request. They are also charged with the responsibility of protecting the financial interests of all policyholders insofar as the insurance contract is concerned. However, borrowing policyholders may, and quite frequently do, interpret their financial interest in the contract in a manner that conflicts with the non-borrowing policyholder's financial interest in the contract. This situation, occasioned by a loan request, is manifested first, in the requirement that the company invest a portion of its assets at suboptimal rates and second, by the transference to persisting policyholders of the financial burden associated with premature termination of the insurance contract. Van Ackerman observed that, in either instance, he believed the company's responsibility to protect the insurance, rather than the financial arbitrage interests of all policyholders should be accorded the greater priority in resolving the conflict.

"Given this line of reasoning," Van Ackerman concluded, "the desirability of managing the policy loan account is irrefutable." He then proceeded to clarify his use of the term, "management."

"If we're going to avoid getting the proverbial cart before the horse, we'd better draw a distinction, at the outset, between what I call 'active' management and 'passive' management. In a passive sense, I would see management of the policy loan account as consisting of developing an *understanding* of the profile of the account and of those factors which influence the time-state disposition of the individual components of the account.

"In a second, 'active' sense, the term, 'management' connotes the taking of action designed to *influence* the time-state disposition of particular policy loan accounts."

"Clearly, we can't expect to be successful in actively managing these accounts until we thoroughly understand what they look like and why they behave as they do. Now, this is a very complex task, so we'd better tackle it one piece at a time. Therefore, Hayden, I would like you to ascertain whether it is possible to differentiate, in a multivariate context, between those policy loans that result in surrender of the policy and those that do not. If we can't accomplish this, then I don't see that there's much hope for our ever successfully influencing what happens to individual policy loan accounts, and we would be well advised to abandon the whole project. If you are successful, though. . .well, then we'll just take it from there and try to see if we can't prevent loan-supporting policies that have a high probability of prematurely terminating from actually doing so."

After the discussion session had ended, Hayden Roberts felt very elated at the success he had had in convincing Van Ackerman to try to come to grips with the policy loan problem. However, as he began assembling data, he became concerned about the unavailability of information relative to most of the variables he intuitively felt would be the best "discriminators" between loan-supporting policies that terminated and those that persisted. In general, he thought that the time-state disposition (i.e., surrender versus persist) of the policy depended upon two things: (1) the utility the policyholder derived from the policy, and (2) the financial outlay required to repay the loan. For example, he thought that the time-state disposition of the borrowed-on policy would be a function of the purpose for which the loan

was requested, as well as of the financial, professional, educational, and family profile characteristics of the borrowing policyholder. The company did not maintain—in accessible form, at least—information on any of these variables. Moreover, Roberts had serious doubts as to the feasibility of ever aggregating such data, let alone keeping it current. Therefore, he admitted the necessity for working under a major constraint; specifically, he would have to use proxy variables.

To identify the most appropriate proxy variables, Roberts first addressed himself to the following query: what considerations exerted the major influence on the policyholder's initial decision to purchase and, subsequently, to maintain a cash value policy? He concluded that the answer to this question was implicit in the nature of the cash value life insurance product. It provided, essentially, two "commodities": (1) economic protection against premature death, and (2) an investment, or savings element. Thus, he reasoned, the *utility* which the policyholder derived from the policy might be inferred from proxies which tangibly reflect upon either or both of these focal points. After scrutinizing the available data, he selected the following proxies for utility:

(1) annual premium

(2) face value of the policy

(3) policy anniversary (i.e., number of years since its inception)

(4) loan value (approximately the same as the policy's cash value)

(5) billing status of the policy (i.e., whether it was paid-up or not)

(6) existence of automatic premium loans.

In similar fashion, he decided to use the following proxy variables for the purpose of providing insight into the *financial sacrifice* required to repay the policy loan:

(1) loan balance

(2) loan balance-to-loan value ratio

(3)   loan balance-to-face value ratio

He felt that these latter three variables reflected, respectively, the absolute outlay required to repay the loan, en toto, and the relative significance of this outlay.

Roberts shared with Van Ackerman his concern over the credibility of these proxy variables. Van Ackerman replied that he appreciated Roberts' concern but added that "if the company were to aggregate and maintain the missing data, the costs incurred in conjunction with the policy loan account would be increased. Then, we would have to ascertain whether these incremental costs could reasonably be expected to be offset by the benefits derived in terms of improved cash planning, reduction of policy termina-

tions, and a reduction in the proportion of assets committed to low-yielding policy loans. At this point, we're not even sure that a workable model is within the realm of reason. Therefore, it's worth a try to see if we can accomplish our objectives with existing data—i.e., at minimum cost. If the results are encouraging, we can make various modifications later."

After several days of steady effort, Hayden Roberts had brought together the data displayed in Exhibit 2. The three-pronged question that now occupied his time was which of several possible analytical techniques to employ, how to organize the data so as to facilitate the analysis, and finally, how to interpret the results of the analysis, once it had been completed.

Exhibit 1:

Money Market Rates
(Percent per annum)

Period	Prime banker's acceptance 90 days	Federal funds rate	U.S. Government Securities			
			3-month bills		6-month bills	
			Rate on new issue	Market yield	Rate on new issue	Market yield
1967	4.75	4.22	4.321	4.29	4.630	4.61
1968	5.75	5.66	5.339	5.34	5.470	5.47
1969	7.61	8.21	6.677	6.67	6.853	6.86
1970	7.31	7.17	6.458	6.39	6.562	6.51
1971	4.85	4.66	4.348	4.33	4.511	4.52
1972	4.47	4.44	4.071	4.07	4.466	4.49
1973	8.08	8.74	7.041	7.03	7.178	7.20
1973-May	7.15	7.84	6.348	6.36	6.615	6.62
-Jun	7.98	8.49	7.188	7.19	7.234	7.23
-Jul	9.19	10.40	8.015	8.01	8.081	8.12
-Aug	10.18	10.50	8.672	8.67	8.700	8.65
-Sep	10.19	10.78	8.478	8.29	8.537	8.45
-Oct	9.07	10.01	7.155	7.22	7.259	7.32
-Nov	8.73	10.03	7.866	7.83	7.823	7.96
-Dec	8.94	9.95	7.364	7.45	7.444	7.56
1974-Jan	8.72	9.65	7.755	7.77	7.627	7.65
-Feb	7.83	8.97	7.060	7.12	6.874	6.96
-Mar	8.43	9.35	7.986	7.96	7.829	7.83
-Apr	9.61	10.51	8.229	8.33	8.171	8.32
-May	10.68	11.31	8.430	8.23	8.496	8.40

Source: *Federal Reserve Bulletin* (June, 1974), p. A29

Exhibit 2:

Summary of Policy and Loan Value Information for a Systematically Selected Sample of 70 Policies which Developed Positive Loan Balances during 1966

Policy Number	Int. Rate	Face Value (000)	Periodic Premium	Billing Period	Billing Status	APL*	Policy Anniversary	Initial Loan Value	Initial Loan Balance	LB**/LV	LB***/FV	Policy Surrendered within 1 year of loan
3283	06	5.0	0	—	Paid-up	No	54	1582.86	570.00	.36	.29	Yes
10341	06	3.0	0	—	Paid-up	No	48	2402.86	2402.33	1.00	.80	No
25257	05	2.5	72.28	Annual	Paying	Yes	34	1535.38	39.50	.03	.02	No
33805	05	1.0	22.52	Annual	Paying	Yes	37	419.81	22.52	.05	.02	Yes
43113	05	1.0	24.88	Annual	Paying	No	34	760.38	759.70	1.00	.77	No
51121	05	1.5	34.74	Annual	Paying	Yes	32	660.85	19.22	.03	.01	No
58370	05	1.0	20.76	Annual	Paying	No	30	343.40	343.40	1.00	.35	Yes
60735	05	1.0	30.86	Annual	Paying	No	29	963.21	500.00	.52	.50	No
65017	05	10.0	134.80	Semian.	Paying	No	27	3907.77	3890.00	1.00	.39	No
80012	05	3.0	21.15	Quart.	Paying	No	25	1251.11	1242.68	.99	.41	No
83872	05	2.5	32.61	Semian.	Paying	Yes	21	787.80	32.61	.04	.01	No
85377	05	5.0	123.45	Annual	Paying	Yes	23	1338.10	123.45	.09	.02	No
87441	05	1.0	0	—	Paid-up	No	23	769.52	200.00	.26	.20	No
88707	05	6.0	15.72	Month.	Paying	Yes	22	2229.21	15.72	.01	.00	No
100075	05	2.0	46.36	Annual	Paying	No	22	590.48	565.42	.96	.28	Yes
102763	05	10.0	268.40	Annual	Paying	Yes	21	3352.38	161.60	.05	.02	No
108045	05	1.5	10.14	Quart.	Paying	Yes	20	602.96	10.14	.02	.01	No
111685	05	4.0	265.00	Annual	Paying	No	19	5447.62	2000.00	.37	.50	No
111755	05	2.5	102.90	Annual	Paying	No	19	1757.00	1700.00	1.00	.70	Yes
112222	05	3.0	62.07	Annual	Paying	Yes	19	840.00	62.07	.07	.02	No
113804	05	3.0	18.27	Quart.	Paying	No	16	681.48	260.00	.38	.09	No
115573	05	50.0	1273.50	Annual	Paying	No	16	14952.38	739.50	.05	.01	No
118402	05	25.0	596.75	Annual	Paying	No	15	6523.81	3500.00	.54	.14	No
118413	05	2.0	13.66	Quart.	Paying	Yes	15	507.65	28.93	.06	.01	No
120041	05	5.0	17.40	Month.	Paying	Yes	15	1073.03	17.40	.02	.00	No

(Continued)

*Automatic Premium Loan
**Loan Balance-to-Loan Value ratio
***Loan Balance-to-Face Value ratio

Exhibit 2: (Continued)

Summary of Policy and Loan Value Information for a Systematically Selected Sample of 70 Policies which Developed Positive Loan Balances during 1966

Policy Number	Int. Rate	Face Value (000)	Periodic Premium	Billing Period	Billing Status	APL*	Policy Anniversary	Initial Loan Value	Initial Loan Balance	LB** LV	LB*** FV	Policy Surrendered within 1 year of loan
121135	05	10.0	358.70	Annual	Paying	No	15	3314.29	1812.25	.55	.18	No
124775	05	10.0	47.54	Quart.	Paying	Yes	13	1856.79	47.54	.03	.00	No
127807	05	5.0	28.75	Month.	Paying	No	13	3384.23	500.00	.15	.10	No
128067	05	3.0	26.15	Quart.	Paying	No	13	894.81	876.10	.98	.29	No
139171	05	1.0	14.11	Semian.	Paying	Yes	13	214.15	14.11	.07	.01	No
139856	05	10.0	358.50	Annual	Paying	Yes	12	2819.05	241.80	.09	.02	No
142548	05	5.0	16.10	Month.	Paying	No	12	697.10	504.24	.72	.10	No
145440	05	1.0	23.72	Semian.	Paying	No	11	380.49	94.00	.25	.09	No
146331	05	4.0	19.05	Month.	Paying	No	11	767.47	581.91	.76	.15	No
149443	05	15.0	213.30	Annual	Paying	No	10	1657.14	500.00	.30	.03	No
150757	05	10.0	336.70	Annual	Paying	No	10	2219.05	1800.00	.81	.18	No
152162	05	20.0	295.26	Semian.	Paying	Yes	10	4019.51	295.26	.07	.01	No
156302	05	3.0	0	—	Paid-up	No	9	235.00	230.41	1.00	.08	Yes
157282	05	10.0	42.67	Month.	Paying	No	9	1787.55	600.00	.34	.06	No
157303	05	2.0	35.19	Quart.	Paying	Yes	7	459.85	285.57	.63	.14	Yes
158051	05	1.5	24.40	Quart.	Paying	Yes	9	585.93	24.40	.04	.02	No
159040	05	2.5	10.28	Month.	Paying	No	9	433.20	294.70	.68	.12	No
159630	05	10.0	17.00	Month.	Paying	No	9	1249.79	1124.00	.90	.11	Yes
161184	05	10.0	306.90	Annual	Paying	Yes	8	1714.29	306.90	.18	.03	No
162147	05	10.0	298.00	Annual	Paying	Yes	8	2228.57	1214.94	.55	.12	No
163842	05	5.0	13.85	Month.	Paying	No	8	672.20	105.00	.16	.02	No
164616	05	10.0	25.81	Month.	Paying	No	8	1573.44	343.79	.22	.03	No
165340	05	12.0	379.80	Annual	Paying	Yes	8	2257.14	379.80	.17	.03	No
168121	05	10.0	194.20	Annual	Paying	Yes	7	1009.52	194.20	.19	.02	No

(Continued)

*Automatic Premium Loan
**Loan Balance-to-Loan Value ratio
***Loan Balance-to-Face Value ratio

Exhibit 2: (Continued)

Summary of Policy and Loan Value Information for a Systematically Selected Sample of 70 Policies which Developed Positive Loan Balances during 1966

Policy Number	Int. Rate	Face Value (000)	Periodic Premium	Billing Period	Billing Status	APL*	Policy Anniversary	Initial Loan Value	Initial Loan Balance	LB** / LV	LB*** / FV	Policy Surrendered within 1 year of loan
169811	05	10.0	20.21	Month.	Paying	No	7	1148.55	500.00	.44	.05	No
170467	05	10.0	398.80	Annual	Paying	Yes	7	1571.43	1124.05	.72	.11	No
171225	05	15.0	57.12	Month.	Paying	Yes	5	448.13	381.80	.85	.03	Yes
171683	05	25.0	95.50	Month.	Paying	No	5	5261.41	2000.00	.38	.08	No
172174	05	3.0	21.72	Quart.	Paying	Yes	5	248.00	245.93	1.00	.08	Yes
173658	05	6.0	9.96	Month.	Paying	Yes	5	261.79	9.96	.04	.00	No
175441	05	5.0	14.47	Month.	Paying	Yes	5	299.59	8.71	.03	.00	No
176003	05	10.0	294.40	Annual	Paying	No	5	323.81	251.00	.78	.05	Yes
176463	05	10.0	19.86	Month.	Paying	Yes	4	640.66	19.86	.03	.00	No
179622	05	50.0	2062.00	Annual	Paying	No	4	6190.48	5182.00	.84	.10	Yes
180123	05	10.0	14.16	Month.	Paying	Yes	4	298.76	84.96	.28	.01	No
180614	05	10.0	13.33	Month.	Paying	Yes	4	438.17	132.32	.30	.01	No
180979	05	5.0	14.79	Month.	Paying	Yes	4	345.23	104.39	.30	.02	No
183810	05	10.0	15.56	Month.	Paying	Yes	3	188.38	15.56	.08	.00	No
184504	05	10.0	18.60	Month.	Paying	No	3	314.52	202.00	.64	.02	Yes
185618	05	5.0	28.08	Quart.	Paying	Yes	3	148.15	51.39	.35	.01	No
187568	05	5.0	10.60	Month.	Paying	Yes	3	165.97	8.36	.05	.00	No
188336	05	2.5	12.63	Month.	Paying	No	3	181.33	104.00	.57	.04	No
190865	05	10.0	15.50	Month.	Paying	No	2	486.31	435.70	.90	.04	Yes
191361	05	3.0	11.73	Month.	Paying	No	2	296.51	95.67	.32	.03	No
191770	05	4.0	39.80	Month.	Paying	No	2	1042.99	194.99	.19	.05	No

*Automatic Premium Loan

**Loan Balance-to-Loan Value ratio

***Loan Balance-to-Face Value ratio

Case 10

Prudential Insurance Company of America

In observing its centennial year in 1975, the Prudential Insurance Company of America, which was the largest insurer in the United States, established new records in almost all areas of its operations, according to Donald S. MacNaughton, chairman and chief executive officer. Although affected by the slow economic recovery in 1975, Prudential's life insurance sales reached an all-time industry high of $30.8 billion. The company's life insurance in force increased from $218 billion to $236 billion, which was an industry record. Total assets also rose to an industry record high of $39.3 billion. Payments to policy holders and beneficiaries, including dividends, also increased significantly, as did the rate of investment earnings and the market value of the company's common stock portfolio.

At a press conference in New York City on February 26, 1976, Mr. MacNaughton observed that while 1975 was a year of continued growth and expansion for Prudential, "We expect 1976 will prove an even better one for the nation and Prudential. Business will be aided by a gradual expansion of consumer spending, moderate housing gains, and an upswing in capital spending. This forward momentum," he explained, "should be aided by the Federal Reserve's more accommodative monetary policy stance and the recent extension of lower income tax withholding rates." However, Mr. MacNaughton mentioned some disturbing signs despite the strengthening economy. "These signs exist," he said, as a result of "the political and economic events of the past two years. They created a skepticism toward America's public and private institutions and a fear of being out of control of one's own future. We at Prudential and all those in a position of leadership in both the private and public sectors must take a large part in restoring the traditional American pride and confidence in ourselves if we are all to prosper together."

Comments on some other lines of Prudential's business were made at the same press conference by Robert A. Beck, president and chief operating officer. He stated that Prudential Reinsurance Company, which was started as a spinoff of the Property and Casualty Subsidiary in 1973, was in early 1976 the nation's seventh largest reinsurer with premium income of over $100 million in 1975. Mr. Beck also reported that in 1975 Prudential purchased a 9.5 percent equity interest in Hambros Limited of London. He further stated that while Prudential Property and Casualty Company doubled its premium income in 1975, it joined in the Property and Casualty industry's extremely high underwriting loss to the extent of $53 million. Mr. Beck stated however, that, "the Casualty Company's growth continues on schedule and we remain optimistic about its long-term future."

THE LIFE INSURANCE INDUSTRY IN THE UNITED STATES

The business of insurance in the United States can be divided into three broad categories: life insurance, health insurance, and property and liability insurance. Altogether the insurance industry provides about 1,-640,000 jobs and is responsible for assets of more than $383 billion, according to an industry publication, *Insurance Facts*. This publication stated that the insurance industry's greatest significance in the American economy is that of an absorber of personal and business risks.

The United States was the world's leading insurance country in the mid-1970s, with slightly more than 50 percent of total world insurance premiums. West Germany ranked second, with just over 9 percent. Japan was third with 8.6 percent and Great Britain was fourth with 5.75 percent of world insurance premiums. The total U.S. premiums involved in this comparison were $103.2 billion for all types of insurance in 1974. In 1975, total U.S. premiums for all types of insurance reached approximately $110 billion.

A relative measure of the level of insurance protection is the ratio of life insurance in force to national income. This ratio measures the significance of life insurance protection in each country in the world. Such ratios have, in general, shown improvement during the past decade, according to *Life Insurance Fact Book 1976*. By that statistical measure, according to the same publication, Japan, in 1976, led all other nations of the world for which data were available. The United States ranked second, followed by Canada. The five other countries in which life insurance in force exceeded national income were New Zealand, Sweden, Australia, the Netherlands, and the United Kingdom. In the United States, life insurance in force in 1974 was 168 percent of national income, measured on market price basis.

Total life insurance in force in the United States at the end of 1975 amounted to nearly $2.14 trillion, covered by 380 million policies (see Exhibit 1). The amount of new life insurance sold in 1975 was $292.5 billion (see Exhibit 2) covered by 27.3 million policies. Both the total number of policies and total amount of insurance sold represented a slight decrease from the previous year. The year 1975 was considered the weakest year for individual life insurance sales in the post-World War II era, according to Standard and Poor's Industry Outlook in April 1976.

The growth in premium income between 1974 and 1975 was relatively strong, however, increasing from $70 billion to $78 billion (see Exhibit 3). This increase in premium income was attributed by the industry to the favorable effect of the pension reform act of 1974 on sales of annuities.

Life insurance benefit payments in the U.S. increased slightly over a billion dollars between 1974 and 1975 (see Exhibit 4). Death payments made up about 40 percent of all benefit payments, with policy dividends accounting for about 20 percent. Annuity payments, disability payments, surrender values, and matured endowments made up the rest of the benefit payments, illustrating that life insurance is important for living benefits as well as death benefits.

Premium income for the life insurance industry as a whole made up 77.5 percent of all income in 1975, and the remaining 22.5 percent came from investments. Investment income is derived primarily from reserves established from premiums on ordinary insurance. In the case of ordinary life policies, premium rates are determined by using assumptions concerning expected investment earnings, expenses, and mortality rates and including a margin for the possibility of adverse experience and for profit and/or dividends to policyholders. Accordingly, earnings and/or dividends paid to policyholders represent the margin included in the premium adjusted for the gains or losses from experience which differs from that which was assumed in the premium calculation.

Life insurance companies had a combined pool of assets in 1976 of nearly $300 billion, which was exceeded only by the nation's commercial banks and savings and loans associations. No other lender could match the $100 billion in corporate bonds that life insurance companies held, which made life insurance companies the largest single source of long-term business capital. Whereas savings and loans were essentially small institutions operating locally and making mortgage loans, life insurance companies could operate almost anywhere and finance almost anything. While life insurance company assets appeared relatively modest compared to the $900 billion in commercial bank assets in 1976, life insurers operated under fewer investment restrictions than did banks.

Corporate bonds accounted for more than 36 percent of the investment portfolios of U.S. life insurance companies in 1975, with mortgages second at just under 31 percent (see Exhibit 5). Over the 10-year period

from 1966 through 1975, the average overall net yield on investment portfolios of the U.S. life insurance industry had risen from 4.73 percent to 6.44 percent, with each year during that period showing an increase over the previous year (see Exhibit 6).

Life insurance companies provided the largest share of private health insurance in the United States. In 1975, life companies paid $14.3 billion of health insurance benefits paid, including $12.4 billion under group contracts and $1.9 billion under individual policies. The overall U.S. total was $15.5 billion, so that $1.2 billion in health insurance benefits were paid by casualty and other health insurance companies, not including Blue Cross, Blue Shield, and similar organizations.

There are two principal kinds of life insurance companies in the industry. Stock companies are owned by shareholders who have an equity in the company's earnings and who elect a board to direct the company's management. Mutual companies are owned by their policy holders, who elect the management of the companies. In general, mutual companies issue only participating policies on which the policyholder receives dividends as long as investment, expense, and mortality experience produce net gains or losses from such experience which do not exceed the margin for adverse experience and dividends included in the premium calculation. Premium rates on participating policies are generally higher than those on non-participating insurance, but the net rate of the dividends may be lower. Stock companies usually offer only non-participating policies, although there are exceptions.

There were 1,790 life insurance companies operating in the United States in 1975. Although stock life insurance companies outnumbered the mutual life insurance companies by eleven to one, the mutual companies dominated the industry with about two-thirds of the industry's total of 287 billion dollars worth of assets and slightly more than half of the insurance in force. Five of the six largest companies, including Prudential, were mutual companies.

Policy reserves of all U.S. life insurance companies from 1971 to 1975 were stated by the *Life Insurance Fact Book 1976* as follows:

1971	$179 billion
1972	$192 billion
1973	$204 billion
1974	$215 billion
1975	$235 billion

These reserves represent funds set aside to meet the companies' future obligations to policy holders and their beneficiaries. Each company is required by state law to maintain its policy reserves at a level that will assure payment of all policy obligations as they fall due. The amount is calculated on an actuarial basis, taking into account the funds expected from future premium payments and assumed future interest earnings, and expected mortality experience.

THE SIX LARGEST LIFE COMPANIES IN THE U.S.

Prudential Insurance Company led the U.S. life insurance industry in 1975, followed by Metropolitan Life, The Equitable Life Assurance Society, New York Life, John Hancock Mutual Life, and Aetna Life, in that order (ranked by total assets). The first five of the six companies were mutual companies, whereas Aetna Life was a stock company.

Prudential had been second in size to Metropolitan for many years, but in 1966 Prudential's assets outgrew Metropolitan's, and in 1974 Prudential's insurance in force exceeded that of Metropolitan for the first time (see Exhibit 7). In 1975, Prudential widened its lead as the nation's largest life insurance company.

An unbroken record of net operating gain during each year from 1970 through 1975 was shown by only three of the six largest life insurance companies (see Exhibit 8), although even in those three companies the gain was not consecutive each year. All of the six largest companies were actively engaged in the accident and health business along with the life insurance business, and all six showed steady increases over the previous six years in their investment income (see Exhibit 8). The investment yields of the six largest companies are shown in Exhibit 6, along with the yields of the entire U.S. life insurance industry. The assets of five of the six largest companies are shown in Exhibit 9 for the years 1970 through 1975. Prudential's assets and other balance sheet items are shown in Exhibit 10.

Of the six largest insurance companies in 1975, five were also involved in property and casualty insurance through subsidiaries or affiliated companies. Metropolitan began operating in the property/liability auto insurance field in 1974 and in 1975 began offering homeowners' policies. Metropolitan planned to eventually offer both home automobile and homeowners' insurance in all states. In 1974, the Equitable Life Assurance Society entered the property/casualty insurance business by acquisition. In 1971 John Hancock initially entered the property/liability insurance field through an affiliation with the Sentry Insurance group. Of the six, only New York Life was not active in the property and liability insurance field in 1975. All of the above companies moving into property and casualty insurance, except Equitable, had debit agent operations. Metropolitan began to phase out its debit operations in 1973 and no longer sold debit policies nor appointed debit agents.

HISTORY OF PRUDENTIAL

Prudential began the business as the Prudential Friendly Society in 1875. The company had originally been incorporated in New Jersey in 1873 under the title The Widows and Orphans Friendly Society, but no business was done for two years, after which time the name of the company was changed. In 1877, the title of the company was again changed to the present, the Prudential Insurance Company of America. On March 30, 1943, the company became completely mutualized upon the cancellation of the remaining 584 shares of capital stock.

John F. Dryden was the principal organizer and driving force behind formation of Prudential, and he served as its first corporate secretary and later as president. The aim of the company was to market a small-sized life insurance policy to working people, selling basically what amounted to burial insurance. This was the beginning of what became known as industrial insurance, which is characterized generally by policies of less than $1,000 face value and for which the insurance agent collects the premiums from the policy holders on a weekly or monthly basis. This system of agent collection of premiums is known as the debit system and it was still used extensively by the Prudential Agency organization as of 1976, even though by then Prudential no longer sold industrial policies. Each District Agent is assigned a territory and the responsibility for collection of all premiums on Prudential insurance which is in force in that territory that has been sold on a debit ordinary or industrial basis. In addition to debit ordinary insurance, the District Agent can sell regular, ordinary, and group insurance, for which all premiums after the first are sent directly to the company by the policyholder. Agents in the Ordinary Agency organization have no responsibility for collecting premiums subsequent to the initial premium and cannot sell debit ordinary insurance. The reason for two separate organizations which sell the same basic insurance products is that the District Agency organization is designed primarily to serve the lower and middle income markets while the Ordinary Agency organization is designed primarily to serve the upper middle and high income markets.

Even though Metropolitan was phasing out the debit system as of 1973, Prudential intended to continue it. Although small industrial policies were no longer sold by Prudential, there were many such policies in existence for which premiums had to be collected. Moreover Prudential's debit agents wrote more than three-fourths of the individual insurance sold by Prudential, and according to the company, "The debit system is designed to serve the mass market. We believe it will be a viable and progressive operation for a long time to come, serving the insurance needs of the lower and middle income groups who make up a majority of the population."

From its modest beginning Prudential enjoyed steady growth over the years. In 1976, Prudential employed about 65,000 people in the United States and Canada, including approximately 26,000 sales representatives. In the previous 20 years the number of full-time employees had increased by about 30 percent. In that same period of time the life insurance sales increased 600 percent, insurance in force 500 percent, and the company had expanded its product line. Both the computer and people were seen as contributing significantly to advances in productivity in Prudential, according to Robert A. Beck, President. "In 1954," he stated, "34 Prudential agents were million dollar producers. In 1974, 4,400 Prudential agents were million dollar producers."

The life insurance annuity premiums from policies in force and newly produced by all Prudential agents reached a total of 5.76 billion dollars in 1975 (see Exhibit 11 and also Exhibit 8). Prudential's investment income to total income was in about the same proportion as the total life insurance industry. The overall net yield on its investment portfolio was slightly above the industry average and was second largest of the six biggest companies, exceeded only by Aetna (see Exhibit 6).

Investments in subsidiaries amounted to about 25 percent of the total of Prudential's total common stock account in 1975. The dollar amount of Prudential's investments in its subsidiaries had increased from 417 million in 1974 to 543 million in 1975 (see Exhibit 10).The investment yields shown excluded separate account business, which consisted of funds in specific investment programs for large policyholders in which the policyholders shared the investment risk and where the funds were not subject to the regulations of state insurance laws for the policyholders of the company in general. Prudential's separate account assets were about 10 percent of total admitted assets in 1975.

ORGANIZATION AND MANAGEMENT

Prudential operated from its home office in Newark, New Jersey until 1948, when a decentralization program was started. By 1975, regional home offices were maintained in Los Angeles, California; Houston, Texas; Chicago, Illinois; Minneapolis, Minnesota; Jacksonville, Florida; Boston, Massachusetts; South Plainfield, New Jersey; Dressier, Pennsylvania; and Toronto, Ontario, Canada. Operations were conducted throughout the United States and Canada, and Prudential was represented in 1975 by more than 3,800 managers and assistant managers and more than 24,000 soliciting agents.

Prudential operations were divided functionally into three major areas: marketing, investments, and administration. Each was headed by an executive vice-president and those three officers together with the chairman and president constituted the executive office. These company executives were responsible to a board of directors of 24 members, all of whom were policyholders. Of these 24, six were "public directors" appointed by the Chief Justice of the Supreme Court of New Jersey, while 16 were elected by the policy owners. The chairman of the board and chief executive officer and the president are ex-officio directors. As a mutual company, Prudential is owned entirely by its policyholders.

There were six committees active in the board of directors in 1975: The executive committee, the finance committee, the committee on dividends, the committee on nominations, the committee on salaries, and the auditing committee. The committee on nominations developed a list of candidates for directorships to submit to the policyholders at the annual election of directors. Thus, the board of directors was in that sense self-perpetuating, subject to the balance of public interest represented by the appointed six public directors (who also must be policyholders) already mentioned. Policyholders were allowed to vote either in person at the annual meeting or by mail with the ballot obtained by writing to the secretary of the company no later than 60 days prior to the date of the election.

Prudential had in 1976 twelve subsidiary corporations as follows:

1. *Pruco, Inc.* was organized in 1970 and was Prudential's wholly-owned holding company subsidiary. In turn, Pruco, Inc. held all of the outstanding stock of nine U. S. subsidiaries:

2. *G. I. B. Laboratories, Inc.* was activated in 1971 as a clinical laboratory which provided services for Prudential as well as for industry and other insurance companies throughout the United States.

3. *P. I. C. Realty Corporation* was engaged in owning, developing, operating, and leasing real property either directly or through participation in joint ventures and partnership in the United States. Building management services were also performed by P. I. C. Realty for certain Prudential and P. I. C. Realty owned buildings.

4. *Pruco Life Insurance Company* was incorporated in the state of Arizona in 1971 as a wholly-owned stock company

for the purpose of transacting life and disability insurance. As of 1975, Pruco Life was engaged in the group health insurance business. Other potential uses for it were being studied.

5. *Pruco Security Corporation* was activated in 1971 as a securities brokerage firm. It virtually ceased business in 1975 following the S. E. C.'s abrogation of fixed commission rates on securities transactions. Because commission rates by the brokerage industry became more competitive after that, it appeared that the usefulness of Pruco Security Corporation was declining and at the end of 1975 a study was being made to determine whether the company's continued existence was necessary.

6. *Prudential Property and Casualty Insurance Company* (PRUPAC). Started in 1970, this company was engaged in personal lines of insurance business consisting of automobile, homeowners, and disaster policies. These were sold, by those Prudential agents who had become properly licensed to sell such business in 44 states in the U. S. as of the end of 1975.

7. *Prudential Reinsurance Company* was activated in 1973 to assume most of the reinsurance operations previously handled by Prudential Property and Casualty Insurance Company. Prudential Reinsurance reinsured a large variety of risks in many parts of the world, including Ocean Marine, Nuclear Power Plants, and high-level catastrophe coverages such as hurricanes.

8. *PruLease, Inc.* was acquired in 1974 and was principally active in the leasing of nuclear energy cores, motor vehicle fleets, and electronic computer hardware as well as other equipment. Its customers were primarily in the public utility industry.

9. *Prudential Health Care Plan, Inc.* was started in Texas in 1975 and operated in the Houston areas as a health maintenance organization qualified under both federal and Texas laws.

10. *P. I. C. Management, Inc.* was owned by PruLease, Inc. and it provided administrative and management services to PruLease.

The following two Canadian companies were directed subsidiaries of Prudential:

11. *P. I. C. Realty Canada, Ltd.,* was activated in 1973 for the same purpose as P. I. C. Realty in the U.S., except that it dealt entirely with property and ventures located in Canada.

12. *Prudential Fund Management Canada, Ltd.,* was the distributor and advisor for the Prudential Growth Fund Canada, Ltd. and Prudential Income Fund of Canada, two Canadian mutual funds. It was organized for that purpose in 1970.

COMPANY OBJECTIVES AND PHILOSOPHY

Prudential's fundamental objective as stated in 1976 was "to maximize use of its human and financial resources in the interest of Prudential policy owners and of society at large, consistent with moral, legal and financial considerations and society's needs and desires." Although risk-bearing was generally considered to be the most significant feature of the life insurance industry, Prudential recognized that its responsibility extended far beyond the basic risk-bearing feature by its broadly stated objective. In recent years Prudential had changed from a life insurance company to a multi-lines company. As stated by the management, it was Prudential's primary function "to market certain financial security products at prices which are reasonable and acceptable to the public, and to efficiently serve those who purchased those products."

Donald S. MacNaughton, chairman and chief executive officer, stated in 1976 his rationale for supporting corporate social responsibility,

> Business has responsibilities to many constituencies (stockholders, policy owners, employees, suppliers, consumers, the general public) and business needs to be responsive to the needs and desires of all of these, not one or perhaps two at the expense of the others.
>
> A business is created by the people, and has, in effect, a franchise granted to it by society which will be continued only as long as the people are satisfied with the way the business performs.
>
> The corporation, therefore, ought to be viewed as a social-economic institution rather than an economic institution which has some incidental social responsibilities.

In a social report issued in 1976, it was stated that Prudential was focusing attention currently in the following areas:

Consumer issues affecting our business

Investment policy and how to make it more socially responsive

Urban problems

Equal opportunity employment and minority assistance.

Mr. MacNaughton described several trends which he believed that could serve as planning assumptions for the future:

> First, the point needs to be made that the social-economic concept of business is not a passing fad. Some people feel that preoccupation with other problems may cause business attention to social issues to be postponed or tempered down or even adandoned. I do not believe this will happen, but if it does, it will be one of the worst mistakes American business has ever made.
>
> I believe also that the timing is good for a real breakthrough in the critical relationship between business and government. Evidence is accumulating that unwise legislation and regulation, together with problems of unworkable enforcement, are adding to the economic problems we're struggling with. There is an opportunity for

business initiative to move into some problem areas with responsive programs of reform . . .

> Finally I don't think the full implications of the change relationship between individuals and institutions have been fully perceived and this poses both challenges and opportunities for business in the near future. Probably the one lasting and permanent effect of the campus revolt of the '60s is that institutions of all sorts will not again have the same unchallenged authority over their constituencies that they used to enjoy. "Because I say so," or its corporate equivalent "Because it's company policy," were never very good reasons, but there was a time when they at least used to get some action. That day is fading fast and we will be increasingly under the gun to supply better reasons to our employees and our customers.

Corporate social responsiveness was stated by Prudential as a concept undergoing change, and corporations could be found at every stage of the evolutionary process. Prudential had identified six stages or categories of corporate responsibility.

Stage 1: A corporation meets its social responsibility merely by being in business.

Stage 2: A corporation meets its social responsibility by performing its economic function so as to produce quality goods and services at the most efficient costs.

Stage 3: In addition to 1 and 2, a corporation has a responsibility to be a good citizen in the localities where it has factories and offices.

Stage 4: In addition to the above, corporate social responsibility calls for making short-term sacrifices, such as hiring and training the disadvantaged in order to make long-term gains.

Stage 5: In addition to the above, the corporation recognizes that society is being subjected to severe strains, and that the corporation must make sacrifices in order to survive.

Stage 6: In addition to the above, the corporation recognizes the responsibility of its power and the need to anticipate society's problems and provide leadership in resolving those problems.

Mr. MacNaughton believed that the insurance industry was in a position to participate significantly in solving the problems of society. In a statement made in 1972, he said, "American society, in its desire to tackle the problems of urban decay, poverty, pollution, and adequate medical care and other major issues of our day, is increasingly looking to the insurance technique as a vehicle for attacking such problems."

Robert A. Beck, who in 1972 was executive vice president of Prudential, at that time stated that, "The pace of change, if anything, will accelerate over time. We will be tested as never before to learn, to personally grow, to stay close to our markets physically and mentally, to be sophisticated in those markets which require it, and to be ever more people and problem-oriented for those markets requiring less technical skill and knowledge. The future of the Agent, the individual marketer of our basic products—life, property and casualty, health and individual equities—will be very bright. He will need to make adjustments to change, anticipate change, even react to change; but he can do what no one or nothing else can do, he can persuade the reluctant or the procrastinating buyer to take action."

Investment objectives in relation to social policy were expressed in 1972 by Frank J. Hoenemeyer, executive vice-president of Prudential. "I believe that the objective of the investment area will continue to be to get the highest possible net yield after reflecting expenses and capital gains and losses. We have, I believe, been very successful in achieving that objective in the past. At the same time we must be aware of the need to divert from that goal when broader social considerations dictate. In the future, we will have to give greater consideration to the environmental and social impact of every investment that we make. I am not suggesting that our objective of achieving the highest possible yield is going to change. It was always understood that we would not do anything that was judged by society to be harmful or illegal in reaching that objective. What is and will be changing in the future is our perception and society's views of what is harmful or disadvantageous. And so society will be paying more attention to what we are doing."

The first major response to changing investment attitudes, which recognized more the importance of the qualitative aspects of life, including the consideration of various non-economic factors, by the life insurance industry and Prudential came in 1967 with the Urban Investment Program. A total of 126 insurance companies pledged one billion dollars to investments for housing and jobs for central city residents of low and moderate income. In 1968 a second billion dollars was pledged. Prudential's share of this program rose to over $330 million before the program was completed. This program produced 116,000 housing units, 60 day-care centers, two industrial parks, 40 nursing homes, $177 million in hospital construction, and $240 million in commercial and industrial ventures that created more than 40,000 non-construction jobs. Higher than average foreclosures were experienced by the investors in this program. As of 1975, 12 percent of the mortgages involved in the program were foreclosed or being foreclosed, and 7 percent (three times the normal rate) had been taken over by government guarantees (such as FHA), according to a *Business Week* article in August 1976. Prudential had experienced $37 million in foreclosures and nearly $32 million turned back to the government under this program. There was disagreement within the insurance industry as to whether the program was worthwhile. An executive of one large participating company said that he didn't think it was worth the time and effort: "It demonstrated. . .that you can't force the private sector into making uneconomic loans, which is what we were doing. The problem of the inner city is bigger than just housing and some office buildings." However, a top executive of another leading participant took a more positive view and said, "The program enabled many people to own their homes, and it created job opportunities. It served its purpose." A spokesman for the American Council on Life Insurance's Clearinghouse on Corporate Social Responsibility was quoted as saying, "We regret losses but, overall, I don't see how we could regret having done it."

Since 1971, those responsible for Prudential's investment portfolios had been instructed not to make any investments in companies that were not socially responsive in such areas as pollution control, job safety, equal employment, and fair housing. In addition, Prudential reported annually since 1972 to the Clearinghouse on Corporate Social Responsibility all social action investments. This included investments specifically for socially desirable purposes which would not normally be made under the company's customary lending standards or in which sound considerations played a substantial part in the investment decisions. Socially desirable projects included but were not limited to: housing for low-income and moderate-income families, health and social facilities for those in inner-city or rural areas, industrial or commercial facilities in areas of chronic unemployment, deposits in minority owned or operated financial institutions, long-term or venture capital minority entrepreneurs, and bonds to finance anti-pollution facilities. In addition, Prudential engaged in a number of other social responsibility programs, including customer relations, customer complaints, public attitude surveys, employee hiring on a non-discriminatory basis, employee training, development and education, job design and enrichment, purchasing from minority suppliers, direct contributions to various charitable organizations and social benefit programs, and special projects of support and participation in various areas of the United States.

PRUDENTIAL PROPERTY AND CASUALTY INSURANCE COMPANY

The first group of Prudential agents began selling automobile, homeowners, and personal catastrophe policies for PRUPAC in June of 1971 in Illinois. Prudential acquired from the Kemper Organization a small inactive company and changed its name to Prudential Property and Casualty Insurance Company, which was licensed in 31 states and the District of Columbia to start with.

Prudential wanted its agents to be able to offer customers as full a line as possible of insurance and financial services. It also wanted its agents to have an opportunity to increase their earnings through a broader line of insurance services.

David J. Sherwood, president of PRUPAC described the outlook for the company in optimistic terms at the time it started business in 1971. The question was raised as to whether the upsurge in automobile accidents, damage repair costs and thefts made it a tough time to get into the automobile insurance market. Mr. Sherwood responded that even though the overall results in the property and casualty industry had been pretty bad in recent years due mainly to the impact of inflation on claims costs, the susceptibility of the automobile to damage, and substantial increase in burglaries and automobile thefts, there were some changes taking place which should improve the picture. He believed that the personal lines insurance could become profitable enough to be self-supporting by the time PRUPAC was fully established in the business. The change he was referring to was the prospect of slowing down in claim costs as inflation decreased and as the automobile industry responded to the increasing pressure for safer cars. He also pointed out that even during the worst period in the history of property and casualty insurance industry, a number of well managed insurers had been able to make consistent underwriting profits. Mr. Sherwood believed that in the long run PRUPAC could outperform most of the other companies in the property and casualty field.

In addition to the reasons mentioned above, Prudential indicated two other motives for entering the property and casualty insurance field. The first was that Prudential had the financial resources to help meet the growing public need for insurance capacity in those lines. The second reason was that Prudential had an established sales force well suited to making complete insurance protection available to households in all parts of the country.

Prior to going into the property and casualty business a thorough study was made by Prudential of the prospects for that business. It was found that automobile and home insurance premiums had kept better pace with inflation than personal life insurance premiums, even though cycles of profit and loss were characteristic of personal property and casualty insurance lines. In the 1950s, the property and casualty insurers in the United States began to diversify into life insurance, with the strategic concept of making their agents representatives of all lines of insurance to the consumer. After many years of effort, the property and casualty insurers had had only moderate success in producing all-lines insurance counselors. Even so, the life insurers were coming back to the concept in the early 1970s because they saw persistent evidence of strong consumer demand for all lines of insurance services from one agent or company. There were some differences between property and casualty agents and life insurance agents. It was believed that the major reason that the property and casualty agents had found it difficult to handle all other insurance needs for their clients was that they rarely stayed in personal contact with their customers and most of their selling was done over the telephone rather than in person (although there were not any specific survey facts to determine the extent of this impression). Life insurance agents, on the other hand, must sell in person. It was believed that this closer contact would enable them to sell other lines of insurance more easily to their life insurance customers than property and casualty insurance agents could sell life insurance to their clients. Prudential believed that the transition would be fairly slow and they were approaching it cautiously.

A simulation of the financial implications of going into property and casualty insurance was started by a small team in the middle of 1969. A twenty-year period was chosen for study. Prudential's top management had become accustomed to very explicit financial data as bases for major decisions on the property and casualty business. As a result of having quantitative illustrations of different assumptions and arrangements available by using a simulation model, the new management of Prudential's property and casualty operation was able to come to very quick agreement on the problem of agency compensation with the managers of Prudential's sales departments once the decision was made to go ahead.

The property and casualty operation was regarded by management as an investment of Prudential's assets. Many of Prudential's investments, especially new projects or new enterprises, showed losses in their early years because of the initial expense. In the long run, Prudential's management expected that the investment in property and casualty insurance would bring a return to Prudential at least as high as what was regarded as the riskiest of investments—that is, common stock. In other words, it was neither planned nor expected that property and casualty insurance would be subsidized by the mutual policyholders of the parent (life insurance) company.

Participation in the property and casualty program was strictly voluntary so far as the

Prudential agents were concerned, but over 90 percent of Prudential agents available for licensing were actively selling property and casualty coverage. Agents were required to have a year's experience selling other lines of insurance for Prudential before they could sell property and casualty coverage. In 1975, 87.5 percent of applications for automobile insurance and 92.5 percent of applications for home insurance met PRUPAC standard of acceptability.

Net written premiums for automobile and homeowners insurance by PRUPAC exceeded 111 million in 1975 (see Exhibit 12). Total earned premiums of $125 million included $37.5 million for long-term disability reinsurance. Underwriting losses in 1975 were $53 million and investment gains exceeded $21 million, for a net loss of more than $32 million (Exhibit 12). Prudential agents wrote 232,000 home owner applications and 289,000 automobile applications in 1975, and by the end of that year 523,000 cars and 369,000 homes were insured by PRUPAC. Volume of claims processed rose from nearly 90,000 in 1974 to just under 200,000 in 1975. In order to maintain sufficient capital, Prudential increased its equity investment in PRUPAC $113 million in 1975 (Exhibit 12). Total assets of PRUPAC at the end of 1975 were over $313 million (see Exhibit 13). Other operating data and Key Ratios for PRUPAC are shown in Exhibit 14.

A strategic question posed by Mr. Sherwood, president of PRUPAC, in the summer of 1976 was, "How fast should PRUPAC grow?" PRUPAC needed more capital in addition to that which Prudential had invested in it up to that point in time, and Mr. Sherwood felt that it was desirable to maintain the industry standard of one dollar in surplus for every three dollars in premium written. PRUPAC had recently been doubling its volume every year, and a 15 percent annual growth rate over a longer period of time was envisioned by Mr. Sherwood. As of 1976 in the automobile field, Allstate and

State Farm each had about 12 percent of the market whereas PRUPAC had less than 1 percent. Mr. Sherwood visualized a position for PRUPAC to be 10 percent of the market eventually and to level off there. In homeowners insurance, Allstate and State Farm each had between 6 and 7 percent in 1976 and Prupac had .5 percent. The position for PRUPAC seen by Mr. Sherwood was to reach 5 to 6 percent of the homeowners insurance market.

The profitability objectives for PRUPAC were expressed as reaching break-even on the bottom line (after taking into account the investment income) by about 1979 and reaching break-even on the underwriting portion of the business by about 1981, or 10 years after PRUPAC began business. Another question posed by Mr. Sherwood was that of how to control the growth of PRUPAC. In mid-1976 the company had 600 employees in the corporate office plus 1,900 in regional offices (not including the Prudential agents who sold the insurance).

Some other current issues discussed by Mr. Sherwood were those of how to handle the increase in damage and repair claims. "We've got to find a way to get out from under this tremendous waste," he stated. "Repair costs have gone up about three times the consumer price index in recent years and medical costs about two times the consumer price index. We think we've just about reached the saturation point." Mr. Sherwood mentioned that PRUPAC was using specialists in crash damage and medical specialists to question doctors on charges. He differentiated between adjusting claims and paying claims. "If we pay too much for a car, people will sell too many of them to the insurance company," he said, and mentioned also that it was not uncommon for garages to load non-insured repairs onto the total insurance bill. "We are working on road and highway safety such as breakable poles. We think air bags will come eventually in some form," he continued. "As a new company, with the backing and stature of

Prudential, PRUPAC will have a stronger voice in the industry and get more response to safety programs," Mr. Sherwood believed. However, he said it was discouraging that there was not more response by the public and by legislatures for automobile safety.

Another new program being considered by PRUPAC in mid-1976 was the mass marketing of group automobile insurance. No one was selling group automobile insurance yet, but if employers contributed and got all risks together in a pool it would facilitate the growth of this kind of coverage. Contributions by employers to automobile insurance were taxable to employees in 1976. Would this change? Mr. Sherwood thought that it was a matter of time. "We want to test group automobile underwriting as a new concept," he stated.

Mr. Sherwood summarized the strategic issues facing PRUPAC in mid-1976 as growth, possible future integration with Prudential, automobile safety with the industry becoming more active, government regulation, and group automobile insurance.

THE PROPERTY AND CASUALTY INSURANCE INDUSTRY

The years 1974 and 1975 were said to be the two most devastating years ever experienced by the property and casualty insurance industry. In 1974 the industry's total loss amounted to $2.7 billion but in 1975 it increased to $4.3 billion. The cyclical performance of the industry over a period of years was illustrated in the operating results of 909 stock casualty and liability companies listed in Best's aggregates and averages (see Exhibit 15). Thirty companies in the property and casualty insurance field became insolvent in 1975. Some of these were large enough to cause significant shock waves within the industry, according to the management of one company which did better.

Another result was that many companies sharply curtailed their writing of insurance for new policy holders, even those type of people once considered reasonably good risks. A number of the companies in difficulty had their top financial rating lowered by A. M. Best and Company.

A major problem was attributed to inflation by many industry observers. Premiums charged for most types of insurance had lagged behind the increase in the cost of good service paid for by insurance dollars. This was especially true in the case of automobile insurance. Liability companies were beginning to get their rates in line with the general price level by mid-1976, and the situation in the industry was looking better, while recovery in the securities markets had improved investment income of the insurers, and the slow down in inflation had reduced the sharp increases of the cost of claims. The result for the policy holder was sharply increased premiums. Automobile owners in New York, New Jersey, and Florida faced increases of about 50 percent in insurance rates despite a no-fault law that was supposed to reduce the cost of insurance.

Two types of inflation were blamed by industry observers for the increasing cost of insurance. Price inflation was only one of the problems. The other was called "social inflation." Courts, regulatory agencies, and legislative bodies were extending liabilities to areas where they hadn't existed before and were establishing new and higher standards for awards to injured parties. This was seen as part of the egalitarian trend in U.S. society, or in other words, the leveling movement which tries to narrow the gap between the rich and the poor. Social inflation was the real threat to the insurance industry, according to a *Business Week* article in September 1976, because it involved a huge unpredictable increase of risks and created obligations that did not exist in an earlier society. Malpractice and product liability were two examples cited. Some industry executives thought that car ownership might go beyond the reach of mass markets just as home ownership was believed to be going. The prospect of annual automobile insurance premiums in the range of $1,000 would certainly prevent some people in the lower income range from owning an automobile if it were required that they carry insurance to do so.

Standard and Poor's evaluation of the casualty insurance industry in 1976 mentioned that the demand for insurance was expanding at a time when the industry found itself in a financial bind due to heavy underwriting losses and that if the industry became unable to furnish the needs of the market it could lead to government intervention. It was stated that underwriting cycles would probably remain an inherent characteristic of the property and liability industry. A hope was expressed that insurers would eventually find some way to protect themselves against unexpected flareups in inflation.

The four largest property and casualty insurance companies in the United States in 1975 were the State Farm group, Allstate, Travelers, and Aetna Casualty and Surety (see Exhibit 16). Total assets of these companies were more than 10 percent of the total assets of all U.S. property and liability insurance companies (see also Exhibit 17). The net premiums written by these largest companies were more than 15 percent of the total net premiums written in the industry (see Exhibits 16 and 17). Best's Aggregates and Averages listed 909 stock companies, 303 mutual companies, 42 reciprocal companies, and 31 large companies in the totals (see Exhibit 18) for the year 1975.

PRUDENTIAL'S FUTURE STRATEGY

Observers in the life insurance industry believed that it was partly because Prudential had no more life insurance worlds to conquer that it was so anxious to diversify. Although the diversification trend really began to take place when Mr. MacNaughton became the chief executive in 1969, Prudential was seen as having previously been willing to break with old practices and assumptions and take some risks in a way that set it apart from an otherwise conservative industry. Prudential's decentralization after World War II was counter to the industry trends at that time. At the same time, Prudential made a fundamental change in its investment strategy, in which it began accepting increased risk to get a higher rate of return on its general account funds. In 1950, Prudential began to channel some of its investment funds into common stocks, which Metropolitan did not do until 1964.

It was considered more central to Mr. MacNaughton's thinking, however, that a fundamental change was taking place in the insurance business, a change that he expected to split the whole industry into two levels: a few broadly diversified giants and a large number of specialized insurers that would sell to selective markets or in limited geographical areas. Mr. MacNaughton acknowledged that Prudential's move into the property and casualty insurance was done less to make money than to protect its district agent selling force. According to an article in *Business Week* in February 1976, Mr. MacNaughton said, "The district agency method of marketing insurance products will not be sustained in the long run if something is not done to increase the number of products available to our agents."

Prudential's diversification movements had come under some criticism by others in the industry. It was accused, for example, of charging lower rates on property and casualty policies than was justified by current industry experience, in order to get PRU-PAC established in that field. As of early 1976, Pruco, the Prudential holding company, had yet to remit any cash dividends to the parent company. Prudential's management believed, however, that in the long run it would prove equally as profitable as its other investments on the average.

International expansion of Prudential was facilitated by the activities of Prudential Reinsurance, which in 1976 had policies in 29 countries outside the United States and written in 25 currencies. According to Robert A. Beck, "PRURE has given us the chance to be international in scope. We are now involved in virtually every major disaster in the world." Many of the companies Prudential had invested in or lent to had gone abroad to do business, and Prudential executives believed that in order to evaluate those companies properly they had to know what was happening abroad. Even more important, the overseas insurance needs of the multinational companies appeared to be an untapped market for the Prudential, which had always had a number of overseas corporate and individual customers (Americans living or doing business abroad). According to Mr. MacNaughton, Prudential could not continue to be a successful domestic company if it didn't know much more about what was going on abroad. He stated that, "If we get so that we don't understand multinational business, then multinational business will eventually find someone else who does."

Prudential's investment in Hambros Limited, consisting of a 10 percent equity interest plus a $25 million loan, had given it a board seat on the London-based holding company with $2.4 billion in assets that owned both a major British life insurance company and one of the world's largest merchant banks. "Hambros is our window on the world," said Frank J. Hoenemeyer, executive vice president in charge of investments at Prudential. In 1976, the Prudential and Hambros were exploring possible joint ventures outside of Britain and North America.

Mr. MacNaughton, according to the *Business Week* article, had Prudential's top managers considering such questions as what geographic and product limitations should be applied to subsidiaries, what portion of surplus should be risked in subsidiaries, and when to close down a subsidiary. Mr. MacNaughton was quoted as saying, "while we are acquiring some expertise on how to get into subsidiaries, we know nothing about how to get out of them."

Mr. MacNaughton was respected as "one of the great leaders of this industry," according to the president of another large insurance company. "He thinks broadly and deeply, and he thinks of things not only as they are today but also as they might be tomorrow."

Both Mr. MacNaughton and Mr. Beck believed that in a free market system (imperfect, by nature) performance (of all participants collectively) is always mixed and that if the U.S. has a bad year it wouldn't mean that all of its institutions would perform poorly. Moreover, they believed that "the best overall results year in and year out are achieved when institutions, no matter what their calling, pay close attention to their individual purposes and responsibilities and attempt to maximize their own achievement."

Exhibit 1:

The Prudential Insurance Company of America
Life Insurance in Force in the United States
(000,000 omitted)

Year	Ordinary No.	Ordinary $Amt.	Group Cert.	Group $Amt.	Industrial No.	Industrial $Amt.	Credit No.	Credit $Amt.	Total No.	Total $Amt.
1940	37	79,346	9	14,938	85	20,865	3	380	134	115,530
1941	39	82,525	10	17,359	87	21,825	3	469	139	122,178
1942	41	85,139	11	19,316	90	22,911	2	355	144	127,721
1943	43	89,596	13	22,413	94	24,874	2	275	152	137,158
1944	46	95,085	13	23,922	98	26,474	2	290	159	145,771
1945	48	101,550	12	22,172	101	27,675	2	365	163	151,762
1946	53	112,818	13	27,206	104	29,313	3	729	173	170,066
1947	56	122,393	16	32,026	106	30,406	5	1,210	183	186,035
1948	58	131,158	16	37,068	106	31,253	6	1,729	186	201,208
1949	61	138,862	17	40,207	107	32,087	8	2,516	193	213,672
1950	64	149,116	19	47,793	108	33,415	11	3,844	202	234,168
1951	67	159,109	21	54,398	109	34,870	12	4,763	209	253,140
1952	70	170,875	24	62,913	111	36,448	14	6,355	219	276,591
1953	73	185,007	26	72,913	112	37,781	18	8,558	229	304,259
1954	76	198,599	29	86,410	111	38,664	21	10,046	237	333,719
1955	80	216,812	32	101,345	112	39,682	28	14,493	252	372,332
1956	83	238,348	35	117,399	110	40,109	32	16,774	260	412,630
1957	87	264,949	37	133,905	108	40,139	34	19,366	266	458,359
1958	89	288,607	39	144,772	104	39,646	35	20,536	267	493,561
1959	93	317,158	41	160,163	102	39,809	38	24,998	274	542,128
1960	95	341,881	44	175,903	100	39,563	43	29,101	282	586,448
1961	97	366,141	46	192,794	98	39,451	45	31,107	286	629,493
1962	99	391,048	49	209,950	95	39,638	47	35,341	290	675,977
1963	102	420,808	51	229,477	93	39,672	52	40,666	298	730,623
1964	104	457,868	55	253,620	92	39,833	58	46,487	309	797,808
1965	107	499,638	61	308,078	89	39,818	63	53,020	320	900,554
1966	109	541,022	65	345,945	88	39,663	69	58,059	331	984,689
1967	113	584,570	69	394,501	84	39,215	70	61,535	336	1,079,821
1968	116	633,392	73	442,778	81	38,827	75	68,357	345	1,183,354
1969	118	682,453	76	488,864	79	38,614	78	74,598	351	1,284,529
1970	120	734,730	80	551,357	77	38,644	78	77,392	355	1,402,123
1971	123	792,318	82	589,883	76	39,202	76	81,931	357	1,503,334
1972	126	853,911	85	640,689	76	39,975	78	93,410	365	1,627,985
1973	128	928,192	88	708,322	75	40,632	78	101,154	369	1,778,300
1974	131	1,009,038	94	827,018	71	39,441	84	109,623	380	1,985,120
1975	134	1,083,421	96	904,695	70	39,423	80	112,032	380	2,139,571

Source: Life Insurance Fact Book, 1976

Exhibit 2:

The Prudential Insurance Company of America
Life Insurance Purchases in the United States
(Exclusive of Revivals, Increases, Dividend Additions and Reinsurance Acquired)

Year	Ordinary Policies (000 Omitted)	Ordinary Amount (000,000 Omitted)	Group Certificates (000 Omitted)	Group Amount (000,000 Omitted)	Industrial Policies (000 Omitted)	Industrial Amount (000,000 Omitted)	Total Number (000 Omitted)	Total Amount (000,000 Omitted)
1940	3,855	$ 6,689	285	$ 691	14,017	$ 3,350	18,157	$10,730
1945	4,343	9,859	681	1,265	11,869	3,430	16,893	14,554
1950	5,279	17,326	2,631	6,068	14,924	5,402	22,834	28,796
1955	7,572	30,827	2,217	11,258*	14,356	6,342	24,145	48,427*
1960	8,734	52,883	3,734	14,645	12,287	6,880	24,755	74,408
1961	8,735	55,016	3,971	17,019	12,327	7,000	25,033	79,035
1962	8,662	56,998	3,498	15,533	11,799	7,046	23,959	79,577
1963	9,046	64,267	3,534	18,152	11,407	7,154	23,987	89,573
1964	9,605	74,012	4,225	23,684	11,059	7,312	24,889	105,008
1965	9,937	83,485	7,007	51,385†	10,492	7,296	27,436	142,166†
1966	10,131	88,693	4,055	26,219	9,764	7,078	23,950	121,990
1967	10,192	94,694	4,353	39,118*	9,404	7,056	23,949	140,868*
1968	10,451	103,944	4,875	39,877*	8,417	6,674	23,753	150,495*
1969	10,588	113,500	5,156	39,329	7,916	6,454	23,660	159,283
1970	10,968	122,820	5,219	63,690†	7,582	6,612	23,769	193,122†
1971	11,281	132,130	5,403	49,407	8,326	7,274	25,010	188,811
1972	11,844	145,479	6,698	55,857	8,123	7,394	26,665	208,730
1973	12,198	162,506	7,065	64,461	7,506	7,224	26,769	234,191
1974	12,763	182,755	7,994	111,622†	6,747	6,680	27,504	301,057†
1975	12,599	189,556	8,348	96,213†	6,352	6,741	27,299	292,510†

Source: Life Insurance Fact Book, 1976

Exhibit 3:

The Prudential Insurance Company of America
Income of U.S. Life Insurance Companies
($ millions)

Year	Premium Receipts				Investment Income	Other Income	Total Income
	Life Insurance Premiums	Annuity Considerations	Health Insurance Premiums*	Total Premium Receipts			
1911	$ 626	$ 4	—	$ 630	$ 182	$ 24	$ 836
1915	776	6	—	782	241	20	1,043
1920	1,374	7	—	1,381	341	42	1,784
1925	2,340	38	—	2,378	551	89	3,018
1930	3,416	101	—	3,517	891	186	4,594
1935	3,182	491	—	3,673	1,013	386	5,072
1940	3,501	386	—	3,887	1,231	540	5,658
1945	4,589	570	—	5,159	1,445	1,070	7,674
1950	6,249	939	$1,001	8,189	2,075	1,073	11,337
1955	8,903	1,288	2,355	12,546	2,801	1,197	16,544
1960	11,998	1,341	4,026	17,365	4,304	1,338	23,007
1965	16,083	2,260	6,261	24,604	6,778	1,785	33,167
1966	17,160	2,416	7,244	26,820	7,353	1,961	36,134
1967	18,094	2,671	7,887	28,652	7,929	2,054	38,635
1968	19,364	2,993	8,730	31,087	8,613	2,163	41,863
1969	20,491	3,762	9,743	33,998	9,354	2,278	45,628
1970	21,679	3,721	11,367	36,767	10,144	2,143	49,054
1971	22,935	4,910	12,897	40,742	11,031	2,429	54,202
1972	24,678	5,503	14,318	44,499	12,127	2,222	58,848
1973	26,373	6,771	15,524	48,668	13,670	2,415	64,753
1974	27,750	7,737	17,123	52,610	15,144	2,256	70,010
1975	29,336	10,165	19,074	58,575	16,488	2,959	78,022

*Includes some premiums for workmen's compensation and auto and other liability insurance.

Source: Life Insurance Fact Book, 1976

Exhibit 4:

The Prudential Insurance Company of America
Life Insurance Benefit Payments in the U.S.
($ thousands)

Year	Death Payments	Matured Endowments	Disability Payments	Annuity Payments	Surrender Values	Policy Dividends	Total
1940	$ 995,000	$ 269,200	$103,500	$ 176,500	$ 652,000	$ 468,100	$ 2,664,300
1945	1,279,600	406,700	87,600	216,400	210,900	466,100	2,667,300
1950	1,589,700	495,100	99,600	319,400	592,300	634,600	3,730,700
1955	2,240,700	613,900	110,000	462,300	895,900	1,059,900	5,382,700
1960	3,346,100	673,100	123,800	722,000	1,633,400	1,620,100	8,118,500
1965	4,831,400	931,100	163,000	1,038,900	1,932,300	2,519,900	11,416,600
1966	5,218,200	981,600	169,300	1,152,600	2,120,600	2,699,900	12,342,200
1967	5,665,300	1,017,100	174,600	1,261,300	2,243,100	2,932,200	13,293,600
1968	6,209,300	967,200	195,600	1,401,000	2,456,400	3,155,500	14,385,000
1969	6,758,100	952,600	204,700	1,558,600	2,721,600	3,328,900	15,524,500
1970	7,017,300	978,300	232,900	1,757,100	2,886,400	3,577,400	16,449,400
1971	7,423,300	990,200	256,800	1,944,400	2,881,600	3,680,900	17,177,200
1972	8,007,000	1,000,400	271,200	2,213,200	3,027,400	4,054,900	18,574,100
1973	8,572,000	1,025,600	316,600	2,597,900	3,417,800	4,382,900	20,312,800
1974	8,885,100	991,400	374,500	2,904,300	3,641,700	4,655,300	21,452,300
1975	9,192,100	946,300	426,000	3,176,800	3,763,200	5,031,800	22,536,200

Source: Life Insurance Fact Book, 1976

Exhibit 5:
The Prudential Insurance Company of America
Distribution of Assets of U.S. Life Insurance Companies

Amount (000,000 Omitted)

Year	Government Securities	Corporate Securities		Mortgages	Real Estate	Policy Loans	Misc. Assets	Total
		Bonds	Stocks					
1917	$ 562	$ 1,975	$ 83	$ 2,021	$ 179	$ 810	$ 311	$ 5,941
1920	1,349	1,949	75	2,442	172	859	474	7,320
1925	1,311	3,022	81	4,808	266	1,446	604	11,538
1930	1,502	4,929	519	7,598	548	2,807	977	18,880
1935	4,727	5,314	583	5,357	1,990	3,540	1,705	23,216
1940	8,447	8,645	605	5,972	2,065	3,091	1,977	30,802
1945	22,545	10,060	999	6,636	857	1,962	1,738	44,797
1950	16,118	23,248	2,103	16,102	1,445	2,413	2,591	64,020
1955	11,829	35,912	3,633	29,445	2,581	3,290	3,742	90,432
1960	11,815	46,740	4,981	41,771	3,765	5,231	5,273	119,576
1961	12,045	48,887	6,258	44,203	4,007	5,733	5,683	126,816
1962	12,598	51,124	6,302	46,902	4,107	6,234	6,024	133,291
1963	12,630	53,453	7,135	50,544	4,319	6,655	6,385	141,121
1964	12,509	55,454	7,938	55,152	4,528	7,140	6,749	149,470
1965	11,908	58,244	9,126	60,013	4,681	7,678	7,234	158,884
1966	11,396	60,819	8,832	64,609	4,885	9,117	7,797	167,455
1967	11,079	64,687	10,877	67,516	5,187	10,059	8,427	177,832
1968	11,096	68,310	13,230	69,973	5,571	11,306	9,150	188,636
1969	10,914	70,859	13,707	72,027	5,912	13,825	9,964	197,208
1970	11,068	73,098	15,420	74,375	6,320	16,064	10,909	207,254
1971	11,000	79,198	20,607	75,496	6,904	17,065	11,832	222,102
1972	11,372	86,140	26,845	76,948	7,295	18,003	13,127	239,730
1973	11,403	91,796	25,919	81,369	7,693	20,199	14,057	252,436
1974	11,965	96,652	21,920	86,234	8,331	22,862	15,385	263,349
1975	15,177	105,837	28,061	89,167	9,621	24,467	16,974	289,304

Exhibit 5: (Continued)

The Prudential Insurance Company of America
Distribution of Assets of U.S. Life Insurance Companies

Amount (000,000 Omitted)

Year	Government Securities	Corporate Securities		Mortgages	Real Estate	Policy Loans	Misc. Assets	Total
		Bonds	Stocks					
Percent								
1917	9.6%	33.2%	1.4%	34.0%	3.0%	13.6%	5.2%	100.0%
1920	18.4	26.7	1.0	33.4	2.3	11.7	6.5	100.0
1925	11.3	26.2	.7	41.7	2.3	12.5	5.3	100.0
1930	8.0	26.0	2.8	40.2	2.9	14.9	5.2	100.0
1935	20.4	22.9	2.5	23.1	8.6	15.2	7.3	100.0
1940	27.5	28.1	2.0	19.4	6.7	10.0	6.3	100.0
1945	50.3	22.5	2.2	14.8	1.9	4.4	3.9	100.0
1950	25.2	36.3	3.3	25.1	2.2	3.8	4.1	100.0
1955	13.1	39.7	4.0	32.6	2.9	3.6	4.1	100.0
1960	9.9	39.1	4.2	34.9	3.1	4.4	4.4	100.0
1961	9.5	38.5	4.9	34.9	3.2	4.5	4.5	100.0
1962	9.4	38.4	4.7	35.2	3.1	4.7	4.5	100.0
1963	8.9	37.9	5.0	35.8	3.1	4.7	4.8	100.0
1964	8.4	37.1	5.3	36.9	3.0	4.8	4.5	100.0
1965	7.5	36.7	5.7	37.8	3.0	4.8	4.5	100.0
1966	6.8	36.3	5.3	38.6	2.9	5.5	4.6	100.0
1967	6.2	36.4	6.1	38.0	2.9	5.7	4.7	100.0
1968	5.9	36.2	7.0	37.1	3.0	6.0	4.8	100.0
1969	5.5	36.0	6.9	36.6	3.0	7.0	5.0	100.0
1970	5.3	35.3	7.4	35.9	3.0	7.8	5.3	100.0
1971	4.9	35.7	9.3	34.0	3.1	7.7	5.3	100.0
1972	4.8	35.9	11.2	32.1	3.0	7.5	5.5	100.0
1973	4.5	36.4	10.3	32.2	3.0	8.0	5.6	100.0
1974	4.5	36.7	8.3	32.8	3.2	8.7	5.8	100.0
1975	5.2	36.6	9.7	30.8	3.3	8.5	5.9	100.0

Source: Life Insurance Fact Book, 1976

Exhibit 6:

The Prudential Insurance Company of America
Investment Yields, U.S. Life Insurance Industry and Six Largest Companies

		Overall Net Yield	Bonds	Stocks	Mortgages	Real Estate (Net)
All U.S. Life Insurance	1966	4.73%				
Companies	1967	4.83				
	1968	4.97				
	1969	5.15				
	1970	5.34				
	1971	5.52				
	1972	5.69				
	1973	6.00				
	1974	6.31				
	1975	6.44				
Prudential	1971	5.80	6.14%	2.88%	6.24%	4.95%
	1972	5.96	6.48	2.55	6.51	4.73
	1973	6.16	6.82	3.28	6.77	4.58
	1974	6.44	7.07	4.44	7.09	4.15
	1975	6.47	7.17	4.60	7.18	3.78
Metropolitan	1971	5.57	5.35	3.04	6.14	7.65
	1972	5.72	5.58	2.67	6.36	8.22
	1973	6.01	6.09	2.85	6.52	9.03
	1974	6.32	6.45	3.86	6.77	9.35
	1975	6.41	6.55	4.22	6.84	10.18
Equitable Life Assurance	1971	5.54	5.55	3.16	6.17	4.51
	1972	5.66	5.75	3.04	6.33	4.23
	1973	5.96	6.36	2.79	6.52	5.85
	1974	6.22	6.62	3.45	6.87	5.74
	1975	6.22	6.92	3.43	7.13	4.96
New York Life	1971	5.25	5.25	3.95	5.77	5.66
	1972	5.49	5.62	3.75	6.04	6.00
	1973	5.79	6.01	3.89	6.40	5.95
	1974	6.00	6.31	4.45	6.69	5.70
	1975	6.16	6.50	4.60	6.87	6.29
John Hancock Mutual	1971	5.25	5.42	2.87	5.95	5.11
Life	1972	5.39	5.80	2.75	6.09	4.86
	1973	5.78	6.28	3.09	6.49	5.14
	1974	6.03	6.57	3.76	6.77	4.82
	1975	6.36	6.99	3.73	7.19	4.02
Aetna Life	1971	5.62	5.45	3.70	5.97	5.64
	1972	5.98	6.06	4.13	6.16	6.28
	1973	6.33	6.47	4.82	6.54	11.61
	1974	6.61	6.76	5.74	6.90	11.28
	1975	6.67	6.96	5.50	7.17	12.33

Note: All ratios are before federal and foreign income taxes. Net yield is for all invested assets and is after deduction of investment expenses and taxes. Real Estate is net after expenses, taxes, and depreciation; mortgages are after servicing fees and premiums (charged off first year). Excludes Separate Account Business.

Source: Best's Insurance Reports

Exhibit 7:

The Prudential Insurance Company of America

Life Insurance in Force (Year End), Net Policy Reserve, (Year End), and New Insurance Issued During Year, for Six Leading U.S. Companies

($ millions)	Year	Life Insurance in Force					Net Policy Reserves	New Life Insurance Issued				
		Ordinary	Group	Industrial	Credit	Total		Ordinary	Group	Industrial	Credit	Total
Prudential	1970	91,119	60,607	5,049	—	156,775	22,976	11,674	5,157	—	—	16,831
	1971	96,463	66,892	4,898	—	168,253	23,928	12,733	4,955	—	—	17,689
	1972	102,300	75,359	4,764	—	182,423	25,307	13,604	6,862	—	—	20,467
	1973	109,040	72,321	4,637	11,430	197,428	26,566	15,280	6,337	—	—	22,835
	1974	116,444	85,895	4,524	11,407	218,270	27,900	17,016	11,427	—	—	29,630
	1975	122,816	98,312	4,417	10,654	236,200	29,405	17,012	12,234	—	—	30,043
Metropolitan	1970	77,934	83,556	5,793	—	167,284	23,205	9,763	5,339	—	—	15,101
	1971	81,425	90,077	5,510	—	177,014	24,162	10,286	6,255	—	—	16,541
	1972	84,737	95,610	5,239	—	185,585	25,116	10,691	4,595	—	—	15,287
	1973	88,332	103,543	4,972	1,347	198,185	26,327	11,763	5,509	—	62	17,335
	1974	92,495	117,281	4,726	1,398	215,901	27,440	13,484	10,643	—	63	24,189
	1975	95,849	124,668	4,579	1,191	226,288	28,825	12,488	9,069	—	9	21,565
Equitable Life Assurance	1970	26,310	50,599	—	—	76,909	11,770	3,291	2,731	—	—	6,022
	1971	27,742	55,035	—	—	82,777	12,321	3,594	4,811	—	—	8,405
	1972	29,387	60,354	—	—	89,741	12,598	4,038	4,663	—	—	8,701
	1973	31,242	65,779	—	487	97,508	13,033	4,533	3,990	—	1	8,525
	1974	33,291	75,155	—	549	108,995	13,747	5,004	5,473	—	30	10,507
	1975	35,017	83,739	—	411	119,167	14,969	4,999	7,814	—	2	12,815
New York Life	1970	39,595	10,683	—	—	50,317	8,355	5,632	1,407	—	—	7,040
	1971	42,865	11,191	—	—	54,058	8,757	6,208	875	—	—	7,083
	1972	46,409	12,133	—	—	58,542	9,156	6,690	1,157	—	—	7,843
	1973	50,541	11,950	—	352	62,843	9,652	7,520	989	—	11	8,519
	1974	55,820	13,776	—	374	69,971	10,167	9,157	2,185	—	4	11,346
	1975	60,335	15,433	—	335	76,105	10,715	8,750	1,702	—	2	10,453
John Hancock Mutual Life	1970	31,658	28,042	1,194	—	60,896	7,968	5,570	2,806	—	—	8,377
	1971	33,630	30,132	1,062	—	64,826	8,272	5,463	2,693	—	—	8,157
	1972	35,568	33,434	937	—	69,941	8,585	5,507	2,895	—	—	8,404
	1973	37,354	34,447	826	2,425	75,056	8,992	5,403	2,382	—	359	8,143
	1974	38,964	38,878	732	2,773	81,350	9,550	5,384	3,737	—	353	9,438
	1975	40,332	43,880	649	2,929	87,784	10,257	5,487	5,557	—	403	11,449
Aetna Life	1970	7,955	51,927	—	—	59,883	5,533	1,254	4,653	—	—	5,902
	1971	8,247	54,658	—	—	62,907	5,786	1,172	3,411	—	—	4,584
	1972	8,748	56,351	—	—	65,101	6,062	1,424	3,754	—	—	5,179
	1973	9,747	60,588	—	1,196	71,506	6,386	2,029	4,026	—	70	6,127
	1974	10,743	66,818	—	1,477	79,039	6,729	2,322	4,488	—	208	7,020
	1975	11,148	72,002	—	1,403	84,555	6,887	2,221	5,155	—	168	7,545

Source: Best's Insurance Reports

Exhibit 8:

The Prudential Insurance Company of America Operating Summary of Six Largest Life Insurance Companies

($ millions)		Life Pre-miums	Annuity Pre-miums	A&H Pre-miums	Invest-ment Income (Net)	Total Income (A)	Death Pay-ments	Matured Endow-ments	Annuity Pay-ments	A&H Pay-ments	Other Benefits Paid	Policy Divi-dends	Net Oper-ating Gain (Loss) (B)
Prudential	1970	2,455	181	850	1,414	5,905	851	167	239	631	364	788	55
	1971	2,569	341	974	1,535	6,732	886	168	276	659	376	844	24
	1972	2,690	446	1,088	1,671	7,198	942	158	324	794	386	863	35
	1973	2,933	418	1,089	1,816	6,767	985	169	363	901	415	899	57
	1974	3,084	401	1,267	1,962	7,215	1,016	156	408	1,044	442	955	91
	1975	3,279	467	1,469	2,076	9,200	1,083	155	453	1,285	462	1,003	71
Metropolitan	1970	2,501	304	901	1,399	5,388	991	183	231	734	414	655	27
	1971	2,577	297	950	1,491	5,730	1,025	191	262	768	432	651	33
	1972	2,692	401	1,028	1,598	6,240	1,108	193	291	747	430	703	72
	1973	2,911	536	990	1,752	6,429	1,145	204	332	795	539	764	(13)
	1974	2,977	350	1,048	1,901	6,613	1,187	204	376	867	583	787	(83)
	1975	3,078	566	1,094	2,020	7,428	1,214	219	416	973	601	791	(21)
Equitable Life Assurance	1970	1,007	151	589	699	2,847	456	31	334	523	155	296	.7
	1971	1,074	365	635	747	3,345	486	31	359	556	154	306	(58)
	1972	1,113	161	705	793	3,483	511	31	401	572	161	334	67
	1973	1,200	203	710	864	3,507	542	31	431	603	189	343	53
	1974	1,278	284	779	928	3,655	567	29	464	667	191	353	(27)
	1975	1,344	338	901	982	5,364	589	30	506	854	185	365	(89)
New York Life	1970	957	40	207	508	1,927	270	43	46	138	169	285	.05
	1971	1,020	58	247	549	2,100	291	43	51	182	162	301	(10)
	1972	1,092	76	279	603	2,271	294	43	57	190	166	312	15
	1973	1,210	88	238	668	2,441	315	44	65	172	190	341	27
	1974	1,386	83	234	722	2,601	326	44	76	173	203	352	30
	1975	1,392	82	276	780	2,832	321	43	86	211	214	369	86

Exhibit 8: (Continued)

The Prudential Insurance Company of America Operating Summary of Six Largest Life Insurance Companies

($ millions)	Life Pre-miums	Annuity Pre-miums	A&H Pre-miums	Invest-ment Income (Net)	Total Income (A)	Death Pay-ments	Matured Endow-ments	Annuity Pay-ments	A&H Pay-ments	Other Benefits Paid	Policy Divi-dends	Net Oper-ating Gain (Loss) (B)
John Hancock Mutual Life												
1970	811	51	343	466	1,935	287	27	112	282	137	185	18
1971	853	47	365	490	2,121	298	28	125	299	135	185	22
1972	896	73	408	523	2,250	315	29	136	299	140	198	24
1973	966	143	375	581	2,183	332	29	153	328	146	208	44
1974	998	123	394	627	2,376	345	27	171	355	153	210	59
1975	1,047	232	431	699	3,018	371	28	196	411	164	230	20
Aetna Life												
1970	569	163	1,066	345	2,247	317	17	132	984	84	40	57
1971	572	143	1,077	376	2,487	324	17	151	977	82	34	74
1972	571	107	965	429	2,431	335	16	170	835	59	39	81
1973	610	121	1,044	485	2,529	346	16	196	904	90	38	76
1974	646	70	1,216	539	2,759	368	15	227	1,058	107	23	43
1975	728	86	1,432	588	3,557	379	16	273	1,301	120	28	47

(A) Total includes other items not shown

(B) Net includes other items not shown

Source: Best's Insurance Reports

Note: Best's Reports are based on accounting practices that are different in some respects from company accounting and reporting.

Exhibit 9:

The Prudential Insurance Company of America
Assets of Five U.S. Life Insurance Companies

($ millions)		Bonds	Stocks	Mortgages	Real Estate	Policy Loans	Total*
Metropolitan	1970	13,117	508	11,088	517	1,288	27,866
Life	1971	13,592	725	11,369	607	1,335	29,163
	1972	14,252	1,350	11,330	622	1,376	30,776
	1973	14,871	1,589	11,658	574	1,426	31,985
	1974	15,467	1,384	11,923	559	1,527	32,728
	1975	17,204	1,523	12,003	660	1,568	35,138
Equitable	1970	5,140	601	6,097	475	942	14,371
Life	1971	5,544	744	6,108	491	985	15,395
Assurance	1972	5,631	970	6,211	522	1,019	16,443
	1973	5,736	886	6,509	530	1,130	17,152
	1974	5,687	741	6,828	580	1,294	17,558
	1975	6,300	915	7,292	681	1,366	19,819
New York	1970	4,994	678	2,877	321	1,436	10,741
Life	1971	5,267	726	2,954	323	1,536	11,268
	1972	5,597	840	3,070	273	1,636	11,912
	1973	5,774	825	3,248	257	1,840	12,472
	1974	5,849	707	3,510	286	2,093	13,002
	1975	6,202	806	3,673	302	2,243	13,862
John Hancock	1970	4,299	511	3,398	475	534	10,048
Mutual Life	1971	4,459	633	3,380	488	564	10,604
	1972	4,619	679	3,459	524	598	11,195
	1973	4,685	568	3,757	510	666	11,447
	1974	4,824	488	4,017	483	757	11,822
	1975	5,237	611	4,206	537	820	12,801
Aetna Life	1970	2,957	106	3,106	91	197	7,215
	1971	3,258	110	3,188	110	204	7,803
	1972	3,666	142	3,272	115	209	8,437
	1973	3,894	117	3,515	130	237	8,934
	1974	4,068	84	3,845	147	274	9,429
	1975	4,340	238	4,156	174	287	10,415

*Includes miscellaneous assets not shown

Source: Best's Insurance Reports

Exhibit 10:

The Prudential Insurance Company of America
Statement of Financial Condition
December 31
(in millions)

	1970	1971	1972	1973	1974	1975
Assets						
Bonds	$11,216	$11,748	$12,378	$12,887	$12,957	$13,836
Preferred stocks	111	116	311	846	996	1,080
Common stocks	1,183	1,643	2,195	2,016	1,581[1]	2,135[1]
Mortgage loans on real estate	10,989	11,053	11,086	11,653	12,306	12,411
Real estate (including Home Offices)	971	1,050	1,092	1,263	1,446	1,678
Loans on policies	1,322	1,419	1,501	1,632	1,812	1,953
Cash and temporary investments	354	336	564	67	309	296
Other investments	142	172	335	232	152	476
Net premiums secured by policy reserves	818	877	961	1,037	1,146	1,208
Investment income due and accrued	311	329	360	369	402	450
Separate Account Business assets	1,677	2,369	3,068	2,916	2,663	3,741
Other assets	40	48	50	46	49	45
	$29,134	$31,160	$33,901	$34,964	$35,819	$39,309
Liabilities and Margin for Protection of Policyowners						
Insurance and annuity reserves	$24,169	$25,761	$27,773	$28,877	$29,999	$32,507
Other policy reserves	453	449	460	465	449	460
Policy and contract claims					520	567
Reserved for policy dividends	595	648	683	711	733	781
Other policy liabilities	1,659	1,935	2,322	2,658	2,387	2,794
Accrued taxes	170	121	139	134	125	113
Other liabilities	69	59	66	72	88	110
Mandatory securities valuation reserve	343	532	816	360	25	174
Margin for protection of policyowners	1,575[2]	1,604[2]	1,642	1,687	1,493	1,800
Additional reserve for fluctuation in securities values and other contingencies	101	51				
	$29,134	$31,160	$33,901	$34,964	$35,819	$39,309

1. Including investments in subsidiaries of $543 million in 1975 and $417 million in 1974.

2. Consists of policy reserve required by New Jersey Statute NJSA 17:34-24 and unassigned surplus.

Source: Company Reports available to the public

Exhibit 11:

The Prudential Insurance Company of America
Summary of Operations and Margin for Protection of Policyowners
(All figures in millions)

	1970	1971	1972	1973	1974	1975
Income:						
Insurance Premiums and Annuity Considerations	$3,930	$4,388	$4,710	$5,006	$5,452	$5,760
Investment Income	1,476	1,595[4]	1,743[3]	1,915[2]	2,095[1]	2,222[1]
Net Realized and Unrealized Capital Gains (losses) on Separate Account Business	(13)	160	368	(606)	(867)	702
Total Income	5,384	6,143	6,821	6,315	6,680	8,684
Application of Income:						
Paid or Credited to Policyowners and Beneficiaries[5]	3,091	3,375	3,597	3,862	4,113	4,666
Increase in Insurance and Annuity Reserves to Provide for Future Payments to Policy Owners and Beneficiaries	1,258	1,659	2,014	1,108	1,119	2,509
Insurance Operating Expense	703	797	843	888	966	1,043
State, Premium and other Insurance Taxes	75	84	91	102	108	117
Sub-Total of Applications	5,127	5,897	6,545	5,960	6,306	8,335
Gain from Operation before Federal Income Tax	257	246	276	355	374	349
Federal Income Tax	187	226	250	253	272	255
Gain from Operation	70	20	26	102	102	94

357

Exhibit 11: (Continued)

The Prudential Insurance Company of America

Summary of Operations and Margin for Protection of Policyowners

(All figures in millions)

	1970	1971	1972	1973	1974	1975
Change in Margin for Protection of Policyowner:						
Net Realized and Unrealized Capital Gains (loss) on other than Separate Account Business	2	(41)	(39)	(57)	(296)	213
Decrease in Additional Reserve for Fluctuation in Securities Values and other Contingencies	—	50	51	—	—	—
Increase in Margin for Protection of Policyowners	72	29	38	45	(194)	307
Margin for Protection of Policyowner, Beginning of Year	1,503	1,575	1,604	1,642	1,687	1,493
Margin for Protection of Policyowner, End of Year	1,575	1,604	1,642	1,687	1,493	1,800

[1]Net of investment expenses, taxes, and depreciation.

[2]Net of investment expenses of $109 million, taxes of $57 million and depreciation of $25 million.

[3]Net of investment expenses of $85 million, taxes of $55 million and depreciation of $22 million.

[4]Net of investment expenses of $78 million, taxes of $45 million and depreciation of $21 million.

[5]Includes dividends: 1971—$844 million, 1972—$864 million, 1973—$898 million, 1974—$927 million, 1975—$1,000 million.

Source: Company Reports available to the public

Exhibit 12:

The Prudential Insurance Company of America
Prudential Property and Casualty Insurance Company
($000 omitted)

	Income Statements, Years Ended December 31				
	1971	1972	1973	1974	1975
Underwriting Income					
Premiums earned	$ 2,254	$52,151	$51,171	$64,688	$124,963
Deductions:					
Losses incurred	954	36,545	38,750	54,146	112,257
Loss expenses incurred	79	1,133	3,580	6,380	12,015
Other underwriting expenses	2,988	22,023	24,764	35,384	53,548
	4,021	59,700	67,093	95,910	177,819
Net underwriting gain or (loss)	(1,767)	(7,550)	(15,923)	(31,221)	(52,856)
Investment Income					
Net investment income earned	1,345	6,152	8,066	10,764	22,410
Net realized capital gain or (loss)	(106)	115	(97)	(1,148)	(1,243)
Net investment gain or (loss)	1,239	6,268	7,968	9,316	21,168
Other income or (expenses)					
Net gain or (loss) from chargeoffs	—	(7)	(70)	(291)	(447)
Finance and service charges	—	—	88	220	489
Adjustments on reinsurance	—	(4,426)	(5,627)	(6,402)	(7,670)
Miscellaneous	—	—	1	(7)	(16)
Total	—	(4,432)	(5,607)	(6,480)	(7,643)
Net income before taxes	(528)	(5,714)	(13,562)	(28,386)	(39,331)
Income taxes	(1)	(75)	(50)	(3,654)	(6,733)
Net income (loss)	(527)	(5,639)	(13,511)	(24,731)	(32,598)
Net unrealized capital gains or (losses)	667	2,600	(5,149)	(5,053)	5,110
Change in non-admitted assets	(24)	(375)	(728)	(389)	(866)
Change in reserves		(418)	(418)	(18)	(2)
Other changes		1		(34)	(22)
Capital: Paid in					1,500
Transferred from surplus			1,500		
Surplus: Paid in	37,026			44,000	111,500
Transferred to capital			(1,500)		
Net changes in capital and surplus	37,142	(3,832)	(18,970)	13,775	84,666
Capital and Surplus, 12-31	39,134	35,302	16,332	30,106	114,772

Source: Annual Statements to State Insurance Departments

Exhibit 13:

The Prudential Insurance Company of America
Prudential Property and Casualty Insurance Company
($000 omitted)

	Balance Sheets - December 31				
	1971	1972	1973	1974	1975
Assets					
Bonds	$ 91,109	$101,353	$101,300	$143,819	$271,328
Stocks: Preferred	—	138	67	—	—
Common	14,597	22,037	18,232	11,078	15,380
Cash and bank deposits	299	799	1,071	1,197	1
Agents' balances or uncoll. prem.	427	2,992	1,806	3,703	8,366
Fund with ceding reinsurers	—	3,879	—	—	—
Reinsurance recoverable	—	—	206	176	155
Accounts receivable—other	2,574	42	149	17	88
Due from affiliated co.	—	—	187	121	297
Fed. income tax due from parent co.	—	76	64	3,678	7,433
Accrued income	339	1,234	1,425	2,007	4,823
Foreign exchange adjustments— net	—	1	1	8	—
Other reinsurance items receivable	—	—	—	—	5,391
Deposits and misc.	6	6	6	10	30
Total Assets	$109,345	$132,557	$124,514	$165,813	$313,293
Liabilities					
Losses	68,792	78,019	88,882	107,359	140,004
Loss adjustment expenses	26	427	930	2,384	5,500
Contingent commissions	—	246	14	—	—
Other expenses	169	409	539	786	1,600
Taxes, licenses, fees	9	40	394	816	1,778
Unearned premiums	657	9,547	9,206	19,985	43,706
Reinsurance funds held	—	—	1,281	—	—
Withheld for other accounts	2	24	125	155	235
Resurance due from unauth. companies	—	—	—	41	1
Excess of liab. reserves	—	418	—	18	20
Foreign exchange adjustments	—	—	—	—	10
Ceded Reinsurance Bal. Payable	548	40	465	504	682
Accounts payable—other	9	709	1,607	2,986	3,392
Outstanding loss drafts	—	92	540	433	1,128
Losses in course of payment	—	653	229	—	—
Other reinsurance payable	—	6,631	3,970	239	—
Cash overdraft	—	—	—	—	744
Total liabilities	70,212	97,256	108,182	135,707	198,521

Exhibit 13: (Continued)

The Prudential Insurance Company of America
Prudential Property and Casualty Insurance Company
($000 omitted)

	Balance Sheets - December 31				
	1971	*1972*	*1973*	*1974*	*1975*
Capital					
Capital paid up	1,000	1,000	2,500	2,500	4,000
Gross paid in and contrib. surplus	37,426	37,426	35,926	79,926	191,426
Unassigned funds (surplus)	707	(3,125)	(22,095)	(52,320)	(80,654)
Total Capital	39,134	35,302	16,332	30,106	114,772
Total Liabilities and Capital	$109,345	$132,557	$124,514	$165,813	$313,293

Source: Annual Statements to State Insurance Departments

Exhibit 14:

The Prudential Insurance Company of America
Prudential Property and Casualty Insurance Company
($000 omitted)

	Personal Lines Operating Results				
	1971	*1972*	*1973*	*1974*	*1975*
Number of Market States (End of Year)	1	5	17	30	44
Average Number of Agents	1,200	1,700	5,600	9,800	13,700
Average Apps Per Agent Per Month	1.8	2.0	2.5	2.4	3.2
Net Written Premium	$ 1,000	$ 5,000	$ 21,500	$ 50,100	$111,300
Earned Premium	$ 500	$ 3,500	$ 14,500	$ 39,400	$ 87,500
Losses	$ 500	$ 2,000	$ 10,000	$ 30,300	$ 77,700
Loss Expense	—	1,000	3,500	6,600	11,600
Loss and Loss Expense	$ 500	$ 3,000	$ 13,500	$ 36,900	$ 89,300
Commissions	$ —	$ 1,000	$ 3,500	$ 7,300	$ 15,500
Marketing Expense Paid to Prudential	—	—	500	1,400	3,100
Corporate, Service Office & Other Expense	3,000	8,000	18,500	26,500	34,700
Total Expense	$ 3,000	$ 9,000	$ 22,500	$ 35,200	$ 53,300
Statutory Underwriting Gain (Loss)	$(3,000)	$(8,500)	$(21,500)	$(32,700)	$(55,100)
Key Ratios					
Auto Loss to Earned Premium	—	—	69.5	71.2	95.9
Home Loss to Earned Premium	—	—	70.6	90.0	71.0
Total Loss to Earned Premium	62.2	62.1	69.8	76.8	88.8
Loss Expense to Earned Premium	16.3	24.8	24.2	16.8	13.2
All other Expenses to Written Premium	269.1	167.4	103.4	70.3	48.0
Combined Ratio	347.6	254.3	197.4	163.9	150.0

Exhibit 15:

The Prudential Insurance Company of America
Operating Results of 909 U.S. Stock Casualty and Liability Insurance Companies

	Investment Income	Percent of Mean Assets	# Investment Profit or Loss	# Underwriting Profit or Loss	Percent to Earned Premiums
1975	3,142,861,849	4.83	6,568,966,246	−2,880,201,864	−8.34
1974	2,890,580,730	4.72	−3,251,012,944	−1,760,721,093	−5.60
1973	2,491,217,215	4.13	−1,440,544,013	225,638,542	0.78
1972	2,068,252,326	3.84	4,723,880,105	914,510,864	3.44
1971	1,784,761,165	3.88	3,417,071,364	679,155,069	2.85
1970	1,438,519,247	3.57	1,250,040,674	−154,048,539	−0.72
1969	1,238,191,069	3.27	−492,256,103	−395,830,131	−2.07
1968	1,100,754,543	3.06	2,279,072,657	−200,881,215	−1.17
1967	987,060,456	3.03	2,301,940,460	10,438,666	0.07
1966	895,858,963	2.87	−552,499,384	102,516,773	0.70
1965	852,040,581	2.78	1,466,357,600	−424,506,694	−3.19
1964	782,167,507	2.69	1,820,959,417	−347,516,590	−2.81
1963	720,635,582	2.69	2,017,133,045	−218,657,390	−1.89
1962	673,401,325	2.62	−230,432,963	2,500,012	0.02
1961	620,612,859	2.57	2,515,706,725	29,773,180	0.28
1960	592,392,261	2.66	655,412,051	65,614,742	0.64
1959	534,478,804	2.55	1,020,646,567	70,865,429	0.74
1958	488,897,254	2.57	2,074,163,163	−92,731,225	−1.05
1957	460,999,407	2.58	−166,342,033	−361,289,939	−4.33
1956	429,795,101	2.45	579,900,785	−135,751,271	−1.75
1955	393,698,785	2.38	1,147,365,136	255,482,374	3.49
1954	363,183,088	2.46	1,583,363,182	384,982,416	5.50
1953	326,091,617	2.37	267,132,361	333,203,439	5.00
1952	294,097,103	2.30	548,975,323	185,123,911	3.08
1951	272,874,450	2.47	544,628,671	13,131,070	0.24
1950	253,079,413	2.52	600,246,330	190,795,816	4.00
1949	215,211,428	2.42	527,598,722	421,133,728	9.51
1948	188,018,235	2.39	151,670,488	199,597,313	4.99
1947	172,123,812	2.44	108,897,608	−48,844,410	−1.44
1946	153,830,808	2.38	−11,548,122	−151,638,020	−5.78

363

Exhibit 15: (Continued)

	Investment Income	Percent of Mean Assets	# Investment Profit or Loss	# Underwriting Profit or Loss	Percent to Earned Premiums
1945	147,499,831	2.47	516,907,056	33,334,347	1.47
1944	141,171,590	2.62	330,954,385	71,725,446	3.37
1943	133,166,468	2.72	331,547,073	152,717,539	7.42
1942	123,360,002	2.71	83,668,088	74,073,158	3.43
1941	127,562,431	2.95	38,969,457	54,752,023	2.96
1940	121,668,886	2.93	57,830,541	70,439,249	4.28
1939	115,804,000	2.88	138,191,000	88,504,000	5.78
1938	115,365,000	2.97	233,182,000	96,561,000	6.40
1937	126,164,000	3.24	285,803,000	85,023,000	5.64
1936	120,470,000	3.21	358,741,000	69,285,000	4.98
1935	107,552,000	3.23	332,306,000	82,664,000	6.35
1934	111,782,000	3.58	24,538,000	58,915,000	4.62
1933	105,814,000	3.17	107,360,000	63,745,000	5.10
1932	124,950,000	3.38	-8,629,000	-3,455,000	-0.24
1931	153,877,000	3.92	59,969,000	-11,200,000	-0.69
1930	163,597,000	3.92	-147,831,000	-22,601,000	-1.30
1929	151,900,000	3.65	84,317,000	30,751,000	1.74
1928	140,401,000	3.76	241,749,000	61,685,000	3.65
1927	123,920,000	3.80	285,070,000	26,296,000	1.59
1926	112,361,000	3.83	158,357,000	-49,260,000	-3.17
1925	115,655,000	4.31	163,251,000	-57,171,000	-4.01
1924	112,505,000	4.59	190,009,000	-47,752,000	-3.57
1923	114,772,000	5.02	70,983,000	-11,751,000	-0.94
1922	113,037,000	5.25	151,288,000	6,811,000	0.58
1921	100,667,000	5.32	114,044,000	-22,753,000	-1.90
1920	105,032,000	5.61	53,433,000	-28,935,000	-2.47
1919	85,732,000	5.38	42,078,000	50,925,000	5.18
1918	63,061,000	4.64	37,009,000	19,872,000	2.34
1917	60,990,000	5.05	15,142,000	5,456,000	0.77
1916	64,227,000	5.89	49,480,000	3,324,000	0.56

*Before Federal Income Taxes, since 1942.

Includes Investment Income.

Source: Best's Aggregates and Averages

Exhibit 16:

The Prudential Insurance Company of America
Financial and Operating Data on the Largest Property and Casualty Insurance Companies

($ millions)		Total Assets	Policy-holders' Surplus	Net Premiums Written	Losses Incurred to Premiums Earned	Expense Incurred to Premiums Written	Under-writing Profit (Loss)	Net Invest-ment Income	Other Invest-ment Gains or Losses
State Farm Mutual Auto	1970	$2,040	$ 564	$1,685	80.3%	16.7%	$ 38	$ 80	$ 2
	1971	2,491	834	1,888	68.3%	16.8%	263	101	54
	1972	2,800	1,101	2,046	69.1%	17.5%	270	119	81
	1973	3,131	1,264	2,184	73.9%	17.3%	191	130	—
	1974	3,407	1,324	2,295	78.0%	18.5%	83	154	(88)
	1975	4,002	1,616	2,582	85.3%	17.4%	(73)	175	185
State Farm Fire & Casualty	1970	380	125	259	63.6%	32.0%	.5	16	—
	1971	461	148	317	60.5%	31.5%	12	18	.5
	1972	580	190	404	55.6%	31.8%	36	24	7
	1973	683	219	497	60.1%	29.8%	31	29	(16)
	1974	769	227	598	63.8%	31.6%	4	36	(27)
	1975	960	283	758	67.8%	30.1%	(16)	45	25
Allstate Insurance Co.	1970	2,548	687	1,639	77.5%	20.6%	3	79	(82)
	1971	3,060	909	1,966	75.0%	20.9%	44	91	120
	1972	3,708	1,181	2,167	75.0%	22.5%	53	106	180
	1973	3,741	959	2,343	76.2%	22.9%	27	125	(303)
	1974	3,658	655	2,522	78.0%	23.8%	(42)	145	(402)
	1975	4,312	889	2,804	87.9%	22.2%	(271)	167	302
Travelers Indemnity Co.	1970	1,342	219	897	69.9%	30.9%	(11)	(47)	(2)
	1971	1,569	287	1,018	68.5%	30.3%	4	54	29
	1972	1,794	365	1,030	67.5%	31.2%	15	58	31
	1973	1,797	287	1,052	67.4%	32.4%	2	65	(94)
	1974	1,878	255	1,201	77.2%	30.7%	(102)	77	(107)
	1975	2,469	357	1,434	81.4%	27.4%	(141)	101	43
Aetna Casualty & Surety	1970	1,853	350	1,047	73.7%	28.7%	(28)	61	(33)
	1971	2,006	483	1,185	70.0%	28.7%	1	74	62
	1972	2,052	535	1,083	69.6%	31.2%	3	76	78
	1973	1,978	360	1,214	67.4%	31.9%	2	72	(149)
	1974	1,791	217	1,166	71.5%	31.5%	(30)	85	(227)
	1975	2,167	389	1,414	76.0%	28.9%	(82)	97	87

Source: Best's Insurance Reports

Exhibit 17:

**The Prudential Insurance Company
of America
Assets, Policyholders' Surplus and Total Net Premiums
Written for all U.S. Property and Liability Insurance
Companies
($ millions)**

Year	Assets	Policy-holders' Surplus	Total Net Premiums Written
1961	$33,690	$14,594	$15,474
1962	34,217	14,144	16,034
1963	37,076	15,747	17,175
1964	39,865	16,990	18,317
1965	41,843	17,112	20,063
1966	42,288	15,556	22,090
1967	46,562	17,501	23,829
1968	51,226	19,107	26,026
1969	52,369	16,719	29,225
1970	58,594	18,521	32,867
1971	67,284	22,749	35,715
1972	78,885	28,211	39,318
1973	83,862	27,091	42,480
1974	82,115	20,898	45,152
1975	94,000	25,000	50,000

(1975 = Preliminary)

Source: Insurance Facts—1976

Exhibit 18:

The Prudential Insurance Company of America
1975 Aggregate Balance Sheet Summaries for Four Groups of U.S. Fire and Casualty
Companies
($ millions)

	909 Stock Companies	*303 Mutual Companies*	*42 Reciprocal Companies*	*31 Lloyds Companies*
Assets: Bonds	$37,459	$13,234	$2,307	$44
Stocks	18,929	3,889	438	3
Other	13,328	2,908	763	36
Total Assets	69,716	20,031	3,508	83
Liabilities: Losses-Adjustment				
Expenses	29,292	8,647	1,515	23
Unearned premiums	15,945	4,340	970	15
Other	6,027	1,315	166	12
Total Liabilities	51,264	14,302	2,651	50
Policyholders'				
Surplus: Capital	2,235	—	—	—
Reserve, Deposits,				
Guaranty	1,366	457	287	8
Net Surplus	14,850	5,273	256	25
Total	18,451	5,729	858	33
Total Liabilities and Surplus	69,716	20,031	3,508	83

Source: Best's Aggregates and Averages

Case 11

The Computech Pension Plan

This case was prepared by Neil E. Seitz with assistance from Fred C. Yeager and William B. Gillespie, Dept. of Finance, Saint Louis University.

In May, 1979, Alecia Snyder was having lunch with Mr. Bryan Kemp, president of Computech, the computer software company with which she had been employed since completing her bachelor's degree in mathematics and computer systems four years before. Mr. Kemp asked Alecia how she was doing in the evening M.B.A. program at Springfield State and she mentioned that they were presently studying pension funds in the financial institutions course. Mr. Kemp asked her what she thought of Computech's pension plan. She replied that she had not really given it a lot of thought, but intended to look at the plan over the weekend. She thought this would be good reinforcement for her classroom exercises.

Mr. Kemp had been meaning to sit down and give some thought to the pension plan himself, but did not feel very knowledgeable in this area. He asked Alecia to prepare a written analysis of the plan with any recommendations for changes. He told her he would instruct his secretary to allow her access to all of the files relating to the pension plan. While this was outside Alecia's normal area of responsibility as a systems programmer, she was pleased with the opportunity to use her newly acquired knowledge and to make a favorable impression on Mr. Kemp.

THE COMPANY

Computech was one of the many small software companies spawned by the rapid growth in computer usage. Much of this growth was stimulated by a key anti-trust ruling requiring large manufacturers such as IBM to price their software services separately from their computer hardware. This allowed companies such as Computech to enter the business of designing information systems and writing computer programs to meet the needs of individual computer users. This was entirely a service industry, with the software companies offering little more than skilled systems analysts and programmers.

Computech had been organized in 1970, when Bryan Kemp and three other employees of a large computer manufacturer resigned to form their own software company. They believed that a small software firm with reduced overhead could more effectively serve smaller businesses. Therefore, Computech specialized in providing programs and systems designs for small- to medium-size businesses.

Because Computech's overhead costs were minimal, and because its concentration on the Springfield market virtually eliminated travel expense, Computech was able to offer its services at lower prices than those offered by the large manufacturers. However, Computech was not alone in this. There were approximately fifteen independent software firms operating in the Springfield area and competing directly with Computech. To succeed in this environment, it was necessary to attract high quality programmers and analysts, and to offer programming and systems analysis services at the lowest possible prices.

Computech had indeed been able to compete successfully in this environment. From the original group of four people, Computech had grown to a total of twenty-four employees in eight years. Mr. Kemp attributed his success to three factors. First, all four of the original organizers had outstanding "human skills" as well as experience and ability in software creation. Thus, they were able to interact effectively with employees and customers. Computech had continued this pattern by always giving consideration to human skills as well as computer skills when hiring employees. Second, Computech had always offered its employees a good working environment and employee benefit package. This was believed to be important for attracting employees and developing loyalty in an industry known for high employee turnover. Third, Mr. Kemp used the same services he sold to his customers. Very soon after the company began operations, Mr. Kemp implemented a management information system which provided excellent cost accounting data. This system contributed to

appropriate pricing policies and provided excellent controls so that costs were kept in line. Thus Computech was competitive in price while providing excellent employee benefits.

Mr. Kemp felt that the company was now at a point where greater attention to long term planning was required. In addition, he felt that there were areas in which increased efficiency could be achieved if he only had the time to do the analysis. If Ms. Snyder's study of the pension plan worked out, he hoped to assign her several other studies relating to financial planning.

THE PENSION PLAN

Shortly after the company was formed, Mr. Kemp realized the importance of developing inducements to attract and keep employees. A company needed to be cost-effective with employee benefits if it was to attract high quality employees. While most software firms offered almost no fringe benefits at that time, Mr. Kemp believed that the addition of fringe benefits would increase the likelihood of attracting and retaining competent personnel. The first benefit which Computech provided was a term life insurance program. This benefit was obtainable at a low cost since most of the employees were relatively young. This benefit seemed to be helpful in recruiting and more benefits were soon added. These included medical insurance and a pension program.

The pension program, which was begun in 1972, was serviced by an insurance company. Like most smaller companies, Computech could not afford to provide portfolio and administrative management for a pension fund covering a relatively small number of people. Each month, Computech forwarded to the insurance company a sum equal to 10 percent of the gross income of each eligible employee. Half of this was contributed by Computech and the other half was deducted from the employee's salary.

While no employee was required to participate, all eligible employees had elected to participate.

Pension fund contributions were used to purchase "units" in the insurance company's portfolio: a bond portfolio and a common stock portfolio. When the employee reached retirement age, the accumulated value of his units could be taken as a lump sum payment or could be used to purchase a fixed or variable annuity, at the employee's option. The variable annuity would provide fluctuating pension payments dependent on financial market returns, while the fixed annuity would simply pay a fixed return based on the number of units owned, the value of these units, and certain actuarial assumptions.

Computech had chosen to have half of the funds used to purchase stock portfolio units and half used to purchase bond portfolio units. The bond portfolio units remained at a constant price of $10. Each year, the beneficiary's bond account was credited with an amount equal to the yield on the pension fund bond portfolio times the value of his account at the beginning of the year, minus an administrative charge of 0.5 percent of asset value. The value of a unit in the stock portfolio changed each month with the values of the stocks in the portfolio. Dividend or interest income was reinvested on behalf of the beneficiary in additional units. Return earned on the stock portfolio each year was computed as

$$\text{Return} = \frac{P_t - P_{t-1} + D_t}{P_{t-1}},$$

where: P_t = price of a unit at the end of the year,

P_{t-1} = price of the unit at the beginning of the year, and

D_t = dividends per unit during the year.

Annual return on the stock portfolio, as well as average yield on the bond portfolio and relevant market information covering a 20-year period, appears in Exhibit 1. Both sets of returns are before the 0.5 percent per year service charge.

While Computech did not have enough employees to consider managing its own pension fund portfolio, certain options to the existing arrangements were available:

1. Change the bond and stock portfolio mix.

2. Change to a different insurance company.

3. Cancel the pension fund and give each employee a 5 percent pay raise. Employees who wanted pension protection could make private arrangements to purchase mutual fund shares or make other investments with tax treatments similar to those for the pension fund contributions.

4. Replace the pension program with a profit sharing program in which employees would be given shares of Computech with a book value equal to some fraction of net profit for the year. For the last three years, this would have resulted in an average cost approximately the same as the pension plan, but it would not have represented as great a drain on cash flows. The four founders presently held all of Computech's stock.

In addition to a possible change in the plan format, Mr. Kemp wondered if certain plan participant eligibility requirements should be changed. Under present rules, an employee became eligible for participation after three years of full-time employment. One-fourth of total wages paid by Computech were paid to employees who worked twenty hours a week or less and one-third of the full-time employees left Computech during their first three years of employment. A recent study of the software industry, conducted by an industry trade association, concluded that half of the employees of a typical software firm changed employers before completing three years of service and only one-fifth of the employees tended to stay with the same company ten years or more. Mr. Kemp wondered whether the present eligibility rules were optimal with regard to cost and with the objective of attracting and maintaining a stable, talented workforce.

Mr. Kemp did not give Ms. Snyder the impression that he was considering any particular change in policy with regard to the pension plan. As near as she could determine, his only interest was in a complete review to determine if the pension plan was the best available for achieving the objectives desired in a cost-efficient manner. Ms. Snyder collected information on the performance of the insurance company's fund in the years since Computech had been involved and for earlier years. She also collected the information on general stock market performance and interest rates that appears in Exhibit 1. She took this material home with her for the weekend to begin examining the problem.

Exhibit 1:

	Equity Portfolio Return	Bond Portfolio Return	S&P 500 Return	Inflation Rate	10 Year U.S. Gov. Bond Rate	6 Month T-Bill Rate
1959	13.89%	4.14%	27.32%	1.5%	4.33%	3.83%
1960	3.36	4.35	.80	1.5	4.12	3.25
1961	18.60	4.52	21.85	.7	3.88	2.61
1962	−14.36	4.68	−2.50	1.2	3.95	2.91
1963	18.34	4.79	15.18	1.6	4.00	3.25
1964	12.66	4.88	19.47	1.2	4.19	3.69
1965	17.75	4.99	11.36	1.9	4.28	4.06
1966	−4.66	5.11	.10	3.4	4.92	5.08
1967	23.42	5.24	11.02	3.0	5.07	4.63
1968	6.12	5.45	10.43	4.7	5.65	5.47
1969	−5.51	5.72	2.37	6.1	6.67	6.85
1970	−3.22	5.95	−11.11	5.5	7.35	6.56
1971	20.25	6.28	21.25	3.4	6.16	4.51
1972	17.07	6.58	13.94	3.4	6.21	4.47
1973	−18.14	7.16	1.44	8.8	6.84	7.18
1974	−30.96	7.59	−18.41	12.2	7.56	7.93
1975	32.06	7.82	8.31	7.0	7.99	6.12
1976	21.19	8.13	22.17	4.8	7.61	5.27
1977	−6.44	8.39	.89	6.8	7.42	5.51
1978	8.68	8.71	3.06	7.8	8.41	7.57

Case 12

FHI Financial, Inc.
Bank Holding Company Diversification

The problem was troubling all three people, each in a different way. Six months ago the Department of Regulatory Agencies denied First Hawaiian, Incorporated's application for a de novo industrial loan license. First Hawaiian, a holding company for the second largest bank in the state, will be appealing this denial next week, the end of May 1975. Wayne Minami, the newly appointed director of Regulatory Agencies, must decide whether to continue the existing ban on bank holding company entry into the industrial loan company market.

The other two key participants in this encounter are Teruo Himoto, spokesman for The Hawaii Consumer Finance Association and also president of Commercial Finance, Limited, and Phillip Ching, vice president of First Hawaiian, Inc. and First Hawaiian Bank.

Himoto and the other members of the Hawaii Consumer Finance Association are determined that bank holding companies must be kept out of the industrial loan market. Their entry would likely lead to unequal competition and could cause serious problems for the more than two hundred industrial loan licensees. The holding company's earlier application was denied and the Governor subsequently spoke out against bank holding company entry, but stopping the appeal still might not be easy. The holding company has apparently strengthened its position considerably.

At this same time, Ching and others at the bank holding company are putting together their appeal position. The 1970 amendments to the Bank Holding Company Act gave them new authority under Federal law and regulations to enter bank related activities, including the industrial loan company market. Many other applications around the country were successful in the last two years. Ching knew that he must prepare effective counter arguments to the points raised in last year's denial ruling. In addition, he must be prepared to respond to arguments raised by the Consumer Finance Association.

FIRST HAWAIIAN BANK

First Hawaiian Bank is the oldest and second largest bank in the state. It is a state bank, chartered under the laws of the state of Hawaii and not a member of the Federal Reserve System. In 1974, the bank reached a major milestone as assets rose above the one billion dollar level. The Bank of Hawaii continues to be slightly larger. Together these two banks control 71 percent of the assets and 70 percent of the deposits held by the state's 8 banks (see Exhibit 1).

First Hawaiian Bank offers a broader range of financial services than any other bank in Hawaii. The bank is an active lender in the commercial, consumer, and real estate loan markets. Demand, savings, and time deposits are accepted. The bank manages the Master Charge credit-card system in Hawaii. Recent customer service innovations include the OTTO automatic 24-hour tellers, the Yes-Check plan which covers checks written above the account balance, and an individual automobile-leasing plan. The trust department handles a full range of trust services, including living trusts, fiscal management of apartments, probates, life insurance, and employee benefit trusts. The enactment of the Employee Retirement Income Security Act of 1974 promises increased participation as a trustee for employee benefit accounts. In the international area the bank works with both U.S. and foreign companies that are trading and investing in the Pacific Basin market.

On July 1, 1974, First Hawaiian Bank was reorganized as a holding company. First Hawaiian, Inc., the holding company, owns all the stock of First Hawaiian Bank except for Directors' qualifying shares. During 1974 the holding company began to issue commercial paper and was temporarily using the proceeds to acquire time certificates of deposit from First Hawaiian Bank. The bank in turn paid dividends to the holding company of $6.098 million during 1974. Total dividends paid by the holding company to its stockholders were $4.110 million.

According to regulations issued by the Federal Reserve System, bank holding companies are permitted to operate industrial loan companies as authorized by state law. Within a week of its formation, the holding company applied to the State Department of Regulatory Agencies for permission to operate an industrial loan subsidiary under the name of FHI Financial, Inc.

HAWAII'S FINANCIAL INSTITUTIONS

Competition in banking in Hawaii is intense. The bank must compete for deposits and loans with seven other banks located in Hawaii and with mainland banks when interest rate differentials arise. The Bank of Hawaii is a regional bank which has a relatively high level of mortgage and other long-term loans outstanding. The major money-center banks in New York and Chicago which concentrate on relatively shorter term loans are better positioned to adjust their interest rates. In 1974, for example, corporate deposits tended to move to the mainland money-center banks and First Hawaiian Bank's deposit growth was modest, producing less funds for lending than was desired. The 1974 Annual Report goes on to note that outside borrowings were also cut due to the cost of money. "During the second half's [1974] general shortage of lendable funds it was necessary to dampen the growth of our real estate loan portfolio but we continued to serve essential needs even when it necessitated outside borrowing."

There is active competition in Hawaii for savings and time deposits. Savings and loan associations, industrial loan companies, and credit unions are all actively seeking funds and they are permitted to pay higher rates of interest than banks for individual accounts. The eleven savings and loan associations are more than twice the national average in asset size. Over the last 10 years Hawaii's banks have experienced a slower growth of savings deposits than each of the other three financial institutions. In 1974 the savings and loan associations actually exceeded the banking institutions in terms of total time and savings deposits. Although they continue to be much smaller, the industrial loan companies have demonstrated a rapid rate of growth (see Exhibits 2 and 3).

Industrial loan companies are often called finance companies or consumer finance companies. Counting all the branches, Hawaii has about 80 companies operating around 230 offices. Some of Hawaii's industrial loan companies are associated with large national firms such as Household Finance, CIT Financial, Beneficial Finance, and GMAC. Others are very small organizations with capital near the $15,000 level required by the state for getting a license.

Industrial loan companies are far less regulated than the commercial banks. Like the banks they make both personal and business loans. In general both the risk and rate of interest are higher on the industrial loan company's loans. The area of rapid growth has been the real estate mortgage loan market (see Exhibit 4). In 1969 these loans totaled $36 million and 12 percent of total assets. At the end of 1974 the real estate loans were $292 million and 41 percent of assets. Much of the real estate loans are second mortgages at simple interest rates of up to 18 percent a year for terms of up to six years. Banks and S & L's are not allowed to make second-mortgage loans. Rising mortgage interest rates have made second mortgages very attractive for homeowners seeking to raise money against a rising equity value in their property.

Almost half the total funds available in industrial loan companies are raised by investment certificates (see Exhibit 4). These deposits are not insured but investors are attracted by the interest rates which exceed those offered by other financial institutions. Another major source of funds is borrowed money, primarily supplied by commercial banks.

BANK HOLDING COMPANY LEGISLATION

Bank holding companies have existed since before 1900 but it was not until 1956 that specific powers were given to the federal reserve board to regulate them. Despite a reduction in the number and importance of bank holding companies following the widespread bank failures during the depression, the Federal Reserve Board contended that holding companies were being used to evade the intent of the Banking Act of 1933. Banks were not supposed to engage in business activities unrelated to banking yet bank holding companies or their affiliates were doing what their subsidiary banks were prohibited from doing.

In 1956 Congressional concern about the growth of bank holding companies led to the passage of the Bank Holding Company Act which gave the Federal Reserve Board the power to regulate bank holding companies. The Act limited nonbanking activities to the performance of services that were "a proper incident to" banking or managing or controlling banks and, in addition, were "of a financial, fiduciary or insurance nature." Surprisingly, the Act applied only to multibank holding companies controlling two or more banks, and one-bank holding companies were excluded.

Exclusion of the one-bank holding companies meant they could engage in unrestricted types of business activity. At first their activities were primarily confined to financial activities but in the late 1960s both the number of one-bank holding companies and their non-financial activities increased greatly. In 1970, in order to preserve the basic separation of bank activities from other business activities embodied in federal law since the Glass-Steagall Act of 1933, Congress passed a series of amendments to the Bank Holding Company Act of 1956. The principal purposes of the amendments were to regulate the one-bank holding companies and to broaden the range of activities in which regulated holding companies could engage.

Section 4 (c) (8) of the amendments established two tests which must be met in order for an activity to be permissible. First, the Federal Reserve Board must determine that the activity is "so closely related to banking or managing or controlling banks as to be a proper incident thereto." Second, it is necessary that the activity "by an affiliate of a holding company can reasonably be expected to produce benefits to the public, such as greater convenience, increased competition, or gains in efficiency, that outweigh possible adverse effects, such as undue concentration of resources, decreased or unfair competition, conflicts of interests, or unsound banking practices."

The 1970 amendments to the Bank Holding Company Act did not change Section 7 which reserves the right of the states to exercise their present and future powers and jurisdiction with respect to banks, bank holding companies, and their subsidiaries.

Bank holding companies were quickly given permission to acquire finance company subsidiaries. From January 1971 through June 1974 the Federal Reserve Board approved applications to purchase 77 existing finance companies and denied only eleven applications. Four hundred thirty-one de novo finance subsidiaries were also authorized.[1]

Writing in the *Banking Law Journal,* Rose and Fraser have summarized several Federal Reserve Board preferences with regard to finance company subsidiaries:

1. Acquisitions of small finance companies or de novo entry are clearly favored over applications which seek to take over a substantial creditor in the market area.

2. There is little competitive overlap between small loan operations and commercial banks. Consumer finance companies make a wider variety of loans and service different risk classes of customers.

3. With holding company management and capital, finance company subsidiaries are able to enter new geographic markets, expand their loan volume, offer larger and more diversified loans, and be more effective competitors.

4. Several applications were turned down because they would result in undue concentration of resources or adverse effects on existing competition in the consumer finance field.

5. All applications must be subjected to the so-called "balancing test." The holding company must show that any potentially adverse effects on competition must be offset by public benefits. This may be shown through new services being offered, reductions in fees charged on loans, or increased access to sources of capital to support future growth.

---

[1] Peter S. Rose and Donald R. Fraser, "Bank Holding Company Diversification into Mortgage Banking and Finance Companies," *Banking Law Journal,* November, 1974, p. 977.

FIRST HAWAIIAN'S APPLICATION FOR A FINANCE SUBSIDIARY

On July 5, 1974, First Hawaiian, Inc., filed an application on behalf of FHI Financial, Inc., a proposed wholly-owned subsidiary which intended to conduct an industrial loan business under chapter 408 of the Hawaii Revised Statutes. The application stated the management of the proposed subsidiary would be directed by the senior officers of First Hawaiian, Inc., which in most instances comprises the senior officers of First Hawaiian Bank. The subsidiary would concentrate in the real estate loan market and, more specifically, in the taking of junior liens on real property. Under current Hawaii statutes, banks cannot make such junior liens, and they may represent a substantial potential for consumer borrowing.

On August 26, 1974, Hawaii Bancorporation, Inc., also filed an application for an industrial-loan subsidiary. It is a one-bank holding company for the Bank of Hawaii, the largest bank in the state.

Chapter 408–8 of the Hawaii Revised Statutes establishes three conditions which must be demonstrated before the application could be approved by the Director of Regulatory Agencies. The conditions are

1. That the financial responsibility, experience, character, and general fitness of the applicant and of the officers or members thereof are such as to command the confidence of the community and to warrant belief that the business will be operated honestly, fairly, and efficiently within the purposes of this chapter;

2. That allowing the applicant to engage in this business will promote the convenience and advantage of the locality or community in which the business of the applicant is to be conducted; and

3. That the applicant has available for the operation of this business at the specified location capital of at least $100,000.

INFORMATION SUPPORTING THE APPLICATION

A hearing was held before the Director of Regulatory Agencies on October 18, 1974. A second hearing was also held on November 15 to consider supplemental information filed by First Hawaiian, Inc. In the section which follows information presented at these hearings and in the application will be summarized or reported in part. Certain issues which primarily dealt with the proposed location will not be included in this case. This case is not concerned with the location of the subsidiary. The question at issue is whether a bank holding company should be authorized to establish an industrial loan subsidiary in the State of Hawaii, regardless of its location within the state.

Prior to the hearings, Phillip Ching, a vice president of both the holding company and the bank, sent the following information to the director of Regulatory Agencies.

1. *Background.* First Hawaiian, Inc., a bank holding company, has filed an application on behalf of FHI Financial, Inc., a proposed Hawaii Corporation, which will be a wholly-owned subsidiary of First Hawaiian, Inc., to conduct an industrial loan business under chapter 408, Hawaii Revised Statutes . . . . The application to conduct an industrial loan business . . . is a permissible activity under the Bank Holding Company Act of 1956 as amended in Regulation Y of the Federal Reserve Board.

2. *Convenience and Advantage to the Community in Which Applicant's Business Is to Be Conducted.*

   a. Growth of industrial loan companies. In the recent past Hawaii has seen a substantial increase in loans made by industrial loan companies which indicates tremendous growth potential. Annual loan growth rates for Hawaii's industrial loan companies, savings and loans, and banks are as follows for the period June 1969 to June 1974. For the industrial loan companies, 21.1 percent; savings and loan, 18.6 percent; banks, 11.5 percent.

b. Real estate loans. FHI Financial intends to emphasize the real estate loan area, particularly the making of second mortgage loans on real property. FHI Financial will, of course, also offer all the services of an industrial loan company dependent on the demands and needs of its clients in the community in which it will conduct its business.

"We believe that the potential for second mortgages in Hawaii is substantial. In view of the fact that we have had in recent years tremendous increase in real estate values, statistics compiled by the Multiple Listing Services of the Honolulu Board of Realtors show the following average prices of residences on the Island of Oahu. For 1971 for the period August to December—because this is the only time that the Hawaii Board of Realtors had started tabulating on single-family residences—average price for that period for single-family residences was $60,160; for condominiums for the same period, $42,616. For the year 1972, single-family residence, $65,704; condominiums, $44,136. 1973, $85,912; condominiums, $49,312. For six months of 1974, the single-family residence average sales price was $85,951; condominiums, $54,902.

"This may result in a wide gap between current market value and current balances on first mortgages thus giving the property owner the capability of making a second mortgage. Refinancing of existing mortgages would be impractical due to current high mortgage interest rates which would make such long-term refinancing costly. High prices for homes represent another potential market for second mortgages due to the fact that in many instances purchasers are unable to meet the substantial down payment for a home, though their income is adequate for the entire debt services. Banks are currently restricted to a maximum loan-to-value ratio on mortgages. First Hawaiian Bank has been forced to turn down mortgage loans which otherwise represent prudent desirable loans solely because they were in excess of the permissible loan-to-value ratio. Entry into the industrial loan field would permit FHI Financial to make such loans which ordinarily would have been made by First Hawaiian Bank or other banks but for the loan-to-value restrictions.

c. Benefit to the community. "We intend to conduct business on the basis which will be of benefit and convenience to the public. We propose to implement innovative programs through FHI Financial such as Pay Any Day of the month program, simple interest calculation, and no prepayment penalty on all loans. It is our understanding that these are not generally available throughout the industrial loan industry, which programs should result in lower borrowing costs to our customers.

"FHI Financial will provide another competitive entity in the industrial loan field. We feel that we will be able to compete effectively with other industrial loan companies. This should result in benefit to the community in better service and competitive pricing of our services."

3. *Financial Responsibility and General Fitness of the Applicant.*

". . . We propose to capitalize FHI Financial at a million dollars fully paid in. We intend to staff FHI Financial with experienced financial officers who will be identified at a later date."

HEARING ON THE APPLICATION

At the opening session of the hearings, John Bellinger, president of First Hawaiian, Inc., made the following statement to start the bank's presentation:

"Mr. Chairman, I just have a brief statement. I would like to go on record in reply to the brief that was filed by the Hawaii Consumer Finance Association, which lists both Bank of Hawaii and ourselves as applicants, that this is our application and Bank of Hawaii is not being heard today. They had a holding company for a couple of years and if they decide to file an application a month after us, that is their problem, but ours is a separate problem and I would prefer that this is handled in that manner. This is our application and should be looked upon as our application and not the two banks'.

"Secondly, I think that with the application we have submitted we can offer to the consumer public better service than they are receiving now. It is obvious that the growth of some of the finance companies and industrial loan companies, in the last five years has been tremendous and that there is room for additional companies. We intend to offer services which we cannot afford in the bank. We will include those we think are convenient to the public, and if our application is approved we will offer the public simple interest loans and also the opportunity of our Pay Any Day Plan.

"We do not believe that our entering this field will in any way damage or hurt the other finance companies. Competition is always healthy. Thank you."

The hearings continued throughout the day. Questions were asked by Mr. Wee, the senior bank examiner, Mr. Honda, the director of Regulatory Agencies, Mr. Wheelan, an attorney for the Hawaii Consumer Finance Association, and several members of the audience. The following are excerpts, occasionally paraphrased, from these exchanges.

Mr. Honda: You say that you do not feel that your entry into the business will hurt others. Whom do you mean by "others"?

Mr. Bellinger: I meant the other finance companies that are objecting.

Mr. Honda: How do you arrive at that conclusion?

Mr. Bellinger: Well, because of the growth of the overall totals of the finance companies in the last five years. I think there will be continued growth and those that are hustling and working for the business will continue to grow. I think that some of those that do not really get in and work are going to maybe stay status quo and not have the growth. We think that there is room.

Mr. Wee: Would this be a vehicle for referring down the second mortgage? In other words, an individual goes to the bank and makes an application for a first mortgage loan and is referred to your subsidiary.

Mr. Bellinger: Probably would.

Mr. Ching: We have stated in our application we intend to stress second mortgages, but we have also stated that as a collateral matter dependent on the clients we will engage in the other activities permitted to industrial loan companies, but our main intent in applying for industrial loan license is to do those things which we cannot do now under the bank. It would be, I think, somewhat imprudent as a general business practice to actively solicit consumer loans in our industrial loan company when in fact we are conducting that business as a bank. We would be fighting against each other in a sense. And so it is our intent to concentrate in the second mortgage area and as a collateral matter as a benefit, you know, where a guy comes in and he happens to be a one-stop shopping in finance, if he happens to need a consumer loan, fine, but we are not going to be pursuing it on an active basis.

★ ★ ★

Mr. Ching: One of the unfair competitive advantages cited by the Consumer Association is that the bank, which now provides lines of credit to some of the financial companies, would begin to favor FHI Financial and this would provide unfair competition. As a matter of practicality, the FHI Financial will be considered an affiliate under the Federal Deposit Insurance Act of the Federal Reserve, and as such, any lines or borrowings by FHI Financial would have to be fully collateralized depending on the class of the collateral whether it be securities or governments or municipals; but, in any event, it would be at least fully collateralized, any loans. Now, we have analyzed this and considered it and we have concluded that this is totally impractical to conduct our business as FHI Financial by borrowing from the bank and we are not looking to borrowings from the bank or First Hawaiian Bank lines to finance the activities of FHI Financial.

★ ★ ★

Mr. Schutte (Bank Attorney): The banks in the State of Hawaii have total assets of $2,875,000,000. Our information indicates that Household Finance consolidated assets are two billion, nine hundred eighty-five million; CIT's consolidated assets of December 31, '73, were three billion, nine hundred sixty-one million dollars; Beneficial Finance at June 30, '74, reported consolidated assets of two billion, three hundred ninety-nine million dollars. And we are turning loose, depending on how you look at it, a million-dollar company in that arena. Or, if you use our consolidated assets, about a nine-

hundred-million-dollar company taking on two and three-billion-dollar companies, so we don't believe solely in competition among equals. We are willing to go in as a pigmy and fight our way along with the giants.

★ ★ ★

Mr. Honda: Where would the proposed finance company be obtaining funds from?

Mr. Ching: Initially, of course, the million-dollar capitalization; but, in addition, First Hawaiian, Inc., has recently gone into the commercial paper market, and we intend to downstream funds to the finance company. Outside bank borrowing from mainland banks would be another source of funds for our finance company's operations. At the present time the commercial paper market is within the state. However, it is our intention to market it outside of the state on a national basis.

Mr. Pingree (Bank Officer): We find that while we are marketing our commercial paper locally, we are really competing for mainland dollars because we found that many of the people who are traditionally in the paper market are using mainland sources, so in that sense in essence when we market our paper locally we are bringing dollars back to Hawaii because that money would traditionally stay on the Mainland in other types of paper.

Mr. Ching: An additional source of funds ultimately will be the issuance of investment certificates and/or debentures as has been the case for other industrial loan companies.

Mr. Honda: So you will be in that sense competing for funds with many of the existing institutions?

Mr. Ching: Certainly.

★ ★ ★

Mr. Schutte (Bank Attorney): I take it that the question addresses itself to will FHI Financial borrow from First Hawaiian Bank. To respond very briefly, the answer is no;

but, here is the answer why the answer is no: First Hawaiian Bank is a State non-member insured bank, deposits which are insured by the Federal Deposit Insurance Corporation. As such it is subject to the Federal Deposit Insurance Act. Section 18 (j) of the Federal Deposit Insurance Act makes Section 23(a) of the Federal Reserve Act applicable to all State non-member banks. Section 23 of the Federal Reserve Act prohibits loans between banks and their affiliates unless certain conditions are met. Affiliates are specifically defined in Section 23(a) as amended now in force to include the subsidiaries of bank holding companies; that is to say, every subsidiary of the bank holding company is an affiliate of every other subsidiary of a bank holding company under Section 23(a).

Section 23(a) says that a bank shall not lend to an affiliate unless: One, there are certain maximum loan amounts observed in terms of percentage of capital to surplus. But the really significant thing is that they cannot lend except on collateral. If the collateral is securities other than U.S. governments, government agencies and municipals, the collateral must equal 120 percent of the amount of the loan. If the collateral is municipal, State and local government obligations, the collateral must be 110 percent of the loan. If the collateral is United States government and government agencies, then the statute simply requires that the loan be collateralized.

I suggest to you, Mr. Director, in response to this question also that if there is a local industrial loan licensee who has got stock exchange, government or municipal collateral sufficient so that he could put up that kind of backing for his bank loan, it is either the richest industrial loan license in the world or it is headed for bankruptcy, one of the two.

A voice: Will you get a loan from the Bank of Hawaii? Can your subsidiary get a bank line from Bank of Hawaii?

Mr. Schutte: Legally, the answer is legally it could. To the best of my knowledge and belief, we do not own Bank of Hawaii or any controlling interest in it so that we wouldn't be an affiliate of Bank of Hawaii. It would be legally permissible; whether our No. 1 competitor would be delighted to give us the money with which to compete with them, I don't know.

Prior to the November resumption of hearings, First Hawaiian submitted additional material which established the following points:

1. It is generally uneconomical to refinance an existing mortgage loan bearing a low rate of interest since the entire loan will be rewritten at current rates. In Hawaii there is both a low percent of second mortgages and a large homeowner equity in homes which provide a tremendous market for second mortgages.

2. All applicants for second mortgages do not receive them and 63 percent of the downtown industrial loan companies are not currently making second mortgage loans. This is hardly meeting the public's need for second mortgage loans.

3. We will be able to benefit the public through lower borrowing costs.

COUNTER ARGUMENTS PRESENTED BY THE HAWAII CONSUMER FINANCE ASSOCIATION:

The Hawaii Consumer Finance Association and its attorneys submitted a statement to the Director of Regulatory Agencies which strongly objected to the First Hawaiian application. The following are excerpts from the conclusion section of this statement.

The proposed entry of the Bank of Hawaii and First Hawaiian Bank into the industrial loan company market poses several serious problems:

1. Bank of Hawaii and First Hawaiian Bank, by virtue of being the two largest banks in the state, have the potential to direct a tremendous amount of business to their proposed industrial loan company subsidiaries. This would tend to monopolize control and related activities within the banking field and the industrial loan company market.

2. Bank of Hawaii and First Hawaiian Bank are regulated by the state and federal governments, and accounts are insured by an agency of the federal government. Industrial loan companies are not insured by any governmental agency, and are only subject to state regulation. It is probable that industrial loan company customers will confuse the identity of these banks and their respective proposed industrial loan companies. The banks and their proposed industrial loan companies have a number of common incidents: common ownership, common directors, common names, etc. These factors will lead customers to believe that the bank and its proposed industrial loan company are one and the same. This gives the bank's proposed industrial loan company an unfair edge in competition. It misleads the customer. It perhaps exposes the bank and its assets to liability arising out of the industrial loan company operations by "piercing the corporate veil."

3. If, as the banks project, there is increased demand for real estate second-mortgage money, an important source of industrial loan company operating funds to meet this demand derives from the banks. Diversion of bank lines from existing industrial loan companies would unfairly and illegally affect the future of existing industrial loan companies to meet this demand.

4. Although the banks' applications for industrial loan company licenses do not specify whether the proposed companies will issue thrift certificates or debentures, state law permits issuance of such debt instruments. The banks take various forms of deposit which yield various returns. The industrial loan companies receive non-demand funds by issuance of certificates or debentures which generally produce higher yields than can be obtained from the banks. The banks will be in a position to divert public monies which would otherwise be deposited with the banks to their proposed industrial loan companies by issuing certificates or debentures.

   The banks may also divert public monies which would otherwise be invested with other industrial loan companies to the banks' proposed industrial loan companies. Such activity would be illegal and unfair to the existing industrial loan companies. The public is aware that bank deposits are insured by an agency of the federal government.

Teruo Himoto, the president of Commercial Finance, Limited, and a director of the Hawaii Consumer Finance Association, also presented a statement at the hearings.

"I appear before this hearing with mixed emotions. I have worked very closely with the two major banks that have applied for industrial loan licenses under Chapter 408, Hawaii Revised Statutes, while employed by three separate companies that I have worked for during the past 23 years. These two banks have been very good to me and assisted me with our financial needs.

"On account of the good business relationship that we have with these two banks, many of the members of the Hawaii Consumer Finance Association are reluctant to testify at this hearing in order that these relationships would not be severed. If none of us spoke up to express our true feelings and thoughts when our very livelihood depended on the outcome of whether or not bank holding companies may be permitted to oprate industrial loan companies and eventually put many of us present industrial loan license operators out of business, we are definitely shirking our responsibility to our investors and the public.

"The management of the industrial loan companies as well as the staff of the Bank Examiner's Office are entrusted with the responsibility of protecting the public monies invested in the various industrial loan companies. We both must make every effort to see that such public funds do not deteriorate through poor management operation or unfair edge in competition by the entries of two giant banks into our industry.

"Why did the Federal and the individual states throughout the country create three major categories of financial institutions; namely, banks, savings and loan associations and industrial loan companies? Each of these financial institutions has a specific function to perform to serve the financial needs of the public. Under the Banking Act, the banks were prohibited from operating a savings and loan or an industrial loan company; so why should they be permitted to operate an industrial loan company under the Bank Holding Company Act? Isn't it one and the same thing?

"Under our free enterprise system, I welcome good healthy competition, but am strongly opposed to unfair competition. As you are all aware these two major banks dominate the market in this small financial community of ours, operating only as a bank. What will happen if they were permitted to enter the industrial loan area and later into the savings and loan industry. Do you think our free enterprise system will be in operation then? The answer is *no!* They will definitely monopolize and control the banking and other financial markets.

"First Hawaiian, Inc. has indicated that the second-mortgage loan market has grown substantially during the past few years and quoted the amount of second mortgages closed in 1973, and the first five months of 1974. Who has provided the funds for such second mortgages? It is the present existing industrial loan companies that have met the needs of the public and will continue to meet these needs of the public.

"Until a few years ago, the industrial loan companies were primarily making consumer loans, such as installment sales contracts, auto loans, character loans and loans on personal property; but when the need for second mortgages arose, we were able to take care of the public demand. We were able to meet the public demand for such needed funds and we are prepared to satisfy the needs of the public for such demands in the future, without the banks entering into this field.

"The public convenience and advantage will not, in any legitimate way, be served by approving the application of First Hawaiian, Inc. The present industrial loan companies have in the past, and will continue to meet the demands of the public. . . . No convenience or advantage will be served granting the application when there would be the potential for unfair competition and monopolistic trade practices. The public convenience and advantage will be much better served if the existing industrial loan companies are permitted to maintain the healthy and strong competitive market which presently exists. Entry of the banks into this market would seriously distort competition and jeopardize the financial health of the industrial loan company industry in Hawaii."

INITIAL DECISION OF THE DIRECTOR OF REGULATORY AGENCIES

On November 27, 1974, the Director of Regulatory Agencies denied the application for an industrial loan license. After considering all the facts, information, and relevant laws, the director determined that

1. Allowing the applicant to be licensed as an industrial loan company under Chapter 408, Hawaii Revised Statutes, through a wholly-owned subsidiary will not promote the convenience and advantage of the locality or community in which the business of the applicant is proposed to be conducted, based on the fact that First Hawaiian Bank, a

principal subsidiary of the applicant, presently possesses under Section 478–4, Hawaii Revised Statutes, the same rights conferred upon industrial loan companies operating under Chapter 408, Hawaii Revised Statutes, as to charge, contract for, receive, collect in advance, or recover interest, discount, and other charges at the same rates and in the same amounts as permitted by law in the case of loans made by industrial loan companies licensed under Chapter 408, Hawaii Revised Statutes.

2. Since applicant's principal subsidiary, First Hawaiian Bank, is not permitted under the present statutes to make second-mortgage loans, applicant should not be permitted to accomplish this through an indirect route.

3. The consumer loan activity of applicant conducted through its subsidiary, First Hawaiian Bank, will not be adversely affected without an industrial loan license.

4. Applicant's earnings will not be substantially affected without an industrial loan license.

5. Approval of the subject application would result in undue concentration of resources due to the resources of applicant's principal subsidiary, First Hawaiian Bank, as of June 30, 1974, being 1.392 times the total resources of all industrial loan companies in Hawaii.

6. Approval of the subject application would create a competitive inequality, to some degree, in the field of mortgage loans where first mortgage loans are made to the borrowers by applicant's principal subsidiary, First Hawaiian Bank, and the second mortgage loans are directed to its proposed industrial loan licensee.

7. At this time, there are no compelling mitigating circumstances of competitive or other hardships which applicant or any of its subsidiaries will suffer vis-à-vis comparable institutions which are chartered by other than state agencies.

"Based on the foregoing, it is ordered that the application of First Hawaiian, Inc. for a license to engage in the business of an industrial loan company through a subsidiary be and is hereby denied at this time."

SUBSEQUENT EVENTS

During the 1975 session of the State Legislature a bill was introduced which would prevent banks and savings and loan associations from getting into the commercial loan business. This attempt to deny entry created considerable controversy in the Legislature.

A spokesman for First Hawaii, Inc., testified before the Legislature that:

1. The Federal Reserve Board permits bank holding companies to operate industrial loan companies in the manner authorized by state law. The bill would prevent other financial institutions from engaging in the industrial loan business.

2. The bill will eliminate potential competition and the possibility of lower borrowing costs to the public.

3. There is a definite need for additional financing alternatives in the second mortgage market.

Late in the Legislative session Governor Ariyoshi sent a letter to the Speaker of the House of Representatives which outlined his support of the bill:

"There is a present prohibition against the enumerated firms from directly engaging in the industrial loan business. I do not believe that they should be permitted to do indirectly through a holding company that which they could not do directly. I am therefore very strongly in support of the concept of the bill to prohibit all banks, savings and loan associations, and trust companies from engaging in the industrial loan business.

"I also believe that this prohibition should apply equally to all legal entities, whether they are organized and doing business in or out of our state. It is therefore my hope that the bill passed by the House will be amended to reflect a total prohibition.

"I want to assure you that I feel very strongly about this matter. I feel equally strongly that such action should be taken during this session of the Legislature. To delay may result in the need to "grandfather" more firms than are presently involved. Your consideration of this matter would therefore be greatly appreciated."

Despite the Governor's support, the bill failed to pass.

From the viewpoint of the bank holding company it was fortunate they were attempting to secure approval for an industrial loan subsidiary rather than a real estate investment trust. Nationally a combination of high interest rates and a slow housing market had pushed many REIT's close to financial bankruptcy. Within the last year the Fed had informally suggested that banks extend credit generously to the endangered REIT's so as to avert a total collapse. The May 19, 1975 issue of *Business Week* reported that the Chase Manhattan Bank subsequently encountered difficulty with its REIT affiliate:

"Of all the banks involved, Chase Manhattan Bank, the $1 billion REIT's sponsor,

advisor, and with $150 million in the credit lines, biggest creditor, has the most at stake. It does not own the trust or have any legal obligation to stand behind it, but Chase's name is on the line. And any default to the public bondholders by the trust could do incalculable damage to the bank, to Chase Manhattan Corp., the bank's holding company parent, and to the holding company's various nonbank subsidiaries."

There are 38 industrial loan licensees in the downtown Honolulu area. The research personnel at First Hawaiian in the latter part of 1974 conducted a poll which asked the question: Are you making consumer and/or second-mortgage loans? Only 14 of the 36 said they are currently making second-mortgage loans. The results of this poll were reconfirmed by a more recent poll.

APPEAL HEARING

As provided for in State statutes, First Hawaiian, Inc., appealed the denial of its application. The three-person appeal board was composed of Wayne Minami, the newly appointed director of Regulatory Agencies, Attorney General Ron Amemiya, and State Comptroller Hideo Murakami.

The appeal hearing was scheduled for late May.

Exhibit 1:

Banks in Hawaii, December 31, 1974
Assets, Deposits, and Capital Accounts
($ million)

	Total Assets	Total Deposits	Total Capital
Bank of Hawaii	$1,061	$944	$82
First Hawaiian Bank	1,008	855	76
Central Pacific Bank	220	202	14
American Security Bank	218	190	18
Liberty Bank	137	119	9
City Bank	133	117	11
Hawaii National Bank	123	109	8
Bank of Honolulu, N.A.	18	16	2
	$2,918	$2,553	$220

Exhibit 2:

**Savings in Hawaii's Financial Institutions
1965–1974
($ million)**

Year	Bank Time Deposits	S&L Withdrawable Shares, Deposits and Investment Certificates	Industrial Loan Investment Certificates	Credit Union Shares	Total Institutional Savings
1965	$ 394.4	$ 378.1	$ 24.7	$114.8	$ 912.0
1966	427.7	399.5	25.9	123.5	976.6
1967	495.4	450.2	33.3	133.4	1,112.3
1968	566.9	502.4	40.6	146.9	1,256.8
1969	592.6	553.3	56.9	162.0	1,364.8
1970	713.9	625.9	99.7	182.6	1,622.1
1971	791.6	780.5	143.8	216.0	1,931.9
1972	891.7	957.6	191.7	248.6	2,289.6
1973	1,022.7	1,080.0	245.9	278.0	2,626.6
1974	1,111.2	1,190.6	319.0	313.2	2,914.0

Sources: *Credit Union Yearbook* and *Bank Examiner Reports*

Exhibit 3:

**Hawaii's Financial Institutions
Percentage Shares of Savings**

Year	Bank	S&L	Industrial Loan	Credit Union
1965	43.2%	41.5%	2.7%	12.6%
1966	43.8	40.9	2.6	12.6
1967	44.5	40.5	3.0	12.0
1968	45.1	40.0	3.2	11.7
1969	43.4	40.5	4.2	11.9
1970	44.0	38.6	6.1	11.3
1971	41.0	40.4	7.4	11.2
1972	38.9	41.8	8.4	10.9
1973	38.9	41.1	9.4	10.6
1974	38.1	40.2	10.9	10.7

Source: Calculated from Exhibit 2

Exhibit 4:

Industrial Loan Companies in Hawaii
Balance Sheet Data on December 31
($000)

	1969		1974	
	$	%	$	%
Assets				
Real estate mortgage loans	$ 35,936	12.3%	$291,566	41.0%
Retail installment contract	27,431	9.4	31,245	4.4
Character loans	49,609	16.9	62,766	8.8
Collateral loans	64,609	22.0	89,029	12.5
Auto & trade financing loans	9,054	3.1	16,878	2.4
All other loans	27,572	9.4	51,250	7.2
Total loans	$214,088	73.0	$542,733	76.3
Judgments & Repossessions	162	0.1	126	0.0
Premises, furniture & fixtures	3,122	1.1	6,184	0.9
Cash	9,474	3.2	22,152	3.1
All other Assets	66,186	22.6	140,408	19.7
Total Assets	$293,031	100.0%	$711,604	100.0%
Liabilities & Capital				
Borrowed money	$100,673	34.4%	$151,761	21.3%
Debentures	47,308	16.1	41,685	5.9
Invest. cert. outstdg.	56,906	19.4	318,978	44.8
Other liabilities	9,997	3.4	52,910	8.2
Unearned interest	26,238	9.0	30,444	4.3
Capital	27,422	9.4	47,835	6.7
Surplus & undivided profits	19,944	6.8	49,996	7.0
Reserve for losses	4,542	1.5	12,995	1.8
Total	$293,031	100.0%	$711,604	100.0%

Case 13

Nello L. Teer Company

This case was prepared by Professor Mark R. Eaker of Southern Methodist University. This case is designed to be used as a basis for class discussion rather than to illustrate either effective or ineffective handling of an administrative situation.

Presented at a Case Workshop and distributed by the Intercollegiate Case Clearing House Soldiers Field, Boston, Massachusetts 02163. All rights reserved to the contributors. Printed in the U.S.A.

It was 6:30 P.M. and Robb Teer, Assistant Treasurer of Nello L. Teer Company, had just called his wife to tell her that he would be home late for dinner. The next day, December 15, 1976, was the submission date for bids on the Dantokpa-Akpakpa Bridge project in Benin (formerly the Republic of Dahomey), and he had still not decided whether to take out an Overseas Private Investment Corporation (OPIC) Construction Insurance Policy. Once the decision on the amount and timing of the coverage was made, Teer would have to cable Howard Frederich, the head of Nello Teer's African office so that the premium could be factored into the company's bid.

COMPANY BACKGROUND

Nello L. Teer Company of Durham, North Carolina, is a full service construction firm, actively involved in projects throughout the world. Founded in 1909 by Nello L. Teer, Sr., the firm remains privately held with two generations of the founder's descendants active in the management of the enterprise.

Among Teer's more prominent jobs have been sections of the Massachusetts and Pennsylvania turnpikes, Broken Bow Dam in Oklahoma, the North Carolina Blue Cross & Blue Shield headquarters building, Chapel Hill, North Carolina, and primary highways of Tanzania, Panama, Nicaragua, Honduras, and Guatemala. Approximately 20 percent of Teer's business is conducted outside of the United States. The company has an average world-wide payroll of 2,500 employees.

THE DANTOKPA-AKPAKPA BRIDGE PROJECT

The Dantokpa-Akpakpa (D-A) Bridge Project was part of a larger effort by the country of Benin to upgrade its primary transportation system. In order to finance the project, Benin had successfully enlisted the assistance of the Agency for International Development in providing the majority of the funding. Local sources would provide the rest, but the AID participation, and the terms of payment outlined in the project's bid specifications meant that exchange risk and default need not be considered by the bidders. However, the possibility of expropriation of materials or loss due to war, civil insurrection, or natural disaster was still a consideration; and it was this type of OPIC coverage (See Appendix 1) that Robb Teer was trying to evaluate.

Robb was aware that he had to consider a number of factors. First, he had to evaluate the political climate in Benin. In order to accomplish that, he spent some time researching Benin at the library as well as soliciting information from various government agencies. (Appendix 2 summarizes the material on Benin.) Second, it was necessary to measure the extent of Teer Company's exposure. This information was essential in arriving at the quantity of coverage. In order to assess Teer's vulnerability, Robb had had the project manager provide a materials flow-chart related to the project.

To this he added his own projections of the outstanding pay estimates and the average bank balance required in country. (See schedule below.)

April 1, 1977-September 30, 1977	$1,600,000
October 1, 1977-March 31, 1978	1,500,000
April 1, 1977-September 30, 1978	1,500,000
October 1, 1978-March 31,1979	1,500,000
April 1, 1979-September 30, 1979	800,000
October 1, 1979-March 31, 1980	200,000

Exhibit 1

TO: Robb Teer
FROM: Howard Frederich
SUBJECT: Materials Flow and Cost Estimates Related to the Dantokpa-Akpakpa Bridge Bid

Equipment and Materials

A. General construction equipment with six-year life and no salvage value. Arrive in Benin on April 1, 1977. $1,651,000

B. Specialized equipment to be written off during the 33 months of construction.   75,513

C. Materials for site preparation and initial construction. Arrive in Benin on April 1, 1977.   422,622

D. Miscellaneous support services and materials to be used during first 24 months of construction.   569,416

E. Miscellaneous expendable equipment to be used at a rate of $20,000 per year beginning April 1, 1977.   100,000

F. Materials incorporated in the job to be used at the rate of $167,000 per year. $100,000 to arrive April 1, 1977, and $400,000 on October 1, 1977.

Although it could only be an estimate based upon the bid specifications and engineering plans, Teer was reasonably confident of the numbers and dates (Exhibit I).

Although the Teer Company had operated overseas for a number of years, their experience with African countries was not extensive. Company policy had been not to utilize this type of insurance for any of the Latin American projects. Within Latin America where the company has had a long-standing presence, the feeling was that the company could accurately assess the climate, and provide sufficient guarantees in the process of negotiating a contract. With regard to Africa, that same confidence was not felt and as a result, Robb was carefully weighing the situation.

Teer was certain that there were other companies interested in the project, so the bidding was expected to be highly competitive. As a result, every effort had to be made in order to minimize the cost of erecting the bridge. A success on this project could pave the way for other work on the Benin highway system. Yet, at the same time Teer Company expected a profit on every undertaking. Therefore, Robb was being particularly careful in assessing the risk to Teer, and the cost of insuring against loss. Too much caution could lead to not getting the job, but too little might eventuate into significant losses.

Robb sat down to go through the background material one more time, not wanting to miss dinner entirely, and knowing that the decision had to be made that night.

Nello L. Teer Company

Appendix 1: The Overseas Private Investment Corporation (OPIC)

The Overseas Private Investment Corporation was created by the Foreign Assistance Act of 1969 and formally established January 19, 1971. OPIC was organized in order to foster two primary goals: to assist in development projects in less developed countries, and to make U.S. firms more competitive in participating in development related projects worldwide. The mechanism for attaining those goals is the provision of insurance services that allow U.S. firms to protect themselves against a variety of risks related to overseas business activity. Since similar insurance was not available through private channels, yet was in many cases provided to foreign firms by their governments, it was believed that U.S. firms operated at a competitive disadvantage. Furthermore, it was believed that the inability of U.S. firms to acquire insurance reduced the overall flow of funds into development related projects.

OPIC provides insurance for qualified projects in approximately 90 less developed countries. Specifically, OPIC is authorized to provide coverage against the following types of risk:

1) Inability to convert local currency into dollars. This applies to profits or earnings, as well as the return of the original investment.

2) Loss of investment due to expropriation, nationalization, or confiscation by a foreign government.

3) Loss due to revolution, war, or insurrection.

OPIC offers a variety of insurance programs of which the Special Incentive Program for U.S. Construction and Services Overseas is specifically designed for contractors engaged in overseas projects. The package provides insurance against all three of the risks outlined above, and coverage can be extended to 90 percent of the amount expected to be at risk during a policy year.

At the time an OPIC policy is applied for, the firm must indicate the maximum amount of coverage that might be required. This is usually done when a $100 registration fee is paid to OPIC. The insuree can then allocate that maximum amount between two types of coverage, current and standby. Current coverage refers to the amount of active insurance in force during a half of a contract period (6 months). Any claims against OPIC can not exceed the current coverage. Standby coverage is the difference between the maximum and the current amounts. It represents the additional amount of current coverage available to the insuree during the life of the policy. Prior to the first day of a half of a contract period, the policy holder elects the amount of current and standby coverage for that period. The total coverage during a period sets the maximum coverage during all subsequent periods.

The premiums are determined by the amount of current and standby coverage. The rate for current coverage is 1.5 percent per annum. Standby coverage carries a premium of 0.75 percent per annum. Premiums accrue from the first day the policy is in force, which also marks the beginning of the first contract period.

In order to qualify for OPIC Construction and Services coverage, a project must be development related and have host country approval. The host country must agree to arbitrate any claims and there must not be any illegal boycott or other restrictions as conditions for doing business.

Nello L. Teer Company

Appendix 2: Benin

Benin (43,483 sq. miles, pop. 3,191,628) is situated along the western African coast between Togo and Nigeria. Formerly a part of French West Africa, the country achieved full independence on August 1, 1960, as the Independent Republic of Dahomey. Initially a constitutional democracy, Dahomey experienced a succession of military governments brought into power through six coups between 1960 and 1972. Currently, the country is governed by a military council headed by Lt. Col. Mathier Kerekou, who assumed power by coup d'etat on October 26, 1972.

On December 3, 1974, President Kerekou declared Dahomey to be a "Marxist-Leninist state." Two days later, the nation's banks, insurance companies, and oil distribution facilities were nationalized. Additional control of business activity has since been mandated in order to "protect the revolution from sabotage." On November 30, 1975, the country was renamed the People's Republic of Benin. Despite several attempted coups, President Kerekou has retained power.

Benin's economy is mainly agricultural. The gross domestic product was estimated to be $80 per capita in 1970. The country has had severe balance of payments problems and has experienced an inability to balance its local budget. Deficits have largely been met by virtue of bilateral aid, primarily from France.

Benin does have one of the more highly educated populaces among African countries. However, economic problems resulting in severe unemployment have led to unrest among the educated citizens and is probably a major factor explaining the political instability.

Appendix

Time Value of Money Tables

Table A-1:
Compound Value of a Dollar (Annual Compounding)
$(1 + i)^n$

Year	1.00	2.00	3.00	4.00	5.00	6.00	6.25	6.50	6.75	7.00
1	1.0100	1.0200	1.0300	1.0400	1.0500	1.0600	1.0625	1.0650	1.0675	1.0700
2	1.0201	1.0404	1.0609	1.0816	1.1025	1.1236	1.1289	1.1342	1.1396	1.1449
3	1.0303	1.0612	1.0927	1.1249	1.1576	1.1910	1.1995	1.2079	1.2165	1.2250
4	1.0406	1.0824	1.1255	1.1699	1.2155	1.2625	1.2744	1.2865	1.2986	1.3108
5	1.0510	1.1041	1.1593	1.2167	1.2763	1.3382	1.3541	1.3701	1.3862	1.4026
6	1.0615	1.1262	1.1941	1.2653	1.3401	1.4185	1.4387	1.4591	1.4798	1.5007
7	1.0721	1.1487	1.2299	1.3159	1.4071	1.5036	1.5286	1.5540	1.5797	1.6058
8	1.0829	1.1717	1.2668	1.3686	1.4775	1.5938	1.6242	1.6550	1.6863	1.7182
9	1.0937	1.1951	1.3048	1.4233	1.5513	1.6895	1.7257	1.7626	1.8002	1.8385
10	1.1046	1.2190	1.3439	1.4802	1.6289	1.7908	1.8335	1.8771	1.9217	1.9672
11	1.1157	1.2434	1.3842	1.5395	1.7103	1.8983	1.9481	1.9992	2.0514	2.1049
12	1.1268	1.2682	1.4258	1.6010	1.7959	2.0122	2.0699	2.1291	2.1899	2.2522
13	1.1381	1.2936	1.4685	1.6651	1.8856	2.1329	2.1993	2.2675	2.3377	2.4098
14	1.1495	1.3195	1.5126	1.7317	1.9799	2.2609	2.3367	2.4149	2.4955	2.5785
15	1.1610	1.3459	1.5580	1.8009	2.0789	2.3966	2.4828	2.5718	2.6639	2.7590
16	1.1726	1.3728	1.6047	1.8730	2.1829	2.5404	2.6379	2.7390	2.8437	2.9522
17	1.1843	1.4002	1.6528	1.9479	2.2920	2.6928	2.8028	2.9170	3.0357	3.1588
18	1.1961	1.4282	1.7024	2.0258	2.4066	2.8543	2.9780	3.1067	3.2406	3.3799
19	1.2081	1.4568	1.7535	2.1068	2.5270	3.0256	3.1641	3.3086	3.4593	3.6165
20	1.2202	1.4859	1.8061	2.1911	2.6533	3.2071	3.3619	3.5236	3.6928	3.8697
25	1.2824	1.6406	2.0938	2.6658	3.3864	4.2919	4.5522	4.8277	5.1191	5.4274
30	1.3478	1.8114	2.4273	3.2434	4.3219	5.7435	6.1641	6.6144	7.0964	7.6123
35	1.4166	1.9999	2.8139	3.9461	5.5160	7.6861	8.3467	9.0623	9.8373	10.6766
40	1.4889	2.2080	3.2620	4.8010	7.0400	10.2857	11.3021	12.4161	13.6369	14.9745
50	1.6446	2.6916	4.3839	7.1067	11.4674	18.4202	20.7227	23.3067	26.2056	29.4570

Table A-1:
Continued

Year	7.25	7.50	7.75	8.00	8.25	8.50	8.75	9.00	9.25	9.50
1	1.0725	1.0750	1.0775	1.0800	1.0825	1.0850	1.0875	1.0900	1.0925	1.0950
2	1.1503	1.1556	1.1610	1.1664	1.1718	1.1772	1.1827	1.1881	1.1936	1.1990
3	1.2336	1.2423	1.2510	1.2597	1.2685	1.2773	1.2861	1.2950	1.3040	1.3129
4	1.3231	1.3355	1.3479	1.3605	1.3731	1.3859	1.3987	1.4116	1.4246	1.4377
5	1.4190	1.4356	1.4524	1.4693	1.4864	1.5037	1.5211	1.5386	1.5563	1.5742
6	1.5219	1.5433	1.5650	1.5869	1.6090	1.6315	1.6542	1.6771	1.7003	1.7238
7	1.6322	1.6590	1.6862	1.7138	1.7418	1.7701	1.7989	1.8280	1.8576	1.8876
8	1.7506	1.7835	1.8169	1.8509	1.8855	1.9206	1.9563	1.9926	2.0294	2.0669
9	1.8775	1.9172	1.9577	1.9990	2.0410	2.0839	2.1275	2.1719	2.2171	2.2632
10	2.0136	2.0610	2.1095	2.1589	2.2094	2.2610	2.3136	2.3674	2.4222	2.4782
11	2.1596	2.2156	2.2730	2.3316	2.3917	2.4532	2.5161	2.5804	2.6463	2.7137
12	2.3162	2.3818	2.4491	2.5182	2.5890	2.6617	2.7362	2.8127	2.8911	2.9715
13	2.4841	2.5604	2.6389	2.7196	2.8026	2.8879	2.9756	3.0658	3.1585	3.2537
14	2.6642	2.7524	2.8434	2.9372	3.0338	3.1334	3.2360	3.3417	3.4506	3.5629
15	2.8573	2.9589	3.0638	3.1722	3.2841	3.3997	3.5192	3.6425	3.7698	3.9013
16	3.0645	3.1808	3.3012	3.4259	3.5551	3.6887	3.8271	3.9703	4.1185	4.2719
17	3.2867	3.4194	3.5571	3.7000	3.8483	4.0023	4.1620	4.3276	4.4995	4.6778
18	3.5249	3.6758	3.8328	3.9960	4.1658	4.3425	4.5261	4.7171	4.9157	5.1222
19	3.7805	3.9515	4.1298	4.3157	4.5095	4.7116	4.9222	5.1417	5.3704	5.6088
20	4.0546	4.2479	4.4499	4.6610	4.8816	5.1120	5.3529	5.6044	5.8672	6.1416
25	5.7535	6.0983	6.4630	6.8485	7.2560	7.6868	8.1420	8.6231	9.1314	9.6684
30	8.1643	8.7550	9.3868	10.0627	10.7854	11.5582	12.3845	13.2677	14.2116	15.2203
35	11.5853	12.5689	13.6334	14.7853	16.0316	17.3796	18.8375	20.4140	22.1182	23.9604
40	16.4396	18.0442	19.8012	21.7245	23.8296	26.1330	28.6530	31.4094	34.4237	37.7194
50	33.1028	37.1898	41.7699	46.9016	52.6496	59.0863	66.2923	74.3575	83.3820	93.4773

Table A-1:

Continued

Year	9.75	10.00	10.50	11.00	11.50	12.00	13.00	14.00	15.00	20.00
1	1.0975	1.1000	1.1050	1.1100	1.1150	1.1200	1.1300	1.1400	1.1500	1.2000
2	1.2045	1.2100	1.2210	1.2321	1.2432	1.2544	1.2769	1.2996	1.3225	1.4400
3	1.3219	1.3310	1.3492	1.3676	1.3862	1.4049	1.4429	1.4815	1.5209	1.7280
4	1.4508	1.4641	1.4909	1.5181	1.5456	1.5735	1.6305	1.6890	1.7490	2.0736
5	1.5923	1.6105	1.6474	1.6851	1.7234	1.7623	1.8424	1.9254	2.0114	2.4883
6	1.7475	1.7716	1.8204	1.8704	1.9215	1.9738	2.0820	2.1950	2.3131	2.9860
7	1.9179	1.9487	2.0116	2.0762	2.1425	2.2107	2.3526	2.5023	2.6600	3.5832
8	2.1049	2.1436	2.2228	2.3045	2.3889	2.4760	2.6584	2.8526	3.0590	4.2998
9	2.3102	2.3579	2.4562	2.5580	2.6636	2.7731	3.0040	3.2519	3.5179	5.1598
10	2.5354	2.5937	2.7141	2.8394	2.9699	3.1058	3.3946	3.7072	4.0456	6.1917
11	2.7826	2.8531	2.9991	3.1518	3.3115	3.4786	3.8359	4.2262	4.6524	7.4301
12	3.0539	3.1384	3.3140	3.4985	3.6923	3.8960	4.3345	4.8179	5.3503	8.9161
13	3.3517	3.4523	3.6619	3.8833	4.1169	4.3635	4.8980	5.4924	6.1528	10.6993
14	3.6784	3.7975	4.0464	4.3104	4.5904	4.8871	5.5348	6.2613	7.0757	12.8392
15	4.0371	4.1772	4.4713	4.7846	5.1183	5.4736	6.2543	7.1379	8.1371	15.4070
16	4.4307	4.5950	4.9408	5.3109	5.7069	6.1304	7.0673	8.1372	9.3576	18.4884
17	4.8627	5.0545	5.4596	5.8951	6.3632	6.8660	7.9861	9.2765	10.7613	22.1861
18	5.3368	5.5599	6.0328	6.5436	7.0949	7.6900	9.0243	10.5752	12.3755	26.6233
19	5.8571	6.1159	6.6663	7.2633	7.9108	8.6128	10.1974	12.0557	14.2318	31.9480
20	6.4282	6.7275	7.3662	8.0623	8.8206	9.6463	11.5231	13.7435	16.3665	38.3376
25	10.2356	10.8347	12.1355	13.5855	15.2010	17.0001	21.2305	26.4619	32.9190	95.3962
30	16.2981	17.4494	19.9926	22.8923	26.1967	29.9599	39.1159	50.9502	66.2118	237.376
35	25.9513	28.1024	32.9367	38.5749	45.1461	52.7996	72.0685	98.1002	133.176	590.668
40	41.3220	45.2592	54.2614	65.0009	77.8027	93.0510	132.782	188.884	267.864	1469.77
50	104.767	177.391	147.270	184.565	231.070	289.002	450.736	700.233	1083.66	9100.44

Table A-2:
Compound Value of a Dollar (Monthly Compounding)

$$\left(1 + \frac{i}{12}\right)^{12n}$$

Year	1.00	2.00	3.00	4.00	5.00	6.00	6.25	6.50	6.75	7.00
1	1.0100	1.0202	1.0304	1.0407	1.0512	1.0617	1.0643	1.0670	1.0696	1.0723
2	1.0202	1.0408	1.0618	1.0831	1.1049	1.1272	1.1328	1.1384	1.1441	1.1498
3	1.0304	1.0618	1.0941	1.1273	1.1615	1.1967	1.2056	1.2147	1.2238	1.2329
4	1.0408	1.0832	1.1273	1.1732	1.2209	1.2705	1.2832	1.2960	1.3090	1.3221
5	1.0512	1.1051	1.1616	1.2210	1.2834	1.3488	1.3657	1.3828	1.4001	1.4176
6	1.0618	1.1274	1.1969	1.2707	1.3490	1.4320	1.4536	1.4754	1.4976	1.5201
7	1.0725	1.1501	1.2334	1.3225	1.4180	1.5204	1.5471	1.5742	1.6019	1.6300
8	1.0833	1.1734	1.2709	1.3764	1.4906	1.6141	1.6466	1.6797	1.7134	1.7478
9	1.0941	1.1970	1.3095	1.4325	1.5668	1.7137	1.7525	1.7922	1.8327	1.8742
10	1.1051	1.2212	1.3494	1.4908	1.6470	1.8194	1.8652	1.9122	1.9603	2.0097
11	1.1162	1.2458	1.3904	1.5516	1.7313	1.9316	1.9852	2.0402	2.0968	2.1549
12	1.1274	1.2710	1.4327	1.6148	1.8198	2.0507	2.1129	2.1769	2.2428	2.3107
13	1.1388	1.2966	1.4763	1.6806	1.9130	2.1772	2.2488	2.3227	2.3990	2.4778
14	1.1502	1.3228	1.5212	1.7490	2.0108	2.3115	2.3934	2.4782	2.5660	2.6569
15	1.1618	1.3495	1.5674	1.8203	2.1137	2.4541	2.5474	2.6442	2.7447	2.8489
16	1.1734	1.3768	1.6151	1.8945	2.2218	2.6055	2.7112	2.8213	2.9358	3.0549
17	1.1852	1.4045	1.6642	1.9716	2.3355	2.7662	2.8856	3.0102	3.1402	3.2757
18	1.1971	1.4329	1.7148	2.0520	2.4550	2.9368	3.0712	3.2118	3.3588	3.5125
19	1.2092	1.4618	1.7670	2.1356	2.5806	3.1179	3.2688	3.4269	3.5927	3.7665
20	1.2213	1.4913	1.8208	2.2226	2.7126	3.3102	3.4790	3.6564	3.8429	4.0387
25	1.2839	1.6480	2.1150	2.7138	3.4813	4.4650	4.7514	5.0562	5.3804	5.7254
30	1.3497	1.8212	2.4568	3.3135	4.4677	6.0226	6.4892	6.9918	7.5332	8.1165
35	1.4189	2.0126	2.8539	4.0458	5.7337	8.1235	8.8624	9.6684	10.5474	11.5061
40	1.4916	2.2241	3.3151	4.9399	7.3584	10.9574	12.1037	13.3696	14.7675	16.3114
50	1.6484	2.7160	4.4733	7.3645	12.1194	19.9359	22.5760	25.5651	28.9491	32.7803

Table A-2:

Continued

Year	7.25	7.50	7.75	8.00	8.25	8.50	8.75	9.00	9.25	9.50
1	1.0750	1.0776	1.0803	1.0830	1.0857	1.0884	1.0911	1.0938	1.0965	1.0992
2	1.1555	1.1613	1.1671	1.1729	1.1787	1.1846	1.1905	1.1964	1.2024	1.2083
3	1.2422	1.2514	1.2608	1.2702	1.2797	1.2893	1.2989	1.3086	1.3184	1.3283
4	1.3353	1.3486	1.3621	1.3757	1.3894	1.4033	1.4173	1.4314	1.4457	1.4601
5	1.4354	1.4533	1.4715	1.4898	1.5085	1.5273	1.5464	1.5657	1.5852	1.6050
6	1.5429	1.5661	1.5896	1.6135	1.6377	1.6623	1.6872	1.7126	1.7382	1.7643
7	1.6586	1.6877	1.7173	1.7474	1.7781	1.8092	1.8409	1.8732	1.9060	1.9394
8	1.7829	1.8187	1.8552	1.8925	1.9304	1.9692	2.0086	2.0489	2.0900	2.1319
9	1.9166	1.9599	2.0042	2.0495	2.0958	2.1432	2.1916	2.2411	2.2917	2.3435
10	2.0602	2.1121	2.1652	2.2196	2.2754	2.3326	2.3913	2.4514	2.5129	2.5761
11	2.2147	2.2760	2.3391	2.4039	2.4704	2.5388	2.6091	2.6813	2.7555	2.8317
12	2.3807	2.4527	2.5269	2.6034	2.6821	2.7632	2.8468	2.9328	3.0215	3.1128
13	2.5591	2.6431	2.7299	2.8195	2.9120	3.0075	3.1061	3.2080	3.3131	3.4217
14	2.7509	2.8483	2.9491	3.0535	3.1615	3.2733	3.3891	3.5089	3.6329	3.7613
15	2.9572	3.0694	3.1860	3.3069	3.4324	3.5626	3.6978	3.8380	3.9836	4.1346
16	3.1788	3.3077	3.4419	3.5814	3.7265	3.8776	4.0346	4.1981	4.3681	4.5449
17	3.4171	3.5645	3.7183	3.8786	4.0459	4.2203	4.4022	4.5919	4.7897	4.9960
18	3.6732	3.8412	4.0169	4.2006	4.3926	4.5933	4.8032	5.0226	5.2520	5.4919
19	3.9486	4.1395	4.3395	4.5492	4.7690	4.9993	5.2408	5.4938	5.7590	6.0369
20	4.2446	4.4608	4.6880	4.9268	5.1777	5.4412	5.7182	6.0091	6.3149	6.6361
25	6.0924	6.4829	6.8983	7.3402	7.8103	8.3104	8.8424	9.4084	10.0105	10.6510
30	8.7448	9.4215	10.1505	10.9357	11.7815	12.6925	13.6737	14.7305	15.8688	17.0949
35	12.5518	13.6922	14.9360	16.2925	17.7719	19.3852	21.1446	23.0633	25.1557	27.4375
40	18.0162	19.8988	21.9777	24.2733	26.8081	29.6070	32.6975	36.1098	39.8774	44.0375
50	37.1176	42.0276	47.5859	53.8780	61.0004	69.0627	78.1885	88.5179	100.209	113.443

Table A-2:
Continued

Year	9.75	10.00	10.50	11.00	11.50	12.00	13.00	14.00	15.00	20.00
1	1.1020	1.1047	1.1102	1.1157	1.1213	1.1268	1.1380	1.1493	1.1608	1.2194
2	1.2144	1.2204	1.2326	1.2448	1.2572	1.2697	1.2951	1.3210	1.3474	1.4869
3	1.3382	1.3482	1.3684	1.3889	1.4097	1.4308	1.4739	1.5183	1.5639	1.8131
4	1.4747	1.4894	1.5192	1.5496	1.5806	1.6122	1.6773	1.7450	1.8154	2.2109
5	1.6250	1.6453	1.6866	1.7289	1.7723	1.8167	1.9089	2.0056	2.1072	2.6960
6	1.7908	1.8176	1.8725	1.9290	1.9872	2.0471	2.1723	2.3051	2.4459	3.2874
7	1.9734	2.0079	2.0788	2.1522	2.2281	2.3067	2.4722	2.6494	2.8391	4.0087
8	2.1746	2.2182	2.3079	2.4013	2.4983	2.5993	2.8134	3.0451	3.2955	4.8881
9	2.3964	2.4504	2.5623	2.6791	2.8013	2.9289	3.2018	3.4998	3.8253	5.9606
10	2.6407	2.7070	2.8446	2.9892	3.1409	3.3004	3.6437	4.0225	4.4402	7.2683
11	2.9100	2.9905	3.1581	3.3351	3.5218	3.7190	4.1467	4.6232	5.1540	8.8628
12	3.2068	3.3037	3.5062	3.7210	3.9489	4.1906	4.7191	5.3136	5.9825	10.8073
13	3.5338	3.6496	3.8925	4.1516	4.4277	4.7221	5.3705	6.1072	6.9442	13.1783
14	3.8942	4.0317	4.3215	4.6320	4.9646	5.3210	6.1117	7.0192	8.0606	16.0695
15	4.2913	4.4539	4.7978	5.1680	5.5666	5.9958	6.9554	8.0675	9.3563	19.5950
16	4.7289	4.9203	5.3265	5.7660	6.2416	6.7562	7.9154	9.2723	10.8604	23.8940
17	5.2112	5.4355	5.9135	6.4333	6.9985	7.6131	9.0080	10.6571	12.6063	29.1361
18	5.7426	6.0047	6.5652	7.1777	7.8471	8.5786	10.2514	12.2486	14.6328	35.5283
19	6.3282	6.6335	7.2887	8.0083	8.7986	9.6666	11.6665	14.0779	16.9851	43.3229
20	6.9735	7.3281	8.0919	8.9350	9.8656	10.8926	13.2768	16.1803	19.7155	52.8275
25	11.3323	12.0570	13.6479	15.4479	17.4845	19.7885	25.3435	32.4513	41.5442	142.421
30	18.4153	19.8374	23.0186	26.7082	30.9872	35.9497	48.3772	65.0847	87.5411	383.964
35	29.9256	32.6387	38.8232	46.1762	54.9178	65.3097	92.3451	130.535	184.465	1035.15
40	48.6302	53.7008	65.4793	79.8347	97.3294	118.648	176.274	261.802	388.701	2790.75
50	128.420	145.371	186.265	238.638	305.707	391.585	642.294	1053.09	1725.92	20283.9

Table A-3:

Compound Value of An Annuity of $1 (Annual Payments, Annual Compounding)

$$1 + (1 + i) + (1 + i)^2 + (1 + i)^3 + \ldots + (1 + i)^{n-i}$$

Year	1.00	2.00	3.00	4.00	5.00	6.00	6.25	6.50	6.75	7.00
1	1.0000	1.0000	1.0000	1.0000	1.0000	1.0000	1.0000	1.0000	1.0000	1.0000
2	2.0100	2.0200	2.0300	2.0400	2.0500	2.0600	2.0625	2.0650	2.0675	2.0700
3	3.0301	3.0604	3.0909	3.126	3.1525	3.1836	3.1914	3.1992	3.2071	3.2149
4	4.0604	4.1216	4.1836	4.2465	4.3101	4.3746	4.3909	4.4072	4.4235	4.4399
5	5.1010	5.2040	5.3091	5.4163	5.5256	5.6371	5.6653	5.6936	5.7221	5.7507
6	6.1520	6.3081	6.4684	6.6330	6.8019	6.9753	7.0194	7.0637	7.1084	7.1533
7	7.2135	7.4343	7.6625	7.8983	8.1420	8.3938	8.4581	8.5229	8.5882	8.6540
8	8.2857	8.5830	8.8923	9.2142	9.5491	9.8975	9.9867	10.077	10.168	10.260
9	9.369	9.755	10.159	10.583	11.027	11.491	11.611	11.732	11.854	11.978
10	10.462	10.950	11.464	12.006	12.578	13.181	13.337	13.494	13.654	13.816
11	11.567	12.169	12.808	13.486	14.207	14.972	15.170	15.372	15.576	15.784
12	12.683	13.412	14.192	15.026	15.917	16.870	17.118	17.731	17.627	17.888
13	13.809	14.680	15.618	16.627	17.713	18.882	19.188	19.500	19.817	20.141
14	14.947	15.974	17.086	18.292	19.599	21.015	21.387	21.767	22.155	22.550
15	16.097	17.293	18.599	20.024	21.579	23.276	23.724	24.182	24.650	25.129
16	17.258	18.639	20.157	21.825	23.657	25.673	26.207	26.754	27.314	27.888
17	18.430	20.012	21.762	23.698	25.840	28.213	28.845	29.493	30.158	30.840
18	19.615	21.41	23.414	25.645	28.132	30.906	31.648	32.410	33.194	33.999
19	20.811	22.841	25.117	27.671	30.539	33.760	34.626	35.517	36.434	37.379
20	22.019	24.297	26.870	29.778	33.066	36.786	37.790	38.825	39.894	40.995
25	28.243	32.030	36.459	41.646	47.727	54.865	56.836	58.888	61.024	63.249
30	34.785	40.568	47.575	56.085	66.439	79.058	82.625	86.375	90.317	94.461
35	41.660	49.994	60.462	73.652	90.320	111.435	117.547	124.035	130.923	138.237
40	48.886	60.402	75.401	95.026	120.800	154.762	164.833	175.632	187.213	199.635
50	64.463	84.579	112.797	152.667	209.348	290.336	315.564	343.180	373.416	406.529

Year	7.25	7.50	7.75	8.00	8.25	8.50	8.75	9.00	9.25	9.50
1	1.0000	1.0000	1.0000	1.0000	1.0000	1.0000	1.0000	1.0000	1.0000	1.0000
2	2.0725	2.0750	2.0775	2.0800	2.0825	2.0850	2.0875	2.0900	2.0925	2.0950
3	3.2228	3.2306	3.2385	3.2464	3.2543	3.2622	3.2702	3.2781	3.2861	3.2940
4	4.4564	4.4729	4.4895	4.5061	4.5228	4.5395	4.5563	4.5731	4.5900	4.6070
5	5.7795	5.8084	5.8374	5.8666	5.8959	5.9254	5.9550	5.9847	6.0146	6.0446
6	7.1985	7.2440	7.2898	7.3359	7.3823	7.4290	7.4760	7.5233	7.5709	7.6189
7	8.7204	8.7873	8.8548	8.9228	8.9914	9.0605	9.1302	9.2004	9.2713	9.3426
8	10.353	10.446	10.541	10.637	10.733	10.831	10.929	11.028	11.129	11.230
9	12.103	12.230	12.358	12.488	12.619	12.751	12.885	13.021	13.158	13.297
10	13.981	14.147	14.316	14.487	14.660	14.835	15.013	15.193	15.375	15.560
11	15.994	16.208	16.425	16.645	16.869	17.096	17.326	17.560	17.798	18.039
12	18.154	18.424	18.698	18.977	19.261	19.549	19.843	20.141	20.444	20.752
13	20.470	20.806	21.147	21.495	21.850	22.211	22.579	22.953	23.335	23.724
14	22.954	23.366	23.786	24.215	24.652	25.099	25.554	26.019	26.493	26.977
15	25.618	26.118	26.630	27.152	27.686	28.232	28.790	29.361	29.944	30.540
16	28.476	29.077	29.693	30.324	30.970	31.632	32.310	33.003	33.714	34.442
17	31.540	32.258	32.995	33.750	34.525	35.321	36.137	36.974	37.832	38.713
18	34.827	35.677	36.552	37.450	38.374	39.323	40.299	41.301	42.332	43.391
19	38.352	39.353	40.384	41.446	42.540	43.665	44.825	46.018	47.248	48.513
20	42.132	43.305	44.514	45.762	47.049	48.377	49.747	51.160	52.618	54.122
25	65.566	67.978	70.490	73.106	75.830	78.668	81.623	84.701	87.907	91.246
30	98.818	103.399	108.217	113.283	118.611	124.215	130.108	136.308	142.828	149.687
35	146.004	154.252	163.012	172.317	182.201	192.702	203.858	215.711	228.305	241.688
40	212.960	227.257	242.596	259.057	276.722	295.682	316.035	337.882	361.338	386.520
50	442.798	482.530	526.064	573.770	626.056	683.368	746.198	815.084	890.616	973.445

Table A-3:

Continued

Year	9.75	10.00	10.50	11.00	11.50	12.00	13.00	14.00	15.00	20.00
1	1.0000	1.0000	1.0000	1.0000	1.0000	1.0000	1.0000	1.0000	1.0000	1.0000
2	2.0975	2.1000	2.1050	2.1100	2.1150	2.1200	2.1300	2.1400	2.1500	2.2000
3	3.3020	3.3100	3.3260	3.3421	3.3582	3.3744	3.4069	3.4396	3.4725	3.6400
4	4.6240	4.6410	4.6753	4.7097	4.7444	4.7793	4.8498	4.9211	4.9934	5.3680
5	6.0748	6.1051	6.1662	6.2278	6.2900	6.3528	6.4803	6.6101	6.7424	7.4416
6	7.6671	7.7156	7.8136	7.9129	8.0134	8.1152	8.3227	8.5355	8.7537	9.9299
7	9.4146	9.4872	9.6340	9.7833	9.9349	10.089	10.405	10.730	11.067	12.916
8	11.333	11.436	11.646	11.856	12.077	12.300	12.757	13.233	13.727	16.499
9	13.437	13.579	13.868	14.164	14.466	14.776	15.416	16.085	16.786	20.799
10	15.748	15.937	16.325	16.722	17.130	17.549	18.420	19.337	20.304	25.959
11	18.283	18.531	19.039	19.561	20.100	20.655	21.814	23.045	24.349	32.150
12	21.066	21.384	22.038	22.713	23.411	24.133	25.650	27.271	29.002	39.581
13	24.120	24.523	25.352	26.212	27.104	28.029	29.985	32.089	34.352	48.497
14	27.471	27.975	29.014	30.095	31.221	32.393	34.883	37.581	40.505	59.196
15	31.150	31.772	33.060	34.405	35.811	37.280	40.417	43.842	47.580	72.035
16	35.187	35.950	37.531	39.190	40.929	42.753	46.672	50.980	55.717	87.442
17	39.617	40.545	42.472	44.501	46.636	48.884	53.739	59.118	65.075	105.931
18	44.480	45.599	47.932	50.396	52.999	55.750	61.725	68.394	75.836	128.117
19	49.817	51.159	53.965	56.939	60.094	63.440	70.749	78.969	88.212	154.740
20	55.674	57.275	60.631	64.203	68.005	72.052	80.947	91.025	102.444	186.688
25	94.724	98.347	106.052	114.413	123.487	133.334	155.620	181.871	212.793	471.981
30	156.903	164.494	180.882	199.021	219.101	241.333	293.199	356.787	434.745	1181.88
35	255.910	271.024	304.159	341.590	383.879	431.664	546.681	693.573	881.170	2948.34
40	413.559	442.592	507.252	581.826	667.850	767.092	1013.70	1342.03	1779.09	7343.86
50	1064.28	1163.91	1393.05	1668.77	2000.61	2400.02	3459.51	4994.52	7217.72	45497.2

Table A-4:

Compound Value of an Annuity of $1 (Monthly Payments, Monthly Compounding)

$$1 + \left(1 + \frac{i}{12}\right) + \left(1 + \frac{i}{12}\right)^2 + \left(1 + \frac{i}{12}\right)^3 + \ldots + \left(1 + \frac{i}{12}\right)^3 + \ldots + \left(1 + \frac{i}{12}\right)^{12n-1}$$

Year	1.00	2.00	3.00	4.00	5.00	6.00	6.25	6.50
1	12.0552	12.1106	12.1664	12.2225	12.2789	12.3356	12.3498	12.3640
2	24.2314	24.4657	24.7028	24.9429	25.1859	25.4320	25.4939	25.5561
3	36.5300	37.0701	37.6206	38.1816	38.7533	39.3361	39.4835	39.6317
4	48.9521	49.9290	50.9312	51.9596	53.0149	54.0978	54.3730	54.6499
5	61.4990	63.0474	64.6467	66.2990	68.0061	69.7700	70.2201	70.6740
6	74.1720	76.4305	78.7794	81.2226	83.7642	86.4088	87.0866	87.7712
7	86.9723	90.0838	93.3419	96.7541	100.329	104.074	105.038	106.013
8	99.9012	104.013	108.347	112.919	117.740	122.829	124.144	125.477
9	112.960	118.223	123.809	129.741	136.043	142.740	144.479	146.245
10	126.150	132.720	139.741	147.250	155.282	163.879	166.122	168.403
11	139.472	147.509	156.158	165.471	175.506	186.323	189.157	192.045
12	152.929	162.597	173.074	184.435	196.764	210.150	213.674	217.271
13	166.520	177.990	190.505	204.172	219.109	235.447	239.767	244.186
14	180.248	193.693	208.466	224.713	242.598	262.305	267.539	272.904
15	194.114	209.713	226.973	246.090	267.289	290.819	297.098	303.545
16	208.119	226.057	246.043	268.339	293.243	321.091	328.557	336.238
17	222.265	242.730	265.693	291.494	320.524	353.231	362.040	371.120
18	236.553	259.740	285.940	315.592	349.202	387.353	397.677	408.339
19	250.985	277.093	306.804	340.673	379.347	423.580	435.606	448.050
20	265.561	294.797	328.302	366.774	411.033	462.041	475.975	490.421
25	340.670	388.821	446.008	514.129	595.509	692.993	720.273	748.836
30	419.628	492.725	582.737	694.049	832.258	1004.51	1053.92	1106.18
35	502.633	607.548	741.563	913.730	1136.09	1424.71	1509.59	1600.31
40	589.891	734.435	926.059	1181.96	1526.02	1991.49	2131.91	2283.62
50	778.053	1029.61	1389.32	1909.35	2668.65	3787.18	4142.59	4535.09

Table A-4:
Continued

Year	6.75	7.00	7.25	7.50	7.75	8.00	8.25	8.50
1	12.3783	12.3926	12.4069	12.4212	12.4356	12.4499	12.4643	12.4787
2	25.6185	25.6810	25.7438	25.8067	25.8699	25.9332	25.9967	26.0604
3	39.7805	39.9301	40.0804	40.2314	40.3831	40.5356	40.6887	40.8427
4	54.9287	55.2092	55.4916	55.7759	56.0619	56.3499	56.6397	56.9315
5	71.1315	71.5929	72.0581	72.5271	73.0000	73.4768	73.9576	74.4424
6	88.4626	89.1609	89.8663	90.5788	91.2984	92.0253	92.7595	93.5012
7	107.000	107.999	109.009	110.032	111.066	112.113	113.173	114.245
8	126.829	128.199	129.587	130.995	132.422	133.869	135.335	136.821
9	148.038	149.859	151.708	153.586	155.493	157.429	159.396	161.394
10	170.724	173.085	175.487	177.930	180.416	180.946	185.520	188.138
11	194.989	197.990	201.048	204.165	207.342	210.580	213.882	217.247
12	220.944	224.695	228.525	232.436	236.430	240.508	244.674	248.928
13	248.706	253.331	258.061	262.901	267.853	272.920	278.105	283.410
14	278.402	284.037	289.812	295.732	301.801	308.022	314.400	320.939
15	310.164	316.962	323.943	331.112	338.475	346.038	353.806	361.786
16	344.139	352.268	360.632	369.238	378.095	387.209	396.589	406.243
17	380.479	390.126	400.071	410.324	420.896	431.797	443.038	454.630
18	419.349	430.721	442.467	454.600	467.135	480.086	493.467	507.294
19	460.926	474.250	488.040	502.313	517.088	532.382	548.217	564.613
20	505.397	520.926	537.030	553.730	571.052	589.020	607.660	626.998
25	778.746	810.071	842.884	877.260	913.279	951.025	990.587	1032.06
30	1161.46	1219.97	1281.89	1347.44	1416.85	1490.36	1568.22	1650.70
35	1697.31	1801.05	1912.02	2030.76	2157.84	2293.88	2439.55	2595.56
40	2447.57	2624.81	2816.48	3023.82	3248.17	3491.00	3753.91	4038.64
50	4968.74	5448.06	5978.08	6564.42	7213.31	7931.70	8727.34	9608.86

Table A-4:
Continued

Year	8.75	9.00	9.25	9.50	9.75	10.00	10.50	11.00
1	12.4931	12.5076	12.5221	12.5365	12.5510	12.5656	12.5947	12.6239
2	26.1244	26.1885	26.2528	26.3173	26.3820	26.4469	26.5773	26.7086
3	40.9973	41.1527	41.3089	41.4658	41.6234	41.7818	42.1009	42.4231
4	57.2251	57.5207	57.8182	58.1177	58.4191	58.7225	59.3353	59.9562
5	74.9312	75.4241	75.9211	76.4223	76.9276	77.4371	78.4689	79.5181
6	94.2503	95.0070	95.7714	96.5435	97.3235	98.1113	99.7112	101.344
7	115.329	116.427	117.538	118.662	119.799	120.950	123.294	125.695
8	138.328	139.856	141.405	142.975	144.567	146.181	149.477	152.864
9	163.423	165.483	167.576	169.702	171.861	174.054	178.544	183.177
10	190.803	193.514	196.273	199.081	201.938	204.845	210.815	216.998
11	220.677	224.175	227.740	231.376	235.082	238.861	246.642	254.733
12	253.273	257.711	262.245	266.876	271.606	276.438	286.418	296.834
13	288.839	294.394	300.080	305.899	311.855	317.950	330.577	343.807
14	327.644	334.518	341.567	348.795	356.208	363.809	379.602	396.216
15	369.984	378.405	387.058	395.949	405.084	414.471	434.030	454.690
16	416.181	426.410	436.941	447.782	458.944	470.437	494.456	519.930
17	466.586	478.918	491.638	504.760	518.297	532.263	561.542	592.720
18	521.583	536.351	551.615	567.393	583.703	600.564	636.021	673.932
19	581.591	599.172	617.381	636.242	655.778	676.016	718.707	764.543
20	647.064	667.886	689.495	711.924	735.204	759.370	810.506	865.639
25	1075.53	1121.12	1168.93	1219.07	1271.66	1326.84	1445.47	1576.14
30	1738.11	1830.74	1928.93	2033.04	2143.42	2260.49	2516.41	2804.52
35	2762.69	2941.78	3133.71	3339.47	3560.07	3796.65	4322.65	4928.31
40	4347.09	4681.31	5043.56	5436.31	5862.17	6324.10	7369.06	8600.15
50	10585.9	11669.1	12870.4	14203.3	15682.4	17324.4	21173.1	25924.1

Table A-4:
Continued

Year	11.50	12.00	13.00	14.00	15.00	20.00
1	12.6531	12.6825	12.7415	12.8007	12.8604	13.1635
2	26.8406	26.9735	27.2417	27.5132	27.7881	29.2149
3	42.7484	43.0769	43.7434	44.4228	45.1155	48.7878
4	60.5852	61.2226	62.5228	63.8577	65.2284	72.6549
5	80.5849	81.6697	83.8945	86.1951	88.5745	101.758
6	103.010	104.710	108.216	111.868	115.674	137.247
7	128.154	130.672	135.895	141.376	147.129	180.521
8	156.347	159.927	167.394	175.290	183.641	233.289
9	187.958	192.893	203.242	214.269	226.023	297.634
10	223.403	230.039	244.037	259.069	275.217	376.095
11	263.146	271.896	290.464	310.560	332.320	471.771
12	307.708	319.062	343.298	369.740	398.602	588.436
13	357.674	372.209	403.426	437.758	475.540	730.698
14	413.698	432.097	471.854	515.935	564.845	904.170
15	476.516	499.581	549.726	605.787	668.507	1115.70
16	546.952	575.622	638.348	709.057	788.833	1373.64
17	625.928	661.308	739.202	827.749	928.502	1688.17
18	714.481	757.861	853.977	964.168	1090.62	2071.70
19	813.771	866.660	984.596	1120.96	1278.81	2539.37
20	925.102	989.256	1133.24	1301.17	1497.24	3109.65
25	1720.12	1878.85	2247.09	2695.83	3243.53	8485.28
30	3129.10	3494.97	4373.28	5492.98	6923.29	22977.8
35	5626.21	6430.97	8431.85	11103.0	14677.2	62049.3
40	10051.8	11764.8	16179.1	22354.4	31016.1	167385.
50	31795.5	39058.4	59196.4	90179.1	137993.	1216971.

Table A-5:

Present Value of a Dollar (Annual Compounding)

$$\frac{1}{(1 + i)^n}$$

Year	1.00	2.00	3.00	4.00	5.00	6.00	6.25	6.50	6.75	7.00
1	0.9901	0.9804	0.9709	0.9615	0.9524	0.9434	0.9412	0.9390	0.9368	0.9346
2	0.9803	0.9612	0.9426	0.9246	0.9070	0.8900	0.8858	0.8817	0.8775	0.8734
3	0.9706	0.9423	0.9151	0.8890	0.8638	0.8396	0.8337	0.8278	0.8220	0.8163
4	0.9610	0.9238	0.8885	0.8548	0.8227	0.7921	0.7847	0.7773	0.7701	0.7629
5	0.9515	0.9057	0.8626	0.8219	0.7835	0.7473	0.7385	0.7299	0.7214	0.7130
6	0.9420	0.8880	0.8375	0.7903	0.7462	0.7050	0.6951	0.6853	0.6758	0.6663
7	0.9327	0.8706	0.8131	0.7599	0.7107	0.6651	0.6542	0.6435	0.6330	0.6227
8	0.9235	0.8535	0.7894	0.7307	0.6768	0.6274	0.6157	0.6042	0.5930	0.5820
9	0.9143	0.8368	0.7664	0.7026	0.6446	0.5919	0.5795	0.5674	0.5555	0.5439
10	0.9053	0.8203	0.7441	0.6756	0.6139	0.5584	0.5454	0.5327	0.5204	0.5083
11	0.8963	0.8043	0.7224	0.6496	0.5847	0.5268	0.5133	0.5002	0.4875	0.4751
12	0.8874	0.7885	0.7014	0.6246	0.5568	0.4970	0.4831	0.4697	0.4567	0.4440
13	0.8787	0.7730	0.6810	0.6006	0.5303	0.4688	0.4547	0.4410	0.4278	0.4150
14	0.8700	0.7579	0.6611	0.5775	0.5051	0.4423	0.4280	0.4141	0.4007	0.3878
15	0.8613	0.7430	0.6419	0.5553	0.4810	0.4173	0.4028	0.3888	0.3754	0.3624
16	0.8528	0.7284	0.6232	0.5339	0.4581	0.3936	0.3791	0.3651	0.3517	0.3387
17	0.8444	0.7142	0.6050	0.5134	0.4363	0.3714	0.3568	0.3428	0.3294	0.3166
18	0.8360	0.7002	0.5874	0.4936	0.4155	0.3503	0.3358	0.3219	0.3086	0.2959
19	0.8277	0.6864	0.5703	0.4746	0.3957	0.3305	0.3160	0.3022	0.2891	0.2765
20	0.8195	0.6730	0.5537	0.4564	0.3769	0.3118	0.2975	0.2838	0.2708	0.2584
25	0.7798	0.6095	0.4776	0.3751	0.2953	0.2330	0.2197	0.2071	0.1953	0.1842
30	0.7419	0.5521	0.4120	0.3083	0.2314	0.1741	0.1622	0.1512	0.1409	0.1314
35	0.7059	0.5000	0.3554	0.2534	0.1813	0.1301	0.1198	0.1103	0.1017	0.0937
40	0.6717	0.4529	0.3066	0.2083	0.1420	0.0972	0.0885	0.0805	0.0733	0.0668
50	0.6080	0.3715	0.2281	0.1407	0.0872	0.0543	0.0483	0.0429	0.0382	0.0339

Table A-5:
Continued

Year	7.25	7.50	7.75	8.00	8.25	8.50	8.75	9.00	9.25	9.50
1	0.9324	0.9302	0.9281	0.9259	0.9238	0.9217	0.9195	0.9174	0.9153	0.9132
2	0.8694	0.8653	0.8613	0.8573	0.8534	0.8495	0.8456	0.8417	0.8378	0.8340
3	0.8106	0.8050	0.7994	0.7938	0.7883	0.7829	0.7775	0.7722	0.7669	0.7617
4	0.7558	0.7488	0.7419	0.7350	0.7283	0.7216	0.7150	0.7084	0.7020	0.6956
5	0.7047	0.6966	0.6885	0.6806	0.6728	0.6650	0.6574	0.6499	0.6425	0.6352
6	0.6571	0.6480	0.6390	0.6302	0.6215	0.6129	0.6045	0.5963	0.5881	0.5801
7	0.6127	0.6028	0.5930	0.5835	0.5741	0.5649	0.5559	0.5470	0.5383	0.5298
8	0.5712	0.5607	0.5504	0.5403	0.5304	0.5207	0.5112	0.5019	0.4928	0.4838
9	0.5326	0.5216	0.5108	0.5002	0.4899	0.4799	0.4700	0.4604	0.4510	0.4418
10	0.4966	0.4852	0.4741	0.4632	0.4526	0.4423	0.4322	0.4224	0.4128	0.4035
11	0.4631	0.4513	0.4400	0.4289	0.4181	0.4076	0.3974	0.3875	0.3779	0.3685
12	0.4318	0.4199	0.4083	0.3971	0.3862	0.3757	0.3655	0.3555	0.3459	0.3365
13	0.4026	0.3906	0.3789	0.3677	0.3568	0.3463	0.3361	0.3262	0.3166	0.3073
14	0.3754	0.3633	0.3517	0.3405	0.3296	0.3191	0.3090	0.2992	0.2898	0.2807
15	0.3500	0.3380	0.3264	0.3152	0.3045	0.2941	0.2842	0.2745	0.2653	0.2563
16	0.3263	0.3144	0.3029	0.2919	0.2813	0.2711	0.2613	0.2519	0.2428	0.2341
17	0.3043	0.2925	0.2811	0.2703	0.2599	0.2499	0.2403	0.2311	0.2222	0.2138
18	0.2837	0.2720	0.2609	0.2502	0.2400	0.2303	0.2209	0.2120	0.2034	0.1952
19	0.2645	0.2531	0.2421	0.2317	0.2218	0.2122	0.2032	0.1945	0.1862	0.1783
20	0.2466	0.2354	0.2247	0.2145	0.2049	0.1956	0.1868	0.1784	0.1704	0.1628
25	0.1738	0.1640	0.1547	0.1460	0.1378	0.1301	0.1228	0.1160	0.1095	0.1034
30	0.1225	0.1142	0.1065	0.0994	0.0927	0.0865	0.0807	0.0754	0.0704	0.0657
35	0.0863	0.0796	0.0733	0.0676	0.0624	0.0575	0.0531	0.0490	0.0452	0.0417
40	0.0608	0.0554	0.0505	0.0460	0.0420	0.0383	0.0349	0.0318	0.0290	0.0265
50	0.0302	0.0269	0.0239	0.0213	0.0190	0.0169	0.0151	0.0134	0.0120	0.0107

Table A-5:

Continued

Year	9.75	10.00	10.50	11.00	11.50	12.00	13.00	14.00	15.00	20.00
1	0.9112	0.9091	0.9050	0.9009	0.8969	0.8929	0.8850	0.8772	0.8696	0.8333
2	0.8302	0.8264	0.8190	0.8116	0.8044	0.7972	0.7831	0.7695	0.7561	0.6944
3	0.7565	0.7513	0.7412	0.7312	0.7214	0.7118	0.6931	0.6750	0.6575	0.5787
4	0.6893	0.6830	0.6707	0.6587	0.6470	0.6355	0.6133	0.5921	0.5718	0.4823
5	0.6280	0.6209	0.6070	0.5935	0.5803	0.5674	0.5428	0.5194	0.4972	0.4019
6	0.5722	0.5645	0.5493	0.5346	0.5204	0.5066	0.4803	0.4556	0.4323	0.3349
7	0.5214	0.5132	0.4971	0.4817	0.4667	0.4523	0.4251	0.3996	0.3759	0.2791
8	0.4751	0.4665	0.4499	0.4339	0.4186	0.4039	0.3762	0.3506	0.3269	0.2326
9	0.4329	0.4241	0.4071	0.3909	0.3754	0.3606	0.3329	0.3075	0.2843	0.1938
10	0.3944	0.3855	0.3684	0.3522	0.3367	0.3220	0.2946	0.2697	0.2472	0.1615
11	0.3594	0.3505	0.3334	0.3173	0.3020	0.2875	0.2607	0.2366	0.2149	0.1346
12	0.3275	0.3186	0.3018	0.2858	0.2708	0.2567	0.2307	0.2076	0.1869	0.1122
13	0.2984	0.2897	0.2731	0.2575	0.2429	0.2292	0.2042	0.1821	0.1625	0.0935
14	0.2719	0.2633	0.2471	0.2320	0.2178	0.2046	0.1807	0.1597	0.1413	0.0779
15	0.2477	0.2394	0.2236	0.2090	0.1954	0.1827	0.1599	0.1401	0.1229	0.0649
16	0.2257	0.2176	0.2024	0.1883	0.1752	0.1631	0.1415	0.1229	0.1069	0.0541
17	0.2056	0.1978	0.1832	0.1696	0.1572	0.1456	0.1252	0.1078	0.0929	0.0451
18	0.1874	0.1799	0.1658	0.1528	0.1409	0.1300	0.1108	0.0946	0.0808	0.0376
19	0.1707	0.1635	0.1500	0.1377	0.1264	0.1161	0.0981	0.0829	0.0703	0.0313
20	0.1556	0.1486	0.1358	0.1240	0.1134	0.1037	0.0868	0.0728	0.0611	0.0261
25	0.0977	0.0923	0.0824	0.0736	0.0658	0.0588	0.0471	0.0378	0.0304	0.0105
30	0.0614	0.0573	0.0500	0.0437	0.0382	0.0334	0.0256	0.0196	0.0151	0.0042
35	0.0385	0.0356	0.0304	0.0259	0.0222	0.0189	0.0139	0.0102	0.0075	0.0017
40	0.0242	0.0221	0.0184	0.0154	0.0129	0.0107	0.0075	0.0053	0.0037	0.0007
50	0.0095	0.0085	0.0068	0.0054	0.0043	0.0035	0.0022	0.0014	0.0009	0.0001

Table A-6:

Present Value of A Dollar (Monthly Compounding)

$$\dfrac{1}{\left(1 + \dfrac{i}{12}\right)^{12n}}$$

Year	1.00	2.00	3.00	4.00	5.00	6.00	6.25	6.50	6.75	7.00
1	0.9901	0.9802	0.9705	0.9609	0.9513	0.9419	0.9396	0.9372	0.9349	0.9326
2	0.9802	0.9608	0.9418	0.9232	0.9050	0.8872	0.8828	0.8784	0.8740	0.8697
3	0.9705	0.9418	0.9140	0.8871	0.8610	0.8356	0.8294	0.8233	0.8172	0.8111
4	0.9608	0.9232	0.8871	0.8524	0.8191	0.7871	0.7793	0.7716	0.7640	0.7564
5	0.9512	0.9049	0.8609	0.8190	0.7792	0.7414	0.7322	0.7232	0.7142	0.7054
6	0.9418	0.8870	0.8355	0.7869	0.7413	0.6983	0.6880	0.6778	0.6677	0.6578
7	0.9324	0.8695	0.8108	0.7561	0.7052	0.6577	0.6464	0.6352	0.6243	0.6135
8	0.9231	0.8523	0.7869	0.7265	0.6709	0.6195	0.6073	0.5954	0.5836	0.5721
9	0.9140	0.8354	0.7636	0.6981	0.6382	0.5835	0.5706	0.5580	0.5456	0.5336
10	0.9049	0.8189	0.7411	0.6708	0.6072	0.5496	0.5361	0.5230	0.5101	0.4976
11	0.8959	0.8027	0.7192	0.6445	0.5776	0.5177	0.5037	0.4901	0.4769	0.4641
12	0.8870	0.7868	0.6980	0.6193	0.5495	0.4876	0.4733	0.4594	0.4459	0.4328
13	0.8781	0.7712	0.6774	0.5950	0.5228	0.4593	0.4447	0.4305	0.4168	0.4036
14	0.8694	0.7560	0.6574	0.5717	0.4973	0.4326	0.4178	0.4035	0.3897	0.3764
15	0.8608	0.7410	0.6380	0.5494	0.4731	0.4075	0.3926	0.3782	0.3643	0.3510
16	0.8522	0.7263	0.6192	0.5279	0.4501	0.3838	0.3688	0.3544	0.3406	0.3273
17	0.8437	0.7120	0.6009	0.5072	0.4282	0.3615	0.3465	0.3322	0.3185	0.3053
18	0.8353	0.6979	0.5831	0.4873	0.4073	0.3405	0.3256	0.3113	0.2977	0.2847
19	0.8270	0.6841	0.5659	0.4683	0.3875	0.3207	0.3059	0.2918	0.2783	0.2655
20	0.8188	0.6705	0.5492	0.4499	0.3686	0.3021	0.2874	0.2735	0.2602	0.2476
25	0.7789	0.6068	0.4728	0.3685	0.2873	0.2240	0.2105	0.1978	0.1859	0.1747
30	0.7409	0.5491	0.4070	0.3018	0.2238	0.1660	0.1541	0.1430	0.1327	0.1232
35	0.7048	0.4969	0.3504	0.2472	0.1744	0.1231	0.1128	0.1034	0.0948	0.0869
40	0.6704	0.4496	0.3016	0.2024	0.1359	0.0913	0.0826	0.0748	0.0677	0.0613
50	0.6067	0.3682	0.2235	0.1358	0.0825	0.0502	0.0443	0.0391	0.0345	0.0305

Table A-6:

Continued

Year	7.25	7.50	7.75	8.00	8.25	8.50	8.75	9.00	9.25	9.50
1	0.9303	0.9280	0.9257	0.9234	0.9211	0.9188	0.9165	0.9142	0.9120	0.9097
2	0.8654	0.8611	0.8568	0.8526	0.8484	0.8442	0.8400	0.8358	0.8317	0.8276
3	0.8051	0.7991	0.7931	0.7873	0.7814	0.7756	0.7699	0.7641	0.7585	0.7529
4	0.7489	0.7415	0.7342	0.7269	0.7197	0.7126	0.7056	0.6986	0.6917	0.6849
5	0.6967	0.6881	0.6796	0.6712	0.6629	0.6548	0.6467	0.6387	0.6308	0.6230
6	0.6481	0.6385	0.6291	0.6198	0.6106	0.6016	0.5927	0.5839	0.5753	0.5668
7	0.6029	0.5925	0.5823	0.5723	0.5624	0.5527	0.5432	0.5338	0.5247	0.5156
8	0.5609	0.5498	0.5390	0.5284	0.5180	0.5078	0.4978	0.4881	0.4785	0.4691
9	0.5218	0.5102	0.4989	0.4879	0.4771	0.4666	0.4563	0.4462	0.4364	0.4267
10	0.4854	0.4735	0.4619	0.4505	0.4395	0.4287	0.4182	0.4079	0.3979	0.3882
11	0.4515	0.4394	0.4275	0.4160	0.4048	0.3939	0.3833	0.3730	0.3629	0.3531
12	0.4200	0.4077	0.3957	0.3841	0.3728	0.3619	0.3513	0.3410	0.3310	0.3213
13	0.3908	0.3783	0.3663	0.3547	0.3434	0.3325	0.3219	0.3117	0.3018	0.2923
14	0.3635	0.3511	0.3391	0.3275	0.3163	0.3055	0.2951	0.2850	0.2753	0.2659
15	0.3382	0.3258	0.3139	0.3024	0.2913	0.2807	0.2704	0.2605	0.2510	0.2419
16	0.3146	0.3023	0.2905	0.2792	0.2683	0.2579	0.2479	0.2382	0.2289	0.2200
17	0.2926	0.2805	0.2689	0.2578	0.2472	0.2370	0.2272	0.2178	0.2088	0.2002
18	0.2722	0.2603	0.2489	0.2381	0.2277	0.2177	0.2082	0.1991	0.1904	0.1821
19	0.2533	0.2416	0.2304	0.2198	0.2097	0.2000	0.1908	0.1820	0.1736	0.1656
20	0.2356	0.2242	0.2133	0.2030	0.1931	0.1838	0.1749	0.1664	0.1584	0.1507
25	0.1641	0.1543	0.1450	0.1362	0.1280	0.1203	0.1131	0.1063	0.0999	0.0939
30	0.1144	0.1061	0.0985	0.0914	0.0849	0.0788	0.0731	0.0679	0.0630	0.0585
35	0.0797	0.0730	0.0670	0.0614	0.0563	0.0516	0.0473	0.0434	0.0398	0.0364
40	0.0555	0.0503	0.0455	0.0412	0.0373	0.0338	0.0306	0.0277	0.0251	0.0227
50	0.0269	0.0238	0.0210	0.0186	0.0164	0.0145	0.0128	0.0113	0.0100	0.0088

Table A-6:
Continued

Year	9.75	10.00	10.50	11.00	11.50	12.00	13.00	14.00	15.00	20.00
1	0.9075	0.9052	0.9007	0.8963	0.8919	0.8874	0.8787	0.8701	0.8615	0.8201
2	0.8235	0.8194	0.8113	0.8033	0.7954	0.7876	0.7721	0.7570	0.7422	0.6725
3	0.7473	0.7417	0.7308	0.7200	0.7094	0.6989	0.6785	0.6586	0.6394	0.5515
4	0.6781	0.6714	0.6582	0.6453	0.6327	0.6203	0.5962	0.5731	0.5509	0.4523
5	0.6154	0.6078	0.5929	0.5784	0.5642	0.5504	0.5239	0.4986	0.4746	0.3709
6	0.5584	0.5502	0.5341	0.5184	0.5032	0.4885	0.4603	0.4338	0.4088	0.3042
7	0.5067	0.4980	0.4810	0.4646	0.4488	0.4335	0.4045	0.3774	0.3522	0.2495
8	0.4599	0.4508	0.4333	0.4164	0.4003	0.3847	0.3554	0.3284	0.3034	0.2046
9	0.4173	0.4081	0.3903	0.3733	0.3570	0.3414	0.3123	0.2857	0.2614	0.1678
10	0.3787	0.3694	0.3515	0.3345	0.3184	0.3030	0.2744	0.2486	0.2252	0.1376
11	0.3436	0.3344	0.3166	0.2998	0.2839	0.2689	0.2412	0.2163	0.1940	0.1128
12	0.3118	0.3027	0.2852	0.2687	0.2532	0.2386	0.2119	0.1882	0.1672	0.0925
13	0.2830	0.2740	0.2569	0.2409	0.2259	0.2118	0.1862	0.1637	0.1440	0.0759
14	0.2568	0.2480	0.2314	0.2159	0.2014	0.1879	0.1636	0.1425	0.1241	0.0622
15	0.2330	0.2245	0.2084	0.1935	0.1796	0.1668	0.1438	0.1240	0.1069	0.0510
16	0.2115	0.2032	0.1877	0.1734	0.1602	0.1480	0.1263	0.1078	0.0921	0.0419
17	0.1919	0.1840	0.1691	0.1554	0.1429	0.1314	0.1110	0.0938	0.0793	0.0343
18	0.1741	0.1665	0.1523	0.1393	0.1274	0.1166	0.0975	0.0816	0.0683	0.0281
19	0.1580	0.1508	0.1372	0.1249	0.1137	0.1034	0.0857	0.0710	0.0589	0.0231
20	0.1434	0.1365	0.1236	0.1119	0.1014	0.0918	0.0753	0.0618	0.0507	0.0189
25	0.0882	0.0829	0.0733	0.0647	0.0572	0.0505	0.0395	0.0308	0.0241	0.0070
30	0.0543	0.0504	0.0434	0.0374	0.0323	0.0278	0.0207	0.0154	0.0114	0.0026
35	0.0334	0.0306	0.0258	0.0217	0.0182	0.0153	0.0108	0.0077	0.0054	0.0010
40	0.0206	0.0186	0.0153	0.0125	0.0103	0.0084	0.0057	0.0038	0.0026	0.0004
50	0.0078	0.0069	0.0054	0.0042	0.0033	0.0026	0.0016	0.0009	0.0006	0.0000

Table A-7:

Present Value of an Annuity of $1 (Annual Payments, Annual Compounding)

$$\frac{1}{(1+i)} + \frac{1}{(1+i)^2} + \frac{1}{(1+i)^3} + \cdots + \frac{1}{(1+i)^n}$$

Year	1.00	2.00	3.00	4.00	5.00	6.00	6.25	6.50	6.75	7.00
1	0.9901	0.9804	0.9709	0.9615	0.9524	0.9434	0.9412	0.9390	0.9368	0.9340
2	1.9704	1.9416	1.9135	1.8861	1.8594	1.8334	1.8270	1.8206	1.8143	1.8080
3	2.9410	2.8839	2.8286	2.7751	2.7232	2.6730	2.6607	2.6485	2.6363	2.6243
4	3.9020	3.8077	3.7171	3.6299	3.5460	3.4651	3.4454	3.4258	3.4064	3.3872
5	4.8534	4.7135	4.5797	4.4518	4.3295	4.2124	4.1839	4.1557	4.1278	4.1002
6	5.7955	5.6014	5.4172	5.2421	5.0757	4.9173	4.8789	4.8410	4.8036	4.7665
7	6.7282	6.4720	6.2303	6.0021	5.7864	5.5824	5.5331	5.4845	5.4366	5.3893
8	7.6517	7.3255	7.0197	6.7327	6.4632	6.2098	6.1488	6.0888	6.0296	5.9713
9	8.5660	8.1622	7.7861	7.4353	7.1078	6.8017	6.7283	6.6561	6.5851	6.5152
10	9.4713	8.9826	8.5302	8.1109	7.7217	7.3601	7.2737	7.1888	7.1055	7.0236
11	10.3676	9.7868	9.2526	8.7605	8.3064	7.8869	7.7870	7.6890	7.5929	7.4987
12	11.2551	10.5753	9.9540	9.3851	8.8633	8.3838	8.2701	8.1587	8.0496	7.9427
13	12.1337	11.3484	10.6350	9.9856	9.3936	8.8527	8.7248	8.5997	8.4774	8.3577
14	13.0037	12.1062	11.2961	10.5631	9.8986	9.2950	9.1528	9.0138	8.8781	8.7455
15	13.8651	12.8493	11.9379	11.1184	10.3797	9.7122	9.5555	9.4027	9.2535	9.1079
16	14.7179	13.5777	12.5611	11.6523	10.8378	10.1059	9.9346	9.7678	9.6051	9.4466
17	15.5623	14.2919	13.1661	12.1657	11.2741	10.4773	10.2914	10.1106	9.9346	9.7632
18	16.3983	14.9920	13.7535	12.6593	11.6896	10.8276	10.6272	10.4325	10.2432	10.0591
19	17.2260	15.6785	14.3238	13.1339	12.0853	11.1581	10.9433	10.7347	10.5322	10.3356
20	18.0456	16.3514	14.8775	13.5903	12.4622	11.4699	11.2407	11.0185	10.8030	10.5940
25	22.0232	19.5235	17.4131	15.6221	14.0939	12.7834	12.4852	12.1979	11.9208	11.6536
30	25.8077	22.3965	19.6004	17.2920	15.3725	13.7648	13.3043	13.0587	12.7272	12.4090
35	29.4086	24.9986	21.4872	18.6646	16.3742	14.4982	14.0831	13.6870	13.3088	12.9477
40	32.8347	27.3555	23.1148	19.7928	17.1591	15.0463	14.5843	14.1455	13.7284	13.3317
50	39.1961	31.4236	25.7298	21.4822	18.2559	15.7619	15.2279	14.7245	14.2495	13.8007

Table A-7:

Continued

Year	7.25	7.50	7.75	8.00	8.25	8.50	8.75	9.00	9.25	9.50
1	0.9324	0.9302	0.9281	0.9259	0.9238	0.9217	0.9195	0.9174	0.9153	0.9132
2	1.8018	1.7956	1.7894	1.7833	1.7772	1.7711	1.7651	1.7591	1.7532	1.7473
3	2.6124	2.6005	2.5888	2.5771	2.5655	2.5540	2.5426	2.5313	2.5201	2.5089
4	3.3682	3.3493	3.3306	3.3121	3.2938	3.2756	3.2576	3.2397	3.2220	3.2045
5	4.0729	4.0459	4.0192	3.9927	3.9665	3.9406	3.9150	3.8897	3.8646	3.8397
6	4.7300	4.6938	4.6582	4.6229	4.5880	4.5536	4.5196	4.4859	4.4527	4.4198
7	5.3426	5.2966	5.2512	5.2064	5.1622	5.1185	5.0755	5.0330	4.9910	4.9496
8	5.9139	5.8573	5.8016	5.7466	5.6925	5.6392	5.5866	5.5348	5.4838	5.4334
9	6.4465	6.3789	6.3124	6.2469	6.1825	6.1191	6.0567	5.9952	5.9348	5.8753
10	6.9431	6.8641	6.7864	6.7101	6.6351	6.5613	6.4889	6.4177	6.3476	6.2788
11	7.4062	7.3154	7.2264	7.1390	7.0532	6.9690	6.8863	6.8052	6.7255	6.6473
12	7.8379	7.7353	7.6347	7.5361	7.4394	7.3447	7.2518	7.1607	7.0714	6.9838
13	8.2405	8.1258	8.0136	7.9038	7.7962	7.6910	7.5879	7.4869	7.3880	7.2912
14	8.6158	8.4892	8.3653	8.2442	8.1259	8.0101	7.8969	7.7862	7.6778	7.5719
15	8.9658	8.8271	8.6917	8.5595	8.4304	8.3042	8.1810	8.0607	7.9431	7.8282
16	9.2921	9.1415	8.9946	8.8514	8.7116	8.5753	8.4423	8.3126	8.1859	8.0623
17	9.5964	9.4340	9.2757	9.1216	8.9715	8.8252	8.6826	8.5436	8.4081	8.2760
18	9.8801	9.7060	9.5367	9.3719	9.2115	9.0555	8.9035	8.7556	8.6116	8.4713
19	10.1446	9.9591	9.7788	9.6036	9.4333	9.2677	9.1067	8.9501	8.7978	8.649
20	10.3912	10.1945	10.0035	9.8181	9.6381	9.4633	9.2935	9.1285	8.9682	8.8124
25	11.3958	11.1469	10.9067	10.6748	10.4507	10.2342	10.0249	9.8226	9.6269	9.4376
30	12.1037	11.8104	11.5286	11.2578	10.9974	10.7468	10.5058	10.2737	10.0501	9.8347
35	12.6025	12.2725	11.9568	11.6546	11.3651	11.0878	10.821?	10.5668	10.3220	10.0870
40	12.9541	12.5944	12.2516	11.9246	11.6125	11.3145	11.?297	10.7574	10.4968	10.2472
50	13.3764	12.9748	12.5943	12.2335	11.8910	11.5656	.2562	10.9617	10.6812	10.4137

Year	9.75	10.00	10.50	11.00	11.50	12.00	13.00	14.00	15.00	20.00
1	0.9112	0.9091	0.9050	0.9009	0.8969	0.8929	0.8850	0.8772	0.8696	0.8333
2	1.7414	1.7355	1.7240	1.7125	1.7012	1.6901	1.6681	1.6467	1.6257	1.5278
3	2.4978	2.4869	2.4651	2.4437	2.4226	2.4018	2.3612	2.3216	2.2832	2.1065
4	3.1871	3.1699	3.1359	3.1024	3.0696	3.0373	2.9745	2.9137	2.8550	2.5887
5	3.8151	3.7908	3.7429	3.6959	3.6499	3.6048	3.5172	3.4331	3.3522	2.9906
6	4.3874	4.3553	4.2922	4.2305	4.1703	4.1114	3.9975	3.8887	3.7845	3.3255
7	4.9088	4.8684	4.7893	4.7122	4.6370	4.5638	4.4226	4.2883	4.1604	3.6046
8	5.3838	5.3349	5.2392	5.1461	5.0556	4.9676	4.7988	4.6389	4.4873	3.8372
9	5.8167	5.7590	5.6463	5.5370	5.4311	5.3282	5.1317	4.9464	4.7716	4.0310
10	6.2111	6.1446	6.0148	5.8892	5.7678	5.6502	5.4262	5.2161	5.0188	4.1925
11	6.5705	6.4951	6.3482	6.2065	6.0697	5.9377	5.6869	5.4527	5.2337	4.3271
12	6.8979	6.8137	6.6500	6.4924	6.3406	6.1944	5.9176	5.6603	5.4206	4.4392
13	7.1963	7.1034	6.9230	6.7499	6.5835	6.4235	6.1218	5.8424	5.5831	4.5327
14	7.4682	7.3667	7.1702	6.9819	6.8013	6.6282	6.3025	6.0021	5.7245	4.6106
15	7.7159	7.6061	7.3938	7.1909	6.9967	6.8109	6.4624	6.1422	5.8474	4.6755
16	7.9416	7.8237	7.5962	7.3792	7.1719	6.9740	6.6039	6.2651	5.9542	4.7296
17	8.1472	8.0216	7.7794	7.5488	7.3291	7.1196	6.7291	6.3729	6.0472	4.7746
18	8.3346	8.2014	7.9451	7.7016	7.4700	7.2497	6.8399	6.4674	6.1280	4.8122
19	8.5053	8.3649	8.0952	7.8393	7.5964	7.3658	6.9380	6.5504	6.1982	4.8435
20	8.6609	8.5136	8.2309	7.9633	7.7098	7.4694	7.0248	6.6231	6.2593	4.8696
25	9.2544	9.0770	8.7390	8.4217	8.1236	7.8431	7.3300	6.8729	6.4641	4.9476
30	9.6271	9.4269	9.0474	8.6938	8.3637	8.0552	7.4957	7.0027	6.5660	4.9789
35	9.8612	9.6442	9.2347	8.8552	8.5030	8.1755	7.5856	7.0700	6.6166	4.9915
40	10.0082	9.7791	9.3483	8.9511	8.5839	8.2438	7.6344	7.1050	6.6418	4.9966
50	10.1585	9.9148	9.4591	9.0417	8.6580	8.3045	7.6752	7.1327	6.6605	4.9995

Table A-8:

Present Value of an Annuity of $1 (Monthly Payments, Monthly Compounding)

$$1\Big/\left(1+\frac{i}{12}\right) + 1\Big/\left(1+\frac{i}{12}\right)^2 + 1\Big/\left(1+\frac{i}{12}\right)^3 + \ldots + 1\Big/\left(1+\frac{i}{12}\right)^{12n}$$

Year	1.00	2.00	3.00	4.00	5.00	6.00	6.25	6.50	6.75	7.00
1	11.9353	11.8710	11.8073	11.7440	11.6812	11.6189	11.6034	11.5880	11.5725	11.5571
2	23.7518	23.5071	23.2660	23.0283	22.7939	22.5629	22.5056	22.4486	22.3917	22.3351
3	35.4508	34.9131	34.3865	33.8708	33.3657	32.8710	32.7489	32.6275	32.5067	32.3865
4	47.0335	46.0933	45.1787	44.2888	43.4230	42.5803	42.3732	42.1675	41.9632	41.7602
5	58.5009	57.0524	55.6524	54.2991	52.9907	51.7256	51.4158	51.1087	50.8041	50.5020
6	69.8543	67.7946	65.8169	63.9174	62.0928	60.3395	59.9120	59.4887	59.0695	58.6545
7	81.0948	78.3243	75.6813	73.1593	70.7518	68.4531	67.8947	67.3426	66.7969	66.2573
8	92.2235	88.6456	85.2546	82.0393	78.9895	76.0952	75.3949	74.7036	74.0212	73.3476
9	103.241	98.7628	94.5453	90.5718	86.8261	83.2934	82.4419	81.6026	80.7753	79.9599
10	114.150	108.680	103.562	98.7702	94.2814	90.0735	89.0630	88.0685	87.0897	86.1264
11	124.950	118.401	112.312	106.648	101.374	96.4596	95.2840	94.1286	92.9931	91.8772
12	135.642	127.929	120.804	114.217	108.121	102.475	101.129	99.8083	98.5122	97.2402
13	146.228	137.269	129.045	121.490	114.540	108.140	106.621	105.131	103.672	102.242
14	156.709	146.424	137.044	128.478	120.646	113.477	111.781	110.121	108.496	106.906
15	167.086	155.398	144.806	135.192	126.455	118.504	116.629	114.796	113.006	111.256
16	177.359	164.195	152.338	141.644	131.982	123.238	121.184	119.179	117.222	115.313
17	187.531	172.817	159.649	147.843	137.239	127.698	125.463	123.286	121.164	119.096
18	197.601	181.269	166.744	153.799	142.241	131.898	129.485	127.136	124.850	122.624
19	207.571	189.553	173.629	159.523	146.999	135.854	133.263	130.744	128.295	125.914
20	217.441	197.674	180.311	165.022	151.525	139.581	136.812	134.125	131.516	128.983
25	265.342	235.930	210.877	189.453	171.060	155.207	151.591	148.103	144.736	141.487
30	310.907	270.549	237.189	209.461	186.282	166.792	162.412	158.211	154.179	150.308
35	354.251	301.875	259.841	225.849	198.142	175.380	170.336	165.521	160.923	156.530
40	395.482	330.223	279.342	239.270	207.384	181.748	176.137	170.807	165.740	160.919
50	472.012	379.089	310.581	259.264	220.197	189.968	183.496	177.394	171.637	166.199

Table A-8:

Continued

Year	7.25	7.50	7.75	8.00	8.25	8.50	8.75	9.00	9.25	9.50
1	11.5417	11.5264	11.5111	11.4958	11.4805	11.4653	11.4501	11.4349	11.4198	11.4047
2	22.2787	22.2224	22.1664	22.1105	22.0549	21.9995	21.9442	21.8891	21.8343	21.7796
3	32.2669	32.1479	32.0296	31.9118	31.7947	31.6781	31.5622	31.4468	31.3320	31.2179
4	41.5586	41.3584	41.1595	40.9619	40.7657	40.5708	40.3771	40.1848	39.9937	39.8039
5	50.2024	49.9053	49.6107	49.3184	49.0286	48.7412	48.4561	48.1734	47.8930	47.6148
6	58.2435	57.8365	57.4336	57.0345	56.6394	56.2481	55.8606	55.4769	55.0968	54.7205
7	65.7238	65.1964	64.6749	64.1593	63.6494	63.1453	62.6469	62.1540	61.6666	61.1846
8	72.6826	72.0260	71.3779	70.7380	70.1062	69.4824	68.8666	68.2585	67.6580	67.0651
9	79.1561	78.3637	77.5826	76.8125	76.0534	75.3049	74.5670	73.8394	73.1220	72.4146
10	85.1781	84.2448	83.3260	82.4215	81.5311	80.6545	79.7915	78.9417	78.1051	77.2812
11	90.7803	89.7022	88.6424	87.6006	86.5765	85.5696	84.5797	83.6065	82.6495	81.7084
12	95.9918	94.7664	93.5636	92.3828	91.2237	90.0856	88.9683	87.8711	86.7938	85.7358
13	100.840	99.4659	98.1189	96.7985	95.5040	94.2348	92.9904	91.7701	90.5734	89.3996
14	105.350	103.827	102.336	100.876	99.4466	98.0471	96.6767	95.3346	94.0202	92.7327
15	109.546	107.873	106.239	104.641	103.078	101.550	100.055	98.5935	97.1636	95.7648
16	113.449	111.629	109.852	108.117	106.423	104.768	103.152	101.573	100.030	98.5231
17	117.079	115.113	113.196	111.327	109.503	107.725	105.990	104.297	102.645	101.032
18	120.457	118.347	116.292	114.291	112.341	110.441	108.591	106.787	105.029	103.315
19	123.599	121.348	119.158	117.027	114.955	112.938	110.974	109.064	107.203	105.392
20	126.522	124.132	121.810	119.554	117.362	115.231	113.159	111.145	109.186	107.281
25	138.350	135.320	132.393	129.565	126.831	124.189	121.633	119.162	116.770	114.456
30	146.590	143.018	139.585	136.284	133.109	130.054	127.113	124.282	121.555	118.927
35	152.331	148.315	144.472	140.793	137.270	133.894	130.657	127.552	124.573	121.712
40	156.330	151.959	147.794	143.821	140.029	136.408	132.949	129.641	126.477	123.447
50	161.058	156.193	151.585	147.216	143.070	139.132	135.389	131.827	128.435	125.202

Table A-8:
Continued

Year	9.75	10.00	10.50	11.00	11.50	12.00	13.00	14.00	15.00	20.00
1	11.3896	11.3745	11.3445	11.3146	11.2848	11.2551	11.1960	11.1375	11.0793	10.7951
2	21.7251	21.6709	21.5629	21.4556	21.3491	21.2434	21.0341	20.8277	20.6242	19.6480
3	31.1043	30.9912	30.7669	30.5449	30.3251	30.1075	29.6789	29.2589	28.8473	26.9081
4	39.6154	39.4282	39.0573	38.6914	38.3303	37.9740	37.2752	36.5945	35.9315	32.8619
5	47.3390	47.0654	46.5248	45.9930	45.4698	44.9550	43.9501	42.9770	42.0346	37.7446
6	54.3478	53.9787	53.2510	52.5373	51.8372	51.1504	49.8154	48.5302	47.2925	41.7487
7	60.7080	60.2367	59.3096	58.4029	57.5160	56.6484	54.9693	53.3618	51.8222	45.0325
8	66.4796	65.9015	64.7668	63.6601	62.5807	61.5277	59.4981	57.5655	55.7246	47.7254
9	71.7171	71.0293	69.6822	68.3720	67.0976	65.8578	63.4776	61.2231	59.0865	49.9338
10	76.4700	75.6711	74.1097	72.5953	71.1260	69.7005	66.9744	64.4054	61.9828	51.7449
11	80.7830	79.8730	78.0978	76.3805	74.7188	73.1107	70.0471	67.1742	64.4781	53.2302
12	84.6969	83.6765	81.6899	79.7731	77.9231	76.1371	72.7471	69.5833	66.6277	54.4482
13	88.2486	87.1195	84.9255	82.8138	80.7808	78.8229	75.1196	71.6793	68.4797	55.4471
14	91.4716	90.2362	87.8399	85.5392	83.3295	81.2064	77.2043	73.5029	70.0751	56.2662
15	94.3963	93.0574	90.4650	87.9819	85.6025	83.3216	79.0362	75.0896	71.4496	56.9380
16	97.0504	95.6112	92.8296	90.1713	87.6297	85.1988	80.6459	76.4702	72.6338	57.4889
17	99.4589	97.9230	94.9594	92.1335	89.4377	86.8647	82.0604	77.6713	73.6539	57.9407
18	101.645	100.016	96.8778	93.8923	91.0502	88.3431	83.3033	78.7164	74.5328	58.3112
19	103.628	101.910	98.6058	95.4686	92.4882	89.6551	84.3954	79.6257	75.2900	58.6151
20	105.428	103.625	100.162	96.8815	93.7708	90.8194	85.3551	80.4168	75.9423	58.8642
25	112.216	110.047	105.912	102.029	98.3797	94.9465	88.6654	83.0729	78.0743	59.5787
30	116.393	113.951	109.321	105.006	100.980	97.2183	90.3996	84.3973	79.0861	59.8437
35	118.964	116.323	111.342	106.728	102.448	98.4688	91.3081	85.0576	79.5663	59.9420
40	120.546	117.765	112.540	107.724	103.276	99.1571	91.7840	85.3869	79.7942	59.9785
50	122.118	119.174	113.672	108.634	104.006	99.7446	92.1639	85.6329	79.9536	59.9970

Index